# MARKETING FOR TOURISM AND HOSPITALITY

The marketing landscape has changed dramatically in recent years, especially for tourism and hospitality practitioners. Marketing for these industries is now a multi-dimensional, collaborative venture driven by technological change and the growing demand for authentic co-created experiences.

*Marketing for Tourism and Hospitality* provides students with a contemporary, accessible and useful resource as they prepare to encounter the complexities and challenges of tourism and hospitality marketing globally. A clear articulation of the changing landscape, a comprehensive introduction to the three underpinning themes of collaboration, technology and experiences, and a plentiful supply of international case material provide students with an enjoyable and digestible resource that is both academically rigorous and practice-oriented, helping them prepare for day-to-day problems in the dynamic world of marketing.

This contemporary, challenging and highly applied text is an indispensable resource for all students of tourism and hospitality degree programmes.

**Alan Fyall** is Orange County Endowed Professor of Tourism Marketing and Graduate Programs' Director at the Rosen College of Hospitality Management, University of Central Florida, USA.

**Patrick Legohérel** is Professor at the School of Hotel and Tourism Management (ESTHUA), University of Angers, France, where he teaches tourist behaviour, marketing strategy, pricing and revenue management in hospitality and tourism, international marketing.

**Isabelle Frochot** is a Senior Lecturer at the University of Savoie, France, where she teaches tourist behaviour, experiential tourism, branding and international tourism.

**Youcheng Wang** is William C. Peeper Preeminent Professor in Destination Marketing and Dean of the Rosen College of Hospitality Management, University of Central Florida, USA.

# MARKETING FOR TOURISM AND HOSPITALITY

## Collaboration, Technology and Experiences

ALAN FYALL, PATRICK LEGOHÉREL,
ISABELLE FROCHOT AND
YOUCHENG WANG

Routledge
Taylor & Francis Group

LONDON AND NEW YORK

First published 2019
by Routledge
2 Park Square, Milton Park, Abingdon, Oxon OX14 4RN

and by Routledge
52 Vanderbilt Avenue, New York, NY 10017

*Routledge is an imprint of the Taylor & Francis Group, an informa business*

*British Library Cataloguing-in-Publication Data*
A catalogue record for this book is available from the British Library

*Library of Congress Cataloging-in-Publication Data*
A catalog record has been requested for this book

ISBN: 978-1-138-12127-0 (hbk)
ISBN: 978-1-138-12129-4 (pbk)
ISBN: 978-1-315-65102-6 (ebk)

Typeset in Stone Serif
by Integra Software Services Pvt. Ltd.

Visit the eResources: www.routledge.com/9781138121294

Printed in Canada

# Contents

## 1 Revisiting traditional approaches to the marketing of tourism and hospitality

### *Alan Fyall and Kenneth Deptula*

## 2 The need for change: the dynamics of the global tourism and hospitality environment

### *Alan Fyall*

# FIGURES

# TABLES

# TOURISM AND HOSPITALITY INSIGHTS

# Contributors

**Alan Fyall** is Orange County Endowed Professor of Tourism Marketing and Graduate Programs' Director at the Rosen College of Hospitality Management, University of Central Florida, and is a member of UCF's National Center for Integrated Coastal Research. He has published widely in the areas of tourism and destination marketing and management including 22 books. Dr. Fyall is a former member of the Bournemouth Tourism Management Board (DMO) and Board of Solent Synergy Ltd in Southern England, and has conducted numerous consulting and applied research projects for clients in the UK, the European Union, Africa, the Caribbean, the USA, Central and South America, and South East Asia. Clients include Grant Thornton, Ernst & Young, the Commonwealth Secretariat, the Malaysian Government, the Supreme Commission for Tourism and Antiquities (Saudi Arabia) and the World Travel and Tourism Council.

Alan currently teaches International Tourism Management and Destination Marketing and Management and to date has examined 27 PhDs in the UK, India, France, South Africa, Australia, Hong Kong, and Malaysia. He has organized a number of international conferences and workshops for academic, professional, and governmental audiences and is frequently invited to deliver key note addresses. He is Co-Editor of Elsevier's *Journal of Destination Marketing & Management* and sits on the editorial boards of many leading journals. His current research interests relate to smart and sustainable tourism and destination resilience in Florida, the Caribbean, and South East Asia.

**Patrick Legohérel** is Professor at the School of Hotel and Tourism Management (ESTHUA), University of Angers, France, where he teaches tourist behavior, marketing strategy, pricing and revenue management in hospitality and tourism, international marketing. He has also been a Visiting Professor at several universities (including Hilton College, University of Houston (USA), School of Hotel and Tourism Management, Hong Kong Polytechnic University (Hong Kong SAR), the University of Guangzhou, and Sun Yat-Sen University (China)).

His work has appeared in both marketing journals (such as the *European Journal of Marketing, Journal of Retailing and Consumer Services, Journal of Consumer Marketing*, etc.), and tourism and hospitality journals (including *Tourism Management, International Journal of Contemporary Hospitality Management, Journal of Travel and Tourism Marketing*, etc.). He also serves on the editorial boards of ten international journals, including *Journal of Travel and Tourism Marketing, Journal of Travel Research, Journal of Destination Marketing and Management*, and *International Journal of Contemporary Hospitality Management*.

Patrick has also published three books in the area of tourism marketing, including *Marketing du tourisme* (4th ed., Dunod, 2018) (co-authored with Isabelle Frochot), and *Revenue Management for Hospitality and Tourism* (GoodFellow Publisher, 2013) (co-authored with Alan Fyall).

Patrick's research interests lie in consumer behaviour – technology acceptance, senior, variety seeking, atmospherics, consumer spending, and price perception. He also specializes in revenue management, both in terms of research interest and publications, and managerial implications (he is director of the master's program in revenue management at the University of Angers, a member of the Revenue Management Club France, undertakes consultancy, and is co-founder of the Remaps conference). He is also a TTRA European Chapter board member, and he was in charge of the Angers TTRA 2017 European Conference.

**Isabelle Frochot** is a senior lecturer at the University of Savoie, France, where she teaches tourist behaviour, experiential tourism, branding and international tourism. Isabelle completed her PhD at Manchester Metropolitan University on the subject of heritage quality perceptions and visitors' segmentation. She has published five books in the area of tourism marketing and published in international tourism journals as well as conferences throughout the world.

Isabelle is a past president of TTRA Europe and has organized several international conferences over the years as well as sitting on the editorial board of the *Journal of Travel Research, Journal of Vacation Marketing, Journal of Destination Marketing and Management, Mondes du Tourisme* and *Journal of Gastronomy and Tourism*.

Isabelle's research interests include tourists' psychographic segmentation techniques, the definition and redefinition of tourists' vacation satisfaction and experiential marketing. Since returning to France, Isabelle has moved her research focus to mountain tourism, conducting various studies on its image and exploring customer satisfaction and experiential dimensions within this context. Her current interests include the study of the tourist experience, with a specific focus on flow, immersion, nesting, and satisfaction. Isabelle is also involved in various publicly-funded projects and consultancy projects in the areas of experience management in mountain and museum contexts.

**Youcheng Wang** is Professor and Dean of the Rosen College of Hospitality Management, University of Central Florida. His teaching area includes destination marketing and management, information system management, technology and e-commerce strategy, and research methods in hospitality and tourism.

Dr. Wang's research interest focuses on hospitality marketing, destination marketing and management, customer relationship management, information search behavior, collaborative strategies, and technology management. He is the author of three books and more than 100 scientific publications. He is the Co-Editor of *Journal of Destination Marketing and Management,* and is on the editorial board of nine international academic journals in the domain of hospitality and tourism marketing and management.

Dr. Wang has consulting experience in the areas of destination marketing and development, technology and e-commerce strategies for hospitality and tourism organizations, collaborative strategies for regional destination marketing and management, and experiential marketing.

Dr. Wang earned his master's from Purdue University and his PhD from the University of Illinois. He is a member of several professional associations including the Travel and Tourism Research Association (TTRA), the International Council on Hotel, Restaurant and Institutional Education (I-CHRIE), the International Society of Travel and Tourism Educators (ISTTE), and Hospitality Financial and Technology Professionals (HFTP). He also serves on the Research Committee of Visit Orlando and the Expert Committee of Shanghai Tourism Development Research Center.

Kenneth Deptula, Amanda Templeton, Ryuichi Karakawa, and James Wollner, are all current or former graduate students at the Rosen College of Hospitality Management, University of Central Florida, in Orlando, Florida.

# Preface

Welcome to the first edition of *Marketing for Tourism and Hospitality: Collaboration, Technology and Experiences*. The marketing landscape has changed dramatically in recent years with marketing practitioners in the fields of tourism and hospitality frequently at the forefront of such changes. The marketing of tourism and hospitality is no longer a static, single-organizational activity, rather it is a multi-dimensional, collaborative venture driven by technological change (more often than not of a mobile nature) and the insatiable appetite amongst consumers for authentic co-created experiences. As such, rather than discuss collaboration, technology, and experiences in isolated chapters, these three trends underpin the entire text and collectively shape what we believe to be a contemporary, challenging, realistic, and highly-applied text for students of tourism and hospitality marketing.

The book has been written for a truly international audience, as reflected by the global dynamics and reach of tourism and hospitality, with first- and second-year undergraduate markets ideally suited to the content and style of the book. The three underpinning themes are integrated throughout the entire text with tourism and hospitality *insights* used throughout to amplify real-life marketing situations, challenges and solutions.

The speed with which the wider environment and markets are changing pose particular challenges to faculty teaching such programs with the pressures of modern-day academia frequently conspiring against the delivery of quality lectures, seminars, and workshops. Pressure to publish, generate income, and entertain "Millennial" students necessitates the need for quality, up-to-date, and relevant textbooks that challenge traditional approaches and provide contemporary and applied solutions to real-life marketing problems. The collective teaching and publishing experience of the authors, the structure and organization of ideas, and the provision of numerous examples and associated online resources available for this text are such that we feel confident that this book will be an indispensable resource for future teaching needs.

For students, the text will provide a contemporary, accessible, and useful resource as they encounter, possibly for the first time, the intricacies and complexities of tourism and hospitality marketing and the very real challenges that lie ahead. A clear articulation of the changing landscape, an accessible introduction to the three underpinning themes of collaboration, technology and experiences, and a plentiful supply of case material provide students with an enjoyable and digestible resource that will challenge them academically as well as prepare them for day-to-day problems in the real and dynamic world of marketing.

We hope you enjoy the book and are excited as we are about the future of tourism and hospitality marketing.

Alan Fyall, Patrick Legohérel, Isabelle Frochot, and Youcheng Wang
July 2018

# Acknowledgments

Completing a book of this nature and magnitude is never an easy task and as such, we are all hugely grateful to a large number of people for their time, advice and contributions over the past two years. In addition to our respective families for persevering with "yet another book", we are all hugely indebted to the following in particular.

To Kenneth Deptula, Amanda Templeton, Ryuichi Karakawa, Jalayer Khalilzadeh, and James Wollner, all current or former graduate students at the Rosen College of Hospitality Management, University of Central Florida, in Orlando, Florida. Without your collective input, this book would have been seriously delayed, with your enthusiasm, willingness to "go find cases" and impressive ability to complete work of such a high standard at such short notice to be commended. You are all a credit to the college and university!

From Patrick, a heartfelt thanks goes out to colleagues and staff of the research department GRANEM (University of Angers, France), for their support, and specifically Gemma Davies, research assistant. For particular chapters, Patrick would like to thank the following: Chapter 12, H.G. Parsa, Barron Hilton Chair and Professor, Daniels School of Business, University of Denver, USA; Emmanuel Meunier, TCI Research; Georges Panayotis, Editor-in-Chief, *Hospitality On*, Paris, France; Ali Kassir, Senior Officer Inventory Management, Marketing and Development, Middle East Airways, Lebanon; Olivier Glasberg, Associate Director, Succès Voyage, Paris, France. Chapter 13, Stéphane Gautier, Hotel Manager, Orléans, France; Jocelyn Kwok, CEO, AHRIM – Association des Hôteliers et Restaurateurs, Mauritius; Michel Dubreuil, Destination Canada, Vancouver, Canada. Chapter 14, Philippe Mugnier, Founding President of ATTRACT, Consulting, strategy, and marketing agency for attractivity, Paris, France; I Gusti Ayu Oka Suryawardani and Agung Suryawan Wiranatha, Doctorate Program in Tourism, Udayana University, Bali, Indonesia; Olivier Bouchereau, Marketing Department, Angers Loire Tourisme, Angers, France; Feriel Gadhoumi, Tunisian National Tourism Office, Tunisia. Chapter 16, Georges Panayotis, Editor-in-Chief, *Hospitality On*, Paris, France (a special thanks to *Hospitality On*, and Georges Panayotis, Editor-in-Chief, for their contribution to Chapter 16); P. Kaye Chon, Dean, School of Hotel and Tourism Management, Hong Kong Polytechnic University, Hong Kong SAR; Leonid Goncharov, CEO, Anticafé company, Paris, France; Céline Bossanne, Huttopia company, France; Juleigh Giberson, BSc and Frederic Dimanche, PhD, Ted Rogers School of Hospitality and Tourism Management, Ryerson University, Canada; Olivier Cohn, CEO, Best Western® Hotels & Resorts France;

Cécilie de Saint Venant, Domaine National of Chambord, France; Julian Hagger, Chief Sales and Marketing Officer, LUX Hospitality, Mauritius. Chapter 17, Amina Hachem, Head of Revenue Management Department at Middle East Airlines, Lebanon; Mona Maamari, Director of Revenue Management Development, Madrid, NH Hotel Group, Spain; Cindy Yoonjoung Heo, PhD, Assistant Professor of Revenue Management. École hôtelière de Lausanne, HES-SO/University of Applied Sciences Western Switzerland. Jad Aboukhater, Director of Revenue Management, InterContinental Carlton Cannes, France; Christophe Imbert, RM expert, Milanamos, France; Agnès Roquefort, Senior VP Global RM, Pricing and Analytics, Data and RM Department, Accor Hotels, France. Chapter 19, Charlotte Reed and Xuan Lorna Wang, University of Surrey, UK; Nathalie Dalmasso, Digital Communication Officer, Côte d'Azur CRT, France, Jean-Jacques Laham, Client Relations Manager, Sodexo Energy and Resources, UK, and Emmanuel Meunier (TCI Research).

From Isabelle, a big thank you goes to: colleagues from the research lab IREGE and teaching department CITHEME, both at Université Savoie Mont Blanc. She also wishes to thank all the contributors on the GlobeVeilleur website for producing interesting and up-to-date information on the tourism and hospitality industry. For the chapters, Isabelle wishes to thank: Florence Boyer (Chargée de communication institutionnelle – Disneyland Paris), Christel Camelis (Université de la Réunion), Amber Cumings (Aussie Specialist Program Executive | Tourism Australia), Ludovic Dublanchet, Pierre Eloy, and François Perroy (Agitateurs des Destinations Numériques), Elsevier, Emerald Group, Annabelle Forget (Assistant Group Head of Legal, Secretarial, and Corporate; LUX Hospitality Ltd), Melitta Franceschini (South Tyrol Museum of Archaeology), Grégory Guzzo (Office de Tourisme de Val Thorens), Olivier Henry-Biabaud (CEO | TCI Research), Alastair M. Jack (Partnership and Promotions Manager, GoToBermuda.com), Teresa Lee (Hotel-Online), Julia Luczak-Rougeaux (Travelonmove.com), Hana McGee (McGee's entertainements), Jean and Boris Moscarola (Sphinx), Sylvain Rabuel (Club Med France Europe Afrique), Katharina Rainer (Marketing and PR, My Experience Fellow), Abel Rupari (customer service representative | marketing and sales | iso central secretariat), Rob Sinclair-Barnes (Strategic Marketing Director – Airlines, Amadeus), Inga Hlín Pálsdóttir (Director, Visit Iceland and Creative Industries), Sage Publications and Taylor and Francis.

Finally, a huge thank you to all our students over the years who have served to stimulate our continuous curiosity and interest in tourism and hospitality marketing and for contributing their part in the co-creation of knowledge in this fascinating, fast-changing, and demanding field. Thank you, we hope you enjoy the book!

# 1 Revisiting traditional approaches to the marketing of tourism and hospitality

## Learning outcomes

**Key terms**

marketing, marketing management concepts, strategic marketing planning, experience economy

By the end of this chapter, students will:

- Understand the meaning of marketing and the origins of the marketing management concepts
- Become familiar with the strategic marketing planning process
- Understand the special characteristics of services generally and tourism and hospitality marketing more specifically
- Be cognizant of the evolution of economies and the emergence of the experience economy.

## Introduction

### What is marketing?

According to the American Marketing Association, "Marketing is the activity, set of institutions and processes for creating, communicating, delivering and exchanging offerings that have value for customers, clients, partners, and society at large" (Kotler & Keller, 2016, p. 26). This all-encompassing definition can be both intimidating and confusing to many. For now, think about marketing as a process in which a company seeks to understand the consumers' needs and desires. Then, with this new understanding, the process culminates with the active education of the consumers about how one's products and services help fulfill their needs and desires. Some view marketing as the promotion of only tangible products; this is incorrect. The truth is, just about everything can be marketed; events, people, ideas, and services are just a few of these entities.

Marketing methods, originating in the early 20th century in western economies, are now omnipresent across the world with the vast majority of economies, even those with high levels of state control, adopting in some shape or form the basic tenets of marketing and market orientation. The world we live in is very complex with a number of quite considerable forces for change disrupting the current status quo to the extent that uncertainty is now the new normal in many countries. What doesn't change though is the need to understand the needs, wants, and desires of individuals and groups of individuals who make up the markets that consume the products manufactured and supplied in order to ensure that those products and services delivered are those that the market wishes to consume. This process of "exchange" where supply ideally matches demand can relate to all exchange scenarios whether the exchange is driven by money, time, or societal need. As long as there exists some degree of freedom of choice as to which products or services the market can choose then the notion of exchange remains central to marketing irrespective of the product or service in question. According to Middleton et al. (2009, p. 24), for the user or buyer marketing is concerned with six key questions:

1. What are the needs, wants and desires of existing and prospective users and their interactions with suppliers?
2. Which products or services do they wish to buy or use and at what price?
3. What information do they obtain to make their purchasing or consuming decisions, how do they process that information and what type of communication influences their decision?
4. Where do they obtain their preferred products and services (i.e. where do they buy them from)?
5. What level of post-sales service is required (if any)?
6. What is their level of satisfaction with their purchase or consumption and how likely are they to make such a decision again?

For the producer or supplier organization, meanwhile:

1. Which products and services do they need to supply and why?
2. How many of the products or services do they need to produce?
3. At what price or cost do these products and services need to be made available for?
4. How should they communicate their products and services to users and buyers?
5. When, where, and how do they make them available to the market?
6. What level of service is required before, during, and/or after purchase has taken place?

What seem like very simple and ordinary questions on the surface, in reality require a management decision process and the adoption of a marketing orientation that ensures that the real needs of the market are met. This approach, which is often referred to as the "marketing concept" is, however, just one of four historical marketing concepts outlined in the next section.

## The historical marketing management concepts

As mentioned above, there are four different trains of thought when it comes to marketing management. All of these concepts aim to fulfill business objectives and achieve financial success. However, each of these concepts have differing means to reach these ends. The four marketing management concepts are the: product concept; selling concept; marketing concept; societal concept.

The "product concept" can most easily be defined by the cliché, "Build it and they will come." This theory assumes that if a quality product is built and sold at a reasonable price, little-to-no marketing effort will be needed to sell the product. This marketing management concept is what is known as a "product-oriented strategy." Management's concentration is on continuously improving their product, rather than on marketing strategies, in the hopes that the quality of the product itself will create demand. This concept's popularity stems from an environment where demand outpaced supply; there was a shortage of manufactured goods and most markets had scarce levels of competition. Often being the only option to consumers, marketing as we know it today was generally deemed unnecessary. The product concept was wildly popular throughout history, ultimately giving way to the next orientation around the 1930s.

The "selling concept" states that consumer demand will not meet a company's goals unless the product is aggressively promoted. Unlike the product concept, this concept assumes that when businesses and consumers are left alone, they will not naturally interact with one another. Those who operate under this business orientation believe that the degree of aggressiveness in advertising and selling tactics will have a positive correlation with sales volume. Thus, their primary objective is to increase profits through mass selling. This concept came about as competition in market places began to grow and supply began to exceed demand. Like the product orientation, this concept was inward looking. This myopic sales-oriented philosophy fails to address the needs, wants, or values of the consumer. The ever-increasing competition and focus on maximizing sales above all else, often leads to price wars, and declining product quality. Even if some companies survive a war of attrition, they ultimately suffer, as consumers begin to perceive the product as "cheap." The selling concept spawned in the midst of the Great Depression and maintained its popularity well into the 1950s. On rare occasions, the concept can still hold relevance in today's environment. In fact, Tourism and hospitality insights 1.1 demonstrates a very good example of where the selling concept continues to thrive.

The "marketing concept," meanwhile, is the concept we will spend the most time focusing on in this book. This concept shifted the strategic mindset for companies. Before, businesses operated on a "Sell what we can make" approach. With the marketing concept, businesses now operated with a "Make what we can sell" tactic. In market-driven economies, the primary focus of the marketing concept is to analyze and satisfy the wants and needs of the consumer. If achieving this, a company should also always be looking to create and increase overall customer value. It must be recognized that

## TOURISM AND HOSPITALITY INSIGHTS 1.1
## SELLING TIMESHARE

The sales process involves all aspects of an encounter between a salesperson and a prospective customer (AIF, 2014). Salesmanship is "the process of effecting the transfer, with a profit to buyer and seller, of goods and services that give such lasting satisfaction that the buyer is predisposed to come back to the seller for more of the same" (Vashisht, 2006, p. 14).

A salesperson must determine the prospects' personal and family vacation goals, overcome any false perceptions the prospects might have, familiarize the prospects with the vacation ownership products and services available, and create a favorable impression of vacation ownership, the developer, and the resort. There is a saying within the vacation ownership industry: "People do not buy vacation products for how they work; they buy for how the product makes them feel" (AIF, 2014, p. 103). Often, prospects often approach the sales encounter with preconceptions based on publicity, comments from friends and acquaintances, and/or prior vacation ownership tours.

Therefore, the salesperson must remember several fundamentals of selling:

1) Know the company: A salesperson should remember that they are the face of the company and must always be able to answer questions regarding the company, policies and procedures, or other queries that prospects may have.

2) Know the product: A salesperson should be knowledgeable about the various aspects of the product as a prospect can have a variety of questions regarding the product throughout the presentation.

3) Know the competitors: It is important for a salesperson to be aware of the strengths and weaknesses of the product as compared to the competition. There is always the possibility that a prospect will be comparing products or have stayed at another vacation ownership property.

4) Know the customer: The discovery process is key to helping the salesperson gather as much information regarding the prospect as possible. This information will help the salesperson overcome objections and offer the right product to match the prospects' needs and wants.

5) Know the selling process: the selling process should be tailored to match the customer's buying process. The salesperson should be able to judge, using discovery questions and trial closes, if the customer is ready to purchase the product (AIF, 2014; Cobos & Templeton, n.d.; Vashisht, 2006).

In addition to the fundamentals of timeshare sales, research has shown that it is important to understand that most timeshare owners are frequent travelers and own vacation real estate at tourism destinations. This means that many of them may have somewhat of an interest in tourism development in the destinations where they own their timeshare (Huang et al., 2008). This makes timeshare owners a special group of tourists who have additional connections with the tourism destination through their timeshares. Having this knowledge, salespersons should be armed with knowledge regarding the local area and foster relationships with local governments and tourism organizations in order to stay informed about the local area (Huang et al., 2008).

**References**

AIF (2014). *Timeshare industry: Resource manual.*

Cobos, L.M., & Templeton, A. (Forthcoming). Sales practices: Getting over the sales slump. In A. Gregory (Ed.), *Current cases in timeshare.* Washington, DC: ARDA International Foundation.

Huang, C., Pennington-Gray, L., Ko, Y.J., & Thapa, B. (2008). Engaging timeshare owners in tourism destination management: Tourism planning and tourism marketing implications. *Journal of Travel & Tourism Marketing, 27*(1), 14–30.

Vashisht, K. (2006). *A practical approach to sales management.* New Delhi: Atlantic Publishers & Distributors.

Source: Amanda Templeton and Liza Cobos.

long-term success for a company relies on customer satisfaction and retention. Unlike the previous concepts which prioritize closing the deal on a one-off sale, the marketing concept puts a special focus on establishing and maintaining relationships with their most loyal buyers. To complete these goals, marketing research and segmentation strategies are heavily relied upon.

Additionally, the company has to convince consumers that their offering fulfills the consumer's needs better than any competitor's product. To do this, companies need to have a solid comprehension of the short- and long-term strengths and weaknesses of their competitors. This understanding will allow the company to then establish short-term tactics and long-term strategies to help counter opposition strengths and take advantage of opposition weaknesses. Examples of potential short-term tactics are slight product alterations, changes in production capacity, or a minor price adjustment. All of these changes could also apply to long-term strategic decisions. In addition, long-term strategies may involve introducing new products, phasing out dated products or repositioning the company within a market.

The onset of this concept marked the first time that businesses had a positive, outward-looking, innovative attitude towards sales and growth. Though the original idea for this marketing orientation strategy was originally proposed in the 18th century, it was not widely adopted by businesses until well into the 1950s, when supply permanently remained higher than demand. The saturation of many industries has caused the marketing concept to rapidly evolve and intensify over the last couple of decades. Today, it continues to be the most widely used marketing management concept.

The "societal concept" goes one step beyond the marketing concept and follows the philosophy of utilitarianism. This concept not only fulfills the wants of consumers and ensures a company's financial success, it also considers the long-term effect a product will have on societal welfare. Effective usage of this concept will benefit a company's overall ethical image with customers, shareholders, and the public in general. A debate exists in the marketing field. Does the societal concept deserve its own management orientation, or is it really just an extension of the marketing concept? Most historians agree that its inception was in the 1970s, though it has only really become popular in the last couple of decades as sustainability efforts have emerged.

It is important to understand that the popularity of these marketing management concepts have a distinct linear progression; as economic environments evolve, so does the importance of strategic marketing. Understanding the progression of these concepts will allow you to better understand the overall gradual migration of our economy from the antiquated agrarian system of old, to the experience economy we live in today. This migration will be discussed in length, later on in this chapter. Before that, it is necessary to outline how a company adopts the marketing management concept previously discussed.

## Strategic marketing planning process

For a company to effectively utilize marketing management, they must go through a very specific process that helps them develop an identity, analyze their market potential, identify and select their target audiences, formulate a strategy, implement tactics and reflect on their efforts to date.

### Strategic context

The first part of the strategic marketing planning process is to create an identity. This will include a corporate vision, which is a road map that suggests their future direction and key initiatives moving forward. It will also include a corporate mission, which tells a company's employees, shareholders, and consumers what the company is and why the company exists. Visions and missions are sometimes used interchangeably but this is incorrect and due to a misunderstanding of their purposes. For example, whereas a vision looks to the future, a mission looks at the here and now. The last part of the strategic context is a list of goals and objectives. Like vision and mission, goals and objectives are also mistakenly used interchangeably. Goals, like vision, speak with emotion about future plans. However, no specifics are given to how these goals are to be achieved. Objectives are written without emotion and should always be measurable. For example:

- Corporate vision: Our vision is to be earth's most customer-centric company; to build a place where people can come to find and discover anything they might want to buy online (Amazon).
- Corporate mission: Build the best product, cause no unnecessary harm, use business to inspire and implement solutions to the environmental crisis (Patagonia).

- Corporate goal: We will exponentially increase our market share in the United States.
- Corporate objective: We will increase our US market share by 2% each quarter for the next three years.

## Marketing audit

This stage of the strategic marketing planning process is all about analysis. The first analysis to be performed is that of the macro-environment (see Chapter 2). The macro-environment effects all businesses. Some examples of macro-environment factors are inflation rates, political instability, and tax rates. Many companies perform what is known as a PEST analysis during this stage. A PEST analysis looks at all of the outside political, economic, social and technological factors that could benefit or disrupt a business in any way.

Logically, the next step is a micro-environment analysis. The micro environment considers factors like suppliers, customers, employees, shareholders, and competitors. This analysis is equally as important as the macro-environment analysis as a good understanding of these factors will certainly help with strategy development.

The next steps are market and portfolio analyses. A market analysis is also known as an industry analysis. It looks at factors like market growth rates, various distribution channels, industry trends and market size. A portfolio analysis is an inward look at the various products being offered in a company. This analysis is important as it helps determine resource allocation and focal points moving forward. It may be determined that some products need to be discontinued while others should be more actively promoted within the company's internal portfolio.

The final analysis in the marketing audit stage is a traditional SWOT analysis. SWOT stands for strengths, weaknesses, opportunities, and threats. Strengths and weaknesses are considered to be internally effecting elements in the company while opportunities and threats are all external factors. While SWOT analysis is widely used in the business world, you can actually perform one on yourself. Whether it is for a business or personal, a SWOT analysis may provide great insights that allow you to carve out a previously unidentified niche market to operate in.

## Marketing strategy formulation and planning

This stage of the planning process is where marketing strategies are truly formed. First, all marketing options are considered. Then, a market position is established. A market position is the perception a product or company has in the consumer's mind in relation to the product or company's competitors. A company's job is to control and establish the position in the consumer's mind, rather than letting the consumer or other external forces, like competitors, establish the position instead. This is an absolutely critical step in the entire process because for some industries, once a product has an established position, it could be impossible or at the very least very costly to move to another position. For appropriate position development to take place, marketers need to first figure out who their target markets will be. Segmentation strategies are used to form homogeneous sub groups; members of these groups will have similar behavioral, demographic, benefit, geographic and psychographic characteristics to one another, allowing very specific targeting and subsequently positioning to take place.

Once the company is happy with the product's positioning, they must also consider whether they want a push or pull strategic approach. A push approach means that the company will be promoting their product by "pushing" it on to prospective customers. In a pull approach, interest for a product is generated by using social media or other tactics, and the consumer creates a demand that requires distribution channels to order and carry the product (thus "pulling" it through the necessary sales channels).

Earlier, we discussed a company laying out measurable objectives for the organization as a whole. Now, it is time for quantifiable objectives to be put on the particular marketing plan. The importance of these objectives to be quantifiable cannot be overstated. Being able to measure a marketing strategy's success or failure will be crucial in the evaluation stage.

## Implementation

The implementation stage is all about the marketing mix. The marketing mix distinguishes a brand's unique selling points. Over the years, the marketing mix has been simplified into the well-known four Ps (Product, Price, Promotion, and Place). The product stage is clearly defining the competitive advantages and uniqueness of the product or service being provided. Once everyone understands what exactly the product or service "is," the marketers can move on to pricing strategies. Things to consider when pricing a product are profit margins, price elasticity, and supply and demand. Once the price point is set, marketers consider promotional options. The goal of a promotion is to distribute information about the product to the target markets via various forms of media. This media can be radio, television billboards, direct mailing, social media, etc. Ideally, these promotional efforts should be quantifiable so that return on investments can be tracked. Lastly, marketers must choose the best places where they will be able to make their product visible to their targeted consumers. Placing can literally mean the physical locations products will be sold from an entire region to specific store shelves. It can also be an intangible placement, for example where a product appears on a website or its usage in a television show. When you think about the implementation goals of the four Ps, just think about having the right product at the right price at the right place at the right time.

## Marketing control

This is the final step in the strategic marketing planning process. In this stage, we evaluate how the implementation of our strategy is being executed. If you remember, we stressed the importance of making objectives quantifiable. One way to monitor and assess the successes and failures of a marketing campaign is to analyze the numbers. Do the resulting numbers surpass, match, or fall short of the objectives laid out in the strategic context and planning stages? Once information is gathered and examined, it is time for the team to return to the beginning of the strategic marketing planning process and start anew, albeit with more data to use this time around.

## Special characteristics of tourism and hospitality marketing

Although the aforementioned marketing planning process can be applied to any industry or sector, the tourism and hospitality industry offers some quite distinct characteristics that are worthy of introduction as introduced by Middleton et al. (2009). These are in addition to the generic service characteristics of inseparability, heterogeneity, intangibility and perishability (all of which are discussed in more depth in Chapter 8). First, within most aspects of tourism and hospitality, seasonality and other major variations in demand patterns are evident. For example, many destinations in the Caribbean, South East Asia, and the Mediterranean are heavily seasonal, based on climate, school vacation patterns, and historical agricultural trends and customs. Although numerous strategies exist to counter seasonality, the extent to which many tourist economies generate the bulk of their income in highly-defined time periods remains a challenge for the wider industry. Second, the high infrastructural cost of many products and the high fixed cost nature of so many tourism and hospitality operations continue to prove challenging vis-à-vis revenue generation and cash flow in certain parts of the year. For example, the cost of getting an aircraft in the air varies only slightly irrespective of how many passengers are on board. Likewise, a major theme park provider is obliged to fund the full visitor experience irrespective of the number of guests to their park(s). This combination of high seasonality and high fixed costs provides a challenging operating environment for tourism and hospitality businesses with much emphasis placed on the generation of marginal sales with a high percentage of such sales representing a much welcome revenue gain at no extra cost. Third, the majority of the tourism and hospitality industry is interdependent in that most visitors use several different products and services, with multiple different owners, when consuming their tourism or hospitality product. In very few destinations around the world does one person, organization, or government own all the airlines, hotels, attractions and restaurants that a visitor would frequent as part of their visit experience. This, in part, explains why collaboration is such an important characteristic of the tourism and hospitality industry and why it features so strongly throughout this book.

In addition to the above, Pride (2016) highlighted a series of generic consumer trends with far-reaching implications for the tourism and hospitality industry. Pride's "Yourism" agenda highlights the trend towards accessible and personalized experiences. For example, consumer trends are such that the mass marketing of old no longer works for many in the tourism and hospitality industry as guests, visitors, passengers, or users expect individual or personalized experiences and a degree of tailored authenticity with "one size" most definitely "not fitting all." There also appears to be a general rejection of authority in many countries with the widespread use of social media encouraging and hastening the bypassing of traditional institutions. This has clearly raised the importance of social media as a communication channel although "fake news" and "fake advertising" are now challenges not experienced in the past. Consumers are also becoming more impatient with Pride arguing that many now have an attention span of about 8 seconds. Not only does this have implications for marketing but it also impacts on all aspects of communication and interpretation. With their uploading of opinions, content, and images on social media, people are now "co-creators" of their experience rather than simply consumers. This represents a fundamental shift for those in tourism and hospitality with the experiential dimension a key theme running through this book. When communicating with consumers, there is also the growing issue of "information overload" with so much information now accessible. The vast majority of the market can only cope with a certain amount of communication before it simply becomes too much and a haze of indecision surfaces. Hence, more than ever is there a need for marketers to be precise with the communication of their message and actual channels of communication and distribution. In light of many of the turbulent trends highlighted in Chapter 2, security is an emerging issue whereby many markets now "play safe" with destinations and brands that represent a low security risk. This already is impacting on some longer-haul destinations and destinations in parts of the world where political instability, natural disasters, or terrorist activity are becoming the norm. Finally, in a world dominated by virtual agendas, there is a growing trend toward consumers seeking a degree of social capital or "sense of belonging" in their pattern of consumption of tourism and hospitality products. This is evidenced by the increasing number of people visiting places of significance whether it be as a result of family connection and places of birth, religious sites, or places deemed significant to their self-worth. Tourism and hospitality insights 1.2 below introduces some of the measures implemented by the French Ministry of Tourism in trying to measure and monitor their country's ability to meet and exceed the experiential demands of international visitors to France.

## TOURISM AND HOSPITALITY INSIGHTS 1.2
## FRENCH MINISTRY OF TOURISM

In an effort to guide strategic direction and enhance their understanding of the visitor experience, the French government established an independent assessment tool in the form of a survey back in 2011. With measurements taken every two years, the French Ministry of Tourism is able to assess the overall degree of hospitality in France at a time of considerable competition both within Europe and beyond. Key competitors to France for leisure travel are Germany, Austria, and Switzerland along with Spain, Italy, Turkey, Greece, and Croatia. The survey is also designed to gather data that facilitates the evaluation of public policies implemented along with the interaction of all key stakeholders. This approach acknowledges and takes into account the holistic and interdependent characteristic of tourism mentioned previously in addition to the recognition of the ever changing demands and dynamics of international visitors. One particular aspect of this research is the analysis of conversation from the "social web" with what tourists are saying on reservation and opinion sites such as TripAdvisor and Booking.com critical in understanding the co-created experiences of visitors. Recent outcomes suggest the intention to recommend and revisit France remains favorable although when compared to the level of service available it remains a particularly expensive destination. In addition, although performing well in the arenas of accommodation, catering and hospitality, public transportation and signage, among others, areas for improvement remain. These include some concerns with regard to shopping, digital services, food value, and the prices of recreational activities. Finally, the survey outcomes suggest higher awareness of the local population to tourism issues will be crucial to the further development of France as a valuable and truly high-experience destination.

**Image 1.1**

Image source: Pexels.

Source: Alan Fyall, adapted from TCI Research report, Emmanuel Meunier, Monitoring the Visitor Experience: Case study of the French Minister of Tourism.

In an attempt to understand the historical context of the origins of the experience economy, the following section introduces the history of economic stages of development.

# The evolution of economies

All economies are continuously evolving. Some are borderline stagnant and take considerable amounts of time to change. Others have advanced rapidly over the last 150 years. Regardless of pace, transformation is certain. Modern economies are in the midst of the "experience" stage, with this stage of marketing development underpinning the very need for this book. This section helps explain historically how so much of the world arrived at the "experience" stage.

## History of economic stages

The agrarian economy is the oldest stage of an economy. It is generally considered to be rural in nature and can be dated back several thousands of years to when subsistence agriculture began. Many great ancient civilizations grew and prospered thanks to the agrarian economy. For example, the Romans grew a surplus of grain to sell and trade across much of their empire, while the people of Southeast Asia did the same with rice. This type of economy extracts undifferentiated products and gives little-to-no thought about the needs of its customers. As time moved forward and international partnerships were formed, the farming and selling of many natural commodities became lucrative.

Industrialization is the second stage of economic development. Economies in this stage have moved past agriculture as a primary source of growth, relying on the manufacturing of goods instead. While this form of economy started in the latter part of the 1700s, it really took off post American Civil War (1865). This stage puts an emphasis on the mass production of minimally differentiated goods, lowered costs, and the increased usage of machinery rather than manual labor.

After industrialization, advanced nations transitioned to the service economy. In this stage, the economy focuses much less on the actual production of goods. Instead, services are provided to help consumers acquire and maintain the goods they desire. Product differentiation is highly valued and the customer's needs are heavily considered. Many of the more advanced economies in the world are in or entering this stage. However, many economists agree that the United States economy has now matured beyond a service economy to what is known as the "experience" economy.

## The emergence of the experience economy?

The emergence of the experience economy has reshaped the way that conventional businesses have looked to position themselves in the consumers' minds. The experience economy views a product/business as a stage and the goal is to create personalized transactions meant to elicit sensations with the goal of being positively memorable. These customized and memorable experiences are intended to build pre-purchase excitement, win a customer over for repeat purchases, and catalyze positive WOM marketing.

Pine and Gilmore write, "An experience occurs when a company intentionally uses services as the stage, and goods as props, to engage individual customers in a way that creates a memorable event" (1998, p. 98). Pine and Gilmore further developed their definition of the experience economy by creating a chart, known as "The Four Realms of an Experience." The outermost layer of this chart claims that there are four ways for consumers to experience a transaction: passive participation; active participation; absorption; immersion.

Within these characteristics are the four Es. The following helps to narrow down and mesh the previous characteristics into one type of participation (Passive Participation or Active Participation) and one type of connection (Absorption or Immersion): escapist; educational; entertainment; esthetic.

These dimensions will be covered in greater length in Chapter 6 of this book. Ultimately, Pine and Gilmore envision the demise of companies that insist on being bound by their goods and services rather than innovate and evolve themselves into the "Experience" economy. Tourism and hospitality insights 1.3 provides a good example of how one very famous hotel company has in part moved from a service to an experiential orientation.

## TOURISM AND HOSPITALITY INSIGHTS 1.3
## THE RITZ-CARLTON – FROM SERVICE TO EXPERIENTIAL MARKETING

The Ritz-Carlton Hotel Company, which operates five-star resorts and hotels, has revolutionized the hotel industry by creating luxury in the hotel setting, such as private baths in each guest house, extensive fresh flowers throughout the public areas, and à la carte dining (Ritz-Carlton, 2108). In 1998, the success of the Ritz-Carlton Hotel Company had drawn attention from the industry and the company was purchased by Marriott International, the largest leading lodging company. The Ritz-Carlton Hotel Company is now an independently operated division of Marriott International (Ritz-Carlton, 2108). The Ritz-Carlton brand's properties now have 91 hotels in over 30 countries and territories (Ritz-Carlton, 2108). One reason for their success is the Ritz-Carlton's brand's high prestige in the global market, as it has been recognized by numerous awards, including Malcolm Baldrige National Quality Award by the United States Department of Commerce (Ritz-Carlton, 2018). It is important to note that such a brand could not have been achieved simply from advertising campaigns or creating a brand logo, but from a long-standing commitment to superior customer service from their employees and their corporate culture that regulate brand environment.

The Ritz-Carlton's "Gold standards," which include a credo, motto, three steps of service, and service values, have contributed to the creation of a unique and strong corporate culture, which has led to superior customer service which, in turn, has consequently made their brand so prestigious. These standards describe expected employee attitudes and processes for serving guests and resolving problems as well as detailed grooming, housekeeping, safety, and efficiency standards (Partlow, 1993). As the motto claims, "[they] are Ladies and Gentlemen serving Ladies and Gentlemen (Ritz-Carlton, 2018)." Each employee is expected to serve customers in an elegant and polite way as they are representatives of the company. Furthermore, the Ritz-Carlton's values are reinforced continuously by frequent recognition for momentous achievement and performance appraisals at numerous occasions, such as orientation, training, and certification processes (Partlow, 1993). In addition to these standards, all employees are empowered to do whatever it takes to improve or fix a guest's "experience." For instance, every employee has the right to utilize $2,000 per day per guest in order to go beyond just ordinary customer satisfaction (Ritz-Carlton, 2013). Through this employee empowerment, employees have confidence that the company will always support their decisions and use their natural abilities to create "extraordinary experiences."

As Jeff Hargett, a senior corporate director, argues "Culture helps create the brand, and brand fortifies the culture. When a culture of teamwork, engagement, and purpose exists, the brand will become legendary, thereby validating the culture (Ritz-Carlton, 2014)." Therefore, a company's brand and culture are interdependent. The Ritz-Carlton has been demonstrating this by creating a corporate culture based on strong customer service which has enabled their employees to provide superior customer experiences, which, in turn, has led to the creation of one of the most prestigious hotel brands in the world.

### References

Partlow, C.G. (1993). How Ritz-Carlton applies "TQM." *Cornell Hotel & Restaurant Administration Quarterly*, 34(4), 16.

Ritz-Carlton Hotel Company. (2013, Aug 5). *Blog: The good, the bad and the beautiful of employee empowerment*. Retrieved from http://ritzcarltonleadershipcenter.com/2013/08/440/

Ritz-Carlton Hotel Company. (2014, Dec 8). *Blog: Dear Ritz-Carlton: brand and culture related?*. Retrieved from http://ritzcarltonleadershipcenter.com/2014/12/brand-and-culture/

Ritz-Carlton Hotel Company. (2018). *Awards*. Retrieved from http://www.ritzcarlton.com/en/about/awards

Ritz-Carlton Hotel Company. (2018). *Factsheet*. Retrieved from http://www.ritzcarlton.com/en/about/factsheet

Source: Amanda Templeton.

It should be mentioned that the article in reference was published in the summer of 1998, so let us analyze how far this "new" economy has come. It is surely evident that the authors were correct in predicting that experience-based encounters between business and consumer would greatly increase in the coming years. The next sections will briefly describe how the experience economy works in the tourism and hospitality industry and then illustrate just a couple of these examples for you, in order to help you with your comprehension of this developing phenomenon. Some of the experience driven transactions in the hospitality and tourism field have been made possible through technological advancements while others have been made through collaboration. This exemplifies the interconnectedness between the three themes of this text with Tourism and hospitality insights 1.4 showcasing the future direction of hotel marketing in the "experiential" age.

## TOURISM AND HOSPITALITY INSIGHTS 1.4
## USER-GENERATED CONTENT: THE FUTURE OF HOTEL MARKETING

With the continued development of social media, customers are increasingly sharing their experiences through user-generated content. Recent trends are showing that social media experts at hotel companies are exploring ways to: 1) influence what guests post on social platforms while on-property; 2) obtain permission to utilize the user-generated content on hotel websites and social media platforms (Hess, 2018). Hotels are finding that guest posts share a more genuine story and can often showcase what the hotel has to offer more successfully than a marketing department.

Hyatt has been at the forefront of utilizing social media, mobile sites, and apps as a means in which to interact with guests. In 2014, Hyatt launched the Hyatt "Control Room" a dedicated social services team created to connect with guests (Dua, 2014). In an interview with *SocialMediaToday*, the Director of Social Strategy and Activation for Hyatt noted that:

> As a brand, we're doing a lot on Twitter and Instagram. We're also testing Snapchat to see if it's a good fit for the brand's target customers. And while it may seem a little out of place, Snapchat actually makes perfect sense...We've been watching the growth and evolution of Snapchat over the last couple of years with interest. We've been looking for an opportunity to test it, and with the Hyatt Regency brand's focus on making it good not to be home, we felt that the geo-filter was a great fit here. With these, we're able to take an existing social behavior – snapping while at a Hyatt Regency hotel – and make it that little bit better thanks to the different geo-filters for each day of the week that our guests can overlay on their images.
>
> (Hutchinson, 2015, n.p.)

For Hyatt, instead of relying on purely promotional material, they have found a way to harness social media to bring user-generated content to the forefront of its marketing tactics and have created a dedicated social media outlet at social.hyatt.com (Hess, 2018; Samuely, n.d). The site boasts over 89,000 Instagram images uploaded by guests staying at one of any of Hyatt's many hotels around the world (Samuely, n.d). Additionally, travelers can browse the site to seek inspiration for their next trip by using the experiential filters. Hyatt guests are encouraged to upload snapshots of their experiences via the #InaHyattWorld hashtag. This builds onto the "World of Hyatt" integrated marketing campaign that utilizes Snapchat glasses to record Hyatt employee perspectives on social media (Kirkpatrick, 2017).

The Director of Social Media for Hyatt commented that "Creating memorable experiences will create UGC; bringing a location into a property will create UGC; caring for our guests will also do the trick. After all, UGC shouldn't just be limited to a sunset. Providing someone a special meal or a phone charger, or fixing something that had the potential to go wrong will often create a moment where a guest will take to social channels to talk about the experience" (Hess, 2018, np).

## References

Dua, T. (2014, July 11). Inside Hyatt's revamped social media strategy. *DIGIDAY*. Retrieved from https://digiday.com/marketing/hyatt-social-media-strategy/

Hess, D. (2018, May 18). Hotels finding ways to influence, share guests' photos. *Hotel News Now*. Retrieved from http://www.hotelnewsnow.com/Articles/286451/Hotels-finding-ways-to-influ ence-share-guests-photos

Hutchinson, A. (2015, Dec 31). Big brand theory: Hyatt Regency uses social to evolve the customer experience. *Social Media Today*. Retrieved from https://www.socialmediatoday.com/special-col umns/big-brand-theory-hyatt-regency-uses-social-evolve-customer-experience

Kirkpatrick, D. (2017, Feb 24). How Hyatt's new "World of Hyatt" platform uses Snapchat spec- tacles. *Marketingdive*. Retrieved from https://www.marketingdive.com/news/how-hyatts-new- world-of-hyatt-platform-uses-snapchat-spectacles/436814/

Samuely, A. (n.d.). Hyatt unlocks branded social media hub to inspire undecided travelers. *Mobile Marketer*. Retrieved from https://www.mobilemarketer.com/ex/mobilemarketer/cms/news/ social-networks/22394.html

Shallcross, J. (2016, March 3). Unbound is Hyatt's hotel group for the social media age. *Conde Naste Traveler*. Retrieved from https://www.cntraveler.com/stories/2016-03-03/unbound-hyatt- hotel-group-for-social-media-age

Source: Amanda Templeton.

## Conclusion

This introductory chapter set out to clarify the meaning of marketing and outline the origins of the four traditional marketing concepts, outline the strategic marketing plan- ning process, and highlight those characteristics that make the marketing of tourism and hospitality products and services so challenging. The examples adopted through- out this chapter highlight the changing face of marketing in tourism and hospitality and underscore how this industry is at the forefront of the experience economy. Pat- terns of consumption and visitation are changing fast with much of the change fueled by the Internet and social media. So much so that the major case study at the end of this chapter on SEO demonstrates how this, more than many other more traditional approaches to marketing, has become an essential strategy for all tourism and hospital- ity businesses irrespective of their size, location, and ownership. For most tourism and hospitality businesses today, a strong web presence is everything with SEO to leverage consumer engagement, commitment. and loyalty.

## REVIEW QUESTIONS

1. What are the four marketing management concepts and to what extent are some/ all of them still relevant in the experience economy?
2. What changes, if any, do you anticipate in the marketing planning process for an independent high-quality boutique hotel with a strong presence on the Internet?
3. Relate the special characteristics of services generally and tourism and hospitality marketing more specifically to a tourism or hospitality product of your choice.
4. Why did the experience economy come about and what do you think the next "economy" is likely to be and with what implications for tourism and hospitality?

## YOUTUBE LINKS

### "Welcome to the experience economy – Joe Pine"

https://www.youtube.com/watch?v=TOjUxGqh7aA

Summary: A thoughtful and easy to digest introduction to the experience economy by one of the authors of the seminal text.

### "Customer service versus customer experience"

https://www.youtube.com/watch?v=bL_D-qyva0c

Summary: A really useful clarification and overview of the differences between customer service and customer experience.

### "Examples of experiential marketing – Disha Kanchan"

https://www.youtube.com/watch?v=qZhbmlbfG5U

Summary: An eclectic mix of real-life examples of experiential marketing that help explain the key differences with previous iterations of the marketing concept.

### "The reason they won't do it is always the reason they should do it"

URL: https://youtu.be/zb1u9vgbLBE

Summary: Shari Levitin discusses handling objections in the sales process of selling timeshare.

## *"Tourism Training Live: SEO strategies and best practices for travel brands"*

URL: https://youtu.be/UoKJSNm39gw

Summary: Tourism Training Live session for travel and tourism industry professionals looking to make SEO a meaningful part of content marketing efforts; it shares practical steps and techniques that can be implemented to make SEO a key part of the marketing success for a tourism business.

### REFERENCES, FURTHER READING, AND RELATED WEBSITES

### References

Fiore, A.M., Jeoung, M., & Oh, H. (2007). Measuring experience economy concepts: Tourism applications. *Journal of Travel Research, 46*(2), 119–132.

Gilmore, J.H., & Pine, B.J. (1998). Welcome to the experience economy. *Harvard Business Review.* Retrieved from https://hbr.org/1998/07/welcome-to-the-experience-economy

Kotler, P., & Keller, K. (2016). *A framework for marketing management* (6th ed.). Uttar Pradesh. Pearson India Education Services

Meunier, E. (2016). *Monitoring the visitor experience: Case ctudy – French Ministry of Tourism.* Paris: TCI Research.

Middleton, V.T.C., Fyall, A., Morgan, M., & Ranchhod, A. (2009). *Marketing in travel and tourism* (4th ed.). Oxford: Elsevier Butterworth Heinemann.

Pride, R. (2016). Yourism – accessible, personalized experiences. Keynote presentation at the University of Surrey, June 2016.

Ritchie, J.R.B. (July, 1984). Assessing the impact of hallmark events: Conceptual and research issues. *Journal of Travel Research, 23,* 2–11.

Su, J. (June, 2017). You need to stop relying on your great services as your core competitive differentiator. *Neural Impact.* Retrieved from http://neuralimpact.ca/blog/need-stop-relying-great-services-core-competitive-differentiator/

### Further reading

Atwal, G., & Williams, A. (2009). Luxury brand marketing–the experience is everything! *Journal of Brand Management, 16*(5–6), 338–346.

Baker, M.A., & Magnini, V.P. (2016). The evolution of services marketing, hospitality marketing and building the constituency model for hospitality marketing. *International Journal of Contemporary Hospitality Management, 28*(8), 1510–1534.

Gentile, C., Spiller, N., & Noci, G. (2007). How to sustain the customer experience: An overview of experience components that co-create value with the customer. *European Management Journal, 25*(5), 395–410.

Jiang, Y., Ramkissoon, H., & Mavondo, F. (2016). Destination marketing and visitor experiences: The development of a conceptual framework. *Journal of Hospitality Marketing & Management, 25*(6), 653–675.

Mossberg, L. (2007). A marketing approach to the tourist experience. *Scandinavian Journal of Hospitality and Tourism, 7*(1), 59–74.

Pan, B., MacLaurin, T., & Crotts, J.C. (2007). Travel blogs and the implications for destination marketing. *Journal of Travel Research, 46*(1), 35–45.

Tynan, C., & McKechnie, S. (2009). Experience marketing: A review and reassessment. *Journal of Marketing Management, 25*(5–6), 501–517.

Williams, A. (2006). Tourism and hospitality marketing: Fantasy, feeling and fun. *International Journal of Contemporary Hospitality Management, 18*(6), 482–495.

## Websites

American Marketing Association
https://www.ama.org/

The Data and Marketing Association
https://thedma.org/

The Chartered Institute of Marketing
https://www.cim.co.uk/

International Marketing Association
https://imacorporate.com/

Internet Marketing Association
https://imanetwork.org/

Social Media Association
http://socialmediaassoc.com/#

# MAJOR CASE STUDY
# SEARCH ENGINE OPTIMIZATION

Gross bookings in the global travel industry reached $1.6 trillion in 2017, making it one of the largest and fastest growing sectors in the world (Hallam, 2018). Noticeable changes in how customers are searching for and booking their travel arrangements are being seen from non-branded searches to mobile searches with all areas of tourism and hospitality able to benefit from SEO campaigns.

SEO is a term used to describe a range of marketing tactics implemented to try and influence the visibility of webpages in the "organic listings" of a search engine's results page (Rowett, 2017). Phrased alternatively, it is the practice of setting up a website to gain better visibility on search engines like Google, Bing, and Yahoo (jenny, 2016). The goal for businesses is to put their website in one of the top spots on Google and/or other popular search engines.

When initiating SEO tactics, it should result in providing webpages with the best opportunity to rank highly in search engine results, and therefore give the business a higher percentage of qualified "click throughs" or "leads" to the website, with the hope that they have a higher percentage of sales conversion than competitor businesses (Rowett, 2017).

Within any industry, SEO should be a main component of the marketing plan, but for the tourism and hospitality industry it's absolutely essential (Rowett, 2017; Santos, n.d.). According to various reports, online SEO is the most popular online planning source for travelers.

## Google's 2014 Traveler's Road to Decision report

- 60% of leisure travelers reported that search engines are the most popular online planning source and the second most popular source for business travelers (55%);
- 57% of leisure travelers always turn to SEO first as the starting point for the travel shopping and booking process (Rowett, 2017).

## Stat counter global statistics

- 2016–2017: Google was most widely used search engine with over 90% of market share.

## Additional stats

- 95% of natural clicks come from page one of Google, Yahoo, and Bing.
- 3% of clicks came from page two, and 2% came from page three.
- One of five Google searches are related to location.
- The number one spot on Google search results gets double the traffic as the number two spot, and the second through fifth spots combined.
- 41% of searches unsuccessful after the first page choose to refine their keyword search phrase or their chosen search engine.
- 80% of completely unsuccessful searches are followed with keyword refinement.

Source: Santos, n.d.

The Internet has provided consumers with access to a plethora of choices, deals, flexible planning, information, and media all provided with the intention to immerse them in the destination before they arrive. This quick, simple, and convenient travel planning has revolutionized the industry by transforming tourism and hospitality into one of the most highly competitive niches, requiring specialized, industry-specific optimization strategies (Santos, n.d.). To thrive and survive, businesses must gain an understanding of what consumers are searching for and learn how they can leverage Internet search technology to maximize not only traffic to their site, but also to the destination itself (Santos, n.d.).

When it comes to SEO, it is important to know that it is not enough to rely solely on keyword-rich text. On-page content is important; however there are a multitude of other, back-end, factors to consider, including title tags, meta tags, image optimization, internal link structure, multilingualism, and foreign search terms (Santos, n.d.).

SEO tips:

(1)  Submit the site to Google Search Console.
(2)  Prove that the https site is secure.
(3)  Use Google Analytics to measure success.
(4)  Optimize meta descriptions and titles.
(5)  Value intent over exact matches.
(6)  Write clear, succinct headlines.
(7)  Stay away from keyword stuffing.
(8)  Stick to the basics on the homepage.
(9)  Focus on the quality of pages, not quantity.
(10)  Think critically about user experience.
(11)  Utilize alt text for all site's images.
(12)  Make sure it is mobile ready.

Off-site SEO tips:

(13)  Create a solid Google My Business account.
(14)  Network with influences in the industry.
(15)  Keep backlinks clean.

Source: Jenny, 2016

**Image 1.2**
Source: Pexels

Recently, it has been shown that presence, or lack thereof, on social media can impact Google rankings. Additionally, Google introduced a feature for businesses called "Google Place Pages," that can dramatically affect search results. Google Place Pages can be claimed by businesses, allowing the business to verify and supplement their business information, including products, photos, videos, hours of operation and more. Not only do the Place Pages take up a major portion of the first page, but they also pull in positive and negative reviews from a variety of sources (Santos, n.d.). Place Pages were designed by Google to help consumers make informed decisions where to go, making it more important than ever before for businesses to maximize their online presence (Santos, n.d.).

Hallam (2018) notes that travel SEO is highly dependent on high-quality link building, as consumers often look for information on neutral websites such as "The Telegraph Travel," "Condé Nast Traveler," and "Lonely Planet," to name a few.

### Thomson holiday rebrand by TUI

An example of the critical importance of SEO can be seen with TUI's rebrand of Thomson Holiday. In addition to an extensive, and expensive, traditional marketing campaign, TUI has cemented partnerships with YouTube, Snapchat, Spotify, The Mail Online, and TripAdvisor (Faull, 2017). The biggest challenge for the rebrand is to push bookings from Thomson.co.uk to TUI.co.uk as over 60% of bookings are digital and over 50% of TUI's web traffic results from SEO (Faull, 2017). TUI began the SEO campaign in 2017 with CRM campaigns, in-flight magazines, retail and online communications and, importantly, launching TUI.co.uk as a content hub. In an interview, a Marketing Director for TUI noted that "Protecting the huge SEO equity from the old Thomson brand is a mighty challenge, therefore an extensive plan across all platforms to maintain traffic to the new TUI website has been put in place" (Faull, 2017, n.p.).

### References

Faull, J. (2017, Oct 18). TUI cements Thomson rebrand with biggest ever marketing push but SEO now the multi-million pound challenge. *THEDRUM*. Retrieved from http://www.thedrum.com/news/2017/10/18/TUI-cements-thomson-rebrand-with-biggest-ever-marketing-push-seo-now-the-multi

Hallam, S. (2018, Jan 22). The importance of SEO in the travel industry. *The Hallam blog*. Retrieved from https://www.hallaminternet.com/travel-seo-importance-seo-travel-industry/

Jenny. (2016, March 23). 15 essential SEO tips for tourism businesses. *Blog*. Retrieved from https://fareharbor.com/blog/2016/03/seo-tips-for-tourism-businesses/

Rowett, P. (2017, March 9). SEO 101: What is search engine opimisation + why it's important for tourism brands. *Tourism eSchool*. Retrieved from https://tourismeschool.com/what-is-search-engine-optimisation-tourism-brands/

Santos, S. (n.d.). Why the tourism industry needs a special approach to SEO. *stikky media*. Retrieved from http://www.stikkymedia.com/blog/why-tourism-industry-needs-special-approach-seo

Source: Amanda Templeton

### Major case questions

1. Why is SEO so important in the tourism industry?
2. Why is showing up on the first two pages of Google critical for tourism businesses?
3. Search TUI and determine how successful the SEO and rebranding campaigns have been since the initial launch.

# 2 The need for change

## The dynamics of the global tourism and hospitality environment

## Learning outcomes

| Key terms |
| --- |
| external environment, internal environment, forces for change, tourism and hospitality industry |

By the end of this chapter, students will:

- Understand the dynamic external environment within which the tourism and hospitality industry operates
- Understand the fast-changing internal environment within which the tourism and hospitality industry operates
- Be cognizant of those particular external and internal forces which are driving the need for change across the tourism and hospitality industry
- Be introduced to a number of tourism and hospitality case study insights that explain how particular facets of the industry are responding to, or even pre-empting, these external and internal forces for change.

## Introduction

The wider external environment impacts all forms of life with those forces at play shaping the way we live, work, and play. Often referred to as the "macro environment," the manner in which wider political and legal, economic, socio-cultural, environmental and technological factors are predicted, understood, managed and planned for, will significantly impact the future success, or otherwise, of the tourism and hospitality industry. With it widely considered to be the world's largest industry, the need to understand what external forces exist and how best to navigate the challenges and opportunities each offer is paramount.

Less than a decade ago, Middleton et al. (2009, p. xiii) advanced a number of underlying external forces for change predicted to impact on the future of the marketing of tourism and hospitality. It is interesting to note that the majority of these forces have stood the test of time in that they remain critical in shaping the future direction of both tourism and hospitality. The external forces introduced include the:

- Growing impact of globalization in the demand for and supply of goods and services driven in part by the continuous and growing flow of capital, people, business, and information across borders;
- Continued, and exponential, growth of the Internet since its emergence in the field of travel in the mid-1990s and the more recent social media revolution, Web 2.0, and the omnipresence of user-generated content;
- Continuous income growth in most developing countries with a parallel growth in the sophistication of consumer demand;
- Economic emergence of China and India, among others, with considerable potential for the re-shaping of trends in tourism and hospitality and a global shift to a more culturally-diverse traveling and consuming population;
- Impact of international terrorism and global instability and its negative impact on international tourism in certain parts of the world;
- Consequences of global warming and climate change caused by the expansion in the world's population, continuous industrial growth and related carbon emission and the use of fossil fuels.

Although only a few years have passed since the above publication, the world has experienced some radical events in a compressed period of time that collectively have conspired to create an even more turbulent external environment for tourism and hospitality to prosper. For example:

- The Financial Crisis of 2007, caused initially by problems in the US housing market, had a devastating ripple effect throughout the world's economies with many countries to this day struggling to come to terms with both the suddenness and scale of the crisis. Although not the only factor contributing to its problems, the prolonged economic recession in many European countries including Spain, the Republic of Ireland, Portugal, and perhaps most seriously Greece, can all be traced back to the financial problems originating in the US at the end of 2007.
- The Arab Spring, which began in Tunisia in December 2010, comprised of a series of democratic uprisings in many countries across North Africa and the Middle East whereby the populations at large rose up against what were considered to be highly corrupt and tyrannical regimes. These uprisings have not delivered peace in any country to date with sustained violence and political instability the sad outcome across many countries with the tourism economies of Tunisia and Egypt, among others, damaged as a consequence.
- Turmoil in Eastern Europe, driven in part by rising nationalism, has seen part of the Ukraine annexed forcibly by forces loyal to the Russian Federation with opposing views and loyalties in the Syrian crisis leading to Turkey and the Russian Federation terminating diplomatic relations.

- The emergence of the "sharing economy" (as introduced in Chapter 1), most notably through tourism and hospitality brands such as Uber and Airbnb, has changed the rules of competitive engagement in many sectors whereby existing players, and especially corporate brands, are being bypassed entirely with transactions and experiences facilitated by mobile technologies and apps. Although popular with consumers, this force for change has been met with fierce resistance in many markets, most notably in Europe.

- The emergence of new pandemics around the world such as Ebola and Zika have caused panic among mostly poor countries where a combination of poverty, poor sanitation, and a polluted environment have resulted in many deaths, deformities, and widespread panic. Each has had a direct impact on global travel with the Zika virus affecting many tourist resorts in South and Central America, the Caribbean and the US.

- The problem of income inequality and inequality of opportunity for many in the developed world is a problem that persists with the Financial Crisis of 2007 contributing much to what now is a deep-rooted economic and social problem which, in turn, hinders the wider population's propensity to partake in tourism and hospitality-related activity. It can also be discussed in the same breath as changing socio-economic and health-related trends which include greater levels of obesity and shortages of affordable housing.

Before discussing many of the above external forces in more depth, von Bergner & Lohmann (2014) outline five key forces that bring together many of those forces introduced. The first, *globalization*, relates to the tourism and hospitality industries' abilities to cope with a changing market situation in a globalized, dynamically-connected world. The many global travel, tourism, and hospitality brands that exist maybe global in their reach but each, depending on what region they are located in the world, are likely to be impacted differently with the same external force serving as an opportunity for one while at the same time serving as a negative for another. *Contribution and effects* represent the second force with the younger generation in particular demonstrating a much deeper awareness of tourism's influence on nature, society, and the economy at large with them also being far more receptive generally as to what is going on than previous generations. Closely related is the third force, that of *balance* whereby the basic principles of sustainability and a greater awareness of the environment are evident in much more of the population than was previously the case with the need to protect and conserve destination's core values being viewed as a priority over old-style development at all costs. The fourth force, that of *adaptability*, relates to the ability of both tourism and hospitality adapting to and surviving in a changing climate while the fifth and final force of *self-control* relates to the ability of those managing tourism and hospitality assets to manage them with respect to market conditions. Although true of all of these five forces, this latter force necessitates the need for strategic planning and professional management across the industry.

Although the above forces impact all industries from pharmaceuticals to automotive and from construction to financial services, tourism and hospitality demonstrate a number of core characteristics that make them particularly susceptible to forces in the wider external environment in that they:

- Are indicative of the service sector with intangibility, inseparability, heterogeneity and perishability with a more recent orientation toward the "experience economy" as introduced in Chapter 1;
- Frequently demonstrate high seasonality and variable patterns of demand;
- Exhibit high fixed costs of operation along with a fixed (perishable) capacity at a certain point in time;
- Demonstrate high degrees of interdependence which, in turn drives the collaborative dynamics of so much tourism and hospitality marketing;
- Are highly variable due to the myriad of factors, including the weather and labor, that are instrumental in terms of their delivery;
- Rely heavily on discretionary income with both, to varying degrees, representing luxury rather than necessity forms of consumption;
- Are equally impacted by exogenous (external) and/or endogenous (inside) forces for change with all forces predictably unpredictable in their breadth, depth, and longevity of impact.

Interestingly, and despite the many aforementioned problems in the world, the volume and value of international tourism continue to grow exponentially as evidenced in Tourism and hospitality insights 1. Much of this can be attributed to tourism in particular migrating from an elite activity to one for the masses, with the sheer volume of international tourism alone necessitating the need to address such forces for change with a renewed vigor and professionalism.

## TOURISM AND HOSPITALITY INSIGHTS 2.1
## UNWTO HIGHLIGHTS 2017

Nations who invest in tourism are starting to witness socio-economic progress in the areas of job creation, enterprises, export revenues, and the development of new infrastructures. It thus comes as no surprise that international tourism has grown from a mere 25 million travelers in 1950 to over 1,235 billion in 2016. Eager to catch up for lost time, new and emerging markets are forecast to grow at 4.4%, double that expected among more established markets. Europe continues to dominate international travel numbers with it containing 49.9% of all international arrivals and 36.7% of total receipts. Although much of this can be attributed to the proximity of borders, European nations see much higher arrival rates than actual international receipts as most tourists travel from nation-to-nation, visiting multiple cultural sites along the way.

In 2016, France was the number one arrival destination. Of its 82.6 million international arrivals, 12.8 million (approximately 15% of them) were British. Interestingly, although recording the highest number of arrivals, this is not the case with revenue with camping and short-term trips contributing to lowering receipts. The US was the second most visited international destination in 2016 with it generating more revenue than the next three destinations combined. Recently, the US tourism industry has specifically tapped into international tourists seeking consumer goods at highly favorable prices when compared to their own countries.

Of the emerging markets in 2016, Mexico was a top arrival nation with Macau, Thailand, and Hong Kong attracting significant receipts. Mexico's market segmentation, combined with a three million-passenger cruise industry, has helped turn it into a top international destination. Macau, on the other hand, is a small Chinese SAR whose industry is focused primarily on gaming. Macau's 2016 international receipts exceeded $29 billion with only 15.7 million international visitors (Kaiman, 2015). While Hong Kong has benefited from China's outbound tourism boom, Thailand has relied on a combination of Chinese and East Asian tourists to maintain its tourism industry that today accounts for over 20% of its total GDP (WTTC, 2017).

European and Asian nations are first and second in arrivals and receipts, while collectively the Americas are third in both categories. Conversely, the trends suggest that by 2030 emerging destinations will see more rapid growth than the more developed ones. The Middle East, Africa, and Eastern Europe are newly emerging markets whose growth will depend on a number of factors related to progress, conflict resolution, and cultural developments.

### References

Kaiman, J. (2015, Jan 28). Macau records higher tourism receipts than UK or Italy. Retrieved from http://www.theguardian.com/world/2015/jan/28/macau-records-higher-tourism-receipts-uk-italy

WTTC. (2017). Travel and tourism: Economic impact of Thailand 2017. Retrieved from https://www.wttc.org/-/media/files/reports/economic-impact-research/countries-2017/thailand2017.pdf

Source: UNWTO (2017), Alan Fyall, James Wollner and Ryuichi Karakawa.

As well as those forces in the external environment, the tourism and hospitality industries also operate within a myriad of internal forces that impact on the way business is conducted. Before examining these internal forces, however, the section below breaks down the external forces for change into five key, and well referred to, headings, namely: political and legal; economic; environmental; socio-cultural; and, technological, with Figure 2.1 providing a broad overview of some of those factors within each heading.

*Political and legal factors*
- National and regional policy
- Employment law
- Environmental legislation
- Foreign trade agreements
- Political and governmental stability
- War and terrorism

*Socio-cultural factors*
- Age profiles
- Social mobility
- Population growth
- Lifestyle trends and changes
- Family structures
- Educational patterns and levels of achievement
- Income distribution
- Social class
- Attitudes and values
- Consumerism
- Immigration and emigration rates
- Work-life balance
- Nationalism and regionalism

*Technological factors*
- Technological developments (hardware and software)
- New technology applications
- Internet and e-technologies
- Government and research
- Computer reservation systems
- Development cycles
- Production technology

*Economic factors*
- Monetary and fiscal policy
- Interest and inflation rates
- Consumer price index
- Commodity prices (i.e., oil)
- Unemployment and labor force issues
- GDP and GNP growth rates
- Economic and business cycles
- Stock markets
- Exchange rates and purchasing power parity
- Taxation rates
- Unemployment levels
- Credit policies and availability

*Environmental factors*
- Climate change
- Greenhouse gas emissions
- Rising sea levels
- Safety, security, and risk minimization
- Waste disposal and recycling
- Protection of the natural and cultural environments

**Figure 2.1 Factors in the external macro environment**

Source: Adapted from Fyall and Garrod (2005).

# The external environment

## Political and legal

Although at first hand, students of tourism and hospitality marketing do not always see the relevance of politics in their studies, politics, political boundaries and political personalities and decisions are critical in shaping the wider macro environment. All destinations, be it at the national, regional, or local level, are accountable to political administrations irrespective of their size, reach, and brand influence with the various components of the tourism system such as hotels, restaurants, transport operators, and attractions all subject to the laws and taxation policies of their governing administration. For example, in Orlando Florida, the Walt Disney Co. and Universal Studios operate some of the largest, most successful and most profitable theme parks in the world. As such they both contribute many $ millions in taxation revenue to the City of Orlando and to Orange County which normally are in excess of $200 million in taxation receipts from all the tourism and hospitality operators within its boundaries per annum! With no state income tax, the millions and millions of visitors to the State of Florida contribute approximately 50% of all tax receipts in Florida through a combination of tourism-specific taxes and county-determined sales taxes; a political decision at the State level which seems to appease the residents of Florida for hosting so many visitors on an annual basis.

At a more national level, political decisions are critical in managing a balance between facilitating the ease with which international visitors can enter a country while at the same time protecting its borders and controlling immigration. Although an issue for many countries, the plight of the mainly Syrian refugees in the summer of 2015 trying to enter the European Union via Greece caused shock and widespread outrage across the world. Although shocking on a humanitarian level, many of the Greek islands are economically-reliant on tourism and the free movement of people across Europe's Schengen Area with the latter, in particular, under threat due to the vast numbers of refugees involved.

The free movement of people across much of Europe contributes strongly to France's leading position as the world's most visited destination by international visitors while the decision to re-instate national frontiers by Denmark and Sweden to curtail the flow of refugees may inadvertently negatively impact their respective numbers of incoming tourists.

Growing nationalism in many parts of the world, but especially in Europe, also offers a myriad of positive and negative outcomes with respect to tourism. For example, Scotland in the UK, Catalonia in Spain, and the island of Corsica in France are all seeking political independence for a variety of reasons. In the context of tourism, benefits may include a distinct cultural identity for each, freedom to "go it alone" in a marketing and branding sense, and the ability to break away from dominant other destinations in their "old" countries. As mentioned previously, the Arab Spring was, in part, a reaction to political systems with severe consequences for the future tourist appeal of destinations such as Tunisia and Egypt. Political stability is a crucial ingredient for tourism success with the ease of product "substitutability" a particular feature of commodity-driven (i.e. low price) destinations. For example, tourism to the Mediterranean region remains hugely popular for northern Europeans but rather than head east to the likes of Turkey, Egypt, Cyprus, and Tunisia the mass market substitutes the "east" for the "west" with Spain and Portugal benefiting considerably with their perceived safety a major draw to tourists seeking cheap sun, sand, and sea. Although global terrorism, wars, and political instability are not caused by political factors alone, clearly, they are a contributory factor with the Russian embargo on its citizens from visiting Turkey for purposes of business and leisure causing widespread disruption to the economic viability of many of its coastal resorts.

One area where political decision making continues to be a positive force for change is with climate change and the protocols, legislation, and policies being implemented to encourage adaptation and mitigation across the tourism and hospitality industries. Intergovernmental bodies such as the United Nations Framework Convention on Climate Change (UNFCCC) and the Intergovernmental Panel on Climate Change (IPCC) are leading the global initiatives on climate change with the United Nations Climate Change Conference held in Paris in December 2015.

At a more local level, political decisions are integral to a myriad of tourism and hospitality organizations with regard to zoning, environmental health, licensing agreements, legalization of gambling and casinos, local labor laws, management of so-called "public goods" such as beaches, parks and other natural environments, local micro-taxes (often levied via parking charges) and decisions pertaining to the organization of events and festivals, parades and local markets (i.e. food fairs, farmers' markets and beer festivals). On a slightly larger scale, many airports are heavily impacted by political decisions due to their public ownership. One highly successful international airport governed by local municipalities is that of Manchester in the UK which is owned by the ten metropolitan borough councils of Greater Manchester. Manchester Airport is now the busiest airport in the UK outside of the London region catering for over 22 million passengers in 2015.

## *Economic*

Ever since the Financial Crisis of 2007, the state of the world economy has been under constant scrutiny by industry and households with the uncertainty created by the financial markets impacting everyone. This is particularly so in the case of tourism and hospitality as both are reliant on discretionary or disposable income, especially in the context of leisure markets. If anything, the robust growth of international travel numbers as shown in Tourism and hospitality insights 2.1 are testament to the durability of international travel and the degree to which it has become a necessity rather than a luxury for so many people around the world. Perhaps more significant is the unequal distribution of incomes and spending power around the world with economic inequality an issue for policy makers in many countries, both in the developed and developing world.

Although not the only contributory factor, financial uncertainty and insecurity has resulted in many markets postponing longer-term decision making and bookings, replacing them with short-term and ad hoc decisions as to when to eat out, when and where to vacation, and which attractions to frequent. The trend toward shorter-term contracts is also contributing to this trend which, in turn, is making planning and forecasting much more challenging. With many markets looking for economic value in their purchases it is perhaps not surprising that all-inclusive resorts, cruising, and discounted accommodation and lodging have proved so popular over the past few years.

One highly dynamic economic factor is the low price of oil and the turbulence among oil-producing countries in failing to agree on levels of supply. For transportation, operators generally and airlines in particular, low oil costs are a welcome boost as they contribute a large percentage of fixed costs. This is good news for travelers and consumers as transportation, especially for international travel, is a significant component of the overall cost. More worrying is that so few commentators forecast the radical decrease in oil prices with even fewer sure about when prices will start rising again. Once again, this uncertainty contributes to nervousness in markets and ferments a continuous short-term mindset in many markets. This is also true about exchange rate fluctuations with many tourist economies in the Caribbean and Central and South America pegged to the US dollar with implications for both inbound and outbound tourism.

Globalization is also a key economic force for change in that the greater global interdependence of economic and cultural activities is shaping both the supply and demand dimensions of tourism and hospitality. The global reach of many of the corporations and brands that dominate the tourism and hospitality landscape is impressive with many tapping into a global "middle class" with similar needs, wants, and aspirations. Merlin Entertainments is a very good example of the modern "global" tourism and hospitality with its products and brands located in Europe, Asia, North America, and Australasia. Merlin brands include Legoland, Madame Tussaud's, and SeaLife, among others, with the company seeking to offer memorable experiences to guests and families worldwide.

## Environmental

Although the environment impacts all industries to varying degrees, its significance to tourism is critical as tourism in so many places is driven by pristine natural environments. Its relationship with tourism is contradictory though in that such pristine environments serve as the catalyst for yet more travel and lust for discovery with new and untouched destinations of appeal to travelers seeking unique and authentic experiences. More than any other environmental concern, however, is that of climate change and its impact on existing and future tourist destinations. Although there remain factions in some countries who still question the legitimacy of the scientific evidence supporting climate change, it is interesting to note that the 1990s were the warmest decade since records began with 1998 being the warmest global year to date. The implications of climate change are already prevalent in a range of destinations with climate change adaptation and mitigation the order of the day. For example, while mountain resorts are experiencing lower snowfalls and shorter seasons, beach and coastal destinations are having to cope with increasing sea levels, beach erosion, and stronger hurricanes and tornadoes. Although mountain resorts can diversify with eco-green mountain trekking a possibility, many coastal destinations have more limited scope for change. Urban centers are not immune from change with many cities experiencing severe (and expensive) flooding, extreme heat, and poor air quality. Geographically, Europe is experiencing warmer wetter winters and warmer drier summers with there gradually being less of a need for northern Europeans to travel to traditional holiday destinations in the south which are becoming too hot to travel to in the traditional summer months. A similar pattern is evident in the United States and the Caribbean with increasing heat indices, beach erosion, the depletion of corals, and increasing health risks all contributing to turbulent forces for change; and all arguably made worse by increased levels of visitation.

On a more positive note, many markets are demonstrating much higher levels of environmental awareness than previous generations with green certification, eco and green brands and transport electrification making considerable headway in many parts of the world. In addition, more sustainable business models are becoming the norm, rather than niche, with walkable cities, cycle-friendly routes, and "slow" travel increasingly proving popular. Partly driven by ignorance and misinformation in the past, new generations are increasingly aware of the true environmental cost of tourism and hospitality and will shape its future by purchasing products, services, and experiences that are consistent with their values and beliefs.

## Socio-cultural

Social and cultural changes around the world are continuous with the need to keep abreast, or even ahead, of change increasingly challenging. In some ways, globalization has contributed to forms of social and cultural homogenization where there has been a gradual conformity in many countries in tastes, needs, and expectations. These, in turn, impact on societal values, perceptions, preferences and behaviors, and frequency of purchase and loyalty to brands among others. One notable trend of late is the increasing popularity of healthy tourism and hospitality products and experiences with healthy eating and the desire for a balance of body, mind, and spirit replacing more traditional and more hedonistic modes of consumption. Interestingly, one of the outcomes of greater affluence in many parts of the world has contributed to a more complex life for many with increasing pressures on daily life. The rise of stress-related illnesses such as depression and eating disorders are indications of a disillusionment with wealth and a desire for more basic forms of living with time rather than wealth becoming the new luxury with desires for simpler and richer experiences. Such trends offer much thought for those operating and marketing tourism and hospitality products and experiences with one questioning the future sustainability of the mass market as it exists today.

Perhaps the most dynamic form of social change in the world is that of demographic change with demography representing the study of population and population change. Population size and composition (i.e. how is the population divided up by young and old, married couples and singles, etc.) directly relate to travel trends with the success of cruising over the past two decades largely attributed to the aging of many Western origin markets such as Germany. At the same time, an aging population brings with it challenges, most notably in the area of pensions. For example, in addition to there being fewer young people to pay for the retirement of the elderly, these younger markets will have less disposable income to spend on travel due to the imposition of higher taxes to pay for increasing retirement costs. Interestingly, by 2050 the population of the 49 least developed nations will double to 1.7 billion while the population of the developed world will remain relatively static at 1.2 billion with the global population increasing to 9 billion in 2050 from its current level of around 7 billion.

For some destinations, such as Florida and the Mediterranean, an aging population is being tapped into vis-à-vis "retirement" tourism in the form of second homes and senior living communities where elderly people live together in warm climates with age-related healthcare. A further, and contrasting trend, is that of growing urban populations with urban centers now having more in common with each other than their own countries. This is leading to the increasing popularity of urban tourism and innovations in hospitality such as boutique hotels, innovative foods, and service.

One particular trend of note is that which relates to the increasing age that people decide to marry. With women now omnipresent in the workplace, and both sexes struggling to pay off student debt and purchase homes that now far-outreach their ability to afford, marriage is being considered much later in life with the number of "singles" particularly significant. For example, Yeoman and Butterfield (2011, p. 9) found that the "average solo vacationer is 42 years of age, with an annual household income of $54,000. More than 25% have a professional or managerial occupation, 53% are male and 47% female, and 38% have graduated from university."

Disney is one such company that understands fully the dynamics of changing demographic patterns with its focus on "major life" events in families such as birthdays, marriages, and religious stages of passage underpinning its marketing of "magical moments." Like many other companies, it is also trying to come to terms with Generation Y (Gen Y) and Millennials which now represent the second largest age "cohort" after the "baby boomers" (see Tourism and hospitality insights 2.2).

## TOURISM AND HOSPITALITY INSIGHTS 2.2
## MILLENNIAL VIEWS OF THE WORLD – SAME WORLD, DIFFERENT VIEWPOINTS

People say that Millennials, or Generation Y, are the most entitled, lazy, selfish, and backward generation to exist; however, that generalization couldn't be more false. Interestingly enough, this generalization includes all Millennials, all over the world. This is the generation who grew up with technology shaping their lives and lived a life centered on human capital and education. As of 2014, the Millennials were the largest and most diverse of all of the generations in the US. Aside from the US population, it's very important to note that the Millennials are the most recent generation to strongly embrace cultural values, suggesting that the populations aren't the same everywhere around the world (Schewe et al., 2014).

Millennials are more connected than any generation before them. They are the drivers of the globalization of this world through their use and adoption of rapid technological growth. Even with this general acceptance and need for technology in each Millennial group across the globe, Schewe et al. (2013) suggest that not all Millennials share the same beliefs. For example, their study found that people who stayed together shared similar beliefs regardless of outside influences. America's Millennials thus had very similar beliefs to those of New Zealand Millennials, while Swedish Millennials demonstrated different beliefs with cultural and collective identities much stronger than any global influences.

**Image 2.1**

Source: Pexels.

Even with the spread of globalization, European Millennials distinguish themselves from their American counterparts. For example, although both may have very similar expectations in life they demonstrate very different views of the world around them, as exemplified by Corvi et al. (n.d.). American Millennials, in general, don't possess the same appreciation for rich cultural, multi-linguistic, traits of the world like Europeans do because of the relative isolationism that Americans have (Corvi et al., n.d.). European Millennials tend to see the world from a worldly perspective, not simply an "American" perspective.

What makes it difficult for marketers to target the Millennial generation as a whole is the diversity within it. The confluence of geopolitical and technological developments since the 1980s is what makes up the "typical" global Millennial. This generation's independent nature, coupled with its desire to differentiate itself from the Generation-X and Baby Boomers enhance the difficulty for marketers of approaching them without first addressing their specific preferences. Their tech-savvy way of living has led them to live a life of convenience, resulting in less brand loyalty than any generation before them. Such trends present some serious challenges for tourism marketers as they try to adapt to the needs of the Millennial generation in the next decade to come.

### References

Corvi, E., Bigi, A., & Ng, G. (n.d). *The European millennials versus the US millennials: Similarities and differences*. Milan: Department of Sociology, University of Milano-Bicocca, Italy.

Schewe, C.D., Debevec, K., Madden, T.J., Diamond, W.D., Parment, A., & Murphy, A. (2013). "If you've seen one, you've seen them all!" Are young millennials the same worldwide? *Journal of International Consumer Marketing*, *25*(1), 3–15.

Source: James Wollner.

One further area of socio-cultural change, and related to Millennials, is that of consumption with a cause in the form of social responsibility. This trend has been evident in the political elections within many countries, including the US and UK, where candidates such as Bernie Sanders and Jeremy Corbyn have begun to change the way in which many voters, and especially young voters, are viewing the world: a world in which future generations are unlikely to be as economically well-off as their parents. This is an interesting conundrum for many in that Western society is built on the assumption that progress is continuous. Historically, earnings and home, and car ownership have steadily increased as did the propensity to take vacations and enjoy higher levels of discretionary spend. With large levels of student debt, increasing costs of home ownership, and fewer opportunities for full-time employment than previous generations, the impact on future spend on tourism and hospitality products and experiences is likely to be impacted significantly with greater levels of insecurity becoming the norm. Interestingly, many innovative trends – such as "crowd working" where employees are paid via online platforms such as Uber, Upwork, and Taskrabbit – are inadvertently contributing to even greater levels of instability and insecurity.

## Technological

Perhaps one of the most fundamental external forces for change is that of technology generally and the Internet in particular. The speed with which the latter has come to almost dominate the world we live in is astonishing with its impact on travel and tourism totally transforming the way in which products, services, and experiences are marketed, consumed, and co-created. Much of this book is attributed to the specific ways in which technology and technological innovations are driving change across tourism and hospitality with Chapter 3 featuring a detailed overview of the forces for technological change. From the emergence of the early global distribution systems in the 1960s to the almost daily proliferation of new consumer-friendly "apps" of today, technology has migrated from a means to deliver strategy to one that now actively drives the strategic direction of the entire industry. Perhaps the most visible impact of the Internet on the strategic direction of the industry was the emergence of low-cost "no-frills" airlines in Europe in the mid-to-late 1990s where the intelligent and creative use of the Internet was the strategic platform for the likes of Ryanair and EasyJet to set the new ground rules of competitive engagement for an entire industry. Although, for the most part, merely duplicating the approach first adopted by Southwest Airlines in the US in the mid-to-late 1990s the timely use of the Internet by their two European counterparts enhanced their speed of growth and turbulent impact on the European aviation industry which, arguably, continues to this day in the form of price competition, innovative cost-cutting services, and travel to routes previously ignored (and deemed unprofitable) by the traditional airlines.

Again in the aviation industry, one significant area of change at the moment is the investment by many companies, and countries, in new and more cost-effective aircraft which are affording the opening of new destinations that previously were considered inaccessible, or simply too expensive, to reach. As such, one of the major influences on airline costs, route selection and profitability over the next decade will be the new aircraft types being delivered. For example, new aircraft types including the A350 and the new variants of the A330 and of the narrow body aircraft, A320s and B737s, will join the A380s and B787s in airline fleets over the next few years with the new aircraft designs saving on fuel, demonstrating an increasing distance and, in turn, improving cost efficiency. In view of the pressures of climate change, these new aircraft are designed to be far more climate-friendly than previous models with minimum emissions in the earth's atmosphere.

The catalytic impact of the Internet across the entire tourism and hospitality landscape is a key feature of this book with it revolutionizing the way we search, evaluate, confirm, purchase and then re-confirm our purchases. So much so that travel, tourism and hospitality reservations, purchases and payments dominate transactions on the Internet. Search engines drive consumer behavior while search engine optimization (SEO) is the ultimate objective of all Internet-based strategies. The likes of Facebook, Instagram, and TripAdvisor may be three of the best-known but new competition emerges on an almost daily basis with more recent "sharing economy" advances (see Chapter 3 for a detailed introduction to this new phenomenon) contributing to the emergence and growth of the likes of Uber and Airbnb, and the catalytic impact they are having on the "traditional" and "pre-sharing" economy. As presented in Tourism and hospitality insights 2.2, the Millennial generation are clearly tapping into these technological innovations and serving to drive their acceptability and widespread use in the marketplace. Older generations are far from excluded, however, from this technological revolution with "Zoomers" in particular being active users of technology (see Hudson 2010).

For the present, and near future "gamification," "virtual and augmented reality," "smart tourism," and the use, management and interpretation of "big data" offer many new challenges and opportunities with those in the tourism and hospitality industries eager to not get left behind as their consumers continue to receive such innovations so quickly and comfortably with levels of "expectation" rising almost daily. As evidenced throughout Parts II and III of this book, it is advances in technology, perhaps more than anything else that drive the collaborative and experiential demands of both consumers and industry that make up the global tourism and hospitality industry.

# The internal environment

The internal or "market" environment relates to those forces in close proximity to the organization, business, or destination that impact directly on their ability to operate effectively and satisfy, and hopefully exceed, the needs, wants, and expectations of customers, visitors, or tourists. Although on the surface not seemingly as dramatic as many of the external forces for change, many of those factors in the internal micro environment (see Figure 2.2) can be just as impactful. Consistent with the landmark studies conducted by Porter back in the 1980s, the primary areas of the internal micro environment are as follows: organization environment; buyers, and suppliers; potential entrants and substitutes; intermediaries; competition, and competitiveness with Figure 2.2 identifying just some of the internal factors impacting on change. The key question with all internal micro-environment factors is where does the balance of power sit with regard to what areas carry more influence than others in shaping the competitive landscape.

## *The company/organizations' environment*

Although numerous forces can impact on individual organizations, the means by which organizations are owned, structured, funded, and connected are all important determinants. The latter is of particular significance in tourism and hospitality with both industries interdependent and dominated by smaller, often family-owned companies which collectively contribute to the wider tourism and hospitality experience. Connectivity and collaboration are central themes running throughout this book with the latter crucial in compounding the power of the increasingly concentrated nature of the industry; this particularly being a trend with the airline companies through their global airline alliances and hotel chains through their collaborative networks and extensive brand groupings. As an example of the concentration of power in the international hotel industry, IHG, Hilton Worldwide, Marriott International, and Wyndham Hotel Group own between them just under 300,000 hotel rooms. While in some countries it is normal for many tourism and holiday organizations and products to be publicly owned, the trend

*External audit – market*
- Market size, growth, and volume trends
- Market characteristics, developments, and trends
- Products and prices
- Channels of distribution
- Communication and industry practices

*External audit – competition*
- Competitors
- Size
- Market share and coverage
- Market standing and reputation
- Production capabilities
- Distribution policies
- Marketing strategies
- Diversification
- Human resource matters
- International connections
- profitability

*Internal audit*
- Marketing operational variables
- Sales by location, type, customer, and product
- Market share and profit margin
- Marketing information and research
- Product management
- Pricing
- Promotion
- Distribution
- Resources and operation

**Figure 2.2 Factors in the internal micro environment**

Source: Adapted from Fyall and Garrod (2005).

nowadays is for increasing privatization and liberalization with those companies mentioned leading the way in the hotel industry with regard to service and experiential innovations, new product development, and effective human resource strategies.

## Buyers and suppliers

Most commentators argue that consumers of today are more knowledgeable, demanding, and "marketing-aware" than was previously the case with marketing professionals year-on-year having a more demanding task to communicate, persuade, and convince the market as to the overall benefits of the product, service, or experience in question. Much of this can be attributed to their growing access to information (mostly facilitated by the Internet) and the power of word-of-mouth and/or electronic word-of-mouth in influencing patterns of behavior. Much of the trend towards healthy eating and reduced sugar in foods can be attributed to such communication along with the need to supply consumers with the origins, health considerations, and feeding policies of farm and sea produce. Instances where the power of consumers and buyers is strong include where a few buyers control a large percentage of a volume market, where there is a large number of small suppliers and where the costs of switching to a new supplier are low. Buyer power is also strong where the product, service, or experience on offer is relatively undifferentiated which, in turn, ensures low barriers to alternative sources of supply. In contrast to the above situation, suppliers tend to be in a strong and influential position where supply is concentrated in the hands of a small number of players, where the costs of switching to a new source of supply are high or where the supplier has a strong and differentiated brand. Influence is also strong where the supplier is in an industry with a large number of smaller disparate customers.

## Potential entrants and substitutes

The ability to protect a position in a particular market is crucial, especially with competition now emerging from all corners of the globe. Perhaps the biggest barrier to entering new markets is with the capital investment required with the ability to build large-scale luxury-end hotels limited to those with the financial resources necessary to compete effectively. Cost advantages can also be achieved through early mover advantage in that those that are first to establish the market often have time to establish a strong foothold and create barriers to entry based on knowledge and experience. Increasingly in today's technological-driven industry, the ability to access the right electronic distribution channels can make a big difference with electronic distributors such as expedia.com, booking.com, hotels.com very much re-writing the rules of engagement with their access to such large markets a key factor. With regard to substitutes, the threat to existing players occurs where there is the emergence of a new product or service that nullifies existing products, where a new product replaces an existing product or service or where there is the threat of a generic substitution. An example of this, albeit extreme, is where the trend for leisure vacations is replaced by the trend toward spending more time in the home and more domestic forms of leisure activity.

## Intermediaries – channels of distribution

The recent decision by Hilton to go it alone in the world of electronic distribution and bypass so-called e-intermediaries is significant as it represents a highly successful global hospitality brand challenging the power of the e-intermediaries head on. Time will tell as to how successful Hilton is but it does demonstrate the scale of the organization or company necessary to even think about such a strategy. The growth of electronic distribution channels and e-intermediaries is such that whereas in previous decades it was the producer, or supplier, who carried the balance of power, it is now the channels of distribution that demonstrate extensive reach across many countries and continents. "Channel" power is thus key in the modern era with the Internet, and its innovative use by distributors, once again serving as a catalyst for change across the tourism and hospitality industries.

## Competition and competitiveness

For organizations and companies to succeed, irrespective of their industry, it is imperative that they meet, and preferably exceed, the needs and wants of consumers more effectively than their competitors. As such, an awareness of what is going on elsewhere and why, an ability to react or "bypass" a competitive threat if needed is essential with knowledge of all current, and potential, competitors necessary. Knowing where future competition is likely to come from is key, as is the ability to withstand the competitive threat when it surfaces. Knowing your size and relative position compared to competition also helps with the ability to know the "best" position in the market critical in ensuring survival in the short-, medium- and longer-term.

As discussed already, competition can, and does, come from virtually anywhere now with increasing liberalization and decentralization of markets contributing to the speed with which changes are occurring. In many ways, such changes increase the number of opportunities albeit at the same time increasing competition and innovation via new competitive forms. For example, is competition obvious from companies selling the same products, similar products, companies competing for discretionary spend or companies, products, services and experiences competing for peoples' time which in many markets, is in diminishing supply? Tourism and hospitality insights 2.3 takes the interesting case of two international tourist destinations, France and Vietnam, and explores their degree of competitiveness in the highly competitive landscape of international tourism.

## TOURISM AND HOSPITALITY INSIGHTS 2.3
## WORLD ECONOMIC FORUM – TOURISM COMPETITIVENESS

### France and Vietnam

In a rapidly globalizing world, the travel and tourism industry has become an even bigger player in the global economy. In 2016, tourism accounted for roughly 10% of the entire globe's Gross Domestic Product (GDP), or approximately 8 trillion dollars (Crotti & Misrahi, 2017). In this regard, the 2017 Travel and Tourism Competitiveness Index presents the competitiveness of individual nations competing in the global travel and tourism industry.

Interestingly, in addition to being the world's most popular international destination, France also ranks second in "competitiveness" behind Spain. Vietnam, on the other hand, ranks 67th with a number of reasons explaining such a difference including social, economic, and geopolitical factors. For example, France's high ranking is attributed to its rich history, culture, and highly recognized progressive development (Attwooll, 2015). Aside from the culture, cuisine, and historical sights, France possesses a very central location in Europe. According to Crotti and Misrahi (2017), France ranked among the top five nations in 12 subcategories that were measured in 2016. In contrast, Vietnam didn't rank in the top five in any of the 12 subcategories in the 2016 assessment.

The 2017 report indicates that more industrialized nations, such as France, rank highest among culture, transportation, healthcare, and infrastructure categories with healthcare frequently damaging emerging destinations' scores, as is the case with Vietnam; although it also scores lowly with tourist service infrastructure and ground and port infrastructure, to name but a few (Crotti & Misrahi, 2017). Vietnam is in fact a nation endowed with abundant resources but to this day continues to struggle with tourist prioritization, infrastructure, and environmental stability. Vietnam remains a heavily polluted and poor country with it investing less in tourism and travel in 2016 than any other developing nation on the competitiveness index. Interestingly, when compared to its former colonial power, France, Vietnam underperforms in nearly every category except for that of price competitiveness (Crotti & Misrahi, 2017).

**Image 2.2**
Source: Pexels.

By more closely interpreting the data in the 2017 Index, Vietnam could better understand exactly where their industry lies within the world landscape and where some of the more "competitive" destinations succeed vis-à-vis infrastructure, cultural, and natural resources, and a strong sense of environmental awareness. The 2017 Index makes clear that Vietnam demonstrates a rich cultural history. However, without the will to promote and strengthen it, their tourist industry will not grow at the rate of competing global competitors.

## References

Attwooll, J. (2015, July 14). 17 reasons why France is so popular. Retrieved from http://www.tele graph.co.uk/travel/destinations/europe/france/11062807/17-reasons-why-France-is-so-popular. html

Crotti, R., & Misrahi, T. (2017). Part 1: The Travel & Tourism Competitiveness Index 2017. *The Travel and Tourism Competitiveness Report 2017*. Geneva: World Economic Forum.

Source: World Economic Forum, James Wollner and Ryuichi Karakawa.

# Conclusion

There is nothing more constant than change – this is truer today than it has ever been with change omnipresent in every corner of the world. Although much attention is often given to technological change, the myriad of external and internal forces discussed in this chapter are all contributing to the dynamism, and some would argue turbulence, in today's global environment. The speed of technological change is truly astounding with the year-on-year growth of social media alone contributing to significant changes in patterns of consumer, visitor, and tourist behavior. For future success in the tourism and hospitality industries, it is thus clear that organizations need to be better in anticipating, responding, and benefiting from change than ever before. The rise from almost nowhere of the sharing economy is the latest in a long line of technological advances that have changed the rules of engagement with the many protests and legal challenges evident around the world a defensive reaction perhaps to the inevitable rise of app-fueled sharing innovations that will contribute to an even more fast-changing, exciting, and diverse industry … and world at large.

In stark contrast to the positive forces of technological change, the apocalyptic forces apparent in the wider political environment continue to cause concern with the political instability in much of the world transforming travel patterns, travel routes, and brand reputations. As a reaction to global instability, the growth of "localism" poses an interesting question in that many markets in many countries are beginning to pursue more local delights and pursuits with the growth of authentic food and wine tourism and smaller, boutique-style hotels just two such trends impacting many destinations.

Driven in part by demographic change and in part by the age of austerity evident in many countries after the financial crisis of 2007–2008, levels of "affordability" and "changing priorities" will drive change with income inequality an economic policy challenge for many countries. Delayed retirements, declining pension pots, and the worrying emergence of the "working poor" will also impact on how people live and spend, especially in Western economies. At the same time, increasing sections of the population will have more knowledge and information than they've ever had before, thus begging the question is it the right knowledge and if so, how will it impact future patterns of behavior? Finally, and perhaps more than any other factor that has been discussed in this chapter, the continuous availability of resources to support our expanding, and varying, needs and wants will be put under extreme pressure, most notably with the continued growth in China and India, albeit slightly slower than has previously been the case, and the insatiable appetite for … tourism and hospitality.

## REVIEW QUESTIONS

1.  How will a greater understanding of the external and internal environments impact on the day-to-day running of a small-, medium- and large-scale hotel?

2.  Climate change and demographic change are two of the biggest forces for change in the external environment. How may they both impact on future patterns of domestic and international leisure travel in the next decade?

3.  The Internet has changed dramatically since its launch in tourism and hospitality in the mid-1990s. How do you think it is likely to shape the way tourism and hospitality organizations operate in the next five-to-ten years and what may be the consequences, positive or negative, for the consumer?

4.  Crises and disasters have a mix of impacts, both short and long term for all kinds of tourist destinations around the world. For one of your favorite destinations, either domestic or international, how do you think its performance has been impacted over the past 20 years by crises and disasters?

## YOUTUBE LINKS

### *"World travel market global trends report 2015"*

URL: https://youtu.be/kkplbmMdqyQ

Summary: For ten consecutive years, the World Travel Mart Global Trends Report by Euromonitor International has been at the forefront of accurately predicting major travel trends around the world, looking at how the travel industry is developing in a rapidly changing landscape. The Global Travel Trends Report offers an insight into to the size and shape of travel and tourism and identifies pressing industry issues, emerging brands, destinations and demographics, growth categories and consumer trends. Analysis by Euromonitor International illustrates how the travel market is set to change and outlines the criteria for success.

### *"What do I need to know in order to understand tourism legislation?"*

URL: https://youtu.be/SFunQYmiuO4

Summary: Learn what tourism legislation is and what it encompasses, how it can affect you when creating and managing a tourism business, and how you can keep up to date with any changes in legislation.

### *"Millennials are the new face of travel"*

URL: https://youtu.be/6FdC9jiiBII

Summary: There's a new travel trend on the horizon thanks to millennials. It's called experiential travel, going beyond the regular tourist attractions. Travelers choose to experience the city through culture, food, and nightlife. The trend is drawing 20-somethings to cities like Seattle, San Francisco, and Austin for unique nightlife and eats. So why the shift in the way to experience these popular cities and others? Travel expert Kendra Thornton explains.

## *"Brazil tourism serves as a bright spot amid current economic trouble"*

URL: https://youtu.be/7JXsk6VeZYA

Summary: Tourism is one sector that has aided in softening the blow of Brazil's economic troubles. With a plunge of the country's currency and the country's plans to host major sporting events, more foreign visitors are discovering Latin America's largest nation. CCTV's Lucrecia Franco reports from Rio de Janeiro.

## REFERENCES, FURTHER READING, AND RELATED WEBSITES

### References

Moutinho, L., Rate, S., & Ballantyne, R. (2013). In C. Costa, E. Panyik, & D. Buhalis (Eds.), *Trends in European tourism planning and organization* (pp. 313–325). Bristol: Channel View Publications.

Schewe, C.D., Debevec, K., Madden, T.J., Diamond, W.D., Parment, A., & Murphy, A. (2013). "If you've seen one, you've seen them all!" Are young millennials the same worldwide? *Journal of International Consumer Marketing, 25*(1), 3–15.

von Bergner, N.M., & Lohmann, M. (2014). The challenges for global tourism: A Delphi survey. *Journal of Travel Research, 53*(4), 420–432.

### Further reading

Amelung, B., Nicholls, S., & Viner, D. (2007). Implications of global climate change for tourism flows and seasonality. *Journal of Travel Research, 45*(3), 285–296.

Beirman, D. (2003). *Restoring tourism destinations in crisis: A strategic marketing approach.* Oxford: CABI Publishing.

Camilio, A., Presenza, A., & Di Virgilio, F. (2015). An analysis of the characteristics and dynamic development of an emergent sustainable hotel business model in Italy: "Albergo Diffuso." In A. Camilio (Ed.), *Handbook of research on global hospitality and tourism management (Advances in hospitality, tourism and the services)* (pp. 1–12). Hershey, PA: IGI Global.

Camilio, A. (2015). *Handbook of research on global hospitality and tourism management (Advances in hospitality, tourism and the services).* Hershey, PA: IGI Global.

Costa, C., & Buhalis, D. (2006). Conclusion: Tourism futures. In D. Buhalis & C. Costa (Eds.), *Tourism business frontiers: Consumers, products and industry* (pp. 241–246). Oxford: Elsevier Butterworth Heinemann,.

Dwyer, L. (2015). Globalization of tourism: Drivers and outcomes. *Tourism Recreation Research, 40*(3), 326–339.

Enz, C. (2010). Competitive dynamics and creating sustainable advantage. Retrieved from Cornell University, School of Hospitality Administration. http://scholarhsip.sha.cornell.edu/articles/349

Fyall, A., & Garrod, B. (2005). *Tourism marketing: A collaborative approach.* Clevedon: Channel View Publications.

Gössling, S., Scott, D., Hall, M., Ceron, J., & Dubois, G. (2012). Consumer behavior and demand responses of tourists to climate change. *Annals of Tourism Research, 39*(1), 36–58.

Hamzah, H., Karim, S., Camillo, A., & Holt, S. (2015). ISO 14001: The challenges in establishing environmental management systems in tourism and hospitality establishments. In A. Camilio (Ed.), *Handbook of research on global hospitality and tourism management (Advances in hospitality, tourism and the services)* (pp. 13–22). Hershey, PA: IGI Global.

Hudson, S. (2010). "Wooing zoomers: Marketing to the mature traveler." *Marketing Intelligence & Planning, 28*(4), 444–461.

Hudson, S., & Thai, K. (2013). The impact of social media on the consumer decision process: Implications for tourism marketing. *Journal of Travel and Tourism Marketing, 30*(1–2), 156–160.

Jones, P. (2006). Hospitality megatrends. In B. Buhalis & C. Costa (Eds.), *Tourism business frontiers: Consumers, products and industry* (pp. 191–199). Oxford: Elsevier Butterworth Heinemann,.

Porter, M. (1980). *Competitive strategy.* New York: The Free Press.

Ritchie, J.R.B., & Crouch, G. (2003). *The competitive destination: A sustainable tourism perspective.* Wallingford: CABI.

Ritchie, B., Molinar, A., & Frechtling, D.C. (2010). Impacts of the world recession and economic crisis on tourism: North America. *Journal of Travel Research, 49*(1), 5–15.

Saha, S., & Yap, G. (2014). The moderation effects of political instability and terrorism on tourism development. *Journal of Travel Research, 53*(4), 509–521.

Song, H., & Lin, S. (2010). Impacts of the financial crisis on tourism in Asia. *Journal of Travel Research, 49*(1), 16–30.

Yeoman, I., & Butterfield, S. (2011). In L. Yeoman, C.H.C. Hsu, K.A. Smith, & S. Watson (Eds.), *Tourism and demography* (pp. 1–22). Oxford: Goodfellow Publishers Limited.

Yeoman, I., Hsu, C.H.C., Smith, K.A. & Watson, S. (2011). *Tourism and demography.* Oxford: Goodfellow Publishers Limited.

## Websites

Euromonitor
http://www.euromonitor.com/

Global Trends
http://www.globaltrends.com/

Hospitalitynet
http://www.hospitalitynet.org

Organisation for Economic Co-operation and Development
http://www.oecd.org/

SKIFT
http://skift.com/

Tourism Futures
http://www.tourism-futures.org/

Travelmole
http://www.travelmole.com

United Nations World Tourism Organization
http://www2.unwto.org/

World Economic Forum
http://www.weforum.org/

World Health Organization
http://www.who.int/en/

World Travel & Tourism Council
http://www.wttc.org/

## MAJOR CASE STUDY
## TOURISM IN BRAZIL: DEVELOPING TOURISM IN A TURBULENT ENVIRONMENT

Brazil, once one of the fastest growing tourism segments in the hospitality and tourism industries, has fallen into a deep recession that is having global implications. According to the UNWTO's *Conference on Shopping Tourism* (2015), parts of the world, including many US and European destinations, are seeing a dramatic decrease in their international tourism receipts due to the lack of the once dependable spending habits of the Brazilian tourists. There are numerous macro-environmental factors that are directly contributing to Brazil's economic recession. In order to better understand these factors, it's important to first understand the very nature of Brazil's economy and how it contributes to global tourism.

The World Travel and Tourism Council (2015) notes that Brazil's recession is actually proving to be a driving force for Brazil's tourism industry, domestically. Brazil's tourism industry is relatively immature given that, until the last two decades, government and private industry leaders snubbed tourism as a major generator of revenue (Sobral et al., 2007). According to Sobral et al. (2007), Brazil's leaders, upon realizing the socio-economic benefits of tourism, have invested billions in infrastructure, marketing, and sustainability in order to highlight the cultural and ecological exuberance that it offers. Carnival, the Amazon Rainforest, São Paulo and Rio de Janeiro are just a few examples of Brazil's tourism attractors. Even though Brazil's recession is resulting in more tourists visiting the country. According to Travel Markets Insider (2016), Brazil's economy is so heavily dependent on the economic activity of its trade partners that any decreased economic activity abroad will have domestic economic impacts.

Brazil's economy is in a severe recession, having contracted by over 3% in the last six months, alone (Gillespie, 2015). The reason for this is that Brazil's economic stability relied so heavily on trade agreements with other emerging economies, most notably China. Brazil's key economic commodities included oil, sugar, coffee, and industrial metals, all of which have seen a dramatic decrease in demand and price (Gillespie, 2015). It's the common philosophy of supply and demand. Those commodities in high demand and a smaller supply have higher prices; whereas those with a low demand and a large supply have lower prices. Brazil has fallen victim to basic economics as the price of oil, alone, has fallen by more than 60% in the last year. China's economic contraction has also led to dramatic decreases in imports from Brazil and has contributed to fuel corruption between Brazil's major state-run oil company, Petrobas, and the Brazilian government (Gillespie, 2015).

As the economic output of Brazil sinks further into a recession, the value of their currency continues to plummet. According to economist Sean Snaith (2016), Brazil's currency has lost 57% of its value, when compared to the US dollar, in the last year alone. This decrease in value is resulting in both a decrease in Brazilian visitors to international destinations and spending albeit now cheaper for international tourists to visit Brazil. The WTTC (2015) predicts that Brazil will have fewer international departures in the coming year; however, their international arrivals will see an increase. This can, in part, be attributed to the 2016 Olympic Games in Rio in August 2016.

If economic problems were not causing enough problems, Brazil also has had to contend with public health issues due to the emergence, and rapid spread, of the Zika virus. Brazil is considered to be the "ground zero" for the Zika virus which is transmitted through the bite of a mosquito (WHO, 2016). One of the biggest impacts that this health concern could have is on the number of tourists generated by the Olympics in Rio de Janeiro. The biggest concern for Brazil in the near

**Image 2.3**

Source: Pexels.

future is likely to be public opinion of the way they handle and potentially contain the outbreak (Petroff, 2016).

Although the Brazilian recession is impacting many tourist destinations worldwide, it is of a particular concern to Florida in the United States. The impacts of the Brazilian recession are having a ripple effect, as it's not only the world's seventh largest economy, but it is also Florida's number one trade partner (Florida Chamber of Commerce, 2015). The import/export value of Central Florida's goods to Brazil alone total over $20 billion annually. As the Brazilian currency continues to lose its value due to continued decreased economic output at home, the cost of goods in Florida will become prohibitive for Brazilian travelers. According to the UNWTO's Conference on Shopping Tourism (2015), Brazilians' spending habits in tourist destinations make up sizable pieces of their overall international tourism revenues. Given the inability of the Brazilian tourists to travel to places like Florida, where they typically come to purchase vast amounts of consumer goods at deeply discounted prices, international and local economies abroad are going to soon feel the impacts of the Brazilian recession.

Brazil's dependency on emerging markets to grow its economy was nothing short of a gamble. In addition, it relied too heavily on a few commodities to generate its economic growth. The consequences of Brazil's deepening recession will be felt worldwide, especially in those markets that rely so heavily on Brazilian tourists' spending. As the real continues to devalue, fewer and fewer Brazilians will leave their country to travel, as it will ultimately become too expensive. The Brazilian recession began from a ripple from China's decreased economic activity. Now it's creating its own ripples that will be felt in tourism destinations all over the world.

## References

Florida Chamber of Commerce. (2015). About the Florida-Brazil partnership: Florida chamber leading effort to expand Florida's trade relationship with Brazil. Retrieved from http://www.flchamber.com/brazil/about-the-florida-brazil-partnership/

Gillespie, P. (2015, Aug 28). Brazil falls deep into recession. Retrieved from http://money.cnn.com/2015/08/28/news/economy/brazil-recession/

Petroff, A. (2016, Jan 28). Zika virus: The last thing Brazil's economy needs right now. Retrieved from http://money.cnn.com/2016/01/28/news/economy/zika-virus-brazil-economy/

Snaith, S. (2016, Jan 29). Sean Snaith: Economy is approaching the next recession. Retrieved from http://www.bizjournals.com/orlando/blog/2016/01/sean-snaith-economy-is-approaching-the-next.html

Sobral, F., Peci, A., & Souza, G. (2007). An analysis of the dynamics of the tourism industry in Brazil: Challenges and recommendations. *International Journal of Contemporary Hospitality Management, 19*(6), 507–512.

UNWTO. (2015). Global report on shopping tourism. Retrieved from http://dtxtq4w60xqpw.cloudfront.net/sites/all/files/pdf/am9-shopping-report_v2.pdf

WHO. (2016). Zika virus. Retrieved from http://www.who.int/mediacentre/factsheets/zika/en/

WTTC. (2015). Travel and tourism economic impact 2015: Brazil. Retrieved from https://www.wttc. org/-/media/files/reports/economic%20impact%20research/countries%202015/brazil2015.pdf

Source: James Wollner.

Major case study questions

1. Why is Brazil such an important inbound and outbound destination in South America?
2. What are the consequences for inbound and outbound tourism of a weak Brazilian currency as compared to the US $?
3. What emerging inbound markets are likely to prove most popular for tourism to Brazil?
4. What is the impact of the recent mega-events held in Brazil in the context of inbound and outbound international tourism?

# 3 Collaboration, technology, and experiences

## Drivers for change in the marketing of tourism and hospitality

<table>
<tr><td>

### Learning outcomes

By the end of this chapter, students will:

- Understand collaboration, those forces driving its growth, and its relevance to and impact on the marketing of tourism and hospitality
- Be cognizant of the emergence of technology and its dynamic role in the marketing of tourism and hospitality
- Be introduced to consumer experiences, co-creation, and the experience and sharing economies
- Understand how collaboration, technology, and experiences are significant drivers for change in the marketing of tourism and hospitality

</td><td>

### Key terms

collaboration,
technology,
experiences,
co-creation,
sharing
economy

</td></tr>
</table>

## Introduction

The previous chapters introduced the historical development of marketing to the present day with three key forces for change driving the current marketing agenda for tourism and hospitality, namely: collaboration; technology; experiences. Since the mid-to-late 1990s, collaboration has been commonplace across many different industries as organizations have struggled individually to cope with the forces at play in the wider environment (see Chapter 2) in order to create customer and consumer value. For many in tourism and hospitality, collaboration is widely viewed as a strategic necessity with both industries characterized by interdependence, a large number of very small players, and fragmentation of markets. Tourism is particularly complex in its dynamics and networks with changing political, social, and economic forces incentivizing collaborative approaches to marketing. As with all industries, however, tourism and hospitality are highly competitive industries so a key question for all organizations is when it is most appropriate to adopt collaborative and/or competitive strategies to seek a competitive advantage in the marketplace? Similarly, the exponential growth in technology both generally and specific to the tourism and hospitality industry has perhaps been the greatest single disruptor over the past two decades. Not only has it changed the way in which we consume products and services (demand side) but it has fundamentally changed the way in which those products, services, and now experiences are put together in the first instance (supply side). This latter point is important in introducing the domain of tourism and hospitality "experiences" and the means by which the industry and its customers, clients, and on occasions resident communities co-create the tourism experience!

Each of the three pillars of this book will now be considered in turn. First, the following section defines what we actually mean by collaboration generally and collaboration in the context of tourism and hospitality.

## Collaboration

### Defining collaboration

Collaboration in a generic sense is defined as "when a group of autonomous stakeholders of a problem domain engage in an interactive process, using shared rules, norms, and structures, to act or decide on issues related to that domain" (Wood & Gray, 1991, p.146). It is thus clear that collaboration is built on a few guiding principles. First, collaboration takes place among autonomous or independently-owned organizations. Degrees of autonomy will vary depending on the strategy being implemented but it is important to stress that collaboration is built on independent organizations working together to achieve a common goal. Second, although independent and with often differing views on some issues, organizations that collaborate believe in working together and the joint decision-making process that it entails. Third, as with any process of joint working, interaction is important with collaboration normally an iterative process whereby consensus is eventually achieved for the pursuit of the common good. Fourth, some governance is required for collaboration to succeed in the form of rules, norms, and governance structures. For the most part, such governance is temporary as collaboration is frequently a short-to-mid-term strategy for the achievement of the fifth and final component, that of the achievement of a common goal.

One of the common problems in understanding collaboration in tourism and hospitality is that so many different terms are used for what is essentially the same thing that is collaboration. For example, co-ordination, co-operation, partnerships, alliances, and joint ventures are all terms commonly used to describe collaboration with many such terms taking on context-specific meaning. Hence, while the airline industry talks about "alliances," restaurants and hotels refer to "consortia" with tourist destinations more often than not using the term "partnership." Irrespective of the term used, there are, however, five key characteristics of the collaboration process:

- Stakeholders are independent;
- Solutions emerge by dealing constructively with differences;
- Joint ownership of decisions is involved;
- The stakeholders assume collective responsibility for the ongoing direction of the domain;
- Collaboration is an emergent process.

By adopting a collaborative approach, organizations are seeking to achieve something that is impossible for them to achieve on their own. This is referred to as "collaborative advantage" where the joint outcomes of collaboration deliver more than what would have been achieved individually. In both tourism and hospitality, the scope for achieving collaborative advantage can be considerable as evidenced in Tourism and hospitality insights 3.1 below on the SkyTeam Global Airline Alliance.

## TOURISM AND HOSPITALITY INSIGHTS 3.1
## SKYTEAM ALLIANCE

There are three mega airline alliances, namely Star Alliance, Oneworld, and SkyTeam, that together control more than 50% of global air capacity and generate more than $380 billion in revenue annually (Airways, 2016). Since SkyTeam Airline Alliance, one of these alliances, was established in June 2001 by four member airlines (Aeromexico, Air France, Delta Airlines, and Korean Air), the number of member airlines has gradually increased to 20. Today, SkyTeam provides travelers with access to 1,074 destinations in 177 countries, operates 16,609 flights daily and carries 730 million passengers annually.

Consistent with their slogan of "Caring More About You," SkyTeam offers several benefits to their travelers by utilizing their huge network. The most significant benefit for travelers is seamless connections. Thanks to SkyTeam's extensive network, their travelers can experience efficient, comfortable, and seamless transfers through their alliance's hubs; their customers can check in for all their flights at once with their baggage checked through to their final destinations. Furthermore, their customers can experience the alliance's joint services and facilities, such as lounges and self-service kiosks (SkyTeam, 2018). In addition, their frequent flyer program is very beneficial to their customers. Signing up for any one of SkyTeam's airline members' frequent flyer programs enables customers to earn and redeem miles from all 20 member airlines. Furthermore, as customers fly more with SkyTeam's member airlines, they can level up in SkyTeam status, thereby obtaining additional benefits, such as priority check-in, preferred seating, and lounge access.

The collaborative alliance not only offers benefits to customers, but it also provides several advantages for airlines. The critical motivation for airlines to join the alliance is access to Sky-Team's huge networks in the global market, as noted above. Once airlines join the alliance, they can increase market reach through alliance partnerships, such as a code-sharing agreement, and airlines can strengthen their brands by gaining exposure in new markets. On top of that, they can enjoy cost savings by sharing airport spaces with other SkyTeam airline members. Through co-location, they can optimize the utilization of their resources, including check-in and ticketing areas, lounge facilities, and even ground handling staff, which consequently leads to significantly reduced costs.

Since their establishment on June 22, 2000, SkyTeam has evolved their services as well as the size of their global network. One example is SkyPriority, which was introduced in 2012 and was the first aligned priority program offered by alliances. Through SkyPriority, SkyTeam provides branded priority benefits, from priority check-in to priority baggage handling, across their global network, in order to make traveling smoother for SkyTeam Elite Plus, First and Business customers. Clearly, an airline will reach more customers, be able to take them to more destinations, and provide them with better services if they are a member of a collaborative alliance, such as SkyTeam.

**References**

Airways. (2016, Apr 8). *The global airline alliances are outdated*. Retrieved from https://airways mag.com/industry/global-airline-alliances-outdated/

SkyTeam. (2018). *Accruing miles across our members is seamless*. Retrieved from https://www.sky team.com/en/frequent-flyers/

SkyTeam. (2018). *A history of excellence*. Retrieved from https://www.skyteam.com/en/about/ history/

SkyTeam. (2018). *SkyTeam airline alliance*. Retrieved from https://www.skyteam.com/en/about/

SkyTeam. (2018). *SkyTeam airline member benefits*. Retrieved from https://static.skyteam.com//con tentapi/globalassets/about-us/pdf/st-14-ff_member-benefits_may.pdf?_ga=2.200749801. 655084096.1524955900-544845747.1524955900

SkyTeam. (2018). *SkyPriority – the world leader in priority services*. Retrieved from https://www.sky team.com/en/skypriority/

SkyTeam. (2018). *Transfers*. Retrieved from https://www.skyteam.com/en/flights-and-destinations/ transfers/

Source: Ryuichi Karakawa.

## Forces driving collaboration

While many of those forces for change in the wider environment, as outlined in Chapter 2, are relevant in explaining the growing role played by collaboration over the past two decades in the marketing of tourism and hospitality, a few particular drivers are worthy of specific mention. First, the continuing competitive nature of global markets indicates that collaboration between organizations, especially smaller ones, will continue to expand. One could argue, in fact, that we already live in a globalized, connected, and collaborative society that is helping to shape the world we live in. With the presence of global trade deals, numerous global networks and political institutions, and distribution channels spanning the globe it appears that both competition and collaboration between organizations is in fact required to survive and grow in what has become a challenging and uncertain world.

With so many advances in information technology, communication methods, and distribution systems in recent years, the ability to go-it-alone has become harder and harder with the need for organizational flexibility critical in adapting to the various advances at play. In the future, it is in fact believed that organizations will no longer only be judged on the quality of their concepts and competencies, but also on their "connections" which relate to their collaborative networks, that is, the alliances and relationships that lever core capabilities, create value for customers, and remove boundaries.

It is interesting to note, however, that in some parts of the tourism and hospitality industry, there is in fact a growing trend toward consolidation and concentration in the global economy.

## Theories of collaboration

So, what are the theories that best explain the existence of collaboration as a strategy for growth? The first explanation is that of "resource dependency" whereby one organization is in need of the resource endowments of others to succeed. Without access to these resource endowments, individual organizations will struggle with their future being impeded. As such, resource dependency suggests that organizations try to reduce external pressures by gaining access to critical resources through collaboration rather than spending much time and money in developing such resources themselves. For many organizations, this may in fact represent a "second-best" strategy as you are in fact balancing the loss of autonomy involved in the collaboration process with the opportunity to gain access to critical resources. A more positive approach to collaboration is that of "relational exchange" whereby "mutual dependency" takes over as many organizations feel more comfortable working together to achieve a common goal rather than going it alone. In this instance, organizations acknowledge and accept the interdependence of the challenges they face and the benefits to be gained from collaborating through reciprocal relationships. Although "self-interest" still exists, unlike resource dependency, relational exchange approaches to collaboration are driven by organizations that believe that their self-interest is best served by the adoption of joint, collaborative working strategies built on trust and commitment. The final explanation for collaboration is that of "transaction cost" theory whereby the actual cost of conducting business is reduced if undertaken in a collaborative manner.

Although a complex issue, the three theories of collaboration above all are premised on the fact that the environment is complex, fragmented and turbulent with it being increasingly difficult for organizations to act independently in achieving desired outcomes. Where the three differ in their explanation is how they distinguish between organizations responding to the challenge. Hence, whereas resource dependency theory views the reaction as one of organizations attempting to achieve "competitive advantage" by accessing resources that lie out of their individual control, relational exchange theory views the reaction as principally one of recognizing the mutual advantages to be gained through collaboration, that is, "collaborative advantage." Finally, transaction cost theory depicts collaboration as being a rational response to the need to control the growth of transaction costs under such conditions.

## Motives for collaboration

Motivations for collaborating vary by organization, although across the tourism and hospitality industry collaboration has predominantly been driven by product or market-related factors. In the latter case, typical motivations include the need to build an expanded customer base, access to new and/or more distant markets, the need to protect existing markets and motivations relating to market research (Fyall & Garrod, 2005). Product-related motivations, meanwhile, include the need to fill gaps in the current product line, to broaden the product portfolio or to differentiate or add value to existing products. Motivations may also include a mix of product-market motives, motives related to market structure as in the need to reduce the potential threat of future competition, or market-entry timing related motives. Finally, motives may be driven by the need to use resources more efficiently, to reduce levels of risk and/or to enhance skill levels more broadly (Beverland & Brotherton, 2001).

With specific regard to the increasing presence of collaboration in tourism and hospitality, a number of explanations are offered. The complex, composite, and fragmented nature of the tourism system contribute their part with turbulence in the wider market environment including the need for many to collaborate to counter the threat, as well as leverage benefit, from the exponential growth and reach of technology in travel, tourism and hospitality more broadly adding to the need for collaborative strategies. Collaboration is never easy, however, with the mix of public- and private-sector organizations integral to successful collaborative efforts. Needless to say, their varying cultures, budgets, strategic imperatives, and timescales often clash making effective collaboration very difficult to achieve. That being said, the opportunities that collaboration can bring are significant with the effort necessary to succeed justifiable in most cases.

## Types of collaboration

When thinking of collaboration, clearly one of the most important questions for organizations to consider are what type of collaboration is most suited to their particular situation? With regard to type, collaboration can be "horizontal" whereby collaboration takes place between organizations at the same channel level (i.e. direct competition), "vertical" whereby collaboration takes place between suppliers of a product and its buyers, or "diagonal" which is collaboration between organizations in different sectors or industries. Similarly, collaboration can be "short-term" and opportunistic with a strictly limited focus, "medium-term" and tactical with a strong sense of self-protection, or "long-term" which involve continuity and a high degree of commitment. One of the most useful means of classifying collaboration types is that advanced by Terpstra and Simonin (1993) who introduce "coverage," "mode," and "form" in addition to "motive." While "coverage" refers to the extensiveness of the collaboration in terms of the markets, marketing functions, or geographical areas with which it is concerned, "form" relates to a collaboration's constitutional characteristics with governance structures and governance styles integral to collaboration effectiveness. Finally, the "mode" of collaboration refers to the intrinsic nature of the relationship among the members involved with these relationships being of a personal and cultural nature.

## Stages of collaboration

In addition to being aware of the types of collaboration available, the stages of the collaboration process are also worth knowing as success is seldom instant. Most forms of collaboration start with "problem-setting" whereby key stakeholders are identified before then attaining a common understanding of the key issues that need to be, and can be, addressed through a process of collaboration. "Direction setting" then follows whereby stakeholders identify and share their individual values and goals before identifying their ambitions and desired outcomes from collaboration. It is at this stage that a sense of coming together is developed among the stakeholders. Finally, there is "implementation" whereby the collaborating stakeholders institutionalize their common agenda and put in place structures and processes to achieve their desired collaborative goals with specific goals set out and tasks assigned to particular members. One additional stage, albeit one that is not widely discussed, is that of "after life." Collaboration is temporary, as outlined in the beginning of this chapter, so clearly knowing what happens when the collaboration has achieved its outcomes is critical. In her study on tourist destinations Caffyn (2000) identified a number of so-called "after-life" options. For example, while some may terminate completely with "mission accomplished," others may continue albeit in a different form with a slightly different purpose. Others may morph into other larger collaborative groupings while others may in fact splinter into smaller, leaner and more region-specific forms of collaboration. Collaboration could, in fact, continue in a more permanent form, for example as a limited company or a trust, while, in other cases, local residents, business or third-party organizations may take over the collaboration.

## Collaboration performance and effectiveness

Two of the biggest challenges for those involved in collaboration in any shape or form are collaboration performance and effectiveness. Owing to multiple stakeholders being involved and success heavily influenced by so many internal and external factors, consensus on performance and effectiveness is hard to find. However, a combination of the following will certainly help:

- Involvement of key stakeholders;
- Good interpersonal relationships and development of trust between stakeholders;
- Recognition of individual and/or mutual benefits to be derived from the process;
- Recognition of a high degree of interdependence in planning and management;
- Inclusive organizational culture and management style;
- Goal (outcome) compatibility among stakeholders;
- Well-planned and well-balanced project;
- Facilitative contractual conditions;
- Previous positive relationships among stakeholders;
- Decisive convenor, leadership;
- High potential payoff relative to cost;
- Balance of management resources and power;
- Carefully chosen partners;
- A perception that decisions arrived at will be implemented.

Although all of the above would be ideal, if the collaboration is clear vis-à-vis scope, intensity, and the degree to which consensus emerges among participants, then collaborative success ought to occur.

# Technology

Technological advances have always been a catalyst for industry change. From Eli Whitney's cotton gin to today's virtual reality revolution, technological advances transform the world. Technology never stops moving forward; in the last 20 years, it has infinitely changed the hospitality and tourism industry. Traditionally speaking, advances in technology are often good for both innovative businesses and most consumers. This continues to hold true for businesses which have been able to forecast and capitalize on these most recent rapid changes. However, the recent explosion in the way we use the Internet, its speed, and the relative ease of access to it on a global scale, has widely contributed to making consumers smarter than ever. For that reason, this section will look at several instances in the tourism and hospitality industry where technological advancements have benefited (and in some cases hampered) both business and consumers while also providing a historical context to technology in the industry.

## *Destination distribution channels and the World Wide Web*

According to Kracht and Wang, a *tourism distribution channel* is, "A system of intermediaries, or middlemen that facilitates the sale and delivery of tourism services from suppliers to consumers" (2011, p. 165). Only 25 years ago, destinations were marketed to consumers via the traditional travel agencies and tour operators. Before the Internet web browser was launched, major hotel chains desired to eliminate the intermediary travel agencies by opening their own retail shops and call centers; this would allow them to sell directly to the consumer. The industry-changing moment came in 1993, when the World Wide Web was launched to the public. At this point, tech-savvy destinations could develop their own websites to reach consumers, making it more realistic than ever to bypass intermediaries.

The independence from intermediaries was still in its infancy when a new middleman would emerge; search engines became the new bridge between consumer and supplier. The search engine was not the only new layer to enter the equation. While traditional brick and mortar travel agencies were being dissolved, online travel agencies began to emerge. Some of the giants that you would still recognize today like Priceline, Expedia, and Travelocity were among the early pioneers. These companies, individually, possessed unique core competencies. Finally, one last player has penetrated the intermediary market in the last several years; metasearch engines not only provide prices from suppliers, they also collect, analyze, and distribute offered pricing by all other intermediaries. This presumably provides value-seeking consumers with a wealth of knowledge to help make purchase decisions. Some of the best-known intermediaries of this variety are SkyScanner and Kayak (see Tourism and hospitality insights 3.2).

## TOURISM AND HOSPITALITY INSIGHTS 3.2
## KAYAK.COM

Kayak is one of the world's leading travel metasearch companies. Kayak offers a leading metasearch service, allowing travelers to conveniently find the best itineraries and prices from hundreds of travel websites at once, including airline tickets, accommodation, rental car services, and vacation packages (Booking Holdings, 2018). In addition to Kayak.com, Kayak manages a portfolio of several metasearch brands: momondo, Cheapflights, Swoodoo, Checkfelix, and Mundi (Kayak, 2018). Kayak now offers services in more than 20 languages in over 60 countries, with the United States as its largest market, processing more than 2 billion consumer queries per year. In 2012, Kayak officially went public, raising $91 million in an IPO (Bloomberg Technology, 2012). The following year, Kayak was acquired by Booking Holdings Inc, the world leader in online travel-related services, but it is still managed independently as a subsidiary of Booking Holdings Inc. In just over ten years, since its establishment in 2004, Kayak has developed into one of the most successful travel metasearch companies in the global market. Their success can be boiled down to three key elements. The first is their business model. Steve Hafner, a founder of Kayak, recognized the elasticity of travelers after working as executive vice president at Orbitz, realizing that only a small percentage of users had actually booked through their website, usually bypassing the transaction fees charged by Orbitz and buying directly from airline and hotel companies (Fast Company, 2008). Therefore, instead of charging customers the transaction fees, Kayak made a cost-per-click model that started selling hotel reservations and flights on Kayak.com and earning commission from suppliers (Forbes, 2016). Another key element to their success was their acquisition of competitors. Kayak acquired Sidestep, a rival travel search company in 2007 and completely migrated Sidestep. com traffic to Kayak.com in 2011, which consequently increased Kayak's scale and improved its search algorithms (Kayak, 2011). Kayak started international expansion by acquiring Swoodoo, a German travel search engine, in 2010 and JaBo software, which operated Checkfelix, a travel search engine in Austria, in 2011 (Tech Crunch, 2010; Tnooz, 2011). The largest recent acquisition was Momondo Groups, which includes Momondo and Cheapflights, two metasearch brands that have strong market presence in the UK, the Nordics, and Russia (Skift, 2017).

The most important reason for their incredible growth is that Kayak has innovated their services in the travel metasearch industry by pursuing their mission: "to help people experience the world by creating their favorite travel tools" (Kayak, 2018). Unlike other travel metasearch sites, Kayak launched the kayak booking path in 2011 in order to improve user experience; users no longer had to leave Kayak's platform and could book directly from Kayak.com (Skift, 2012). In 2013, Kayak added a fare forecast function to its flight search results, such that users would be able to see price predictions, whether the fare would rise or fall, and its confidence level (Skift, 2013). Kayak's most recent innovative service is a voice-powered hotel booking service that allows customers to book hotels via Amazon's smart speakers (Skift, 2017). In the current highly competitive travel metasearch industry with aggressive rivals, including Tripadvisor, Trivago, Skyscanner, and Google, Kayak will keep innovating their business.

## References

Bloomberg Technology. (2012, Jul 19). *Kayak software raises $91 million, prices IPO above range.* Retrieved from https://www.bloomberg.com/news/articles/2012-07-19/kayak-software-raises-91-million-prices-ipo-above-range

Booking Holdings. (2018). *2017 annual report.* Retrieved from http://ir.bookingholdings.com/static-files/d0dcbba1-c150-4a1f-9d1b-858cbfc8180a

Fast Company. (2008, Sep 1). *The success of Kayak.com.* Retrieved from https://www.fastcompany.com/958590/success-kayakcom

Forbes. (2016, Jul 5). *He cofounded Kayak, sold it for $2 billion, and is back with Lola, which uses human travel agents.* Retrieved from https://www.forbes.com/sites/forbestreptalks/2016/07/05/he-cofounded-kayak-sold-it-for-2-billion-and-is-back-with-lola-which-uses-human-travel-agents/#43ba9b231e42

Kayak. (2011). *SideStep integration with Kayak.* Retrieved from https://www.kayak.com/news/sidestep-integration-kayak/

Kayak. (2018). *About Kayak.* Retrieved from https://www.kayak.com/about

Skift. (2012, Aug 22). *Kayak steps beyond metasearch and into direct bookings.* Retrieved from https://skift.com/2012/08/22/kayak-expands-direct-booking-with-expedia-hertz-avisbudget-and-getaroom/

Skift. (2013, Jan 15). *Kayak adds fare forecasts to flight results, tells you if you should buy now or wait.* Retrieved from https://skift.com/2013/01/15/kayak-adds-fare-forecasts-to-flight-results/

Skift. (2017, Feb 7). *Pliceline buys Momondo for $550 million to expand in Europe*. Retrieved from https://skift.com/2017/02/07/priceline-buys-momondo-for-550-million-to-expand-in-europe/

Skift. (2017, Jul 11). *Kayak and Amazon Echo now offer voice powered hotel booking*. Retrieved from https://skift.com/2017/07/11/kayak-and-amazon-alexa-now-offer-voice-powered-hotel-booking/

Tech Crunch. (2010, May 6). *Kayak swoops on German travel search engine Swoodoo*. Retrieved from https://techcrunch.com/2010/05/06/kayak-swoops-on-german-travel-search-engine-swoodoo/

Tnooz. (2011, Apr 5). *Kayak buys Austrian travel search engine Checkfelix*. Retrieved from https://www.tnooz.com/article/kayak-buys-austrian-travel-search-engine-checkfelix/

Source: Ryuichi Karakawa.

Not all consumers accept or adapt to new technology the same way. For some, the learning curve is too great to initially comprehend. This may be because they have already fallen behind with previous advances that have now led to the current one. In 2010, those who still did not have an email address or own a PC were surely less likely to purchase a smart phone. Meanwhile, some consumers reject new advances because they are content with the status quo. They may initially view the new technology as unnecessary and perhaps even nonsensical, perhaps underestimating its ultimate value in society. Then, there are the traditionalist consumers. These consumers tend to believe that things were "better how they used to be." For example, since professional sports have adopted "replay review" technology, games, though they may take longer, have been made much more accurately officiated. Still, despite the obvious advantages to the system, traditionalists will likely continue to be the biggest opponents to this technology. While many may resist or adapt to advancements slower than others, there will always be forward-thinking individuals who fully embrace the progressions. These buyers/users often have the advantage of educating themselves long before other consumer segments and thus reap some of the greatest benefits of the new technology.

Reaction to the World Wide Web and its ensuing changes to distribution channels in the tourism and hospitality industry were no different. While there was obviously a large learning curve for many, a great number of people began seeing the advantages the Internet brought to travel. With the expansion of the World Wide Web came the growth of consumer options. Whereas before brick and mortar agencies may have been pushing few destinations that best suited their business, the Internet let the potential purchaser see the world's vastness. However, with a great expansion of travel options, comes a more time-consuming search. Before, choosing between the Bahamas and the Dominican Republic at a travel agency, may not have been such an arduous task. Suddenly, choosing where to visit out of 26 Caribbean countries can become a major process. This led the way to some of the intermediaries we see today that help facilitate this process more easily compared to the early days of the Internet. As you can imagine, all of these options and newly opened doors would go on to change the entire landscape of travel in terms of anthropological needs, psychological needs, and business models.

As the world opened up for many previously green travelers, destination management organizations (DMOs) and developing tourism markets began tapping into consumer segments they were previously unable to penetrate. Countries longing for a piece of the tourism market share finally saw their chance. However, many of these struggling and developing nations still saw themselves at a disadvantage. More developed countries and larger international companies are naturally better suited to quickly adopt technological change. For example, Marriott's financial situation and ability to attract top of the line talent in emerging fields like website development and SEO, assuredly proved to be a competitive advantage over the 12 room Oasis Marigot in St. Lucia. Still, lesser known destinations and smaller lodging options capitalized on the Internet boom. For example, in 1998, Morocco welcomed 3.2 million tourists (UNWTO, 1999). Just 16 years later, that number has spiked to almost 10.3 million visitors to the African kingdom (UNWTO, 2016). Managing the demand for an increase in tourism opens up many new collaborative business opportunities between locals, multinational corporations, and governments. For example, in order for 7 million more people from around the globe to visit one area, transportation networks and alliances need to be formed, lodging infrastructure needs to be built, and experience based businesses need to be created. The exponential growth in tourism can in large part be accredited to the World Wide Web, but that was just the first stage of major technological change.

## Tourism and Web 2.0

In the past, suppliers were the feeders of information to the consumers. Without today's technology, consumers were forced to weigh out the trustworthiness of companies who were bound to be naturally biased in order to further their specific business agenda. To help alleviate these biases, an entire industry of what amounts to "reviewers" was born; you may be familiar with Frommer's, Fodor's, Michelin, or Lonely Planet. Before the origination of Web 2.0, consumers enjoyed the literature provided by these intermediaries, developing their destination itineraries based on the reviews. However, in time, many of these intermediaries' credibility came into question. Consumers began to consider the very real possibility of quid pro quo. For example, O'Connor et al. (2011) describe the instance of a restaurant in Brussels, which had yet to open, but already received a Michelin star. It is conceivable that a restaurant, airport, attraction, or even destination, could exchange money or other favors in return for a great review in globally recognized literature. As consumers once again began to lose faith in the medium delivering the message, they decided to turn to one another for travel recommendations. Today, consumers trust the reviews of their peers more so than traditional marketing channels. Web 2.0 can be defined as, "A new generation of Internet-based technology (sites, applications, services and processes) that allow people to collaborate and share information in ways that were previously unimaginable" (O'Connor et al., 2011, p. 227). It is this emergence of this second generation of Internet advancement that has led to *P2P Marketing* and review sharing that we know today. Web 2.0 has made it difficult for companies to formulate strategies that are able to persuade buyers.

The advent of Web 2.0 has also contributed to the rapid reduction of mass travel. The plethora of information provided by peers enables travelers to delve into particular itinerary details that best fit their wants and demands. Conventional tour guides cannot handle the extremely diverse desires of today's tourist. Therefore, prospective travelers will continue to rely on reviews from likeminded consumers who have had experiences similar to what the potential buyer seeks. In short, P2P marketing allows individuals to comfortably fit into very narrow homogeneous market segments. Originally, marketers heavily pondered ways to reestablish credibility in the Web 2.0 era and how to disseminate information to consumers on these new social network platforms. However, companies soon understood the true value in Web 2.0 was in marketing intelligence. Past accumulation of research data was very costly and time consuming. Marketers would have to set up focus groups, design questionnaires, conduct phone interviews, rely on receipt responses, and other forms of traditional collecting methods. Now, they often need to look no further than social network forums to receive the most candid customer opinions. Full social network discussions take the place of a six-person focus group without the cost associated with said group. Of course, this vital information allows businesses to formulate new strategies and make consumer driven adjustments to features and quality of their products and services.

**Image 3.1**

Source: Pexels.

## Tourism and big data

Much of this research accumulation may not be possible without the last stage of Internet development, big data analytics. *Big data* "refers to the ever-increasing volume, velocity, variety, variability and complexity of information. For marketing organizations, big data is the fundamental consequence of the new marketing landscape, born from the digital world we now live in" (SAS Institute, 2017). This data, as previously stated, can drive new strategies and product improvements. Another benefit of big data is their ability to establish deeper customer relationships and extend the customer lifecycle. Buying patterns, locational movements, and purchasing behavior can all be tracked at an unparalleled rate. Some challenges with big data are still being dealt with. The word "big" does not really do the amount of data available justice. Therefore, figuring out which data to use can be a burdening task. Though it can be a heavy workload, choosing the right information is imperative; quality over quantity is certainly applicable for marketers in big data.

Tourism in particular is a major beneficiary of big data. Tracking flight searches, lodging history, and destination inquiries, allows DMOs to discover insights never before imagined. DMOs also have the benefit of using posted pictures to segment their markets. For example, a company responsible for attracting people to the Swiss Alps could choose to bypass social media users who only post photos of holidays on white-sand beaches in the Caribbean. On the other hand, an Italian DMO may find it prudent to track Americans who regularly check into "Little Italy" boroughs across the United States. For tourism to fully engage in big data analytics, they should consider focusing on *holistic integrated marketing*. Liu and Song write, "With the vigorous growth of the amount and applications of big data, traditional tourism data and methods are going to be interfacing with the novel data and methodologies: for example, call centers are going to be interfacing with online consumer reviews; loyalty programs are going to be linking with booking histories; and "property preferences" are going to be combined with social media chatter" (2017, p. 20). Moving forward, the hospitality and tourism industry will garner a deeper understanding of big data, ultimately using it to make faster, cheaper, and more targeted decisions.

## TOURISM AND HOSPITALITY INSIGHTS 3.3
## BIG DATA IN TOURISM AND HOSPITALITY – MASTERCARD

Big data is becoming one of the most frequently-used buzzwords in today's tourism industry. Given its robust characteristics, volume (amount of data), velocity (speed of data), and variety (variety of data types and sources), big data provides valuable insights for practitioners' decision-making processes by allowing them to track and analyze consumer behaviors, such as transaction, purchasing patterns and recommendations (Song & Liu, 2017). In addition to benefiting businesses, big data can provide better targeted services and products to travelers through personalized marketing and targeted product designs (Pries & Dunnigan, 2015).

However, there are several challenges for businesses and DMOs regarding the utilization of big data: identifying the right data, interpreting the data to find meaningful insights, aggregating and managing it, and maintaining its security (Song & Liu, 2017). In order to overcome these obstacles and leverage big data to drive tourism revenue, Mastercard, a technology company in the global payments industry, provides one of the leading services: Mastercard Tourism Insights. With the vast transaction data (more than 160 million transactions per hour from more than 210 countries and territories), sophisticated data analytics and expertise, Mastercard Tourism Insights affords practitioners the following valuable information: a 360° view of travel cycles (pre- to post-trip), as well as aggregated and timely insights. With insight on pre- to post-trips, practitioners can gain a better understanding of travelers' plans, interests, and preferences, such that practitioners can wisely invest in channel marketing (Mastercard, 2017). Provided with all the aggregated and anonymized spending data coupled with social sharing, perceptions, sentiments and experiences, practitioners no longer have to deal with irrelevant data. On top of that, unlike static reports and surveys that can soon become outdated, Mastercard Tourism Insights provides timely data, in such a way that practitioners can stay on top of changeable market trends and travelers' preferences. Through these valuable insights, Mastercard helps tourism practitioners gain market share as well as enhance travelers' experience.

**Image 3.2**

Source: https://www.pexels.com/photo/coding-computer-data-depth-of-field-577585/.

Mastercard has been working with a number of cities, including London, Singapore, and Mexico City. With international tourism representing a significant source of income and jobs for these cities, data and insights derived from Mastercard Tourism Insights help tourism practitioners better understand the kinds of experiences their travelers are looking for. Mastercard Tourism Insights's most recent project is the Smart Dublin program (SmartCitiesWorld, n.d.). In this project, Mastercard, through a partnership with Dublin City Council, explores spending and tourism patterns, through aggregated and anonymized transaction data, in order to help the city understand the spending patterns of tourists for their future marketing strategies (SmartCitiesWorld, n.d.). As emerging economies' share of tourism is growing and expected to reach 57% by 2030 (UNWTO, 2017), global competition is rising. Therefore, timely and deeper insights utilizing big data, such as those provided by Mastercard Tourism Insights, are becoming a necessary tool for tourism businesses and DMOs in order to tailor their marketing efforts to travelers' trends and needs.

### References

Mastercard. (2017). *Leveraging big data to drive tourism revenue.* Retrieved from file: ///Users/assistant2015/Downloads/tourism-insights-summary%20(1).pdf

Pries, K.H., & Robert Dunnigan, R. (2015). Big aata analytics: A practical guide for managers. Abingdon: Taylor & Francis.

SmartCitiesWorld. (n.d.). *Mastercard and Dublin city team to track spending patterns.* Retrieved from https://www.smartcitiesworld.net/news/news/mastercard-and-dublin-city-team-to-track-spending-patterns-2308

Song, H., & Liu, H. (2017). Predicting tourist demand using big data. *Analytics in Smart Tourism Design, 13.* doi:10.1007/978-3-319-44263-1_2

UNWTO. (2017). *UNWTO tourism highlights 2017 edition.* Retrieved from https://www.e-unwto.org/doi/pdf/10.18111/9789284419029

Source: Ryuichi Karakawa.

# Experiences

## *Tourism and the experience economy: an industry understanding*

Tourism is a leading industry in terms of the experience economy. This is largely due to the fact that tourism destinations are already clearly unique and differentiated from other competitor options, unlike other industries. For example, a Canadian couple looking to spend a week on the beach in the Caribbean will have two very different perceptions, opinions, and options when choosing between Jamaica and Cuba. On the other hand, if the same couple is looking to buy household items from a retail chain, their expected and consumption experiences between Walmart and Target will not be so highly differentiated. Tourism destinations have a customized stage already in place. However, it is important for destinations to realize that the physical location itself is not at the forefront of importance in the experience economy. Fiore et al. write, "What tourists primarily seek and consume at destinations is engaging experiences accompanied by the goods and/or service components of the destinations. Hence, entire tourist destinations are beginning to be positioned as 'experiences'" (2007, p. 119). Experiences are varied, however, in that tourists are seeking four different types of experiences: entertainment, esthetic, educational, and escapist. Knowing your audiences' needs and desires is a fundamental staple of marketing. It is the job of marketing managers to assess the potential value of each type of experience seeker and determine which or if all should be targeted for their destination. The following sections take a closer look at the adoption of experiential approaches to marketing in a range of sectors including lodging, events, and sport.

## Hospitality and the experience economy: lodging

Currently in the hospitality and tourism industry, tourists and travelers can stay in many different styles of lodging. Major hotels, resorts, bed and breakfasts, hostels, Airbnb, and a stranger's couch via social networking sites like "Couch Surfing" are all viable lodging options. Many would consider there to be a very distinct difference between a "traveler" and a "mass tourist" though. For example, travelers are much more likely to stay in a hostel or utilize "Couch Surfing" when traveling. These experience seekers looking to completely immerse themselves in cultures may be best described as "escapists." On the other end of the spectrum, mass tourists looking to stay at a globally recognized all-inclusive resort are likely to fit into the "entertainment" mold. In between, we have the tourists who are seeking an esthetic experience. They are looking for a deeper experience than a mass tourist but will want to only passively participate and immerse themselves in local culture in a low-risk capacity. These consumers may be perfect for the bed and breakfast industry. This is just one example of how complex the experience economy can be for marketing managers in the hospitality and tourism industry.

## Tourism and the experience economy: hallmark events

Tourist destinations are often confronted with the challenge of convincing prospective travelers that their place is better than another. The experience economy teaches us that eliciting sensations and creating a memorable experience are absolutely paramount for success. Therefore, it is not coincidental that at the same time consumers began to yearn for a more unforgettable experience. Destinations have shifted to an increased focus on the development of hallmark events. Hallmark events can be defined as, "Major one-time or recurring events of limited duration, developed primarily to enhance the awareness, appeal, and profitability of a tourism destination in the short and/or long term. Such events rely for their success on uniqueness, status, or timely significance to create interest and attract attention" (Ritchie, 1984, p. 2). These events help define the culture and uniqueness of a destination, separating them from competitors in the market. The experiences that a good hallmark event creates, often leave guests with personalized memories that they could not have gotten somewhere else. Today, hallmark events like Tampa Bay's Gasparilla or Miami's Ultra Music Festival are great examples of the tourism industry operating in the experience economy.

## Hospitality and the experience economy: sport

New American sports stadiums, especially those designed for baseball, have mastered the experience economy. Citizens Bank Park, in Philadelphia, can keep a guest entertained for the entire duration of the game without the guest even viewing a single pitch. The abundance of retail stores, restaurants, interactive games, photo opportunities, artwork, and historical landmarks makes it conceivable that a novice sports fan may not ever see their seat. In the past, it was only the field that was seen as the stage. This limited the sensations, level of participation, and connectivity that guests would feel, thus limiting the stadium's target market. This new strategy, as compared to the old, uninviting, cement bowls of the 1970s, has greatly increased the interactivity for guests and thus greatly diversified the crowds that we see in sports stadiums today.

## The future of the experience economy: anything is possible

When experience meets collaboration and technology, there is no limit to the creativity that one may witness in this new economy. Before moving on, consider one futuristic track that could eventually become our reality, to illustrate just how experiential our now basic travels could become. It is not far-fetched, that in the future, airline flight passengers could receive personal virtual reality headsets. These headsets, at first may act as personal movie theaters, giving individual passengers a personalized experience as they have the ability to sift through an entire collection of media to view. Eventually, these headsets could take passengers to their destination well before their actual arrival. As the experience economy moves forward, airlines could collaborate with resorts, enabling passengers to "walk around" and view all of the amenities, stroll the white sands, and perhaps even check in and book excursions all while 35,000 feet in the air. In this example, the sky is literally the limit. The future is on its way and the experience economy is going to be around to see it.

## Conclusion

This chapter set out to introduce the three pillars running through the entire book, that of collaboration, technology, and experiences. All three are integral to the future development, marketing, and management of tourism and hospitality albeit with some subtle differences in each of the many sectors. For international airlines, the continuation of the global airline alliance model continues to go from strength to strength as evident by the case example of SkyTeam in Tourism and hospitality insight 3.1. The rapidly changing world of technology is central to all development in hospitality and tourism with travel distribution, guest experience, and visitor satisfaction having been transformed over the past two decades in light of the emergence and omnipresence of the Internet across the globe. The use of technology and specialized data analytic skills are driving forward many parts of the industry as evidenced with the case study of Mastercard Tourism Insights, with all major airlines, hotels, theme parks and many destinations today exploring competitive advantage through data and its analysis. Finally, the redefinition of the customer/guest/tourist experience is driving change across the industry as co-created experiences are now becoming the norm across all aspects of the industry. Without doubt the industry continues to change at break-neck speed with collaboration, technology, and experiences likely to continue to serve as significant industry drivers of change long into the future.

## REVIEW QUESTIONS

1. How have collaborative strategies been adopted in different sectors of the hospitality and tourism industry?
2. To date, what have been some of the benefits (and drawbacks) of the adoption of innovative technologies in the hotel sector?
3. How have international airlines gone about trying to enhance the traveler "experience"?
4. What is "co-creation" and what factors/features need to be implemented at the destination level to ensure a successful co-created destination experience is achieved?

## YOUTUBE LINKS

*"The industry's first keyless check-in was launched at Starwood group hotels"*

URL: https://www.youtube.com/watch?v=9MX7Mo4fDdY

Summary: Starwood Hotels and Resorts Worldwide has launched "SPG Keyless" – the keyless entry system for its loyalty program members. It is the first keyless system in the hospitality industry that allows guests to use their mobile phones as a room key. Through the loyalty program app, guests can access the key without checking in at the front desk.

*"The world's first hotel staffed by robots opened in Japan"*

URL: https://www.youtube.com/watch?v=C6bQHUlq664

Summary: "Hen na hotel" in Japan opened as the world's first hotel stuffed by robots. Having robots fill human jobs helps the futuristic hotel reduce the labor costs by approximately 70% and provide rooms at a low price. CBS's Seth Doane reports from Tokyo.

### "Digital Key comes to New York Hilton Midtown"

URL: https://www.youtube.com/watch?v=7C1rU2eWKkQ

Summary: With Hilton's Digital Key you the customer are in control of your hotel experience by using the HHonors app. This enables customers to book direct for great prices, to check in, choose the exact kind of room you want, and use your cellphone as your door key.

### "Using data to help drive tourism growth"

URL: https://www.youtube.com/watch?v=c3Zdif9tmx8

Changing consumer behavior and increased competition create challenges to generating tourism growth. Mastercard Tourism Insights accesses multiple data sources to bring you actionable insights throughout the entire traveler journey. These insights can inform marketing investments and help tourism bureaus be more competitive in identifying and attracting high-value tourists.

### How Kayak is Using AI for Travel Planning

URL: https://www.youtube.com/watch?v=orUQsPTuMRQ

Summary: Steve Hafner, Kayak's chief executive officer and co-founder, talked with Bloomberg's Emily Chang on "Bloomberg Technology." He discussed his strategy regarding the utilization of Artificial Intelligence technology for travel planning. He said that Kayak is finding ways to make their platform more convenient for millennial and younger generations. He also discussed his perspective regarding Priceline.com's (a Kayak.com's competitor) aggressive acquisition.

"SkyPriority exclusive services by SkyTeam"

URL: https://www.youtube.com/watch?v=gvKsnRQptyA

Summary: SkyTeam offers "red-carpet treatment" that unites the most exclusive airport benefits of all alliance members into an alliance-wide network in order to provide consistent and smooth experiences across the globe. Priority check-in, boarding, baggage handling, priority lanes at ticket offices, transfer desks, security and immigration are automatic for SkyTeam Elite Plus, First and Business Class travelers.

## *"Why Hilton's Digital Key means staff can focus on customer delight"*

URL: https://www.youtube.com/watch?v=8muzfDM0dTo

Summary: Hilton's Digital Key enables customers to use their mobile phones to open their hotel rooms. Hilton Honors (Hilton's loyalty program customers) can choose their desired room, check in on their mobile devices and have the option of using a Digital Key during their stay. Hilton argues that it also allows their staff to focus more on customer service by utilizing their reduced check-in time.

## REFERENCES, FURTHER READING, AND RELATED WEBSITES

### References

Beverland, M., & Brotherton, P. (2001). The uncertain search for opportunities: Determinants of strategic partnerships. *Qualitative Market Research: An International Journal, 4*(2), 88–99.

Caffyn, A. (2000). Is there a tourism partnership life cycle? In B. Bramwell & B. Lane (Eds.), *Tourism collaboration and partnerships: Politics, practice and sustainability* (pp. 200–229). Clevedon: Channel View Publications.

Fiore, A.M., Jeoung, M., & Oh, H. (2007). Measuring experience economy concepts: Tourism applications. *Journal of Travel Research, 46*(2), 119–132.

Fyall, A., & Garrod, B. (2005) *Tourism marketing: A collaborative approach.* Clevedon: Channel View Publications.

Kracht, J., & Wang, Y. (2011). Distribution channels in destination marketing and promotion. In Y. Wang & A. Pizam (Eds.), *Destination marketing and management: Theories and applications* (pp. 165–183). Oxford: CABI.

O'Connor, P., Wang, Y., & Li, X. (2011). Web 2.0, the online community and destination marketing. In Y. Wang & A. Pizam (Eds.), *Destination marketing and management: Theories and applications* (pp. 225–243). Oxford: CABI.

Ritchie, J.R.B. (July, 1984). Assessing the impact of hallmark events: Conceptual and research issues. *Journal of Travel Research, 23*, 2–11.

SAS Institute. (2017). Big data, big marketing. Retrieved from https://www.sas.com/en_us/insights/big-data/big-data-marketing.html#

Terpstra, V., & Simonin, B. (1993). Strategic alliances in the triad: An exploratory study. *Journal of International Marketing, 1*(1), 4–25.

United Nations World Tourism Organization. (1999, May 19). *Tourism highlights 1999 edition.* Retrieved from http://www.e-unwto.org/doi/pdf/10.18111/9789284403011

United Nations World Tourism Organization. (2016, August 09). *Tourism highlights 2016 edition.* Retrieved from http://www.e-unwto.org/doi/book/10.18111/9789284418145

Wood, D.J., & Gray, B. (1991). Towards a comprehensive theory of collaboration. *Journal of Applied Behavioural Science, 27*(2), 139–162.

### Further reading

Homburg, C., Jozi⊠, D., & Kuehnl, C. (2017). Customer experience management: Toward implementing an evolving marketing concept. *Journal of the Academy of Marketing Science, 45*(3), 377–401.

Kirillova, K., Lehto, X.Y., & Cai, L. (2017). Existential authenticity and anxiety as outcomes: The tourist in the experience economy. *International Journal of Tourism Research, 19*(1), 13–26.

Knobloch, U., Robertson, K., & Aitken, R. (2017). Experience, emotion, and eudaimonia: A consideration of tourist experiences and well-being. *Journal of Travel Research, 56*(5), 651–662.

Morgan, M., Lugosi, P., & Brent Ritchie, J.R. (2010). *The tourism and leisure experience.* Clevedon: Channel View Publications.

Paulauskaite, D., Powell, R., Coca-Stefaniak, J. A., & Morrison, A. M. (2017). Living like a local: Authentic tourism experiences and the sharing economy. *International Journal of Tourism Research, 19*(6), 619–628.

Pine, B. J., & Gilmore, J. H. (1998). Welcome to the experience economy. *Harvard Business Review, 76,* 97–105.

Schmitt, B. (1999). Experiential marketing. *Journal of Marketing Management, 15*(1–3), 53–67.

## Websites

The Leading Hotels of the World
https://www.lhw.com/get-inspired/destination-experiences

Mastercard Tourism Insights
https://www.mastercardadvisors.com/en-us/solutions/mastercard-tourism-insights.html

OneWorld
https://www.oneworld.com/

Skift
https://skift.com/

SkyTeam
https://www.skyteam.com

Star Alliance
http://www.staralliance.com

Travel Weekly
http://www.travelweekly.com/

WTTC
https://www.wttc.org/

## MAJOR CASE STUDY
## TECHNOLOGY IN HILTON WORLDWIDE

Hilton Worldwide is one of the leading global hospitality companies, with more than 4,900 hotels, resorts, and timeshare properties comprising in excess of 804,000 rooms in 100 countries and territories as of the end of 2016 (Hilton Worldwide, 2017). During the nearly 100 years since its foundation in 1919 by Conrad Hilton, it has defined the hospitality industry and established a portfolio of 14 world-class brands, spanning from luxury and full-service hotels and resorts to extended-stay suites and focused-service hotels. The brand portfolio includes the flagship Hilton Hotels and Resorts, Waldorf Astoria Hotels and Resorts, Conrad Hotels and Resorts, Curio-A Collection by Hilton, DoubleTree by Hilton, Embassy Suites by Hilton, Hilton Garden Inn, Hampton by Hilton, Homewood Suites by Hilton, Home2 Suites by Hilton, Hilton Grand Vacations, Canopy by Hilton, Tru by Hilton as well as a newcomer, Tapestry Collection by Hilton (Hilton Worldwide, 2017). Hilton HHonors, its award-winning customer loyalty program that introduced in 1987, has now approximately 60 million members across the globe (Hilton Worldwide, 2017).

Since its early stage, Hilton has been a pioneer and leader in innovative technology in the hospitality industry. In 1927, it opened its first hotel with cold running water and air-conditioning in public areas and became the first hotel in the world that installed televisions in guest rooms in 1947 (Hilton Worldwide, 2018). In 1955, Hilton created its first central reservation office called Hilcron, making it possible for guests to reserve rooms at any Hilton by telephone, telegram, or Teletype (Hilton Worldwide, 2018). In 1995, 40 years after the launch of HILcron, the first Hilton website was created (Hilton Worldwide, 2018). The process had been a struggle in an industry not widely known for advanced technology; however, Hilton has kept making steady progress toward superior customer satisfaction and loyalty by adopting extensive use of innovative technology, which is a part of Hilton's ongoing efforts to enhance its long-term competitiveness in the hospitality business.

Technology has revolutionized the ability for all kinds of businesses to personalize their services in the 21st century, and Hilton has spurred its technology utilization accordingly. One of their remarkable technology implementations in recent years is "OnQ," its proprietary customer-information system introduced in 2004. This new integrated technology platform put employees on stage in front of customers to perform "on cue," giving them the information that they need to deliver the most efficient service ("Hotels," 2003). For example, a repeat guest is immediately recognized by the system in the check-in process, warmly welcomed by a front-desk employee and asked if he/she still want a non-smoking, king-bed room on a high floor level, as he/she had a month ago at the other Hilton group hotel. In addition, if there was a mistake during the previous stay at a Hilton property, the mistake would be noted in the system next time he/she visit any Hilton properties, and the front-desk personnel are not only supposed to apologize again, but should also offer him/her something extra ("Hotels," 2003). OnQ consolidates all the personal information that guests provide to Hilton at any touch points, from the front desk to call centers, in order to create a "Guest Profile Manager." Profiles are created for any guest who is either a loyalty program member or simply has visited a Hilton property at least four times within the last year ("Hotels," 2003). Their stay history and any prior complaints logged during previous visits are combined with profiles, and together act as the front-desk employees' "personal assistant," enabling them to provide a more enhanced level of service based on real-time access to the guest profiles ("Hotels," 2003). In an effort to build and enhance customer loyalty across all brands within the Hilton portfolio, OnQ was developed with more than five years of effort and the approximately US$50 million of investment ("Hotels," 2003). Hilton became the first hotel company that employed a single technology platform across all brands by sharing guest information between the front desk, reservations, and the Hilton HHonors program (Griffy-Brown, Chun, & Machen, 2008). Hilton has certainly boosted its competitiveness by offering exceptionally personalized services using OnQ.

The most recent innovative update by Hilton is the introduction of "Digital Key," the industry-leading Hilton HHonors app that provides the loyalty program members with more choice and control over their entire travel experience. Digital Key gives loyal guests the option to not only choose their preferred rooms, make special requests and check in prior to arrival, but also completely bypass the hotel check-in counter and access their rooms directly using the Hilton HHonors app on their smartphones (Hilton Worldwide, 2015). The Digital Key project was an unprecedented technological development for Hilton, taking seven years to rebuild the whole technological infrastructure and costing them $550 million (CNBC, 2014). As the first step, digital check-in and digital room selection were introduced in July 2014. Within a year after the introduction of those functions, HHonors members digitally checked-in more than 5 million times and the HHonors app was downloaded more than 2 million times (Hilton Worldwide, 2015). Customer feedback on digital check-in was overwhelmingly positive, with 93% of guests responded that they were satisfied or extremely satisfied with the experience (Hilton Worldwide, 2015). With the introduction of Digital Key in 2016 as the next step, HHonors members are now able to use their smartphones as their room key to enter more than 170,000 rooms at 250 US properties within the Hilton Hotels and Resorts, Waldorf Astoria Hotels and Resorts, Conrad Hotels and Resorts and Canopy by Hilton brands (Hilton Worldwide, 2015). Through the app, HHonors members are offered the ability to better control and customize their stay with Hilton, which ultimately gives an additional convenient and security for them. "We are reshaping the way guests dream, book and stay with us – helping earn their loyalty and affinity for our brands," Geraldine Calpin, global head of digital at Hilton Worldwide noted (Hilton Worldwide, 2014).

Hilton always looks for ways to provide their guests with a better experience. With the recent partnership with Uber, Hilton loyalty program members can now seamlessly access their hotel and ground transportation reservations through the Hilton HHonors and Uber apps (Hilton Worldwide, 2016). It is also collaborating with IBM to pilot a new Watson-enabled robot concierge for a better customer experience (Skift, 2016). Hilton will keep innovating and sharpening its services with cutting-edge technology for the time being.

## References

CNBC (2014, July 29). *Hilton Hotels goes high-tech* Retrieved from http://video.cnbc.com/gallery/?video=3000296709&play=1

Griffy-Brown, C., Chun, M.W.S., & Machen, R. (2008). Hilton Hotels corporation self-service technology. *Journal of Information Technology Case and Application Research*, *10*(2), 37–57. doi:10.1080/15228053.2008.10856135

Hilton Worldwide. (2014, Nov 3). *Hilton Worldwide truly opens doors: Company to roll out mobile room keys in 2015 at hundreds of U.S. hotels across four brands*. Retrieved from http://news.hilton worldwide.com/index.cfm/news/hilton-worldwide-truly-opens-doors-company-to-roll-out-mobile-room-keys-in-2015-at-hundreds-of-us-hotels-across-four-brands

Hilton Worldwide. (2015, Aug 11). *Hilton introduces digital key, further enhancing industry-leading HHonors App*. Retrieved from http://news.hiltonworldwide.com/index.cfm/news/hilton-intro duces-digital-key-further-enhancing-industryleading-hhonors-app-

Hilton Worldwide. (2017). *2016 Annual Report*. Retrieved from http://www.corporatereport.com/hilton/2016/ar/_pdf/Hilton_2016_AR.pdf

Hilton Worldwide. (2018). *History and heritage*. Retrieved from http://www.hiltonworldwide.com/about/history/

Hilton Worldwide. (2016, March 30). *Hilton and Uber expand partnership, unveil app integration for simplified travel*. Retrieved from http://news.hiltonworldwide.com/index.cfm/news/hilton-and-uber-expand-partnership-unveil-app-integration-for-simplified-travel

Hotels. (2003). *Hilton Hotels Corp. takes lead with OnQ*. London: Reed Business Information, Inc.

Johnson, R.L. (2004, Aug). *Hilton's customer-information system, called OnQ, rolling out across 8 hotel brands; seeking guest loyalty and competitive advantage with proprietary technology*. Retrieved from http://www.hotel-online.com/News/PR2004_3rd/Aug04_OnQ.html

SKIFT (2016, March 9). The Tiny Hilton robot concierge that hints at IBM's ambitious plans for travel. *Digital*. Retrieved from https://skift.com/2016/03/09/the-tiny-hilton-robot-concierge-that-hints-at-ibms-ambitious-plans-for-travel/

Source: Ryuichi Karakawa.

## Major case study questions

1. What benefits have Hilton accrued over the past two decades by being a pioneer in the adoption of innovative technologies?

2. What is the relationship between the adoption of innovative technologies and repeat business? How does (can) it work and what benefits (and possible drawbacks) does it bring?

3. What is the DigitalKey and how may it transform Hilton business in the future?

4. What may be some of the benefits of collaborative technological developments with the likes of Uber?

# Collaboration marketing

## Partnerships, networks, and relationships

## Learning outcomes

By the end of this chapter, students will:

- Understand the rationale and dynamics of different forms of collaboration marketing
- Appreciate the differences between partnerships, networks, and relationships in the context of collaboration marketing
- Be introduced to a number of case examples of collaboration marketing in practice across tourism and hospitality with specific emphasis on destination partnerships, airline alliances and hotel consortia.

**Key terms**

partnerships,
networks,
relationships,
consortia

## Introduction

Although the lack of resources to achieve strategic objectives individually is often portrayed as the most common argument in favor of collaboration, the reality is somewhat different as was demonstrated in Chapter 3. To broaden understanding of the existence, benefits and drawbacks of different forms of collaboration marketing, this chapter explores in greater detail the particular instances of collaboration marketing in the areas of destination partnerships, airline alliances and hotel consortia. Although sharing some common agendas and characteristics, each has come about for slightly different reasons and experience a myriad of sometimes similar and sometimes quite different challenges. Collaboration marketing is now such an important and pervasive facet of the tourism and hospitality industry that it is imperative that understanding of the particular dynamics of each mode of collaboration is clear. Partnerships, alliances and consortia have been widespread across the industry over the past few decades with them continuing to shape the future of the industry.

# Partnerships

## *Partnerships defined*

Partnerships are a vital component of the business world with their importance critical in so many aspects of the tourism and hospitality industry. A partnership can be defined as a business enterprise where two or more parties collaboratively offer their resources and assets in order to reach their mutually desired goals. These resources and assets can range from money, equipment, land, skills, and particular industry expertise among other things. In partnerships, contracts are generally put in place that explain the responsibilities of each party and their respective stakes in terms of risks, rewards, profits, and losses.

The history of business partnerships stretches as far back as medieval times (if not further). Before logistics companies were prevalent, merchants would find partners they trusted to help deliver one another's cargos when one party was ready to embark across a trade route. This basic form of a partnership, built on trust, would help cut shipping costs and widen the geographic position of a business entity. Several hundred years later, those fundamental reasons for forming a partnership still exist, albeit with more complex conditions attached to them.

In general partnerships, all parties assume fairly equal liability for any potential debts incurred during the duration of the enterprise. In some instances, limited partnerships are formed. In this type of agreement, some parties will give up their managerial roles in exchange for a lesser responsibility for liabilities. Lastly, silent partners may exist in a partnership. These silent partners are often financial investors who want no part of the operations of a business and thus have no debt liability; their investments are expected to yield a gainful return via a share of the profits a business accumulates.

## *Partnerships in tourism: trends with benefit*

In recent decades, the world has shifted from regional commerce to an increasingly global economy. International tourism marketing, in some ways, has done the opposite. In many regions of the world, destination marketing organizations (DMO) have seen their funding reduced significantly, creating new opportunities for local tourism associations (LTA). These associations, as their name indicates, cater to the development of more local destinations than the traditional DMO. This allows associations to form partnerships with businesses that will often share a more focused mutual goal, rather than a partnership that spans a multitude of regional destinations (Fyall & Garrod, 2017).

The mutually shared goals to develop a localized region can be both economically and socio-culturally beneficial to the area being developed. In some instances, traditional DMOs may struggle to garner local support for initiatives and marketing campaigns.

With more localized partnerships with an LTA, research has found that the social capital is higher (Fyall & Garrod, 2017).

## Partnerships in tourism: frequent issues

While partnerships can offer a wide range of benefits, problems can also arise. Different members of partnerships should always have a mutual goal. However, how they view the current business climate and their interpretations of the mutual goal may not run parallel with one another. For example, previous research has suggested that, "Private, public and voluntary organizations were found to live in 'separate worlds', with great differences in businesses, tasks and worldview" (Gibson, Lynch, & Morrison, 2005, p. 91). On paper, it may make sense for these three organizations to join forces, but if their perspectives and visions are not synchronized, development towards goals will be slowed. If differences are not worked out, the partnership could be greatly fractured or even terminated leaving goals unfulfilled.

Frequently, in the tourism industry, goals are not only economically driven; both public and private organizations often have a socio-cultural responsibility as well. Therefore, ensuring the success of partnerships in the tourism industry is arguably more important than many other industries because the sustainability of local populations, their values, and their traditions could be at stake. In most circumstances, public organizations are much more likely to primarily focus on community development. At the other end, private organizations are likely to hold commercial development as their number-one priority. This is one prime issue that tourism development partnerships need to work out to everyone's mutual benefit in order to cohesively achieve their goals.

## Partnerships in tourism: an emerging threat

The new role of LTAs has them taking on much of the responsibility formerly held by DMOs with particular challenges for them never before experienced. Like many public organizations, bureaucracy and a lack of industry-specific expertise from those in leadership roles, have the potential to create suboptimal conditions. The inability to maximize results could lead to outside threats taking market share away from the partners within an LTA. With regard to the potential of inefficient operations, Fyall and Garrod (2017, p. 688) warn, "There is a danger that there will be a vacuum in destination marketing which could potentially be filled instead by the burgeoning number of e-intermediaries." Only the future will determine what happens but the warnings are most definitely present for those in the traditional sphere of destination marketing.

## Public private partnerships (PPPs) in tourism

The importance of public private partnerships (PPPs) in today's international tourism climate cannot be overstated. These pivotal partnerships have been essential to the development of sustainable tourism. With both sides having the ability to offer unique resources, many destinations have reaped the benefits of fruitful collaborations.

Private sector involvement can come in many forms. These include but are not limited to: marketing efforts, infrastructure development, new product expansions (attractions fall under this title), environmental and cultural protection projects, and quality service improvements (Smith, 2011). While the private sector uses its specific areas of expertise to deliver high-quality projects, the public sector is generally involved with financing, approving, and strategizing projects. One example, could be a local coastal destination government who sees value in repainting buildings that have been weathered by coastal storms and the constant barrage of sea winds. The public sector will develop the time frame and budget for this project. Their partner, from the private sector, will be in charge of the actual labor necessary to get the job done. This partnership will add value to the attractiveness of the destination, hopefully adding to its long-term economic sustainability.

The establishment of PPPs occur for a variety of complex reasons, beyond the scope of this introductory section. It is true that many PPPs are naturally formed on the basis of a traditional partnership. A public organization looking to better a destination will hire a willing private entity who is also looking to better a destination while generating revenues for the business. However, sometimes, governments can coerce private companies into taking on projects that may not be ideal for them. While this tactic is not always necessarily ethical, the public organization feels that the ends justify the means. Of course, if a government wants to be more principled and attract private companies for partnership in other creative ways, they have the tools to accomplish that too. For example, tax breaks, eased restrictions, and zoning exemptions are all ways to entice private companies to volunteer their services for a project (Smith, 2011). Ultimately, a PPP's mutual goal is sustainable tourism that helps local community development and preservation.

## Tour operators: partnerships as a necessity

In many of the world's top destinations, tour operators participate in a highly competitive and oftentimes saturated market. Key to their survival, is the procurement and development of partnerships. Partners play a critical role in supplying tour operators with the clientele necessary to keep them in business. As discussed in this book, retail travel agents and destination concierges used to play an indispensable role in the travel industry. For tour operators, they used to be the most attractive partners to acquire due to their perceived local expertise and trustworthiness by prospective travelers. Hotel guests and vacationers planning their itineraries would be steered by these concierges and agents in the direction of tour operators that they were amalgamated with. Then, with the advent of the World Wide Web, online travel agents became the most prized partner to obtain. This is because, with the wealth of data accumulated on the web, online agents could help operators appeal to specific target markets, maximizing their

## TOURISM AND HOSPITALITY INSIGHTS 4.1
## COLLABORATIVE DESTINATION MARKETING IN ACTION – BRAND USA

The United States has been leading the tourism industry; it has continually topped the list of international tourist receipts, US\$ 206 billion, and was ranked second in international tourist arrivals, at 76 million, in 2016 (UNWTO, 2017). However, surprisingly, this comes after the United States experienced a "Lost Decade of Tourism" between 2000 and 2010, in which its share of international arrivals dropped from 17% to 12% and it lost approximately 467,000 related jobs, \$606 million in spending by international visitors and \$37 billion in tax revenue (Dow, 2011). The critical reason for this momentous decline is considered to be that the United States didn't have a nationally coordinated collaborative marketing effort, while other countries, including Australia, France, Spain, and the UK, were spending tremendous amounts on marketing (Brand USA, 2017). In response to this decline, Brand USA, the destination marketing organization for the United States, was established and it began operations in May 2011 in order to "increase incremental international visitation, spend, and market share to fuel the nation's economy and enhance the image of the USA worldwide" (Brand USA, 2017).

Image 4.1

Source: Pexels.

As the destination marketing organization for the United States, it is critical for Brand USA to cooperate and collaborate with more than 700 partner organizations in order to increase awareness of the USA as a destination (Brand USA, 2017). Deploying cooperative marketing platforms and programs, through which their partners can participate and make contributions, accounts for the majority of Brand USA's marketing efforts. One significant example is the VisitTheUSA and GoUSA websites that are designed to attract international travelers and influencers to the United States through fascinating content and valuable information on one of the best destinations in the world (Brand USA, 2017). In these digital marketing platforms, partners can participate in developing page contents and showing off their superior services, helping travelers imagine their US trips (Brand USA, 2017). In addition to cooperative marketing platforms and programs, Brand USA provides trade outreach programs, such as large-scale trade shows that provide their partners access to thousands of leading travel buyers and influencers and mega-fam trips promoting US destinations, travel brands, and attractions (Brand USA, 2017). Through these trade outreach programs of Brand USA, US travel awareness and interests in the global market as well as their partners connecting with the travel industry's most influential professionals can be promoted (Brand USA, 2017).

Since fiscal year 2013, according to the results of a study led by Oxford Economics, one of the world's leading providers of economic analysis, Brand USA's marketing efforts generated "5.4 million incremental visitors who spent $17.7 billion on travel and fare receipts with US carriers, resulting in $38.4 billion in total sales, which support[ed] over 51,580 new jobs" (Brand USA, 2017). After the "Lost Decade," Brand USA has shown a successful example of destination marketing organizations by cooperating and collaborating with tourism industry partners in order to increase international visitors and their spending as well as improve the image of the United States as a destination.

## References

Brand USA. (2017). *Frequently asked questions, what is brand USA?* Retrieved from http://www.theb randusa.com/faq

Brand USA. (2017). *Partner opportunities, powerful marketing to reach international travelers.* Retrieved from http://www.thebrandusa.com/system/files/pictures/Partner%20Programs% 20brochure.pdf

Brand USA. (2017). *ROI study, overview.* Retrieved from http://www.thebrandusa.com/research-analytics/roi-study

Brand USA. (2017). *Who we are.* Retrieved from http://www.thebrandusa.com/about/whoweare

Dow, R. (2011, Nov 21). *America's lost decade of tourism. The Wall Street Journal,* Retrieved from https://www.wsj.com/articles/SB10001424052970203699404577042440873063450

UNWTO. (2017). *UNWTO Tourism highlights, 2017 edition,* Retrieved from https://www.e-unwto.org /doi/pdf/10.18111/9789284419029

Source: Ryuichi Karakawa.

return on marketing dollars and time invested. Ultimately, one of the most overlooked collaborations, takes us back to the beginning of this entire section on partnerships. In the travel world, it is advisable for tour operators to actually partner with one another too. Developing package deals can drastically lower the stress of vacationers planning their trips. A vacationer may originally feel overwhelmed with the idea of planning seven different excursions for each day of their holiday. Suddenly, thanks to the effective partnership amongst tour operators, vacation planners can book one package deal that encompasses all of their holiday desires. To understand the importance of partnerships in tourism, we need to look no further than tour operators and how they interact and partner with National Tourist Boards. Tourism and hospitality insights 4.1, for example, represents a very good example of a collaborative destination branding campaign while Tourism and hospitality insights 4.2 highlights a collaborative partnership between Virgin Atlantic and Mastercard.

## TOURISM AND HOSPITALITY INSIGHTS 4.2
## VIRGIN ATLANTIC WORLD ELITE MASTERCARD

If you are an avid traveler, Virgin Atlantic World Elite Mastercard should be one of your reward credit card options. The card is quite valuable for travelers, allowing them to obtain significant Flying Club miles for their spending: 3 miles per \$1 spent directly on Virgin Atlantic purchases and 1.5 miles per \$1 spent on all other purchases with no limit on the number of miles earned (Virgin Atlantic, 2018). In addition to obtaining miles from purchases, cardholders can earn up to 20,000 bonus miles from their first purchase, 15,000 additional miles every anniversary after qualifying purchases and up to 5,000 bonus miles when they add additional authorized users to their account (Virgin Atlantic, 2018). Flying Club miles can be used to purchase flights in approximately 100 destinations, to upgrade seats or to redeem miles in other ways (i.e. hotels, car rentals, travel packages and gift cards) (Virgin Atlantic, 2018).

In addition to earning miles, cardholders can earn tier points; customers can get 25 tier points per \$2,500 spent and additional tier points when customers fly with Virgin Atlantic or partner airlines (Virgin Atlantic, 2018). As customers earn points, they move to higher statuses (from Red to Silver to Gold). The benefits of a higher status include bonus miles, priority boarding, seat upgrades and airport lounge spas.

There are actually even more card benefits. From international travelers' point of view, the most significant benefit may be the lack of foreign transaction fees (Bank of America, 2018). Traveling abroad with anticipation of significant expenditures, the benefit of not having foreign transaction fees is extraordinarily valuable, considering the fact that other credit cards charge approximately 3% on all foreign transactions. Clearly, Virgin Atlantic World Elite Mastercard is a great choice for international travelers.

**References**

Bank of America Corporation. (2018). *Virgin Atlantic World Elite Mastercard*. Retrieved from https://www.bankofamerica.com/credit-cards/products/virgin-atlantic-credit-card/

Virgin Atlantic Airways Limited. (2018). *Virgin Atlantic Black Credit Card*. Retrieved from https://www.virginatlantic.com/us/en/flying-club/credit-card/black-card.html

Source: Ryuichi Karakawa.

# Alliances

## *Alliances defined*

Alliances are to the airline industry what partnerships are to the tourism industry. As you will soon learn, alliances are an integral and fundamental element of air travel. An airline alliance can be defined as an agreement between two or more airlines with the intention of bettering each party through mutual cooperation (see the earlier Tourism and hospitality insights 3.1). Later in this section, we'll give a quick overview on how these parties benefit one another. Like tourism, there is a great number of airline alliances, most of which are small. These small alliances are mostly for the purpose of code sharing, which is when "two or more airlines agree[ing] to use the same designator code or flight number for connecting services in order to attract more business by extending their networks through partner carriers" (Malver, 1998, p. 19). However, the commercial airline industry does have a few major global alliances that have a stronghold on the entire sector.

## *Alliances: the history of the big three*

There are currently six airline alliances worth mentioning, but only three that truly wield the power. Here is a list of the six big alliances, with the first three dominating the skies: 1. Star Alliance; 2. Oneworld; 3. SkyTeam; 4. Vanilla Alliance; 5. Value Alliance; 6. U-Fly Alliance. Star Alliance, Oneworld, and SkyTeam will be the focal points of this section. These three global alliances have been dominant since before the turn of the millennium. Star Alliance was the first to form in 1997; the original agreement was between five airlines, namely Thai Airways International, Lufthansa, United Airways, Scandinavian Airlines, and Air Canada. Twenty years later, the Star Alliance has grown exponentially. It now has 28 members, sending an extraordinary 18,400 flights in the air every day from any of the 1,300 airports they call home. Their flight network takes them to 191 countries, or, 98% of the world's sovereign nations (Star Alliance, 2017).

The Star Alliance may be the most important collaboration effort in the world. The Oneworld alliance was formed in 1999 and is the fierce rival of their predecessor (see Major case study at the end of this chapter). Unlike the Star Alliance, whose original five were not all already established global airlines, the Oneworld group was founded by three well-known, reputable, carriers. These original carriers were American Airlines, Qantas, and British Airways. Soon after the original founders, two more renowned airlines joined the group. European carriers Iberia and FinnAir linked with the collaboration and thus the airline alliance battle was born. As of late 2017, the group stands at 13 members, accounting for 12,738 daily departures to 158 different countries and over 1,000 destinations (Oneworld, 2017). While these numbers are smaller than the other two major alliances, Oneworld has cornered the frequent international flyer market, particularly business travelers.

Last, we take a quick glance at the youngest of the big three, SkyTeam. SkyTeam was founded in 2000 by four airlines that ensured the fledgling alliance would cover a very wide geographic area (see Tourism and hospitality insights 3.1). In only 17 years, the young alliance has already surpassed Oneworld in membership, boasting 20 associates. This alliance now carries 730 million annual passengers, on 16,609 daily flights, to 177 different countries (SkyTeam, 2017). Their catchphrase, "The smoothest way to travel," gives consumers a confidence that SkyTeam will provide the most hassle-free booking and travel experience out of the big three alliances.

## Alliances: the benefits within

Like so many other business collaborations, an airline's core benefits in joining an alliance are strategic positioning, cost reductions, and improved operating efficiency. Twenty years after the first major alliance was formed, airlines are now, more than ever, eager and even dependent on joining an alliance in order to thrive. If the opportunity to join an alliance presents itself, it would be virtually unthinkable for management to reject. Fyall and Garrod (2005, p. 228) state that, "Today's global airline alliances are so fully integrated into the core businesses of airlines that membership confers a significant market advantage on alliance participants." In this time of economic globalization, joining an airline alliance is like a gambler hedging their bet. Rather than having to rely solely on regional economies, being a part of a global network ensures that an airline's market portfolio is diversified, allowing strong markets to compensate for markets experiencing economic struggles.

The competitive position that a singular airline holds is often only as valuable as the economy it operates in. Service quality and price are the two major components considered by consumers. Agusdinata and Klein write, "During economic upturns customers will be more service sensitive and during economic downturns they will be more price sensitive" (2002, p. 205). Therefore, in times of recession, low-cost carriers will have a distinct advantage in the regional market. At the other end, luxury airlines that provide top notch experiences and service will be the beneficiaries during times of economic prosperity. By being a part of an airline alliance, both types of airlines are able to contribute and survive regardless of the economic situation. Alone, these airlines are polar opposite in position, potentially unable to combat the niche carriers that fall between the two strategies; together they can apply pressure from both ends.

Cost cutting and improving operating efficiency are always goals for any business. Airlines are able to accomplish those goals when they join an alliance and partake in the hub and spoke network amongst partners. When airlines work together, they are able to use one another's stations at various airports. By not having to build stations of their own, they have the ability to save millions in capital investments. In addition, operating as an alliance will limit the number of planes competing at a destination. For example, if airline A and airline B are not in an alliance and both wish to have flights from Philadelphia to Miami on a Tuesday afternoon, each plane may end up half full. By operating in an alliance, only Airline A will offer the flight, resulting in a higher load. Meanwhile, Airline B can now allocate its resources to a new emerging destination to garner new market share. Theoretically, this should ultimately benefit both airlines and the alliance as a whole.

Another key advantage to being a member of an alliance, is that it can work as an industry think tank. Working out problems as an independent airline can be costly in both dollars and time. If the issues an airline faces cannot be solved, it could lead the airline to ruin. By being a part of a collaboration effort, members are able to incorporate several different perspectives and various resources in order to solve a problem. These collaborative efforts help increase the stability of an alliance in two more ways.

Collaboration efforts should benefit all parties involved. Usage of collective knowledge should not only improve the strategies of each independent airline, but give a competitive advantage to the alliance as a whole. Distinct competitive advantages in a dense market can be greatly rewarding for an airline. These benefits help to reassure independent parties that their partnership is a worthwhile endeavor. This will hopefully create a loop effect where the independent airlines feel emboldened by their collaboration; therefore, they will return to the think tank often, ultimately ensuring greater stability for the alliance.

By constantly returning back to partners to help strengthen operations and achieve goals, the independent airlines become more dependent on one another. This dependency undoubtedly stabilizes the alliance. Suddenly, instead of lone airlines loosely working together for code-sharing purposes, a strong bond is formed. This bond instills a new level of trust, proving membership is a team effort rather than a catalyst of opportunism (Agusdinata & Klein, 2002).

## *Alliances: disadvantages*

While the key benefits of reduced costs, improved efficiencies, and reduced macro risks can be realized by airlines who hold alliance membership, these are not obtained without some peril. In addition, airlines can also provide consumers with greater loyalty benefits, easier bookings, better service, more service options and theoretically cheaper fares. However, it is possible that an industry controlled by three major alliances will not be totally beneficial for the consumer. Let us briefly consider some of the major disadvantages from both perspectives.

## *Alliances: membership disadvantage*

While being in an airline alliance should help cut spending, the initial costs to join can oftentimes be burdensome for a carrier. In order to be considered for membership, an airline will have to acquiesce to the demands and standards that an alliance holds. These standards primarily exist to help uniformity and operational efficiency for its members. However, making the operational adjustments necessary to meet specific requirements could create up-front costs for a prospective carrier, forcing management to consider taking on an increased financial risk in the hopes of a future payoff. This is a reason that we continue to see some airlines operate as a lone wolf in an industry ruled by packs.

## *Alliances: consumer disadvantage*

An industry forecasted for a continuous reduction in competition has never been an ideal scenario for consumers. Many believe that the antitrust immunity granted to airlines in the 1990s has led us to this three-alliance oligarchy we are experiencing today. The immunity was supposed to help passengers save money while increasing the convenience factor with better services. Instead, some would argue that it has done the opposite. As we noted earlier, when once competing airlines A and B form an alliance, airline B no longer needs to offer the same flights as airline A. If we consider basic supply and demand economics, multiple layers come into play, all of which are to the detriment of the traveler. First, with only one flight for consumers, they are essentially at the mercy of whatever price airline A chooses to charge. Then, passengers are also pitted against one another; only one flight means limited seats, which increases the value of every space on that flight. When flights quickly sell the bulk of their seats but demand still exists, airlines can increase the price for the remaining seats. While the prices go up, the services can actually deteriorate. In some cases, where no competition exists, airlines offer bare minimum services.

This is not the only way that service may eventually be negatively affected for travelers. A goal for these airline alliances is to experience relative homogeny. This will help them promote consistent branding and streamline their operations even more than they already have. Ed Perkins (2012, para. 9) believes that, "Unfortunately, any moves to standardize on these matters will probably descend to the lowest common denominator, which is a very bad result for consumers." Airline alliances will argue that their goal is to make traveling more convenient and cost efficient for travelers. However, these are just a couple of examples of what many objectors believe is leading to increasingly absent services and disproportionate increases in price.

# Consortium

## Hotel consortium: defined

Consortium is the word most often used when referring to collaboration in the hotel lodging industry. Consortium is usually an agreement between various hotels that allow the partners to pool, acquire, and utilize resources at cheaper costs. However, consortium can also refer to hotels partnering with non-hotel companies. For example, in what is known as a referral consortium, hotels can collaborate with an airline in order to enhance bookings. The popularity of hotel consortia as a business strategy for independent hotels has greatly increased in recent decades.

## Hotel consortium: its popularity explained

As evidenced throughout this book so far, it should now be clear that technology and globalization are together a catalyst for collaboration. This is once again relevant for hotel consortia. The limitless opportunities of the Internet and the expanding brand equities of major hotel chains have engendered immense challenges for independent operations. With a grossly disparate advantage in marketing resources, major chains have the ability to dominate independent operations in terms of search engine optimization (SEO). This dominance leads to a continuous accruement of brand notoriety and a far greater positioning for online bookings. Larger hotel chains have left the smaller lodging operations with very few options. One option is for an independent hotel to affiliate with a major chain. In this option, the individual operation has the opportunity to ride off the coattails of the conglomerate. By associating with a major chain, the smaller hotel's brand can benefit from an improved image and reputation. An affiliation can also lead to an increase in marketing power or make once infeasible financial ideas feasible. Major chains also tend to have a greater expertise in the management of operations, so local managers and staff may get advanced training they may not have otherwise received. However, many times, this form of collaboration strips the identity and power of the small hotel. Lengthy contracts lock-in small operations rendering them helpless, as they suddenly lack control and strategy input while paying royalties to their "partner." For hotels that strive to maintain autonomy, this option is far from ideal (Fyall & Garrod, 2005).

A second option would be for a smaller hotel to position itself in a niche market. Imagine a forest with one small tree with its own little place but surrounded by much larger trees. The much larger trees all bear very similar fruits that are as delicious as one another. Though the tree in the middle is small, it produces a unique fruit unlike any of the larger, surrounding trees. Most people will visit the larger better-known trees for their fruits; but the small tree will still attract a distinctly different clientele for its own. In the hotel lodging industry, the small tree often represents a boutique hotel. In order for a boutique hotel to compete amongst the giants, it needs to have certain qualities and deliver exceptional, personalized service. Location and word-of-mouth marketing are also pivotal when it comes to the survival of these small gems. If everything is not done to perfection, there is a great likelihood of failure. Boutique hotels are high-risk and many small hotels do not meet the multitude of requirements necessary for success; these independent lodgings should seek the third operating option, consortium.

## Hotel consortium: the benefits

The final option to stand up to the growth of major chains is forming/joining a hotel consortium. By joining a consortium, a hotel has the opportunity to experience many advantages that otherwise would have eluded them. The most common, tangible advantages of consortium are either financial, operational, or marketing related with an expected increase in hotel visitors. In most industries, sales are the best way to mask inefficiencies; for the hotel lodging industry, an increase in occupancy rates can do the same. While this rise in revenues is great for business, the hotel will also have the benefit of reduced administrative costs. In many consortia, mundane, time-consuming, office work is organized and analyzed via data software at a consortium headquarters. A discount in asset acquiring costs can also be expected for members. Many consortia will have a central purchasing facility. Since this facility can simultaneously put in purchase orders for many different hotels, the bulk buy can be expected to be cheaper than an independent hotel procurement. These are just some of the financial benefits associated with joining a hotel consortium.

Compared to individual hotels, the consortium cohort will have much more progressive processes and innovative systems put in place. When becoming a member, the individual hotel can now learn and employ these new systems, improving operational efficiency. Earlier in this chapter, we discussed how airline alliances collaborate and form a think tank for new ideas that will benefit all. Lodging consortia have the opportunity to do the same; oftentimes combining skills, data, and unique areas of expertise. Newer technologies may also be more readily available for members. The last important operational benefit to consider is strength in numbers; a consortium provides leverage when negotiating with suppliers and intermediaries (Fyall & Garrod, 2005).

Operational efficiencies and cost reductions are not the only benefits of consortium; marketing benefits also exist. With membership comes the power to expand geographic influence. By sharing some advertising and media costs, members can reach and stimulate consumer markets that were previously deemed unattainable. By boasting a homogeneous theme-based marketing strategy, the involved members will share a strengthened brand image. Positive associations, familiarity, and trust all have the opportunity to build when so many groups, ranging across multiple market segments, carry the same marketing message. This can lead to new referrals and bookings from fellow members in other markets. For some small hotel groups, the prolific marketing advice they receive from professionals in a consortium could be transformational for their brand.

## Hotel consortium: the issues

Ideally, the great perks of consortia should always outweigh the drawbacks. However, there are costs incurred by members which may be an entry barrier for some. In order for a consortium to collaborate to its full potential, there will naturally be costs associated with marketing projects, coordination efforts, and streamlined administrative processes. Each member is expected to contribute their fair share of assets for the betterment of the group. If the return on the contribution does not yield optimum results, then the consortium suddenly becomes cost ineffective.

Members may also incur operational costs. When hotels operate independently, they can experience entrepreneurial freedoms that allow expressive creativity and innovations. Once independent operations are lost, the reins of conformity begin to tug on some of those organizational freedoms. Some owners and management undoubtedly become weary, aggravated, and feel vulnerable when they lose their decision-making powers. If extreme differences of opinion persist on a normal basis, conflict within the consortia may arise. If the relinquished powers in exchange for the benefits of standardization of products and systems do not balance, doubts of membership value may begin to set in.

Lastly, consortium participants must expect marketing costs. Independent hotels have the advantage of quickly reacting to external opportunities and threats. If they see a chance to capitalize on a prospect or minimize an issue, their small team can swiftly do so. In a consortium, lengthy protocols must take place before a final decision can be made. In addition, the cohesion of the brand can also strip a unique facility from some competitive market positions and individual identity. If the overall brand image proves to be less equitable than the distinct character previously held, then membership could hinder the public's perception of the hotel. Tourism and hospitality insights 4.3 provides a contemporary example of the dynamics of the Leading Hotels of the World consortium which operates at the higher luxury end of the hotel lodging scale.

# Conclusion

Although on the surface collaboration marketing seems straightforward, this chapter demonstrates many of the challenges particular to the various sectors within the wider tourism and hospitality industry. The chapter outlined many of the benefits and

## TOURISM AND HOSPITALITY INSIGHTS 4.3
## LEADING HOTELS OF THE WORLD

Leading Hotels of the World (LHW) is one of the largest and most prestigious luxury hotel consortia in the world (LHW, 2018). Influential and forward thinking European hoteliers established the company in 1928, with 38 initial member hotels, such as Hotel Negresco in Nice and King David Hotel in Jerusalem (LHW, 2018). Since its establishment as a reservation service organization, LHW has evolved into a highly recognized luxury brand and marketing company that provides extensive sales, promotional activities, advertising, marketing, and public relations (Maresco & Lyons, 2005). The company currently represents more than 375 fine hotels and resorts, with over 54,000 rooms, in 75 countries (LHW, 2018). To become an LHW member, hotels must meet stringent quality standards, evaluated by an 800-point inspection, including all aspects affecting guests' comfort, convenience, and satisfaction (LHW, 2018). Approximately 95% of their member hotels are independently managed and, therefore, are quite unique in their history as well as service and architecture styles (Elite Traveler, 2013).

For the majority of independent hotels, unlike international brand chains such as Marriott International and Hilton Worldwide, marketing power is extremely limited due to several reasons, such as lack of marketing costs and scale economy. Since its early stage, LHW has been offering solutions for this issue to individual luxury hotels. The Leading Hotels of Europe, the first predecessor of LHW, was established in 1928 by an entrepreneurial group of European hoteliers who came together in order to attract the lucrative market of American travelers to their European hotels (Elite Traveler, 2013). Therefore, the first LHW office was opened in New York City in order for hotels to cooperate with travel agencies in the United States (Elite Traveler, 2013). In the mid-1970s, LHW invested in the technological development of a reservation system in order to increase member sales; they became the first adapter to use a computer-satellite based reservation system in the hotel industry and they obtained a toll-free phone number, which was considered to be cutting edge for both travel agents and consumers at the time (Elite Traveler, 2013). Another benefit to independent hotels is LHW's two-tiered customer loyalty program, Leaders Club, that provides several benefits to frequent customers (Elite Traveler, 2013). Through this loyalty program, LHW can retain customers for their member hotels and member hotels can share their customers' preferences in order to increase customer satisfaction, which consequently leads to increased customer loyalty. Their most recent innovative update is the world's first cognitive travel platform, which leverages IBM Watson's natural language-processing services to provide travelers hotel recommendations based on specific needs (LHW, 2016). Phil Koserowski, the Vice President of interactive marketing, said that, through this platform, customers can effortlessly research and find hotels that meet their desires and needs for their trips (LHW, 2016).

The hotel industry has seen many mergers and acquisitions for more efficient marketing, such as the Marriott International/Starwood Hotels and Resorts merger and the AccorHotels/Fairmont Hotels and Resorts merger, and these trends are anticipated to accelerate (Questex, 2017). In such a highly competitive market with global mega hotel brands, individual hotels will be placed in difficult positions. Therefore, LHW and their further strategic collaborative marketing will be required in order to preserve the unique individuality of luxury hotels.

### References

Elite Traveler. (2013). *The Leading Hotels of the World celebrate 85 years*. Retrieved from https://www.elitetraveler.com/tv/elite-traveler-meets-tv/elite-traveler-meets-distributors-and-partners

LHW. (2018). *Company overview*, Retrieved from https://www.lhw.com/corporate/about-us

LHW. (2016, Mar 2). *LHW taps IBM Watson to launch trip discovery tool on LHW.com*, Retrieved from https://www.lhw.com/press-center/wayblazer-lhw-march-2016

Maresco, P.A., & Lyons, B. (2005). Achieving growth in the luxury market. *Strategic Finance, 86*(11), 47–52.

Questex. (2017, Oct 12). *Mergers and acquisitions in hospitality expected to accelerate*, Retrieved from https://www.hotelmanagement.net/transactions/mergers-and-acquisitions-hospitality-expected-to-accelerate

Source: Ryuichi Karakawa.

drawbacks of different forms of collaboration marketing, with the reader now being familiar with the individual situations evident with destination partnerships, airline alliances, and hotel consortia. Collaboration marketing is now such an important and pervasive facet of the tourism and hospitality industry that it is imperative that understanding of the particular dynamics of each mode of collaboration is clear. Partnerships, alliances, and consortia have been widespread across the industry over the past few decades with them continuing to shape the future of the industry.

### REVIEW QUESTIONS

1.  In the specific context of an LTA, what are some of the reasons social capital might be higher for local stakeholders as opposed to stakeholders in a regional structure?
2.  What are some of the e-intermediaries that pose a threat to LTAs?
3.  What are some of the financial benefits an independent hotel may gain by joining a consortium?
4.  What are some of the operational benefits you can imagine a small hotel gaining by joining a consortium?
5.  What are some of the benefits and drawbacks of membership of one of the three major global airline alliances?

### YOUTUBE LINKS

"McAmerica: the success secrets of brand USA"

URL: https://www.youtube.com/watch?v=6DNViKt50mE

Summary: The United States of America is an extremely indispensable and inimitable national brand that no country has such strong branding; they have continually topped the number of international tourist receipts with the second largest number of tourist arrivals. Al Jazeera investigated the success secrets of Brand USA. They had discussions with representatives who constructed USA branding and disseminated messages as brand ambassadors.

## "Ted Teng, President & Chief Executive Officer, The Leading Hotels of the World"

URL: https://www.youtube.com/watch?v=f0m315d3jW8

Summary: Ted Teng, President of The Leading Hotels of the World discussed the strategies through which they will strive to deliver both high service quality and revenue to their members for the next 80 years and beyond. He described The Leading Hotels of the World as a museum that curates unique and high-quality hotels and introduces them to customers all over the world. He also talked about several industry trends, including distribution channels and influencers in an era of multimedia consumers.

## "74th IATA AGM – Star Alliance media briefing"

URL: https://www.youtube.com/watch?v=wSWDfdZezv8&t=277s

Summary: At the 74th IATA (International Air Transport Association) Annual General Meeting in Sydney, Jeffrey Goh, CEO of Star Alliance, introduced their strategic repositioning, from increasing alliance members to improving the seamless travel experience, especially for customers who travel with several airlines. He identified utilizing digital technologies to offer smoother and better travel experiences as a key component for their strategic repositioning.

### REFERENCES AND RELATED WEBSITES

References

Agusdinata, B., & Klein, W. (2002). The dynamics of airline alliances. *Journal of Air Transport Management, 8*(4), 201–211. Retrieved from https://doi.org/10.1016/S0969-6997(01)00052-7

Fyall, A., & Garrod, B. (2005). *Tourism marketing: A collaborative approach.* Buffalo, NY: Channel View Publications.

Fyall, A., & Garrod, B. (2017). Collaborative destination marketing at the local level: Benefits bundling and the changing role of the local tourism association. *Current Issues In Tourism, 20*(7), 668–690.

Gibson, L., Lynch, P.A., & Morrison, A. (2005). The local destination tourism network: Development issues. *Tourism and Hospitality Planning & Development, 2*(2), 87–99. doi: 10.1080/14790530500171708

Malver, H. (1998). *Service in the airlines: Customer or competition oriented?*. Stockholm: Stockholm University.

Oneworld. (2017). Oneworld at a glance. Retrieved from https://www.oneworld.com/news-information/oneworld-fact-sheets/oneworld-at-a-glance

Perkins, E. (July, 2012). Seven surprising benefits of airline alliances. *SmarterTravel*. Retrieved from https://www.smartertravel.com/2012/07/11/seven-surprising-benefits-of-airline-alliances/

SkyTeam (2017). Facts and figures. Retrieved from https://www.skyteam.com/en/about/

Smith, A.L. (2011). Public-private partnerships (PPP's) for sustainable tourism. *Inter-American Development Bank*. Retrieved from http://www.oas.org/en/sedi/desd/itc2011/pres/Arthur_Smith.pdf

Star Alliance (2017). Destinations. Retrieved from http://www.staralliance.com/en/destinations

## Websites

Airline Trends
http://www.airlinetrends.com/

Atout France
http://us.france.fr/

Brand USA
https://www.thebrandusa.com/

Flight Network – Best Tourism Organizations
https://www.flightnetwork.com/blog/20-worlds-best-tourism-organizations/

Hopper Guide to Airline Alliances
https://www.hopper.com/articles/860/a-guide-to-the-three-major-airline-alliances-star-alliance-oneworld-and-sky-team

Hospitality.net
https://www.hospitalitynet.org/list/1-10/consortia.html

Oneworld Alliance
https://www.oneworld.com/

SkyTeam
https://www.skyteam.com

Star Alliance
http://www.staralliance.com/

State Tourism Organizations
http://www.statelocalgov.net/50states-tourism.cfm

Travel Weekly
http://www.travelweekly.com/

TripSavvy
https://www.tripsavvy.com/what-is-a-consortium-3252390

Visit Britain
https://www.visitbritain.com/

# MAJOR CASE STUDY
# STAR AIRLINE ALLIANCE

Since its establishment by five airlines in May 1997, as the first truly global airline alliance, Star Alliance has defined and led the airline industry. Star Alliance today comprises the following 28 airlines, including many of the world's leading aviation companies as well as smaller regional airlines: Adria Airways, Aegean Airlines, Air Canada, Air China, Air India, Air New Zealand, ANA, Asiana Airlines, Austrian, Avianca, Avianca Brazil, Brussels Airlines, Copa Airlines, Croatia Airlines, EGYPTAIR, Ethiopian Airlines, EVA Air, LOT Polish Airlines, Lufthansa, Scandinavian Airlines, Shenzhen Airlines, Singapore Airlines, South African Airways, SWISS, TAP Portugal, Turkish Airlines, THAI and United Airlines (Star Alliance, 2018). Consistent with their vision "to be the leading global airline for the high-value international traveler" (Star Alliance, 2016), Star Alliance today is the largest global airline alliance, offering over 4,700 fleets for more than 1,317 destinations in 193 countries worldwide. The Star Alliance network reaches 98% of the world's countries (Star Alliance, 2018). Its acceptance by the market has been recognized by several awards, including the Air Transport World Market Leadership Award and Best Airline Alliance by *Business Traveller* Magazine. In addition, Star Alliance was nominated Best Airline Alliance in 2017 by SKYTRAX World Airline Awards for two consecutive years (Star Alliance, 2018).

Star Alliance, as mentioned in its Mission statement, has contributed to "the long-term profitability of its members beyond their individual capabilities" (Star Alliance, 2016) by facilitating cooperation and integration of member airlines while allowing them to retain their individual styles and identities. One of the key benefits of Star Alliance's cooperation and integration is their joint marketing activities. Significant marketing benefits were reaped through Star Alliance's huge global reach and the connectivity of their combined networks (Fyall & Garrod, 2005). One significant example of their joint marketing activities is their Frequent Flyer Program (FFP), through which customers can earn and redeem miles across all Star Alliance member airlines (Star Alliance, 2018). As customers gain benefits and reach certain status levels from their individual airlines' FFPs, they can also obtain Star Alliance statuses (Star Alliance, 2018). With a Silver or Gold status from Star Alliance, customers can obtain additional benefits, including priority services (i.e. wait-listing, airport standby, check-in, and boarding) and worldwide lounge access (Star Alliance, 2018). In order to improve the FFP award ticket-booking process, Star Alliance developed an alliance-wide computer system that allows member airlines to book all other member airlines' available seats in real time (Fyall & Garrod, 2005). These joint marketing activities are beneficial for all member airlines because they increase customer loyalty to the alliance and encourage customers to repeat-purchase on flights offered by partner airlines as well as their own.

Joint operations of Star Alliance have also contributed to "the long-term profitability of its members." One of the principal joint operation examples is their extensive code sharing. Code-sharing agreements within the alliance has enabled member airlines to provide a seamless service to many destinations. As member airlines join huge alliance networks, they are able to provide services to their customers at a wider range of destinations, to obtain access to attractive airports and to offer niche routes on which the number of customers would be so small that each airline would not be able to offer its own service (Fyall & Garrod, 2005). For instance, All Nippon Airways (ANA), the largest airline company in Japan, expanded its network globally through code-sharing agreements with other Star Alliance members and dramatically increased its arrival and departure slots at Narita Airport (Tokyo) as well as revenue from international networks, after they became a member of Star Alliance in 1998 (ANA, n.d.). Sharing baggage handling, ground maintenance, and facilities is also a beneficial joint activity for reducing their costs as well as enabling member airlines to further enhance their customer service. Star Alliance brought member airlines together at selected airports so they could share services like common check-in, transfer, and baggage facilities. They call this service "move under one roof" (Star Alliance, 2018). For instance, all their member airlines were placed together in the same terminals in Miami, Seoul, and Singapore. These initiatives make customers' travel more convenient (Star Alliance, 2018). In addition, a further example of joint operations is procurement and the use of collective buying power. Because of its size, Star Alliance can utilize its higher bargaining power that offers airline members cost-efficient opportunities. The most frequent example is joint fuel purchase agreements that enable airline members to manage fuel supply efficiently.

Since its establishment back in 1997, Star Alliance has driven innovation in the airline industry and developed the leading airline alliance for international travelers. During their two successful decades, Star Alliance has always looked for ways to provide their customers with seamless travel experiences as well as contribute to the long-term profitability of its member airlines through cooperation and integration. On May 14, 2017, its 20-year anniversary, Star Alliance announced their new strategy for the next decade that would harness digital technology to further enhance the travel experience of their customers (Star Alliance, 2018). With their recent partnership with Accenture, Star Alliance launched a Digital Service Platform (DSP) that will allow customers to utilize member airlines' individual websites and applications to obtain all the information they need to travel (Star Alliance, 2018). Star Alliance will continue to roll out better customer experience, enabling customers to receive an improved digital experience, through their members' continued joint activity.

## References

Ana Holdings Inc. (n.d.). *Alliances that create value – the ANA group's alliance strategy for its international business.* Retrieved from https://www.ana.co.jp/group/en/company/pickup/pickup_alliance.html

Fyall, A., & Garrod, B. (2005). *Tourism marketing: a collaborative approach.* Clevedon: Channel View Publications.

Star Alliance. (2016). *Reference guide 2016/2017.* Retrieved from https://portal.staralliance.com/cms/publications/reference-guide/star-alliance-final-web.pdf/@@download/file/Star_Alliance_FINAL_web.pdf

Star Alliance. (2017, May 13). *Star Alliance celebrates 20 years of connecting people and cultures.* Retrieved from http://www.staralliance.com/en/news-article?newsArticleId=PR_ 20TH&groupId=20184

Star Alliance. (2018, Feb 8). *Star Alliance creates digital services platform with accenture.* Retrieved from http://www.staralliance.com/en/news-article?newsArticleId=DSP& groupId=20184

Star Alliance. (2018). *30 seconds about us, Star Alliance leads the way.* Retrieved from http://www.star alliance.com/en/about

Star Alliance. (2018). *Earn and redeem, Making travel even more rewarding.* Retrieved from http://www.staralliance.com/en/earn-and-redeem

Star Alliance. (2018). *Star Alliance member airlines 28 airlines working in harmony.* Retrieved from http://www.staralliance.com/en/member-airlines

Star Alliance. (2018). *We move under one roof, so you move less.* Retrieved from http://www.staralliance.com/en/connectingyou

Source: Ryuichi Karakawa.

Major case study questions

1. Why is it that so many international airlines choose to join global airline alliances rather than operate individually?

2. What are the primary service and experiential benefits offered to passengers by the Star Alliance?

3. What may be some of the negatives of global airline alliance membership?

4. What future opportunities do you think exist for enhancing the traveler experience by Star Alliance?

# Technology and marketing

## Social media and beyond

## Learning outcomes

By the end of this chapter, students will:

- Understand the importance of the role of technology in tourism and hospitality marketing
- Be cognizant of some of the applications of technology in tourism and hospitality marketing
- Understand the reasons underpinning technology adoption in different tourism and hospitality scenarios
- Be introduced to the role of social media in tourism and hospitality marketing and understand the dynamics of user-generated content
- Understand the current and future role of big data analytics in tourism and hospitality marketing.

### Key terms

technology, social media, user-generated content, adoption, marketing operations

## Introduction

Technology has penetrated all aspects of our life. The involvement of technology has reached a level in that modern life is almost impossible without it. Marketing is not an exception in this situation and managing marketing systems in corporations need the managers to be involved in technology as heavily as possible. Everything in marketing plans and marketing systems from the marketing mix elements to mass and target marketing are all now highly interwoven with technology. To a certain extent, marketing operations in the contemporary business world are impossible to conduct without utilization of technology. In this chapter, we discuss some of the applications of technology in hospitality and tourism marketing. Although various technologies are explained throughout the chapter, the main focus of this chapter is on social media and Web 2.0.

From a general business perspective, technology is involved from the beginning to the end of marketing operations. In the beginning, technology helps organizations not only to reduce the cost of production, but also to speed up the new product development process. At the end, the whole experience of the customer is carefully monitored using various sources such as social media and big data analytics. Technology increases the accuracy of product and service delivery. Error-free processes in any stages from design to after-sales support are also possible thanks to technology. That being said, due to the incredible scope, accessibility, speed, and magnitude of the effect that technology provides, any small human mistake can become a fatal one. For example, Intercontinental Hotels mistakenly priced rooms at one of its four-star hotels near Venice, Italy, for €1 per night instead of the actual price of €150 per night. Internet users booked 1,400 room nights before the mistake was realized. Intercontinental Hotels honored the reservations at a cost of €90,000 to the company!

Technology has a core role in the service delivery chain as it integrates multiple layers and processes of service delivery. It is as useful for the company as it is for the customers. Technology can remove most of the traditional barriers in service production and consumption. On the supply side, marketing information systems as part of management information systems (MIS) have benefited considerably by using technology in all aspects of data collection, process, storage, analysis, and distribution. The quality of information available to marketing managers by MIS is not comparable to 20–30 years ago. The level of uncertainty in managerial decision-making has decreased significantly thanks to technology. On the other hand, customer relationship management (CRM) is dramatically changed as a result of technological advancements. Technology in many forms has influenced CRM, from traceable footprints in digital ecosystems to managing mega databases utilizing big data analytics. Nowadays, a truly customized relationship is possible thanks to information and communication technology (ICT). Technology helps CRM to manage all customer contact points from the first contact to the moments-of-truth and to the services and supports after sale. From a business perspective, CRM supported by technology is critical in customer satisfaction by providing customized and even personalized services and products, thus creating and maintaining a competitive advantage.

Technology has also made it possible for small companies to compete with billion-dollar companies, which would not have been possible without the Internet and social media. Owing to inexpensive direct marketing capability that is provided by technology, small- and medium-sized enterprises (SMEs) can now carefully conduct market studies with high accuracy, segregate the market into operationalizable segments, carefully select the target market(s), study them, and offer an appropriate solution to satisfy their needs and wants. In other words, technology has provided accessibility and opportunities for so many SMEs in so many different ways. In addition, using technology-supported data and intelligence to develop customer profiles and perform target marketing is becoming common business practice, and hospitality and tourism companies which used to spend billions of dollars to create up-to-date systems of customer profiling can now carry out the whole profiling process with just a few clicks by using certain big data algorithms. Further explanations of big data analytics are provided toward the end of the chapter.

Examples of technology use in a hospitality and tourism context can be a separate book in itself. Nevertheless, some of the most popular applications are listed here.

- Computerized point-of-sales (POS) systems: A point-of-sale system is a combination of software and hardware that allows sellers to take transactions and simplify key day-to-day business operations which can provide valuable information regarding the operations of the hospitality business for decision-making purposes, in addition to managing the business transaction processes. For example, in the restaurant industry, traditionally, the restaurant POS system is where a customer makes a payment in exchange for goods or services. Payment terminals, touch screens, and a variety of other hardware and software options are used to enable the transaction. Today, however, the restaurant point of sale is often referred to as the restaurant point of service, given that restaurant POS is no longer just about processing sales. For example, by using POS, restaurants can track the popularity of their menu items through various time intervals during a day. They also can identify patterns in food and beverage consumption due to various events. Modern restaurant POS systems provide a platform that sits at the heart of any food and beverage operation, large or small, helping to enhance the customer experience and streamline business operations. Every restaurant POS system allows food and beverage operators to process orders and maintain financial control of their business, through cash management and integration with payment service providers. As margins get tighter in the food and beverage industry, successful operators need a restaurant POS to do much more. An integrated restaurant POS today will also offer: reporting and analytics, inventory management, labor management, gifts and loyalty, and loss prevention, etc.
- Property management systems (PMS): PMS are computerized systems that facilitate the management of hotel properties and are used for reservation, availability and occupancy management, check-in/out, guest profiles, report generation, maintenance, inventory control, safety and security, energy control, customer relationship management and personnel management all through a single piece of software. The PMS can be connected with other applications such as the hotel point of sale (POS) or the central reservation system (CRS). The interface to a CRS is an additional option in order to transfer availability, reservations, and guest profile information for chain hotels. Additionally, various interfaces are available to create further links to internal and external systems such as room key systems, restaurant and banquet cash registers, minibar, telephone and call centers, revenue management, etc. Today, most next-generation property management systems are moving away from client/server configurations and favor web and cloud technology and offer their software to clients using a software-as-a-service model.

# Technology acceptance

The expansion of technology and its exponential growth necessitates having some understanding of the expansion mechanisms. Technology diffusion follows a similar model to new products dispersion known as the Bass model with the classic s-shaped cumulative diffusion curve (Figure 5.1 (a & b)). The Bass model or Bass diffusion model was developed by Frank Bass. It consists of a simple differential equation that describes the process of how new products get adopted in a population. The model presents a rationale of how current adopters and potential adopters of a new product interact. The basic premise of the model is that adopters can be classified as innovators or as imitators and the speed and timing of adoption depends on their degree of innovativeness and the degree of imitation among adopters. The Bass model has been widely used in forecasting, especially new products' sales forecasting and technology forecasting (Bass, 1980).

There are three parameters influencing the diffusion process. The external parameter (parameter of innovation ($p$)) is the primary force initiating the diffusion process. $P$ is usually very minimal and less than 0.4. This external influencer can be a force external to the organization such as the pressure from the environment, promotion related to the technology, other companies' usage, and especially leading companies' usage. The

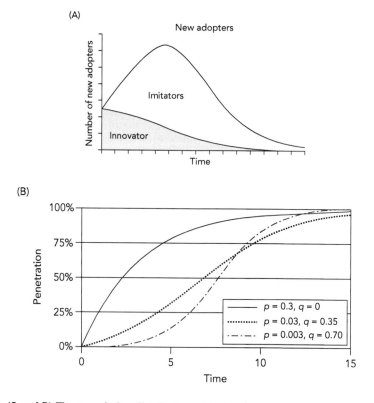

**Figure 5.1** (A and B) The cumulative distribution of technology acceptance

internal parameter (parameter of imitation or social contagion ($q$)) takes the diffusion into the next level by strengthening and rushing the dispersion to its maximum. The internal parameter/influencer can be any internal force within the organization or a reflection of the natural characteristics of the technology. For example, due to the nature of the product, a theme park is more technology sensitive compared to a regular resort or a restaurant. As a result, their (i.e., the firm and its employees) readiness to accept different technologies are different. In addition, different technologies have different levels of attractiveness to organizations and their employees. For example, a new TV is more attractive to a sports bar compared to a jazz bar and the acceptance rate for the TV is going to be much higher for sports bars. Finally, organization size (diffusion ceiling ($m$)) is a critical influencer affecting technology diffusion. Different organizational sizes require different logistics requirements and infrastructure preparation to adopt a technological innovation. While large organizations have more resources for more expensive technologies, the dispersion of technology is also time consuming and the majority might be achieved much later time-wise.

The technology diffusion model is based on mathematical models, which were mainly used for studying epidemics and contagious diseases. While these models are considered as popular models in general studies investigating technology diffusion, technology acceptance studies in the hospitality and tourism context, however, utilize the technology acceptance model (TAM) and the unified theory of acceptance and usage of technology (UTAUT) in most technology adoption investigations. Although these models are mostly related to the theory of technology acceptance, which is not within the scope of this chapter, they help us to better understand the mechanism by which technology usage becomes popular in hospitality and tourism settings. Based on these theories, various factors such as effort expectancy, performance expectancy, social influence, facilitating conditions, attitudes, and behavioral intentions are determinants of technology use in an organization. Effort expectancy is the amount of effort the person is expected to invest in order to use a specific technology. In other words, effort expectancy means how easy a technology use is perceived. Performance expectancy deals with the amount of utility (usefulness) that use of a specific technology creates. In other words, performance expectancy can be perceived from a hedonistic aspect (i.e., how fun is the use of technology) or from a utilitarian aspect (i.e., how useful is the use of technology). Social influence and facilitating conditions are also among the factors influencing the adoption and use of technology. Social norm is the general acceptance of a specific technology in society, which can be reflected by peer pressure in relation to the use of the technology. For example, if a specific technology becomes the norm in society, non-users of the technology will feel the pressure that they also should start using the technology. Facilitating conditions, on the other hand, refer to the efforts to provide infrastructure for the popularity of a technology. Attitudes and behavioral intentions are the final steps to start using technology and can be under the impact of the above-mentioned variables.

Some of the examples of technology adoption are the use of radio-frequency identification (RFID) and near-field communication (NFC) technologies. RFID technology is among the most popular technologies in the hospitality and entertainment industry. By using electromagnetic fields, RFID automatically identifies and tracks labels that are attached to objects (e.g., wristband). The door key cards in hotels and resorts, wristbands and cards in theme parks, game chips in casinos, and various objects in cruise ships, are all examples of vast usage of RFID in hospitality. A specific type of high-frequency (HF) RFID is known as NFC technology, which is a more secure type of data exchange compared to RFID. Unlike RFID, NFC operates at a very short distance (i.e., usually less than 10 cm) and is capable of being both a reader and tag simultaneously. While RFID is among the most popular technologies among suppliers (businesses), NFC is an example of technology adoption among customers. NFC has been successfully embedded in newer generations of smart phones, which makes these phones a no-contact wallet. Apart from ease and convenience, NFC can provide various facts about the product that customer is paying for. NFC has revolutionized e-commerce in a way that a new area of mobile payment (MP) is added to e-commerce that is growing exponentially. Unlike some of the East Asian countries such as Japan and South Korea, NFC-MP is not as popular in North America yet. Apart from facilitating conditions such as infrastructures, which are not as developed as the above-mentioned East Asian countries, trust and security are important factors in that North Americans are less inclined to use NFC-MP. In addition to previous factors such as effort expectancy, hedonic and utilitarian performance expectancy, social influence, and facilitating conditions, some other factors such as risk, trust, and security are also influential in customers' decision in relation to the use of NFC-MP.

## Internet and Web 2.0

The most important impact of technology on operations is on communication regarding both the quality and amount of the available information. ICT has revolutionized the hospitality and tourism industry more than any other technology. Hence, a great deal of this chapter is related to ICT and its impact on hospitality and tourism. ICT is any technology that is involved in stages of information/data collection, accumulation, analysis, communication, and dissemination. There are various criteria to evaluate the efficiency and effectiveness of an ICT system such as accuracy of the information, up-to-the-minute information, and volume of processed data, among others. The information provided as an outcome of an ICT system should be accurate in order not to misguide the decision makers (i.e., managers from the supply side, consumers from the demand side). Inaccurate information can create wrong directions, which might lead to wrong decisions that might result in large monetary losses. The accurate information should also be on time as the expiration date of the information is so critical in defining the utility of the information. In other words, outdated information is as useless as an inaccurate source of information.

The introduction of the Internet in the 1990s and its popularity in 2000s made information the most critical asset for any given company around the world. The hospitality and tourism industry is no exception to this rule. Information and the quality of its communication can make or break a company. The second revolution after the Internet became popular was related to the advent of Web 2.0. The term Web 2.0 emerged in late 2004, almost a decade after the launch of the Internet. Web 2.0 originated in the work of Tim O'Reilly of O'Reilly Media. However, despite much media hype, a formal, agreed-upon, definition has yet to be developed, partly because the term means many different things to many different people. Technically, Web 2.0 can be defined as a new generation of Internet-based technology (sites, applications, services, and processes) that allow people to collaborate and share information in ways that were previously unimaginable. In other words, Web 2.0 provides the infrastructures for an interactive communication channel between consumers and suppliers. Although Web 2.0 is facilitated by technological developments, its growth has had more to do with a fundamental shift in user behavior than any particular technological development. One of the major developments as a result of Web 2.0 is the advent of social media websites. These websites were purely developed based on participatory efforts of their members. Although Web 2.0 enables Internet users to produce and even sell web-based information, Web 2.0 sites tend to be participatory, encouraging contributions and feedback from anyone who is interested, thus blurring the line between the content creator and the content audience.

**Image 5.1**

Source: Pexels.

This interactive nature of social media websites offers users the same spirit of physical society as these websites tend to be conversational, using two-way or multi-way interaction between participants rather than a broadcast approach. They are community-focused, facilitating the interaction of groups of people with similar interests, and they are connected, amalgamating links and content from many different sources to add synergistic value to the resulting service, product, or message. Therefore, the concept of Web 2.0 can be considered as a huge virtual community where people can participate and interact based on commonality of interests. Individuals are increasingly seeking clues from one another, rather than from institutional sources like corporations, the media, political bodies, or even religions. While in the past, consumers looked to such authorities for their information, now they are increasingly looking at the collective wisdom of their peers as the ultimate authority. This paradigm shift in consumer behavior is considered as the main force shaping future markets based recommendation networks as e-WoM (electronic word of mouth) travels much faster than traditional WoM.

## TOURISM AND HOSPITALITY INSIGHTS 5.1
## SOCIAL MEDIA DERAILS STRIKES IN FRANCE

Strikes in France are not uncommon. The most current notable strike is that of French rail workers. Workers are fighting the opening up of state railways to competition, as of 2023 in conjunction with EU requirements, and the consequent phasing out of contracts that include early retirement and automatic pay raises. The workers have been staging massive rail strikes in the hopes of causing a crippling and noticeable change to the country. France has a long history of paralyzing labor strife, such as protests over pension reform in 1995. However, the impact of this year's walkout at SNCF, the national rail system, has been limited (Benoit & Nussbaum, 2018). With the efficiency of the Internet, people are able to work from home (which has been further encouraged by the French government for its workers). Instead of mass chaos, technology has lessened the impact of the strikes to the economy and how the country functions (Benoit & Nussbaum, 2018; Schofield, 2018).

Contrary to strikes in the past, technology is allowing for the quick and efficient sharing of information regarding rail schedules. SNCF has been providing detailed information to commuters via the website as to trains will be running. This information has allowed commuters and companies, to make travel arrangements and work schedules (Schofield, 2018). It has not been uncommon for exams and meetings to be reorganized via group emails based on up-to-date information from the SNCF website. Social networking and the sharing economy have also assisted in lessening the impact of the strike, as people are utilizing alternative means of transportation to combat the rail strikes (Schofield, 2018). Ride-sharing companies are seeing an increase in app usage on strike days and the intercity bus line, FlixBus, is seeing online bookings jumping by 60% on strike days. While technology is lessening the effects of the strike, it has not eliminated the damage done.

Strikes are still responsible for creating slowdowns in daily commuting, grain shipments, freight shipments, and tourist bookings (Benoit & Nussbaum, 2018). The tourism industry is seeing the impacts of the strikes as train operations between France and other European countries (Italy, Spain, Switzerland, Britain, Belgium and Germany notably) have been affected (Macpherson & Charlton, 2018). The French Foreign Ministry is unsure how the strikes will affect the tourism industry as a whole (Macpherson & Charlton, 2018). However, the hotel industry has reported bookings down by 10% in April 2018, with anticipated May and June bookings to also be lower than normal (Benoit & Nussbaum, 2018). Like local commuters, travelers are sharing information via online travel forums and utilizing car-sharing apps to work around the strikes (Macpherson & Charlton, 2018). Ultimately, only time will tell just how the impact of the strikes will be. However, it is certain that without the utilization of technology the effect could be much worse.

### References

Benoit, A., & Nussbaum, A. (2018, April 24). France's rail strike has boosted buses and ride-sharing. *Bloomberg*. Retrieved from: https://www.bloomberg.com/news/articles/2018-04-24/france-turns-to-buses-ride-sharing-to-ease-rail-strike-s-impact

Macpherson, M., & Charlton, A. (2018, April 4). Tourists, commuters seek workarounds to French train strikes. *AP News*. Retrieved from: https://apnews.com/6a6329d6a1fa4fdbb1354fb0a3f1ae0d

Schofield, H. (2018, May 16). How tech took the bite out of France's rail strikes. *BBC News*. Retrieved from: https://www.bbc.com/news/world-europe-44122561

Source: Amanda Templeton.

Considering the unique characteristics of virtual community and examining all discussions about the definition of online community from different perspectives, a framework is suggested by Wang et al. (2002) (Figure 5.2). According to Wang et al.'s conceptual model, place, symbol, and virtual are considered as the unique characteristics of a virtual community including hospitality and tourism virtual communities. At an operational level, virtual community requires the presence of groups of people who interact with specific purposes, under the governance of certain policies, and with the facilitation of computer systems.

In offline worlds, community is a physical venue where people can develop and maintain social and economic relationships and explore new opportunities. Community is formed based on certain commonalities such as location, lifestyle, identity, character, etc. Web 2.0 provides the same opportunity for online communities. Similar to the physical community, a virtual community can be perceived as a social organization where like-minded souls meet. When creating a community, people tend to attach a symbolic meaning to the community. It is the symbolic dimension of a community that provides meaning and identity for the community members. Community is a

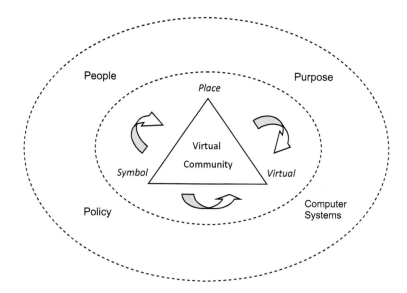

**Figure 5.2** A conceptual model of virtual tourist community (adapted from Wang et al., 2002)

complex system of ideas and sentiments. Virtual community exists because participants define it and give it meaning. Virtual community has its own cultural composition; it has its own collective sense, and its own virtual ideology and symbol. In this sense, virtual community is a very personal thing and only the members themselves can tell whether they feel a part of the community. For example, as a virtual community, TripAdvisor provides a platform (place or to be more precise, space) to build multiple communities of individuals interested in travel and symbolizes various forms and purposes related to travel and tourism. In spite of similarities between online communities and offline ones, being virtual is one of the most important features that distinguishes them. The notion of virtual community is inherently unique because computer-mediated communication (CMC) creates the context within which social relations occur and affects our view of community, especially in a virtual way. In other words, community cannot be seen in virtual or real form but real communities can be shown with physical members and other physical characteristics such as buildings, etc. Virtual communities are completely facilitated by CMC with no physical constraints. Since the term "virtual" is associated with "unreal," it is argued that what happens online is like a community, but is not really a community. However, if one agrees that communication is the core of any community, a virtual community is real no matter where it exists.

Theoretical notions of virtual community can only be made feasible by four operational elements: people, purpose, policy, and computer system. Therefore, a more comprehensive and complete understanding of the virtual community requires an examination of the four elements in different contexts depending on the nature of the community. The growth of virtual community supported by Web 2.0 technologies such as blogs, user reviews, and social networks, provides great opportunities for both business organizations and their customers. Companies can use Web 2.0 sites to create new types of services, to enhance their existing products, and to create new divisions and capabilities. On a macro level, for tourism destinations, these sites can broaden their marketing horizon and have a great impact on marketing, sales, product and service development, supplier network, information quality, and distribution channels.

Irrespective of whether information regarding hospitality and tourism is distributed through an intermediary or directly from the supplier, it generally has a few sources that either come from the supplier itself or from other intermediaries such as third-party websites, newspapers, magazines, guidebooks, etc. Given that all these sources pursue commercial goals, the credibility of these information sources and their producer agencies is questionable. The very marketing and advertising nature of these sources makes them highly biased. As a result, the information obtained from these sources produces very little added value to customers. Compared to these resources, information provided by recommendation-based systems relying mainly on user-generated content (UGC, also known as consumer-generated media or consumer-generated marketing) is mostly produced for the purposes other than commercial. Ideally, customers need a more credible source – a need that is being serviced by the growth of Web 2.0. Since UGC is created by consumers to be used by other consumers, it is considered as the most trustworthy unbiased source of information for decision-making. As this information comes from consumers without any commercial interests, other consumers can trust it.

Given the importance of information in the hospitality and tourism distribution process, this change has important implications. Hospitality and tourism firms' sales are heavily dependent on their perceived quality in the eyes of consumers and UGC is playing a critical role in determining the quality of these businesses. Considering the scarcity of resources such as time, society is coming to realize that the risk of bad consumption experience makes information such a valuable commodity for consumers. Customers, in their decision-making process, face numerous consumption options that can be overwhelming. Existence of a trustworthy distribution system is a necessity for customers to overcome the hurdle of consumption choice. The role of UGC in customer empowerment is thus undeniable. Nowadays, more than 100 million websites contain UGC. This empowerment on the other hand, can become a nightmare for company public relations. For example, the experience of #shareyourstory by McDonald's was a total failure for the company that resulted from a lack of accurate environmental information. McDonald's started a marketing campaign without knowing the true nature of their products in the eyes of customers and #shareyourstory became a place to share scandalous complaints. Nevertheless, it should be noted that unlike a decade ago, nowadays, not all UGCs are produced to help customers as deviant behaviors start appearing in UGC area as well. In other words, some abusive customers have started using empowerment as a result of Web 2.0 to say negative things about businesses and receive financial and economic gains. These types of behavior are also spreading fast throughout the networks of customers in social media. One of the critical areas for companies currently is to be able to identify fake reviews from genuine ones. Companies spent a large portion of their research and development budget to develop machine learning and artificial intelligent algorithms to identify these fake reviews.

Online social media (also known as social networking sites (SNS)) are virtual spaces where individuals interact with each other and engage in a dyadic, mutual, and reciprocal relationships. As previously stated, social media is the most notable achievement of Web 2.0 and the birthplace of UGC. Knowing about them helps companies to understand the mechanisms and procedures of this kind of media and accordingly plan for their marketing on these sophisticated platforms. Most SNSs allow users to build personal web pages, which are known as profiles and then connect with friends and relatives to communicate and share content. The "friends" concept in SNS can be a reflection of physical community as well as individuals that people have no contact with in real life. Subgroups typically form around highly specific interests, with each member taking part in multiple subgroups. Such networks (subgroups) have their origins in supporting interactions among immediate neighbors in a community. The connection to immediate neighbors is the reflection of the concept that your friends' friends are your friends. This concept in network science is known as transitivity or clustering. As a result of transitivity, these subgroups are very coherent and densely connected. In other words, people are connected to multiple members forming various star-circles and triangles. Transitivity is a reflection of physical society with an exception that the rule of physical distance between neighbors is not imposing any limitation to virtual subgroups, and similarity in interests and knowing individuals are the most important rules for the formation of virtual subgroups. Individuals have multiple interests that do not necessarily match those of everyone else in one subgroup. As a result, subgroups become connected to each other by individuals who share various interests. These connections play the role of long distant connections known as random rewiring in network science. This random rewiring, similar to physical communities shortens the distance among individuals and causes a phenomenon known as small world with a difference because virtual small world distances are shorter compared to the real world small world. The small world phenomenon facilitates information exchange, discussions, and joint activities related to local events, issues, and concerns. Moreover, the context of these events, issues, and concerns has been transformed because of the expansion of electronic communications and use of the web which is no longer limited by physical locations. Communities of individuals with similar interests and concerns can now be formed virtually and can interact primarily in the online environment. Small worlds also create less centralized networks that are resilient to many environmental threats. In other words, these online platforms are stronger than physical communities, especially when it comes to their durability and survival.

Facebook is one of the better-known SNSs around the world. Mark Zuckerberg launched it in 2004; at that time, it was targeted exclusively at Harvard students but proved such a huge hit that within two weeks, half of the student body had signed up and other Boston area schools began demanding their own Facebook network. Within four months, Facebook had added 30 more college networks and the social networking trend was born. Facebook continued to grow, opening up to high school students in September 2005, to work networks at the beginning of 2006 and finally to anyone with an email address in September 2006. Among various SNSs, Facebook is one of the most addictive websites. Facebook users visit the website multiple times a day. In addition, typical users spend an average of 19 minutes a day on the site. On the other hand, most of the younger generation is migrating to other platforms (mainly to Instagram, which is owned by the same company as Facebook) mostly because of two main reasons. The first is related to the nature of Instagram. As a photo sharing website, it is apparently becoming a more attractive way of communication for the younger generation. Second, as Facebook is becoming popular among the older generation (parents of the younger generation), the younger generation is not interested in being on the same network as their parents. As of today, Facebook has 2.19 billion active monthly users.

## TOURISM AND HOSPITALITY INSIGHTS 5.2
## HOW TECHNOLOGY IS HELPING KEEP COMMUNICATION FLOWING DURING NATURAL DISASTERS

Destinations affected by natural disasters such as hurricanes and earthquakes often have a crisis management plan in place. Crisis communication has seen changes recently due to the influence of social media, which was showcased in both Florida and Texas with Hurricanes Irma and Harvey.

Emergency management officials have recognized that social media is a means through which to target a larger audience and many emergency management officials and local emergency managers have taken a more proactive approach to utilizing social media outlets (FEMA, 2018).

FEMA has adapted a variety of social media outlets such as Facebook, Instagram, and Twitter, both on national and regional specific levels. When Florida was declared a major disaster, FEMA utilized digital communication specialists to monitor social media to monitor references to the organization on social media, share survivor posts with experts to answer questions, and post information to the FEMA Facebook and Twitter pages (FEMA, 2018).

In Florida, first responders and government officials heavily utilized social media to communicate with residents and coordinate relief efforts (MacMillan, 2017). The Florida tourism office utilized Facebook to send targeted messages to visitors and residents advising them to take the appropriate storm precautions. Alphabet Inc. and Google worked in partnership with the state to quickly update road closures within the state on Google Maps (MacMillan, 2017). Twitter was utilized by various agencies to communicate the risks and location of the storm. The Coast Guard in Florida realized that social media could help to alleviate stress on dispatchers, who were receiving over 1,000 calls per hour (Meadows-Fernandez, 2017).

Following Hurricane Irma, local officials in Florida have tapped into new technology to communicate with different groups of residents. One county is working with Nextdoor, a neighborhood social media site, to create a map of every residence inside the county and unincorporated area. The map would then allow the county to send notices to those residents who would be affected by delayed services, such as trash, after a storm (MacMillan, 2017).

In both Florida and Texas, residents were asked to use Zello, a smartphone app that works as a digital walkie-talkie and has since reached the top of the iTunes store charts. In Houston, Zello was utilized by volunteers in relief coordination efforts. The app is also used by police officers in some parts of Texas, as the app is secure and works in areas with minimal cell coverage (MacMillan, 2017; Meadows-Fernandez, 2017). Another popular app being utilized is GasBuddy, an app that crowdsources prices at the pump allowing users to determine where fuel is available (MacMillan, 2017). Facebook's safety-check tool was used in both states, and is being more commonly used across a variety of disasters, to allow users to mark themselves as safe within their profiles. Crowd-Source Rescue is a smaller site that works on off an online platform to connect users who need rescuing and those with the resources to help; CrowdSource Rescue was utilized in Hurricane Irma to coordinate over 7,000 rescues (MacMillan, 2017).

## References

FEMA. (2018, April 16). Social media and emergency preparedness. *FEMA*. Retrieved from https://www.fema.gov/news-release/2018/04/16/social-media-and-emergency-preparedness

MacMillan, D. (2017, Sept 11). In Irma, emergency responders' new tools: Twitter and Facebook. *The Wall Street Journal*. Retrieved from https://www.wsj.com/articles/for-hurricane-irma-information-officials-post-on-social-media-1505149661

Meadows-Fernandez, R. (2017, Sept 15). What Harvey and Irma taught us about using social media in emergency response. *PacificStandard*. Retrieved from https://psmag.com/social-justice/what-harvey-and-irma-taught-about-using-social-media-in-emergency-response

Source: Amanda Templeton.

## TOURISM AND HOSPITALITY INSIGHTS 5.3
## ENHANCING THE TRAVEL EXPERIENCE – SOCIAL MEDIA AND BEYOND

Technology in the travel and tourism industry is being used in more ways than imaginable.

### Social media

*Instagram:* Instagram is not only being used to upload travel pictures but is also a valuable tool for travelers to research pre and post vacation. Hashtags are being used to view destination stories and images to lead travelers to locations that they may have not been aware of (Levi, 2018).

*Facebook:* Many travelers are utilizing Facebook's recommendations feature to glean information from friends regarding must see things to see and do, as well as where to stay and eat. In addition, the "check-in" feature on the page can provide ways for individuals to meet up with friends or to ask for input from others who have also "checked-in" to that location (WebCrayons, 2018).

## Apps

*Dating apps:* Bumble, Tindr, and other apps are no longer being used solely for love connections, rather many "dating" apps have a "friend/socialization" feature that connects people with common interests. It is becoming more common for travelers to utilize the apps to make friends and connect with locals to enhance a vacation experience with knowledge about the destination (WebCrayons, 2018).

*Other:* Apps and web marketing companies are diverse globally. Some countries have banned the use of commonly utilized North American social media apps like Instagram and Whatsapp. Travelers instead use apps such as Hike or Momo to stay connected. It is recommended that travelers research before they travel (WebCrayons, 2018). Apps such as Meetup offer the opportunity for users to find groups with similar interests and meet individuals traveling, or who have traveled, to a common destination (WebCrayons, 2018).

## Internet of things (IoT)

Internet of Things (IoT) is the concept of connecting any device with an on and off switch to the Internet (and/or to each other). This can include everything from cellphones, coffee makers, washing machines, headphones, lamps, and any other wearable devices (Morgan, 2014). It is anticipated that by 2020 there will be over 26 billion connected devices; being a giant network of connected "things" (including people), the relationship(s) will be between people-people, people-things, and things-things (Morgan, 2014).

A study of IoT by Tata Consultancy Services found that companies in the travel industry led all industries in their investment in IoT, with organizations spending an average of $128 million per organization (Adobe et al., 2016). IoT is being utilized in all aspects of the travel industry from airline companies such as Lufthansa, using it to provide passengers with an app so that they can track their luggage via a link on mobile boarding pass, to lodging companies like Virgin Hotels, who offer an app allowing guests to interface with their room's thermostat or control the TV (Adobe et al., 2016; GlobalData Technology, 2018). Other companies such as Marriott are experimenting with a live "like" button, which allows guests to provide real-time feedback regarding property amenities, designs, and procedures (Adobe et al., 2016).

## References

Adobe, Epsilon, & Skift. (2016, Dec 19). How the Internet of things will impact travel 2017 and beyond. *Skift Take*. Retrieved from https://skift.com/2016/12/19/how-the-internet-of-things-will-impact-travel-in-2017-and-beyond/

GlobalData Technology. (2018, March 8). Top 6 technology trends to watch out for in the travel and tourism industry in 2018. *GlobalData*. Retrieved from https://www.globaldata.com/top-6-technology-trends-watch-travel-tourism-industry-2018/

Levi, E. (2018, March 21). 6 ways social media can enhance your adventure travel. *ADWEEK*. Retrieved from https://www.adweek.com/digital/6-ways-social-media-can-enhance-your-adventure-travel/

Morgan, J. (2014, May 13). A simple explanation of "the Internet of things." *Forbes*. Retrieved from https://www.forbes.com/sites/jacobmorgan/2014/05/13/simple-explanation-internet-things-that-anyone-can-understand/#56e4637e1d09

WebCrayons. (2018, May 8). 6 ways social media can enhance your adventure travel. Social media marketing. Retrieved from https://www.webcrayons.biz/blog/6-ways-social-media-can-enhance-your-adventure-travel/

Source: Amanda Templeton.

The reaction of hospitality and tourism companies to the social networking phenomenon have been two-fold – to leverage the trend and contribute to the creation of specialized communities and SNSs, and to participate in existing public SNSs such as Facebook with the aim of building brand loyalty. Among the specialized communities, brand names such as TripAdvisor, Yelp, and WAYN can be identified. Companies might use social media with any strategies such as communication only, promotion only, or mixing communication and promotion. Some SNSs naturally are more appropriate for some marketing tactics compared to others. For example, YouTube as a video sharing website is more appropriate for communication/promotion but it is difficult to pursue a two-way interaction as the comment section in YouTube is not as well developed as other social media like Facebook. Traditionally, Twitter is mostly used by public relations of companies. Despite many appropriate attributes of Twitter, the word limit is a serious problem in story telling by Twitter. In the era of physical communities, organizations were looking for opinion leaders among the people and opinion leaders were most of the time celebrities. Many customers on social media era are celebrities themselves. They (i.e., customers) produce content, distribute content, and they become popular for their content although for a short time. Social media is the platform for short-lived fame. In this evolved environment, there are other ways of identifying opinion leaders and being an opinion leader is not exclusive to celebrities anymore. Companies need to find the influencers in this era of social media to conduct successful marketing plans. In understanding the social media discourse, it is critical to pay attention to customer privacy, tracking online behaviors, and the business of selling information of customers to various stakeholders. These issues are briefly explained at the end of next section.

## Big data analytics

Technology is continuously evolving and influencing our capability to live a more convenient life. The most recent advancement of technology, which is also affecting the operations and consumption of hedonic products and services, is known as big data analytics. Big data analytics is the ability to collect, process, analyze, and transform large data sets of terabyte, petabyte, exabytes, zettabytes, and yottabytes. These datasets usually include millions of rows (observations) and tens of thousands of variables. Using big data analytics enables artificial intelligence (AI) to precisely predict customer behavior and decision-making. With the technology advancement in the areas of computation and computational power, analysis of such datasets takes from a few seconds to a few hours and the result is usually astonishingly exact and accurate. Since it is not possible to store such a large dataset on personal computers, a cloud storage system is suggested as a solution. This approach also has started a new computational movement known as cloud-based computation, in which the algorithm for the analysis of data is developed on a remote computer and sent using an application program interface (API) and results are returned to the computer running the algorithm. In this way, great deal of time can be saved by using a cloud-based computation instead of a single computer's multi-core central processing unit (CPU). Big data analytics can be employed to tackle problems as complicated as flight delays. Another application of big data analytics is to identify determinant factors of customer satisfaction through analysis of the content of the review websites from a restaurant or hotel at business level to destination management at the macro level. It is critical to note that big data is not only introduced with its volume; in fact, there are five Vs that collectively define big data analytics and volume is only one V, although the most critical one. Other Vs are velocity, variety, value, and veracity. For example, the second important characteristic of big data is velocity. The mega databases are growing in volume at an incredible pace. For instance, while you are reading this text, about 4 million videos are watched on YouTube, half a million individuals are tweeting, and 5000 aircrafts are flying in the sky. Velocity is not only dealing with the rate of increase in data volume but also the timing of the data. Big data is real-time data meaning that the events are occurring at the moment that analyses are carried out. Being real time is also an important feature of big data analytics as it can provide insights in the moment for the managers to make the best possible decisions for the situations in hand. For example, the data produced with the RFID sensors used by the guests in a theme park recording guests' movements and attraction selection can be used simultaneously to manage the long queues of visitors to some of these attractions. The third important V is the variety of the data available for big data analysis. Big data comes in all forms and types; it can measure very objectively time, date, sales' volume, amount of money, number of likes or subjective measures like customer satisfaction. It can be a simple categorical variable like gender or a compound construct like customers' attitudes to something. It can be structured numerical values such as the height of an individual or unstructured textual entries such as tweets of a product user. In fact, only 5% of the existent data is estimated to be structured and 95% is unstructured data such as video clips, online reviews, audio files, etc. Unstructured data needs further processing and transformation to become usable for big data analytics. In addition, it is important that both the source of the data and the timing of the analysis create added value. Some data are more expensive to obtain while others are free to be accessed by everyone. The selection of data, method, technician, and process are important factors in the final cost of big data analytics. Whether the process is continuous or repeated multiple time intervals in a year, it is also going to be an important determinant of expenditure. In the end, companies should be able to balance the cost of obtaining information for decision-making and the level of environmental uncertainty associated with the benefits of the outcomes of the decisions they make. Finally, veracity is the fifth factor defining big data analytics. Data is continuously in production, and there are various sources from which these data can be obtained. Not all available sources, however, collect and process the raw data with the same accuracy. For example, data recorded by CCTVs around a specific geographic location about individuals walking in and out of shopping mall is more accurate compared to data collected from satellites. Validity of the data source is also a key component in veracity. In order to have valuable results, data should be provided with a valid source, collected using valid methods, and analyzed using valid instruments.

Dependent on the situation and usage, data can be equally valuable for both suppliers and consumers. For example, at a macro level, a destination management organization (DMO) might use the online reviews from various sources such as TripAdvisor to evaluate the perceived image of a destination. The same data can be employed in decision-making to make interventions in order to enhance the image and to evaluate the results of the interventions to assess the success of intervention strategies. At a micro level, a business such as a hotel or restaurant might use similar data from online reviews to evaluate their operations or define the determinants of their customers' satisfaction. On the other hand, big data analytics can be used through a specific user interface like Google to provide the cheapest available flights to a specific destination for individual customers. Use of big data analytics is expanding rapidly in various areas from a hotel's efficiency in energy consumption or predicting a hotel's occupancy rate to forecasting the number of visitors to a city. Nevertheless, the extensive use of big data is also creating some concerns regarding customers' privacy. What type of data can be collected or what type of permissions should be attained in order to track customers' physical and virtual activities are unsolved problems in the area of big data analytics. With accurate data collection and the right types of analysis, more than 90% of the behaviors of individuals can be accurately predicted. The question is whether individuals are willing to be monitored in such a manner for the commercial purposes of various companies.

## Conclusion

Technology is not going to replace the role of humans in service; in fact, "high tech" and "high touch" go hand in hand. There are numerous instances of technology use in hospitality and tourism and this chapter only briefly touches upon some of the most critical ones. In order to have a better understanding of how technology spread both among the businesses and amongst customers, this chapter has provided some explanations and examples of diffusion using various models and theories such as the Bass model and the TAM and UTAUT theories. Few individuals might argue against that claim that ICT has the greatest impact on hospitality and tourism compared to other technologies. This chapter offered a brief history of development of Web 2.0, social media as the virtual community of future societies, and UGC uses and misuses.

Owing to the rapid changes of the technological environments, we have not discussed some potential future usage of technology, particularly, the role of augmented reality (AR) and AI in future hedonic tourism and hospitality consumptions. AR is expected to revolutionize the future of the experience economy. Notions such as experience without physical presence and the role of human consciousness and freedom of choice because of using AI and AR are all important topics outside the scope of this chapter that should be carefully investigated in the future. The current approach to application of technology is based on the dominance of human agency in using technology. Strategic decisions are still to be made by the human agent and ICT systems in their most sophisticated forms like AIs are only to assist the decision makers. The question, however, is what is going to happen in the future? What if AI becomes the dominant player and strategic decision-maker? Although asking this question may seem more like a science fiction movie, it is much closer than it appears to be. The discourse about the impact of technology appears to be more urgent to prepare us for embracing emerging technologies to improve business efficiency and effectiveness.

## REVIEW QUESTIONS

1. How integral is the role of technology in all parts of the tourism and hospitality industry? Are there any parts where technology is less important?
2. Briefly outline some of the new and emerging applications of technology in one particular sector within the wider tourism and hospitality industry?
3. For a specific sector of your choice, what reasons may underpin the adoption (or not as the case may be) of technology? For the same sector, what specific markets are likely to be more proactive in their adoption of new technologies and why?
4. How has social media broadly, and user-generated content in particular changed the face of tourism and hospitality marketing in recent years? How do you see things changing in the future and with what impacts for tourism and hospitality marketing?

## YOUTUBE LINKS

*"Episode 122: communicating in chaos: the role of social media during Hurricane Harvey, Part 1"*

URL: https://vimeo.com/239736109

Summary: As Hurricane Harvey swept through Houston, leaving devastation in its path, many brands, individuals, and even traditional news outlets turned to social media for information, support, and help. Our Operations Manager Nyla Spooner, who formed a

Hurricane Harvey relief and recovery Facebook Group, sat down with Web and Social Media Manager for Cox Media Group, Bill Tatar, to have a conversation about how social media has fundamentally changed the way we communicate during and after a natural disaster. For more, visit twicemediaproductions.com/blog.

### *"Social media's role during Hurricane Irma"*

URL: https://youtu.be/rq-Y3FCtz0s

Summary: Social media used for preparation and reaction

### *"French train strikes hits international travel"*

URL: https://youtu.be/mzX55qnU6kM

Summary: International and commuter train services in France were affected on Wednesday as day two of a three-month strike hobbled one of the world's most-traveled rail networks.

### *"Social media can make your travel better"*

URL: https://youtu.be/RjmU86UCmy8

Summary: Using social media can get you the best of everything.

## REFERENCES, FURTHER READING, AND RELATED WEBSITES

### References

Bass, F.M. (1980). The relationship between diffusion rates, experience curves, and demand elasticities for consumer durable technological innovations. *Journal of Business* (July 1980), S51–S67.
Wang, Y., Yu, Q., & Fesenmaier, D.R. (2002). Defining the virtual tourist community: implications for tourism marketing. *Tourism Management, 23*(4), 407–417.

### Further reading

Armstrong, A., & Hagel, J. (1996) The real value of on-line communities. *Harvard Business Review,* May–June.
Boyd, D., & Ellison, N. (2007) Social network sites: Definition, history, and scholarship. *Journal of Computer-Mediated Communication,* 13(1),210–230.
Buhalis, D. (1997) Information technology as a strategic tool for economic, social, cultural and environmental benefits enhancement of tourism at destination regions. *Progress in Tourism and Hospitality Research, (3),* 71–93.
Calhoun, C.J. (1980) Community: Toward a variable conceptualization for comparative research. *Social History, 5,* 105–129.

Carroll, J., & Rosson, M. (2003) A trajectory for community networks, *The Information Society, 19*, 381–393.

Cooper, C.L., & Argyris, C. (1997) *The Blackwell encyclopedia of management: Marketing.* Oxford: Blackwell.

Cox, C., Burgess, S., Sellitto, C., & Buultjens, J. (2008) Consumer-generated web-based tourism marketing, Australia, Collaborative Research Centre for Sustainable Tourism Pty Ltd.

Dearstyne, B. (2007) Blogs! mashups and wikis: Oh, My! *Information Management Journal*, July/August,25–33.

Dwyer, P. (2007) Measuring the value of electronic word of mouth and its impact in consumer communities. *Journal of Interactive Marketing, 21*(2), 63–79.

Fuchs, M., Höpken, W., & Lexhagen, M. (2014). Big data analytics for knowledge generation in tourism destinations – a case from Sweden. *Journal of Destination Marketing & Management, 3*(4), 198–209.

Gandomi, A., & Haider, M. (2015). Beyond the hype: Big data concepts, methods, and analytics. *International Journal of Information Management, 35*(2), 137–144.

Gunter, U., & Önder, I. (2016). Forecasting city arrivals with Google Analytics. *Annals of Tourism Research, 61*, 199–212.

Hsu, C.H.C., & Powers, T.F. (2002). *Marketing hospitality.* New York: Wiley.

Kahn, M.E., & Liu, P. (Peng). (2015). Utilizing "Big data" to improve the hotel sector's energy efficiency. *Cornell Hospitality Quarterly, 57*(2), 202–210.

Khalilzadeh, J., Ozturk, A.B., & Bilgihan, A. (2017). Security-related factors in extended UTAUT model for NFC based mobile payment in the restaurant industry. *Computers in Human Behavior, 70*, 460–474.

Kotler, P., & Armstrong, G. (2012). *Principles of marketing.* Boston, MA: Pearson Prentice Hall.

Liu, Y., Teichert, T., Rossi, M., Li, H., & Hu, F. (2017). Big data for big insights: Investigating language-specific drivers of hotel satisfaction with 412,784 user-generated reviews. *Tourism Management, 59*, 554–563.

Middleton, V.T.C., Fyall, A., & Morgan, M. (2009). *Marketing in travel and tourism.* Burlington, MA: Elsevier.

Milan, R. (2007). *10 things you can do in response to traveller reviews.* Retrieved from http://www.hotelmarketing.com/index.php/content/article/070920_10_things_you_can_do_in_response_to_traveler_reviews/

Nicholas, D., Huntington, P., Jamali, H., & Dobrowolski, T. (2007). Characterising and evaluating information seeking behaviour in a digital environment: Spotlight on the "bouncer." *Information Processing and Management: An International Journal, 43*(4), 1085–1102.

O'Connor, P. (2008a). Electronic distribution. In P. Jones (Eds.), *Handbook of hospitality operations and IT* (pp. 139–166). Oxford: Butterworth-Heinemann.

Pan, B., & Yang, Y. (2017). Forecasting destination weekly hotel occupancy with big data. *Journal of Travel Research, 56*(7),957–970.

Pokryshevskaya, E.B., & Antipov, E.A. (2017). Profiling satisfied and dissatisfied hotel visitors using publicly available data from a booking platform. *International Journal of Hospitality Management, 67*, 1–10.

Salehi-Esfahani, S., & Ozturk, A.B. (in press). Negative reviews: Formation, spread, and halt of opportunistic behavior. *International Journal of Hospitality Management.*

Sheth, J.N., & Malhotra, N.K. (2011). *Wiley international encyclopedia of marketing.* Chichester: Wiley.

Sigala, M., & In Gretzel, U. (2018). *Advances in social media for travel, tourism and hospitality: New perspectives, practice and cases.* New York: Routledge.

Sun, T., Youn, S., Wu, G. & Kuntaraporn, M. (2006) Online word-of-mouth (or mouse): An exploration of its antecedents and consequences. *Journal of Computer-Mediated Communication, 11*(4), 1104–1127.

Sweeney, J., Soutar, G., & Mazzarol, T. (2008) Factors influencing word of mouth effectiveness: Receiver perspectives. *European Journal of Marketing, 42*(3/4), 344–364.

Tasci, A.D.A. (2009). A semantic analysis of destination image terminology. *Tourism Review International*, 13(1), 65–78.

Tredinnick, L. (2006) Web 2.0 and business: A pointer to the intranets of the future? *Business Information Review*, 23(4), 228–234.

Vaughan, D., Jolley, A., & Mehrer, P. (1999) Local authorities in England and Wales and the development of tourism Internet sites. *Information Technology and Tourism*, 2(2), 115–129.

Watts, D.J., & Strogatz, S.H. (1998). Collective dynamics of "small-world" networks. *Nature, 393* (6684), 440.

Xiang, Z., Schwartz, Z., Gerdes, J.H., & Uysal, M. (2015). What can big data and text analytics tell us about hotel guest experience and satisfaction? *International Journal of Hospitality Management*, 44, 120–130.

Xue, F., & Phelps, J. (2004) Internet-facilitated consumer-to-consumer communication: The moderating role of receiver characteristics, *International Journal of Internet Marketing and Advertising*, 1(2), 121–136.

Yoo K., & Gretzel, U. (2009) *Comparison of deceptive and truthful travel reviews*. In W. Höpken, U. Gretzel, & Law, R. (Eds.), Information and communication technologies in tourism, ENTER 2009 (pp. 37–47). New York: Springer.

## Websites

Expedia
https://www.expedia.com/

KAYAK
https://www.kayak.com/

TripAdvisor
https://www.tripadvisor.com/

Trivago
https://www.trivago.com/

Travelocity
https://www.travelocity.com/

Yelp
https://www.yelp.com/

## MAJOR CASE STUDY
## SOCIAL MEDIA AND ITS IMPACT ON CHANGING
## TRAVEL/CONSUMPTION PATTERNS

There are today 3,196 billion social media users, approximately 13% up year-on-year (WE ARE SOCIAL, 2018). An average of 500 million tweets are tweeted on Twitter and 95 million photos are uploaded to Instagram every day (SocialPilot, 2018). As the numbers show, social media has become a part of people's lifestyle with it having huge impacts in many areas, both personal and business-related across the world. The tourism and hospitality industry is no exception. Indeed, social media in the industry now plays a pivotal role in many aspects, including consumer behavior, customer service, and customer loyalty.

The most significant effect that social media has had on the tourism industry is in consumer behavior. First, social media motivates people to travel and affects their holiday choices. Fifty-two percent of Facebook users said that their friends' photos on social media inspire their travel plans (Smart Insights, 2017). This is because the majority of consumers see reviews from their friends and family as their most credible source, as the following data demonstrates: 92% of consumers said that they trust earned media, such as word-of-mouth and recommendations from their friends and family, while only 47% of customers said that they trust paid media, such as television, magazines, and newspaper ads (TNOOZ, 2012). In addition, travelers often search for travel information on social media since it enables them to easily find others' photos, ratings, and reviews. In fact, when booking trips, 89% of millennials plan activities based on content posted by others (Entrepreneur Media, 2017). Furthermore, it is important to note that social media has a huge impact on how travelers book. Only 48% of travelers who used social media to research their trips stuck with their original plans; 33% of travelers changed their hotels, 10% changed their resorts, 5% changed airlines, and 7% even changed their destinations (Smart Insights, 2017). During and after their trips, travelers don't even turn off social media; they share experiences, posting their pictures and comments on social media. In fact, 72% of travelers post their photos and 70% of them update their Facebook statuses while they are traveling (Smart Insights, 2017). More surprisingly, over 97% of millennials share their travel photos and videos on social media, influencing others' travel decisions (Entrepreneur Media, 2017). After returning home, travelers continue to use social media; 55% of travelers like Facebook pages specific to their travel choice, 46% post reviews of their hotels, 40% post reviews of the activities experienced and 40% post restaurant reviews (Smart Insights, 2017).

Owing to the development of social media, tourism-related companies have also transformed how they provide customer services and market to target consumers. The majority of tourism-related companies have official social media accounts in order to communicate with customers as well as promote their brands and services. When customers contact companies on Twitter, more than half of them expect a response (Entrepreneur Media, 2017). In addition, the number increases to 75% when customers contact companies with complaints (Entrepreneur Media, 2017). JetBlue is an exemplary company that effectively utilizes social media to change their customers from unsatisfied to delighted by offering efficient service resolutions (Buffer Social, 2015). When a customer tweeted his complaint about the TV for his seat being broken during his four-hour flight, JetBlue apologized to him for their service failure and offered compensation for his trouble within just 23 minutes through Twitter, which completely changed his attitude toward the company, as the following his tweet proves, "One of the fastest and better Customer Service@JetBlue!" (Buffer, 2015). Social media has also had a huge impact on how companies' loyalty programs are constructed. Since some companies understand that individual customers' posts about their service evaluations are extremely influential on other customers' purchase decisions, they offer compensation to customers for spreading positive information (Entrepreneur Media, 2017). Marriott's reward program is a good example as their customers can obtain loyalty points by sharing their experiences on social media, such as by checking in on Facebook and posting pictures on Instagram (GuestRevu, 2018). By encouraging customers to share their good experiences on social networks in such a way, the company has been able to increase their positive brand awareness (GuestRevu, 2018).

As discussed above, social media has been transforming many aspects in the tourism industry. Customers plan their trips by researching information on social media and they, themselves, become a type of media that influences other customers' travel preferences and decisions by posting their experiences during and after their trips. Accordingly, companies have changed how they provide customer service and communicate with travelers. In addition, they leverage social media in order to build positive brand awareness and increase brand loyalty.

## References

Buffer. (2015, Dec 29). *14 amazing social media customer service examples (and what you can learn from them)*. Retrieved from https://blog.bufferapp.com/social-media-customer-service#

Entrepreneur Media. (2017, Mar 3). *5 ways social media has transformed tourism marketing*. Retrieved from https://www.entrepreneur.com/article/286408

GuestRevu. (2018). *3 Innovative loyalty programs to be inspired by*. Retrieved from https://blog.guest revu.com/3-innovative-loyalty-programs-to-be-inspired-by

SocialPilot. (2018). *171 amazing social media statistics you should know in 2018*. Retrieved from https://www.socialpilot.co/blog/social-media-statistics

Smart Insights. (2017, Jun 9). *How social media and mobile technology impact travel*. Retrieved from https://www.smartinsights.com/social-media-marketing/social-media-mobile-technology-impact-travel/

TNOOZ. (2012, Jul 2). *Impact of social media on the travel industry*. Retrieved from https://www.tnooz.com/article/impact-of-social-media-on-the-travel-industry-infographic/

WE ARE SOCIAL. (2018, Jan 30). *Digital in 2018: world's internet users pass the 4 billion mark*. Retrieved from https://wearesocial.com/blog/2018/01/global-digital-report-2018

Source: Ryuichi Karakawa.

Major case study question

1.  For a company of your choice within the wider tourism and hospitality industry, identify how social media today plays an integral part in shaping:

    a.   consumer behavior
    b.   customer service
    c.   customer loyalty.

# 6 Experiential marketing
## A question of co-creation

### Learning outcomes

By the end of this chapter, students will:

- Understand why experiential marketing is essential to designing tourists' experiences
- Acquire a deeper understanding of the main pillars of a successful and memorable experience
- Understand how a tourist experience can be developed
- Appreciate the different service components that can be cultivated to provide a memorable experience.

**Key terms**

experiential marketing, experience economy, sensorial marketing, authenticity, storytelling, surprise, involvement, emotions

## Introduction

Experiential marketing is not just a buzzword or marketing's latest fashion trend. A strong body of literature that aims to investigate how consumers perceive their consumption experience supports experiential marketing. It adopts the idea that beyond goods and services, customers are actually looking for an experience where they will live, feel, and sense it rather than just buying and taking home a product/service. Considering that what takes place during the consumption itself is what customers are really looking for has changed our vision of marketing. Whilst traditional marketing vision stands for products and services, in the tourism and hospitality context, it is clear that the experience itself is what consumers have come to seek. And if this experience relies on a physical provision, it is the sensorial and experiential elements that take place during the stay that actually drive consumers.

As will become evident throughout this chapter, this vision of marketing has necessitated a re-conceptualization of traditional marketing models, encouraging researchers and managers alike to revise all the concepts involved in the decision and experience process. It is also important to consider that the experience is a longitudinal process that starts well before the experience takes place right through after the consumption of a service, to consider even long-term impacts. Furthermore, it has also been recognized that companies should move away from considering themselves as products and services providers to include the consumer in this process and co-create value with those consumers.

This chapter will first present the basic tenets of experiential marketing, looking at the origins of theories and concepts, and will then develop how sensorial marketing developed. The newer theories that emerged from the 2000s onwards, starting with the Experience Economy, will then be treated and the key components of a memorable experience will be addressed.

# Experiential marketing

## *The origins of experiential thinking*

Whilst sociologists and psychologists have long established the role of senses and emotions in human behavior, its incorporation into marketing theories has been slower and experiential marketing is, in marketing terms, a rather recent matter of interest. Experiential marketing can serve as a rich and useful framework to understand some specific aspects of products and services marketing but it is a topic that has many links with other theories and concepts attached to various disciplines. In the case of the tourist experience, human geography, sociology, psychology and environmental psychology along with leisure sciences are fields that have contributed tremendously to the understanding of the experience.

Within the marketing literature, the origins of experiential marketing can be traced back to the seminal work of Holbrook and Hirschman (1982) on hedonic consumption. The basic tenet of their approach was not to reject traditional marketing models but rather to point to the fact that in some specific goods categories, consumers seemed to obey different decision-making processes and behavior. Those specific hedonic categories included art, music, leisure and, of course, tourism and hospitality.

One of the main differences observed by experiential researchers lay in the rationality of individuals observed: in hedonic consumption contexts, individuals seemed to behave as irrational human beings. Indeed, is it rational to spend $100,000 on a work of modern art, pay to jump from a plane in a free fall, or even pay to lie on a beach and simply relax for a week? If one were to follow traditional marketing decision models, these expenditures would not make any sense. Traditional models advocated the rationality of human beings, with individuals aiming at maximizing their utility and using decisions based on weighting multiple attributes (see Table 6.1 for differences between traditional marketing models and the experiential approach). In experiential marketing, consumers do not seem to obey these rules: they do not seem to behave rationally; they do not really seek to maximize their utility but rather their pleasure, and they seem to react to multi-sensorial stimulations rather than well-defined attributes.

**Image 6.1**

Source: Pexels.

**Table 6.1** Variables used in traditional approaches compared to experiential theories

|  | Traditional approaches | Experiential approach |
|---|---|---|
| Stimuli | Verbal | Non-verbal |
|  | Tangible | Sensorial |
| Consumer objective | Maximise utility | Experience lived |
|  | Extrinsic objectives (to consume in order to achieve an objective) | Intrinsic objective (product consumed for itself) |
|  | Utilitarian criteria | Esthetical and symbolical criteria |
| Goal | Maximise utility and value | Maximise emotional benefits |
| Decision | Formulate preferences with multi attributes comparisons | Holistic perception and difficulty to elaborate concise expectations |
| Mediating variables | Attitudes | Emotions, feelings |
| Post-purchase evaluation | Satisfaction | Pleasure, memory... |
| Involvement | Level of involvement (high/low) | Involvement type (portion of the hedonic component) |

Source: Author.

A cornerstone of experiential marketing lies in the recognized importance of emotions (rather than cognitive processes) as a driving force of behavior. The other difference lies in the evaluation and outcomes of consumption. Whilst traditional models favored multi-attribute modeling and evaluation processes addressed via the satisfaction construct, experiential views emphasize the necessity to move to other constructs. For instance, Holbrook and Hirschman (1982) encouraged researchers to turn towards the concepts of pleasure and memory as more realistic outcomes of the consumption experience.

The other element that seems to characterize hedonic experiences is the rather holistic evaluation of the experience: rather than identifying and weighing different attributes, consumers develop a global and approximate evaluation of the service provided that includes various encounters and senses experienced into one global evaluation, for example a family staying for a week in an all-inclusive resort in the Dominican Republic. During that whole week, the family will experience a vast range of services: sports activities for different age ranges and abilities, catering facilities, accommodation, entertainment, spa, countless contacts with staff, meeting up with other consumers. All these experiences will amount to a vast number of encounters of various kinds. It is humanly impossible for those consumers to remember and evaluate all those encounters. Moreover, while on holiday, one wants to relax and not enter into a deep-thinking process. As a result, those holiday consumers will form a global evaluation of that holiday that will resume, globally, how the family feels after spending this holiday in this resort. It would be pointless to try to translate all those elements into a range of specific attributes.

As mentioned previously, Holbrook and Hirschman (1982) saw the main implication of their work in the domain of the arts, culture, and leisure consumption. In the tourism and hospitality field, this approach is particularly relevant since it provides many answers to an unusual consumption phenomenon that carries specific characteristics.

## What makes tourism a topic so receptive to experiential marketing?

Tourism is a unique consumption phenomenon. It involves people moving to destinations for a certain length of time in a context very different from their everyday life. More importantly, tourism consumption shares the characteristics of any service (these are detailed in Chapter 8), of which there is no ownership and consumers will mostly take home souvenirs. Even though tourism services rely in part on a tangible provision (hotels, restaurants, planes, sites to visit, etc.), it is an experience that conveys, in its heart, feelings, sensations, and emotions that no other services can provide for such a long period of time. This long period means that tourists will develop holistic evaluations of services, combining multiple encounters into one global feeling about how the holiday was. Memories are probably the best evaluation criteria that can be developed of the outcome of the experience. In this holistic evaluation, both service provision and the emotional outcomes are important components.

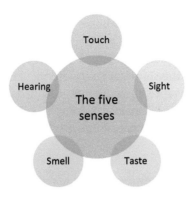

**Figure 6.1 The five senses**
Source: Author.

Tourism services carry both experiential and utilitarian values that need to be addressed. Experiential marketing theory brings a good understanding of the latter since it provides a framework whereby the holistic, emotionally-based, non-rational behaviors can be explained. To understand this complex process, various disciplines have been able to bring their share of knowledge based on 60 years of tourism research which has looked in detail at the experience and all its components and intricacies.

The production of knowledge in this area is therefore vast and multi-disciplinary and in order to provide guidance through it, experiential marketing theories provide a very useful framework. Whilst Holbrook and Hirschman produced their articles in the early 1980s, this scientific production was so much ahead of its time that it took several decades for researchers and consultants to develop this idea into meaningful and practical managerial concepts. From the 1980s to the 2000s, most of the studies concentrated on sensorial marketing. Then, from the 2000s onwards, more defined managerial strategies emerged (named the experience economy). In order to understand the depth of experiential marketing, the next section will address the five senses and how they have been embedded in service provision. The following section will then look at experiential principles from a more conceptual viewpoint where the key components and processes of the experience will be addressed.

## Sensorial marketing

Experiential marketing is too often associated, and limited, to a very commercial vision of service delivery whereby it is reduced to a multi-sensorial experience. As we will address later, senses are only one element of the experience but we shall concentrate on this aspect first.

Sensorial marketing is based on the idea that a link exists between purchase behavior and the atmosphere within a shop setting, atmosphere that is created by managing the five senses through different service concepts and design. The basic principle is that, beyond the product being sold, it is the atmosphere that is produced within the shop that will be conductive to a purchasing behavior.

The first author who investigated atmosphere was Kotler (1974) who insisted on the importance of shop atmosphere to sell a product efficiently and impact positively on purchasing behavior. For instance, a chocolate shopkeeper will have conveniently set up a system to send back to the shop the chocolate smell coming out of its production room at the back. Bakers in France all know that using extractors to diffuse the smell of fresh bread and croissants into the street will bring in more consumers. Free tastings of products can also reinforce this process along with a thematized shop that goes in line with the positioning of the products.

More importantly, the shop experience will come to reinforce the branding strategy of the product and ultimately loyalty. By using one or more of the five senses, sensorial marketing aims to create an affective link between the consumers and the shop outlet and brand.

Developing a specific atmosphere has also been reinforced by the need to differentiate shopping outlets in an intense and competitive environment. For instance, one would not just buy a pair of jeans at any shop but would specifically go out of his/her way to reach an Abercrombie & Fitch shop where more expensive jeans would be sought for their make but also for the sheer experience of buying them at this shop. Abercrombie & Fitch for instance have recruited a very attractive salesforce, music, and lighting that can be compared to a nightclub atmosphere. The shop also preys on smell by spraying perfume all over the shop and its sales force. As a result, visitors will queue to visit this

**Image 6.2**
Source: Pexels.

shop and it has become a key brand on American campuses. In tourism and hospitality settings, similar reasoning is at play, and most of those settings will aim to develop an atmosphere by developing several components that will create an atmosphere of the place. Tourism and hospitality insights 6.1 on mountain resorts shows how this can be achieved in this specific context.

## TOURISM AND HOSPITALITY INSIGHTS 6.1
## MOUNTAIN RESORTS IN THE FRENCH ALPS: THE "CHALET AMBIENCE" LABEL IN MÉRIBEL

In the Alps, mountain resorts wish to provide an authentic feel despite the fact that many modern resorts were built in the 1960s or 1970s. This is particularly the case in France where most of the high-altitude resorts are of a modern composition.

Nonetheless, consumers reach those resorts for their holidays with, in their mind, a very specific image of mountain resorts. Mountain imaginary has been fueled, from early childhood, with romanced images of Alpine villages (of the Heidi type) with a set of chalets located warmly around the church, the whole image covered by snow, not forgetting pine trees. The notion of the village is quite important here but also the typical chalets are an important component.

For modern resorts, it can be a challenge to match this preconceived image as most of them need to fulfill the need of mass tourism and provide accommodation for large numbers of visitors with buildings of several floors rather than chalets. Some resorts have managed to keep to the chalet style (even if it is on a large scale), but overall this is not the norm. Equally, some of those resorts were built in some areas where no previous villages existed (Val Thorens or Avoriaz for instance), so those resorts don't even have an historical basis in terms of architecture. The architecture of those resorts is therefore important, trying to match as much as they can this idealized mountain image. As a result, resorts are gradually encouraging the development of chalet-type accommodations and are cladding the façades of their buildings with wood. Other elements that they can develop further are shop décors, the sale of local products in shops and at the market, keeping white snow inside the resorts (no heated pavements), and lighting up buildings in a "Christmas fashion."

Theming the buildings' interiors is important for consumers. Hotels and private resorts within ski resorts have developed a mountain feel within their buildings. This includes the materials used (wood and rocks) and the fabrics (warm covers, animal skins, mountain themed embroidery, wood paneling, the ideal being a fire place with a fire crackling). However, most accommodation is privately owned and the individual owners have no obligation or motive to theme their interiors. In order to solve this problem, one resort, Méribel, has decided to include esthetical criteria within its quality scheme.

Evaluating theming within an accommodation is quite a subjective feeling, therefore writing the specifications has been a tricky mission. To promote the "chalet ambiance," the Méribel label invites owners to consider criteria of comfort but also esthetic, homogeneous, and harmonious elements that all contribute to a "chalet ambiance." Those can be developed with modernity in mind or be very traditional. For instance, the floor surface, needs to imitate wood or be made of traditional tiling (slate is a typical mountain material), and plastic has to be avoided. The walls are expected to have real wood paneling along with decorative plaster. Thin wood panels, wall carpet, old wall paper, and old material have to be categorically avoided. Doors have to be made of real wood, and of the same color and make as other doors in the apartment, and also match the window frames. Curtains, bed covers, cushions, sofa covers should all be in warm and harmonious colors and inspire a mountain feel. They should also be fairly thick to engender a soothing comfort feeling.

As one can see, setting standards to match an atmosphere is a difficult task especially since the notion of mountain atmosphere can take very different forms, from a clichéd version to a very modern one. The idea for Méribel is to encourage accommodation owners to contribute also to the theming of the resort so that the outside of the buildings reflect the inside. The mountain atmosphere matches visitors' preconceived images. It also acts as a reminder that they are indeed spending their holiday in a different environment (and thereby reduces possible cognitive dissonance). The mountain atmosphere is based on a very global vision of the Alps. For instance, some of the styles used in those resorts are derived from different Alpine countries and the mountain look is a mix that does not necessarily match very local styles. Mountain resorts are by definition very cold and the mountain style also plays on the cold-warm effect: after a long day skiing or a walk outside in the evening, tourists want to come back to a flat that is (physically) warm but also that inspires warmth through its materials (a thick blanket, wool, etc.).

Source: Isabelle Frochot.

## Auditory marketing

Auditory marketing aims to use sounds and music to create an atmosphere within a retail outlet. Carefully planned, it will reinforce the positioning of the shop, not only in line with its branding/communication strategy but also with its targeted consumer base. The music can easily be changed and adapted to the season to reflect different moods (at Christmas, during summer, etc.). Music also affects consumer moods. The recognized advantages of auditory marketing are multiple. Music has an impact on the time spent within the shop and the rate of purchase. This has been experienced in shops, where each brand will be based on a different piece of music but more importantly the level of sound and the rhythm of the music is positively correlated to the rate of purchase.

## Tactile marketing

Tactile marketing covers all the instances where a consumer will have a direct and physical contact with the shop products and staff, including the thermic atmosphere of the retail outlet. This is a notion that has been well developed in the tourism and hospitality industry where the comfort, especially in terms of accommodation, is an element that has received much attention. Indeed, touching an object gives consumers an impression of its quality: the comfort of a bed, the feel of the sheets, the softness of a carpet are all elements that will not only provide a feeling of soothing comfort but also indicate product quality.

Autotelic touch also happens when a consumer touches an object that gives him the desire to keep doing it: cuddling a nice blanket, the silky feel, etc. This is typically cultivated in a cold atmosphere where the nice and soft feeling of warmth is provided by wrapping oneself in a thick furry blanket.

## Olfactive marketing

Olfactive marketing has been the object of intense interest since of all senses, smell is the sense that stays the longest in memory. Smells are strongly associated to emotions: a smell can elicit strong feelings and be directly associated with some specific souvenirs that one can remember vividly. The example of remembering the distinctive smell of one's grandmother's house is often given. This smell is unique and sends individuals back to fond memories of their childhood. Thereafter, whenever they are confronted by similar smell, memories of their grandmother and the positive emotions associated to it will return rapidly to their mind. Proust describes in one of his novels how eating a specific biscuit ("Madeleine") sends him straight back to memories of his childhood. Smells are therefore a direct pathway to some long-stored memories. Whether they send back individuals to comforting memories of their childhood or to any other types of memory, they are a useful marketing tool. Scents are more directly linked to memories since they are directly connected to the limbic system which hosts emotions and memories.

Retail stores have quickly understood that they could use scents to their advantage and to strengthen their branding strategy. Typically, a brand will create a smell that will be used in their different sales' offices so that any time a consumer comes in contact with this smell he will associate it with the brand and then eventually any emotions associated with the brand will be revived by a contact with this specific smell. Using the same smell in different brand units is also particularly useful as it will unify the different shopping outlets. For example, Singapore Airlines has created an aroma called Stefan Floridian Waters which has been used as the flight attendants' perfume, in the hot towels served before take-off, and has become the distinctive smell of Singapore Airlines' planes and brand.

Environments that deal with large numbers of customers need to develop pleasant smells in order to cover any unpleasant odours and make the whole universe of traveling more pleasant. For example, the Hong Kong Railway and the London Underground both use aromas to make the traveling experience more enjoyable. Equally, airport lounges have invested in aromas to pacify customers. Smells can vary throughout the year, each smell being able to be associated with a different season, and travel agents use them conjunctly with promotions of specific destinations and periods. Each smell will have some specific connotations, for instance the Coca-Cola smell for a promotion on travel to the US and the smell of jasmine for Tunisia, etc.

## Gustative marketing

Another dimension associated with tastes is gustative marketing. This aspect of marketing is well developed in tourism where food is a necessary provision of the tourism offer. At least three times a day, tourists will need to feed themselves. Gastronomy is a way to experience culture and taste new food and new ways of cooking. Sharing a meal with local hosts is also a way to increase the feeling of welcome and acceptance in a country.

Taste is a complex area that has deserved specific attention from highly specialized consultant agencies. Research protocols have been developed to test how various products taste and the food industry invests vast amounts of money in identifying the best

**Image 6.3**

Source: Pixabay.

tastes for their products. Beyond the simple like/dislike component of taste, its associated colors also impact upon its appreciation. For instance, when the colors are hidden from a consumer, then his/her taste is much less easily identified. The texture of the food, the containers in which it is presented, and the packaging, all influence the perceptions of the product's attributes.

Foods can also act as memory boosters. For instance, when tourists try out products while on holidays (olive oil in Italy, haggis in Scotland), eating again those products once back home, will evoke pleasant memories of their holidays.

## Visual marketing

The vision is the sense that humans have developed most with more than 80% of perceived stimuli coming from visual sources. Various dimensions can be used in terms of visual impacts. For instance, colors influence behavior and perceptions of a product. Colors will have emotional resonance as well as cognitive impacts (symbolic meanings for instance such as the red carpet in front of a hotel). Colors will also have an impact on other sensorial elements such as the taste, and perception of time, etc.

The use of colors can have different objectives: attracting passer-by attention (color choice, intensity of light); create interest in the shop or more simply develop a feeling of well-being (create a positive atmosphere within the shop/spa/hotel with the aim of enticing consumers to stay longer).

The sight is a sense that will most certainly be used more intensely in years to come due to new technologies. Augmented reality offers the possibility to superimpose new information and images on top of reality and eye-tracking technologies are offering exciting opportunities as Tourism and hospitality insights 6.2 demonstrates.

## The evolution of experiential marketing: identification of the main characteristics of the experience

Beyond sensorial marketing, experiential marketing brings an even deeper understanding of the main components of the experience. After Holbrook and Hirshman's initial contribution, other authors have looked into experiential theory, aiming to refine and conceptualize further its main components. This production started in the late 1990s/early 2000s with the works of Pine and Gilmore *The Experience Economy* (1998); Schmitt (1999) *Consuming Experience*, and Hetzel (2002) *Planète Conso*, among others.

## TOURISM AND HOSPITALITY INSIGHTS 6.2
## EYE-TRACKING IN THE MUSEUM

In 2015, the Louvre museum in Paris tested a new eye-tracking technology with the Suricog startup. The museum wanted to boost consumers' immersion in a work of art (a 17-meters wall paper from the decorative art collection). They equipped some of their visitors with eye-tracking glasses. The system could then identify which parts of the wallpaper visitors were looking at and play some music accordingly. For instance, if a consumer was looking at a bird then bird song would play; other sounds included a crackling fire, nature sounds, etc. The objective was to give another dimension to the interactions between visitors and "static" art. The objective of the museum was to develop a mobile phone app working along the same principles.

Source: T.O.M http://www.tom.travel/2017/05/11/leye-tracking-sinvite-musee-enrichir-lexperience-de-visite/

### The basic tenet of the experience economy

Pine and Gilmore produced a book called *The Experience Economy* in 1998 which became fundamental in giving a new boost to experiential theories. This book stated first and foremost that companies now had to consider that, beyond delivering products and services, what they were really aiming to produce was an accompanying experience necessary to sell the product: "In today's service economy, many companies simply wrap experiences around their traditional offerings to sell them better" (Pine & Gilmore, 1998, p. 98). Experiences are seen as a new category of offer that characterizes 21st-century enterprises. In this line of thought, the company is seen as a stage where consumers emotionally engage themselves, the ultimate objective being the production of emotions and, more importantly, memories.

The typical example cited by Pine and Gilmore was the production of coffee and the success of Starbucks. Whilst coffee has a certain cost (as a commodity), society gradually learned to package it to sell in shops and then it was sold in cafés. Eventually, companies such as Starbucks or Costa (in the UK) came on the market and added another layer to coffee-drinking by wrapping it up in a whole experience: the comfy sofas, nice music, free WiFi, the staff calling customers by their first names, a broad range of coffee options in different sizes and flavors, etc. Pricewise, companies such as Costa or Starbucks, are able to charge a premium price for coffee that is much superior to traditional coffee bars and even more so to the price of making a similar coffee at home.

Similarly, Nespresso has conveniently produced a new way of drinking coffee. First of all, it has eased the coffee making process at home or work. The company has simplified the "messy" process of making coffee by producing various capsules of different intensity and flavors and by producing a machine that is able to produce coffee for them. More importantly, it is the coffee experience that has been revisited through their shops: smartly designed, they allow consumers to taste for free different coffees before making their purchase. Their shops are also cleverly designed, playing on lights, colors, staff to provide a real and distinctive experience. Those shops have a sense of luxury where the customer is shown a lot of respect and consideration.

We can see with both these examples that the simple experience of drinking a cup of coffee has been totally revisited and magnified to produce a whole experience accompanying the sale of the product and allowing those companies to charge a premium price for what is, in reality, a fairly simple process and product.

## The key components of a successful experience

Beyond looking at the experience surrounding specific products, the theories of experiential marketing aimed to list the key components that can lead to a successful experience. Among those, Pine and Gilmore identified five key components to design memorable experiences:

- *Theming the experience:* This element is a central component; its objective is to provide a theme that will harmonize all the elements within the service encounter. The theme acts as a directing line that will make sense of the consumption universe in which consumers are immersed and will create a stage for the experience. Unifying those impressions will allow consumers to feel nested in the service universe, be carried along by it, and will also help the firm to differentiate itself from competitors. Hard Rock Cafés, Starbucks, Disney Resorts are all examples of successful theming. In the tourism and hospitality industry, theming has been extensively used to unify hotels, restaurants, and resorts. The Ötzi case study below shows how a theme can be developed in a museum around a specific topic whether it pertains to the lifestyle or the scientific aspects associated with a mummy.
- *Harmonize impressions with positive cues*: "to create the desired impressions, companies must introduce cues that affirm the nature of the experience to the guest" (Pine & Gilmore, 1998, p. 103).
- *Eliminate negative cues:* "Experience stagers also must eliminate anything that diminishes, contradicts, or distracts from the theme" (Pine & Gilmore, 1998, p. 103). Overdoing the service by interrupting conversations (hotel front desk) or providing information when one does not need it or is doing something else, is also seen as a negative element. For instance, reps in holiday resorts will prompt tourists to participate in group activities and events. The risk of confusion between suggesting and interfering with the holiday mood requires subtlety to ensure that those reps don't burden the tourist with unnecessary information and solicitation.
- *Mix in memorabilia:* Consumers are always keen to take home an item that will intuitively carry remembrance of a fond event. This is very characteristic of the tourism industry where souvenirs have always formed a "must do" component of the holiday.

- *Engage all five senses:* The five sense have already been addressed in this chapter. Pine and Gilmore suggest that an experience will be even more effective and memorable if more senses are stimulated.

## TOURISM AND HOSPITALITY INSIGHTS 6.3
## THE ICEMAN

In 1991, in the Italian Alps close to the Austrian border, two hikers walking in the Ötztal Alps found a body that had been displaced by the glacier. The corpse was in incredibly good condition and had literally been mummified. At first, they thought that it was the corpse of an anonymous alpinist but six days later, Konrad Spindler, Professor of Ancient and Early History at Innsbruck University, inspected the find and from the type of ax that was lying next to the body, he decided that it was at least 4,000 years old. C-14 analysis (radiocarbon dating) conducted by four different scientific institutions then corroborated the age and identified that this iceman must have lived between 3350 and 3100 BC.

All the scientific work produced to identify and date the mummy was important since several rumors circulated that could have reduced the credibility of the find. Therefore, in order to validate the credibility of the find and to deal with international press enquiries, an early Alpine history research institute was established in Innsbruck.

The mummy was in fact a "wet mummy" whereby humidity was retained in individual cells offering researchers plenty opportunities to conduct detailed scientific investigations. The fact that it was not disturbed by burial rites (unlike Egyptian mummies), and that it came with complete clothing and various items of equipment, made the find one of incredible richness. Because the mummy was preserved with all its equipment, the scientists obtained a lot of knowledge from this find. Ötzi was carrying with him an extensive set of items that allowed him to be self-sufficient when away from home for long periods.

Once the scientific investigation was completed, it was decided to put the corpse on display in a museum in Bolzano (South Tyrol).

Building a museum around a single corpse/mummy is a difficult task and getting the public interested in the object was complex but the curators were particularly good at capturing the interest of the find itself and, beyond the mummy, understood what could be gained from analyzing its lifestyle.

In order to develop interest in Ötzi, the museum curators decided to build the story over several floors. Using the five senses for such a topic can be a difficult task since the corpse is old and most of the items that were used by it cannot be touched. The museum decided to develop different aspects surrounding the corpse on different floors and much of the information provided is based on an account of the actual find, the scientific analysis that followed then the mummy and equipment, and all the knowledge that can be derived from this find.

On the first floor, the epic history of the discovery of the corpse is detailed; the scientific battle that took place around it gives some idea of the complexity for scientists, several thousand years later, to clearly identify its origins. The tone of the museum visit is thereby given, directing the visitors through the different floors as if they were leading a police enquiry. The whole museum is driven towards identifying what was found and then all the inferences that can be drawn about Ötzi's lifestyle at that time.

On the second floor, visitors can see the corpse (preserved at a very low temperature) and all the clothes, shoes, and weapons that were found with him. A full-size model of Ötzi (including hair) gives a good idea of what he actually looked like to visitors. Storytelling again is very strong on this floor, presenting the different items of clothing and equipment used by Ötzi to make the various clothes, the incredible shoes, the weapons and how ember was carried around. The whole lifestyle of Ötzi is then uncovered, by giving sense to this corpse and providing, through storytelling, a vision of the universe in which this individual evolved. Surprisingly, Ötzi had several tattoos on his body.

The museum then dedicates a space to Ötzi's lifestyle. Which cultural group did he belong to? Which society? What was the religion during the copper era, its economy, its houses and village structure, the extraction and use of copper, etc.

The last floor is devoted to his health: his diet and several unexplained facts, for instance the vast amount of animal fat found in his stomach. The enquiry about his death is very interesting. Years after the mummy's find, new x-rays identified that he had been wounded by an arrow, leading to intensive bleeding that probably led to his death. Unhealed wounds on his hand and a cerebral trauma all show that Ötzi was involved in a fight not long before he died.

The interest in Ötzi is kept alive by constant new findings. Indeed, every time new scientific evidence is uncovered, the media distribute it on an international scale. Therefore the interest in Ötzi remains fresh and on the news constantly. For instance, in January 2016, a bacterium called Helicobacter pylori was discovered in his stomach. This bacterium can cause stomach ulcers and the spread of this bacterium gives very interesting information has to how the population spread across the world. In this case, Ötzi carried a Eurasian strain (and not the African one) which gave scientists precious information about migration from both Asia and Africa.

Altogether, this museum is a very good example of experiential tourism, especially in regard to storytelling, in other words, making sense of an "object" for the visitor. The museum builds a true story around the mummy by bringing in scientific investigations and linking them with the existing knowledge that archeologists already had of the copper era in this area of the Alps. By building the visit as an enquiry, the museum curators have also managed to create customer interest and sustain that interest throughout the visit.

Source: Isabelle Frochot/http://www.iceman.it/

Schmitt (1999) produced the Strategic experiential modules (SEM) to create successful experiences. According to Schmitt, those experiences need to show five characteristics:

- *SENSE:* Sensory experiences. Schmitt also advocates relying on the five senses for a satisfactory experience. Those five senses need to come together to provide consistency (an underlying concept that one can clearly identify) but with freshness every time. In other words, a consistent message with diversity of expressing it throughout time.
- *FEEL:* Affective experiences. The objective here is to elicit emotion and, more importantly, know which tools/event can be used to prompt those emotions. Care should be brought to make sure that consumers are also willing to empathize with the situation given.
- *THINK:* Cognitive experiences. Those experiences are in direct connection with consumers' intellect. The objective here is to create cognitive, problem-solving experiences by playing on consumers' surprise, intrigue, and provocation. Again, this is very present in the tourist experience, where intellectual challenge is often tested through learning about history and culture and now magnified through various treasure-hunts, geo-catching games that aim to test one's own intellectual capacities. The previous case study about the iceman museum highlights this point.
- *ACT:* Physical, behavioral and lifestyle experiences. These experiences aim to target consumers' physical abilities and encourage them to even consider alternative ways of doing things. Holidays provide many opportunities to try new activities, new sports that can provide tourists with cognitive experiences of long-lasting memories.
- *RELATE:* Social-identity experiences (relating to different groups or cultures). This experience is linked to the desire for self-improvement, to be perceived more positively by others, and relate to a broader system (such as discovering a new culture). Again, this is very present in tourism consumption whereby traveling will often stimulate the desire to know more about the culture of the country visited, rely on one's own culture, and the world in which one lives. This experience also relates to the Consumer Culture Theory vision of tribes and the necessity to belong to a tribe as a new way of finding an identity in contemporary societies.

According to Hetzel (2002) individuals are increasingly seeking a universe that takes them away from their daily life and makes them dream by transporting them to a different universe. In this process, esthetic elements and atmosphere are conceived as key components of the experience. Hetzel identified four pillars of experience that constitute what he called the "experience wheel":

- *Create surprise:* The experience should provide something unusual in order to create a radical break with everyday life and thereby make the consumer free to fully live the experience he is participating in. In tourism, it is an interesting notion to develop since the need to get away being the first motivation of any tourism consumption; it is a notion that needs careful attention. Cultivating that feeling of being away from home, severance from daily routines is often a key component to a successful holiday.

- *Offer something extraordinary:* Hetzel (2002) stressed the importance of offering an experience of a giant nature, spectacular, magic, and authentic. All these notions are central in the tourist experience and indeed the tourism offering cultivates those elements with great care. The example of the ghost tour in Prague below provides some elements of this nature.
- *Stimulate the five senses:* Again, nothing new here, all experiential marketing approaches always stress the need to stimulate those senses. Hetzel (2002) emphasizes the necessity to ensure that consumers need to undergo strong sensorial experiences.
- *Create a link with consumers:* Hezel (2002) underlines the need to establish a strong and personal relationship with consumers. The notion of proximity seems to be essential to this element. The case developed on AirBnB shows how contemporary consumers are increasingly in need of "real" contacts with a country through the interactions they develop with their hosts.

## TOURISM AND HOSPITALITY INSIGHTS 6.4
## GHOST TOURS IN PRAGUE

Ghost tours have become a fairly common feature of guided tours in cities across Europe. These guided tours aim to provide visitors with a very different vision of a city. Traditional guided tours provide visitors with a formal vision of a heritage site, complete with historical knowledge and chronological references. Guided tours take a different approach to a visit by introducing storytelling based on the dark sides of a tourist site. Ghost stories and legends, visiting cemeteries, spooky stories all contribute to creating a hairy feeling to the delight of participating tourists. By introducing surreal and unexplained phenomena, the ghost tour aims to provide another side of a heritage site. The tours however, do provide usually a minimum of history about a destination, so that visitors are not frustrated and develop the feeling that they have retrieved some useful historical information about the site.

In Prague, McGee's company offers ghost guided tours presented as follows:

> Prague is one of the most supernatural cities in Europe, with a history rich in magic, murder and the mysterious. For many years it has been a magnet for students of the occult, and in the 16th and 17th centuries it was a meeting point for alchemists and astrologers during the reign of Emperor Rudolf II. The architecture of Prague is replete with esoteric symbols, which can reveal many secrets to those who know how to read them.
>
> Whether you are a believer or a sceptic, interested in the unexplained, or simply looking for an informative and entertaining evening, McGee's Ghost Tours will show you the darker side of Prague. Our guides will take you through the narrow lanes and cobblestone alleys, to the ancient churches and monuments of Prague, where you will hear about the alchemists, murderers, executioners, and unfortunate souls who lived there. Some of them are said to linger in these places, and who knows, perhaps you will be lucky enough to see them?

**Image 6.4**

Source: Isabelle Frochot/https://www.pexels.com/photo/light-sky-space-abstract-40748/

The tour takes place towards the end of the afternoon, when darkness sets in. The guide, dressed in a dark cape and hat leads his group of visitors through different side streets. The stops are always associated with a specific building and the ghost stories/legends are then shared with visitors. The tour lasts one hour and includes seven different stops. The rating for those tours on Tripadvisor is 4.5/5. The positive comments go towards the capacity of the guide to share his stories with his tour participants and his capacity to raise chilly feelings from his various stories. Visitors also appreciate the fact that they discover another side of Prague. The guide does not lead them through the usual tourist attractions (Charles' Bridge, the Old Square, etc.). The guide takes them instead through side streets with unknown monuments which also have an interesting story (an old hospital, a hidden chapel, etc.). In this sense, visitors feel that this visit is complementary to the other visits they will undertake during their trip.

For a video of McGee Ghost tours of Prague: https://www.youtube.com/watch?v=hEbpm9Pymbo

Source: http://www.mcgeesghosttours.com/

**Figure 6.2 The key experience components**

Source: Author.

In summary, those different approaches to the experience provide some interesting insights into the main components of the experience. Whilst all their visions might be different in some parts, one can retain that all approaches put a strong focus on the necessity to develop the five senses through the experience, develop an element of surprise, and involve consumers. The authors of this book propose an approach that combines the majority of approaches by suggesting that a successful experience should display at least three of the following key elements: develop an element of surprise/ unusual/extraordinary; involve consumers within the consumption process, develop some of the five senses and create sense. One supplementary process that allows for those elements to take place, called immersion, will be developed in Chapter 10.

## Conclusion

This chapter has provided readers with a detailed introduction to experiential marketing. This different marketing approach is particularly suited to the context of tourism and hospitality where the highly esthetical, symbolical, and emotional dimensions of consumption have long been recognized. Tourists seem to behave with less utilitarian rationality than in everyday life, and aim to maximize their pleasure, feeling of detachment, and "otherness" so distinctively that it makes this area of research a unique topic where experiential marketing brings a useful framework and concepts.

The chapter detailed the origins of experiential marketing with the valuable work from Holbrook and Hirschman up to the notion of the experience economy produced by Pine and Gilmore in 1998. The various works produced in this area have helped to establish that a successful and memorable experience should be based on five key components: the use of the five senses, theming the consumption universe, developing consumers' involvement, create surprise, and make sense of the surrounding universe.

Experiential marketing therefore cannot be reduced to a commercial vision of creating a specific service atmosphere based on the five senses and clever theming. There are also other processes that can elicit emotions and strong memories and that need to be integrated when designing tourism and hospitality services.

Experiential marketing also has to be understood within the evolution of the tourism economy, as Chapter 1 has detailed, and also needs to integrate new trends in tourism consumption as will be addressed in the following chapter.

## REVIEW QUESTIONS

1. What are the main objectives of experiential marketing?
2. How does experiential marketing differ from traditional marketing?
3. Why are tourism and hospitality good "candidates" for experiential marketing?
4. What are the key ingredients of a successful tourism or hospitality experience?
5. What are the key elements that can be developed within sensorial marketing?

## YOUTUBE LINKS

### "Building the tourist experience – Thompson Okanaghan Tourism Association"

URL: https://www.youtube.com/watch?v=QVI6aYfx1iQ

Summary: A video from the Thompson Okanagan Tourism Association (Canada) explaining the strategy behind creating tourism experiences rather than simply marketing properties. They look at the different assets provided by the destination (from water, snow, culture to food and wine) and elaborate on their strategy to develop experiences from those resources.

### "London's best tourism experience"

URL: https://www.youtube.com/watch?v=weB-Der3wpI

Summary: This video from the Zoological Society of London presents London's voted Best Tourism Experience in 2010. By watching the video, one can clearly see how the strategy of the zoo is to develop an experience with animals by putting visitors close to the animals, interacting with them, whenever possible, and learn about the animals' life through various educative shows.

## *"Jo Pine explanation of the experience economy"*

URL: https://www.youtube.com/watch?v=amU9Kqomb4I

Summary: This 14-minute video details Jo Pine's vision of the experience economy by explaining its basic principles through various examples to emphasize the importance of the experience economy. Jo Pine discusses the fact that services are becoming commoditized and companies need to go further: experiences are a distinct economic offer and the only way for a company to survive in the future.

## *"Six inspiring new examples of experiential marketing"*

URL: https://econsultancy.com/blog/66431-six-inspiring-new-examples-of-experiential-marketing/

Summary: An article that details a range of videos highlighting various experiential marketing offers from Carslberg to Bud Light house of Water and Bates Motel. These examples will help readers understand how some experiential marketing ideas have succeeded in boosting the image of the brands concerned.

## *"Starbucks marketing"*

URL: https://www.youtube.com/watch?v=9HVMhm59Ibs

Summary: This video analyses the success of Starbucks' rise and analyzes how Starbucks manages to develop a specific vision of its service through an experiential approach. It analyzes all the side products that have helped in asserting the brand and its limits. It then explains how Starbucks cultivated a different positioning from its direct competitors.

### REFERENCES, FURTHER READING, AND RELATED WEBSITES

### References

Hetzel, P. (2002). *Planète conso: Marketing expérientiel et nouveaux univers de consommation.* Paris: Éditions d'Organisation.

Holbrook, M., & Hirschman, E. (1982). Hedonic consumption: Emerging concepts, methods and propositions. *Journal of Marketing, 46*(3), 92–101.

Kotler, P. (1974). Atmospherics as a marketing tool. *Journal of Retailing, 49*(4), 48–64.

Pine, J., & Gilmore, J. (1998). *The experience economy.* Boston, MA: Harvard Business School Press.

Schmitt, B.H. (1999). *Experience marketing: How to get customers to sense, feel, think, and relate to your company and brands.* New York: The Free Press.

## Further reading

Arnould, E.J., & Price, L.L. (1993). Rivermagic: Extraordinary experience and the extended service encounter. *Journal of Consumer Research, 20*(1), 24–45.

Carù, A., & Cova, B. (2007). *Consuming experiences.* Abingdon: Routledge.

Csikszentmihalyi, M. (1991). *Flow: The psychology of optimal experience.* New York: Harper & Row.

Filet, S. (2017). *Tourist experience and fulfilment: Insights from positive psychology.* Abingdon: Routledge.

Frochot, I., & Batat, W. (2013). *Marketing and designing the tourist experience.* Oxford: GoodFellow Publishers.

Kim, J.H., Ritchie, J.R.B., & McCormick, B. (2012). Development of a scale to measure memorable tourism experiences. *Journal of Travel Research, 51*(1), 12–25.

Loeffler, B., & Church, B. (2015). *The experience: The 5 principles of Disney service and relationship excellence.* Hoboken, NJ: Wiley.

Larsen, J. (2007). Aspects for a psychology of the tourist experience. *Scandinavian Journal of Hospitality and Tourism, 7*(1), 7–18.

Otto, J., & Ritchie, J.R. (1995). Exploring the quality of the service experience: A theoretical and empirical analysis. *Advances in Services Marketing and Management, 4*, 37–61.

Ritchie, J.R.B., Tung, V.W., & Ritchie, R.J.B. (2011). Tourism experience management research: Emergence, evolution and future direction. *International Journal of Contemporary Hospitality Management, 23*(4), 419–438.

Tinsley, H.E., & Tinsley, D.J. (1986). A theory of the attributes, benefits and causes of leisure experience. *Leisure Sciences, 8*(1), 1–45.

Tung, V.W.S., & Ritchie, J.R. (2011). Exploring the essence of memorable tourism experiences. *Annals of Tourism Research, 38*(4), 1367–1386.

## Websites

The Experience Economy
https://hbr.org/1998/07/welcome-to-the-experience-economy

Top Ten Experiential Examples for Travel
https://diousa.com/blog/top-ten-experiential-examples-for-travel/

Full management of your customer relationship
https://www.experience-hotel.com/

Experiential marketing
https://www.mmgyglobal.com/services/deploy/experiential-marketing

# MAJOR CASE STUDY
# LUX HOTELS

LUX* Resorts and Hotels is part of the LUX group whose head-office is in Mauritius (see Chapter 16, Major Case Study). Previously known as Naïade Resorts Ltd, it was founded in 1987 and now operates in several islands. It moved from Naïade Resorts Ltd to LUX* Resorts and Hotels on December 2011. In Mauritius, LUX* Resorts and Hotels owns three hotels (LUX* Belle Mare, LUX* Le Morne, and LUX* Grand Gaube). In Reunion, LUX* Resorts and Hotels owns one hotel, the LUX* Saint Gilles and in the Maldives it owns two hotels: Lux* South Ari Atoll and LUX* North male Atoll (opening in 2016). LUX* is now expanding further across the world with one hotel in China (LUX* Tea Horse Road in the greater Shangri-La region) and another one opening in 2017, the LUX* Dianshan lake. Other projects include the United Arabs Emirates with the opening, in 2017, of the LUX* Al Zorah and the lux* Al Zorah residences.

In terms of performance, in 2014, the group reached an average occupancy rate of 72% with a RevPAR (Room Revenue per Available Room) reaching 12%. In 2014, total revenue reached 4.2 billion Rs and EBITDA (Earnings before Interests Tax Depreciation and Amortisation) increased by 18% from 774 m to 91.7 million Rs. The group has just under 3,000 employees across the world.

LUX* Resorts and Hotels has opted for a positioning on luxury, but with a strong contemporary component, the brand aims to be seen as a 21st-century brand. Its objective is to stage "exceptional experiences in different locales – whether on the Beach, in the City or in Nature – by banishing thoughtless patterns and being more simple, fresh, and sensory than our competitors." Therefore their vision is one of simplified luxury, modern, vibrant, to the point:

"LUX* is a brand that celebrates the lighter side of luxury with a unique approach to crafting the finest holiday experience for guests."

The company mission is: "Helping people celebrate life" with the idea of providing a seamless experience where everything has been thought of for the consumer and delivered in the smoothest fashion possible: "LUX* banishes thoughtless patterns to create a truly unique vacation experience. One that is lighter, brighter."

Their vision is that "each moment matters" and therefore that LUX* Resorts and Hotels will pay attention to the smallest details and develop them into a memorable experience. Luxury is a positioning adopted by many large hotel groups throughout the world, and it was important for LUX* Resorts and Hotels to choose a different positioning: "Since luxury means different things from person to person, we focus on perfecting the priorities, while peppering the environment and your experience with pop-up treats and uplifting moments."

LUX* goes beyond the traditional hotel rating schemes (the number of stars), using the guiding principle that surprises are what drive memorable experiences along with top-class employee service. The open hand is a symbol of their values with each finger depicting a different value: people, passion, integrity, leadership, and creativity. The values are then developed into a range of beliefs that qualify employees' behavior: consideration for people, serving with passion, insistence on integrity, responsibility of leadership, and entertaining with creativity.

LUX* Resorts and Hotels strategic choices include the promotion of the offer's diversity and more hotels opening soon, a stronger presence on social networks, employees' involvement and most importantly a differentiation strategy with the famous "50 reasons to go."

*Reasons to go LUX\** explores the stories behind the 54 scenes that make up the LUX* show, everything from coffee to space-age mattress design, to the way our industry is impacting the planet. Don't worry, it's not all one great big advertorial. If you want to book a holiday then we have a website just for that.

Luxury needn't be heavy and hard to digest. We write features and craft films about stories from all over the world to give you just a little taste of why. And maybe brighten up your day too.

LUX* Resorts and Hotels has perfectly understood how to apply the pillars of experiential marketing at specific levels of their service delivery. Those 54 scenes detail different experiences that have been thought through to make sure that consumers will come home with some outstanding and memorable experiences. The main four pillars of experiential marketing can be found across those experiences.

The first one is *surprise*, and indeed LUX* Resorts and Hotels have been extremely judicious at thinking of experiences that can bring a big element of surprise in the day-to-day stay of their customers. Surprise can be created by either taking a fairly common experience and by changing its location/context, or alternatively it is created by providing something that is totally unexpected.

The second one is *making sense of the place* by creating links between a luxurious resort and the destination within which it is located. LUX* Resorts and Hotels thereby tries to identify elements from the local culture that have an exotic feel to the visitors and will be enjoyable to use/consume. They also try to give more sense and humanity to those resorts by bringing a more personalized vision of local culture and customs.

The third component refers to the *involvement of consumers into the experience*, making sure they become the actors of the experience by either doing something new or not, but in any case something that they need to participate in too in order to increase their enjoyment and the memorability of the experience.

The fourth component, which we have not addressed so far in the main text of this chapter, is one of *magic*. This element is in fact very important in tourist experiences, although very little research has been conducted on this aspect. This notion of magic is often associated with childhood memories and thereby directly touches consumers' emotions. The idea is therefore to provide them with experiences that are associated, in their memory, with very comforting and enjoyable times of their early childhood, a time where they lived for the present and most probably encountered fewer worries.

Source: Isabelle Frochot/LUX Annual Report (2014) at http://www.luxresorts.com/media/2599211/lux-annual-report-2014.pdf; http://www.luxresorts.com/fr

Major case study questions

1.  Take a look at the experiences listed as the reasons to go LUX*. The webpage (http://www.luxresorts.com/en/reasons-to-go-lux) lists more than ten experiences. Each experience is described in a few lines and supported by a video. Select three experiences and for each of them identify the key components of that experience and clearly identify which of the following experience pillars is being used: surprise, making sense of the place, involvement and/or magic. Please note that some experiences might involve more than one pillar. You need to analyze how the use of those pillars will create a memorable experience.

2.  Take another tourist experience of any type and analyze how you could apply those principles to boost its experiential dimension. For instance, whether you choose a hotel, a guided tour, a nature walk, or a campsite, think how one or several of the four pillars can be developed to improve the pleasure and memorability of the experience.

# 7 New trends in tourism and hospitality consumption

## Learning outcomes

By the end of this chapter, students will:

- Understand what are the key motivators underpinning tourism demand
- Be able to identify the main push factors that drive consumers' demand
- Appreciate the pull factors that explain the diversity of behavior observed in the tourism market
- Recognize the key trends that will fuel tomorrow's demand
- Understand the principles of segmentation, especially psychographic segmentation.

**Key terms**

push factors,
pull factors,
social needs,
uniqueness,
environment,
psychographic
segmentation

## Introduction

This chapter starts by looking at the key trends underpinning tourist consumption in the 21st century. It first addresses the evolution of contemporary living conditions, as tourism is an inverse mirror to those frustrations and is often seen as a way to escape them. The first part addresses the pull motivations which attract visitors to some specific destinations and products, while the second part focuses on the evolution of customers' expectations and will list the key trends that will shape tomorrow's demand for tourism products.

The notions of playfulness, wellbeing, uniqueness, environment sensitivity, authenticity and the shared economy will demonstrate how demand is evolving and which products will be expected in the long term. The chapter concludes with a case study on Amadeus that explores how suitable segments translate into efficient tourism products.

# The notion of motivation and its specificities in tourism consumption

Motivations represent the key components to understand tourist behavior. They create, direct, and fuel the driving force that underpins the whole consumption process, from decision-making right through post-satisfaction and loyalty. Motivation is also an interesting key concept because it federates many other variables that influence behavior (cultural norms, social class, reference group, etc.). Motivation is a concept that has been heavily studied in tourism marketing and is divided into two important categories: on one side push motivations refer to what motivates individuals to travel; on the other side pull factors refer to what attracts them to specific destinations/tourists' products.

## *Push factors*

Push factors have been the object of intense academic interest in the 1960s and 1970s when researchers started to analyze the core reasons behind the emergence of tourism. Tourism was then seen as a way to escape contemporary societies. Dann (1977) saw tourism as anomic, meaning that tourism consumption was seen as a way to escape from a meaningless life and society. Dann also perceived tourism consumption as an ego-enhancement activity which would allow individuals to compensate for the status deprivation they could experience in daily lives. Krippendorf (1999) even ascertained that holidays could almost be prescribed by doctors as they represented a safety valve for contemporary societies, absorbing individuals' stress and frustrations with their daily lives. In other words, industrialization caused both the reasons and the means for mass tourism to emerge.

## TOURISM AND HOSPITALITY INSIGHTS 7.1
## ABSOLUTE RELAXATION AND ALL-INCLUSIVE PRODUCTS

Following from the pull factors mentioned at the start of this chapter, the need for relaxation is such that contemporary consumers are increasingly looking for stress-free products. Resorts have recognized this need for some time and have become very imaginative in providing products that have no constraints and leave tourists free to fully enjoy their holiday. Reflecting on the fact that tourism consumption is the inversed mirror of society, resorts have designed services and amenities that precisely offer possibilities for tourists to experience completely different rhythms and activities from the quotidian. For instance, one element that tourists particularly long for, is the possibility of waking up undisturbed by an alarm o'clock: they want to restore themselves and dream of long sleep ins. For those tourists, the 7 to 9 am slot for breakfast is perceived as inappropriate. As a result, resorts are offering late breakfasts (up till 11) and also all-day snacking for those who do not want to comply with the restaurant schedule. A vast choice of physical activities (from aqua gym to golf) are offered where nothing is compulsory. Most tourists will only participate in a small range of these activities but it is important that they feel that they have an extensive choice.

Equally, since the need to reinforce family ties has been an increasing demand from tourists, resorts have offered services that allow for each member of a family unit to enjoy their own part of the holiday. For instance, resorts offer to mind the children two nights a week so that parents can enjoy an evening together. Activity clubs, and adolescent clubs also contribute to each sub-group of the family unit engaging their level of interest too.

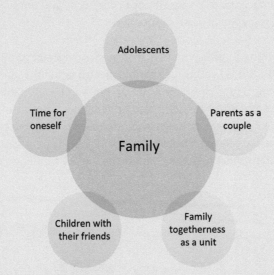

**Figure 7.1** Family dynamics

The ultimate element of total relaxation is to have no worries regarding holiday expenditure. In this regard, all-inclusive holidays have expanded very rapidly over the last two decades. All-inclusive vacations offer the possibility of setting a budget from the start, avoiding having to make budget decisions during vacations and thereby freeing the mind to have a totally relaxing holiday.

Source: Isabelle Frochot.

As society developed and urbanization expanded, more stressful living conditions emerged:

- Workwise, while previous generations most probably stayed with the same employer all their life, contemporary workers are used to changing jobs several times throughout their working life. Trust between employers and superiors has also suffered with increasing outsourcing of production to developing countries and CEOs' salaries considerably higher when factory workers are still being paid comparatively low salaries, are on fixed-term contracts with no guarantee of permanent employment, etc.

- The economy is also showing signs of weaknesses and the 2008 Financial Crisis showed that it was quite a fragile system. Both the insecurity of the employment sphere and the global economy have thereby created a certain amount of tension in societies.
- The general social climate has become less secure due to terrorist threats especially in big urban capitals such as London, Brussels, or Paris.

Living in big urban centers is another cause of stress. By 2030, 70% of the world population will be living in urban populated areas. Urban areas are very attractive places to live in and concentrate a vast amount of services and employment opportunities. However, their geographical scale means that:

- Commuting times have vastly increased (on average a minimum of two hours daily);
- Air pollution is becoming a serious health issue in some locations;
- Noise and light disturbances are becoming objectionable;
- Pressure and stress are increasing due to the amount of crowding (queuing, traffic jams, lack of space, reduced accommodation sizes, etc.);
- Families have fewer opportunities to spend time together, sometimes simply due to different schedules throughout the day and individualized rhythms;

**Image 7.1**

Source: https://www.pexels.com/photo/air-air-pollution-chimney-city-221000/

- On a personal level, life seems to be more destabilizing than for previous generations. The divorce rate is increasing and split custody of children is challenging family time.

Altogether, the above factors have created a certain level of instability. While urban areas are also interesting, vibrant, and dynamic places, they have in themselves created the need to escape from them on a regular basis if one wants to survive in them (Tourism and hospitality insights 7.1 highlights some of those elements). The recent media uptake on positive psychology shows that contemporary societies are increasingly refocusing on enjoying the instant and simple things, and leisure time is where they can just do that.

Holidays come as a response to those needs and have been increasingly invested in the need to experience happiness and to restore oneself. It is also an important time to create (or recreate) family togetherness as parents and children have the opportunity to spend quality time together.

This need for escape fuels other expectations of the holiday. For instance, the sheer speed of contemporary lives leads consumers to use holidays as a perfect period to engage in introspection. The distance from everyday life, the relaxing atmosphere, and the complete change of scene are conductive to rest, reflection, and re-evaluation of one's capabilities. Undertaking new activities, perfecting one's skills, learning new skills all contribute to defining or redefining an image of the self.

Traveling also means getting away from everyday social norms. The pressure of the social norms associated with one's status, social class, and national culture can become quite oppressive and constraining at times. The holiday context can then be seen as an escape where those pressures can disappear and tourists can behave with a freedom and lack of judgment that they would not usually have to comply to. This can be a very positive thing: tourists experience a real feeling of freedom conductive

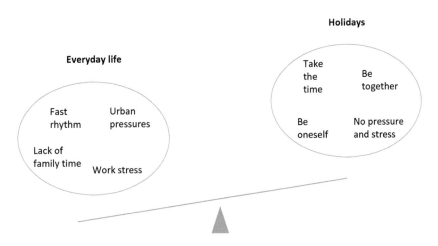

**Figure 7.2 Holidays as opposed to everyday life**

of deep pleasure, rest, and reflection. At the other end, release from one's own social pressures should not conflict with the norms of the country that the tourist is visiting. Negative examples of lack of compliance include excessive drinking, drug taking, dressing inappropriately, etc.

Whilst some of those elements might come as evidence, they do have strong implications in terms of marketing. First and foremost, they have implications for the conceptualization of tourism products whether they impact the types of products or experiences: it is essential for tourism providers to design products and services that cut consumers free from their daily life.

On top of the contemporary needs detailed above, each generation will develop its own attitude to travel. Generation Y, also known as Millennials, for instance, have developed specific expectations of their travels as the Tourism and hospitality insights 7.2 shows.

## TOURISM AND HOSPITALITY INSIGHTS 7.2
## GENERATION Y'S ATTITUDE TO TRAVEL

Generation Y, Millennials, were born between 1978 and 1994 and will outpace the Baby Boomer population by 2030 (78 million compared to the Boomers' 58 million). This generation is tech-savvy but also has an attitude to travel that is quite different from their parents. They are used to traveling and they consider their holidays as a right.

### Key characteristics of Millennials

*Instantaneity*: Millennials seek immediate gratification whether in terms of WiFi access as much as in easy information access on websites, etc. This now generation also expects real-time reporting and they rely on social networks both to get that information and to communicate with their communities. Their booking pattern has also been reduced to 75 days (93 days for previous generations). Equally, they expect very fast feedback/confirmation from the companies they are booking with. Indeed, free WiFi is a must for this generation.

*Flexibility*: This means that those consumers like quick and easy service: very formal service delivery can be perceived as slow and unnecessary. Millennials won't worry about check-in kiosks, or lack of table service. Smartphone applications will give information and direct them, etc. Increasingly, brands also learn to communicate actively on their social networks, whether they are Facebook, Instagram or Twitter. As an example, those customers will enjoy hotels that look trendy, with a contemporary style but not necessarily with luxurious and large rooms. They might appreciate smaller rooms, if they have a nice hotel with plenty of lobby space to socialize/work, and social areas.

*Peer review*: Millennials have long bypassed traditional marketing activities to seek information from their peers directly on Internet. Therefore, reviews such as those on TripAdvisor are becoming crucial in their decision-making since authenticity and trust are their key ingredients.

*Social interactions*: Millennials are highly sociable individuals but the codes that they use to communicate are evolving with technology. For instance, their need to communicate on Facebook, collect "Likes" for their current activity, indicate their location, etc., are all part of a way of communicating with their friends. Beyond the online world, this generation is keen to spend time together, socialize, and party. This can be seen in the increasing socializing opportunities that backpackers create and new generation youth hostels encouraging events in their bars, etc.

*Authentic local experience*: Millennials seek to discover the true nature of a destination. They might visit some of the unavoidable key icons of a destination (the Empire State Building, the Eiffel Tower or Buckingham Palace), but they also want to discover the true side of a country (typically Airbnb and couch surfing offer such opportunities). They also want to feel that they are supporting sustainable issues.

### References

Neault C. (2014) Generation Y, the new face of business travel. *GlobeVeilleur*, June 30. http://touris mintelligence.ca/2014/06/30/generation-y-the-new-face-of-business-travel/

Source: Lee T. (2013) Top 10 Trends of The Next Generation of Travel: The Millennials, hotel. OnlineSearch.

## Pull factors

Countless studies exist on the analysis of tourist motivations and we will simply summarize in this chapter the main key motivations that have been identified in the academic literature.

As we will notice, these studies group together pull and push factors. For instance, the need for regression, compensation, and escape all relate to the need to get away from contemporary societies (push factors). There are many studies of tourist motivations' and overall, they tend to point to four key motivations components (Figure 7.3).

- *A need for relaxation*: As mentioned previously, the need for escape finds its roots in contemporary living conditions in modern and urbanized societies. Therefore, the need to relax always comes at the top of the list of the most important motivations (just after the need to get away).
- *Cultural discovery*: This motivation encapsulates the need for tourists to discover new information about the destination visited. This expectation can cover the need to discover the destination's history and cultural traditions. It can also include local crafts and local products (including food and wine). Cultural discovery can be done independently (with a guide book, mobile phone applications) or guided (organized tours, guided visits, museum visits). The cultural interest can have formal dimensions (for instance, visiting museums) or might translate into a more informal need for a mix of information and entertainment.

**Table 7.1** Key motivations according to Crompton (1979) and Krippendorf (1999)

| Crompton (1999) | Krippendorf (1999) |
| --- | --- |
| • Escape everyday environment | • Travel is recuperation and regeneration (from stressed and ill bodies) |
| • Explore and evaluate oneself | • Travel is compensation and social integration (compensates for what we miss in everyday life) |
| • To relax | • Travel is escape from the everyday world |
| • For prestige | • Travel is communication (contacts with people) |
| • For regression | • Travel broadens the mind |
| • To reinforce relation-ships with one's family | • Travel is freedom and self-determination (own decisions, no obligations) |
| • To facilitate social interactions | • Travel is happiness (the most memorable days of the year, etc.) |
| • Novelty | |
| • Education | |

Source: Author.

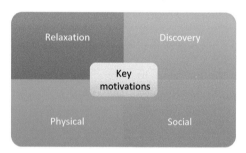

**Figure 7.3 Key motivation components**

- *Social needs*: The need for social interaction has today become one of the essential expectations of a holiday. As there are fewer opportunities for quality socializing than in the past (working rhythms, individualism, etc.), holidays have become a new platform for developing quality social relations. These relate primarily to the family unit which needs more quality time where discussion and time together can "finally" take place. At another level, reinforcing relationships with friends is also another holiday component. Bonding with groups of friends of the same sex has developed into a fairly healthy market (stag and hen nights, shopping weekends, sporting events, preparing and running a marathon, etc.). Tourism and Hospitality Insights 7.3) provides some indication of those markets. Social connections also include meeting up with the local population, learning about their customs, and sitting down together to share a meal for example. The truth is that in many modern forms of packaged tourism, social contact might take place but between tourists themselves, often on cruise ships or in holiday resorts.

## TOURISM AND HOSPITALITY INSIGHTS 7.3
## GIRLFRIENDS' GETAWAY

In 2013, American Express took note of a sharp rise in trips involving women-only groups. According to Marybeth Bond, author of the Gutsy Traveler blog, between 2008 and 2014, US businesses specializing in women-only travel increased by 230%.

As a result, the tourism industry has gradually developed women-only packages that aim to cater for the specific needs of that market. As an example, the Hotel Spa Watel in Canada offers a girls' night out package that includes: an overnight stay, a bottle of sparkling wine, a 30-minute Swedish massage each and a 60-minute facial each, two bathrobes during the stay, full access to Jacuzzis, steam bath and sauna, heated indoor and outdoor pools and beach access.

The adventure tourism market is also responding to this market by offering specific packages for women as well. For instance, Le Germain Hotel in Baie-Saint-Paul (Canada), offers a full weekend of hiking. The package includes: welcome cocktail, one night in a quadruple occupancy Dortoir room, breakfast, one yoga session including rental of a yoga mat, "Chef's Inspiration" lunch box, access to the thermal experience at Spa du Verger, no set checkout time

Source: Neault C. (2017) Girlfriend getaways, Tourism Intelligence Network: http://tourismintelligence.ca/2017/04/10/girlfriend-getaways/

- *Physical needs*: Holidays can contain a strong physical component associated mostly with the practice of sport. Whether it is a sport high in adrenaline (bungee jumping, sky diving, etc.) or one of a milder nature (running, rambling, etc.), sport is an important component as it can help to unwind and restore one's body. It also creates a feel-good factor, endorphins are released by the brain usually in stressful situations but also more simply through sport. This creates a feel-good feeling and reduces stress, anxiety, and depression. Overall, endorphins produce pleasure and euphoria. Beyond the physical impact of sport, and the fact that tourists might increase their abilities, sport can also have a strong social component: practicing with companions and sharing a similar passion.

# New trends in the tourism sector

## Playfulness

Playfulness has always been a key component in the delivery of leisure and tourism services. Since tourism consumption is primarily a need to escape and relax, playfulness allows individuals to unwind, relax, and even regress. Individuals who are increasingly disillusioned with contemporary society are seeking in their leisure and tourism consumption, a way to escape from it all. Whilst some individuals will engage in activities with a

## TOURISM AND HOSPITALITY INSIGHTS 7.4
## DIGITALIZATION AND CONSUMPTION BEHAVIOR

Digitalization has clearly modified consumers' behavior as far as tourism is concerned.

New channels bring about new behavior: within a few years, we have witnessed the emergence of a myriad of new communication channels. SMS, Twitter, Chat, Messenger, WhatsApp and other instantaneous messaging services have introduced new rules in terms of reactive speed. Well before this, we had to wait a few days to receive an answer by mail. Nowadays, we are more inclined to wait a few minutes on those channels.

Instantaneous reply is now expected in the digital sphere whether it refers to the time one needs to access a web page, receive an answer to a crucial question before one can validate the purchase, or our expectations with regard to speed of delivery.

*Hyper-connected consumers*: With 4G coverage, WiFi and Bluetooth connections, the smartphone allows consumers to keep constant connectivity with our numeric lives, both personal and professional. This "electronic lead," that we find difficult to shake off, has pushed us to reply to various solicitations within a time span that gets shorter and shorter by the day so thereby feeding our craving for instantaneity.

*A seamless and fluid service*: The most important companies offer access 24/7 with business never stopping in the globalized web. Most consumers are used to this offer, and tend to expect a similar response even with a small business. Nowadays, for a small tourism business it becomes increasingly difficult to switch off the Internet to sleep for a few hours, weekends, and even less so for a few days off.

*Artificial intelligence (AI) coming to rescue humans*: In this digital world where humans cannot compete with machines, artificial intelligence and chat bots seem to be the only ones that can deliver the service expected by consumers. Even at low levels of AI, performances are already quite efficient, and consumers are increasingly getting used to talking daily with Siri, Alexa, Google Home, or any other system. Robots are starting to appear at the front desk of some hotels, and can even prepare and serve cocktails on cruise ships!

*Emotional intelligence remains capital*: Even if companies are increasingly tempted to revert to machines, the tourist experience remains largely the result of other human encounters, some storytelling, and personal recommendations from local inhabitants. Whether it is used to validate and inform, or to live the memorable experience, human interactions benefit emotional resonance and are still perceived as superior experiences for the majority of travelers.

The objective is therefore to keep on using technology in order to guarantee a seamless service, easy to use so that the technology becomes transparent (we are now using the terms ambient-interface). AI has to be conceived as a way to enhance the delivery and experience delivered by humans. For instance, booking platforms developed on the Internet have now developed strategies to accompany their consumers at every step of their travel plan. On the contrary, providers preferring human interaction over technology, or who don't integrate technology to help with simple tasks which are necessary to consumer satisfaction, are likely to go out of business and disappear.

Source: Contribution from Ludovic Dublanchet, Pierre Eloy and François Perroy, co-founders of Agitateurs de Destinations Numériques – a French Consultant Agency: https://www.agitateurs.com/

high level of specialization (also known as serious leisure), others will simply want to unwind and enjoy themselves without setting themselves high performance objectives.

Playfulness can be encountered in very different tourism products and services. When hearing the word "playfulness," what might spring to mind intuitively are all the tourist attractions that directly resemble children's play activities: theme parks, video games, ball games, etc.

Beyond playfulness, what contemporary consumers also expect is to be entertained. However, edutainment (a neologism combining education and entertainment) aims to provide some educative elements, where consumers will learn new facts about a site/museum/ destination visited, and even provide this knowledge in an entertaining manner. Edutainment might be criticized since it sometimes provides more entertainment than much educative value. However, edutainment has been a very interesting tool to open tourist sites to a wider public. For instance, museum attendance is very much influenced by social class. For instance, the free access to some museums has not erased class differences; most consumers feel that museums have been conceived for "educated" people and that a preliminary level of knowledge is necessary to be able to appreciate a museum.

**Image 7.2**

Source: https://www.pexels.com/photo/people-walking-on-wooden-floor-inside-green-walled-building-34633/

## TOURISM AND HOSPITALITY INSIGHTS 7.5
## PLAYFULNESS IN AQUAPARKS

Playfulness can take very different forms and has been integrated in the conceptualization of products very differently from one area to another. For instance, spas and swimming pools have merged into new types of aquatic leisure centers (aquaparks) where the slides, wave machines, lagoons, waterfalls, and all sorts of spa effects (jacuzzis, showers, different types of saunas, etc.) have been added to make the water look more playful. These aquaparks attract half-day and full-day visits. They add to the fun of the water by providing facilities that either reflect the relaxing and soothing dimension of water (the spa side) or its playful dimension (waves, etc.). Across the world these aquaparks are expanding rapidly, ranging from purely aquatic fun (Disney's Typhoon Lagoon) to parks combining this with a more relaxing dimension.

Source: Isabelle Frochot.

It is also true that edutainment fits in with contemporary consumers' demands, particularly those who are impatient and want fun, easy-to-use and immediate information. Edutainment demystifies the access to knowledge and gives the impression, at least, that it is more fun and easier to access knowledge. In the museum/heritage sites sector, edutainment has been a key factor for redevelopment and innovation and has truly allowed wider access to heritage tourist sites.

### Wellbeing

Wellbeing has become a term used even in daily life and includes various services and activities. In fact, wellbeing encompasses both the physical condition of an individual and his/her mental/psychological state. Wellbeing has often been associated with medical spas where specific waters had been recognized for healing some illnesses. Those medical spas have been in place for a very long time since the Greeks already discovered their virtues in 6th century BC and they were later on developed by the Romans. In Europe, thermal spas gained vast popularity in the 19th and 20th centuries and led to the development of resorts. Whilst the popularity of other forms of tourism emerged (the seaside for instance in the 19th century), spa resorts decreased in popularity.

For the last 30 years, a gradual revival of spa resorts has emerged, and most spas, including the most ancient European ones, have invested in new technologies to provide top-class services. To rejuvenate their product, most spas have also enlarged their positioning, keeping their medical dimension but, at the same time, developing a secondary market aimed at relaxation and wellbeing in the general sense. This secondary market has allowed many spas to keep afloat and has led to the opening of new offers either based on the benefits of mineral or sea waters and even grapes (Caudalie). More generally, the spa option has become a common feature within hotels.

Europe remains the main market for wellness tourism, and its growth has exceeded tourism growth in all regions since 2013. The biggest increase in demand comes from the Asia-Pacific region (The Global Spa and Wellness Economy Monitor, 2014).

In the tourism industry, wellbeing can be the main focus of a holiday (primary wellness travelers) or an add-on product within the holiday (secondary wellness travelers). In any case, it has become the norm and most tourism products will contain a form of wellness service. Considering the evolution of living conditions, it is certain that the popularity of wellbeing will keep on increasing in years to come and will represent a large component of the future tourism options.

## Uniqueness

The need for unique experiences has a direct link with the push factors developed earlier in this chapter. For example, if people are tired and disillusioned with the societies they live in, a holiday experience will be considered worthwhile if it has allowed them to experience a specific and unique event. Uniqueness creates both surprise and strong emotions. It focuses attention on the moment being lived and, on top of that, contributes to strong memories that will be remembered in the long term. In Chapter 6, the element of surprise was identified as a key component of the experience. Surprise focuses the attention of individuals on the moment. Surprise also creates deeply-rooted feelings of happiness. Surprise can be induced by creating something totally unexpected or by moving a service to a different context. Chapter 6 gave several examples of surprises, and especially in the major case study on Lux* Hotels and Resorts.

Uniqueness creates surprises but uniqueness also serves other functions. Uniqueness creates a feeling of satisfaction since consumers feel that they have received something tailor made for them or that, at least, they are part of the happy few who can receive this specific service. Tourism and hospitality insight 7.8 details peak walk high up in the Alps. Intuitively, consumers also know that unique experiences feed into memories that they will "take home" and retain in the very long term. If this unique moment is shared (and it often is), then it reinforces the value of a memory because it will not only serve as a pleasant reminder of the holiday, but it might also serve as a reinforcement of the bond between people. For instance, a holiday experience that has created a strong family bond through what was seen and the emotions felt (for instance watching elephants in Africa, for the first time) will create long-lasting memories. Every time this memory will be recalled, either orally, by looking at pictures of the event or watching a video, the intensity of the emotions felt then and the uniqueness of what was seen will come back all at once and reinforce family togetherness. Many examples exist in tourism, from accommodation in ice hotels and igloos, to all forms of glamorous camping or glamping (tents in zoos, tree houses, etc.).

**Image 7.3**

Source: https://www.pexels.com/photo/black-and-grey-canopy-tent-near-rocky-mountains-735837/

## TOURISM AND HOSPITALITY INSIGHTS 7.6
## PEAK WALK, GSTAAD

In 2015, the resort of Gstaad decided to give access to a high-altitude experience to any tourist, not just mountaineers. A suspension bridge was built over the glacier 3000 connecting two mountain peaks. From this peak walk, visitors can experience what it feels like to be walking on high-altitude paths and they can enjoy breathtaking views of the Matterhorn, the Mont Blanc Massif, the Eiger, Mönch, and Jungfrau. The bridge is 108 meters-long and 80 centimeters wide. It is open all-year around and is free of charge.

Source: Isabelle Frochot/http://www.gstaad.ch/en/service/media/press-releases/press-releases/news/detail/News/adventurous-peak-experience-on-the-peak-walk-by-tissot.htm

### The environment

Consideration for the environment is an essential component of the future tourism offer. It is impossible, within a short paragraph, to relate the diversity of issues pertaining to the environment but we can provide some pointers.

The UNWTO defines sustainable tourism as: "Tourism that takes full account of its current and future economic, social and environmental impacts, addressing the needs of visitors, the industry, the environment and host communities." The impacts of tourism have long been identified and analyzed. They include social, economic, and environmental impacts. Each of them has led to the integration of a new set of practices in the tourism industry such as integrating more fully local communities and genuine contacts with tourists (social impact), integrating local employees within the tourism industry (economic impact). or reducing environmental impacts.

In terms of the environment, the general indicators across the world suggest that the general population needs to commit itself more fully to sustainable behavior. This is necessary in the case of tourism, which impacts on the environment at different levels, through the implementation of tourism infrastructures but also through the impact of transport. Nonetheless, the willingness to pay for more sustainable products is a difficult question and visitors tend to be willing to pay only a small premium for those products.

Whilst a proportion of tourist demand can seek truly sustainable products, this proportion is in fact rather small on the grand scale of tourism demand. Another question that needs to be raised, is the capacity that 21st-century consumers might or might not have in consuming truly sustainable products. Indeed, the ability that urban-based consumers have in accepting the sustainable environment can be limited: consumers often come from several urban generations and have lost, to some extent, intuitive knowledge about the environment and nature. As a result, the environment often needs to be "packaged" to be consumed by those consumers. This implies that interpretation and intermediation have become key components of this missing link and some companies now strive to develop products that provide a "simplified" access to nature. The latest venture from Disney (Tourism and hospitality insights 7.7) gives an indication of this new market.

## TOURISM AND HOSPITALITY INSIGHTS 7.7
## DISNEY: NATURE VILLAGE

In the Marne la Vallée area, Disney has opted for the opening of a new park in 2016, the result of a venture with Center Parks, a key actor in the provision of nature-based resorts. Both actors aim to combine their expertise to provide a park that will be entirely based on sustainable principles.

The park is not far from the current Disneyland Resort in Marne la Vallée (near Paris) and aims to welcome visitors on a longer term basis than the current park (where visitors stay on average three days and two nights). The object of this park is to offer accommodation that is based on sustainable principles and is organized around an aquatic area.

The park has dug in the ground to use geothermal energy and use this warm water for a lagoon. This energy will also be reused to heat some of the park amenities. The project has a strong emphasis on zero carbon emissions and zero waste (strong recycling policy). It also aims to promote sustainable transport (no cars used within the site, slow transport is promoted, and public transport infrastructure has been improved). Local and sustainable materials are used within the construction of buildings with a special emphasis on wood. Food will be sourced locally as much as possible (25% of food will be produced within a 100 km radius, 20% will come from organic farming, 30% from seasonal food and some food will be produced on site via a heated greenhouse and a local farm).

Water usage will be planned so that most of the water is reused and rainwater is heavily used to feed the basins. In this park, Disney has also devised an educative approach by providing services aiming to improve contact with nature. The built site uses only 10% of the surface area. The ecological corridor will be maintained. Biodiversity is considered and a fauna and flora observatory will monitor the evolution of local species. Excursions will be organized to discover the local heritage and nature, and to learn about the program "One Planet Living." A farm will introduce visitors to the concept of organic farming.

Overall, this park will necessarily attract more consumers to the Disney Parks nearby. More generally, it is designed for 21st-century tourists who are sensitive to the notion of both nature and sustainability. On this site, the notion of nature has been built so that the notion of sustainability is embedded in the project but the site also aims to provide a "simplified" version of nature, where the best of the natural environment is staged without its discomforts. Visitors coming to this site are not real eco-tourists in the sense that they could not live with discomfort (such as a camping site or a truly wide area). They are somewhat urban-based inhabitants with a strong sustainable sensitivity.

Source: Isabelle Frochot/http://www.villagesnature.com/wp-content/uploads/2014/10/Dossier-de-presse-Villages-Nature-Juin-2014_BD.pdf

## Authenticity

Authenticity is a complex notion that has always been intimately linked to tourism consumption. Authenticity is, in theory, what tourists have come to seek: discovering a destination, its people, and its cultures in the most genuine form possible. However, tourists seeking true authenticity are not representative of all tourists. In fact, most tourists might sometimes comply with what is given to them in terms of authenticity. The notion of authenticity has been studied for a long time by tourism academics who have demonstrated how a tourism experience seen as authentic will allow consumers to escape from their daily lives and find more sense by consuming something that they see as authentic.

Contemporary societies have cut individuals from their roots and alienated them from the "simple life" that previous generations often experienced. Therefore, authenticity is most often fantasized as an idealized past (Goulding, 2001; Wang, 1999). Contemporary inhabitants are seeking evidence of their roots and are looking for true connections with the rural spheres, nature, agriculture. In other words, they are seeking connections with an idealized past where life was thought to be simpler and better. Nostalgia is therefore a strong component of this fantasized perception of authenticity. This implies that tourists bring with them preconceived ideas of what authenticity should be like or, at least, that they rely on images that they intend to see at the destination. The roots of those images are extremely varied. They can be found in early childhood (books, tales, recurring images, school programs, etc.), movies, national culture that will promote specific images, national and regional stereotypes, etc.

Urry (1990) showed how tourists will even aim to adapt the reality to their preconceived images. Tourists therefore tend to ensure that they don't encounter cognitive dissonance (i.e. purchasing a tourist service that would turn out not to match what they initially expected). As a result, once at the destination, tourists will spot elements that will confirm that the destination matches their preconceived images in the surrounding landscape.

Moreover, reality shows that destinations' authenticity is often a pale version of reality but that most tourists will comply with it simply because they do not have expert knowledge of what the true authenticity should look like.

## Consumer resistance and the shared economy

Consumer resistance is a topic that has attracted increasing attention from sociologists and marketers for some time. The idea behind resistance is that consumers develop deviant behavior that can be contrary to what a brand desires. One of the most common actions is the boycott whereby consumers decide to stop buying a product due to various defects often brought up by consumers' associations. For instance, Adidas has been boycotted by *Viva!* for using kangaroo skins on its football boots. Clothes retail companies such as H&M or Primark have been criticized because of their employees' working conditions and third-world workers producing their garments. Tourism has also been the object of several boycotts. For instance, some hotels have been boycotted due to their treatment of workers. On a different level, various circuses, zoos, and sea life centers have been attacked for their bad treatment of captive animals. Equally, destinations have even been boycotted from within.

Perhaps, in a more simplistic way, consumer resistance can be seen in the simple sharing of information over the Internet, information that is shared beyond all companies' marketing efforts. TripAdvisor for instance is a good example of this form of resistance whereby consumers actively seek to exchange information freely between them that will indicate to other consumers their evaluation of a tourist service.

More profoundly, resistance can also be seen when consumers are deliberately searching services and connections to a destination that go well beyond traditional tourism services. The current decade is witnessing the fourth generation of mass tourists, who have a vast experience of the tourism industry, whether it is experienced by themselves or shared with their parents/grand-parents. They understand

## TOURISM AND HOSPITALITY INSIGHTS 7.8
## AMADEUS' VISION OF THE KEY NEW EVOLUTIONS IN THE TRAVEL MARKET

The latest report from Amadeus "Future Traveler Tribes 2030" introduces the segments of customers who will make up tomorrow's travel market. A summary of their key trends identified in this report are as follows:

*The demographic and economic landscape*: In the forthcoming decades, some emerging countries will witness significant population growth, leading to an increase in the number of travelers worldwide. While emerging markets will rise economically, developed economies (observing reduced growth and lower fertility rates) will slow down encouraging a redistribution of economic power and consumer spending. Advanced economies will witness the high proportion of older consumers, leading societies and industries to adapt to age-based expectations and behavior.

*The consumer landscape*: The general frontier between leisure and work will be blurred with flexible working practices leading to "bleasure" a mix between work and play. The digital space will open up more opportunities for search engines offering bundles of choices (allowing easier comparisons) and big data will allow companies to tailor their offers much closer to individual needs. Perfect price discrimination will allow companies to target new and less affluent markets. Online professional networking will become essential and digital word-of-mouth will revolutionize advisory sources and feed into a strong peer economy. Eco-ethical concerns will become an avoidable feature of consumers' choices.

*The technological concern*: Most consumers will be connected (5G) by 2030 and the reduced cost of devices will imply that access and use of data will increase exponentially. Artificial intelligence will grow in efficiency and virtual reality will allow travelers to "preview" products and destinations more efficiently.

Source: Isabelle Frochot/Amadeus (2015) Future Traveler Tribes 2030 – Understanding Tomorrow's Traveler, Foresight Factory. Copyright © 2015 Foresight Factory

perfectly how it works and can book their holidays and share information. Twenty-first-century consumers do not wish to follow the crowds but make their own way to the hearts of destinations. For instance, free guided tours, "couch surfing," and "woofing" are all attempts to unzip a destination and meet the locals as they are. Through this exchange, what consumers are seeking are more genuine contacts and also a different type of information about a destination: they want to know about the daily life of a destination's inhabitants, where they live, a local market, a local coffee shop, etc. Of course, this is also the case of Airbnb, where consumers have come to seek a different experience.

## Conclusion

This chapter has investigated the key trends that are shaping tourism and hospitality demand today and tomorrow. Holiday taking will always respond to a need to leave

**image 7.4**

Source: https://www.pexels.com/photo/architecture-bed-bedroom-ceiling-271743/

behind the burdens of everyday life and this should always be in the mind of developers and marketers as much at a destination level as well as within accommodation and catering provision. Digital innovations will most certainly impact tourism demand in the long run but one should not forget that current economic and urban living conditions also shape this demand. Experiential marketing needs to observe evolutions and make sure it always anticipates tomorrow's demand.

## REVIEW QUESTIONS

1. What are the key trends that will shape tomorrow's demand for tourism products and destinations?
2. To what extent are the current living conditions impacting the type of demand observed in tourism?
3. How does your answer to question 2 translate into new offerings within tourism products?
4. What are the main pull factors for traveling?

## YOUTUBE LINKS

*"Nicaragua authentic tourism – life-changing experience"*

URL: https://www.youtube.com/watch?v=UFhyRJ6dbrE

Summary: This video aims to bring to life the types of emotions one might experience while traveling across Nicaragua. it concentrates on emotions and memories. The video aims to portray Nicaragua as a lifetime experience and how it will fill visitors with long-term memories of their trip.

## "Keeping cultural authenticity in Santa Fe"

URL: https://www.youtube.com/watch?v=syOlHb2LDsQ

Summary: This presentation led by Dr. Andrew Lovato explores "Hispanic and New Mexican cultures of yesterday and today through his research and writings. In his home town of Santa Fe, the interplay of local culture and commercially-driven influences has created the adobe Disneyland that many tourists have come to love." Dr Lovatro questions the commodification of culture and how authenticity can be preserved to avoid the "Disneylandization" of Sante Fe?

## "Why sustainable tourism?

URL: https://www.youtube.com/watch?v=JFbbKbdqoJg

Summary: This short three-minute video presents an overview of sustainable tourism: how the rise of global tourism has not necessarily implied more profit for destinations. It encourages the development of sustainable projects and responsible behavior from companies. It encourages partnerships and presents the types of projects that can encourage a more sustainable approach.

## "Sustainable tourism in New Zealand"

URL: https://www.youtube.com/watch?v=Icl9akLqkuk

Summary: This eight-minute video introduces the concept of sustainability in New Zealand. Tourism represents 9% of New Zealand GDP and protecting natural resources is a key element of their strategy. It introduces the notion of conservation, using natural resources but also encourages local retribution from the tourism economy.

### REFERENCES, FURTHER READING, AND RELATED WEBSITES

References

Dann, M.S. (1977). Anomie, ego-enhancement and tourism. *Annals of Tourism Research*, IV(4), 184–194.

Goulding, C. (2001). Romancing the past: Heritage visiting and the nostalgic consumer. *Psychology & Marketing*, 18(6), 565–592.

Krippendorf, J. (1999). *The holiday makers – understanding the impact of leisure and travel.* Oxford: Routledge.

MacCannell, D. (1999). *Tourist: A new theory of the leisure class.* Berkeley, CA: University of California Press.

Rokeach, M. (1973). The nature of human values. *Political Science Quarterly, 89*(2), 399–401.

Urry, J. (1990). *The tourist gaze.* London: Sage.

Wang, N. (1999). Rethinking authenticity in tourism experience. *Annals of Tourism Research, 26*(2), 349–370.

## Further reading

Amadeus. (2015). Managed travel 3.0: An insight from the inside, Report. http://www.amadeus.com/images/corporations/managed-travel/amadeus_managed_travel_30_Oct2015.pdf

Amadeus. (2015). Future traveler tribes 2030 – Understanding tomorrow's traveler. Future Foundation. Retrieved from http://www.amadeus.com/documents/future-traveler-tribes-2030/amadeus-traveler-tribes-2030-airline-it.pdf

Blue & Green Tomorrow. (2013). The guide to sustainable tourism. www.blueandgreentomorrow.com

Echtner, C.M., & Prasad, P. (2003). The context of third-world tourism marketing. *Annals of Tourism Research, 30*(3), 2003, 660–682.

Frochot, I.V., & Morrison, A. (2000). Benefit segmentation: A review of its applications to travel and tourism research. *Journal of Travel and Tourism Marketing, 9*(4), 21–45.

Hubspot. (2016). An introduction to marketing psychology, *Britanny Learning.* Retrieved from http://blog.hubspot.com/marketing/marketing-psychology-introduction.

MacCannell D. (1973). Staged authenticity: Arrangements of social space in tourist settings. *American Journal of Sociology, 79*(3), 589–603.

UNWTO. (2013). *Sustainable tourism for development guidebook.* Retrieved from http://icr.unwto.org/content/guidebook-sustainable-tourism-development.

## Websites

Hospitality trends in 2018
http://www.accorhotels.group/en/Actualites/2018/02/08/hospitality-trends-2018

Six hotel trends to watch in 2018
http://www.accorhotels.group/en/Actualites/2018/02/08/hospitality-trends-2018

European Union Short-Term Tourism Trends, Volume 2, 2018–2
http://publications.unwto.org/publication/european-union-short-term-tourism-trends-volume-2-2018-2

Ten travel trends for 2018
https://www.intrepidtravel.com/travel-trends-2018/

OECD tourism trends and policies
https://www.oecd-ilibrary.org/docserver/tour-2018-en.pdf?expires=1529268397&id=id&accname=guest&checksum=D226A227AAC2C7BE8A48AB1E7EEE3466

## MAJOR CASE STUDY
## AMADEUS SEGMENTATION

In 2015, Amadeus and the Future Foundation (now named Foresight Factory) carried out a research report looking into peoples' motivations to travel. The study looked at the current trends affecting society, and then carried out a process of market segmentation to produce six consumer tribes taking into account those changes: "Demographic, economic, consumer landscape and technological changes to come have been at the forefront of our minds in developing these tribes (...), building a three-dimensional image of future travelers to focus on the deep-seated values and ideals that will truly impel their travel" (p. 26). In other words, the tribes refer to which type of experience and benefits consumers are seeking in their travels, their motivation is the key variable. It is understood that the tribes are not mutually exclusive and some consumers might correspond to more than one tribe, or behave like different tribes at different times of the year.

*Simplicity searchers*: Those consumers are not seeking to challenge themselves. They want to escape their daily lives and routines but they seek comfort at the destination and pamper themselves. The real notion of traveling, discovering new cultures and broadening their horizons is not a key element of their holidays. They tend to use third parties and systems to simplify their choices of traditional packages, or "bundles of choices."

> They will be attracted to packages which offer the ability to dip a toe in the waters with the assurance of their safety and enjoyment, and a structure for their experience in place. A sense of adventure will be less important than "the basics," whether that be the simple pleasures of good food and good weather, or taking in the iconic cultural landmarks spurned by more seasoned explorers.
>
> (p. 32)

These consumers need reassurance regarding their choice. The often choose the easiest options (rapid transport, avoid long flights, etc.) and will favor user-friendly and non-invasive forms of technology. The integration of native languages will be an important component of service provision.

*Cultural purists*: Cultural purists want to use their travels to immerse themselves in a totally different culture. They are looking for a complete break from their everyday lives and accept the temporary adoption a new way of leaving. They are truly independent travelers, expecting to escape the masses and rely only sparingly on tourist information: word-of-mouth and small-scale social networks are their preferred sources. They don't want to fall in the tourist traps and they want to live their holiday spontaneously. They tend to be highly educated, curious, and open-minded which means that they will be open to unusual propositions. Since they are seeking niche experiences, they might be receptive to specialized travel agencies:

Cultural purists find satisfaction in their minority status, and are attracted to niche propositions. From "food tourism" to "flower tourism," "last chance tourism" to "music tourism," the amount of nomenclature for travel driven by intimate connected communities clustering around a specific interest or need has grown rapidly in recent years, and it is the cultural purist mentality which is driving this growth.

(p. 39)

*Social capital seekers*: Those customers are truly active digital consumers who aim to live and breathe through their social networks. They are very attracted to traveling, but to them travel carries social capital in the sense that it allows them to find content and update those contents with worthwhile material:

All experiences must have tangible and shareable outputs. This could mean providing "highlight reels" from trips, or other attention-grabbing, aesthetically-pleasing souvenirs. In the abstract, the ideal will be for the traveler to have enhanced the range and strength of his social signal upon his return. The success of the holiday will be made or broken on this.

(p. 46)

Their objective is therefore to share their holiday experiences with their networks. Those networks will even be used to validate their travel choices and they will rely heavily on user-generated websites. Those consumers understand how the Internet functions and in exchange for their online coverage of a brand will expect some feedback (better deals, discounts, VIP access, etc.). Good Internet connections are expected wherever they go.

*Reward hunters*: These consumers have a busy working life and regard their holiday a reward for their efforts. They are wealthy and they are concerned with their health: "We can expect this tribe to seek out wellness experiences dedicated solely to their own relaxation and self-improvement alongside hedonistic excess and extreme self-indulgence, whether gastronomic or party-fuelled" (p. 49). These consumers will seek extra levels of service and personalized help: concierge services, personal assistants, VIP experiences, etc. They expect to gain some wellbeing through their holiday, leave an out-of-the-ordinary experience, unique and memorable and, overall, they want to gain serenity from their trip.

*Obligation meeters*: These consumers have a main objective that will motivate their trip:

What can be called "soft" travel objectives – such as enjoyment, relaxation, skill-acquisition, and to an extent popularity-building, but a significant proportion of flights will be made necessary or desirable by "hard" objectives – to meet this client, to attend this seminar, to have this surgical procedure, to shop at this store, to be at this event, to catch up with this person.

This tribe illustrates "bleasure," where the flexibility of working patterns allows individuals to mix work commitments with holidays. Events and festivals are also attractive elements for this tribe. Obligation Meeters are keen on services that are connected, very efficient, and simplify the different steps of traveling. As frequent flyers, they will enjoy various facilities at airports, including concierge services.

*Ethical travelers*: This tribe reflects consumers' concern for the environment and their willingness to question their traveling and the impact it has on the planet.

In the era of increased Corporate Social Responsibility, demands for greater behind-the-scenes access and accountability from big business, increased pressure to demonstrate tangible results of corporate ethical claims, and the consumer desire for some kind of reward for their ethical choices will come from some segments of the population, and will be particularly important in ensuring the goodwill of Ethical Travelers.

(p. 62)

Their concerns are not just the environment. They are also sensitive to the trajectory of their spending, respecting local destinations. Those tribes are truly looking for authentic destinations off the beaten track.

Source: Isabelle Frochot/Amadeus (2015) Future Traveler Tribes 2030 – Understanding Tomorrow's Traveler, Foresight Factory. Copyright © 2015 Foresight Factory.

## Major case study questions

1. What are the benefits to be gained from a tourism or hospitality organization of your choice by adopting a segmentation strategy based on the above so-called "tribes"?
2. What may be some of the limitations of such a strategy?
3. How sustainable (longevity) do you think each of the so-called tribes are vis-à-vis the fast-changing pace of modern society?
4. What trends, if any, have been omitted in the establishment of these different segment groups?

# 8 Service characteristics and processes

## Learning outcomes

By the end of this chapter, students will:

- Understand the specificities of services and their implications in terms of services' marketing and design
- Understand how strategies need to take on board the specific dynamics of services
- Appreciate the evolution towards a comprehensive management of services through the service design perspective
- Be introduced to a number of case studies that demonstrate the intricacies of tourism service provision and illustrate the various competencies necessary to provide quality service.

### Key terms

service characteristics, services marketing, service quality, service design, consumer journey, persona, service blueprint

## Introduction

Unlike products, services are rather complex elements and processes that have no physical evidence but yet take an essential place in 21st-century societies' consumption. All parts of human life now integrate services, whether it is for assistance in managing a house, minding children, or servicing one's car. Tourism is necessarily a service in itself but it is increasingly composed and elaborated with innovative new service deliveries. Indeed, contemporary consumers seek more than ever innovative services while they are traveling. In consequence new types of services, service design initiatives have evolved and need to be addressed. This chapter first aims to present the main characteristics of services and then focus on the notion of service quality that emerged in the 1980s and remains a crucial component of service delivery. The chapter then integrates recent evolutions in terms of service design, introducing the notions of customer journey and service blueprint.

# The original approaches to services marketing: services' main characteristics

Originally, marketing has been developed mostly in relation to product provision. Its objective was to understand consumer and market needs and design effective strategies to sell, price, communicate, and market specific products to different segments. Marketing is a large field that has accumulated a vast amount of knowledge over the years but yet, practitioners and academics alike have felt that this conceptualization of marketing was too narrow to accommodate the specificities of services. Consequently, the field of services marketing emerged and established itself as a specific marketing stream, based on the obvious and unavoidable differences between products and services.

## The product dynamic

- When a consumer buys a product off-line, he/she usually goes to the shop, views the product, receives advice from the sales person, can handle and sometimes test the product.
- The product that has reached the shop has been the object of various quality control processes that ensure that the product is default-less.
- If the product shows some defects, the consumer has a guarantee and can bring back the product to the shop or might even have a temporary product to replace it.
- Once the product is purchased, it becomes the property of the consumer, who can even sell it if necessary.

## The service dynamic

- When a consumer purchases a service off-line, he can also go to a physical shop but the service cannot be tested, neither can it be seen before experiencing it.
- The nearest the consumer can go to getting evidence about the service is to go through the catalogue, *3D Glasses* or watch a video (although this is still rarely the case) and he/she can rely on the travel agent's advice.
- Once the purchase is made, the service will take place away from the shop location and if a problem arises during the trip, no after-sales service is really feasible (at best some reimbursement, vouchers or upgrades will be offered).
- The consumer does not own the service and once back home, the consumer has no "physical proof" of his purchase apart perhaps from a suntan and some souvenirs or memories.

With this short description, one can easily see that services have characteristics that differentiate them fundamentally from products and those need to be fully understood to be able to provide a satisfactory consumer experience. The description of services above has pointed to five key differences that will de detailed thereafter: intangibility, heterogeneity, simultaneity of production and consumption, lack of ownership and perishability.

## Services are primarily intangible

Whilst this might seem obvious, it is a characteristic that has several implications for marketers. Travel agents, tour operators, and destinations sell a product that can only be really understood and experienced once the purchase has been made and the consumer is experiencing the service. Since a visit is an abstract concept, a sales person can only provide cues about the technical elements of a trip (comfort, different trips included in the holiday, facilities at the hotel/resort, etc.), but will not be able to detail all the inherent qualities of a service. It is a disadvantage in so far as it is difficult to give a clear explanation of the intrinsic properties of the holiday. As we have seen, all the "technical" and physical dimensions of the service can be enumerated and even demonstrated and guaranteed through photos, videos, and quality schemes, but the emotions and sensations felt while at the destination is not something that one can easily describe.

For this "soft" side of tourist service description, other elements come into play. First of all, the travel agent is (or was) perhaps the one that was best suited to give detailed, personal, and emotional elements about a trip/destination. However, a travel agent will talk much more positively and in a more sensitive way about a tourist service if he/she has visited the destination. Therefore, familiarization trips for travel agents and journalists remain a strategic tool that has proved its efficiency. Tourism and hospitality insight 8.1 provides an example of an online training scheme that allows travel agents to gain intimate and inside knowledge about the destinations he/she aims to sell.

If consumers do not use a travel agent, the problem remains in the sense that to finalize their purchase, consumers will need to have sufficient information about the product to project how attractive it is and to what extent it fits their needs. The website of the destination/company needs to provide information and in different formats (text, photos, videos, reviews, 3D glasses that can be tested at a travel show, etc.) but consumers will also seek non-commercial information (guide books, UGC websites, etc.) that will help them in getting a closer vision of the service.

## Services are inherently heterogeneous

Heterogeneity remains a complex question in tourist service provision. Primarily, services are heterogeneous because they rely heavily on humans and humans can be inconsistent in their service delivery. We have all been confronted by a new member of staff who does not yet know how the service functions totally, or by

## TOURISM AND HOSPITALITY INSIGHTS 8.1
## AUSSIE SPECIALIST PROGRAM

The objective of the Aussie Specialist Program is to provide travel agents globally with the knowledge and skills to best sell Australian holidays. The digital platform with inspiring content offers agents a range of helpful resources to increase their destination knowledge and confidence in selling Australia. The key benefits of becoming a qualified Aussie Specialist include:

- Recognition as an Australian expert to customers
- An opportunity to increase sales to Australia
- Access to sales resources, training modules, and webinars to continue their learning
- Latest Australian news, product updates, and monthly e-newsletters
- Exclusive access to the Aussie Specialist Club with:

    - Travel Club Offers for their own trips to Australia
    - Aussie Store to order marketing collateral
    - Invitations to attend training events
    - Opportunities to join families to experience the country first hand
    - Aussie Specialist shared photos via #aussiespecialist

Sales resources include interactive maps, itinerary suggestions, fact sheets, image and video galleries, useful websites and frequently asked questions. Agents joining the program (which is free) gain extensive destination knowledge through completing five training modules to qualify and must pass various activities which test their comprehension throughout each module. Once qualified, there is no need to renew the Aussie Specialist qualification, as long as the agent engages with the program within a two-year period to remain active. They can also use the Aussie Specialist logo in their marketing collateral and are listed as a local expert via australia.com, where consumers can "find a travel agent near them" to book their Australian holiday.

Beyond the first five modules, agents can continue their training and choose from the comprehensive library of modules, be it state specific or special interest including Discover Aboriginal Experiences, Great Walks of Australia, Restaurant Australia, Ultimate Winery Experiences of Australia and much more. The site and program have been built following extensive research with travel agents and there are over 47,000 registered users around the world from over 80 countries.

The program was one of the first of its kind though many destinations now offer online agent training programs. To view a video and gain further insight into the Aussie Specialist Program, visit: https://www.aussiespecialist.com/en

Source: Isabelle Frochot/https://www.aussiespecialist.com/en-gb.html

**Image 8.1**
Source: Pexels.

staff who is not particularly welcoming. Staff training and empowerment is a key tool to ensure that any consumer will experience a consistent experience when coming into contact with the service staff. Staff training, as a minimum, is an essential element to ensure that staff members are compliant with the ethos of the company and have been provided with skills and information to provide an efficient service.

In the tourism context, other variable elements might interfere with the service delivery. Chapter 2 presented the general context within which the tourism industry evolves. Tourism takes place in countries that are far away, often subject to various natural and political disasters and with different service cultures (that tourists might find difficult to adapt to). On top of those elements one key component of the tourism delivery, the weather, can heavily affect the experience to the detriment of providers. Whilst providers cannot change the weather conditions, they can however be reactive and create procedures to provide consumers with alternative activities if the weather turns bad. Whilst companies and destinations cannot control the weather they can attempt to provide some form of refund policy based on the weather (see Tourism and hospitality insight 8.2 for two particular examples).

In the previous paragraph, we saw that services are primarily intangible but all services necessarily integrate a variable proportion of tangible component. One approach to diminish the heterogeneity of service provision is to maximize the tangible dimensions of service delivery. Some companies have made the choice to reduce to the minimum the proportion of intangible components since those are the most variable elements and thereby the ones a company can least manage. Most services can be represented among a continuum (Figure 8.1):

## TOURISM AND HOSPITALITY INSIGHTS 8.2
## GUARANTEEING A GOOD HOLIDAY DESPITE THE WEATHER CONDITIONS

### The sun guarantee

Of all industries, the tourism industry is perhaps the one that is most prone to the weather. This is necessarily an element that cannot be controlled by the industry but one that can be tempered by tourism actors.

Some tour operators, aware that the sun is the main ingredient sought after in some destinations, have developed a sun guarantee. Consumers can subscribe to this guarantee which promises a partial or total refund if the weather is poor. For instance, Aon, an insurance company, has developed a "Weather engine" solution specifically for the tourism industry. The client's tour operator transmits to Aon the details of the trips and destinations purchased by customers claiming a refund. Aon can then check the validity of the claim according to the weather report. Aon's Weather Engine is tied to the national forecast data that identify how long the sun shines during a specific holiday. Aon uses the METNEXT Sun Index® indicator that details the length of sunshine each day between 10 am and 6 pm. Sunshine is defined as a period during which the solar radiation has a high intensity (>120W/m2).

Overall, on average 5% of consumers benefit from a weather-bond discount.

### Bermuda Hotel Association hurricane guarantee

Of a different nature, tourists can also be exposed to various storms. Bermuda has launched a "hurricane guarantee." This guarantee is offered to individual tourists staying in a hotel belonging to the Bermuda Hotel Association. A hurricane is defined as a storm from category 1 to 4, with winds above 74 mph. The guarantee does not include tropical storms. The service is operated by CI$^2$ Aviation Services.

The terms of guarantee are as follows:

1.  In the event that a hurricane is predicted by the Bermuda Weather Service within 150 miles of Bermuda and within three days, the guest will be permitted to cancel their reservations without penalty. Deposits can be refunded or applied to any future booking if the guest is unable to recover the same amount via his/her travel insurance (a copy of the guest's travel insurance may be requested by member hotel management). Group booking cancelations will be handled on an individual basis in accordance with the group contract.

2.  In the event that a member hotel is not able to continue its operations due to damage incurred by a hurricane (as determined by the Bermuda Weather Service), the member hotel will invite the guest to return for a complimentary stay within one year from the reopening of the member hotel.

Source: Isabelle Frochot/https://www.gotobermuda.com/article/bermuda-hotel-association-hurricane-guarantee

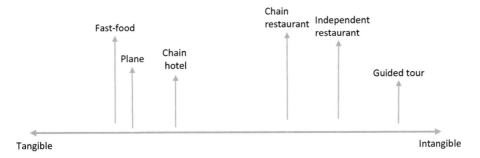

**Figure 8.1** The tangible/intangible service continuum

Source: Source: Author.

To illustrate this continuum, we shall examine two examples, a fast-food restaurant and a traditional, independent restaurant.

A fast-food restaurant:

- has a set menu that does not evolve much over time and it has the same menu at all its premises.
- uniforms, décor, theming, communication, etc., are also the same across the premises.
- to reduce variability, the restaurant has decomposed the production process of each of its items (fries, burgers) and created machines that cook them with an exact timing.
- all the service elements (trays, cups, packaging) are branded and are the same across all the premises.
- food suppliers are the same so that one burger eaten at one end of the country will have the same taste as one at the other end of the country.
- consumers go to the counter to get their order, bring the food themselves to their table, and clean their table after eating.
- the premise offers a take-away service and the drive means that consumers can quickly obtain their take-away.

## A traditional restaurant

This type of restaurant aims to differentiate itself from competing actors by providing a unique and distinctive experience:

- Menu changes regularly according to seasonal products.
- The chef develops his own recipes and brings his personal touch to the food intake.
- The décor and theming of the premises are unique and bring a special atmosphere that does not equal any other premises.
- Members of staff are part of the service and atmosphere of the site: with knowledge and competency they can help visitors to choose from the wine and food menu.

- The view, the location might also be part of the restaurant and contribute to its unique dimension.
- Service is handled by a member of staff who takes the order, delivers the food, and cleans the table without the consumer doing any of those tasks.

One can clearly see that it is more important to provide constant quality in the first model, the fast-food restaurant. All the processes are controlled and the only variable element might pertain to the staff (which cost less in the fast-food example) and other consumers (customer numbers would vary from day to day).

In the second example, the traditional restaurant creates competitiveness through its uniqueness and its elaborated service. Here, quality is more challenging to control (if the restaurant needs to replace a chef, it needs to keep the same positioning; the chef might not be as competent for each of the dishes served; the staff might have variable skills in regard to the intricacies of the food and wine menu; the restaurant takes a risk with its experience-scape choices – some consumers might not like it, etc.). The experience is totally different: in the first case it is a "no-surprise" experience but has the benefit of providing the same meal experience every time. In the second example, consumers enjoy a meal that might differ from day-to-day and will benefit from a personalized service in a unique services-scape. Both cases are economically viable. They have just chosen, on the one hand, to make the service tangible to a maximum (fast-food) to reduce variability. On the other hand, the traditional restaurant has chosen to take more risks by increasing its variable components but it might thereby achieve a reputation and charge prices that will make its model viable and more profitable.

## Simultaneity of production and consumption

Another key service characteristic is a complex one: the service is produced at the same time that it is consumed. Earlier we saw that products are produced outside the shop and consumers' knowledge. When the staff provide a service, the consumer is in the "first row" watching and benefiting from that service. The consumer usually wants this service to happen at the time he/she requests it and does not want to wait till it is "in stock." This puts the tourism provider under heavy pressure to ensure that the service is delivered accurately and in a timely manner. For instance, a family traveling to Morocco, having booked a day-trip in a four-by-four vehicle to the Atlas Mountains will be extremely disappointed if, on the day, the car or the driver are not available and the family cannot undertake this long sought-after trip. In this case, the best option for the provider is to find a replacement solution as soon as possible to make sure the same trip takes place that day or within the holiday boundaries. Eventually, if no solution is available, the provider will at least identify another upgraded service that can replace the missing service (the trip to the Atlas Mountains). It is certain that since no after-sales service exists, the provider has to be extremely reactive. Reimbursements and vouchers are always an option at hand but really a second-based choice since what the consumer wants is a service at the time requested, not a compensation that will not replace the frustration of not having achieved what one wanted when on holiday.

## Services do not lead to ownership

One crucial question with tourism consumption to some consumers is what they own for having spent a fairly large amount of money. In normal life, consumers tend to be wise and rational about their money spending but when it comes to holidays, money can be spent in larger amounts (and with much less scrutiny) with no ownership of any durable goods at the end of it. The value of tourism consumption has to be found somewhere else. Chapter 7 has elaborated in detail the motivations that stimulate tourism demand. Beyond those expectations, the outcome of tourism consumption is an interesting question that will be debated in Chapter 9.

Tourism satisfaction is first and foremost associated with consumers' initial expectations and the outcome of it translates into long-lasting memories that actually have tremendous value to consumers. So, when returning from a holiday, consumers will "own" a new self (more developed and more rested) and memories that will be fondly remembered of the holiday group, shared on the Internet and potentially discussed again over the years. Tourists might buy a few souvenirs, as material reminders of those memories, but these souvenirs are only small in comparison to the scope and intensity of memories that holidays procure. In their experienced economy approach, Pine and Gilmore (1999) insist on the importance of producing memories. For each experience, they recommend that the service company provides either items to bring home as a souvenir or opportunities for taking pictures that will procure a positive reminder of the holiday.

## Services are perishable

A service that is not sold at a set date is a service lost forever. If a plane leaves an airport with only 80% of its seat capacity, the 20% empty seats are definitively lost. They might be sold again later that same day or the following day, but in any case, they are lost on this flight. The same goes for other forms of transport and in fact most service precision components (accommodation, tourist' attractions, etc.). Early-birds and late promotions are means that have been developed by the industry to manage these difficulties and allocate capacities more efficiently. In this regard, revenue management is a very effective technique that has proved its efficiency and will be developed in Chapter 17.

The analysis of the five services' characteristics are essential in understanding the basic elements with which a provider has to comply in order to develop an efficient service. Beyond those characteristics, the academic literature has devoted a lot of effort to

**Image 8.2**
Source: Pexels.

assess how services' quality can be evaluated and this will be the object of the following section.

## The quest for quality

Since the mid-to-late 1980s, quality has become a strategic question as it has been recognized as a key factor of business success (Berry, 1986). Service quality became a focus for any marketing strategy and high levels of quality were seen as a means for an organization to achieve a competitive advantage and position itself more effectively in the market place, facing increasingly demanding consumers (Lewis & Mitchell, 1991). Research also showed that the benefits of good service quality were related to customer loyalty and the attraction of new customers, positive word-of-mouth communication, employee satisfaction and commitment, enhanced corporate image, reduced costs, and increased business performance (Smith & Lewis, 1988). The search for quality arguably became one of the most important trends of the 1980s. Total quality management approaches, norms such as ISO and quality control initiatives became prominent and are still a strong component of enterprises' performance (see Tourism and hospitality insights 8.3 on ISO requirements). These developments were beyond typical grading schemes, and aimed to develop systems that would not only identify defects but also aim at correcting them.

## TOURISM AND HOSPITALITY INSIGHTS 8.3
## ISO AND SERVICES REQUIREMENTS

ISO is a norm recognized internationally that aims to create a common reference within sectors in order to harmonize quality within this sector: "A standard is a document that provides requirements, specifications, guidelines or characteristics that can be used consistently to ensure that materials, products, processes and services are fit for their purpose." (https://www.iso.org/standards.html).

The standard decomposes all the processes involved in the delivery of a service and ensures that quality control mechanisms are in place and that corrective procedures are set to consistently improve the system.

ISO has over 21,000 International Standards. By using this standard, companies aim to reduce their rate of errors and increase their productivity. Owing to its international reputation, the standard gives the company instant recognition for their quality procedures and allows them to bid on international markets. Beyond quality management, the standards also address environmental management and occupational health and safety. In tourism, norms have been specifically developed for tourist information and reception services, wellness spa, tourist services for public use provided by natural protected area authorities, recreational diving services, etc.

New standards can be set in accordance with ISO which designs those standards by consulting experts and stakeholders in the sector targeted.

ISO has been criticized for the heavy bureaucratic and administrative burden that its procedure entails. However, its international recognition does bring an instantly recognized credential for the company that obtains this standard.

Source: Isabelle Frochot/https://www.iso.org/standards.html

Probably what occupied most academics in this field was to identify how quality could be evaluated, considering the five services' characteristics previously identified. To date, the most thought-provoking initiative was brought by Parasuraman, Zeithaml, and Berry who developed a scale that was deemed universal to measure service quality (1985, 1990). Their idea was that, regardless of the types of services, consumers tended to use similar criteria to evaluate their quality. Hence, they produced a scale aimed at measuring those criteria, which was meant to be universal. This scale, called SERVQUAL attempted to identify the key components of the service quality and motivated an intense debate on services' quality evaluations. The scale included, within each dimension, a set of items (for a total of 22) that could be produced in the shape of a questionnaire.

The five SERVQUAL dimensions were named and described as:

- Tangibles: Physical facilities, equipment, and appearance of personnel
- Reliability: Ability to perform the promised service dependably and accurately

- Responsiveness: Willingness to help consumers and provide prompt service
- Assurance: Knowledge and courtesy of employees and their ability to convey trust and confidence
- Empathy: Caring, individualized attention the firm provides to its customers

SERVQUAL remains a reference in terms of quality evaluation even if the scale is not perfect, no other researcher has been able to produce a better approach since then. Whilst the work of those scholars has been undoubtedly acknowledged by both practitioners and academics, it has also encountered some criticisms. Perhaps the largest criticism came from the incapacity to replicate exactly the scale in other service contexts. As a result, several researchers engaged in projects dedicated to adapting the scale in other settings.

For instance, the scale has been developed for airline services, travel agencies, hotels, recreation services and parks (references to those works are listed in the Further Reading section at the end of this chapter). A scale adapted to heritage visits, HISTOQUAL, is detailed in Tourism and hospitality insights 8.4. Taken together these studies seem to bring more confusion than clarity: although they are helpful in advancing knowledge on service quality in a tourist/leisure/hospitality context, they fail to identify a generic scale for those services. Perhaps the truth to be learned from this work is the incapacity to develop generic scales and that services carry intimate specificities that need specific tools to measure their quality.

Some studies even identified that the notion of indirect service provision (guiding through directions, signposts, leaflets) was important in tourism services, which are often consumed on the consumer's own behalf. Even if not mentioned as such, the idea of co-construction started to emerge with the notion of indirect service (Lovelock, 1983).

## TOURISM AND HOSPITALITY INSIGHTS 8.4
## HISTOQUAL

Evaluating quality in a heritage context is perhaps less common than in other sectors such as accommodation or catering. Nonetheless, heritage sites welcome every year vast numbers of visitors and need to cater for their needs. HISTOQUAL was created to respond specifically to the need of historic houses services. It was adapted from SERVQUAL. The same scale-producing procedure was followed and a new set of quality items specific to the historic house context was developed through interviews with consumers on-site. Next, a large data collection was undertaken (780 consumers surveyed) from which the final scale was produced.

The scale refining procedure created a scale with 22 items.

**Table 8.1** Histoqual

| Factors | Items |
| --- | --- |
| F1 Responsiveness | - Staff are always helpful and courteous<br>- Staff are willing to take time with visitors<br>- Visitors are made to feel welcome<br>- Level of crowding is tolerable<br>- Staff are well informed to answer customers' requests<br>- Visitors feel free to explore, there are no restrictions to access<br>- The property and grounds are opened at convenient hours<br>- Staff are always available when needed |
| F2 Tangibles | - The property is well kept and restored<br>- The general cleanliness and upkeep of the property and grounds is satisfying<br>- The grounds are attractive<br>- The site has remained authentic<br>- Direction signs to show around the property and grounds are clear and helpful<br>- The garden and/or park contain a large variety of plants<br>- The interior of the house offers a lot of interesting things to look at |
| F3 Communication | - The written leaflets provide enough information<br>- The information on the property and grounds is detailed enough<br>- Visitors are well informed of the different facilities and attractions available at the property<br>- Foreign language leaflets are helpful |
| F4 Consumables | - The restaurant offers a wide variety of dishes and refreshments<br>- The shop offers a large variety of goods<br>- The restaurant' staff provide efficient service |
| F5 Empathy | - The property considers the needs of less able visitors<br>- Facilities for children are provided |

Source: Reprinted from HISTOQUAL: An adaptation of SERVQUAL to historic houses, *21*(2), 157–167, Frochot, I., & Hughes, H. Copyright (2000) with permission from Elsevier.

For a historic house manager aiming to evaluate quality, the best option is to design a questionnaire based on this range of 22 items. The questionnaire can be completed after the visit and include questions such as "Do you perceive that the staff have been helpful and courteous?" The visitors are then invited to rate each of those questions on a 1 to 7 Likert scale from "totally agree" to "totally disagree." One option for "Does not apply" needs to be provided for each question, in order not to force visitors to answer. Some might prefer to use a 6-rank Likert scale to avoid a middle position.

In order to evaluate the importance of these elements in the visitor experience, it will be useful for managers to describe concretely those five dimensions in one sentence (Responsiveness, Tangibles, Communication, Consumables and Empathy) and request visitors to allocate 100 points among them. This will give the managers some useful information about the importance attached to those elements and to what extent they might vary according to the types of visitors.

To be able to use the survey strategically, it is also necessary to include other elements that will assist the attraction in driving strategic decisions. For instance, the questionnaire can collect data on the origin of visitors, their group structure, their nationality, etc. It can also investigate the parts of the property visited, the different services used, the information sources used, the amount spent, the distance traveled, etc.

Source: Reprinted from HISTOQUAL: An adaptation of SERVQUAL to historic houses, *21*(2), 157–167, Frochot, I., & Hughes, H. Copyright (2000) with permission from Elsevier.

# Service encounters and service design

One element we have not addressed yet are the various elements that make up a service delivery. Services involve a wide range of actors and settings, especially in the tourism area where consumers engage in consumption over several days and will come across a variety of employees, local inhabitants, and multiple encounters within the service delivery context (the experience-scape). Within the experience-scape, the consumer goes through those various contacts that have also been named encounters. Those encounters include all the interactions that consumers will have with a company.

In the 1980s, Eiglier and Langeard identified the servuction model, a system whereby consumers were pictured as being in direct contact with the front-office staff and other consumers, while evolving in the physical window of the company. The servuction model also portrayed the invisible part of the firm where all the organization, staff training, and general managerial and strategic objectives were taken. Their conclusion was that any service evaluation necessarily had to take on board all those elements.

From the 2000s onwards, researchers and consultants have focused more clearly on the managerial implications of those encounters through the approach known as service design. Service design draws in several areas of competences and is a mix of an

**Image 8.3**

Source: Pexels.

in-depth understanding of the user experience, marketing considerations, and project management.

- Service design is planning and organizing people, communication and material elements, and service infrastructures to improve its overall quality.
- Service design aims to align the organizational structure and process with consumers' needs.
- Service design is user-centered and should always engage its analysis from consumers' needs.
- From the analysis on consumers' needs, the service designer then investigates the design of various elements, including technology, processes, information and communication.
- Owing to the complexity of services (components, distribution options, technological interface for instance), the objective of service design is also to unify this complex environment to provide a comprehensive and balanced service delivery to the final consumer (a management that would consider all service elements and processes in isolation from each other would be inefficient).
- Service design approaches are always based on an extensive analysis of consumer demand, of its variability, and integrates end-consumers as contributors in the service improvement process.
- All stakeholders should be involved in this process so that all the needs of the various human and organizational needs are integrated into the analysis.
- The service design process aims to improve the service value received by consumers.

## Service design tools

The service design approach has developed some methodological tools to improve companies' service delivery to their customers, and achieve a whole organizational process that accompanies it. Those tools aim to:

- improve the understanding of consumer needs through designing a consumer's persona.
- understand the sequences and the important touch points of the consumer experience by designing a customer journey map.
- provide a holistic vision of the consumer experience by designing a blueprint.

### Consumers' personas

Consumers' personas aim to provide a factual and illustrated profile of a specific customer who is representative of a broader segment. Principles of segmentation won't be addressed again in this chapter as they have already been discussed in Chapter 7 and will feature again in Chapter 13. In summary, a persona is a fictive person that represents the main characteristics of a segment. With this representation, it is easier to provide a factual and easy-to-read vision of a segment and it engages companies to understand how

**Table 8.2** Blueprint for museum visit

Physical evidence
Customer action
Front-stage interactions
Back-stage interactions
Support process

Source: Author

they can target and conceive services for this target consumer. Personas draw in different information components about a segment including socio-economic data but also the experience thought by consumer (much akin to benefit segmentation presented in Chapter 7). In other words, a persona will also present consumers' psychographic elements such as their main motivation, values, and desires. Tourism and hospitality insight 8.5 provides an example of a persona.

## TOURISM AND HOSPITALITY INSIGHTS 8.5
## CONSTRUCTING PERSONAS

Neault (2017) suggests integrating the following components in the construction of a persona:

- provide a picture and a name
- an age range
- a residence
- level of education
- main occupation
- media habits
- main interests
- purchasing behavior
- main motivations

**The construction of persona requires four stages**

1. Collect data on consumers (surveys, exploit CRM data, survey frontline staff and managers, google analytics, social networks, etc.).

2. Analyze the information collected.

3. Construct a robot portrait by telling the story of this persona with the data detailed above and by making sure that the inner motivations of this individual are clearly expressed and detail his purchasing process and main media usage.

4. Diffuse the persona profile to all members of the organization.

As an example, the following personas are drawn from Fáilte Ireland to describe its main markets.

**Images 8.4 and 8.5**

Source: Reproduction authorized by Fáilte Ireland

### References

http://www.failteireland.ie/International-sales/International-sales/Social-energisers/Social-Energiser-personas.aspx

Neault C. (2017). *Créez vos personas en 4 étapes fáciles.* http://veilletourisme.ca/2017/06/13/creez-vos-personas-4-etapes-faciles/

Source: Isabelle Frochot.

## *Consumers' journey map*

The journey map is a very useful tool that helps enterprises visualize the different steps of the consumer experience: the journey map represents all the interactions that consumers have with an enterprise. Those contacts are multiple and should all be integrated in the analysis, they include the direct contact with the enterprise but also all the contacts that took place before the experience (physically or online), and also after the experience (after-sales service, word of mouth, etc.). The journey map looks at all those touch points and at their frequency. It then provides managers with a powerful tool indicating areas of improvement.

In order to get a more precise vision of the consumer journey analysis, Figure 8.2 details, in its broad lines, how the customer journey might be analyzed in the context of a hotel service.

In reality, the journey map can be more detailed and aims to overview all the touch points. From there onwards, an evaluation can be undertaken which allows companies to evaluate each of their steps: where is the enterprise performing well and what are the pitfalls? How can those elements be improved? If the pitfalls are associated with outside agents, what can be undertaken to improve them?

The customer journey is an interesting approach but one that needs to be supplemented by a vision of what those steps entail in terms of the service company organization and management. For the analysis to be complete, the company then needs to investigate what those touch points refer to in terms of its organizational structure:

**Figure 8.2 The customer journey template**

Source: Author.

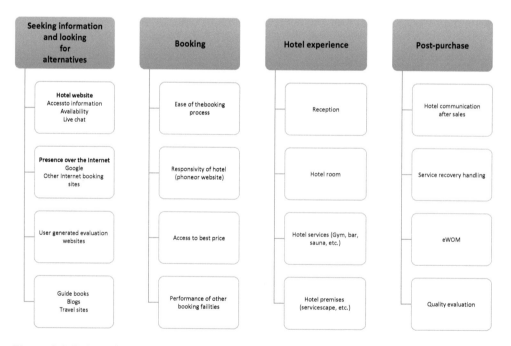

**Figure 8.3 A simplified consumer journey analysis**

Source: Author.

Which services are in charge of those elements? How can a company solve the pitfalls collectively (through its different back office services working together)? The blueprint is a management tool that condenses this information in a very useful model.

## The blueprint

The blueprint helps to identify and differentiate the various encounters that a consumer will come across and also identify who holds the responsibility for each encounter. Figure 8.4 shows a concise representation of this customer journey in a restaurant experience.

The blueprint is designed at different levels. We shall illustrate those elements with the service delivery experienced by Mr. and Mrs. Brown seeking a travel agency to purchase a cruise to the Caribbean.

- *Physical facilities:* All the physical elements that are important for delivering the service. Physical elements refer to all those elements that are physically visible (employees' uniforms, shop setting, furniture, etc.). Because services are partly intangible, those elements are important because they give good quality cues to consumers. Imagine if Mr. and Mrs. Brown entered the travel agency to find the floor dirty, untidy desks, poor lighting, and the travel assistant hooked on his personal mobile phone? These do not send positive cues about the quality of the service being sold.
- *Customer actions:* Steps, choices, interactions, activities undertaken by consumers at each stage of their experience process (seeking information, purchasing, experiencing and post-experiencing). In the case of Mr. and Mrs. Brown, they might have conducted a primary search on the Internet, sought information from blogs or the company has been recommended by some friends. They then found this travel agency, took time to locate it in their town, and visited it together.
- *Front-stage interactions:* Any activities, services, tasks undertaken by a frontline employee. The front-stage window of the blueprint looks at all the direct actions that will take place between the consumer and the frontline staff. Mr. and Mrs. Brown are in contact with a travel assistant and within facilities that provide the conditions for a good service delivery (lighting, seats, a good computer to find the options, etc.). They receive information from a travel assistant. They might even watch a video, and the components of a cruise may be explained to them: countries visited, insurance offers, services included in the package, etc.
- *Backstage interactions:* All the steps and actions that are directly invisible to the consumer but directly connected to the experience. Those elements might pertain to process elements: the agent has been trained to master global distribution systems, for instance. The travel assistant serving Mr. and Mrs. Brown might have also been trained either by the cruise company or his own organization so that he is

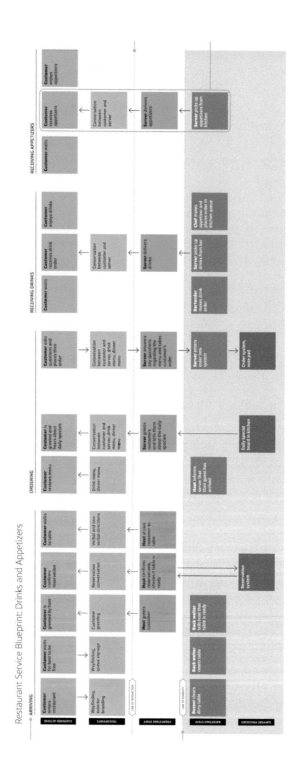

**Figure 8.4 – The blueprint model**

Source: https://newflux.fr/2017/02/02/un-guide-pour-utiliser-le-blueprint-comme-methode-de-conception-de-service-design/

knowledgeable about the products sold. He might even have been lucky enough to have undertaken a familiarization trip. He might wear a uniform provided by the firm, etc.

- *Support processes:* Steps and internal actions that are backstage and support the whole service process.

## The different levels of service provision

As we have seen, each service is composed of a range of service encounters. However, whilst some of those are totally necessary to the service delivery, others are secondary and can therefore be the object of strategic choices. Christopher Lovelock (1992) developed the flower of service model which describes a core service surrounded by two layers of services: facilitating and supplementary services as described thereafter.

Any service is always composed of a core service:

- The core service represents the main service delivered by the company. It is the primary purpose of the service delivery.
- The core service defines what inherently a consumer comes to purchase and the main service that he/she will come out with.
- It is the service that a consumer buys: a plane flight takes a consumer from destination A to destination B; a hotel provides a sleeping experience for one night and a restaurant provides a meal.
- The core service is the main goal of the service company, it cannot be changed but a company might choose to develop other core services within its general offer. For instance, EasyJet offers, as its primary core service, airline flights, but also has a car rental service.

There is now a range of services that will assist the delivery of the core service: the facilitating services which are listed below

- Facilitating services are a combination of goods and services that enable visitors to buy and use the core service.
- The core service cannot be delivered without the facilitating services.
- Lovelock (2009) includes in facilitating services:
    - Information (sign boards, notices, indications of changes, direction signs, order taking, billing and payment, etc.).
    - Order taking: filling out applications, seat, table, or room reservations.
    - Billing: accurate, complete, clearly explained and detailed, legality of the document.
    - Payment: cash and credit card handling, discounts, loyalty cards, etc.

Finally, the supplementary services represent all the additional services and benefits consumers receive.

- Facilitating services are not compulsory for the whole service to be delivered.
- According to Lovelock (2009) included in supplementary services are: consultation, hospitality, caretaking, and exceptions:

    - Consultation: Helping consumers to clarify their own demand, provide advice, counseling, and offering management/technical advice.
    - Hospitality: Greeting, reception, waiting facilities, facilities, food and beverage, packaging.
    - Caretaking: Also known as safe keeping, this element refers to an organization's arrangements for the safe keeping of customers' possessions. It might include baby care, parking facilities, transportation, storage, pick up, cleaning, etc.
    - Exceptions: Any services that are different from customers' routines and that need responses from both frontline and backstage employees to find a quick and satisfactory solution to customers' request.

Differentiating between facilitating and supplementary services is a useful approach to understand how companies can make strategic choices by positioning themselves differently on those elements.

## Strategic choices with service components

As stated previously, companies cannot modify their core concept but they can act on both facilitating and supplementary services. With regard to facilitating services, those can be down-sized in order to save costs. In order to reduce costs, the service can also be delegated to the consumer. For instance, fast-food restaurants save staff costs by encouraging customers to come and place their order at the counter rather than staff taking the order at the table.

Supplementary services are elements that a company can choose not to deliver or it might choose to charge the customer for that service (whilst it might be free of charge in other companies).

These strategic choices on both facilitating and supplementary services have to be carefully planned so that the choices made are in line with the positioning of the product and the brand. If a company chooses to develop a low-cost offer in parallel to its mainstream services, it is preferable to develop a brand for each offer in order not to confuse consumers.

The best way to illustrate the differences between these three levels of service is to compare the service provision of a low-cost airline with a mainstream airline on a short-haul flight (see the major case study at the end of this chapter).

# Conclusion

This chapter has provided a clear insight into the complexities and richness of services, aiming to understand how their specific components create unique management situations compared to physical products. From this recognition, the chapter encourages the reader to consider the managerial implications of tourism and hospitality services' specificities. Quality remains an essential component of service provision. Even if it does not seem to be directly related to experiential marketing considerations, a service not delivering quality is a service that will impact overall consumer satisfaction.

The chapter provided a range of tools that manager can use to improve their service delivery from quality scales to service design elements such as persona design, customer journey, and service blueprint. Service design is comparatively a new field and no doubt will evolve in the years to come. Our understanding of services processes and outputs increases day by day and new technologies will increasingly provide methods and tools that can assist managers in getting closer to the consumer experience.

## REVIEW QUESTIONS

1. The intangibility of services remains a complex problem for their management. Identify three examples of tourism and hospitality companies that have tried to make their service more tangible to guarantee constant quality.
2. Heterogeneity of services are equally a crucial component, especially with regard to employees' variable performances. What are the new advances in this domain that can help in order to provide a better consumer service for frontline staff?
3. Several examples of SEVQUAL applications were given in this chapter, could you design one that would be applicable to a museum service provision?
4. Service design is becoming a key approach to service delivery improvements. What are the new technologies that can facilitate this approach?

## YOUTUBE LINKS

### "Five dimensions of service quality"

URL: https://www.youtube.com/watch?v=Gxf6UfF5PpY

Summary: This nine-minute videos looks at the five service dimensions inspired by SERVQUAL: tangibles, assurance, responsiveness, empathy and reliability. It provides an interesting and specific focus for employees and how they create a climate for the service delivered. The video then looks at the role and place of quality in business success. The video takes the form of a PowerPoint-based lecture and includes an interview with Richard Branson on his quality and consumers' perspective vision.

## *"SERVQUAL model"*

URL: https://www.youtube.com/watch?v=YVGvIJlTjak

Summary: This 3.5-minutes video brings the attention of the viewer to the five quality gaps that were identified by Parasuraman, Zeithmal, and Berry when they developed the SERVQUAL scale. It addresses an element not overviewed in the chapter and points out the internal problems that might arise in a company's organization which might explain why service quality fails. For more information, readers can then read the original paper on quality gaps in the Further Reading section (Parasuraman, Zeithaml, & Berry, 1990).

## *"How to map the customer journey in seven steps | astute solutions"*

URL: https://www.youtube.com/watch?v=3bdjeBDHdrM

Summary: This simple and refreshing video provides an illustrated introduction to the customer journey with an illustrated vision of a cupcake shop. The video reviews all the steps of the customer strategy journey from recognizing consumer needs. It integrates the emotional dimension inspired by the consumer journey.

## *"How to create a journey map | methods"*

URL: https://www.youtube.com/watch?v=A2LFJF1SUBg

Summary: This 3.5-minute video provides a clear and concrete overview of the specific steps involved in a journey mapping procedure. The video concretely shows with a very specific focus on each step of journey mapping, how to build a map and integrate different elements. The aim of this video is to provide a model but leave some flexibility to the viewer so that it can be applied to any service context.

## *"REAL customer journey mapping (that works) – John Lincoln, ignite visibility"*

URL: https://www.youtube.com/watch?v=tGZryr0P5gA

Summary: This 10-minute video, provides an overall look of the whole strategy associated with journey mapping. The video focuses specifically on the digital touch points and how companies can develop a knowledge of those elements to target their consumers more effectively with a seamless service. The video is powerful in showing how companies can identify their consumers, from the initial contact point to then develop a service design in line with the needs of those consumers.

## *"Flower of service complete"*

URL: https://www.youtube.com/watch?v=yAzKSFXT3mk

Summary: This two-minute video is very useful in understanding the flower of service that was presented in this chapter. The video details all the components of the flower of service by using the example of Amazon. It explains how some of the flower categories are then subdivided into different services for this company.

## REFERENCES, FURTHER READING, AND RELATED WEBSITES

### References

Berry, L. (1986). Big ideas in services marketing. *Journal of Consumer Marketing, 3*(2), 47–51.

Frochot, I., & Hughes, H. (2000). HISTOQUAL: An adaptation of SERVQUAL to historic houses. *Tourism Management, 21*(2), 157–167.

Grönroos, C. (2015). *Service management and marketing: Managing the service profit logic.* Hoboken, NJ: Wiley.

Lewis, B.R., & Mitchell, V.W. (1990). Defining and measuring the quality of customer service. *Marketing Intelligence & Planning, 8*(6), 11–17.

Lovelock, C.H. (1983). Classifying services to gain strategic marketing insights. *Journal of Marketing, 47*(Summer), 9–20.

Lovelock, C.H. (1992). Cultivating the flower of service: New ways of looking at core and supplementary services. *Marketing, Operations, and Human Resources: Insights into Services,* June, 296–316.

Parasuraman, A., Zeithaml, V.A., & Berry, L.L. (1988). SERVQUAL: A multiple-item scale for measuring consumer perceptions of service quality. *Journal of Retailing, 64*(Spring), 12–40.

Parasuraman, A., Berry, L.L., & Zeithaml, V.A. (1990). An empirical test of the extended gaps model of service quality. *Marketing Science Institute Working Paper,* 90–122.

Pine, B.J., & Gilmore, J.H. (1999). *The experience economy: Work is theatre and every business a stage.* Cambridge, MA: Harvard Business Press.

### Further reading

Bitner, M.J. (1990). Evaluating service encounters: The effects of physical surroundings and employee responses. *Journal of Marketing, 54*(April), 69–82.

Fick, G.R., & Ritchie J.R. (1991). Measuring service quality in the travel and tourism industry. *Journal of Travel Research, 29*(Fall), 2–9.

Grönroos, C, (1984). A service quality model and its marketing implications. *European Journal of Marketing, 18*(4), 36–44.

Hamilton, J.A., Crompton, J.L., & More, T.A. (1991). Identifying the dimensions of service quality in a park context. *Journal of Environmental Management, 32,* 211–220.

Hudson, S. (2008). *Tourism and hospitality marketing: A global perspective.* London: Sage Publications.

Knutson, B., Stevens, P., Wullaert, C., & Patton, M. (1991). LODGSERV: A service quality index for the lodging industry. *Hospitality Research Journal, 14*(7), 277–284.

Lewis, B.R. (1993). Service quality measurement. *Marketing Intelligence & Planning, 11*(4), 4–12.

Mok, C., Sparks, B., & Kadampully, J. (2009). *Service quality management in hospitality, tourism, and leisure.* Binghamton, NY: Routledge.

Morrison, A. M. (2010). *Hospitality and travel marketing* (4th ed.). Australia: Delmar Cengage Learning.

Osterwalder, A., Pigneur, Y., Bernarda, G., Smith, A., & Papadakos, T. (2014). *Value proposition design: How to create products and services customers want.* Hoboken, NJ: Wiley.

Otto, J., & Ritchie, J.R. (1996). The service experience in tourism. *Tourism Management, 17*(3), 165–174.

Parasuraman, A., Zeithaml, V., & Berry, L. (1985). A conceptual model of service quality and its implications for future research. *Journal of Marketing, 49*(Fall), 41–50.

Reid, R.D., & Bojanic, D.C. (2010). *Hospitality marketing management* (5th ed.). New York: John Wiley & Sons.

Saleh, F., & Ryan, C. (1991). Analysing service quality in the hospitality industry using the SERVQ-UAL model. *The Service Industries Journal, 11*(3), 324–343.

Shaw, M., & Morris, S. (2000). *Hospitality sales: A marketing approach* (1st ed.). New York: John Wiley & Sons, Inc.

Shostack, G.L. (1985). Planning the service encounter. In J.A. Czepiel, M.R. Solomon, & C.F. Surprenant (Eds.), *The service encounter* (pp. 243–254). Lexington MA: Lexington Books.

Shostack, G.L. (1984). Designing services that deliver. *Harvard Business Review, 62*(1), 133–139.

Stickdorn, M., & Schneider, J. (2014). *This is service design thinking: Basics, tools, cases.* Amsterdam: BIS Publishers.

Weiermair, K. (2000). Tourists' perceptions towards and satisfaction with service quality in the cross-cultural service encounter: Implications for hospitality and tourism management. *Managing Service Quality: An International Journal, 10*(6), 397–409.

Zeithaml, V.A., Bitner, M.J., & Gremler, D.D. (2012). *Services marketing: Integrating customer focus across the firm.* New York: McGraw Hill.

Zeithaml, V., Parasuraman, A., & Berry, L. (1985). Problems and strategies in services marketing. *Journal of Marketing, 49*(2), 33–46

## Websites

What is service design?

https://trydesignlab.com/blog/what-is-service-design/

What is service design and why is it important for tourism?
http://www.ireland-guide.com/article/what-is-service-design-and-why-is-it-important-for-tourism.12053.html

How service design helps travel brands woo seemingly irrational customers
https://www.tnooz.com/article/how-service-design-helps-travel-brands-woo-seemingly

Service design tools
http://www.servicedesigntools.org/tools/35

Service blueprints – communicating the design of services
https://www.interaction-design.org/literature/article/service-blueprints-communicating-the-design-of-services #

## MAJOR CASE STUDY
## COMPARING SERVICE PROVISION OF LOW-COST CARRIERS (LCC) AND A REGULAR AIRLINE

In line with the analysis of service components presented in this chapter, this major case study encourages the reader to analyze how different levels of service can be reconceptualized to reduce the cost of the service and provide a low-cost offer. The following tables indicate how a service can be broken down and then how a low-cost airline can work on those elements to reduce the cost of its service.

First of all, the following table details all the service components that make up a service flight offer.

**Figure 8.5** Service structure of mainstream airlines

| Core service | Facilitating services | Supplementary services |
|---|---|---|
| Airline transport from A to B | Checking-in customers and their luggage<br>Passport control<br>Security check<br>Departure lounge<br>Luggage (cabin bags and hold luggage, number of bags)<br>Airport<br>Tickets: direct sales over Internet (own website + resellers), by phone, over the counter or through travel agents<br>Printed tickets or e-tickets | Luggage connection for two flights or more<br>Choice of seats<br>Food and drink<br>Magazines, in-flight entertainment (radio, movies, etc.)<br>Different classes (Business class/economy class, etc.)<br>Private airline lounges in airport<br>Loyalty programs<br>Boarding order according to ticket class<br>Duty free shops<br>Duty free sales on flight<br>Low plane turnover<br>High labour costs<br>Cleaning staff |

Source: Author.

Once this list has been assembled, the company needs to investigate what is under its control and what is not. For instance, security checks are operated by airport services and passport checks are undertaken by toll services; those services cannot be changed (although eye and print recognition might ease the identity-check process). Then the cost facilitating services will be reduced by the low-cost airline.

**Figure 8.6** Facilitating services

| Facilitating services – regular airlines | Low cost strategy |
| --- | --- |
| Checking-in customers | Self-check-in online |
| Checking-in luggage | Self-check-in of luggage |
| Passport control | Not under airline control |
| Security check | Not under airline control |
| Departure lounge | Not under airline control (style and size dependent on airport) |
| Luggage (cabin bags and hold luggage, number of bags) | Strict luggage allowance. Fees for hold luggage |
| Main airport | Secondary airports (lower airport taxes, quicker turnaround) |
| Tickets: direct sales on Internet (own website + resellers), by phone, over the counter or through travel agents | Online sales, very limited or no use of resellers |
| Printed tickets or e-tickets | |

Source: Author.

Regarding facilitating services, the main strategy of low-cost airlines (and bearing in mind that they cannot totally suppress those services) is to either delegate the task to consumers with new self-service technologies or to charge for the facilities concerned. The charge for luggage is recent and has another advantage for LCCs. Less luggage reduces the fuel consumption of the aircraft.

**Figure 8.7** Supplementary services

| Supplementary services – regular airlines | Low cost strategy |
| --- | --- |
| Flight connections for two or more flights | No flight connections |
| Seat allocation choice | Charge for seat allocation |
| Food and beverage | Charge for food and drink |
| Magazines, in-flight entertainment (radio, movies, etc.) | No in-flight entertainment apart from the company's magazine |
| Different classes (Business class/economy class, etc.) | No different classes |
| Boarding order according to ticket class | Some companies provide a speedy boarding option |
| Private airline lounges in airport | No private lounges |
| Loyalty programs | No loyalty program |
| Duty free sales on flight | Duty free sales on flight |
| Low plane turnover | High plane turnover |
| Labour cost – high | Labour cost – lower |
| Cleaning staff | Cabin crew undertake the cleaning between flights |

Source: Author.

Contrary to facilitating services, supplementary services can be reduced to near zero or charged to the consumer. The choice of most LCCs is to reduce to zero the cost of different service components (no connecting flights, one level of service for all passengers, no lounges). For the rest of the services, their cost can be reduced by charging the consumer directly (e.g. seat allocation, extra luggage, food and drinks, etc.).

As well as these strategies, other strategic choices allow LCCs to reduce the overall cost of their flights. For instance, most airlines use only one type of aircraft. This reduces the cost of staff training (pilots, flight attendants, and mechanics, cheaper access to spare parts and bulk orders can improve price negotiations). LCC fleets tend to consist of newer aircraft which means more efficient fuel consumption. When LCCS order their aircraft, they ask for the maximum number of seats to be installed. As there is only one class of service on board, a LCC is able to install 15% more seats than a regular airline in a similar aircraft.

Source: Author.

## Major case study questions

1. By following this reasoning, investigate how you could develop a similar low-cost product for a two-star hotel. Start by listing the facilitating and supplementary services, then design a low-cost strategy that aims to reduce the cost (physical and staff) of your service.
2. Investigate to what extent you can remove, reduce, delegate, or charge for some of these services without damaging the consumer experience.

# 9 Looking beyond quality

## Learning outcomes

By the end of this chapter, students will:

- Understand clearly the role of expectations in the formation of satisfaction
- Be familiar with the variability of expectations with the notion of zone of tolerance
- Appreciate how service elements contribute differently to satisfaction
- Understand the complexity of the notion of satisfaction in a tourism and hospitality experiential context with the notion of service value
- Appreciate the place of consumers within the service production with their role as co-creators.

## Introduction

The previous chapter investigated the characteristics of services and looked at the notion of quality and how service components can be managed. Whilst this approach is invaluable, it is not the only way a manager might conceive service management. Indeed, services are complex entities that can open possibilities for various types of strategies. The first part of this chapter looks beyond traditional service quality approaches. It challenges the expectations–performance traditional tenet, introduces the notion of zone of tolerance, and the role of satisfiers/dissatisfiers and the importance-performance analysis.

The second part of the chapter challenges traditional approaches to quality by presenting different approaches that indicate that quality is only one component of satisfaction and that other elements need to be integrated for a full understanding of consumer satisfaction. Those "alternative" approaches to quality are particularly pertinent in the context of experiential consumption where emotions dominate the experience and calls for a new conceptualization of the consumer model. The notion of consumer values will be addressed along with the co-construction concept.

# Challenging normal service traditions

## Challenging the expectancy-disconfirmation measures

Chapter 8 investigated the notions of service and service quality and presented the SERVQUAL scale, the most prominent scale to measure service quality to date. Most service quality approaches are based on the disconfirmation paradigm, with an underlying understanding that quality is evaluated by comparing expectations with perceptions.

The general tenet behind this evaluation procedure is that if expectations are higher than perceptions then consumers are likely to be dissatisfied (i.e. they did not obtain as much as what they were expecting). On the reverse, if expectations are inferior to the perceived quality of service, then consumers are satisfied (see Tourism and hospitality insights 9.1 on expectations and hotel classification schemes).

## TOURISM AND HOSPITALITY INSIGHTS 9.1
## HOW ARE EXPECTATIONS DRIVEN BY HOTEL CLASSIFICATION SCHEMES?

Hotel classifications have been in use for some time and create a standard that helps consumers orientate their choice and have a preconceived idea of the standard they can expect from a certain category of hotels. The Globe Veilleur Newsletter reports on a study conducted by the University of Cantabria (Spain) investigating how consumers shape expectations according to the classification of a hotel. Their results indicate that the luxury-end hotels demonstrate higher expectations. The results also show that, on average, hotels fail to match consumer expectations apart from the lower levels of quality (Table 9.1).

Table **9.1** Expectations/perceptions alignment according to hotels' classification

| Hotel categories | Expectations* | Perceptions* |
| --- | --- | --- |
| 4 and 5 stars | 6,76 | 6,45 |
| 3 stars | 6,18 | 5,89 |
| 2 stars | 6,35 | 6,01 |
| 1 star | 6,08 | 6,20 |

Notes

* Scores translate a rate of agreement on a 1 to 7 scale
Source: Péloquin C., Réseau de veille en tourisme, Chaire de tourisme Transat: http://veilletourisme.ca/2005/01/13/la-classification-des-hotels-vs-les-attentes-de-la-clientele-lavis-de-michael-nowlis/

**Image 9.1**

Source: Pexels.

This study reveals two elements. First, it points to the limits of grading schemes. Indeed, classification schemes tend to focus on tangible elements mostly. This might explain why perceptions match or surpass expectations for one-star hotels where the service is mostly based on a functional/basic service and where expectations are set at a low level. However, for higher level hotel services, the grading scheme seems to fail to identify less functional and measurable elements and sends a message that translates into expectations being systematically lower than perceptions (hence potentially leading to dissatisfaction).

Quality schemes appear to fail to meet customer expectations. They appear to be unable to translate accurately hedonic components of the service offer. This is problematic since, as the grading of hotels increases, consumers will expect more hedonic components. As a result, for a one-star hotel, where expectations are mostly based on functional and basic elements, hotels match or even surpass the level of (lower) expectations. When moving up in grading levels, consumers still have expectations at a functional level but also expect other dimensions of service delivery that are more rarely integrated into grading schemes. In a way, this explains the success of other "grading" schemes such as guide books or user generated content (UGC) such as TripAdvisor that give a more detailed and in-depth analysis of other qualitative dimensions that are more of an experiential nature.

Expectations are a danger zone and should be carefully watched, whatever the hotel has advertised and communicated previously will highly influence its consumers' expectations. In the case of this study, the four major areas where the hotel failed to deliver adequate service were:

- Quality of service: Discrete staff, efficiently solving problems, attentive and fast service, etc.;
- Personnel characteristics: Courtesy, professionalism, personalized attention, etc.;
- Tangible elements: Room comfort, food quality, attractiveness of the surrounding area, security issues, etc.;
- Other attributes: Peaceful surroundings, information about nearby activities, range of services on offer at the hotel.

Source: Péloquin C., Réseau de veille en tourisme, Chaire de tourisme Transat: http://veilletourisme.ca/2005/01/13/la-classification-des-hotels-vs-les-attentes-de-la-clientele-lavis-de-michael-nowlis/

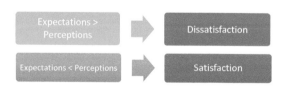

**Figure 9.1** The expectations/perceptions dynamics

# Are expectation measures really appropriate?

Over the years, academics have debated the practicalities of using the disconfirmation indicator. Although this issue is still disputed, perceptions-only scores, or comparative measures, somehow seem to perform as well or even better than the expectation-minus-perception score. Indeed, reality tends to show that separating those two scores is perhaps more complex than at first sought: expectations in themselves impact how consumers perceive a service. For instance, a consumer having specific preconceived expectations about the delivery in a restaurant will shape his/her perception of that service with regard to those preconceived expectations. So, in the end, separating both scores and calculating a difference is probably misleading. This also simplifies quality surveys since the original SERVQUAL methodology advocated conducting a survey before the service (evaluating expectations), tracing consumers, and administrating another perception survey after the service (evaluating perceptions). This survey procedure was somewhat difficult for both surveyors and consumers.

Tourism and hospitality insights 9.2 details an example of a comparative measure used by a consultancy agency which provides interesting results to analyze the digital hospitality at a destination level.

## *The variable facets of expectations*

Consumers have different levels of expectations when evaluating a service and this level of expectation varies according to various elements and circumstances. Moreover, expectations are rarely a precise and definite value. They evolve within a zone of tolerance. Within a zone of tolerance, consumers will evaluate the service performance equally. But this zone will have different widths expanding or reducing, according to circumstances. Outside the zone, consumers either enter satisfaction or dissatisfaction. Several major influences can impact the zone of tolerance:

- The zone of tolerance depends on *previous experiences*. For instance, a consumer who will have used a specific type of resort will have, through his/her cumulated experience, shaped an idea of what is to be expected from those types of services.
- Expectations are influenced by *advertising*, so an advertising campaign that overstates positive elements about a destination/a hotel will inflate expectations. If, once at the destination, the consumer feels that it is under-performing, he/she will have a lower perception than expected which will lead to dissatisfaction. Other sources of information: TV documentaries, UGC websites, guide books will all contribute to shaping expectations at a specific level and they also need to be taken into consideration when analyzing satisfaction/dissatisfaction. In other words, it is essential to consider that advertising will raise expectations at a specific level and the more precise the advertisement, the narrower the zone of tolerance.

## TOURISM AND HOSPITALITY INSIGHTS 9.2
## EVALUATING DIGITAL HOSPITALITY

TCI Research is a consultancy company working with the tourism and hospitality industry. TCI Research produces a Competitive Index Survey that aims to assess destinations' competitiveness based on a 30,000 tourist-based survey from more than 30 countries. Part of this survey is the evaluation of digital hospitality.

The TRAVELSAT Index reads as follows:

**Table 9.2** Travelsat Index

| | |
|---|---|
| **250 to 400** | **Exceptional** |
| **150 to 250** | **High:** the experience exceeds expectations |
| **100 to 150** | **Acceptable:** the experience does not always exceed expectations |
| **0 to 100** | **Poor:** inconsistency in the quality of services provided and/or does not meet expectations |
| **-50 to 0** | **Very poor:** major quality issues, risks tarnishing the reputation of the destination |

Source: Travelsat (2018)

The TRAVELST index is based on a consumer evaluation of respondents' impressions of the availability, accessibility, and quality of the content and services offered via various mobile devices. The indicator does not apply to criteria of satisfaction relating to prices. The TRAVELSAT survey finds that overall, the satisfaction index with the quality of digital hospitality stands at just barely over 100 – indicating that it is acceptable, but does not always exceed expectations.

Once the evaluation is conducted, the indicator is then reanalyzed by segmenting the results according to various socio-economic and behavioral variables.

For instance, an analysis by age shows that the TRAVELSAT index performs differently according to age ranges. Figure 9.2 shows that Generation Y travelers (23 to 34 years old) appear to evaluate quality slightly higher than older generations (who are presumably less accustomed to those devices).

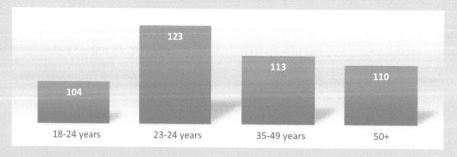

**Figure 9.2** Travelsat scores per age ranges

An analysis per destination also shows that countries perform at different levels in relation to digital hospitality quality. For instance, New Zealand, Australia, the United States, and Canada are performing better than other destinations, including Europe (see Figure 9.3). Inconsistency of quality seems to be one of the major factors explaining lower scores.

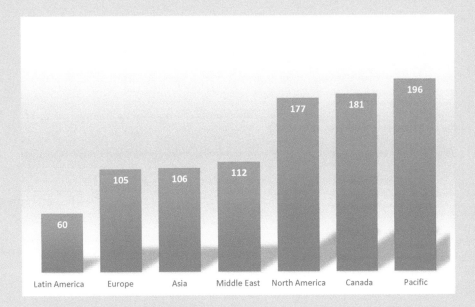

Figure 9.3 Level of satisfaction by destination

On another level, TRAVELSAT analyzed the digital hospitability quality for various activities (Figure 9.4). In terms of satisfaction, the positive information is that most consumers rate the service provision as acceptable (scores above 100). However, overall the scores are not very high since none of them is rated as "high" or "acceptable." Some very specific activities seem to display higher ratings, for instance golf, theaters, and theme parks display higher scores. But equally, activities that require practical information (maps, timetables, etc.), especially when visitors are at the destination, display fairly low ratings (skiing or hiking for instance).

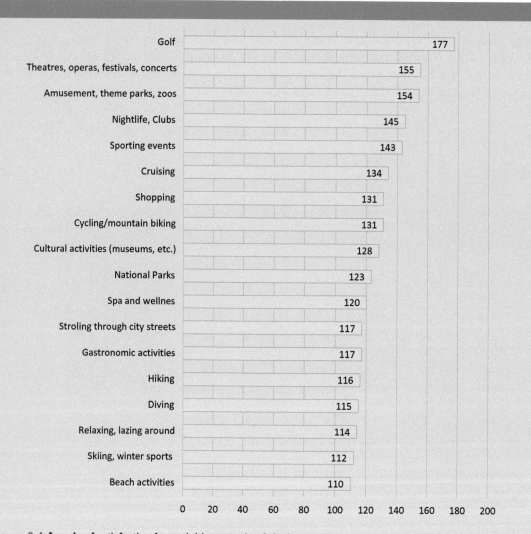

**Figure 9.4** Levels of satisfaction by activities practiced during a stay

Considering that most visitors will search information at the destination, that mobile use is increasing drastically and that mobile applications provide rich tools (geo-localization for instance), these results show that there is still a large scope for improvements in digital hospitality via mobile phones. Nowadays, the majority of tourists do not visit tourist information centers upon arrival, therefore providing them with useful, relevant, efficient and up-to-date mobile information is of utmost importance as a prime welcoming message when receiving tourists at a destination.

Source: TCI Research: http://tci-research.com/travelsat/and Racine A. (2013) Evaluating the quality of digital hospitality, Globe Veilleur: http://tourismintelligence.ca/2013/02/26/evaluating-the-quality-of-digital-hospitality/

- *Existing competition will be another influential factor:* If there is intense competition and several other enterprises are offering similar and better services for a similar range of prices, then consumers' zones of tolerance will narrow. For instance, bus services across the world are improving their service rapidly. If a new company is established with more comfortable seats, free WiFi, and free movies on individual screens, then consumers will become accustomed to this type of service and even expect it from other companies.
- The *price* charged for the service: If the price is particularly low, then consumers will have a higher zone of tolerance. This is typically the case with no-frills low-cost airlines which offer a very limited customer service, and reduce their core service provision to a strict minimum (flying from one destination to another at a very low price). Because the price is so low, consumers accept lower levels of service provision and thereby expand their tolerance zone.
- The zone of tolerance is *time-and-context dependent:* For instance, consumers might have high expectations regarding the speed of delivery of a service but at different times, they will intuitively know that they cannot expect the same speed of service. For instance, a family going to a theme park during the week and outside the main holiday season will not expect the same waiting times as during the main holiday season.
- If the reasons for a service failure are *outside the provider's control* and especially if it is of a natural origin (earthquake, hurricanes, tsunamis, etc.), then consumers will tend to be more tolerant. As a result, their zone of tolerance will be wider. If, however, the fault is within the provider's control, then the zone of tolerance will be narrower. It is the case of airlines as is detailed in Tourism and hospitality insights 9.3.
- The level of *consumer involvement:* If a consumer is highly involved with a product then his/her zone of tolerance will be narrower. For instance, if a consumer goes on a kitesurf holiday once a year, and kitesurfing is the most important sport for that person, then this consumer will have very high expectations regarding this holiday. Since this service is particularly important to him/her, the consumer will have searched through more information and compared more alternatives and will feel fully involved with his/her choice.

This last element is particularly important from a managerial point of view. Managers need to understand where they need to concentrate their efforts and identify potential areas that are unsatisfactory to their consumers. Tourism and hospitality insights 9.4 demonstrates how expectations also need to be associated with their respective importance. Whether it is associated with consumers' experience, personal motivations or circumstances, managers need to understand what key components matter most to them, in order to direct their marketing efforts efficiently.

The chapter has so far investigated how different elements impact the expectations and perceptions of the service delivery. This approach is particularly useful since it goes beyond traditional quality approaches to integrate the fact that, depending on the situation, consumer pre-dispositions, and the context, service components will take

## TOURISM AND HOSPITALITY INSIGHTS 9.3
## EU COMPENSATION RULE

Over the years, consumers have increasingly suffered inconveniences at the hands of tourism providers who want to make sure that their premises are fully occupied and thereby overbook their services to compensate for consumers who do not show up on the day. Overbooking has been common practice for some years but it gradually reached a stage of consumer dissatisfaction that motivated authorities to intervene and regulate the situation. On February 11, 2004, the European Parliament voted in favor of Regulation (EC) No. 261/2004. The EU considered that denial of boarding, cancelations or long delays of flights would cause serious trouble and inconvenience to passengers. The EU saw its responsibility: "The Community should therefore raise the standards of protection set by that Regulation both to strengthen the rights of passengers and to ensure that air carriers operate under harmonized conditions in a liberalized market: It thereby decided that, in the light of consumers' interest, it would impose on airline companies to compensate for denied boarding, canceled and delayed flights".

Compensation only comes into play if the delay or canceled flight is within the company's responsibility. If the problem is caused by something outside its control (weather, strikes) then the compensation is not operational.

The rule applies:

- If a flight is within the EU and is operated either by an EU or a non-EU airline;
- If a flight arrives in the EU from outside the EU and is operated by an EU airline;
- If a flight departs from the EU to a non-EU country operated by an EU or a non-EU airline.

This regulation establishes common rules for compensation and assistance to passengers in the event of denied boarding, cancelations or long delays.

Right to compensation:

Where reference is made to this Article, passengers shall receive compensation amounting to:

a.  €250 for all flights of 1,500 kilometres or less;
b.  €400 for all intra-Community flights of more than 1,500 kilometres, and for all other flights between 1,500 and 3,500 kilometres;
c.  €600 for all flights not falling under (a) or (b).

In determining the distance, the basis shall be the last destination at which the denial of boarding or cancelation will delay the passenger's arrival after the scheduled time.

Governments, states, consumers' associations, NGOs are often key actors in raising issues and imposing laws that help the whole industry to improve. The EU considers that, when the problem is under the company's responsibility, consumers should not have to expand their zone of tolerance to inconceivable levels and asked to accept situations that clearly are not acceptable. When quality is often seen as an enterprise-bound question, it is in fact also in the hands of authorities at various levels in order to guarantee that companies behave accordingly.

Source: Isabelle Frochot/https://eur-lex.europa.eu/legal-content/EN/TXT/?uri=legissum:l24173 © European Union, http://eur-lex.europa.eu/, 1998–2018

## TOURISM AND HOSPITALITY INSIGHTS 9.4
## THE IMPORTANCE-PERFORMANCE MODEL TO INFORM STRATEGIC DECISIONS

Beyond evaluating quality, it is also essential for companies to understand which elements matter most to their consumers. Indeed, it is one thing to understand how consumers evaluate the quality of a service, but providers also need to appreciate what are the important criteria for their customers in order to take strategic decisions. One of the simplest approaches to evaluate those two dimensions is importance-performance analysis (IPA) (Martilla and James, 1977), a two-dimensional scheme that combines both the quality perception and the importance attached by consumers to those items.

When undertaking an IPA, the provider needs to undertake a survey that measures both the quality perception and the quality importance then plot those findings on a map. From these results, the providers can then identify what are the positives and what are the danger zones of their service delivery:

- Keep the good work: Identifies the best service provision elements, whereby consumers perceive that the company is performing well and those elements are important to them.

- Improvements needed rapidly: The danger zone groups elements where the criteria listed are important to consumers but the company is providing poor quality. Those elements need to rapidly improve.

- Needs to be improved – no urgency: Points to elements that also need improvements but since they are less important to consumers, there is less urgency to deal with them.

- Does not necessitate further improvement: These are elements where the firm performs well but are unimportant to consumers. This is a zone where the company invests time and effort for a result which, in time, has little impacts on consumers' perceptions. Therefore, those efforts tend to be wasted and should not need such investment.

Source: Isabelle Frochot.

different routes towards consumer satisfaction. The following section brings yet another approach to satisfaction, one that is particularly rich and brings more depth to the understanding of how elements might have a different impact on satisfaction.

## How service components impact satisfaction differently

In the early 1980s, a stream of researchers investigated the possibility that all attributes, within a service delivery, might not have the same linear contribution to satisfaction. In other words, some service delivery components would impact satisfaction or dissatisfaction with variable forces. This vision had already been advanced by Herzberg, Mausner, and Snyderman in 1959, on a study of employees and bi-factorial contribution to satisfaction. Their study showed that motivation factors (how employees fulfill themselves through work) only contributed to employees' satisfaction whilst hygiene factors (the quality of the employee situation at work) contributed only to dissatisfaction. Then in 1984, Kano, Seraku, Takahashi, and Tsuji identified other possible options for contributions to satisfaction. These authors, by investigating different components of the user experience to the global satisfaction, identified four different processes:

- *One-dimensional quality* elements: These items contribute to either satisfaction or dissatisfaction when they are evaluated positively or negatively. These service items are performance indicators. For instance, a plane being on time might be part of these factors.
- *Must-be quality elements:* These elements only contribute to dissatisfaction when they are evaluated negatively but not to satisfaction when they are evaluated positively; in other words, they are noticed through their absence. These are also commonly named dissatisfiers. For instance, the cleanliness of a hotel bathroom is a component that is expected and is considered to be normal. If a hotel bathroom turns out not to be cleaned to the correct standard, then it will create dissatisfaction. However, a clean bathroom, since it is expected, will not create satisfaction.
- *Attractive quality elements:* Also known as satisfiers, they are elements that will impact satisfaction if they are present but will not impact dissatisfaction in their absence. Typically, these elements are those that are unexpected which come as a plus. Their absence would go unnoticed (precisely because they are not expected), but their presence can create a real boost in satisfaction. Elements of surprise, and generally speaking experiential components often fall in this category. Typically, during a holiday if a resort manages to organize an unannounced event with a local guide sharing some anecdotes and stories about the destination, preferably in an attractive authentic setting, this would create a satisfier. More generally, supplementary elements that are free and unannounced can easily produce a satisfying effect.
- *Indifferent quality elements*: These elements only have a minor impact on satisfaction or dissatisfaction.

In the Kano et al. study (1984), their results on an analysis of TVs show that the remote-control was perceived as a satisfier. Image resolution was a necessary quality component, bi-lingual possibility an indifferent quality dimension and the after-sales service a one-dimensional quality element.

The major case study at the end of this chapter provides an interesting adaptation of this model to a tourism context with a study on Reunion Island and the Dominican Republic.

# Complexity of satisfaction in an experiential context

In experiential consumption situations, one might question what is most important to consumers. Consumers are more likely to be in an experiential-mode, than a rational one, therefore their evaluation procedures might be much more associated with key hedonic encounters than general service provision. Their emotions might also play a key role that was not adequately addressed in the quality studies previously reviewed. This is an old debate in academia but one that cannot be ignored. For instance, Oliver (1981, 1993) has shown that satisfaction is based on disconfirmation of expectations but also on positive and negative effects elicited by the consumption experience. West-brook and Oliver (1991) also showed that two types of emotions were significantly linked to high satisfaction levels. These were the pleasure linked to surprise over the consumption experience and pleasure coupled with high interest.

In Chapter 7, the concept of motivation was introduced and its importance in determining consumers' choice was addressed. In experiential consumption, those motivations can also serve as a guide for understanding how satisfaction is derived from the experience. For instance, if a consumer expressed as a prime motivation the need to get away and to indulge in a very relaxing holiday, this consumer will evaluate his/her holiday based on those prime motivations. Therefore, those elements have to be integrated into consumption evaluations and the concept of values brings an interesting approach to grasp those elements.

## Service value

Value is a general concept that compares the benefits and costs of a service to a consumer. The benefits can be vast, especially in an experiential context, and include all the elements, attributes, services that a consumer will gain from using the service. The costs are necessarily associated with the price paid for the service. However, costs can also include the time taken to book the service (amount of Internet searches for instance, delay in booking the service, etc.), the risks associated with the booking procedure, etc.

In services, researchers have established that the notion of value includes all the benefits that a consumer is gaining from a service provision. Researchers recognize that values have to be conceptualized as a multi-dimensional concept, and that, especially in an experiential concept, values extend way beyond the functional properties of a service. To begin with, values can be differentiated in three broad categories: functional, hedonic, and social:

- *Functional value* is defined as the utility derived from the functional, utilitarian, or physical performance that reflects the quality of the physical outcome of using a service (Sánchez-Hernández, Martínez-Tur, Peiroe, & Ramos, 2009). For instance, a consumer booking a week's holiday in a four-star resort in Florida will have a set of functional elements from which the functional value is derived: for instance, the quality of the bedding, cleanliness of the room, quality of the restaurant (décor and food served), quality of staff service, etc. To a large extent, the studies presented in Chapter 8 on SERVQUAL evaluate those elements.
- Then the second value category, *hedonic values,* translates rather the affective and symbolical dimensions, the feelings and emotions generated by the service consumed. Various categories of affective values exist. According to Sheth, Newman, & Gross (1991), the types of emotions elicited range from security and excitement to anger, romance, passion, fear, or guilt. Needless to say, this dimension is essential in any type of experiential context and it is particularly dominant in tourism experiences. In the example given in the previous paragraph, one can easily see how the week's holiday in a Florida-based resort, beyond its functional components will also (and primarily) produce a whole range of other values covering notions of excitement, passion (between individuals or by practicing a favorite activity), deep-relaxation, etc.
- A third dimension is associated with *social contacts:* the perceived value is associated with the possibility of enhancing social self-concept and increasing social contacts with outsiders as much as insiders (family, friends, etc.).

Values, and especially hedonic values, are in fact more complex than presented here and various researchers have attempted to interpret this diversity by producing more detailed sets of values. One typical reference in this line of thoughts is a study conducted by Sheth, Newman, and Gross (1991) who identified five types of consumption values:

- functional (utilitarian and physical performances);
- social (association with social groups);
- emotional (feelings and affective states aroused from the experience);
- epistemic (curiosity, novelty, desire for knowledge);
- conditional (how the context justified a choice as being the correct one).

Lai (1995) produced a typology of different types of values adapted from Sheth et al. (1991):

- functional (utilitarian performance);
- social (associations between the product and a social class);
- affective (product capacity to elicit feelings);

- epistemics (knowledge desire and curiosity);
- conditional (capacity to adapt to the constraints of the situation);
- hedonic (pleasure);
- esthetical (beauty and personal expression);
- holistic (coherence of the product with other products purchased).

The logical next question is: How to operationalize this notion of value from a marketing and managerial viewpoint?

## The means-end-chain approach

The differences between functional and hedonic approaches to satisfaction are complex and difficult to resolve. The truth is that neither approach can be rejected. Even if tourist products are hedonic, a consumer always integrates, to a smaller or larger extent, the functional components of a service delivery when he/she evaluates it.

So far, we have addressed in this chapter one way to address this issue. With the notion of value, we can envisage that functional components contribute, among others, to the overall value of an experiential service.

Another way to envisage this relationship is not in a longitudinal approach but rather as a process. Hence functional components can also be seen as a means to achieve some ends. The means would be represented by all the functional components of the service delivery and the ends by the values presented in the preceding section. The means-end-chain as proposed by Gutman (1982) was defined as follows:

> Means are objects (products) or activities in which people engage (running, reading). Ends are valued states of being such as happiness, security, accomplishment. A means-end chain is a model that seeks to explain how a product or service selection facilitates the achievement of desired end-states.
>
> (Gutman, 1982, p. 60)

## The means-end-chain model

Gutman's model is based on several assumptions whereby values (or desired end-states) are portrayed as playing a dominant role in the choice process. The model assumes that all consumers are capable of associating particular consequences to specific actions and this might be achieved with specific questioning techniques such as laddering. The means-end-chain model suggests that:

- Values sought by an individual will lead his/her desires for products that will provide certain consequences;
- Consumers will opt for products which will provide them with the maximum of desired consequences while minimizing the undesired consequences;

- These consequences are assimilated as benefits, in other words, the advantages consumers derive from the consumption of products and services;
- The benefits can be of a psychological and sociological nature;
- Values being ordered by importance; it follows that consequences linked to important values will be perceived as more important than those leading to less important values;
- Therefore, values will direct both the selection of specific attributes and their relative salience in relation to these end-states;
- The marketing implications resulting from this model includes market analysis and segmentation, product planning, and promotional strategy.

It is important to note that this model investigates values with a different meaning from those presented in the previous section.

- Those values are inspired by the work of Rokeach (1973): "A value is an enduring belief that a specific mode of conduct or end-state of existence is personally or socially preferable to an opposite or converse mode of conduct or end-state of experience" (p. 5).
- Rokeach identified 18 instrumental and 18 terminal values whereby terminal values were defined as relating to the end-states of existence such as security and happiness while instrumental values related to modes of behaviors such as courage, honesty, and so on.

## TOURISM AND HOSPITALITY INSIGHTS 9.5
## THE MEANS-END CHAIN FOR A GROUP STAY AT A SKI RESORT

The notion of togetherness has become increasingly important in tourism consumption and it is essential for providers to understand which service components respond to this specific need. The need for togetherness goes back to the terminal value of family security, happiness, and true friendship (taking care of loved ones) and to the broader instrumental value of being loving and cheerful. To achieve this togetherness, families/groups of friends need to rent accommodation (concrete service attribute) where there is enough space to accommodate each member of the family/group (functional benefit) and where there is enough space to spend quality time together (psychological benefit).

**How can this analysis translate into concrete implications for providers?**

In the case of French ski resorts, most of the accommodation is provided in rented flats. When conducting interviews with tourists who come in groups (at least two families together or two groups of friends), it is interesting to identify what are the key qualities of the accommodation they are looking for, qualities that can contribute to the feeling of togetherness. These groups need to find accommodation that can accommodate all of their group; as a result, they seek to rent large properties (of more than three bedrooms) or at least accommodation located in the same building, or ideally on the same landing. Whilst this might seem a detail, it is not. These tourists want to spend time together so large dining tables and good cooking facilities (being able to cook for more than four individuals) are important to them. When investigating the booking process of these groups, interviews reveal that finding large properties was a key criterion when booking. So, when a group decided to book accommodation for its winter holiday, it was the availability of such accommodation that was crucial in influencing their decision. So far, no resort has guaranteed twin flats (with the same landing) or large properties as a selling advantage on their booking website . The first resort that will be able to understand fully the needs of those groups and offer large properties to rent will secure a lot of bookings.

Source: Frochot I. and Kreziak D. (2015) Étude de l'expérience client à Val Thorens, Déconnection, immersion et réenchantement à 2300m, unpublished report.

- This list was also named the Rokeash Value Survey (RVS) (Rokeash, 1973) and is operationalized by asking respondents to rank each set of values by order of importance.
- Rokeach argued that, once learned, values were ordered hierarchically into a value system and each would be allocated different weights.
- Values are portrayed as emanating from culture, society, and personality influences and are conceived as more stable over time than attitudes since they are considered to be more central to an individual's cognitive system.

Whilst the means-end-chain model is particularly useful, it can be cumbersome to use and collect data. As a result, a reduced version of the model is being used whereby consumers are segmented according to their main motivations (psychological consequences one may say) and then their perception of quality is investigated.

McCool and Reilly (1993) produced an interesting study in which motivations and the importance consumers attach to some attributes were investigated. The authors stated that:

Since expected benefits are the outcomes of the visit to a park, we would expect visitor behavior to be consistent with those benefits. Behavior would reflect the visitor's way of organizing the components of the setting the visitor controls to achieve those benefits.

(McCool and Reilly, 1993, p. 4)

The study investigated consumer ratings of the attributes of state parks in the Montana region. The research identified four benefit segments (enthusiasts, passive players, escapists, and group naturalists) which appeared to differ significantly in terms of the importance customers attached to the park's attributes such as the degree of naturalness, little evidence of others, water access, and little development. Tourism and hospitality insight 9.6 illustrates how quality perception and importance changes according to motivation segments.

## Co-creation and value in use

Whilst quite intuitive, the notion of co-creation has been developed from the early 2000s onwards with service dominant logic or SDL (Vargo & Lusch, 2004). The idea behind the SDL is to reconsider the place of the consumer in the service process. Indeed, over the years, most marketing strategies considered that a company serving a consumer but not really a company working with the consumer would create a service with a higher value. In this line of thought, various stakeholders have specific knowledge and skills and are therefore involved in the conception of services and products.

## TOURISM AND HOSPITALITY INSIGHTS 9.6
## HOW BENEFITS SOUGHT TO INFLUENCE THE PERCEPTION OF QUALITY

In Chapter 8, a scale evaluating quality for historic houses was presented. The study identified that, in this context, consumers could be categorized along four segments based on benefits. Benefits are another approach to segment consumers according to the experience they are seeking at the destination. The results identified that consumers could be placed into four segments:

- *Casual historians:* Seeking to gain some knowledge but with a casual approach to their visit which they also see as a leisurely outing;

- *Browsers:* Like and consume each side of the properties visited. A large part of them own a loyalty card which explains this behavior;

- *Historians:* Very keen knowledge seekers. They seek learning and understanding and only the heritage side of the property is of interest to them (the park, shopping facilities, etc. are very much secondary);

- *Family trippers:* Only interested in the outdoor facilities to spend time with their young children, and also enjoy the restaurant and shopping facilities.

**Image 9.2**

Source: Image: https://www.pexels.com/photo/architecture-india-agra-delhi-62348/

In that same study consumers were encouraged to evaluate the five quality dimensions identified with the HISTOQUAL scale (Chapter 8). Table 9.3 details those results.

Table 9.3 Means of importance scores of service quality dimensions for each benefit cluster

| Factors | Casual Historians | Browsers | Historians | Family Trippers |
| --- | --- | --- | --- | --- |
| **Tangibles** | 4.68 | 4.80 | 4.72 | 4.71 |
| **Communications** | 3.53 | 3.48 | 4.29 | 1.96 |
| **Consumables** | 3.04 | 3.12 | 2.08 | 3.20 |
| **Responsiveness** | 2.95 | 2.94 | 3.06 | 2.81 |
| **Empathy** | 2.39 | 2.76 | 2.15 | 3.03 |

Source: Frochot, I. (2004). An investigation into the influences of the benefits sought by visitors on their quality evaluation of historic houses' service provision. *Journal of Vacation Marketing, 10*(3), 223-237.

As a reminder, these key dimension definitions were as follows:

- *Responsiveness:* Willingness to help consumers and provide prompt service;

- *Tangibles:* Physical facilities, equipment, and appearance of personnel;
- *Communications:* Information and guidance provided about the site;
- *Consumables:* Subsidiary services such as the restaurant and shop;
- *Empathy:* Individualized attention provided to customers.

Overall, what the study indicates is that visitors value first and foremost the tangible dimension. Then, communication elements are most important for consumers who are very attached to the historical dimension of the site (historians) and these same consumers pay the least attention (of all the segments) to the consumables and empathy dimensions. Family trippers are most in need (beyond tangibles) of consumables and empathy because, with young children, they are in need of special assistance and specific services.

What these types of studies indicate is really quite intuitive: a consumer, depending on his motivations or benefits, will seek different elements to achieve them. These elements will be different according to the range of motivations displayed by the individual.

Source: Frochot, I. (2004). An investigation into the influences of the benefits sought by visitors on their quality evaluation of historic houses' service provision. *Journal of Vacation Marketing, 10*(3), 223–237.

User generated content websites integrating consumer feedback, specific co-creation workshops, and focus groups are all strategies that can be developed to encourage co-creation. For instance, LEGO encourages its fans to submit designs and discover other fans' creations on their community website. When projects reach 101,000 votes then can be adopted by LEGO and selected as a new LEGO product that will be sold.

The SDL approach also considers that the value of a service is revealed when it is consumed. The idea behind the SDL approach is that:

- a service gains value in the eyes of the consumer because it is co-created;
- the company sells a product or service that calls for some competences on behalf of the consumer;
- the involvement of the consumer in producing this service creates higher value than a product/service that is simply "bought." For instance, a ready-made dessert pack for making a cake will achieve higher satisfaction if the consumer adds an egg and milk to produce the cake. The consumer will have the satisfaction of having "baked" the cake and perhaps might even have shared this experience satisfactorily with his/her children.

## Conclusion

This chapter challenged the well-established approaches to service satisfaction as they are known and have been reviewed in Chapter 8. These theories cannot be rejected altogether since they have provided useful tools to measure quality. However, consumers' quality perceptions are rather complex and the notion of zone of tolerance, satisfiers/dissatisfiers and comparative measures bring a useful insight in their ways of evaluating a service. The active role of consumers in service delivery also needs to be integrated in this reasoning. If involving consumers is one of the key components of experiential services' delivery, then the notion of co-construction is very important.

## REVIEW QUESTIONS

1.  Provide three examples of how expectations shape satisfaction across the tourism and hospitality industry.
2.  Why do expectations vary so much between the different sectors of the tourism and hospitality industry?
3.  What is co-creation and how does it contribute to a satisfactory tourism or hospitality experience?
4.  How has user generated content changed the face of consumer decision making in the different sectors of the tourism and hospitality industry?

## YOUTUBE LINKS

### *"Understanding customer services: customer expectations"*

URL: https://www.youtube.com/watch?v=kl4sblpQj44

Summary: This video presents clearly what customer expectations are and how they are influenced by different sources of information. It also investigates how companies can inherently provide a service that matches those expectations. It includes looking at timetable issues, financial, and legal issues and understands that there might be some conflicting expectations.

### *"Five essentials for creating a differentiated customer experience"*

URL: https://www.youtube.com/watch?v=jsL_eX8jQWA

Summary: This video provides a different vision to satisfying customers and goes well beyond service quality traditional approaches to focus on what brings customer delight. Notions of kindness, pro-activeness, providing extra-benefits, showing gratitude and putting oneself in consumers' shoes (empathy) are presented. This video provides a mix of some service quality learning combined with the more recent advances in experiential marketing, as presented in Chapter 6. It is a refreshing vision of customer care and how to bring about delight.

## *"Discovering the Kano model"*

URL: https://www.youtube.com/watch?v=Gm-UgLKxdzk

Summary: This video provides a detailed analysis of the Kano model. It explains the four categories of requirements. Performance requirements are those resulting in satisfaction when fulfilled. Basic requirements detail those elements that are "must-be" and that will create dissatisfaction in their absence but won't create satisfaction in their presence (because they are expected). Excitement requirements are the WOW factors, innovative elements that create surprise and will satisfy by their presence but won't dissatisfy by their absence.

## *"Means-end-chain (MEC) 2014 examples AIC"*

URL: https://www.youtube.com/watch?v=qL604JVmVFE

Summary: This video provides a detailed explanation of all the steps in the means-end-chain model from the benefits right through to the value. Where the video is interesting is in its capacity to provide clear examples detailing how the means-end-chain can explain some behavior observed in the market. The examples given are mostly about products but the analysis of the benefits and how they relate to higher order values is interesting. It looks at products such as hair spray, flavored potato crisps, mouthwash, FedExDelivery, pickup trucks or perfumes. It will be an interesting exercise to produce the same level of thinking for various tourism and hospitality products.

## *"Laddering works LLC"*

URL: https://www.youtube.com/watch?v=X84T-waZuyo&t=57s

Summary: This video explains the strategic usefulness of using the laddering technique to gain consumer intelligence. Eric Holtzclaw explains how laddering helps managers to get consumer minds to go back to the source of their decision. Why do they buy a product? What does a purchase relate to in their lives? What do they like or dislike about services' features?

---

### REFERENCES, FURTHER READING, AND RELATED WEBSITES

#### References

Gutman, J. (1982). A means-end chain model based on consumer categorization processes. *Journal of Marketing*, 46(2), 60–72.

Herzberg, F., Mausner, B., & Snyderman B. (1959). *The motivation to work*. New York: John Wiley & Sons, Inc.

Kano, N., Seraku, N., Takahashi, F., & Tsuji, S. (1984). Attractive quality and must-be quality, *The Best on Quality*, 7, 165–186.

Lai, A.W. (1995). Consumer values, product benefits and customer value: A consumption behavior approach, in NA. In F.R. Kardes & M. Sujan (Eds.), *Advances in consumer research*, vol. 22 (pp. 381–388). Provo, UT: Association for Consumer Research, Pages.

Llosa, S. (1997). L'analyse de la contribution des éléments du service à la satisfaction: Un modèle tétraclasse. *Décisions Marketing, 10* (January–April),81–88.

Martilla, J.A., & James, J.C. (1977) Importance-performance analysis. *Journal of Marketing, 41,* 77–79.

McCool, S.F., & Reilly M. (1993). Benefit segmentation analysis of state park visitor setting preferences and behavior. *Journal of Park and Recreation Administration, 11*(4),1–14.

Oliver, R.L. (1981). Measurement and evaluation of satisfaction process in retail store. *Journal of Retailing, 57,* 25–48.

Oliver R.L. (1993). Cognitive, affective and attribute based of the satisfaction response. *Journal of Consumer Research, 20,* 418–430.

Rokeash, M. (1973). *The nature of human values.* New York: The Free Press

Sánchez-Hernández, R.M., Martínez-Tur, V., Peiró J.M., & Ramos, J. (2009). Testing a hierarchical and integrated model of quality in the service sector: Functional, relational, and tangible dimensions. *Total Quality Management & Business Excellence, 20*(11), 1173–1188.

Sheth, J.N., Newman, I., & Gross, L. (1991). Why we buy what we buy: A theory of consumption values. *Journal of Business Research, 22*(2), 159–170.

Vargo, S.L., & Lusch, R.F. (2004). Evolving to a new dominant logic for marketing. *Journal of Marketing, 68,* 1–17.

Westbrook, R.A., & Oliver, R.L. (1991). The dimensionality of consumption emotion patterns and consumer satisfaction. *Journal of Consumer Research, 18,* 84–91.

## Further reading

Alegre, J., & Garau, J. (2010). Tourist satisfaction and dissatisfaction. *Annals of Tourism Research, 37*(1), 52–73.

Baker, D., & Crompton, J. (2000). Quality, satisfaction and behavioral intentions. *Annals of Tourism Research, 27*(3), 785–804.

Bigné, J.E., Andreu, L., & Gnoth, J. (2005). The theme park experience: An analysis of pleasure, arousal and satisfaction. *Tourism Management, 26,* 833–844.

Bitner, M.J., Booms, B.H., & Tetreault, M.S. (1990). The service encounter: Diagnosing favourable and unfavourable incidents. *Journal of Marketing, 54,* 71–84.

Callan, R.J. (1998). The critical incident technique in hospitality research: An illustration from the UK lodge sector. *Tourism Management, 19*(1), 93–98.

Danaher, P.J., & Arweiler, N. (1996). Customer satisfaction in the tourist industry: A case study of visitors to New Zealand. *Journal of Travel Research, 34*(1), 89–93.

Gregory, A.M., & Parsa, H.G. (2013). Kano's model: An integrative review of theory and applications to the field of hospitality and tourism. *Journal of Hospitality Marketing & Management, 22*(1), 25–46.

Gronroos, C. (2015). *Service management and marketing: Managing the service profit logic.* Hoboken, NJ: Wiley.

Johnston, R. (1995). The zone of tolerance: Exploring the relationship between service transactions and satisfaction with the overall service. *International Journal of Service Industry Management, 6*(2), 46–61.

Johnston, R. (1995). The determinants of service quality: Satisfiers and dissatisfiers. *International Journal of Service Industry Management, 6*(5), 53–71.

Li, H., Ye, Q., & Law, R. (2013). Determinants of customer satisfaction in the hotel industry: An application of online review analysis. *Asia Pacific Journal of Tourism Research, 18*(7), 784–802.

Lovelock, C., & Wirtz, J. (2010). *Services marketing: People, technology, strategy.* Englewood Cliffs, NJ: Pearson.

Matusitz, J., & Breen, G. M. (2009). Consumer dissatisfaction, complaints, and the involvement of human resource personnel in the hospitality and tourism industry. *Journal of Human Resources in Hospitality & Tourism, 8*(2), 234–246.

Oliver, R.L. (1980). A cognitive model of the antecedents and consequences of satisfaction decision. *Journal of Marketing Research, November,* 460–469.

Oliver, R.L. (1992). An investigation of the attribute basis of emotion and related affects in consumption: Suggestions for a stage – specific satisfaction framework. *Advances in Consumer Research, 19,* 237–244.

Racherla, P., Connolly, D.J., & Christodoulidou, N. (2013). What determines consumers' ratings of service providers? An exploratory study of online traveler reviews. *Journal of Hospitality Marketing & Management, 22*(2), 135–161.

Sharma, G., & Baoku, L. (2013). Customer satisfaction in Web 2.0 and information technology development. *Information Technology and People, 26*(4), 347–367.

Sparks, B.A., & Bradley, G.L. (2014). A "triple A" typology of responding to negative consumer generated online reviews. *Journal of Hospitality & Tourism Research, 41*(6), 719–745.

Tribe, J., & Snaith, T. (1998). From SERVQUAL to HOLSAT: Holiday satisfaction in Varadero, Cuba. *Tourism Management, 19*(1), 25–34.

Wan, Y., & Chan, S. (2013). Factors that affect the levels of tourists' satisfaction and loyalty towards food festivals: A case study of Macau. *International Journal of Tourism Research, 15,* 226–240.

Wang, Y. (2016). More important than ever: Measuring tourist satisfaction. *Griffith Institute for Tourism Research Report Series Report No. 10,* 1–32.

Zhou, L., Ye, S., Pearce, P.L., & Wu, M-Y. (2014). Refreshing hotel satisfaction studies by reconfiguring customer review data. *International Journal of Hospitality Management, 38,* 1–4.

## Websites

Understanding quality management principles
https://www.sixsigmaonline.org/six-sigma-training-certification-information/understanding-quality-management-principles/

Customer expectations vs. customer satisfaction
https://www.rezdy.com/blog/customer-expectations-vs-customer-satisfaction/

Turning expectations into customer satisfaction
https://knowledge.insead.edu/customers/turning-expectations-into-customer-satisfaction-2606

What is consumer value?
https://bizfluent.com/about-5522239-consumer-value.html

The elements of value
https://hbr.org/2016/09/the-elements-of-value

Seven of the best value proposition examples we've ever seen
https://www.wordstream.com/blog/ws/2016/04/27/value-proposition-examples

## MAJOR CASE STUDY
## SATISFACTION AND DISSATISFACTION WITH REUNION ISLAND AND THE DOMINICAN REPUBLIC

In 2014, Camelis, Maunier, and Llosa produced a very interesting analysis of the service provision on Reunion Island and in the Dominican Republic. Their analysis was inspired by Kano's et al. model and primarily by Llosa's tétraclasse model (1997).

Their vision was to investigate the tourist experience at a destination level, taking on board both private and public components and including local contacts, accompanying persons, etc. In this Tetralasse model, the authors divide the encounters into four categories, according to their contribution to overall satisfaction:

- *Key elements:* Have a high contribution to satisfaction positively and negatively; they are crucial components.
- *Secondary elements:* Contribute mildly to satisfaction whether evaluated positively or negatively.
- *Plus elements:* Contribute to satisfaction when evaluated positively, but do not generate dissatisfaction in their absence. They create a state of enchantment. They are unexpected elements that contribute to satisfaction.
- *Basic elements:* Do not create satisfaction when present but create dissatisfaction when absent (they represent an accepted minimum).

This study investigated these four components through a qualitative study first identifying critical incidents with 107 tourists and identifying 39 elements of the tourist experience. These critical incidents concerned three types of elements: private tourism services (hotels, restaurants, leisure activities), destination-based elements (landscape, architecture, cleanliness, etc.) and human components (local population, other tourists etc.).

**Table 9.4** Items measured

|  | Items | Measure | Scale |
| --- | --- | --- | --- |
| **Destination based elements** | Fauna and flora<br>Landscapes<br>Climate<br>Pollution<br>Historic and cultural sites<br>Architecture<br>Cleanliness<br>Signage | I enjoyed fauna and flora<br>I enjoyed landscapes<br>Climate was overall favourable<br>I did not suffer from pollution<br>I appreciated historic and cultural sites<br>I enjoyed the architecture<br>I appreciated sites' cleanliness | Don't agree at all (1) –<br>Totally agree (7) |

*(Continued)*

**Table 9.4** (Cont.)

| | Items | Measure | Scale |
|---|---|---|---|
| | Roads' network<br>Public transports<br>Sites' accessibility<br>Atmosphere<br>Time difference | On the road, directions were clearly indicated<br>I appreciated the quality of the roads' network<br>I was satisfied with public transports<br>Sites were accessible easily<br>I appreciated the general atmosphere<br>I coped well with the time difference | |
| **Service providers elements** | Overall flight-in satisfaction<br>Overall flight-back satisfaction<br>Overall satisfaction with accommodation<br>Price for value of accommodation<br>Overall satisfaction towards catering services<br>Price for value of catering services<br>Overall satisfaction towards entertainment<br>Price for value of entertainment<br>Reliability of rented vehicles<br>Taxi<br>Shopping<br>Shop keepers attitude | I was overall satisfied with the flight-in<br>I was overall satisfied with the flight-back<br>I was overall satisfied with accommodation<br>Accommodation had good value for price<br>I was overall satisfied with catering services<br>Good price for value of restaurants<br>I was overall satisfied with leisure and entertainment facilities provided<br>Price for value of entertainment facilities<br>Reliability of rented vehicles<br>I was overall satisfied with taxi services<br>I enjoyed shopping<br>I appreciated shop keepers attitude | Don't agree at all (1) – Totally agree (7) |
| **Human factor elements** | Meeting with local population<br>Hospitality<br>Local culture<br>Local traditions and folklore<br>Local level of living | I have enjoyed communicating with local population<br>I appreciated the inhabitants' hospitality<br>I have enjoyed immersing in the local culture<br>I enjoyed local traditions and folklore | Don't agree at all (1) – Totally agree (7) |

*(Continued)*

**Table 9.4** (Cont.)

| | Items | Measure | Scale |
|---|---|---|---|
| | Security<br>No racism<br>Guides<br>Other tourists present<br>Meeting up with other tourists<br>Behaviour of other tourists<br>Family/friends presence<br>Family and friends pleasure felt<br>Health of friends and family | The difference in standard of living did not perturb me<br>I feel totally in security on the island<br>I did not suffer from segregation or racism<br>I enjoyed the guides accompanying us<br>I enjoyed other tourists'' presence (number and density)<br>I enjoyed meeting up with other tourists<br>I appreciated the other tourists' behaviour<br>I enjoyed spending this holiday with my family/friends presence<br>I enjoyed the fact that my Family and friends seemed to enjoy their holiday<br>I was relieved that none of the travel party felt ill or had an accident | |
| **Global satisfaction** | SATI1<br>SATI2<br>SATI3<br>SATI4 | What is your overall satisfaction with your trip at the Reunion Island?<br>In comparison to your expectations, your holiday at the Reunion Island was…<br>Your holiday at the Reunion has…<br>After your holiday at the reunion Island, you felt.. | Very unsatisfied (1) - very satisfied (7)<br>Much worse than expected (7) -much better than expected (1)<br>Really pleased me (7) – really not pleased me (1)<br>Very unhappy (1) – Delighted (7) |

**Source**: Camelis, C., Maunier C., & Llosa, S. (2014). Faut-il envisager différemment la gestion de la satisfaction et de l'insatisfaction des touristes ?. 1ère Conférence Annuelle AFMAT, 21 Mai, Aix en Provence.

Those 39 elements here then converted into a questionnaire administrated to 190 tourists in Reunion Island and another 153 tourists visiting the Dominican Republic. Those consumers had to have visited one of the two islands in the previous 12 months and for holiday purposes.

The results of the study identify the four categories of elements as follows:

- *Key elements:* They are in a majority linked to the human factor (meeting up with the local population, local traditions and folklore, accompanying persons). Of all elements, travel companions are the most impactful element on satisfaction. Those elements are stable across the two tourist islands investigated and contribute highly to the satisfaction, whether they are evaluated positively or negatively.

- *Basic elements:* The landscapes and the hotel and catering value-for-money elements contribute significantly to dissatisfaction when they are evaluated negatively. But they have a low impact when evaluated positively. In other words, those elements are part of the basic expectations from consumers and they are regarded as normal (i.e. it is normal that a restaurant should serve quality food or that the landscape should be pretty to look at, etc.). So, if those elements are up to expectations they go unnoticed and do not impact satisfaction since they are considered as normal. Inversely, if the landscape is disappointing, if the level and quality of service in key tourist experience elements are deficient (typically hotels and restaurants), then they will highly influence consumers.
- *Plus elements:* For the Dominican Republic, those elements referred to the historical and cultural sites and architecture, cleanliness of the destination and availability of transport. Those elements are unexpected from consumers; therefore, their level of expectations is slow and when they are performing well, they create a real positive surprise and impact satisfaction highly (enchantment). Positive interactions with other tourists also constitute a "plus" element.
- *Secondary elements:* Accessibility to tourist sites, flights, signage, and a safe destination. Those elements are comparatively less important than the other categories.

When looking at the impact of satisfaction and dissatisfaction, the elements that are most stable are those related to dissatisfaction. There are clearly some key and unavoidable elements impacting this dissatisfaction (Table 9.5).

However, regarding satisfaction, elements are quite different between the two islands.

Beyond the differences between the two islands, those two tables mostly show that factors contributing to satisfaction are different from those contributing to dissatisfaction.

**Table 9.5** Top ten elements contributing to dissatisfaction

| | The Reunion Island<br>Experience elements Loadings | The Dominican Republic<br>Experience elements Loadings |
|---|---|---|
| 1 | Landscapes 1,236<br>Other tourists' behaviour 0, 953<br>Accompanying persons 0, 931<br>Guides 0, 859<br>Satisfaction accommodation 0, 859<br>Meeting local population 0, 741<br>Hospitality 0,611<br>Fauna and flora 0, 387<br>Architecture 0,387<br>Pleasure accompanying people 0, 387 | Presence accompanying people 1,844<br>Pleasure accompanying people 1,844<br>Landscapes 0,905<br>Accommodation value for money 0,788<br>Traditions and folkloric events 0, 685<br>Accompanying persons' health 0,593<br>Fauna and flora 0,436<br>Meeting local population 0,375<br>Atmosphere 0,202<br>Hospitality 0,188 |

**Source**: Camelis, C., Maunier C., & Llosa, S. (2014). Faut-il envisager différemment la gestion de la satisfaction et de l'insatisfaction des touristes ?. 1ère Conférence Annuelle AFMAT, 21 Mai, Aix en Provence

**Table 9.6** Top ten elements contributing to satisfaction

| | The Reunion Island<br>Experience elements Loadings | The Dominican Republic<br>Experience elements Loadings |
|---|---|---|
| 1 | Accompanying persons' health 0,125<br>Local culture 0,047<br>Hospitality 0,04<br>Local level of living 0,033<br>Shopping 0,03<br>Racism 0;023<br>Meeting local population 0, 018<br>Satisfaction with leisure activities 0,014<br>Accompanying persons 0, 931<br>Traditions and folkloric events 0, 002 | Public transports 0,095<br>Historical and cultural sites 0,084<br>Destination cleanliness 0,084<br>Meeting local people 0, 063<br>Guides 0,052<br>Leisure activities price for value 0,048<br>Traditions and folkloric events 0,037<br>Taxi 0,036<br>Accompanying persons' health 0,027<br>Return flight 0,027 |

**Source**: Camelis, C., Maunier C., & Llosa, S. (2014). Faut-il envisager différemment la gestion de la satisfaction et de l'insatisfaction des touristes ?. 1ère Conférence Annuelle AFMAT, 21 Mai, Aix en Provence.

Major case study questions

1.  If you were the DMO manager in Reunion or the Dominican Republic, you would be encouraged to design a strategy that provides solutions for the elements impacting dissatisfaction. Which strategies/initiatives can be developed to counteract those elements? Then, identify some specific actions that could be developed by those islands by looking at initiatives developed elsewhere across the world and adapting them to the context investigated.
2.  Investigate the sources of satisfaction and understand how those elements could be encouraged even more, or at least maintained.

# Delving deep into the experience

## Learning outcomes

By the end of this chapter, students will:

- Understand how to communicate on an experience
- Comprehend that an experience needs to be prepared by transferring skills to consumers and allowing tourists to anchor themselves at destinations
- Recognize what are flow and optimal experiences and measure their role and importance within the consumer experience
- Understand the place of tourism experiences within the global frameworks of wellbeing, quality of life and happiness.

**Key terms**

preparing to experience, communication, appropriation, optimal experiences, flow, wellbeing, quality of life

## Introduction

Whilst experiential marketing is concerned with managing and developing a satisfactory experience, this chapter looks in more detail at the elements that are constructing the experience, starting from the pre-experience through the dynamics of the experience itself and to the impacts of the experience. Chapter 6 looked at different elements that constitute a memorable experience while Chapters 8 and 9 looked into how services are constructed, evaluated, and orchestrated. This analysis would not be complete if one does not look into how consumers take in an experience, the dynamics that take place at an individual level, keeping in mind a longitudinal vision of this experience. This chapter aims to do just that by arguing that an experience can be constructed and prepared before it takes place. A provider can produce disconnection (one of the prime motivators of contemporary consumers) and boost this disconnection through the construction of optimal experiences, and experiences impact individuals well beyond the tourist encounter. With this chapter, the reader will gain valuable insight into the experience from the eyes of the consumer: What does a tourism experience contribute to individuals' lives? What are the dynamics that are important to consumers and what do these mean for managers trying to deliver successful experiences?

# Preparing for the experience

Whilst the first advances in experiential marketing concentrated on the experience components as outlined in Chapter 6, a lot of work has now been undertaken to understand also how providers can communicate and prepare for the experience.

## Communicating on the experience

Experiences by definition are lived and breathed by consumers. The element of surprise is also a key component of their success. It is therefore complex for a company to communicate on an aspect of its service provision that is largely ineffable, can only take form once lived, and that should not be disclosed in advance. An experience is also a promise that the service will be memorable and will differentiate a company from its competitors.

The communication on an experience needs to emphasize the element of surprise, very much like a trailer for a movie. It has to give hints of elements that the consumer will experience when consuming it without giving concrete information.

Most certainly the best communication tool that can be used to communicate on experiences is through videos.

*   Videos are the best way to provide a clear and vivid vision of the experience. What are consumers likely to experience, at which emotional level is the experience, its pattern, and what will consumers get out of it? The consumer needs to get an indication of the emotional state in which he/she will be/feel once the experience is lived and consumed.
*   The consumer needs to understand if this experience will be in tune with his expectations and values. It is therefore important that this information is given clearly.
*   Positioning is again a key component: understanding consumers' expectations, the situation in which they are (a corporate/team building experience will have a different positioning that one lived with one's family), the age range, etc. In Chapter 7, we investigated psychographic segmentation techniques that allow managers to understand what consumers are expected to get out of their experience. This is a key element that should always guide the communication strategy.

At the end of Chapter 6, the major case study on Lux* Hotels and Resorts invited the reader to study the website of this company to discover the types of experiences that can be lived in this resort. Here again, through the range of videos, the consumer can get a glimpse of the type of events that might take place throughout his/her stay. Not all the experiences are transcribed into videos. The videos only last a few seconds, but overall, they give a clear indication as to how this company includes experiential components in its offer. It helps the viewers to understand its experiential positioning without revealing all its key components and all its surprises. It sets the tone, does not reveal all the experiences, and keeps the interest of the consumers going.

## TOURISM AND HOSPITALITY INSIGHTS 10.1
## GHOST STORIES

As an example, Ghosts and Gravestones is a company based in Boston that runs ghost tours of its location. Its objective is to base its products on sensations, thrills, and chilling ghost stories.

Watch their inviting video on: https://www.youtube.com/watch?v=4OuRkkqMMu8

The tune of the speaker, the background music, the pictures depict an experience that would not leave anyone indifferent. The focus is clearly put on eliciting chilling emotions among participants, with guides that are here to take visitors on a specific journey. Guides are trained to be intimidating but not scary individuals to set the tone of the visit. The visitors are seen undertaking the visit in a mini-bus, therefore giving a concrete vision to the experience being set out for them. The tourists shown in the video are clearly enjoying their tour. The playful component of the tour can be sensed through the different videos' settings and aim to reassure the consumer. The video is here to create a desire, say something about the arrangement of the tour, yet without being too specific about the stories and the constitution of the tour. The consumer can also clearly see whether he/she feels that this product will match his/her expectations.

Source: Isabelle Frochot.

Lately, companies have also invested in 3D glasses that allow their consumers to visualize a setting as if consumers were in the place. Mountain resorts have invested in those glasses for promotional shows and this helps them to allow consumers to have a clearer experience of their resort: how it feels to be at the top of the resort, looking up and down and around. It allows consumers to gain a better idea and get closer to the emotions they would feel if they were physically in that destination.

## *"Training" consumers before an experience*

Preparing for the experience is a notion that is rather new in the field of experiential marketing and one that is crucial to the success of the experience. By definition, in the tourism and hospitality industry, most consumers are not from the area they are visiting and this can contribute to various difficulties.

When tourist consumption involves some specific skills, for instance in a lot of outdoor activities, the provider will usually check the competencies of the consumer before the experience. This often involves an evaluation of how good a person is at rock climbing, high altitude mountaineering, or surfing that is evaluated with various official grades, evaluations, or at least a very clear description of the level expected from the consumer. This is important for security reasons but also because the activities are practiced in groups, and require the whole group to be at the same level.

When fewer physical activities are involved, evaluation of a level of competence is not so important, although multi-cultural skills are a necessary component of traveling. As a result, some tour operators have elaborated some codes of conduct to help tourists by providing them with traveling advice.

Codes of conduct aim to:

- Help travelers understand how they should behave when traveling.
- Encourage visitors to adopt more responsible forms of behavior that will create less tension and or negative impressions locally.
- Develop empathy so that tourists' behavior is more in tune with local customs.
- Encourage tourists to behave in a more respectful/sustainable way; in other words respect also the local environment.

## TOURISM AND HOSPITALITY INSIGHTS 10.2
## APUS PERU'S TRAVELERS' CODE OF CONDUCT

Apus Peru is a travel agency specializing in adventure trekking in Peru. They have produced a code of conduct to encourage their consumers to comply with environmentally- and socially-sustainable practices. They see this code as particularly important because the agency offers "off the beaten track" trekking and tour experiences, which often take their clients through remote areas vulnerable to environmental damage and cultural change. The guidelines are designed to minimize participants' impact on the areas visited, explain acceptable and respectful behavior, and awareness of cultural differences as far as local culture is concerned.

Day to day...

*Be sensitive to local customs*

Conduct that may be acceptable at home may not be acceptable in the Andes! Please be aware that things like recreational drug use, nude sun bathing, loud conversations in public places, and boisterous public behavior are not appropriate here.

Be aware of your own cultural values, and how they affect your judgement of others. In the Andes, different concepts of time, personal space, and communication norms exist. These are not wrong or inferior, just different.

If you encounter some of these cultural differences and notice yourself getting frustrated, try to take a step back and remember that you are the one visiting this new landscape.

*Be a positive cultural ambassador*

Often our perception of other cultures is skewed by TV and other media. Now is your chance to let everyone know what it is *really* like in your home country! Look for those special moments where you can really connect with someone, whether that's the person next to you on the bus or the person serving your meal, and learn from each other. These are some of the most rewarding experiences you will have on your trip!

Cultural exchange is great, but be careful about what you choose to share. Photos of your home or on holidays could end up emphasizing difference rather than highlighting similarity and promoting solidarity.

### Be respectful and responsible

- *Churches* are first and foremost places of worship for local residents. Please be quiet and respectful when you visit them.
- *Photography*: Do you like your photo being taken without your permission? Always *ask first* before taking someone's photo!
- *Do not support* businesses that utilize forced or child labor.
- *Archeological artifacts and endangered species*. It is *illegal* to remove archeological objects or artifacts made from exotic or endangered species. *Do not* purchase or take any such items!
- *Say no* to sex tourism and human trafficking of any kind, especially that involving children and teens.

### Be flexible

One of the best things about traveling to new places are the unexpected and often serendipitous things that can happen. Travel with an open mind and you will *not* be disappointed! When plans change, go with the flow – you never know what amazing new experience it might lead to!

### Be a good shopper

Many visitors to Peru come with the expectation of finding really good deals. While in the urban centers it is often OK to bargain, don't forget that the handful of soles you might be saving may actually make a difference to the seller and their livelihood. In remote communities, haggling is not done and can actually seem insulting to the seller. If you are offered a price for something, it is expected you will pay that price.

### Giving gifts

Visitors to Peru are often painfully aware of the different standard of living that many Peruvians experience, and feel compelled to do what they can to help. This is a very noble and understandable sentiment, but you must be very careful about what and how you give gifts as they can create undesirable side effects, like corruption, jealousy, and a begging mentality where none existed before.

### Gifts to avoid

- candies and chocolates
- loose change

- anything packaged – packaging will inevitably become litter
- fridge magnets (most rural families do not have refrigerators)

*Recommended gifts*

- fresh and dried fruit – oranges, peaches, apples, raisins
- bread
- hats, t-shirts
- shampoo, toothbrushes and toothpaste (though the packaging will become litter)
- Spanish-language reading books or picture books. Please be sure to give books to the local school. Your guide can accompany you to meet with the teacher. Do not give books to individuals.

Other recommendations include:

- Practicing environmental minimum impact (complying with law, regulations and restrictions)
- Follow the international "Leave No Trace" rules (bio-degradable soap and rechargeable batteries for your flashlights and cameras; travel and camp on durable surfaces, etc.)
- Solid waste (collect any litter, bring your own refillable bottle water, take all rubbish with you, collect all organic food waste in a green bag)
- *Say no* to plastic water bottles and bags
- Encourage minimal use of energy and water

Image 10.1

Source: Isabelle Frochot/https://www.apus-peru.com/responsible-travel/travellers_code_of_conduct.html

Beyond sustainable and responsible behavior, tourism service providers have also come to realize that in many situations, tourists are unaware and lack knowledge about local practices and customs. This aspect has often been disregarded at tourism destinations because most providers assume that consumers will have the "skills" to consume a destination. But sometimes very simple elements are unknown to tourists and because they don't have that inside knowledge, they are likely to live a less memorable experience. This is an important element to take into consideration since most contemporary visitors live in urban areas and have often lived there through several generations. This means that those consumers have the basic skills to enjoy some encounters. The extended case study/exercise at the end of this chapter encourages the reader to develop strategies to transmit those skills to visitors.

Beyond the "simple" notion of skills, tourism actors might also want to investigate how consumers can feel more at home in a new holiday environment. To understand this process, the concept of appropriation produces an interesting analysis.

## Tourists' appropriation

- A consumer needs to identify and feel more at ease with their new setting and thereby feel more comfortable with a new place (whether it is a destination, a hotel, a resort, etc.).
- Appropriation refers to the process that allows tourists to feel "at home" and more relaxed in a new experience universe.

Appropriation has been explored by Carù and Cova (2006) in a study that investigated how new consumers got themselves immersed into a classical music concert. They studied consumers attending a classical music concert for the first time to understand how they managed, or not, to appropriate this new experience context. They modified the conductor's guidance: in the first part of the concert the conductor arrives and introduces the piece that is going to be played. He is dressed informally, explains the storyline, and indicates the role that each instrument will play (one will represent birds songs and another one the wind in the leaves, etc.). In other words, the conductor supplies the codes that will help this new audience make sense and feel more at ease with the concert. In the second part, the conductor comes back dressed formally, turns his back to the audience and the orchestra begins to play. The researchers then interviewed the consumers to find out to what extent they felt at ease with the concert. Did they get "into it" and how did they react to the two performances by the conductor. Through this study, Carù and Cova (2006) identified three appropriation steps: (i) nesting (recreating home); (ii) investigating (exploring surrounding space); and, (iii) stamping (the personal meaning assigned to the experience).

- *Nesting* refers to the human need to feel "at home" in new situations: "the individual feels at home because part of the experience being faced has been isolated, a part that is already familiar because of one's accumulated experience and existing foothold in it" (Carù & Cova, 2006, page 6). Nesting equals a search for and identification of anchorage points and can be experienced through physical and mental sensations. In Carù and Cova's study (2006), the referents given by a conductor in his introduction to a classical music concert helped consumers identify points of anchorage.

- *Investigating:* Refers to any action that, from the nest, will see consumers exploring physically and identifying other products/services that will create new points of anchorage and control called "signposts" (Carù & Cova, 2006, p. 7). This process involves observing, describing, and exploring and by doing so, consumers feel more comfortable because they have extended their territory. In Carù and Cova's study (2006) the consumers mention that the conductor's directions given before the concert help them to "find their way" through the concert by being able to understand which sounds come from which instruments and what they refer to in the music's storyline.

- *Stamping:* Refers to the personal meaning consumers attach to their experience. In the case of concerts this might remind consumers about concerts (of any type) they used to attend as a child with their grandfather, etc.

## Boosting the experience: flow and optimal experiences

The need for contemporary consumers to get away from everyday life, stresses, and frustrations has been mentioned on a number of occasions in this book. Once at the destination, tourists want to immerse themselves into this new setting, and this immersion might be improved via the strategies developed in the previous section.

However, we have also reviewed different approaches to experiential marketing that clearly point to the central place of positive emotions and to the importance of creating long-lasting memories. As we have seen, those elements can be created by designing experiences that are able to reach consumers and resonate with them. One way to understand which key experiences impact consumers is to investigate the notion of optimal experiences.

Optimal experiences are particularly interesting parts of the tourist experience because they are able to create intense emotions and create long-lasting memories. Moreover, they are clearly boosters to disconnection. Optimal experiences create a positive "shock to the system" that helps consumers disconnect even more.

## TOURISM AND HOSPITALITY INSIGHTS 10.3
## SYLVAIN RABUEL CEO CLUB MED FRANCE EUROPE AFRICA

Le Club Med has been in existence since 1957 but has evolved significantly in terms of positioning and client offer.

What are the specificities of consumer demand for your offer nowadays?

S. Rabuel: Gérard Blitz, the Club Med founder, used to say that "What is important in life is to be happy. The time to be happy, it's right now. The place to be happy, it's here [au Club Med]." This mission is still present in Club Med today, but to achieve this, we have had to adapt and especially "premiumrise" our products to stay in line with the evolution of consumers' comfort expectations. Beyond this aspect, our customers expect to feel restored by their holiday, get back in touch with themselves, and reconnect with their families. They also expect to use this privileged holiday time to indulge in their preferred activities or to discover the world. We aim to create listening Club Med a location where consumers can fulfill their various expectations. When we achieve this, the holidays experienced by our consumers will transform them; they will come back different and more able to confront their daily life.

Beyond the notion of experience, you also use the notion of "client consideration"?

S. Rabuel: I am absolutely convinced that our clients want to feel considered for what they are, and for their idiosyncrasies. Nowadays, the reference to big data has started a trend to consider them as targets rather than king consumers who have a private life that needs respecting. Tomorrow, I think that they will have the power to decide with whom they will share their data and to operate a conscious choice. Within Club Med, we have tried to be pioneers of the consideration economy which implies:

- Guaranteeing to our consumers the control over their personal data;
- Provide an individualized and reactive answer to their needs;
- Co-create the future of our enterprise with our consumers.

**Which innovations have you developed in response to the evolution of this demand?**

S. Rabuel: We aim to collect information that helps us to provide a quality consumer journey. In our agencies, we offer our clients an immersive experience to gain a better vision of our destinations with virtual reality glasses, thereby arousing positive emotions long before their departure. Beyond our digital innovations, we have just launched 70 Club Med signatures: various services and considerations in order to provide an individualized, unique and reactive answer to consumers' needs. For example, with the signature 63, "Prepare children from head to skis," we give our clients the opportunity to dress their children for skiing.

**It is particularly complex to understand the subtleties of consumer demand evolution. How do you develop your consumer intelligence?**

S. Rabuel: The consumer consideration concept has encouraged us to develop collaborative initiatives where consumers are involved into the design process of our brand in the future. We have launched clubmakers.fr platform that allows our clients, but also our collaborators, to suggest ideas and to vote for those that they feel are most appropriate and that we will develop in the long run. We have also modified our governance and have opened our departmental meetings: nine consumers (fairly loyal to primo-consumers), will participate in our meeting, because they know their own needs, to have a direct input in co-constructing tomorrow's Club Med. We have already had two of those open committees and we are planning to pursue this initiative.

Source: Interview with Sylvain Rabuel, CEO of Club Med France, Europe and Africa, December 2017.

**Image 10.2**
Source: https://www.pexels.com/photo/beach-beautiful-blue-clear-water-279574/

Optimal experiences have been studied for some time and can have different meanings. The first part of this section will detail flow experiences, then we will move on to the broader notion of optimal experiences.

### *Flow as a key experiential component*

As early as 1968, Maslow identified a concept named the peak experience. Peak experiences are defined as moments of highest happiness and fulfillment, which can be achieved through the consumption of activities such as art, intellectual insight, aesthetic perceptions, nature experiences and so forth. If religious experiences and exotic travel can produce peak experiences, Maslow also suggested that peak experiences may be felt by ordinary people in somewhat normal common circumstances. Optimal experiences are not so much triggered by the activity itself but by the ecstatic feeling that is experienced while doing it.

The concept of flow, fairly similar in nature, was introduced later. This concept, borrowed from psychology, has been historically associated with the work of Csíkszentmihályi (1991) who produced a detailed analysis of the flow concept and its mechanisms. Flow, as conceptualized by Csíkszentmihályi (1991), is a mental state that develops when an individual performing an activity is fully immersed and totally focused, fully involved, and enjoys the activity. Flow is a holistic sensation that people feel when they act in total involvement.

One of the prime elements that condition the occurrence of flow is the congruence between an activity, one's level of skills, and the perception of the challenge of the activity. The challenges experienced in an activity must also be high for flow to occur. For instance, cooking a plate of pasta will rarely create flow (although it is probably at the skill level of the domestic cook). However, skiing in powdery snow will create intense feelings of flow (as long as it matches the skier's level of skills). The main characteristics of flow have been defined as follows (Csíkszentmihályi, 1991):

- Intrinsic enjoyment;
- Loss of self-consciousness;
- Skill/challenge balance (notion of optimum level);
- Intense focused attention;
- Immersion in the activity;
- Clear goals;
- Immediate but not necessarily ambitious feedback;
- Sense of control over the environment and actions;
- Momentary loss of anxiety and constraints;
- Enjoyment and pleasure.

Activities are seen as being conducive to flow if they have been designed to ease the access to this state: 'they have rules that require the learning of skills, they set up goals, they provide feedback, they make control possible' (Csíkszentmihályi, 1991, p. 72). The intensity of such an experience leads people to totally forget their surrounding environment (including the notion of time) and the intrinsic reward of the activity could lead people to seek experiences at great cost, for the simple objective of doing it. The notion of intensity of the experience is important though: "flow is likely to occur when a context exists that pushes individuals to near their physical and mental limits, without overwhelming them" (Celsi, Rose, & Leigh, 1993, p. 12).

However, there is clearly an important distinction to be made between short-lived pleasures and those that impact consumers more deeply. Csíkszentmihályi (1991) differentiates the notions of pleasure and enjoyment. Enjoyment is usually conceived as an optimal experience. Pleasure, on the other end, is considered as a reflex response

## TOURISM AND HOSPITALITY INSIGHTS 10.4
## FLOW IN OUTDOOR ACTIVITIES: MOUNTAIN BIKING

Would a mountain bike experience create a flow experience? Let's imagine Mr. Taylor who has booked a long weekend in the Loch Lomond National Park in Scotland with two friends who also practice mountain biking. The group of three friends has been practicing mountain biking for some years and have similar levels of competence. As soon as he starts, a combination of the effort needed to power the bike, pacing his effort, making sure he stays on the path, mean that the biker will be fully absorbed in his activity. This focused attention will mean that Mr. Taylor will be completely immersed in this activity and will no longer think about either work or personal problems. Mr. Taylor does not necessarily want to undertake this activity with a competitive spirit. There is no reward and it is not a race. He might want to challenge his friends from time to time, but the element of competition is out of his experience. His goals are clear. They had already studied the paths in the park and had set up the routes they would take during their long weekend. He has enough experience to feel in control of his bike and he is satisfied that the group of friends have chosen a level of difficulty similar to his.

The flow increases itself through a feeling of deep enjoyment and pleasure. Obviously, the activity contributes heavily to this feeling but the company of his friends plus the amazing surrounding of the National Park are also part of it.

If Mr. Taylor had been an inexperienced cyclist, he would have been left behind by the group. He might have felt anxious (not feeling in control, fear of falling, and not being fit enough, etc.). He might have felt frustrated by slowing down his friends, and this negative feeling will have been overwhelming. Equally, if the level of the paths taken were clearly below his level, he would have still enjoyed it (the cycling, friends' company, and the surroundings) but he would have experienced few flow episodes.

Does this example mean that flow is directly associated with competencies? According to the definition of flow provided by Csíkszentmihályi (1991), it is indeed a prerequisite. However, providers can develop strategies to bypass this difficulty. They can provide training for their consumers but they also use technology to ease this process. Indeed, technological advances have allowed the development of electric bikes. With these bikes, consumers, even inexperienced ones, are able to reach, master, and conquer paths and hills they would have been incapable of mastering previously. The advent of electric bikes is a real booster to the experience and a technological advance that is able to make cycling available to a wider range of tourists that are currently not necessarily considering cycling as a tourist transport mode or activity (senior citizens, women, families with children, etc.). It can also be an even bigger provider of flow episodes for those consumers since some of them might consider cycling again and feel very satisfied with their achievement when they had stopped practicing it.

Source: Isabelle Frochot.

genetically imbedded in human beings. For instance, a human being will experience an instant pleasure from relieving his anger by eating some food, felling warmer by lighting a fire, etc. Usually this type of pleasure is considered as evanescent: one might experience great pleasure from relieving anger with a good meal but this pleasure will be short lived. Enjoyment seems to be related much more vividly to optimal experiences and is more interesting because it is longer lasting and impacts memories more deeply. Since we have already identified that one of the key outcomes of experiential marketing is to create memorable experiences, and taking on board the impact of experiential digital WOM, it is essential for practitioners and academics to fully understand those experiences.

Is flow necessary to provide a successful experience? While some researchers argue that consumers need an extraordinary event to create an intense and unforgettable experience (Arnould & Price, 1993), others indicate that not all experiences need to be extraordinary to procure a pleasurable experience (Carù & Cova, 2006). This aspect is worth mentioning since, in the case of tourism, consumers seek at times calm and relaxing moments, therefore, flow is not the only feature of their holiday experiences. Flow would also be tiring if experienced over a long period and on a very recurrent basis. It is therefore more interesting to consider that flow occurs only in some episodes during the holiday. Moreover, one can clearly see that some intense holiday experiences are not always extraordinary in the purest sense of the word. For instance, connecting with one's children by building a sandcastle and defending it from the incoming tide for hours, might be lived as a key experience and a strong connecting moment. An encounter with a local person, who welcomed the family to his farm and taught them to make blueberry jam might also be an extremely fulfilling experience. It is out of the ordinary but probably not extraordinary in the sense that has been given to flow experiences. Those experiences develop deep feelings of joy, togetherness, and strong emotions but in fact they are quite banal. It is what emanates from them that makes them extraordinary. The notion of optimal experiences refers to those encounters.

## Optimal experiences

Optimal experiences is a term often used for flow experiences, but it might be more accurate to consider that flow is one type of optimal experience. Flow has been studied in various contexts but it is often associated with the practice of an activity. Because the notion of flow requires some form of skill, thereby it is very much connected to an activity that, indeed, requires competences. Some authors have investigated the possibility that other elements could provide optimal experiences.

Campbell (1987) indicated that pleasure can transform itself into enjoyment but only under certain conditions. Campbell argues that this process happens only if:

*   Intensity of attention is produced by the experience;
*   Consumers develop a sense of achievement;
*   Consumers gain psychological growth from the experience.

This approach is interesting to understand the visitor experience, since, indeed, most tourism providers will acknowledge that: a) they are unable to provide constant experiences of flow, b) this would also be tiring for visitors, and c) clearly all optimal experiences do not fully match the description of flow. This is a very interesting question really because if one follows Campbell's vision, it does explain that some key experiences can be qualified as optimal even if they don't match all the flow experiences' characteristics.

This would explain that for instance a cooking class organized for tourists in Thailand might provoke an optimal experience:

- People are in full attention, trying to understand how the recipe unfolds (ingredients, equipment, cooking strategies) with the objective to be able to reproduce the recipe once back at their home;
- Tourists will develop a sense of achievement: they have succeeded, let's say, in mastering the process for cooking a Thai green curry;
- Tourists might also experience psychological growth in terms of self-confidence;
- They might also develop a feeling of having developed a closer connection with the destination.

This type of optimal experience is interesting because it is rather simple to organize, does not bear resemblance to the physical activities presented previously, and is conductive of enjoyment. Obviously, the notion of skills is somehow still present (if the cooking class was set at a very high level of competencies, most participants would switch off and in any case the instructor is here to transmit some of those skills), but expectations of skills are positioned at a very low level.

Tourism and hospitality insights 10.5 displays analysis of a group of consumers, identifying key optimal experiences during a five-day stay and provides an interesting insight into the elements contributing to the experience.

## After the experience

Traditional marketing has generally established that the major elements to consider in the post-purchase stage were related to quality and satisfaction evaluations (usually orchestrated with quantitative questionnaires after consumption and those will be addressed in Chapter 11). Post-purchase evaluations were also concerned with studying and analyzing loyalty behavior, aiming to identify ways and devices to boost loyalty. With the advent of the Internet, the notion of word of mouth has taken a brand-new dimension and the digital resonance of consumers' experiences cannot be ignored and needs to be monitored, encouraged, and driven.

## TOURISM AND HOSPITALITY INSIGHTS 10.5
## THE LA PLAGNE STUDY

This study investigated how the consumer experience evolves throughout a holiday. This study was conducted with ten tourists who were interviewed every evening of their stay, during a five-day stay. With this research protocol, the researchers wanted to investigate how a consumer experience evolves and changes, as the holiday unfolds, and what are the contributing components to this change. Presented here are the results focusing specifically on optimal experiences.

The stay involved skiing as the main activity but the group investigated undertook a snow shoeing experience on the second day. The experience was a key highlight of the holiday since first and foremost, all the participants in the group were at the same level of competencies. Even if the balance of challenge and skill was much lower, it did not stop participants from achieving flow. The other important dimension was the fact that participants were in a different setting: a field of powdery snow, away from the resort. Participants could finally see what they called "real snow." Whilst they were surrounded by snow at the resort, during the snowshoeing experience, the fact that they could touch powdery snow, and make their own prints in the snow, created intense emotions. There was a strong element of magic (and even discovery) associated with powdery snow. The social dimension of group bonding was evident in this experience. When comparing the snowshoeing to the ski experience, one can see that the characteristics of flow could be found but again well-defined goals did not clearly appear.

On day three, a new episode of flow took place, when the weather cleared up. Whilst this might seem evident, the quality of the skiing was identified as an important component but more importantly, it was the view (that participants finally discovered on that day) that became the main component of their enjoyment: "*When I arrived at the top of the resort and suddenly discovered the view, I got taken over by the magnitude of the landscape, its sheer beauty and magnitude, it just took over me*" (Marie-Charlotte, day three). In this instance, not all characteristics of flow could be found. This episode created a lot of emotions and pleasure (the sheer joy of looking at a beautiful and overwhelming landscape) but flow characteristics such as skill/challenge balance, clear goals, and sense of control were clearly absent from this episode. Moreover, with this good weather, participants split into small groups of friends to ski, and the social connections that took place on this day was clearly a strong contributor to their enjoyment.

Most interestingly, but unsurprisingly, when those consumers were interviewed one year later, only those two experiences stood out in their memory.

This study goes to show how flow can be identified in some experiences but the notion of optimal experiences is most probably more interesting. Flow is one of those optimal experiences but experiences with clear esthetical values (landscape) or bonding between group members turned out to be as intense as optimal experiences.

Whether they might be qualified as flow or optimal experiences, they are key drivers to a vacation and need to be investigated to understand how providers can create a tourist offer that includes them.

Source: Frochot, I., Elliot, S., & Kreziak, D. (2017). Digging deep into the experience: Flow and immersion patterns in a mountain holiday. *International Journal of Culture, Tourism and Hospitality Research, 11*(1), 81–91.

Beyond those elements of loyalty and digital resonance, the tourist experience has also been investigated in relation to its place and impacts on consumers' existence. Decades of research can provide very useful pointers, and we have chosen to present in this section a few concepts only: quality of life, wellbeing, and eudaimonia.

## Quality of life (QOL)

Quality of life is a holistic concept that looks at individuals' and societies' perceived quality of various components fueling their everyday lives. Various definitions and indicators measuring QOL exist and won't be discussed here. Usually they include measures of life satisfaction such as physical health, education, employment, finance, family, etc. The media and politicians always like to report on various indicators. For instance, the World Happiness Report has pointed to the quality of life observed in Nordic European countries such as Norway, Denmark, Iceland, and Finland.

Among the existing studies, Richards (1999) identifies that vacations contribute to QOL through their capacity to generate social interactions, personal development, and improve individual identity. Lyu et al. (2018) identified that cruise vacations have a direct effect on life satisfaction, although this impact is rather short lived.

Whichever indicators might be used, researchers call for caution with measures that could be restrictive in their capacity to evaluate the real meaning of quality of life and it is commonly accepted that measures of QOL are much more appropriate when allowing an element of subjectivity: "an individual's subjective evaluations of the degree to which his or her most important needs, goals and wishes, have been fulfilled" (Frisch, 2000, p. 220). QOL should integrate some element of subjectivity and should refer to a more general feeling of contentment with one's life, how individuals view their life and how they feel about it (Andereck et al., 2007). Hence, the definition of QOL is often interchanged with that of subjective wellbeing which we will address thereafter.

## Wellbeing

Wellbeing can be conceptualized as an objective concept and "relates to the idea of fulfillment of materialistic demands and access to physical, environmental, social, and other resources" (Hartwell et al., 2016, p. 5). The capacity to fulfill those aims is necessarily conditioned by resources: 'In essence, stable wellbeing is when individuals have the psychological, social, and physical resources they need to meet a particular psychological, social, and/or physical challenge' (Dodge et al., 2012, p. 230).

To name a few, various studies have identified clear links between vacations and elements of wellbeing:

- Gilbert and Abdullah (2004) demonstrate that having taken a vacation recently was clearly associated to a higher sense of wellbeing, after the holiday but also before. Hence, the holiday anticipation phase is also conductive of a sense of wellbeing.
- Westman and Eden (1997) demonstrated the impact of vacations on the reduction of burnout.
- Strauss-Blasche (2000) confirmed the improvement of moods and sleep quality during a vacation.

## Subjective wellbeing

Beyond the notion of wellbeing, that of subjective wellbeing (SWB) is also commonly used. SWB encourages the development of measures that can move away from classic indicators such as level of income or career success to reconsider wellbeing as a subjective perception of what will make an individual feel happier in his/her life. It is often interchanged with the concept of life satisfaction and happiness. Subjective wellbeing questions the extent to which individuals are contented overall with their life and what really makes them happy.

In a study on tourists in Macau, Lam and So (2013) demonstrated that leisure satisfaction is directly conductive of life satisfaction that then brings about positive word of mouth. Their study shows that it is through the increased appreciation of subjective wellbeing that consumers become more active providers of word of mouth.

Gilbert and Abdullah (2004) characterize SWB with three components: lack of negative emotions, high positive emotions, and life satisfaction. Their study indicates a small increase in SWB after a vacation.

In a review of the SWB concept, Laing and Frost (2017) list the key qualities of wellbeing including: personal growth, authenticity (being true to oneself), positive relationships, environmental mastery (identifying an environment that suits one's personal needs and abilities), and excellence.

Overall, studies investigating QOL and SWB are deeply rooted in the notions of eudaimonia and within the field of positive psychology.

## Eudaimonia and hedonia

- *Eudaimonia* refers to Aristotle's concept describing deep wellbeing in life, and is associated with living a virtuous life, reaching excellence, and allowing individuals to reveal their full potential.
- Eudaimonia is often contrasted to *hedonia* which focuses more on the pleasure of an activity, enjoyment, life satisfaction and lack of discomfort.

We shall end this discussion here and one will have clearly understood that all the concepts addressed in this section have a strong overlap. More importantly, it is not the objective of this book to discuss the importance of vacations in individuals' lives. However, these theories can bring an extremely interesting view in understanding the mechanisms at stake in the achievement of highly satisfactory experiences. With these approaches, one can see how the mechanisms and principles addressed in the studies of wellbeing can be adapted to the context of tourists' experiences. The approaches detailed in positive psychology are particularly interesting in that regard since they bring pointers to the mechanisms that can help individuals increase a sense of deep satisfaction (Filep et al., 2017). As an example, two prevailing models can bring some interesting cues to help developers enhance the impact of their tourism experiences:

- PERMA model: Seligman (2011) has developed mechanisms and exercises that would help individuals naturally fight depression rather than reverting to medical assistance. The PERMA model stipulates that to achieve a deep feeling of satisfaction with life, individuals need to cultivate: positive emotions, engagement, relationships, meaning and achievement.
- Another model currently used is that of DRAMMA (Newman et al., 2014), which lists five characteristics of subjective wellbeing: autonomy, mastery, meaning, affiliation and detachment-recovery (detachment from everyday life and work and the possibility of recuperating).

**Image 10.3**

Source: https://www.pexels.com/photo/casual-cliffs-enjoyment-environment-590510/

Inspired by those approaches, Tourism and hospitality insights 10.6 shows how a tourist destination might use some of these mechanics to increase tourists' wellbeing while at the destination.

## Transformation

To finish, one of the outcomes of those key experiences is the impact that they can have on human beings. This element has been studied under the concept of transformation which investigates to what extent a tourist experience might impact consumers at different levels (physically, mentally, etc.). Whilst most of the marketing literature has focused on satisfaction, quality, and loyalty in previous decades, experiential marketing is getting more interested in combining some of the knowledge addressed in the previous section to understand how some experiences transform visitors. The vision here is to look beyond producing satisfactory holidays to produce vacations where consumers can experience a deep sense of change and a transformation that will stay with them. If the outcome of experiential marketing is to create long-lasting memories, then the concept of transformation can help providers understand how these can be formatted.

## TOURISM AND HOSPITALITY INSIGHTS 10.6
## POSITIVE TOURISM – MY SERENITY IN VAL THORENS SKI RESORT

The resort of Val Thorens has chosen to develop an approach inspired by positive psychology as part of their experiential marketing strategy. Their concept is to use and simplify some key mechanics developed in the positive psychology field and redeploy a simplified version to the holiday context.

    The resort has produced a small booklet that first introduces how happiness can be achieved in everyday life, what are the origins of stress and how to identify them, and a simple method that tourists can use during their stay. The booklet also explains in simple terms how some experiences can reduce stress and improve happiness. For instance, contemplating a mountainous landscape reduces heartbeat and stress, etc.

    Then the booklet encourages visitors to learn to take a step back and appreciate what they are living. On a page of the booklet, consumers are encouraged to write in one column what did not go well during the day and what stood out positively. Then tourists single out three key positive experiences during the day and think about them before they go to sleep, thereby improving sleep quality and decreasing stress levels (a simpler version would be to write down simply the three outstanding experiences of the day, similar to what is encouraged in the PERMA approach). Then another section of the page is dedicated to improving tourists' feelings of personal efficacy in order to boost self-confidence. Tourists are encouraged to write down parts of their day when they felt they had improved themselves/gained new competences.

Source: Isabelle Frochot/http://www.valthorens.com/presse/h2018/My_Serenity_Fr.pdf

In a study on life changing vacations, Kirillova et al. demonstrate how "a transformative tourist experience necessarily implies a greater awareness of existential concerns and heightened sensitivity to existential anxiety, which encourages a tourist to seek a more authentic lifestyle" (2016, p. 11).

Lately, the use of physical measures has come as a new approach to evaluate this transformation. Various indicators can be used such as heartbeat or transpiration. In 2015, Kim and Fesenmaier investigated travelers in Philadelphia, monitoring their electrodermal activity. The study identifies strong variations of emotions along the trip and that this is both continuous and discrete: all along the trip there are higher levels of emotions, and strong peaks are observed with specific activities.

Research in neurosciences, especially on serotonin and dopamine is also bringing some interesting insights. For tourism experience designers, it is certainly a field of research that can provide another vision and understanding of the processes taking place within an individual, the factors impacting them and how providers/destinations can translate this information into the design of new experiences.

## Conclusion

This chapter has aimed to bring a more detailed vision of the processes at stake within the experience. These components are newer in the experiential marketing horizon but they can find their inspiration in theories and models that have been developed for some time, especially in the psychology field. Whilst some of these notions might seem remote from the preoccupations of tourism managers, they bring a very interesting, detailed, and analytical vision of the components that trigger deep experiences. The notion of optimal experiences is particularly important since those key experiences accelerate tourists' disconnection and fuel memories. Beyond those experiences, the more general knowledge brought about by studies on wellbeing, quality of life, and the general approach in positive psychology are equally important since they bring some interesting pointers to mechanisms, elements, exercises that can be redeveloped within tourist experiences and boost their impact. The start of the chapter also pointed to the necessity to provide tourists with skills that will improve their connection with a tourist universe and experience. This awareness is more recent and is another element to take into consideration if tourism providers want to ameliorate tourists' access capacities to an experience. The following case study will encourage readers of this book to elaborate a strategy in relation to those essential components.

### REVIEW QUESTIONS

1. Explain why it is essential to introduce consumers to an experience. How does it impact the quality of the experience?
2. Why is the notion of appropriation such an important element in tourist experiences?

3. Why are optimal experiences key components of the tourist experience?
4. Define the notion of wellbeing and explain how it can be related to the tourism experience.

## "Interpretation tips for tour guides – interpreting culture, the environment, history and heritage"

URL: https://www.youtube.com/watch?v=HkhTY7UWi4M

Summary: This video is presented by two tour guides who review the key interpretation principles as developed by Sam Ham. It gives pointers to the main elements that need to be present in a guided tour: theme, organization, relevance and enjoyment.

## "Flow by Mihaly Csíkszentmihályi/animated book review"

URL: https://www.youtube.com/watch?v=8h6IMYRoCZw

Summary: This video presents the concept of flow as it is related to the larger notion of happiness. It points to the limits of belonging in relation to happiness and points to the power of flow experiences. It differentiates flow from anxiety, boredom, and apathy. The video makes some connections with TV viewing or Facebook, to point out which activities really create flow.

## "Quality of life survey: top 25 cities"

URL: https://monocle.com/film/affairs/quality-of-life-survey-top-25-cities-2017/

Summary: This video shows how quality of life indicators are used and portrayed in the media to provide lists of the "best cities" according to their criteria. This video is aimed to people wanting to move to those cities but they give an indication of the different components that individuals might consider when they envisage moving to a city. It is evident that any improvements that are undertaken in urban centers will necessarily also impact the tourist experience.

References

Arnould, E.J., & Price, L.L. (1993). Rivermagic: Extraordinary experience and the extended service encounter. *Journal of Consumer Research, 20*(1), 24–45.
Campbell, C. (1987). *The romantic ethic and the spirit of modern consumerism*. Oxford: Blackwell.

Carù, A., & Cova, B. (2006). How to facilitate immersion in a consumption experience: Appropriation operations and service elements. *Journal of Consumer Behaviour, 5,* 4–14.

Celsi, R., Rose, R.L. and Leigh, T.W. (1993) An exploration of high-risk leisure consumption through skydiving. *Journal of Consumer Research, 20*(1), 1–23.

Csíkszentmihályi, M. (1991). *Flow: The psychology of optimal experience.* New York: Harper & Row.

Dodge, R., Daly, A.P., Huyton, J., & Sanders, L.D. (2012). The challenge of defining wellbeing. *International Journal of Wellbeing, 2*(3), 222–235.

Filep, S., Laing, J., & Csíkszentmihályi, M. (2017). *Positive tourism.* London: Routledge.

Frisch, M., Cornell, J., Villanueva, M., & Retzlaff, P. (1992). Clinical validation of the quality of life inventory: A measure of life satisfaction for use in treatment planning and outcome assessment. *Psychological Assessment, 4*(1), 92–101.

Gilbert, D., & Abdullah, J. (2004). Holidaytaking and the sense of well-being. *Annals of Tourism Research, 31*(1), 103–121.

Hartwell, H., Fyall, A., Willis, C., Page, S. Ladkin A., & Hemingway, A. (2018). Progress in tourism and destination wellbeing research. *Current Issues in Tourism, 21*(16), 1830–1892.

Kirillova, K., Lehto, X., & Ca, L. (2016). Tourism and existential transformation: An empirical investigation, *Journal of Travel Research, 56*(5), 638–650.

Laing, J.H., & Frost, W. (2017). Journeys of well-being: Women's travel narratives of transformation and self-discovery in Italy. *Tourism Management, 62,* 110–119.

Lam, D. & So, A. (2013). Do happy tourists spread more word-of-mouth? The mediating role of life satisfaction. *Annals of Tourism Research, 43,* 624–650.

Lyu, J., Mao, Z., & Hu, L. (2018). Cruise experience and its contribution to subjective well-being: A case of Chinese tourists. *International Journal of Tourism Research, 20*(2), 1–11.

Newman, D.B., Tay, L., & Diener, E. (2014). Leisure and subjective well-being: A model of psychological mechanisms as mediating factors. *Journal of Happiness Studies, 15,* 555–578.

Richards, G. (1999). Vacations and the quality of life: Patterns and structures. *Journal of Business Research, 44,* 189–198.

Seligman, M.E.P. (2011). *Flourish.* New York: The Free Press.

Strauss-Blasche, G., Ekmekcioglu, C., & Marktl, W. (2000). Does vacation enable recuperation? Changes in well-being associated with time away from work. *Occupational Medicine, 50*(3), 167–172.

Westman, M., & Eden, D. (1997). Effects of a respite from work on burnout: Vacation relief and fade-out. *Journal of Applied Psychology, 82*(4), 516–527.

## Further reading

Anderek, K.L., & Vogt, C.A. (2000). The relationship between residents' attitudes toward tourism and tourism development options. *Journal of Travel Research, 39,* 27–36.

De, S., & Bispo, M. (2016). Tourism as practice. *Annals of Tourism Research, 61*(November), 170–179.

Dolnicar, S., Yanamandram, V., & Cliff, K. (2012). The contribution of vacations to quality of life. *Annals of Tourism Research, 39,* 59–83.

Edensor, T. (2007). Mundane mobilities, performances and spaces of tourism. *Social & Cultural Geography, 8*(2), 199–215.

Holt, D.B. (1995). How consumers consume: A typology of consumption practices. *Journal of Consumer Research, 22* (June), 1–16.

Kim, J.J., & Fesenmaier, D.R. (2015). Measuring emotions in real time: Implications for tourism experience design. *Journal of Travel Research, 54*(4), 419–429.

Larsen, J. (2007). Aspects for a psychology of the tourist experience. *Scandinavian Journal of Hospitality and Tourism, 7*(1), 7–18.

McCabe S. (2002) The tourist experience and everyday life. In G.M.C. Dann (Ed.), The tourist as a metaphor of the social world (pp. 61–75). Wallingford; Cabi Publishing.

O'Shaughnessy, J., & O'Shaughnessy, N.J. (2002). Marketing, the consumer society and hedonism. *European Journal of Marketing*, *36*(5/6), 524–547.

Otto, J.E., & Ritchie, J.B.R. (1996). The service experience in tourism. *Tourism Management*, *17* (3), 165–174.

Schouten, J. & McAlexander, H. (1995). Subcultures of consumption: An ethnography of the new bikers. *Journal of Consumer Research*, *22*, 43–61

Tussyadyah, L.P. (2014). Toward a theoretical foundation for experience design in tourism. *Journal of Travel Research*, *53*(5), 543–564.

Wang, N. (1999). Rethinking authenticity in tourist experience. *Annals of Tourism Research*, *26*(2): 349–370.

## Websites

Green hotelier: talking point
http://www.greenhotelier.org/our-themes/community-communication-engagement/talking-point-educating-guests-more-sustainable-tourism/

Huffington Post: "Flow" experiences: the secret to ultimate happiness
https://www.huffingtonpost.com/lance-p-hickey-phd/flow-experiences-happiness_b_811682.html

Positive psychology center
http://ppc.sas.upenn.edu/

Positive psychology: living in the glow: what is it and how to enter the flow state?
http://positivepsychology.org.uk/living-in-flow/

Mindfulness for wellbeing and peak performance
https://www.futurelearn.com/courses/mindfulness-wellbeing-performance

Tourism intelligence network
http://tourismintelligence.ca/2014/04/14/enhance-your-product-with-dynamic-nature-interpretation-activities/

# MAJOR CASE STUDY
# VISIT YOUR DESTINATION

Earlier in this chapter, we investigated the idea that consumers need to be "trained" before an experience. We are not referring to sporting activities where a level of competence is clearly required. We will instead analyze in this exercise the capacity and necessity that destinations have to develop communication schemes that pass destination skills onto consumers.

Those skills are composed of practice elements that are often associated with the specificities of a destination and culture.

To illustrate those different elements, two examples are given. For the first illustration, please log onto the *Iceland Academy* website. This website was created by Visit Iceland to provide tourists with useful advice on their country. Their idea was to communicate their specificities, whether those relate to their settings, their culture, or practices. Visit Iceland intended to share those elements with tourists in order to help them access a better experience and also to encourage them to be more respectful towards their environment and culture.

- *Driving in Iceland:* This video gives some clues about driving on Icelandic roads. The advice given refers to dealing with snowy conditions and speed limits. It also communicates on-the-bridge specificities: more crashes are caused by non-Icelandic drivers on narrow bridges.

Website: https://www.inspiredbyiceland.com/
icelandacademy/driving-in-iceland/

- *The best outfits:* this video provides advice to visitors about what to pack in their suitcases. One might think that those indications are evident but they are not necessarily for consumers who are not Icelandic. These tourists fail to fully understand the northern location of the destination, and are not necessarily keen hikers, thereby not fully equipped. The video provides information about the range of clothes that are necessary to feel comfortable in Iceland. One element, for instance, is to avoid wearing jeans outdoors, because if it rains, they don't dry out quickly. Once wet, they stick to the legs, and become rigid, etc. One can clearly see how even just a small detail can dampen the mood on an outing.

Website: https://www.inspiredbyiceland.com/icelandacademy/pack-warm/

- *Northern Lights:* This video provides useful advice to assist consumers in catching the Northern Lights on their cameras. The video provides information about the best camera settings to catch the Northern Lights, how to best access the sites, and some hints about the long wait that tourists might face. In Chapter 2, we addressed the importance of souvenirs in experiential marketing and this is a clear illustration how to best cultivate them.

## Hiking and learning to hike

Studies in the Alps show that, in summer, visitors do not have the most basic skills to enjoy their experience. What could be a nice and enjoyable hike might turn out to be unpleasant because consumers are unprepared and inexperienced:

- Tourists might have the wrong shoes (and quickly get blisters);
- Tourists do not take enough water (and quickly get thirsty);
- They do not appreciate the pleasure of hiking early in the morning (so they start hiking under a scorching sunshine at midday);
- They cannot read maps or signs properly (so get lost);
- They do not understand why there are no dustbins along the paths (they do not know that in the mountains you take your litter back with you), etc.

Locals could have the tendency to make fun of these clearly inexperienced tourists. But one might want to look at their experience differently and with empathy. These tourists need someone who will take the time to explain those elements to them in order to make their experience much more enjoyable. Again, to visitors or locals accustomed to the mountains, those elements are obvious. To a tourist visiting this destination for the first time, nothing is obvious and they need pointers. Whether it is through a leaflet, a signpost, or on videos, this information needs to be shared with visitors. This aspect is really part of welcoming and should be integrated into a strategy: making visitors feel at home by privileging them to "in-house" information just as you would do for family members visiting your area.

## Major case study question

Following the examples given by the Iceland Academy, you are encouraged to develop a similar approach for a destination that either you live in, or that you know very well. It would be best to base your analysis on a destination that has some natural or specific elements that might require some inside knowledge.

### First step

Analyze what the consumer experience is at this destination by putting yourself in the shoes of a tourist visiting it for the first time and having had no previous experience of this type of environment. Identify what are the pieces of information, skills (even the most basic) that you would need to engage in for a fulfilling experience. Look at practices that perhaps you automatically do, and that a tourist might not know. Look at habits, practices, elements that local people intuitively know and that would be useful to have for those novice visitors. You might want to investigate blogs about this destination, and some TripAdvisor comments might come useful. It would be best to interview local tourism actors and local inhabitants and question them about what tourists systematically seem to do incorrectly; and even interview some tourists.

*Second step*

Draw a list of the key elements that you would like to pass on to first-time visitors to this destination in order to enhance their experience.

*Third step*

Choose two of those elements and for each of them and design a non-condescending, constructive, and clear message.

*Fourth step*

Create two videos of two minutes maximum each to pass on this message to future tourists. Mobile phones can create good quality footage and you can find some free access software to produce videos. In order to construct your video, you will first need to have clearly set out your objectives and the message you want to transmit. Then you should design a story board that details every step of your video and its whole construction (if you need a tutorial go to https://www.youtube.com/watch?v=bMX65SveVuI).

Source: Isabelle Frochot.

# Consumer intelligence searching
## Emerging tools, methodologies, and techniques

## Learning outcomes

By the end of this chapter, students will:

- Understand what are the steps involved in designing a research/consultancy project
- Understand that in each of these steps, choices have to be undertaken to fit with the objectives of the project
- Identify clearly the differences between quantitative and qualitative data collection approaches
- Identify different techniques that can be used to collect data, including data available on the web as much as new technologies allowing a more intimate encounter with tourists' experiences.

## Introduction

Consumer intelligence is fundamental to all marketing processes. Understanding consumers' needs, profiles, behavior online or offline, habits, etc., is an essential component of all marketing decisions. We live in an era where there has never been so much information available. Overall, companies keep on conducting market research to collect data on their consumers, but the era of big data gives managers countless possibilities to collect or capture data on their consumers. We can question, observe, follow, trace offline and online, collect detailed information, and target messages more precisely. Yet, consumers evolve fast. Fashion trends and deeper trends modify their behavior and expectations. The opening up to new markets also means that multicultural differences need to be fully understood in order to provide a satisfactory experience. Hence enterprises spend more money every year on their consumer intelligence gathering. Academics produce extensive knowledge that provides a clearer vision of the concepts and general evolution observed in tourist experiences, and the strategic choices that companies and destinations can make.

Yet, despite this existing and extensive knowledge and intelligence, the understanding of the experience itself is still somewhat in its infancy. First and foremost, this field is comparatively new. It emanated in the early 1980s with real interest only emanating from the 2000s onwards. Second, the experience touches different fields and it is complex to federate and comprehend all this extensive knowledge. For instance, psychologists, sociologists, human geographers, marketers, neuro-psychologists, doctors can all contribute to the understanding of the experience. However, being able to concentrate, digest, and understand the complementary knowledge gained throughout those fields is somehow complex. Third, experiences touch emotions, feelings, and subconscious elements that are intricate to grasp by researchers with traditional market intelligence techniques.

Whilst most market research still uses traditional qualitative and quantitative techniques, new approaches are also emerging that will be addressed in this chapter. First, we will review the different approaches that can be developed to gain consumer intelligence. Then, we will expand onto the newer techniques that are increasing due to technical and digital innovations.

## Academic research and consultancy

The research world is extremely vast and we will only address here its most important characteristics. In the beginning, it is important to make the distinction between research that is conducted in academia, and research that is more applied and informative. Both those approaches are necessary, interesting, valuable and rich, but their purpose is different.

Academic research aims to provide an understanding and a conceptualization of various variables and phenomenon. Its objective is to provide a fundamental understanding of those elements and how they are related to each other. So, for instance, academic research will aim to provide holistic models as much as a very precise understanding of specific variables. So, on one side, academic research might provide a general model looking at the links between different variables. For instance, investigating how satisfaction is related to loyalty and eWOM. Those type of research are very important in providing a general framework through which consumer behavior can be analyzed and understood. On the other side, academic research will conduct projects that aim to understand the structure of a specific variable and how it can be measured. For example, a research project might analyze what are the key components of satisfaction (emotional, functional, etc.) and develop a scale to measure this concept.

Academic research does not provide descriptive analysis of phenomena; its objective is to provide a fundamental understanding of those elements. As a result, academic research projects are lengthy, require a strong methodology, undertake in-depth analysis, and are also evaluated on their capacity to contribute to existing knowledge. Publishing in academic journals has become a fairly competitive process and it is incredibly difficult to publish in the top journals. For instance, *Tourism Management, Annals of Tourism Research*, or *Journal of Travel Research* only accept on average 10% of the articles sent to them. Overall, between the start of a research project, its data collection and analysis, submission of the paper to a journal and finally its publication, it is likely that three to five years will have gone by. It does not mean that this research is not relevant to the industry. It has to be understood as research that provides structural knowledge in order to comprehend the phenomenon at stake. However, this research does not aim to provide a practical, empirical vision of a phenomenon.

History tends to show that academic research is very much ahead in time compared to consultancy. On average, it takes the consulting world at least 15 years to embrace existing academic research and work it into measures and approaches that will be more accessible for the industry. For example, experiential marketing originated in the early 1980s in academia, and became more popular with consultants from 2000 onwards. Both academic and consultancy research are important. They fuel different objectives that are both necessary for knowledge to evolve.

Consultants provide services for a specific request coming from a company or a destination. Their results have to be available much more quickly than in academia. They

**Image 11.1**

Source: Pexels.

can also develop their own models and provide regular measures of some specific aspects of the tourism industry (for instance a ranking of the best destinations, a report on new trends, etc.). Consultancy knowledge is not free and is available for its paying clients, although consultants will make part of their work freely available. Academic knowledge is understood by many to be free, but it is published in books or journals that can be quite expensive (especially academic journals).

## Highlights

- *Primary research:* Aims to produce data to answer some specific research needs. It is directly linked to the objectives of the research and its outcome will be to provide the information necessary to answer those objectives/hypotheses.
- *Secondary research:* Aims to find information that is already out there in the press, reports, books, articles, etc. The idea is to provide a state-of-the-art version of everything that is known about a specific aspect of tourism and hospitality consumption at a certain date in time. A large part of the tourism industry is public and various reports/studies are made available on Internet either by public entities (destinations, etc.) or by major players (Amadeus, PhocusWright, etc.).
- *Tertiary research:* This approach is slightly different and refers to the use of any work that has been related by a third party. For instance, a conference report or a book review are a personal analysis of existing information. It is useful because those reviews often gain invaluable time in accessing information, but one should always remember that they have been reprocessed by an individual and might carry some form of subjectivity.

# How to conduct a research project

The steps laying the path to a research project are quite straight forward but they need to respect certain rules.

## Step 1: literature review

The literature review aims to produce a state-of-the-art synthesis of existing knowledge in a specific field. The objective is to seek and identify the knowledge that is in line with the topic investigated. The material included in the review are primarily academic articles and books but can also include industry reports, websites, etc. The literature review is only composed of secondary information, and eventually tertiary, but never primary information; it only includes existing knowledge.

## Step 2: identify objectives and hypotheses

First and foremost, the most important dimensions of a research/consultancy project are to identify clearly the objectives of the project. What does it aim to uncover?

The objective gives the general direction to the project and once it has been settled, it needs to be translated into various sub-objectives that the data collection will come to prove or reject. These are called hypotheses and their main purpose is to identify the different information that, together, will bring an answer to the general objective. Hypotheses are generally written as a statement that is then accepted or rejected by the results that are identified in the study.

## Example of objectives and hypotheses

The following example concerns a student's master's dissertation that focused on the consumer journey map. Journey maps have been extensively used in service encounters and provide a very interesting insight into how consumers evolve through the premises of a service provider. The dissertation overviewed the notion of service journey in the literature review, explaining its premises, its components, and the methods used to develop it along with its managerial implications. The dissertation is questioning to what extent this concept can be applied to a destination, in this case a seaside resort. In other words, it aims to understand and analyze better the implications that shifting the focus from a service provider's enclosed premises (a restaurant or a hotel), to a broader and diversely managed area (a holiday destination) might incur. The literature review also overviews the concept of destinations: its definitions, its main components, its public and private actors, and its governance. The objectives and the hypothesis come at the end of this literature review section.

*Objective of the research: How can a customer journey approach become a strategic tool to improve the service provision at a destination level?*

- Hypothesis 1: Destination journey maps need to integrate all the tourism actors.
- Hypothesis 2: The design of a customer destination journey map requires consumers' participation.
- Hypothesis 3: Customer journey maps need to integrate all components of the journey such as direct and indirect services.

Then, through data collection, the dissertation author can bring answers to those hypotheses, which means accepting or rejecting them, and provide evidence and reasons for those decisions.

For instance, hypothesis 1 was totally accepted and even subdivided into different responses. For instance, the student identified that different public and private actors were involved in the journey map, that they did necessarily not know each other well, and that they did not appreciate their consumer journey fully. The necessity for those providers to analyze the consumer journey, for example by undertaking a journey in pairs (as mystery shoppers) was seen as a powerful approach to designing the journey.

Hypothesis 2 was accepted, but the student insisted on the difficulties encountered when trying to motivate consumers to take part to the study. Therefore, consumer willingness is an element to take in account: rewards and easily used technological devices could become essential components to the success of consumer participation.

Hypothesis 3 was accepted but the dissertation results pointed to the various managerial responsibilities of the different elements constituting the journey map. For instance, if the actors have a direct role to play in the consumer service, signage, or road upkeep, information pre-arrival turned out to also be key indirect service elements facilitating the consumer journey. Each of those elements refers to a different service within the tourist information center, the town hall services, etc.

The dissertation concluded that customer journey maps can be valuable. They identify key points of impact, zones that should deserve improvement, but they can be complex to design at the scale of a destination. The student showed how and where the difficulties might emerge and the solutions that could be developed.

## Step 3: design methodology

The methodology refers to the approach chosen by the researcher/consultant to address the research question and hypothesis previously reviewed.

Within the methodology should be addressed:

- The context chosen for the study: general context (geopolitical situation, turnover of an enterprise, a brief history, geographical limits if applicable, range of enterprises selected, etc.). This first part aims to set the scene in order to contextualize the project undertaken and make sense of the results that will be identified. The choices made will need to be justified to give more depth to the results and avoid potential criticism (if only the companies from one hotel category have been chosen, this is acceptable as long as it is justified).
- Associated with this context and in line with the statistical techniques that will be used, a sampling strategy has to be developed. The sample size might be constrained by some statistical techniques where a minimum is required. If several sites are selected, a set minimum size per site will be identified, etc. The sample size, in terms of individuals interviewed, will be larger in quantitative techniques than in qualitative ones. In qualitative research, of the interview type, the principle of data saturation will be used: a topic will be considered to have been awarded when a researcher eventually keeps on finding no new information and is comfortable with what he/she has already identified.
- The approaches used will also have to be justified. For instance, according to the hypothesis set out previously, the researcher will decide to develop a quantitative or qualitative data collection (or a combination of both). There are no right or wrong answers in terms of choice of methods. The only good answer is that the

method chosen is the best one to uncover adequate results that will bring answers to the objectives of the study.

- Another strategic choice has to be operated in relation to the techniques that will be used to analyze the data. If a quantitative data collection has been undertaken, a choice of statistical analysis will need to be made: again, it has to be undertaken in relation to the objectives of the study and the data that will be collected. If a qualitative data collection is undertaken, various choices can be made from a computerized quantitative analysis of the corpus to a manual analysis as will be discussed later.

## Step 4: sampling strategies

- *Sample bias:* Researchers should be careful with the possibility that their research protocol might induce a bias in the data collected. Depending on the place of data collection, the times of the day, the week, and the year, the data might drastically differ. When studying a tourism market for instance, the data collected at mid-, low- and high- seasons will yield different results since they are likely to reach different types of clienteles. Equally, conducting a survey in the street during office hours will only reach one type of clientele that a survey conducted every day and at every hour will not reach (it will reach a broader category of the population).
- *Contextual bias:* If investigating the experience, it might also be interesting to take note of the weather on the day when the data is collected. The point of data collection will also have an impact. For instance if collecting data from bed & breakfast, hotels, and Airbnb accommodation in a set area, consumers who are staying with friends and family do not participate. In a country like France, where more than 50% of domestic tourists do not rent commercial accommodation, it would mean not surveying half of the domestic tourist population. This is a considerably large bias. Equally, if leaving the questionnaire on a counter or in a hotel room, it is often the same types of people who tend to answer them, thereby influencing the data collected.
- *Sample representativeness:* One way to avoid bias is to guarantee that a sample is representative of a population studied. For instance, if a tourist population is composed of X% of retirees, and X% of working adults, the sample will aim to match similar proportions through a stratified sample. Finally, if only studying one population, a filter question at the start of the questionnaire will help the researcher to ensure that he/she reaches the correct population to be studied.
- *Response rates:* Generally speaking, people are increasingly tired of answering questionnaires of various sizes and non-response is rather high especially when undertaking quantitative questionnaires. If a reward or a competition will motivate some consumers, overall the response rates tend to reach a maximum of 10 to 15%. This is rather low and thereby implies sending out a large number of questionnaires. Questionnaires sent by mail have similar shortcomings.

- *In situ data collection:* Experience shows that for tourism experiential studies, collecting data when consumers are on holiday is rather effective. First, it might be interesting to spot times when consumers are captive and inactive to submit the survey. Typically, a long queue at a Rome museum, a transit time on a chairlift, a departure lounge in an airport, will provide researchers with consumers who are available to answer questionnaires.
- *Panel data:* larger consultancy firms have established panels of consumers that can be vast and cover consumers of all types of profiles. When the consultancy company designs a survey, they can then choose, within their panels, a specific range of consumers (for instance 50+ teachers, etc.) to answer a specific range of questions. Those panels, with whom the consultancy company has built a relationship, display a much higher response rate. Consultants might also run a large survey (omnibus) within which private companies will be able to purchase a few questions and be privy to the results collected on those issues.
- *Big data:* Big data is a vast term that englobes all the techniques, tools, and processes that allow enterprises and destinations to manage large data sets in order to produce intelligence on consumers. With big data sources, one can measure consumers' behavior, purchases, mobility, etc.

## Step 5: conduct data collection

- Data collection is perhaps not the hardest step in a research project but it can be time consuming. Considering the low response rate, the range of surveys sent out will have to be quite high. The collection might involve interviewers catching respondents, typically in the streets, which is equally time consuming.

## Step 6: produce results

- The results part of a report is the key findings of the study. It needs to be presented so that it clearly answers the objectives of the study. Lengthy, wordy reports are tiresome to read, illustrating the findings with graphs, figures, pictures are essential to keep the interest of the reader. Illustrations are also useful, for instance in a segmentation study, personas might be valuable in illustrating the findings of the study.

## Step 7: implication of results and recommendations

- Whilst the previous section provides an overview of the results as they stand, this section requires the necessity for researchers to distance themselves from the study in order to grasp the overall picture of the information identified, and understand its implications for the company/destination investigated. The results' analysis section needs to go back to this literature and identify to what extent the results found in this research project corroborate or not the original literature review. It is important to identify how and to what extent the results help to strengthen, supplement, or reject existing theories and models.

- *Managerial implications* are a must-do in research projects. It is essential, especially for academic work such as research reports, dissertations or articles, to provide some key managerial implications of the results presented. These can relate to new strategic options, the development of new markets, the improvement of some service features, territorial strategies that should be undertaken, etc. They should clearly be set out and targeted towards the main actors that will read the report.
- *Executive summary:* A report, whether it is research or consultancy-based is heavy to read, no matter how neatly it is written. Most readers, especially if they are in a managerial function, will not have the time to read it completely. An executive summary is therefore necessary: a one or two-page summary of the study that provides the framing of the study and its key findings.

# Quantitative research approach

As was already addressed previously, quantitative research is the approach that has been most used in consumer research. It is an approach that aims to describe phenomena, measure, and draw links between different variables. Quantitative research is extremely rich in offering an overall vision and provides managers with data to assist them make informed strategic decisions. Quantitative research is undertaken over samples that are rather large in order to provide a good and rich vision of the objects investigated. The emergence of big data and the access to endless information about consumers has also helped enterprises gain valuable and detailed access to consumers' intimate knowledge.

The most common tool used in quantitative research is the questionnaire. It can be printed and left on a counter for consumers to fill in (with the bias previously mentioned), administrated by an interviewer or sent most usually via email or post.

## Questionnaire design

Questionnaires are both an easy and challenging task. The basic rule in questionnaire design, like any research project, is that the objectives of the study should be very clearly set out. The hypothesis will call for a data collection that aims to bring sufficient data to answer those needs.

If one has never designed a questionnaire, it might be useful to go through the following steps:

- Develop a list of all the information that is necessary to collect in order to respond to the objectives of the study. Pay attention to the format that will be most appropriate for the study. For instance, if one is investigating usage, is it by month or by year? Does the context matter etc.?
- It is extremely important that the wording used in the questionnaire reflects that used by the consumers.

- Most questionnaires usually consist of closed questions with a set choice of answers. It is important to decide whether these questions will have the option of unique or multiple answers.
- Choice questions are useful when it comes to collecting factual information about individuals (age, socio-economic status, etc.), but their scope is necessarily limited and they reduce the types of statistical analysis that can be applied. Scales can be more interesting when it comes to evaluating an opinion or indicating a strength of importance (see Tourism and hospitality insights 11.1).
- Whichever the option taken, a "does not apply" option always needs to be integrated. If this option is not given and the questionnaire is administrated through a screen/online option, consumers might feel obliged to give an answer whilst they have no answer to give (they might not have used a specific service for instance).
- Open questions are always interesting because they give respondents the opportunity to express themselves openly on elements that either have not been addressed in the questionnaire or that need clarification. It can also be the opportunity to engage with the respondent and let him or her develop some suggestions about the service investigated. Open questions do not have a high response rate. Most respondents fail to reply to them, but the few who do tend to provide

## TOURISM AND HOSPITALITY INSIGHTS 11.1
## HANDBOOKS OF SCALES

Whichever the study a consultant/researcher is engaged with, it is rare that a topic has not yet been addressed in research. It is always useful, and highly recommended, that the researcher should check what are the known scales that can be used in relation to the topic investigated.

Handbook of scales are there to guide researchers to the most common scales that have been developed and used to measure a construct. The scales are selected based on their recognition in academic journals (where they have been published and cited). Many handbooks exist and each of them tends to concentrate on a management and marketing area. Those handbooks are extremely useful since they provide researchers with an overview of the tools available, and are validated academically, so that they can be used to develop their own evaluation instrument.

As an example, Zarantonello & Pawels-Delassus published the *Handbook of Brand Management Scales* (2016) which lists scales that assess brand personality, brand authenticity, consumer-brand relationship, and brand equity. For each of those variables, an introduction frames the variable at stake with a definition of the construct, then a structure of the scale, how it should be used, the scale development process, and managerial implications. For instance, the chapter dedicated to brand authenticity presents four scales measuring: brand authenticity, brand extension authenticity, consumer-based brand authenticity, consumer-brand relational authenticity.

Source: Zarantonello, L. & Pawels-Delassus, V. (2016). *Handbook of brand management scales*. Abingdon: Routledge.

valuable comments. Open questions need to be analyzed via a text analysis (similar to what will be addressed in qualitative data analysis). More simply, if there is a recurrence in the information collected, the answers can be classified into categories and then counted, as one would do for quantitative data.

- Some argue that quantitative research is more objective than qualitative approaches. However, quantitative questionnaires can also influence respondents either through the wording of the question or through its format. A respondent will answer the questions that are being included in a questionnaire and will not answer questions that have not been included in the questionnaire. For instance, asking respondents to rate a range of quality items will provide answers on those elements and give a nice and neat quality scale. However, if those same respondents had been asked to indicate what were the elements that actually mattered to them, the researcher might have come up with a very different answer. For instance, the service quality scale addressed in Chapter 8 evaluates quality on a range of 20 to 25 items. Those scales are particularly useful to monitor quality in a service setting but do not necessarily translate how tourists really evaluate those elements. Regarding holiday experiences, consumers tend to elaborate holistic perceptions and will evaluate quality on broad and general evaluations often relying only on four or five key elements.

- A questionnaire should always be pretested before being used for data collection. Once the data collection has started, there is no possibility of going back and modifying the questionnaire (or if one does, then all the first questionnaires already administrated are invalid). The researcher needs to choose a small sample, let say 30 to 50 individuals, and ideally complete the questionnaire face to face with the respondents. This is the best way to see and prompt respondents to see if they clearly understand the questionnaire, if they, at times, get confused or not, if the question format is appropriate, etc.

## Quantitative data analysis

When working on a questionnaire, data then needs to be collected, avoiding the sampling bias that was addressed at the beginning of this chapter. Collecting can be long and tedious, especially if the data collection is processed via operators who screen and stop consumers in the streets. It is of course much easier to send a questionnaire via the Internet. Email lists, social networks contacts, and panels allow for a specific targeting of consumers. They can also allow researchers to target specific communities, for instance a photography club or an association of volcano specialists, thereby allowing the research to gain consumer intelligence for niche tourism markets. The other advantage of Internet data collection lies with the easiness of processing the data: when a consumer answers a questionnaire online, the results are fed immediately into a computer system and be analyzed quicker. Data analysis is then undertaken, and we shall only outline here the main techniques that can be used and this depends on the nature of the data collected.

## The types of variables

- Categorical variables do not offer a choice of order in the responses given: the data is the result of the consumer choice to a closed question such as marital status, age category, etc.
  - Categorical variables can be binary if only two choices are offered (whether you are a male or female for instance)
  - Categorical variables are nominal if the consumer is offered a choice such as ethnicity, social class, etc.
- Ordinal data encourage the respondents to provide an answer that gives an indication of strength, for instance the number of previous visits (more than four times/between 2 and 4/less than 2/never).
- Continuous variables are either interval or ratio.

Analyzing closed questions: this is the easiest task, and the most basic analysis is to provide some indication of proportions by producing percentages, counts, and presenting these with graphs that allow the reader to quickly grasp this information. The results provided need to be backed up by some statistical analysis which depends on the type of data and which dynamics the researcher aims to identify within the data collected.

---

## TOURISM AND HOSPITALITY INSIGHTS 11.2
## FOCUS ON THE MAIN STATISTICAL TESTS*

- Chi-square = strength of association between two categorical variables;
- Pearson correlation = tests for associations between two continuous variables;
- Spearman correlation = tests the strength of the association between two ordinal variables;
- ANOVA: tests differences between group means;
- Simple regression: tests how a change in a variable predicts the level of change in an outcome variable;
- Multiple regression: tests how a change in two or more variables impacts the level of change in an outcome variable;
- Principal components analysis (PCA) and factorial component analysis: discovering the underlying structure in a set of data;
- Typologies: groups techniques, such as k-means analysis, that arranges data into groups that are cohesive (as close as each other) and as distant as possible from each other. Those can be hierarchical or not;

- Structural Equation Modeling (SEM): allows the modeling of relationships between several variables, including latent variables.

*This table is a quick simplified presentation of different techniques that are quite complex and can only be applied under certain conditions. For more information on statistical techniques please refer to specific methodology books.

Source: Isabelle Frochot.

The analyst needs to remember that most readers are not familiar with statistical techniques and he/she will need to provide clear results that can be easily understood. Supplementary information can be left in the annex section. If writing a research report, it is important that the reader can check that the statistical techniques have been used scientifically and the methodology and the annexes' sections will provide this information. In a consultant report, the focus is concentrated more on the results and implications. Statistical information will also be there to guarantee the rigor of the study but will take comparatively less space in the final report.

Quantitative surveys have always reassured managers and academics through the information that they provide, the size of the samples, and their deep statistical analysis. Quantitative techniques remain a key approach used both by consultants and academics, but over the years, qualitative research has also gained recognition.

## Qualitative research approach

The big advantage of qualitative research is its investigation flexibility and its capacity to investigate in depth a phenomenon. In other words, qualitative enquiry allows the researcher not only to gain a valuable detailed insight into consumers but also to be able to choose to investigate some elements in particular details.

Qualitative approaches are vast and can include various techniques and methods. Most commonly, qualitative research is undertaken via interviews or focus groups.

### Interviews and focus groups

- Interviews and focus groups are based on an exchange between the researcher and the respondent(s).
- Interviews take place face to face, in a specific location dedicated to data collection or in situ, when consumers are experiencing a service.
- Qualitative research can be time consuming and requires a lot of effort from the interviewing team. Indeed, it requires skilled interviewers who have been trained and can conduct efficiently an interview/focus group.

- Qualitative research is also time consuming. It involves a lot of face-to-face time.
- Moreover, before being analyzed, the data collected have to be transcribed.
- Some often think that qualitative research is easier than quantitative research because it does not necessitate the mastering of complex statistical techniques. However, often it requires more time in terms of data collection, transcription, and interpretation. It also requires specific skills: skills for conducting the interviews and for interpreting the data.

Qualitative research has often been criticized for its subjectivity. This subjective dimension is often associated with the fact that the interview guide leaves scope for adaptation and because the interviewer is present and can potentially influence the answers given by the interviewees. This risk is certainly present and justifies the necessary training of the interviewers. Nonetheless, we have already addressed the fact that quantitative research, and particularly surveys, can also influence the type of answers given.

The other criticism that is often addressed towards qualitative techniques lies with its broader framing, but this is what makes it valuable: it gives the interviewer the possibility of expanding questioning in areas that quantitative research might not have allowed for. In other words, qualitative research has the defects of its qualities.

Perhaps one of the subtlest aspects of qualitative research is the interviewer's ability to pick up what is not said. For instance, in the study detailed in the interview guide (Tourism and hospitality insights 11.3), one key fact that came out of the focus groups was the inability of the consumers surveyed to project themselves in a forest context as a holiday destination. The interviewers had to hear this resistance and develop emotional intelligence to sense consumers. They could then dig further into their minds with supplementary questioning aiming to understand what were the limiting factors and what were the elements (accommodation, interpretation, activities, services, etc.) that had to be developed to encourage consumers to envisage the forest as a "destination."

The size of the samples involved in qualitative research is much smaller than in quantitative approaches. To identify a sample size, one key principle is that of data "saturation," which corresponds to a threshold point where the researcher feels that he/she hears information that has already been collected and that the subject is surrounded. Although this might appear as a vague recommendation, it is evident to the persons collecting data.

## Interview guide

Whether the researcher engages in interviews or focus groups, the main tool is an interview guide.

- The interview guide lists the main elements that will need to be addressed during the interview.
- An interview guide will drive the questioning in order to uncover information that is necessary to answer the hypothesis that has been set out in the research project.
- When an interviewer starts the interviewing process he/she needs to master fully the interview guide because the consumers investigated are unlikely to provide answers in the same order as the interview guide. For instance, when the interviewer asks question 2, the consumer might answer this question and provide other elements of information pertaining to questions 3 and 4. Therefore, the interviewer needs to be able to navigate through his interview guide and ensure that, at the end, all the necessary information has been collected.

It might be useful to insert some pictures that will be presented to the interviewees. Pictures help consumers to be more concrete with their ideas, express themselves more clearly, reject some pictures, and explain why they are doing so, etc.

---

## TOURISM AND HOSPITALITY INSIGHTS 11.3
## INTERVIEW GUIDE EXAMPLE ON NATURE AS A LEISURE/TOURISM DESTINATION

The objective of the research was to investigate how consumers perceive the forest, and gain information as to how they might, or might not, consider a forest as a holiday destination.

Table 11.1 Interview guide to investigate forest as a tourist destination

| THEMES | QUESTIONS | OBJECTIVES |
|---|---|---|
| **1. Visitors' profiles** <br> Their outdoor leisure practices | Who are they (name, profession) <br> Where do they come from? (do they live in an urban, suburban area? How close are they or not from nature? Has it been an important component of their lives?) | ⇨ **Collect information about visitors' profiles and breaks the ice** |
| **2. Expectations towards nature** | - Do they often spend time in natural spaces? (investigate what "often" means to them) <br> -Which activities do they practice in those spaces? (hiking, mountain biking, walking. . .) <br> With whom? (family, friends. . .) <br> On which occasions? | ⇨ **Understand the motivations and specificities of natural areas and their associated leisure practices, (without, yet, investigate forests)** |

*(Continued)*

**Table 11.1** (Cont.)

| THEMES | QUESTIONS | OBJECTIVES |
|---|---|---|
| Pictures: a set of four pictures of nature areas is shown to consumers (one picture of a lake in nature, one with a forest path, a field, and a hilly/natural landscape). Ask visitors in which universe do they see themselves most practicing leisure? For which occasions and with whom? Choose a picture that seems to attract less attention and ask visitors why this image is not chosen. | | |
| → **The forest** | When was the last time you went in a forest? With whom? How long did you stay there? What attracts you in a forest? What is unique do this type of area or can you find the same elements in other areas? Would you qualify this area as a leisure or a holiday destination (or both?); Why? What do you find most attractive in a forest ground / What does a forest evokes for you? (R: colors, elements, odors, etc.) | ⇨ **Understand the expectations associated specifically to the forests** |
| → **The forests in Champagne & Bourgogne** | Have you ever heard about Champagne & Bourgogne forests? Where would you locate them? At which driving distance from Paris/Dijon/Lyon would you place them? (Show a map of the country and see if visitors can locate the area) | ⇨ **Understand to what extent French inhabitants can locate this area on a map and whether they overvalue or undervalue the driving time to reach it** |
| → **Leisure stays in forest** | We are going to imagine that you are taking a three days holiday in a forest park, can you describe the ideal stay you could have? (R: types of activities, with or without a guide, accommodation, catering services, etc.) How would you describe a typical visitor who chooses to spend three days in a forest area? | ⇨ **Appreciate visitors' expectations for a stay in a forest** |
| | If they struggle prompt them by encouraging them to discuss: contemplating fauna/flora on their own (with or without infrastructures), guided walks (and which type), outdoor physical activities including outdoor yoga, gastronomy centered on forest products, discovering mythology, counts, stories, tales about the local and forestry heritage, discover some know-how associated to the forest (honey or pottery workshops), artistic activities, forest retreats (detoxifying, spiritual, meditation..), wellness activities (spa, massages..), unusual accommodation (tree houses..) | **Identify the various services and structures that are necessary to answer consumers' needs** |

(Continued)

**Table 11.1** (Cont.)

| THEMES | QUESTIONS | OBJECTIVES |
|---|---|---|
| → **National Parks** | Which image do you have of a national park? (what does it mean, how would you define it?) Are you aware of the rules that apply within a National Park? How do you perceive them? Should National Parks have a free access? | ⇨ **Understand how much people know about National Parks, which advantage or limits do they perceive in terms of their usage of those sites?** |
| → **Integral reserve** | The National Park is considering to leave an area as an integral reserve: do they know what this means? (If they don't, the interviewer explains what it stands for) Would this area be detrimental to their experience? Do they see a value in it? | ⇨ **How much do participants know about the integral reserve?** |

Source: Frochot I. Coppel M., Do Santos M. and Bertelot L. (2018) An analysis of the positioning of the Champagne & Burgundy new national park as a holiday destination, Unpublished Report, Université Savoie Mont Blanc.

Source: Isabelle Frochot.

## *Interviews or focus groups?*

So far, we have invariably mentioned interviews and focus groups but they serve different purposes. Interviews allow the researcher to investigate in depth a phenomenon that has personal resonance for an individual (or a family unit) and the interview process will not benefit from sharing/debating that information with other consumers. Interviews are very flexible and can be easy to organize especially if a researcher wants to investigate consumers during their holiday. Experience shows that, in a holiday context, response rates can be as high as 90% when tourists are invited during their holiday to participate to an interview on the spot (Frochot, Elliot, & Kreziak, 2017).

Focus groups are used when the researcher feels that a group exchange over several issues will bring a richness of information. By exchanging views, the group effect will encourage consumers to express themselves more thoroughly.

- Focus groups consist on average of 10 to 12 people (no more) around a table with an interviewer leading the discussion and an assistant moderating/interrupting when necessary.
- Focus groups can be challenging to manage, and it is an art managing dominating individuals and ensure that all participants have spoken.
- Focus groups need to be videoed in order to facilitate transcription matching individuals to the information they gave.

- It is common for refreshments to be available after the focus group meeting, where people will continue to talk.
- Focus groups are more difficult to organize than interviews since consumers need to be recruited in advance, a room needs to be booked, as well as tokens of appreciation for participants, etc.

## How to interpret qualitative data

As we have already mentioned, interpreting qualitative data is time consuming and requires strategies. Qualitative data analysis can be undertaken either manually or with software. Software is useful because it provides a rapid and comprehensive analysis of large corpus of words. However, the researcher needs to master his/her data and usually a manual analysis is always necessary, at least as a first step.

Regardless of the approach developed, because qualitative research aims to investigate a consumer in depth, the analyst needs to immerse himself in the data, make sense of the large corpus, and then transform this analysis into a fairly structured meaning of the data. This emerges from the data gradually and the analyst will need to extirpate himself from the data from time to time to start making sense of it. So, the analysis is conducted on an iterative basis, going backwards and forward to the data. This process is called crystallization whereby the analyst suspends his reading and analytical process in order to start identifying patterns in the data before immersing himself/herself again in the data.

The most common technique used to analyze qualitative data is content analysis which unfolds following a series of steps:

- A first read through the data to gain overall knowledge of the complete corpus collected.
- The researchers need to design a coding strategy and decide how they will analyze the text: isolate paragraphs, sentences, or words.
- The major codes and themes characteristic of the corpus will be identified in agreement with the researchers involved. This aspect is important since it will guarantee the internal validity of the research process. Often the researchers undertake the coding of two to three interviews. They then compare their coding strategy to identify the level of cohesion between them, and refine their common coding strategy.
- The corpus then needs to be coded and themes need to be allocated. This coding process allows the researcher to allocate elements of the corpus (sentences for instance) to different themes.
- A table will be useful at this stage with several columns: the verbatim that has been selected, a summary of its content, the general theme to which it is associated, and a code name.

- It is important to isolate the verbatim as expressed by the consumers for the validity of the research, but also because some of the verbatim will be displayed in the final report.
- At this stage, software can be useful: it allows the researcher to highlight parts of the corpus and assign those parts to a specific theme. This will simplify the analysis. Once the coding is finished, the software can assist the researcher in combining and extracting specific elements. For instance, the software can identify: all the corpus associated with a specific theme, for instance the weather (how consumers perceive a day of bad weather on a seaside holiday). It can also process the verbatim categorized by age, location, time, etc. If the data collection is vast, the use of those software is particularly useful and gains invaluable time in the analysis without losing the value of the verbatim.
- Automatic qualitative data analysis can be undertaken with other types of software to undertake data analysis straight from the verbatim provided. This approach provides an overall categorization of data that is most often conducted in words. The software can allow researchers to categorize words, identify associations of word, count frequencies, and differentiate them according to locations, times, etc.

## *Other types of approaches*

Other forms of qualitative research exist that can bring an interesting insight into the consumer experience.

**Image 11.2**

Source: Pexels.

## Observation

Observation is a technique that has been used by tourism and hospitality researchers for some time. It has its limits but remains a pertinent approach especially if one integrates the new opportunities that technology offers. It can allow researchers to count flows of tourists, observe their behavior (sometimes by changing some elements such as in nudge marketing), etc.

## Travel diaries

Traditionally the closest approach that researchers have developed for studying the experience as it unfolds was to use diaries. Diaries were given to consumers with some specific instructions. Visitors would then fill in the information as they went through their holiday.

Researchers would then collect valuable information about what consumers did and how they perceived various elements constituting their experience. The information is collected sequentially: one would be able to gain insight into what consumers engaged in, day after day, and how they constructed their experience and evolved along it. Spatial locations could also be recorded, thereby providing the researchers with an interesting insight into consumers' sequences throughout their experience.

# Into the experience: visual research

## Photographs

Another approach that has been used by researchers is asking tourists to restitute their experience through the production of pictures taken during a holiday. This approach usually involves researchers giving a camera to consumers and collecting the pictures that they have taken during their tourism activity (with or without instructions). The range of pictures collected and associated comments or, best, the possibility of interviewing tourists to let them comment on the pictures they took brings a valuable insight into their daily experience.

Lately, Vu, Li, Law, and Zhang (2017) have investigated the possibility of using pictures to recreate diaries. The authors used geo-tagged travel photos gathered on social media and succeeded in recreating travel patterns, giving a useful insight into tourists' experiences.

# Videos

Videos are becoming a key component of 21st-century communication and, in that regard, they should also become an important part of researchers' toolboxes. Videos provide an insight into some dimensions that are out of reach with traditional qualitative methodologies.

They bring the depth of physical expressions, locate the subject within a specific context, and give a visual account of consumer' emotions. For instance, elements of embodiment are visually present: body language, facial expressions, physical reactions, all bring a richness that is lost in translation when using traditional interview-based research.

The other strength of videos lies in their capacity to portray the subject investigated within the consumption context. In this context, many clues can be found about the general atmosphere of the location, noise levels, weather, architecture, etc. In tourism, this is a precious resource since it would not make sense to dissociate tourists' reactions from their servicescape.

Videos are particularly pertinent to the study of the tourist experience because it is largely ineffable: the tourist experience is laden with strong emotions and sensations that can prove difficult to articulate. Videos can point to some details that would usually go unnoticed when analyzing qualitative interviews. These details might simply be the use of some specific words but, more importantly, the context in which those are used (situated words). The body language accompanying the discourse gives much richer clues as to how tourists voice their answers. Facial expressions, arm and hand gestures, and the general body position constitute a rich set of clues to understand verbatim. Facial expressions are particularly useful to confer more depth and meaning to the words tourists use.

If it is not through a structured research approach, videos are also freely available online and allow researchers to have access to a vast array of materials that they can analyze for research purposes.

## Mobile ethnography

Mobile ethnography is a new approach that has emerged with the development of new technologies. Ethnography is an approach that has been used for a long time to investigate peoples and cultures and is extremely valuable but it is also a time-consuming approach. With the emergence of new technologies, the tourism industry quickly realized that mobile devices opened new possibilities that were extremely valuable in accompanying and studying the experience as it unfolds: mobile devises have a compass, GPS, geo-localization services, cameras, recorders, video facilities, etc. Mobile ethnography also gives the opportunity to enter the intimacy of the tourist experience by collecting data about tourists' movements, their views, and major touch points (through pictures, recorded comments, videos, etc.). See the video on the netnography in the YouTube links section.

# Conclusion

This chapter has introduced a detailed vision of the framework and steps that characterize a research project. All the steps involved in designing and setting up a project are essential and should not be overlooked. The results of a study will only have powerful strategic implications if the objectives of the project have been clearly set out, adequate

## TOURISM AND HOSPITALITY INSIGHTS 11.4
## MY EXPERIENCE FELLOW: NEW TECHNOLOGY AND SERVICE DESIGN

*My Experience Fellow* is a telephone application developed by More than Metrics, an Austrian-based company. The mobile phone is particularly useful since it is an object that consumers carry with them daily, and through its geo-localization, it brings an interesting insight into consumers' movements during their experience at a destination. For each participant, the application collects personal socio-economic information. Each touchpoint is geo-localized and participants can add videos and pictures associated with those touch points. Participants can then evaluate their experience (satisfaction rating of a touch point, importance within their experience, emotions felt, etc.).

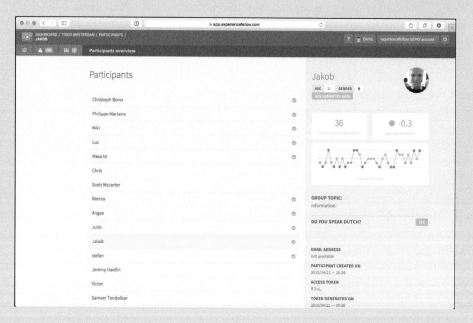

**Image 11.3** **Participants' profile page**

Source: Isabelle Frochot/https://www.experiencefellow.com/

Once participants have registered their experience, the information uploads on a website and the enterprise can access a profile page summarizing participants' information collected for each of those touch points (see Image 11.1). The system then provides a journey map that is extremely valuable. An emotional curve allows the company to evaluate how consumers rate their emotions along their journey. For each touch point, consumers can also give a written description of their experience, upload videos, and pictures that can help understand their perception of this touch point (Images 11.2 and 11.3).

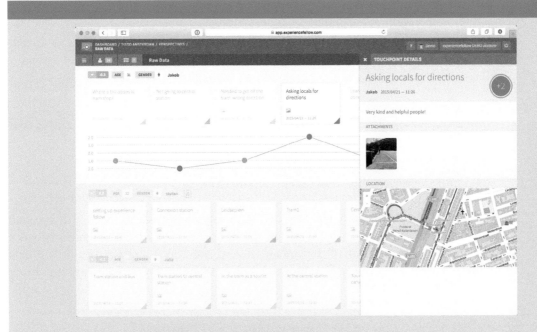

**Images 11.4 Consumers' individual journey maps**

Source: https://www.experiencefellow.com/

When collating this information over the whole sample of consumers, companies can then identify what are the main contributors and the inhibitors to the experience by analyzing data per touch point.

Source: Experience Fellow (2016) Research customer experience, a quick start guide, customer experience manual – version 1.1 2016/2017 http://www.experiencefellow.com

research methods have been developed, and an accurate data collection has been settled. Market studies/research also require a range of skills. Especially if moving towards quantitative analysis or the use of software, then some specific skills need to be mastered. Collecting data can also be challenging. Individuals are increasingly reluctant to answer surveys and their availability regarding data collection remains complex. New technologies are bringing new dimensions to data collection that should not be disregarded. They produce interesting tools to investigate the experience closer to the consumers and open new dimensions to experiential studies.

## REVIEW QUESTIONS

1. What are the differences between the types of data that can be collected (primary, secondary, tertiary)?
2. List the key differences between quantitative and qualitative research methods.

3. List the key steps that are involved in a research project and summarize each of them in two lines maximum.

4. How can new technologies (Internet, smartphones, and other technologies) provide new opportunities to investigate the consumer experience in more detail?

### YOUTUBE LINKS

#### "Qualitative and quantitative research – an introduction"

URL: https://www.youtube.com/watch?v=RYmLE8UqCXU

Summary: This video provides an easy and simple introduction to the research goals to inform strategic decisions. It focuses mostly on the differences between qualitative and quantitative research. It investigates the characteristics of the data collected with each research approach. It investigates surveys, focus groups, interviews, and observations.

#### "How to do a research interview by Graham R. Gibbs"

URL: https://www.youtube.com/watch?v=9t-_hYjAKww

Summary: This video provides an interesting insight into the process of interviewing. First Graham Gibbs lists the 12 key characteristics that make a good interview and how the interviewer needs to address the exchange with the consumer. Then he gives two examples: first an interview is shown and then it is shown again with specific comments indicating where the interview went well and wrong. Then an example of a good interview is shown.

#### "Welcome to Google Analytics for beginners"

URL: https://www.youtube.com/watch?v=GG5xBwbje1E

Summary: This video shows how companies can use online information to analyze the levels of acquisition, behavior, and conversion of their consumers. Online advertising campaigns can be analyzed for instance by identifying geographical locations of the purchases. Online purchasing behavior can also be analyzed on mobile applications, online point of sales systems, video game consoles, etc.

#### "Netnography: social media for cultural understanding by R.V. Kozinets"

URL: https://www.youtube.com/watch?v=SLC_sw4a1mM

Summary: Netnography is ethnography applied to the Internet and allows for a cultural understanding of consumer behavior. The video demonstrates how the Internet is an ongoing system of market intelligence. It demonstrates how much information is out on the Internet, how it can be strategically used, and how powerful it can be to fuel marketing strategic decisions.

## REFERENCES, FURTHER READING, AND RELATED WEBSITES

### References

Frochot, I., Elliot, S., & Kreziak, D. (2017). Digging deep into the experience: Flow and immersion patterns in a mountain holiday. *International Journal of Culture, Tourism and Hospitality Research, 11*(1), 81–91.

Vu, H.Q., Li, G., Law, R., & Zhang, Y. (2017). Travel diaries analysis by sequential rule mining. *Journal of Travel Research, 57*(3), 399–413.

Zarantonello, L., & Pawels-Delassus, V. (2016). *The handbook of brand management scales.* Routledge.

### Further reading

Altinay, L., & Paraskevas, A. (2008). *Planning research in hospitality and tourism.* Burlington, MA: Butterworth-Heinemann.

Baggio, R., & Klobas, J. (2017). *Quantitative methods in tourism: A handbook.* Clevedon: Channel View Publications.

Barbour, R. (2008). *Introducing qualitative research: A student guide to the craft of doing qualitative research.* London: Sage.

Blumberg, B., Cooper, D., & Schindler, P. (2014). *Business research methods* (4th ed.). Reading: McGraw-Hill.

Brunt, P., Horner, S., & Semley, N. (2017). *Research methods in tourism, hospitality and events management.* London: Sage.

Creswell, J.W. (2013). *Qualitative inquiry and research design.* London: Sage.

Creswell, J.W. (2016). *Essential skills for the qualitative researcher.* London: Sage.

Creswell, J.W. (2008). *Research design: Qualitative, quantitative, and mixed methods approaches.* London: Sage.

Dwyer, L., Gil, A., & Seetaram, N. (2012). *Handbook of research methods in tourism: quantitative and qualitative approaches.* Northampton, MA: Edward Elgar Publishing.

Easterby-Smith, M., Thorpe, R., & Jackson, P. (2015). *Management research* (4th ed.). London: Sage.

Eurostat. (2017). *Tourism statistics: Early adopters of big data?* Brussels: Statistical Papers.

Hillman, W., & Radel, K. (2008). *Qualitative methods in tourism research: Theory and practice.* Clevedon: Channel View Publications.

Kozinets, R.V. (2002). *Netnography redefined* (2nd ed.). London: Sage.

Kozinets, R.V. (2002). The field behind the screen: Using netnography for marketing research in online communities. *Journal of Marketing Research, 39* (February), 61–72.

Nunkoo, R. (2018). *Handbook of research methods for tourism and hospitality management.* Northampton, MA; Edward Elgar Publishing.

Ritchie, B.W., Burns, P., & Palmer, C. (2005). *Tourism research methods.* Wallingford: CABI Publishing.

Saunders, M., & Lewis, P. (2012). *Research methods for business students* (7th ed.). Harlow: Pearson Education Limited.

White, B., & Rayner, S. (2015). *Dissertation skills: For business and management students* (2nd ed.). London: Thomson.

Veal, A.J. (2017). *Research methods for leisure and tourism: A practical guide* (4th ed.). Prentice Hall.

## Websites

Eurostat
http://ec.europa.eu/eurostat

Research methods on hospitality and tourism
https://writepass.com/journal/2012/12/research-methods-for-hospitality-and-tourism-managers/

UNLV Libraries: management research in the hospitality and tourism industry
https://digitalscholarship.unlv.edu/cgi/viewcontent.cgi?referer=https://www.google.fr/&httpsredir=1&article=1763&context=thesesdissertations

Sheffield Hallam University: review of established methods in event research
http://shura.shu.ac.uk/5375/3/Crowther%2C_bostock%2C_perry_-_Review_of_established_methods_in_event_research_%28published%29.pdf

# MAJOR CASE STUDY
# INDIVIDUAL RESEARCH PROJECT

Now that you have understood the main directions that you can take in a research project, we shall apply this knowledge to a concrete example.

You are going to conduct a research project investigating the strengths and weaknesses of a hotel service experience. You will conduct this project without collecting primary information through either quantitative surveys or interviews. Instead, we invite you to search for consumer strategic information on the Internet.

In whichever part of the world you are located, select a hotel company, one that has at least three different hotels. Choose a category of service (two, three, or four stars) and only study hotels in the same category.

Make sure that you can collect consumer information on those hotels (whether it is through consumer reviews on blogs or other websites such as TripAdvisor or Booking.com). You should have at least ten reviews for each of the three hotels you have chosen. If you have more, it is even better.

## Step 1: coding strategy

Identify a coding strategy that will help you analyze the reviews collected. Have a first read through the reviews, then code three reviews, and if you are working in pairs, then compare your codes with each other.

At this stage you might still be hesitant. Indeed, what is important to collect? Remember that throughout this book we have seen that services are evaluated on their quality, a component of the experience that is very much related to functional elements of the delivery. Those might be associated with physical and logistical elements but also to human components of the service delivery.

But we have also seen that experiential marketing understands the experience much beyond those functional elements, therefore you also need to identify those components. Any element that seems to stand out from the norm (creating surprise for instance), or that translates some form of involvement into the experience, positive emotions and/or authenticity will be interesting to include in your coding strategy.

Once your coding strategy is settled, go through the reviews and code each of them.

With this analysis, you should be able to identify what seems to stand out both in terms of positive and negative elements for the hotels investigated.

## Step 2: managerial recommendations

First and foremost, what are the key strategic elements that you learn regarding the experience within those hotels? What are their strengths and weaknesses, as seen by their consumers? What are primarily the key areas that you could identify as being the main strengths of the hotel and those that need improvement. You might not be able, strictly speaking, to evaluate the relative importance of those elements. But if some distinctive elements seem to stand out and, in proportion, seem to constitute a large part of the comments, then you can consider that those elements are extremely important (negatively or positively).

Then once this analysis has been conducted, identify if some elements seem to stand out more in some hotels than others. In other words, within the same hotel chain can you identify similar service delivery strengths across different hotels or does the independent management of each hotel seems to produce a different type of service experience?

Can you then address managerial recommendations for the hotel chain concerned, overall for its service delivery and more precisely for each hotel you have chosen to analyze?

## Step 3: benchmark

Once your analysis of the previous brand provided the strategic results you were expecting, then look further and identify if other hotels, in the same category, seem to be more efficient or less efficient than the brand you have just analyzed. For instance, if you live in Denmark and you have analyzed three-star hotels of a specific brand, then choose other three-star hotels in a similar location and then identify if they differentiate themselves significantly or not from the brand you have

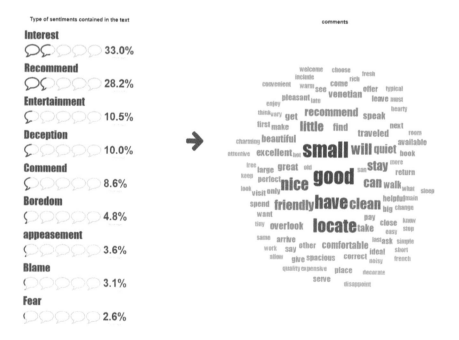

**Figure 11.1** Word clouds

Clic on the word cloud to see the associate verbatim

**Figure 11.2 Lexical proximities**

evaluated. What do you learn? Is the brand that you have investigated performing correctly compared to hotels of a similar category in your country, what can be learned from its competitors?

If you are working in a different area from hospitality, you can conduct a similar analysis for instance for restaurants, or for some visitor facilities, etc.

If one wanted to develop the analysis further, below is an example of data mining undertaken over the Internet for hotels, only from consumer feedback (with Sphinx software).

Those clouds directly show what are the key words that have been used in the reviews collected. The size of the word matches their range of occurrence in the text. Those clouds can be quite useful in PowerPoint presentations as they have a straightforward visual impact.

These types of simple analysis help you to identify at a glance what are the key words that stand out from a collection of reviews collected over the Internet.

Another type of words analysis might involve drawing a map of:

- Lexical proximities: which words were used in connections with which other words?
- Semantic analysis: restitution of the main concepts used in the text and their corresponding range of words.
- Types of sentiment: what are the words used to illustrate consumers' frame of mind?

For each of the theme of those comments, the software is able to identify what are the key words associated with those sentiments.

Whilst software cannot fully replace human intelligence, when it comes to analyzing qualitative data (in the case of netnography and for the type of analysis undertaken in this exercise), software can provide very interesting approaches to go through a large amount of data, extract, and analyze them very efficiently.

Source: Isabelle Frochot.

# 2 Marketing strategy

## Learning outcomes

By the end of this chapter, students will:

- Identify key steps of the strategic decision process
- Understand the importance of a strategic approach, even for small- and medium-sized companies
- Be introduced to different strategies and to a number of case study scenarios that explain how tourism and hospitality companies take long-, mid-, and short-term decisions

### Key terms

strategy, strategic decision-making process, marketing strategy, short-, medium- and, long-term

## Introduction

Marketing strategy and market segmentation are the key elements of the strategic decision-making processes. In this chapter, the principles of the strategic decision-making process are outlined through examples of various approaches used by companies in the tourism and hospitality industry with market segmentation and positioning to be considered in Chapter 13.

## General framework and stages in the strategic approach

A strategic analysis is based on the analysis of the competitive situation and internal diagnostics for a company, organization, or entity. When defining their strategy, companies' owners and managers (normally at the corporate level) have to go through several steps of analysis. One of them, is to define or refine the key factors for success in their market. The analysis of customer needs, such as strategies and practices of competitors and changes in the sector, provides the evidence for the identification of the key factors for success. Such factors can include a particular skill (managerial, technological, etc.), access to key resources (raw materials, financial, etc.) or key partners (suppliers, distributors, etc.), high-performance systems (information systems and monitoring, distribution, revenue management, etc.), and/or location (points of sale, etc.). In small- and medium-sized companies, the psychological profile of the owner/

manager may have a significant impact on the company and might be considered as a key element for success or failure. In this particular case, it will help to understand the level of risk accepted by the manager, and taken by the company (Legohérel et al., 2004).

The competitive situation: Porter's (1985) theories outline the forces that determine sectoral competition: competition between suppliers, the arrival of new competition in the sector, new products and services or alternative products, suppliers and their bargaining power, consumers and their bargaining power.

The internal diagnostic is based on an assessment of the strengths and weaknesses of the organization, integrating various dimensions (human, financial, technical, etc.). It is recommended to process to a comprehensive internal and external analysis before making strategic choices. The SWOT analysis relies on both an internal diagnostic composed of strengths and weaknesses and an external analysis composed of opportunities and threats. This analysis takes data from the macro environment and the micro environment (see Chapter 2), composed of customers, competitors, distribution channels, and suppliers, and therefore identify all the phenomena that may affect the company's business.

- Opportunities are external phenomena likely to have a favorable influence on the activity or profitability. Its value is linked to its appeal and likelihood of success of the company, which depends on the skill and proficiency in the key success factors.
- Threats are problems with an unfavorable trend or a disturbance of the environment in the absence of an appropriate marketing response, leading to a deterioration of the company's position. The severity is related to the impact on the profitability of the company, and the probability of occurrence.

Tourism and hospitality insights 12.1 presents the SWOT analysis for a luxury hotel in the historical city center of Bordeaux (France) and the new strategy decided by the owner of the hotel.

Strategic analysis helps define the main business operations, namely the strategic business areas (SBA) or strategic business units (SBU). The SBA/SBU are homogeneous clusters of activity or products and services. They are defined as product-market pairs sharing the same technology, markets, and competition. Companies try to expand activities in the product-market pairs representing a significant economic opportunity. Various tools, such as the BCG Matrix (named after the Boston Consulting Group), help set up strategic analysis.

These methods are based upon data collection concerning the market (e.g. growth rates), the competition (e.g. relative market share), results (e.g. products and services, the organizations), and competitive advantage (e.g. strength of the competitive

## TOURISM AND HOSPITALITY INSIGHTS 12.1
## SWOT ANALYSIS: FIVE-STAR LUXURY HOTEL, BORDEAUX, FRANCE

In 2010, the owner of the hotel Regent Bordeaux, not fully satisfied with the way the hotel was managed by the Rezidor franchise, decided to carry out an analysis of the hotel. The main results of the SWOT analysis were identified as follows:

Strengths
- Ideal location in the city center of Bordeaux, a UNESCO World Heritage city
- The oldest four-star luxury property in Bordeaux
- The world capital of wine
- Great hotel capacity
- Innovative program of events
- Dynamic hotel

Weaknesses
- Low international awareness
- Weak positioning (significant drop in prices)
- Unstructured communication
- Low impact of being part of an international group
- Long delays for opening of a spa and car park
- No air conditioning in public areas
- Limited size of the superior rooms
- No connecting rooms and twin rooms

Opportunities
- Creation of a more international offer focused on luxury
- Dynamic city for international events
- Close proximity of prestigious vineyards
- High-speed train line with Paris only three hours away
- Nearby operation of low-cost airlines

Threats
- Three other luxury four-star hotels nearby
- Decreased purchasing power due to global recession
- Lack of external communication as a luxury destination

In 2011, a new strategy was determined. The former Regent Bordeaux became the Grand Hotel de Bordeaux & Spa. Behind this name change lies a strategic change and consequently an evolution of the product. "We have become independent again, being in the fold of Rezidor under the name The Regent since its creation in 2008, but this group did not take into account the needs of individual customers and was only interested in the group" recalls, the new CEO of the hotel.

The hotel achieves 70% of its business from individuals, mostly international, 10% of whom are Chinese. To better accommodate this demanding clientele, the hotel opened a new spa on three floors and soon after opened a tea room, sushi bar, and an Asian art gallery. For customers seeking wine tourism, the Grand Hotel relies on its four wine experts to manage demand and organize private local vineyard tours. Wine tourism, a highly popular form of tourism, is expected to increase significantly in the years to come with the hotel now strategically well placed to benefit from its popularity.

Following this period of changes, the hotel kept improving the high standards and luxury positioning of the hotel. In September 2015, the owner hired a famous British chef, Gordon Ramsay, to take care of the two restaurants. And in October 2015, the hotel became member of a new hotel group and change is name for: InterContinental Bordeaux-Le Grand Hôtel.

Source: Patrick Legohérel.

advantage and options to reach this goal). The data analysis helps account for the profitability of each activity under consideration, helping with the decision as to whether or not, and where, to make investments. The return on marketing investment is crucial for any company as it is the net return from a marketing investment divided by the cost of the marketing investment. This is how profits generated by investments in marketing activities are evaluated. Tourism and hospitality insights 12.2. contributes to our understanding of the strengths and weaknesses of restaurants, and some of the reasons for their failures.

At a more advanced stage, companies institute a customer analysis (market segmentation) designed to identify consumers' needs and expectations and to analyze client profiles. This study focuses on both qualitative and quantitative dimensions.

Positioning involves identifying the specific characteristics of a company, brand, product, or service relative to the competition. It is based on the decisions made regarding both the product-market pairs and the client targets, taking consumers' needs and expectations into account.

Companies can thus determine the strategic segments and marketing segments they will focus upon. Activities need to be positioned in relation to one another, and care

# BUSINESS INSOLVENCY AND RESTAURANTS: A COMPREHENSIVE REVIEW OF MACRO AND MICRO FACTORS

*A robust, effective, and efficient bankruptcy system rebuilds companies, preserves jobs, and facilitates economic growth with dynamic financial markets and lower costs of capital. For more than 35 years, the U.S. Bankruptcy Code has served these purposes, and its innovative debtor in possession chapter 11 process, which allows a company to manage and direct its reorganization efforts, is emulated around the globe.*

(American Bankruptcy Institute 2014)

Business insolvency is the heart of any business. Unfortunately, the process of business insolvency is often misunderstood as the terminal step in a business lifecycle, when in fact it is the beginning of a strategic sometimes deliberate transformation process that leads a more agile and responsive organization best suited for the emerging socio-political, economic and business climate. The process of business insolvency can also be described as an instrument of Darwinian natural selection process that keeps the industry healthy and vibrant as a whole. Albeit, for the natural selection to occur and continue, some of the firms have to be discontinued, voluntarily or involuntarily, in the best interest of the industry as whole. Thus, from a macro perspective, business insolvency is a necessary step to keep any industry healthy, vibrant, relevant, and live. From a marketing perspective, all dynamic industries tend to embrace business insolvency as a tool for repositioning. From an organization ecology perspective, business insolvency is a naturally occurring phenomenon that eliminates the weakest links in business chains. Without the process of business insolvency, most industries will experience a chronic lethargy in revenues and financial performance as weakest links continue to drain the resources and keep the prices artificially low. From a legal and organizational transition perspective, business insolvency allows for gradual and methodical change in business leadership, hopefully, resulting in renewed growth and dynamism. As it is obvious, at the macro level, there are significant benefits of business insolvency.

Restaurants are a significant part of American life. According to the National Restaurant Association (2015), total revenues for the restaurant industry exceed $640 billion with nearly 1,000,000 operating restaurants in the US; providing jobs for over 13 million people. The sizeable economic impact of the restaurant industry can be measured by the 4% contribution it makes to the Gross Domestic Product in the United States. In addition, the restaurant industry has been expanding at a steady rate of 2 to 4% over the past three decades. In 2009, despite the economic downturn, the restaurant industry grew by 2.5% (NRA, 2009). The restaurant and foodservice industry continues to be one of the largest private sector employers in the United States with a projected increase of 1 million jobs by the year 2020 (www.restaurant.org). In 2010, the restaurant industry added 24,000 new jobs and nearly 84,000 jobs in first three-quarters of the 2010 (www.restaurant.org). With one-in-three Americans having worked in this industry at least once in their life time and two-in-five agreeing that ordering food from restaurants makes them more productive in their daily life, restaurants are an integral part of American society.

In spite of its sustained growth over the past three decades, the restaurant industry has experienced one of the highest business failure rates. According to the Dunn and Bradstreet report (2001), the restaurant industry has one of the highest business failure rates among the retail and service industries. Erroneously, American Express has estimated that 90% of restaurants fail in the first year. A study by Parsa et al. (2005) showed that restaurant failures are in fact under 30% during the first year of operation, and although individual failure rates may rise by the third year of operation, they do not achieve the levels reported by American Express. Other studies using data from California have shown that restaurant failures are also less than 30%. The National Restaurant Association of US recognizes a 30% failure rate as the norm in the restaurant industry.

Even the well-established and commonly accepted 30% failure rate during the first year of operations is still unacceptable as it has significant economic impact. If the restaurant failure is 30% during the first year of operation, then 9,000 restaurants fail every year in America. According to the National Restaurant Association, average revenues per year per restaurant are about $580,000. Then there is a potential loss of $5.20 billion in the form of lost restaurant revenues to the national economy. In addition, restaurant failures also lead to the loss of nearly 40,000 jobs per year as estimated from the National Restaurant Association statistics. The annual restaurant failure rate of 9,000 units per year would also precipitate the loss of invested capital of $3.2 billion per year in failed restaurant units at a rate of 60% of estimated annual sales considered as the initial investment. Thus, many restaurant entrepreneurs and their investors are also expected to experience extensive economic hardships as a result of restaurant failures. These facts clearly indicate that restaurant failures are a significant factor to consider for their economic impact and its impact on lives of American entrepreneurs.

Factors that contribute to restaurant failures can be divided into two major types, namely macro factors and micro factors.

Some of the relevant and critical macro factors that contribute mostly to restaurant failures include the economy, legislation (national, regional, and local), regional and local planning (urban and rural), climatic factors (natural disasters), changing cultural patterns, evolving food habits, changes in consumer lifestyles, intensity of the competition, and technology.

At the same time, unit level micro factors also contribute to restaurant failures. Selected micro factors are presented here such as need for working capital, location, concept, name, experience of the owner, quality of life of the owner, entrepreneurial (in)competence, leadership style, brand building, restaurant genetics in design and layout, internal controls and the role of fixed costs.

## References

National Restaurant Association. (2009). Retrieved from http://www.restaurant.org/pressroom/press release/?ID=1879.

Parsa, H.G., Self, J., Njite, D., & King, T. (2005). Why restaurants fail? *Cornell Hospitality Quarterly*, *46*(3), 304–322.

Source: H.G. Parsa, Barron Hilton Chair & Professor, Daniels School of Business, University of Denver, USA.

must be taken to maintain balance within the portfolio of brands held by the same company.

Strategic actions operate on a medium- to long-term perspective. They are different from marketing policies that involve translating the strategic area-based decisions into operational measures. SBAs are not frozen, and management needs to be able to call the set policy lines into question when market conditions (e.g. competitive situation, consumer demand) or the macro environment change.

## The strategic line of approach

The key decision for any company is normally the selection of a guideline, a strategic line of action that they commit to in the medium or long term. A modification of the strategy may be decided upon when the market conditions or the internal situation of a company are significantly modified. Such modifications have been frequently observed in the tourism sector in the last couple of years, as the sector has had to face significant structural and dynamic challenges as evidenced in Chapter 2. Companies make strategic choices in terms of their circumstances and with the dual goal of economic efficiency and risk distribution. Is it possible to remain independent in an environment dominated by strong commercial networks? Choices have to be made between independence, inevitably linked to some measure of isolation, and the constraints of collaboration (see Chapter 4), particularly the financial constraints. Another strategic choice is the following: is it possible for tour operators to specialize in one destination? If the latter is hit by a disaster, the company may not continue its activity with another product. Truly generalist or multi-specialist tour operators can thus spread their risks more effectively.

Organizations such as companies or institutional structures establish a new strategic plan regularly with three-to-five year plans commonplace. For instance, the Best Western hotel group establishes three-year strategic plans. Tourism and hospitality insights 12.3 and 12.4 explain the importance of a dominant strategic model in the context of international hotels.

## Strategic approaches

Managers can select from several kinds of non-exclusive strategic approaches:

- Development strategy
- Growth strategy
- Diversification strategy
- Alliance and networking strategy
- International strategy

## TOURISM AND HOSPITALITY INSIGHTS 12.3
## THE FRANCHISE MODEL IN EUROPE'S HOTEL INDUSTRY

The opening up of Europe's emerging markets, both in the south and in the east, has further encouraged franchise development, which is expanding faster than other business models. Franchise operations enable more complete coverage of a market to reach the necessary critical size much quicker than other models. However, franchise development is not always straightforward. For example, there is frequently a need to respect standardization and building standards, the setting of limits on territories that are already mature and where the creation of a new supply runs up against the availability of real estate and construction costs. Each hotel group involved in the franchise race has had to soften its rules, preserving only the brand's core values, or create new, less restricting brands to attack the immense conversion market of pre-existing properties, whether branded or not.

Already well-established on their respective native territories, European hotel groups have tried to block the way for new groups to expand, most notably American ones which have networks in Europe that remain incomplete. To do this, the barriers to entry were made as high and discouraging as possible. In many ways, this approach has been successful in that American brands that have large franchise networks in Europe are rare, with the exception of Holiday Inn/Holiday Inn Express and Best Western, with the latter's cooperative model quite specific.

However, is the positioning fixed? Hilton Worldwide, Marriott International, Wyndham Hotel Group, Choice Hotels and some others have not had their last word. For example, it is their very intention to have a better footprint in Europe with its high average daily rates, even if it means concluding original partnerships, or even temporarily mobilizing capital. Global franchise leaders, backed by the strength of their loyalty programs, are successfully pulling down barriers on the "old" continent. Privileged hunting grounds are no longer so secure as once before for the Europeans!

A major question for all hotel groups in the future is, however, the extent to which the hotel brand is strong enough and whether it generates enough clientele compared to the seemingly non-stop growth of online distribution. Some franchisees are pulling out their calculators to battle nose-to-nose with franchisers about revenues and the real values of the brand in light of the restrictions and investments they must make. With so many disruptors and dynamism in the market, the answer is not as easy as it was only a decade ago.

Source: Groups and brands opened to franchise (2015, July–August). *Hospitality-On*, 238–239.

## TOURISM AND HOSPITALITY INSIGHTS 12.4
## HOTEL FRANCHISING STRATEGY: ACCOR

Accor is the indisputable franchise leader in Europe. It has long understood the importance of the franchise and has developed close, nearly fusional, relationships with franchisees in France, its primary market. And yet, throughout the 1980s, 1990s and even the first years of the 2000s, the development strategy of the Accor Group relied on a balance between growth through subsidiaries, management contracts, and franchise, reserved for its economy brands Ibis and Etap Hotel (and Formula1), and its midscale brand Mercure. The change occurred with the arrival of Gilles Pélisson at the helm of Accor in 2006. This change was brought on in particular by pressure from franchisees that had had trouble establishing a contact with his predecessor, who was an excellent manager, but a poor communicator with operators.

> Gilles Pélisson (…) began a strategic turnaround, later named asset right, a softer version of the asset light strategy requested by investment fund shareholders. The tone was set: the group limited its capital use, recuperated net proceeds from sales of existing assets to redistribute, in great part, to shareholders, and incited franchisees to be ambitious about accompanying the development of the group in France as well as abroad. To show his determination, he created a new brand "All Seasons," on the non-standardized economy segment, to attract unbranded properties and make Accor's troops of franchisees grow quickly. Dialogue was re-established with associations of franchisees whom he warmed up to, seducing them with marketing efforts based on the concepts. Mercure also underwent rejuvenation to get away from an obsolete image and its excessive diversity. (…) The clear repositioning of each brand was the priority at the beginning of this mandate.

However, diverging attitudes regarding the support given to this strategy and the impatience of investment funds of the group's stakeholders contributed in part to Gilles Pélisson's surprise departure. This came as a surprise but further reinforced the change in the economic model adopted upon his arrival. Denis Hennequin, his successor, previously Head of McDonald's Europe, an expert in franchising, confirmed the primacy of this development model. The new President and CEO acted quickly, dealing a blow big enough to unite the economy brands around Ibis to make it a spearhead in the effort to conquer the world, backed by old franchises and especially new ones. The new Ibis family, Ibis Budget (ex-Etaphotel), and Ibis Styles (formerly All Seasons) thus surpassed the 1,500 hotels mark worldwide and 1,200 in Europe-Africa-Middle East in one fell swoop. And the adventure continued as it reached 205,000 rooms worldwide as of January 1, 2015.

The surprise departure of Denis Hennequin in April 2013 didn't change the group's orientation. The strongman on the Board of Directors, Sébastien Bazin, representing the shareholder Colony Capital, was soon to become the operating head of Accor Group. He further accelerated the group's transformation by clearly separating its real estate activities (HotelInvest) and management activities, marketing, and franchise (HotelServices). The latter division's strategy turned to the implementation of a model focused on generating income, with an offer adapted to owners, priority given to more profitable contracts, and optimized cost management with a goal to optimize the economic performance of Accor and its partners.

Aware of the importance of distribution and the need to increase the diversity of the offer for clients, Sébastien Bazin crossed another milestone in June 2015 that he will need to justify to franchisees, by creating an ACCORHotels platform that is open to unbranded hoteliers that wish to take advantage, at a lesser cost, of the group's digital strength and sales tools.

At the end of 2014, of the 3,717 properties under operation, 2,211 were under management contracts, (including 1,354 owned or rented by HotelInvest) and 1,506 under franchise contracts, a proportion that increases regularly.

Source: *Hospitality-On*, 238–239, July–August 2015.

## Development strategies

According to Porter (1985), the competitive advantage that is needed for companies to develop their activity falls within a dual goal: the companies' ability to control costs and the market's ability to absorb the supply. Three key strategies are evident as per below:

*Pricing domination strategy*: Companies seek to control costs in order to offer selling prices lower than those of the competition. They seek to have a substantial market share.

*Differentiation strategy:* Companies offer a different product from those offered by the main competitors by differentiating either the good or the service and/or the price (superior to average market prices) proposed to consumers.

*Concentration of supply strategy:* The majority of sales and marketing efforts are focused upon one segment (sometimes a homogeneous micro-segment) or one type of product. For instance, a tour operator may focus on one destination and highly specific positioning such as the Seychelles or Mauritius, on the luxury end of the scale. Companies choosing to specialize seek to reach and achieve recognition for their high competence level. The specialization may cover a geographic area, a product, or a client base.

Development strategies involve creating and fully utilizing a basic competitive advantage that represents the driving force of the companies' development (cost control and low price, differentiating element, specialization). Other strategies may contribute to development (e.g. increasing the market share) or to the strengthening of a company's position on the market (e.g. improved distribution control or cost control) with examples of strategies used in the tourism industry highlighted below.

## Growth strategies

The purpose of such strategies is to increase the size of a company and/or to strengthen its market position, through for instance, improved control of the service providers downstream or upstream of the service production process.

Internal growth involves developing the company's current activity. External growth involves integrating an existing product on the market. Several economic entities are grouped, either through complete integration (merger) or through financial consolidation (equity holding) or through take-over without merger (acquisition).

Growth is said to be horizontal when the entities grouping together provide the same services (e.g. when two hotel chains establish ties); it is vertical when a company incorporates suppliers and service providers upstream or downstream (e.g. a hotel group takes over a distribution network). Through the integration, growth is achieved along with business complementarity, control of the various functions, and reduction of the production costs. Integration also strengthens the independence of the new structure.

The merger between Air France and KLM illustrates this strategy in the air transport sector. In the spring of 2004, Air France had successfully concluded its tender offer for KLM. The new group operates as a holding company maintaining two distinct brands. Air France-KLM became the first airline in terms of traffic and the world leader in turnover. Besides the desire to save money, the issue of the merger lay in a broader range of services, the sharing of both airline networks codes allowed customers to benefit from flights exploiting the two hubs and all destinations served by both airlines. Other commercial approaches have been operationalized such as the harmonization of tariffs or the approximation of databases and customer loyalty programs in relation to the SkyTeam alliance.

## Diversification strategies

These strategies involve exploring new business, new strategic segments, or new clienteles. Diversification occurs when a hotel group develops tour operator activities or a mass-catering group branches into high-end commercial catering activities.

For instance, the German group TUI, a leading European tourism company and present in 18 European countries, has chosen to develop a diversification strategy as the group focused on, up until the early 2000s, two main activities: tourism and maritime logistics. For this development, TUI chose external growth through mergers, acquisitions, and numerous collaborative alliances (see Chapter 4) in the tourism sector, permanently withdrawing in the industrial activity of maritime logistics. After these operations of diversification and external growth, TUI focused on internal growth. In France, TUI acquired the French tour operator Nouvelles Frontières, then the trademark of another company with a strong reputation in France, Havas Voyages to strengthen its position on the French market. These purchases have enabled the German group TUI to grow rapidly, covering various segments and quickly acquiring a strong reputation on the French market, before continuing its development through internal growth.

Excess diversification may lead a company to adopt the opposite strategy of refocusing. When a company ventures into activities that are not fully controlled or when the new targeted segments are not fully satisfactory, one solution can be to refocus on its core business. After many years of growth and/or business diversification, certain large groups have now opted for a refocusing approach.

## Alliance and networking strategies

Alliances and commercial networks constitute an opportunity for many companies in the tourism sector. These strategies provide various advantages, including extending services. Alliances in the air transport sector give each company a global spread through integrating its partners' offering (see Chapter 4). Customers are able to go from one destination to another with one ticket only and will benefit from wide-

## TOURISM AND HOSPITALITY INSIGHTS 12.5
## HOW SIGNIFICANT IS A GLOBAL ALLIANCE FOR A MEDIUM-SIZED AIRLINE COMPANY? THE CASE OF MIDDLE EAST AIRWAYS (MEA)

Globalization and deregulations have always created opportunities and threats to the air transport industry players. A traditionally dynamic environment, oftentimes marked by fierce competition, forced airline executives to think globally and to build a strategy aimed at developing international networks, providing differentiated services that target higher customer satisfaction and changing demand.

In the airline industry, competition exists when two or more commercial air carriers are authorized to perform the same service. One of the most important developments in the international airline industry in recent years has been the rapid expansion of global airline alliances among airline competitors. Large airlines are spreading their wings by including airlines of various sizes from all parts of the world into their alliances. These have involved cooperation between two or more airlines in a wide range of commercial and operational areas, for example, scheduling, purchasing, marketing, and frequent flyer programs. As of today, there are three competing strategic international alliances in the industry as outlined in Chapter 4. In each multilateral alliance, participants decide with which airlines they establish code-share agreements, and which routes they include in the agreement. Although alliance members cooperate on many aspects, they may nonetheless remain competitors. Nevertheless, within the alliances there are also subgroups of airlines granted with antitrust immunity.

MEA was a model in restructuring its services to compete with high quality airlines such as Emirates, Qatar Airways, Turkish Airlines, and others. MEA has one of the most modern fleets in the world. Its all-new fleet gives you the world's most sophisticated cabin and represents the ultimate operational efficiency, extended cabin space and increased flying range. Large, modern and environmentally compatible, the MEA fleet comprises aircraft of almost every size with state-of-the-art technology used throughout.

Tactical alliances for MEA are no longer a successful strategy, as competitors became stronger and an industry of low-cost carriers has been developing in the Middle East market. The threat of losing market share and seeing profitability decrease was real for MEA. That was the time for considering strategic alliances as a way to safeguard MEA's position and to prevent its customers from being dissatisfied by a low value proposition. MEA knew that entering an alliance could not be achieved without a business model based upon organizational excellence, one that follows complex passenger needs and pursues high quality services. MEA needed to add value to customers, generating extra demand and reaching a scope larger than the Gulf and the major European markets, to expand its competitive advantage.

Middle East Airlines – Air Liban (MEA) signed an agreement to officially join SkyTeam. This agreement came into force in 2012, making MEA the second alliance member in the Middle East, along with Saudi Arabian Airlines (Saudi Arabia's national carrier). Welcoming MEA into SkyTeam enabled the alliance to strengthen its presence in the Middle East. This new membership responds to the alliance's ambition of enhancing its global expansion and increasing access to the Middle East, a region undergoing strong economic development. MEA were to offer customers access to a global network of destinations, and the SkyTeam Frequent Flyer Program and lounge network around the world.

This membership was designed to further strengthen SkyTeam's presence in the Middle East, following on from Saudi Arabian Airlines that signed an agreement to join SkyTeam in 2012 on 10 January. The MEA and Saudi Arabian Airlines networks, which complement those of other SkyTeam airlines, provides customers with ease of access to Middle East destinations not yet served by the alliance members. Passengers are now able to access, via the main hubs of Saudi Arabian Airlines (Riyadh, Jeddah, and Damman) and MEA (Beirut), new destinations in the Arabian Peninsula, Indian, and African sub-continent such as Alexandria, Aden, Colombo, and Islamabad.

The signing of this agreement also strengthened historic ties between Air France and MEA, as the two airlines have been operating the Paris-Beirut service on a code-share basis since February 1999. On this route, MEA passengers can already earn miles and use award tickets. MEA's future membership of SkyTeam will ensure its continuing global expansion and allow it to fully benefit from Air France and MEA's complementary networks in Europe and the Middle East.

On May 10, 2011, MEA signed the adherence agreement to become an effective member of SkyTeam. Until June 28, 2012, the target date for full membership, MEA had restructured its processes, testing them at different organizational and departmental levels, to adhere to the joining require-ments, ranging from inventory management to revenue accounting, customer experience, and air-port management.

As a company focused on profit maximization, one of the notable results stemming from its net-work expansion was cost reduction. MEA passengers now have access to a worldwide network of 926 destinations in 173 countries, easy connections via some of the best hubs in the world (Amster-dam Schiphol, Paris Charles de Gaulle, Madrid Barajas, Atlanta Hartsfield-Jackson, New York JFK, Rome Fiumicino, Beijing, Seoul Incheon, Moscow Sheremetyevo et al.). In addition to certain bilat-eral elements of coordination in maintenance and ground handling, MEA decreased its inventory level as a result of pooling certain spare components for aircrafts.

As members operating overlapping networks with MEA (such as Alitalia on FCO and MXP) increased, marginal cost for MEA decreased and a better service was provided for connecting pas-sengers. The SkyTeam alliance allowed for increased transportation services for Lebanese and for-eign travelers, with more destinations added, and this created a decrease in unit cost for MEA, especially because MEA uses larger aircraft (such as the A330-200) to be compensated with higher traffic density. Additionally, MEA has a potential gain in aligning with SkyTeam because the new destinations added to its network were planned keeping into consideration lower production costs with respect to adding new routes in a standalone scenario. Irrespective of such element, the coordinated internal process of pricing, fare structure and demand tracking have a positive effect on MEA's profitability.

On the marketing side, it is apparent that brand loyalty to MEA increased, with more tickets being sold through MEA's distribution channels in any location covered by SkyTeam. The shared value chain of the Frequent Flyer Programs under the SkyTeam umbrella has made MEA's Cedar Miles more attractive, whereby MEA passengers can now earn mileage on routes whenever flying on any of the alliance partners. MEA also recognized the benefits of the joint advertising/promotional campaigns SkyTeam carries out worldwide, providing wider visibility to MEA's name and brand.

At a service quality level, gains are as well numerous. As SkyTeam includes larger and well known airlines such as Air France, Air Europa, Alitalia et al., which stand out for superior customer service, a similar positioning will positively reverberate upon MEA's passengers, resulting in MEA's service quality gaining a better reputation. This is the starting point for MEA to capture a larger share of HVCs (High Value Customers), especially those who are quality/time –sensitive.

This differentiation in service is a key weapon for fighting in the global market. A single check-in service is now provided for the entire journey; this includes IATCI (Inter-Airline Through Check-In), with baggage tags and boarding passes issued to the final destination, lounge access (to 490 locations) all over the globe for Premium (First Class, Business Class, and Elite Plus) customers, "Earn & Burn" capability with all alliance members, dedicated priority check-in and priority bag-gage tag for all premium customers. Not to be forgotten as well, MEA's frequent flyers are now able to obtain multi-carrier award seats, redeeming online their miles across all SkyTeam carriers with one single award ticket. Finally, customer complaints are handled by the receiving airline, regardless of the operating or marketing carrier status.

From the financial point of view, MEA's entry into SkyTeam proved beneficial. Rather than relying exclusively on its domestic economy, preoccupied with various political and economic issues, the alliance provides a sense of diversification that connects different economies and reduces the return on equity and cash flow fluctuation risks. This results in a decrease in both working capital needs and financial distress risks. Leveraging the new extended network, MEA is able to allocate resources more effectively (aircraft, crews, etc.) where returns are higher and supplies are scarce. Furthermore, the negotiating power with suppliers has become stronger, enabling MEA to get better procurement deals in fuel, spare parts, maintenance, catering, airport charges, cabin crew training, etc.

In general, by joining SkyTeam Global alliance, MEA extends to Cedar Miles members a bouquet of recognized benefits throughout Sky Team network. Irrespective of their class of travel, Cedar Miles top tier members (Silver, Gold, and Platinum) will enjoy the highest level of luxury.

- *Priority at service point:* Cedar Miles top tier members benefit from priority services at airports including premium check-in, immigration and security fast track when available, and priority boarding.
- *Extra baggage allowance:* Cedar Miles top tier members are allowed to carry an extra baggage allowance on all SkyTeam flights upon presentation of their membership cards.
- *Priority baggage tag:* Cedar Miles Gold and Platinum members will get a priority baggage tag to ensure fast delivery of their luggage at destination.
- *Lounge access:* Cedar Miles Gold and Platinum members traveling on an international flight operated by a SkyTeam carrier have access to the airport lounge with one guest.

MEA is now preparing to partner with UX (Air Europa) to add more destinations for Lebanese customers. The need to become a more efficient company and a better-quality provider was the core motive behind MEA's ambition to align with SkyTeam. By standardizing certain processes, sharing best practices, and adopting state-of-the-art technologies in various fields, as well as by understanding customers' preferences from different backgrounds and perspectives, MEA can now serve its customers better, especially those who are demanding global access to the world markets. MEA is now back in the global game!

Source: Ali Kassir, *Senior Officer Inventory Management, Marketing & Development*, Middle East Airways

ranging services (e.g. luggage handling, access to VIP lounges, and links between loyalty schemes). These strategies also enhance commercial visibility and allow greater distribution capacities. Independent hoteliers who join a voluntary hotel chain gain access to a national or even international distribution network and to the commercial recognition of the voluntary network brand image. Finally, pooling resources, as is usually the case with alliances, brings cost savings (e.g. common reservation system, shared technical services, such as aircraft maintenance for airline companies). Tourism and hospitality insights 12.5 explains how a medium-sized airline (Middle East Airways) benefited from the support of a large network (Skyteam Alliance).

## International strategy

In this chapter, we will consider the strategic decision to develop a business on an international level. International marketing (and the related issues of globalization versus adaptation of the marketing mix), will be considered separately in Chapter 14. International development is one of the key options many companies consider. Getting bigger, operating on a larger scale, and on specific targeted markets, contributes to the development of many tourism and hospitality groups. Tourism and hospitality insights 12.6 explains the strategic development of a Chinese group in the French market.

## Conclusion

The tourism and hospitality industry is comprised mainly of small and medium-sized companies in many markets/countries (including major European and Asian markets). Bigger and international companies and groups have emerged in the 1980s and 1990s, first in North America and Europe, and now in Asia. Theoretically, any company must define a strategy. But, of course, the situation is far different between an international hotel group with a business developed worldwide and a family business operating on a local scale. The (very) small business tries to do its best to understand the customers, adapt (more or less) to new trends and guest expectations, and also to understand the local competition. It should be noted that for the last two decades or so, the level of knowledge and expertise of managers has improved, and the tourism industry has gained real professionalism. Even when we consider the fundamental need for a small company to have financial resources, when the entrepreneur asks his/her bank to borrow money for investment, he/she must demonstrate the robustness of his/her business plan, and therefore have a strategy, or at least, a vision of the short-term future of his/her enterprise.

On a larger scale, small-sized companies and bigger international groups have a well-defined strategy, usually defined for a three-to-five-year term, in order to compete and develop their business on markets. However, it is getting more and more difficult to predict the future, and obtain correct forecasting about markets, consumption trends, economic growth, structure of markets, risk levels (due to high uncertainty – political, economic, environmental risks, etc.). In the meantime, we have on a monthly basis, examples of strong strategies implemented by tourism companies at an international level: some try to benefit from Asian growth, some merge with competitors to get bigger and stronger, some apply a franchising model to get stronger commercially, some experiment with new models such as low-cost airlines, hotels, car rental companies. Tourism and hospitality enterprises have many options and definitely have to consider carefully their strategy, their vision of the market, and of their business in order

## TOURISM AND HOSPITALITY INSIGHTS 12.6
## INTERNATIONAL EXPANSION OF JINJIANG IN FRANCE

A major current trend worldwide is the strong rise of Chinese hotel operators that develop through their organic/internal growth, buyouts of operators, hotel real estate buyouts or investments, or strategic agreements with the world's largest companies. In France, the most popular international tourist destination in the world, the Asian market represented 4.9% of overnight stays in 2015.

In 2015, the Louvre Hotel Group (LHG), which is placed fourth in the ranking of European hotel groups, was purchased by one of China's largest operators, JinJiang. After a phase of organic/internal development in its own market, the JinJiang Group started to grow through acquisitions and buyouts of brands already established in their market. Shanghai JinJiang International Hotels Group (owned by JinJiang International Holding) is the largest hotel group and Chinese tour operator, operating in several sectors: hotels, restaurants, transportation, logistics and travel agencies.

The French LHG Group was founded in 1976 and has always grown steadily when in 2009 it merged with another European group, Golden Tulip Hospitality. In February 2015, JinJiang International completed the acquisition of LHG from the investment fund Starwood Capital, in order to strengthen the development of tourism between France and China, and the international expansion of the brands of both groups. A partnership between the two groups had been set up in 2011 to increase their visibility.

In the medium term, the absorption of LHG by JinJiang will create:

- A portfolio combining a full range of international brands tailored to the tastes and needs of customers worldwide;
- Strong complementary synergy between LHG and JinJiang in terms of brand portfolio, geographic footprint and customer base;
- J-Club loyalty program introduced by JinJiang International covering the entire value chain, from hotels to transportation;
- Future synergies with a view to developing the central reservation system;
- Future synergies with a view to strengthening the global strategy of procurement;
- Asset portfolio optimization worldwide after the merger;
- Acceleration of global brand strategy: the group wants to develop megabrands whose objectives are: strong concept with simple, consistent and delivered claims; recognizable identifiers; visibly different stay experience; consistency of concept delivery wherever present. Thanks to strong concepts and their recognizable identifiers, the brands Campanile and Golden Tulip were chosen as megabrands in economic and midscale segments.

JinJiang is continuing with its growth or buyout strategy or acquisition of interests in different groups in France (i.e. stake in the Accor Group) and China (i.e. buyout of the Chinese hotel group Plateno Hotel Group). The LGH is therefore in a group based on the pooling of expertise and activity, such as IT architecture and purchasing.

Source: Patrick Legohérel.

to deal with the competition which is getting tougher due to the diversity offered to consumers (so many destinations, hotels, carriers, leisure activities, etc.), and the challenges of the broader economy.

### REVIEW QUESTIONS

1. What are the main strategic options for companies in tourism and hospitality wishing to expand?
2. In today's fast-changing and dynamic external environment, is there still a need for tourism and hospitality companies to proceed to in-depth analysis (including SWOT) prior to making strategic decisions?
3. Do small- and medium-sized companies have to consider strategic decision-making to the same extent as larger companies?
4. What are the benefits of a joining and collaborative alliance for a hotel/airline of your choice?

### YOUTUBE LINKS

*"Starwood Hotels' director of marketing on his customer-centric marketing approach"*

URL: https://www.youtube.com/watch?time_continue=204&v=PFpTMBqffw8

Summary: Interview with Andrew Watson, Marketing Director of Starwood Hotels. In his interview with Hot Topics, in association with Syniverse, Andrew Watson discusses how Starwood stays ahead in a disruptive hospitality industry to remain a true innovator amongst the competition. Furthermore, Andrew Watson discusses strategies to engage further with customers through technology and how brands are creating world-class experiences through these new methods.

## "Digital marketing differentiation strategy – Starwood hotels and resorts"

URL: https://www.youtube.com/watch?v=U83j2km26vE

Summary: Starwood Hotels and Resorts APAC Digital Director Janice Chan talks us through how she uses digital, and especially mobile technology, to deliver differentiated brand experiences for her nine luxury hotel brands.

## REFERENCES, FURTHER READING, AND RELATED WEBSITES

### References

Parsa, H.G., Self, J.T., Njite, D., & King, T. (2005). Why restaurants fail. *Cornell Hotel and Restaurant Administration Quarterly, 46*(3), 304–322.

Legohérel, P., Callot, P., Gallopel, K., & Peters, M. (2004). Personality characteristics, attitude toward risk and decisional orientation of the small business entrepreneur: A study of hospitality managers. *Journal of Hospitality and Tourism Research, 28*(1), 109–120.

Porter, M.E. (1985). *Competitive advantage: Creating and sustaining superior performance.* New York: Free Press.

Porter, M.E. (1996). What is strategy? *Harvard Business Review*, November–December, 61–78.

### Further reading

Ansoff, I.H. (1957). Strategies for diversification. *Harvard Business Review*, September–October, 113–124.

Buytendijk, F. (2006). Five keys to building a high-performance organization. *Business Performance Management*, February, 24–29.

Canina, L., & Carvell, S. (2007). Short-term liquidity measures for restaurant firms: Static measures don't tell the full story. *Cornell Hospitality Report, 7*(11), 1–18. Retrieved from www.chr.cornell.edu

Day, G.A., & Wensley, R. (1988). Assessing advantage: A framework for diagnosing competitive superiority. *Journal of Marketing*, April, 1–20.

Dubé, L., Renaghan, L.M., & Miller, J.M. (1994). Measuring customer satisfaction for strategic management. *Cornell Hotel and Restaurant Administration Quarterly, 35*(1), 39–47.

English, W., Josiam, B., Upchurch, R., & Willems, J. (1996). Restaurant attrition: A longitudinal analysis of restaurant failures. *International Journal of Contemporary Hospitality Management, 8*(2), 17–20.

Fields, R. (2007). *Restaurant success by the numbers.* Berkeley, CA: Ten Speed Press.

Harrison, J.S. (2003). Strategic analysis for the hospitality industry. *Cornell Hotel and Restaurant Administration Quarterly, 44*(2), 139–152.

Kwansa, F., & Parsa, H.G. (1990). Business failure analysis: An events approach. *Hospitality Research Journal, 14*(2), 23–34.

Lee, D.R. (1987). Why some succeed where others fail. *Cornell Hotel and Restaurant Administration Quarterly* (November), 33–37.

Parsa, H.G., King, T., & Njite, D. (2003). Restaurant ownership turnover: Results from a longitudinal study and a qualitative investigation. *International CHRIE Conference*, Palm Spring, CA, August 6–9.

Parsa, H.G., Self, J., Sydnor-Busso, S., & Yoon, H. (2011). Why restaurants fail? Part II: The impact of affiliation, location, and size on restaurant failures. *Journal of Foodservice Business Research, 14*(4), 360–379.

Parsa, H.G., Gregory, A., & Terry, M. (2010). Why do restaurants fail? Part III: An analysis of macro and micro factors. *Emerging Aspects Redefining Tourism and Hospitality (EARTH)*, *1*(1), 16–25.

Parsa, H.G., van der Rest, J.P., Smith, S., Parsa, R.A., & Bujisic, M. (2014). Why restaurants fail? Part IV: Rate of restaurant failures and demographic factors, results from a secondary data analysis. *Cornell Hospitality Quarterly*, *56*(1), 80–90.

Porter, M.E. (1980). *Competitive strategy: Techniques for analysing industries and competitors*, New York: Free Press.

Strotmann, H. (2007). Entrepreneurial Survival. *Small Business Economics*, *28*(1), 87–94.

## Websites

Accor Group
http://www.accorhotels.group/en

Air France – KLM
http://www.airfranceklm.com/en

Bordeaux – France's best city
https://www.telegraph.co.uk/travel/destinations/europe/france/aquitaine/bordeaux/articles/reasons-to-visit-bordeaux-on-a-city-break/

Boston Consulting Group Matrix
https://www.businessnewsdaily.com/5693-bcg-matrix.html

Harvard Business Review
https://hbr.org/2013/11/what-makes-strategic-decisions-different

HotTopics
www.hottopics.ht/events/starwood-hotels-director-marketing-companys-customer-centric-marketing-approach/

Middle East Airways
https://www.mea.com

# MAJOR CASE STUDY
# THE STRATEGY OF SUCCÈS VOYAGE

The following case study explains the development of a medium-sized French tour operator well known for innovation and customer experience.

Founded in 1993, Succès Voyage has always been dedicated to organizing business and leisure travel. This travel agency brings together a business platform on a human scale and high-end travel concierge services providing tailor-made support, anticipating customers' every need.

Succès Voyage maintains privileged relationships with its providers. These were reinforced in 2010 through the setting up of technology tools providing customers with optimization and cost reduction solutions. Finally, an innovating marketing policy was introduced. First, in 2011, Succès Voyage created a new consumer loyalty tool, the Unimiles Loyalty Programme, enabling customers to travel more often. Second, 2013 saw the launch of a new luxury brand: a lifetime of traveling: As You Go traveling (*Au fur et à mesure*).

## The marketing concept of a new brand

Succès Voyages introduced a new customer approach and launched a new, differentiating concept, based upon experiential luxury. For customers, the key question is no longer where they wish to go but why and with whom.

## The underlying principle

Nowadays, traveling is part and parcel of customers' life. It is widely accessible and consequently has lost its appeal as an exceptional event. Flying and booking hotel rooms have become more accessible. Traveling brings magic moments, but also major disappointments, as is easily seen from viewing sites showing customer assessments of hotel services. Some of the underlying reasons for such trends include:

*   There are no countries left to discover. Means of transport and easily available information have robbed people of the possibility of total discovery;
*   High-end hotels have become standardized in that services are the same everywhere;
*   Travelers are more in search of an experience with luxury accommodation no longer enough;
*   Destinations and countries can no longer rely on their own intrinsic features;
*   The quality of traveling varies according to the traveler.

## As you go through life

The main concept of this new traveling collection, As You Go, is thus the story of everyday life moments that are prolonged. The desire to travel is directly influenced by these life moments in that life is punctuated by various stages and family, social, or sentimental needs.

### Why travel?

Everybody needs to spend time with their children, surprise their significant other, "pick up the pieces," strengthen relationships with those they see too rarely, live another life, or simply step back and take a break.

### With whom?

Travel companions are key determinants of expectations and choices. People travel differently when they are with or without their children, in groups, with their teenagers when separated from their spouse, or even when children have left the nest after graduating. Hence, As You Go offers a collection of trips that are mere suggestions for people to interpret in terms of their own history; this is tailor-made travel through a lifetime.

### Traveling as you go: beyond the tailor-made experience

Just like people's lives, traveling is full of emotions and memorable moments, Succès Voyages provides customers with the opportunity of prolonging certain emotions or changing direction.

*   Feel like changing your mind?
*   Feel like dropping out of a pre-designed itinerary even if it's been self-set?
*   The family is disappointed after the first couple of days?
*   The place is pure magic, everybody's happy; what a shame we have to leave so soon.
*   Quite simply put – feel like changing your need?

The As You Go collection brings customers the ultimate flexibility they need to be able to live each moment to the full. To this end, the travel experiences included in this new collection are stamped "flexi-friendly," with no changed fee or additional costs.

### The strategic choice made by Succès Voyage

The company has chosen to develop its activity-based competitive advantage, relying on its ability to create added value with greater sustainability than its competition. To this end, it selected a strategic line of action based on the notions of difference and focus. In the luxury travel market segment, the new brand As You Go stands out by making available different services that offer a unique and attractive perceived value. These differences involve all the features of the service and are based on a new, client need-based approach. The development tool is based on the notion of clients who have different needs and wish to find products or services that meet their specific expectations.

*   A differentiation strategy aimed at the high end of the market segment that increases the client's perceived value through closely fitting the client's needs;

- The success of this differentiation strategy is based upon unfailing consistency in its implementation: the salespeople's expertise closely corresponds to the product they sell and the services they offer;
- Highly customized services on offer (high-end travel concierge services).

*Its product:* it offers real added value;
*The new brand: As You Go* has an evocative and distinctive quality (as you go through life, as you travel);
*Its communication:* it is dynamic and adapted to the needs of the target client base;
*Its distribution:* it is direct, without intermediaries, thus ensuring a client-focused relationship through expert salespeople.

One example of the As You Go collection is as follows:

Making the children happy – Live out your passion to the full – Belize
One of the great sorrows of modern life is the lack of the unexpected, the absence of adventure.

(Théophile Gautier)

## Paul and Margot playing Indiana Jones

Unknowingly, the budding adventurers will revise their geography, history, and science lessons live! It is in the Toledo region, south of Belize, the tropical rainforest is at its thickest, hiding an amazing network of caves with wonderful crystal-clear water to dive into. Welcome to Maya country. Ceiba trees, benevolent and mysterious, are the gates to the Mayan universe. Each new find will make the young explorers rack their brains: at Lubaantun, monumental stones stand with no cement; at Uxbenka, a tomb is found, and the quest for the crystal skull is launched. As they move into the earth's womb, on the outskirts of villages, through the papaya plantations, parents won't recognize their teenagers!

## Off-the-ground base camp

No need for backpacks or tin plates; the on-stilts cottage boasts a permanent maître d'hôtel (oh yes, adventure can be enjoyed in comfort, not to say luxury!). Nestling in the Machaca reserve itself, is a promontory offering breathtaking views of nature – and what kind of nature! The forest is an inextricable tangle of vegetation over Mayan ruins and a cable car links this area with the river.

## The adventurer's kit bag

Canoes, mountain bikes, and a full range of equipment is available to quite literally explore the area, day or night, on the lookout for jaguar, ocelot, or tapir! A few bubble-filled digressions (quite literally – snorkeling in West Snake Caye) remind everyone that the Sapodilla Cayes Marine

Reserve is on the UNESCO World Heritage list, one of the world's greatest coral reefs. Who said Indiana Jones could not rest a little in-between two scuffles with relic looters?

Source: Olivier Glasberg, Associate Director, Succès Voyage. In I. Frochot and P. Legohérel (Eds.), *Marketing du Tourisme*. Paris: Dunod Editor, 2014.

Major case study questions

1. Why is Succès Voyage such an appropriate example of experiential marketing?
2. What may have been some of the challenges encountered by Succès Voyage in developing this new strategic approach?
3. How sustainable is such a strategy in light of the speed with which competitors can mirror that adopted by Succès Voyage?
4. Are there any other tourism or hospitality companies that you are aware of that have adopted a similar strategy to Succès Voyage and with what results?

# Market segmentation, targeting, and positioning

## Learning outcomes

By the end of this chapter, students will:

- Understand the main stages of the segmentation process (segmentation, targeting, and positioning)
- Be aware of the various categories of segmentation criteria and their respective contribution to relevant market segmentation
- Understand the importance of positioning for companies and destinations facing fierce competition both on the domestic and worldwide markets
- Be introduced to a number of case study scenarios and examples that illustrate various market segmentation, targeting, and positioning approaches.

## Introduction

The purpose of market segmentation is to help companies embark on effective and relevant actions in their markets. Seeking to reach all market segments through common marketing activities is not judicious when a client base is heterogeneous. On the other hand, providing each client with tailor-made services is unrealistic and economically unprofitable. It is only in a few high-end markets, such as tailoring or the luxury hotel sector, that it is feasible and appropriate to allocate resources individual to the company's best clients.

In most cases, market segmentation corresponds to the needs of a business model and its concomitant effectiveness that: show the targeting strategies of one or several groups of clients (segments); unite similar characteristics into one group (individual profiles, purchasing behaviors, etc.); isolate characteristics in between groups/segments. The first step of the market analysis is referred to as *market segmentation*. This is where companies establish an operational marketing plan adapted to the targeted groups of clients (product/service meeting the clients' needs, suitable communication plan, attractive and target-appropriate price range, and distribution network providing optimum contact with the target clients). The second step of the process, called *market targeting*, consists of evaluating each market segment's attractiveness and the expected economical or financial contribution. Once, one or several segments have been targeted, companies will decide on the value the consumer will associate with their product. The *positioning* of the market offering, must not only create value for the customer, but also help to differentiate the product/service from their competitors. At a time when tourism and hospitality companies and destinations are facing fierce competition, it is crucial to create significant value that is clearly identifiable by targeted customers.

Segmentation is an important tool for creating consumer-centric and design services that will be able to answer to customer needs and thereby create value for them. As such it is a central tool for Customer Relationship Management (CRM). Segmentation offers companies the possibility of developing strategic advantages over their competitors as it encourages them to focus on one or several segments, fully understand the needs of those customers, and serve them more efficiently than their direct competitors. However, segmentation is also a costly approach, therefore following several guiding principles is necessary.

## Market segmentation: implementing segmentation

The first step involves considering all consumers in a given market and examining the main differences that exist between consumer groups, based on various segmentation criteria. A statistical analysis then leads to determining homogeneous groups of people who share similar characteristics. In terms of the relative potential of each segment (individual profiles, economic potential), one or several segments are selected. With limited capacity (financial, human, technical), organizations are not necessarily able to focus their efforts on all the identified segments, which creates the need to establish priorities. Once the segmentation process is completed, organizations work towards adapting their operational marketing plans for each targeted segment.

In the tourism sector, companies focus their efforts on market segments comprising travelers sharing common characteristics. Their goal is to maximize the efficiency of their marketing policy, in order to make best use of their limited marketing and budget resources and to achieve the greatest possible economic impact.

Marketing segmentation and positioning is a major concern, not only for large companies, but also for small and medium-sized ones as evident in Tourism and hospitality insights 13.1.

## TOURISM AND HOSPITALITY INSIGHTS 13.1
## HOTEL SEGMENTATION

The hospitality market is eclectic with a very wide offer which is easily accessible on the web. It's crucial more than ever to propose the right product (meeting customer expectation) to catch its fair share of the market, to increase customer loyalty and preferences, and to maximize profit. I own and run a 25 room, two-star hotel, with limited services (bed and breakfast) in Orléans (French Loire Valley) and I have to create a different and dedicated offer if I want to be competitive in my market. Orléans represents a 50%/50% market share between business and leisure with a high season in summer with many foreign visitors passing through or visiting the area (cycling tours, visits to Loire Valley châteaux, and vineyard visits).

*Positioning:* We understand from customer behavior that the three main successful market positions are premium, low-cost, or niche. Regarding my situation, I've chosen to be on a niche market which is much more accessible for a small property. I would like to be *an affordable boutique hotel*: city center, design and decoration, family atmosphere, additional free amenities. The idea is to offer an authentic and dedicated consumer experience at a reasonable price and meet specific customer expectations (family and businesswomen).

*Segmentation:* I need to focus on my main demand groups that is leisure and business, so I will target families for their summer leisure trip and women traveling for business during the week in winter. Of course, I will welcome every other segmentation but will avoid groups due to the size and the atmosphere of the hotel.

*Targeting:* I'm building a website highlighting specificities for each target group.

*Leisure:* Family rooms for up to four people, reduced prices for specific services, breakfast for children, free cots, bottle warmers, high chairs.

*Business:* High speed Internet, parking (charged), carefully decorated rooms, tea and coffee facilities, and advice for nearby take-aways and restaurants.

Being focused on my positioning and trying to understand these customer expectations allows me to propose a slightly different offer on the market and to attract customers where price is not the first option. The mix between specific and dedicated services, a central location, and a good e-reputation give me the opportunity to increase my REVAPR by 15% over that of the market.

The relevant segmentation, targeting, and positioning give the hospitality sectors an opportunity to increase profitability by selling their offer at higher rates because it creates value for the segmented customer you've chosen to focus on. Value is created through the customer reviews that recognize that your answer agrees with their specific guest expectations, creating a virtuous circle. Specific target group attention means customer satisfaction, increases your e-reputation, and influences the next buyer group. Being focused on a chosen group of customers allows me to build positive word of mouth through the main Online Travel Agent (OTA) and allows me to justify a higher rate that can make the difference between my hotel and my competitors' in terms of final choice.

Away from a main site like Paris or New York City where demand is often much higher than the hospitality offer (explaining, in a way, the success of Airbnb in these destination), the hospitality industry is encouraged to create value by focusing their services on a specific segment on a right positioning (low-cost, premium, or niche) and then encourage positive word of mouth to build a powerful marketing communication.

Letting the customer do the marketing for us will increase profitability. The Internet gives the consumer so many choices that we also need to offer customization and specificity in the tourism industry, as the web-mature customer seeks to find the right product for each specific need.

Source: Stéphane Gautier, hotel manager, Orléans, France.

## Market segmentation: segmentation principles

In order to conduct segmentation, the segments identified should respond to different categories:

- *Be identifiable:* Is it easy for the company to access the data necessary for the type of segmentation sought after? Does the segmentation require a new data collection? Which information needs to be collected to direct the future marketing mix?
- *Each segment should be measurable:* Each segment should be measured through specific variables such as purchasing power, shopping basket, size, profiles, etc.
- *Segments should be substantial:* If the company is going to make the effort to develop a different marketing mix, it needs to make sure that the segment is large enough for the whole strategy to remain profitable. Substantiality implies that each segment is evaluated both as a combination of size and spending (i.e. a smaller segment might still be of interest if it is made up of individuals ready to spend more than the other segments, or who come at different times of the year, etc.).
- *Each segment must be reachable:* the company will investigate how each segment can be efficiently reached. For example, communication channels are essential to understand how to communicate with each segment.

On top of those principles are two other principles, pertaining to statistical procedures, but which also have strategic implications which refer to the construction of the segments:

- *Internal cohesion:* If a new marketing mix is developed for the segment, it will necessarily be costlier so the company has to make sure that the segments identified are close enough in needs to be receptive to this marketing mix. Statistical techniques used to segment data usually use this principle.
- *External differentiation:* For a segmentation strategy to be efficient, each segment has to be as far from the next one as possible. In other words, if the company will design a different marketing mix for each segment, it needs to make sure that this marketing mix will respond specifically to the needs of one specific segment. If it attracts partially several segments, then the segmentation strategy has not been efficient.

Once segments have been identified, the company can operate several strategic choices:

- *Undifferentiated marketing:* This marketing considers that, regardless of the segments that might exist in the market, the company aims to cover them all with its products. This is therefore not a segmentation strategic approach since the entire market is targeted together. This strategy was characteristic of companies at the start of the industrialization era when shops offered much less diversity of products and mass production was the norm. In the 21st century, those strategic approaches are quite rare. To remain competitive, companies have specialized in specific consumer needs and those needs are indeed more diverse than in the past. There is perhaps one exception in the low-cost industry. Indeed, if taking the example of Ryanair, the low-cost Irish airline, its strategy has always been to provide a service whose main advantage lies in its price. The notion of customer service is virtually absent and so is any notion of class differentiation and price-privileged service.

- *Differentiated marketing:* This is the opposite strategy to the previous one in the sense that an enterprise will aim to develop one or several products that are aimed at two segments at least. The enterprise will have several products and services that will target those different segments. This strategy is necessarily costlier as a different marketing mix is necessary for each segment. On the other end, sales will be higher. This is an approach that requires a careful strategic vision, as it does carry an inherent risk, the risk of aiming to serve several segments well.

- *Concentrated marketing strategy (or niche marketing):* Within this strategy, a company will aim to target only one segment. This is often the case in small companies who decide to specialize in the very specific needs of one segment. Small travel agents for instance can develop highly specialized skills on specific markets. Their strategy is to become very efficient and competent representatives for the needs of that specific market. It often concerns small markets which can develop high loyalty if the enterprise shows its capabilities in understanding and serving customers' needs. For instance, a travel agency can specialize in a specific interest such as ornithology (bird watching) or volcanoes. By developing expertise on those topics (knowledge about the best areas and seasons to visit places, identifying local guides and accommodation, etc.) and by developing a good understanding of their customers' needs, they become highly efficient and recognized on that market.

- *Individual marketing:* If we consider the core concept of segmentation, we should admit that the best marketing mix is the one provided to each customer, fully adapted to his needs, expectations, characteristics, behaviors, etc. Does it make sense? No, almost all situations, the investment requested to build relevant marketing for a target market is important, and one can expect a return on investment that is it is for the consumers to cover all expenses, and some profit for the business. Let's consider that in some specific context, we may be close to a kind of individual segmentation, when companies accept fully addressing individual guests' needs. For instance, in a palace/luxury hotel, managers pay close attention to high value guests and fulfill almost all of their requests. Can we consider that we are facing a "segment" made up of one guest? Not really. Even if the hotel agrees to modify the room to meet the guest's requests, or prepare a special menu for him, this guest is staying in a hotel targeted towards a larger group of people. And the marketing effort made to tailor the whole place for all customers will satisfy more or less all guests, including a few higher contributing ones.

It is always possible to segment a market with various variables, so it is important to be careful that the segmentation is not just another consultant trick but that it has a reality in terms of significantly different consumer behavior and expectations towards some enterprise products.

## Market segmentation: segmentation criteria

For segmentation to be effective, the necessary information must be collected regarding the customers' main characteristics. Straightforward variables such as socio-demographic, economic, and geographic characteristics are usually used to identify customer profiles. For instance, such criteria as "with or without children" or "children's age" enable significant differentiations in the tourism market. Families will seek appropriate amenities and forms of entertainment and have to follow the school calendar. Age is another significant variable. A younger clientele (those under 20 or in the 20–30 age range) will have specific, multiple, changing expectations. Target marketing and an appropriate service offer depend upon thorough knowledge of these population segments. For instance, a ski resort may decide to target primarily a young population. It should then position its image and adapt its services in terms of the expectations of this clientele. Young customers, however, are said to represent a segment that is more difficult to understand and control than the older generations. Other criteria often used are social class, lifestyle, and personality. These provide a lot of information regarding customers, but they are rather complex, particularly in terms of data gathering and interpreting.

The criteria based upon purchasing and/or use behaviors are said to be highly appropriate as they involve homogeneous behaviors of groups of people. These criteria are thus widely used by tourism sector professionals for their market segmentation. Accurate market segmentation leads to a productive customer breakdown through accounting for the variations in people's purchasing behaviors. The following section reviews the main categories of segmentation criteria.

## Socio-demographic, economic, and geographic market segmentation

Traditionally, segmentation was undertaken on different variables that could describe consumers as who they were (in socio-economic terms) rather than what they expected from life. As a result, traditional segmentation approaches would segment consumers from one or a combination of several variables such as: age, life-cycle, generation, gender, household composition, nationality, etc. Other socio-economic factors could also be used such as level of education (which, in tourism consumption, is a key variable), social class, occupation, income, etc.

Below, we shall consider the example of two important segmentation criteria in the tourism and hospitality industry:

- Life-cycle and age
- Gender

## Life-cycle stage and age

Customers may have different statuses, such as couple, family, "single," and of course different age categories. These two criteria might be associated to better identify specific groups of customers. For instance, couples without children may or may not stay in your resort during the school holiday period and a young couple (in their late twenties or thirties – without children) will very likely have different needs and expectations from a couple in their fifties or sixties (with grown-up children, and unaccompanied).

The family is a significant criterion in the tourism sector as these customers have specific and well identified needs and expectations, naturally most of them due to the presence of children. Interestingly, some operators sometimes decide to separate families from other guests who are looking for a more "quiet and peaceful" atmosphere. It is not easy to prevent one or other groups, either young families or guests without children, from staying in your hotel (which might be a legal issue in some countries, as is the case for many segmentation criteria, once you start refusing some guests and accepting others). Companies get round this problem when they have several properties at the same destination, simply by adapting an offer to families and one for guests without children.

Another criterion, related to personal situations and life-cycle is the "alone" segment which has started to attract the attention of tourism companies. This segment is now well identified and is made up of financially healthy customer, looking to enjoy life, travel, and have some fun. This "alone" status was not previously well accepted socially, but now the "alone" customers are no longer afraid of joining a group of tourists. Some specific offers have even been created with the "alone" segment in mind and some small and medium-sized agencies have developed their business in this niche market. For example, in France, Covoyageurs offer packages not only for single customers, looking to travel with others rather than on their own; but also for grand-parents traveling with grandchildren and for single parents traveling with their children, who want to share their experience with others, and, in the meantime, enjoy services provided by the company.

Targeting consumers based on the age criterion has long been considered as a good means of segmenting markets. Senior citizens (largely the over sixties but dependent on one's definition of senior) are a very important group and are more or less associated with the Baby-boomer generation. In leisure activities, nearly one-third of customers are seniors. Demographic data of the main outbound markets all over the world (in North America, Western Europe, China, Japan, and Australia) show evidence of an ageing population.

An estimation of 13 European markets (across different countries) shows that the 50–74 age group represents 29.5% of the population and the over-fifties represent 39% of the population, but will increase to 44% in 2030.

Seniors are often at ease physically and financially and they have time for leisure, if they are retired. For the new generation of seniors, who have been more and more used to traveling (for family and/or business purposes) they are still willing to travel for pleasure in the "senior period" of their life. They are not afraid of technology: most seniors make online purchases and look for information online before booking (using, for instance, comparison websites).

One interesting approach when segmenting seniors, is not to consider their chronological age, but rather to investigate the perception they have about their age. Which age do they feel they have (cognitive age) and what age do they wish they still had (ideal age). Senior behaviors are strongly correlated with their age perception and their global situation as seniors often perceive themselves as younger than their chronological age. However, this age perception is not the same depending on the cultural environment. For example, Le Serre et al. (2012, 2017) show that French (Western) seniors tend to see themselves as younger than Chinese (Asian) senior travelers. Another interesting segment is that of Millennials as evidenced in Tourism and hospitality insights 13.2.

## TOURISM AND HOSPITALITY INSIGHTS 13.2
## THE MILLENNIALS (ALSO CALLED DIGITAL NATIVES)

Depending on which generation group a traveler belongs to, their behaviors are different. We note:

- Baby-boomers are the generation born just after the Second World War;
- The X generation is made up of people born between 1960 and 1980;
- The Y generation (also called Millennials or Digital Natives) are people born between 1980 and 1999, who grew up with the Internet and mobile telephones;
- The Z generation, the youngest, were born after the year 2000. They are immersed in the social networks, applications, and mobile phones. They don't know that electronic

devices haven't always been mobile! The mobility (ATAWAD (AnyTime, AnyWhere, Any-Device)), access to unlimited information, instant contacts, continuous social contacts, etc., are characteristics written into their genes.

Millennials tend to travel more than the other generations, as much for personal reasons as for professional ones. According to the same study carried out on Internet users in France, the UK, and Germany, these people are more attentive to the prices and photographs in adverts than the X generation and Baby-boomers (Source: *L'Echo Touristique*, July–August 2017, Expedia study).

**Image 13.1**

Source: https://www.pexels.com/photo/group-of-people-enjoying-music-concert-325521/

Millennials are therefore a very interesting generation for the tourism industry due to their professional requirements for traveling but also for their pleasure-seeking travel. Travel is for them a form of escapism, to experience new things, and to share them. One of the principal characteristics of the Digital Natives, is their permanent use of technology, not only for their travel arrangements (they compare and buy on line more than the Baby-boomers and the X generation), but also while traveling, in order to stay connected with the daily social environment and to share their experience with others. This generation is partly constituted of young employed people without children, who purchase many short holidays, and who have sufficient financial capacity and those without school-aged children and have few scheduling constraints.

However, professionals need to keep in mind that these customers also represent a challenge: they seek new experiences, variety (and are therefore difficult to maintain loyalty), and a real traveling experience (they are demanding as far as the services offered and what is provided are concerned). They use technology not only for sharing their experience, but also for judging the service and diffusing their opinions (via written text or photographs, etc.) whether they be negative or positive. This generation makes very independent purchasing decisions (they are more swayed by the opinions of friends and family than adverts and official information), and holiday bookings (the majority of their purchases are carried out on line). Technology is considered as a need which must not fail them during their stay (a Millennials without a WiFi connection is like a fish out of water!). In fact, more so than for the precedent generations, following the rapid consumption trends (the quest for authenticity, sharing – such as couch-surfing, of free tour guides, etc.), and the ever increasing desire for the personalization of offers (which appeared at the end of the 1980s and the beginning of the 1990s), where more or less attention was paid by professionals to these Millennial travelers.

Source: Patrick Legohérel.

## Gender

Dividing a market into different groups based on gender is more or less significant, depending on the product or service offered on the market, but also on the period. Let's consider the interesting situation of businesswomen in hotels, on the upscale segment. Formerly, women were confined to taking care of the family, children, and home. They started to be more involved in professional activity, but without the same status as men in private companies and public organizations. Thanks to positive developments of society (in many parts of the world), women have reached all levels of management and various job profiles (including top management). A consequence is that business segment of upscale hotel group, which almost exclusively consisted of men for decades, started to reach a different mix in the early 2000s, when businesswomen made up 40–50% of the clientele. Aware of this evolution, hotel groups started to consider gender-based segmentation.

Hotels are looking to understand better the particular needs of businesswomen and other female travelers in order to adapt, or even exclusively reserve, products and services for this target group, representing a strongly growing economic opportunity. According to Travel Industry Association Research, women represent 43% of the business segment and 75% of them choose the hotel where they will stay. The number of trips a woman makes increases with more women reaching higher management. Now hotels recognize the specific requirements of female travelers and integrate the notion of gender segmentation in view of a better adaptation of products and services.

The typical profile of the female customer is a customer that is considered demanding, and women travelers tend to be younger and better qualified than their male counterparts. They prefer to dine alone at the hotel rather than going out and they like to feel "at home." Also, women are often members of loyalty programs. During their free time, throughout their business trip, they take the time to go shopping or go on cultural visits. The majority of women choose and reserve their hotel room via the Internet.

In the early 2000s, Grange City Hotel in London, decided to allocate 68 rooms out of 300 to their women guests, and the Hilton Park Lane (where 50% of the guests where women) offered a"women-*only executive floor*." Cigar boxes and mini-bars were taken away to make space for large cupboards, make-up mirrors, and hair dryers with cables long enough to be able to dry one's hair in front of the television, a spyhole in the door, a security chain on the door, and women-only service personnel. They made available healthy snacks and low-calorie menus which are typically sought after by female customers.

Today, all hotel groups pay attention to their female segment and some hotels still offer women's executive floors. For instance, the Hamilton Crowne Plaza in Washington (http://hamiltonhoteldc.com/rooms/womens-floor/) offers special services on the women's executive floor, but itis not exclusively dedicated to women. The Aquincum Hotel in Budapest (http://www.aquincumhotel.com/business-woman-room/) offers floors exclusively dedicated to their female guests.

## Psychographic segmentation

Psychographic segmentation is a very different approach from traditional segmentation since it allocates buyers to different groups based on either their lifestyle, psychological values, personality traits, or social class.

### Personality traits

Are you impulsive or do you take time to make decisions? Are you organized or disorganized? Are you authoritative or rather open to listening to others? These are some examples of character traits showing a large diversity of variables that compose someone's personality. Personality analysis is used in marketing to understand individuals' behavior, but can quickly become complex and make the identification of a large group of consumers difficult.

### Social class

Societies are divided into groups, based on financial circumstances, social image, power, and social position of individual group members. A hierarchy more or less exists within these groups, leading to a categorization of lower-, middle, or upper-class (with a variety of sub groups between the three main categories). Similar behaviors can be identified between members of a given group and these similarities may be relevant in order to create the marketing mix.

### Lifestyle segmentation

Lifestyle segmentation includes variables that collect information on how individuals go about their life. Typically, lifestyles are evaluated using a scale measuring activities, interests, and opinions (the AIO models). As such, the technique aims to understand how consumers envisage their life in terms of their place in society, their activities, their political opinions, their interests, etc. AIO give a global picture of individuals as one would see them in their daily life and within their society. This approach is supposed to translate quite accurately consumers' expectations and preferences in terms of consumption.

### Values as segmentation

Values is another approach used in psychographic segmentation. Those values were first developed by Milton Rokeach (1973, p. 5): "A value is an enduring belief that a specific mode of conduct or end-state of existence is personally or socially preferable to an opposite or converse mode of conduct or end-state of experience."

Rokeach, associated deeply-rooted values with beliefs and attitudes. Those deeply-rooted values were divided into two broad categories: instrumental and terminal values. Terminal values related to the end-states of existence, in other words the goals that one would want to achieve in one's life. These end-states of existence values are: security, happiness, true friendship, inner harmony, freedom, wisdom, etc. Instrumental values referred to preferred modes of behavior and can be considered as means to attain instrumental values. This instrumental perspective groups values such as: courage, honesty, cheerfulness, forgiveness, responsibility, politeness, and so forth. This list is also called the Rokeach Value Survey (RVS) and was operationalized by asking respondents to rank each set of values by order of importance. Rokeach argued that, once learned, values were ordered hierarchically into a value system in which each value would be allocated different weights.

Values are issued from culture, societal and personality influences and are conceived as more stable over time than attitudes since they are more central to an individual's cognitive system. Since this original article, various researchers have used values and the use of this construct has enlarged drastically.

### Behavioral segmentation

Consumers could also be segmented through their product/service usage: heavy/intermittent/low users; loyalty, consumption timing, etc. Behavior variables are often considered as highly significant and relevant criteria for building market segments as many different criteria can be considered. Below are some of these criteria.

## User status and rate

Consumers can be identified through the level and or status of their consumption. Are they users, non-users, ex-users of the product? How many products, or how much of a product/service do they use – in terms of expenses, the level of quantity purchased, or purchase and consumption frequency. Some criteria are of great interest for tourism and hospitality companies and destinations. For example, markets can be divided into heavy, medium, or light spenders. For destinations, this information helps one to understand, not only who are the high contribution consumers, but also identifying travelers willing to spend money at destinations (direct expenditure), which is a significant fact when analyzing the benefit for local companies at destinations (Legohérel & Wong, 2006), and the economic impact of the tourism activity. For a company, targeting the heavy spenders also makes sense: selecting the traveler who is willing to pay a high price for his/her room is a relevant fact (guest selection based on the revenue management processes). But more important, is how much guests are willing to spend in your restaurants and bars, at your spa, at your golf course, at your on-site shops, etc. Identifying the global contribution of your guest not only makes sense in order to increase revenue (Legohérel et al., 2013), but might also be considered as a relevant segmentation approach.

Another example of highly significant standard criteria in tourism, is the first-time visitor versus the repeat-visitor. These two segments could have very different behaviors. For instance, when visiting a destination for the first time, most tourists concentrate on the main places and sites of this destination. When visiting France, most (almost all) first-time visitors concentrate on Paris, and visit some of the main monuments (the Eiffel Tower, the Louvre, the cathedral of Notre Dame, the palace of Versailles, the Champs Elysées, etc.). However, when visiting France for a second or third time (or more), many visitors are willing to discover other areas, such as the Loire Valley with its many châteaux, the wine areas (including the famous Bordeaux, Burgundy, and Champagne areas), the mountains (the Alps, etc.) and the coast (Normandy, Brittany, etc.) areas, or also the French Riviera in south-eastern France, for example. Tourism authorities in charge of these regions and tourism sites, require knowledge about the degree of usage visitors already have in the main destination (i.e. the country, France, and the place that attracts the most tourists, Paris). Moreover, some tourists may have a "basic" touristic behavior when coming for the first time (and visit the main places), but may well change their behavior when coming on return visits and have a different approach to the destination. They might decide to visit less touristy places, engage differently with the local population, and seek to discover local culture, etc.

## Loyalty status

A market can be segmented using loyalty status and it is more efficient for a company to keep customer loyal rather than prospecting for new customers all the time. Loyalty programs were first developed on a large scale when airlines expanded their frequent flyer programs in the early 1980s. At that time, major established airlines were fighting against many newcomers on the market, after the turmoil caused by the Airline Deregulation Act (1978). Major airlines could offer travelers a whole trip whatever the destination in the US, or for any international destination, but many smaller companies had a limited number of destinations to offer. Rewards for loyal travelers were given in the form of commercial gifts, such as free air-miles. Now, almost all companies, small-, medium-sized, international hotel groups, airlines and alliances offer loyalty programs.

The challenge is to keep one's customer loyal, which proves to be more and more difficult. A non-loyal customer, or one with a "zapping behavior" is explained by the fact that the consumer is confronted with a huge diversity of products and services, and moving from one product to another or from one brand to another is so easy. Consumers are also more curious and often seek variety, diversity, and change. When a guest, who stayed for a couple of days in your hotel, answers "very satisfied" to all the questions in a survey, but "no" when asked whether he/she is willing to return to your hotel, you might be surprised and disappointed. Are you accountable? Probably not. The customer may just consider that he/she had spent an enjoyable stay in your hotel and simply wants to discover something else next time, which makes keeping customers loyal to places, products, or brands a real challenge. However, segmenting your market using loyalty can contribute greatly to your business.

### Benefit segmentation

Benefit segmentation was primarily introduced in 1968 by Haley who aimed at developing an instrument that would provide a better understanding and prediction of future buying behavior than did traditional market segmentation techniques. As a practitioner, and having admitted the limits of traditional techniques such as geographic, demographic, or volume-based segmentation for advertising purposes, Haley (1968) was mainly concerned with the development of new market segmentation tools.

Although, he did not deny the advantages of traditional techniques in guiding promotional tools (media purchase, identification of users and non-users, geographical identification and so forth), he criticized their inability at predicting behavior.

Haley introduced benefit segmentation as a market segmentation technique whereby market segments would be identified by causal factors: "The belief underlying this segmentation strategy is that the benefits which people are seeking in consuming a given product are the basic reasons for the existence of true market segments" (Haley, 1968, p. 31).

Although the concept in itself might not have been revolutionary, the main development brought by Haley was to motivate marketers to analyze their consumer markets from a different perspective and consider the benefits sought as a primary source of purchasing behavior. Haley strongly believed that the benefits sought were the best translators of the reasons why people would buy a product rather than another, or prefer a specific brand. Haley was also determined to develop a technique that would have practical implications, for instance, the benefits identified could be used directly as promotional messages.

While Haley studied benefits of a tangible nature, years later the notion of benefits was expanded to integrate experiential benefits: what the consumer ought to gain from the experience. This is particularly true in tourism research where benefit segmentation proved to be particularly well adapted. The example of historic houses below illustrates in detail how this technique can be used in a tourism context. For a review of its applications in the tourism sector, see Frochot and Morrison (2000).

## Multiple segmentation bias

Some segmentation strategies aim to group several of those variables under a multivariable segmentation approach such as the PRIZM classification provided by Nielsen. The objective of multiple segmentation basis is to better identify target groups, defined on the basis of various categories of criteria, including socio-demographic, economic, and geographic criteria, life style, and behavioral data.

Nielsen PRIZM classifies American households on segments based on a combination of sociological, geographical and demographic variables. The basic tenet that underpins this approach is that from a statistical perspective, individuals are highly influenced by the place where they live.

All these variables remain interesting and useful at explaining different behaviors and have always produced efficient segmentation strategies. However, if they are pertinent at decrypting some behavioral commonalities in segments, they remain very descriptive. For instance, they do not bring an explanation as to why and how differently some consumers perceive some products. For instance, consumers within the same age group, or social class, or income level might have very different expectations towards a product. Experiential marketing theories also show that an experience is highly personal that needs to be understood with more subtle segmentation strategies than the traditional ones mentioned above.

## International segmentation

Although international marketing is to be introduced in Chapter 14, in this section, we remind readers that for any company or destination engaged in international activity, segmenting markets on the basis of similarities between consumers from the main markets is the first relevant step. Often, the criterion considered is therefore geographic location, as the customers' country of origin helps to define one's markets ("Where do your guests come from?"). Each group of customers associated with a country is often also regarded as a segment. We then speak about the

Japanese market/segment, the French market/segment, assuming that all consumers from each segment have similar needs and buying behaviors. This criterion makes sense, as it seems logical that a Chinese tourist will have different expectations and will behave in a different manner from a Spanish tourist. However, we must keep in mind that to achieve accurate and meaningful segmentations, other criteria must be considered such as the cultural environment (partially correlated with geographic location, but not only), economic factors, and the macro-environment (political, legal, administrative factors, etc.).

## Market targeting and positioning

As explained earlier in this chapter, the decision regarding the selection of the segments targeted by a company is based on the estimated financial and or economic power and expected benefit from each segment. As it is not relevant, or feasible to target all segments, a company will target the most valuable segments, or more specifically just one or two segments. These decisions will always have been in line with the strategy decided by the management of the company (see Chapter 12). Apart from the key factor (i.e. benefit expected from each segment), other factors (including: competitors' strategies, range and diversity of consumers' profiles, products or services themselves, etc.) may be considered when deciding a concentrated, differentiated, or undifferentiated market targeting strategy. Sometimes, products may not be that easy to adapt to different markets due to the product itself (technical issues, legal issues, etc.). However, services are usually easier to adapt and modify to a specific context/segment.

Once segments will have been identified, market positioning consists of assuring a logical relationship between the marketing strategy, positioning, and the market targeted. For example, the Club Med group (created in the 1960s), which offers attractive resorts ("Les Villages") all over the world, decided in the early 2000s to move to a "high standard/luxury positioning" but to continue targeting families (one of their main/first target segment). The first decision (i.e. move to a high standard/luxury positioning) was made with the evolution of the market in mind and is based on a marketing strategy analysis. The second decision (i.e. to carry on targeting families), is based on marketing segmentation analysis. The results of both (i.e. target families with high financial capacities) will pave the way for a marketing mix decision. Whatever the segments, a marketing mix has to be developed for each target segment (concentrated or differentiated marketing).

The aims of positioning are twofold:

- *Strategic positioning:* Decided by the company in order to give the product a significant advantage on targeted markets. Each company expects their product/service or destination to obtain a greater advantage than competitors.

- *Marketing positioning:* Shapes the way consumers perceive the service or product. Consumers may have a global image of the product/service, but they sometimes concentrate on attributes perceived as more important than others.

A gap may occur between positioning decided by the company, and consumers' perception of the positioning. When Club Med moved to an upper-scale segment, it took many years for consumers from the upscale segment to understand that this product could meet their expectations in terms of high quality services and standards expected. The company had a long history on the French and European markets, with a strong notoriety of the brand. What had been an advantage for 30 years then became a weakness for the company (known as a midscale lodging company, with its villages built for mass tourism in the 1970s and the 1980s). It took nearly eight years for the company to fill the gap between the new strategic positioning decided in 2002 and the perception by upscale consumers of really high quality services delivered by Club Med.

Companies and destinations can follow various positioning strategies, and consider various criteria in order to differentiate themselves from their competitors.

- A specific or original product: Kentucky Fried Chicken (KFC) is known for its original product, fried chicken, symbolized by the bucket.
- A specific ambiance or service design: Motel One is known for its designed hotels.
- A specific concept – adopted by many companies: for example, the boutique hotels. All over the world, boutique hotels are made for guests who want a more charming place than standardized hotels, sometimes, highlighting local cultures, artists, products, etc.
- A specific concept – emblematic of one company: the Jo&Joe hotels developed by Accor group, a product in between a hotel and a private apartment, created for the Millennial generation.
- An economy/midscale or upscale/luxury positioning: most companies and destinations in the world, more or less try to define segments using this type of positioning. For example, destinations focus on upscale markets, the objectives being to attract high contributing customers, but sometimes also to avoid mass tourism (fewer tourists help destinations to be more sustainable); Mauritius (see Tourism and hospitality insights 13.3 is one of these destinations. In the same vein, many ski resorts in the Alps have raised the quality of their services (hospitality, services at the destination, etc.) in order to have a better image, to be perceived as an upscale resort and attract, not fewer, but rather exclusively high contribution travelers. Some of them also trying to attract a majority of foreign visitors, such as Russian guests, looking for high quality ski resorts.

Once the company or the destination has decided on the competitive advantage which will be used to build positioning, it not only has to be effective, which means that it will drive the marketing mix implementation, but also it has to be promoted to the segments targeted: Consumers must know the advantage they can benefit from when staying in your hotel or at your destination. Of course, the real advantage for the consumer, is when they come to your restaurant, hotel, theme park, or arrive at your destination, but for the customer to fully consider the competitive advantage you offer, in order for him to make his decision to purchase, he must be aware of this advantage at that point! It means that he must get the information, whatever the context or the media, during the buying decision process. If the guest has previously experienced your product or service, he has already considered this information in his decision process, and he is therefore willing to do so again. But for all potential first-time visitors, it is necessary to promote your image, along with the competitive advantages customers will benefit from when buying your product or service.

How do you inform customers about competitive advantages? A basic recommendation is to say that you have to communicate and clearly explain to consumers the benefits they can get from your product and services, and avoid confusing them. The positioning and differentiating image must be based on one or two main criteria/arguments. For example, your destination might be environmentally friendly, and family oriented, or for upscale segments. Two main criteria are fine and they will help your targeted segments to understand who you are. However, if you add two or three more criteria, it might then be confusing and consumers will not retain any of the message you are trying to communicate. This is why tourism authorities and managers should be careful not to over-communicate. Also, even if commercial advertisements are always a little bit over-optimistic and positive, do not go too far from reality. You can promise a great experience, but never over-promise as customers may then become frustrated and dissatisfied.

Delivering the chosen position is made through communication, but also with the help of the staff, with the support of all partners of the company (for example, if you are part of a network or an alliance). Brand (see Chapter 18), is an interesting tool for communicating positioning, not only on a large scale (brand campaigns are usually made using mass media), but also on a long term. The name (brand) itself, may have a specific meaning. But when a short slogan with some specific visuals are associated with the brand, consumers will then easily understand the main message destinations or companies want to promote, these one or two (no more) main ideas being your competitive advantages.

## Conclusion

In an every increasingly competitive context, destinations and tourism and hospitality companies must have an efficient strategy regarding markets. This manufactures itself on the one hand in the form of a choice of target markets, presenting the best economic opportunities available. For this to work effectively, perfect knowledge of consumers allows the identification of the most pertinent segmentation criteria. On the other hand, the positioning of the company or destination turns out to be very important, with a view of being perfectly identifiable by tourists (by meeting their expectation

## TOURISM AND HOSPITALITY INSIGHTS 13.3
## MAURITIUS – DESTINATION TARGET MARKETING AND POSITIONING

Mauritius has been following an impressive trend. Over the years, Mauritius tourism has grown consistently and constructively. From 935,000 arrivals in 2010, the country attracted more than 1 275 000 visitors in 2016, and is expected to have hosted more than 1,360,000 visitors by 2017. Since 2014, the tourism sector has outperformed the whole economy with double-digit growth rates in both 2015 and 2016 (Source: AHRIM – Association des Hôteliers et Restaurateurs – Ile Maurice, Report 2017). Growth in tourism arrivals went up by 10.8%, between 2015 and 2016. Monsieur Jocelyn Kwok, CEO of AHRIM (interviewed in November, 2017, at Port Louis, Mauritius) confirmed that the tourism sector is still expected to grow, and that in the meantime, the hospitality sector, which has been a developing sector for a long time in Mauritius, keeps on improving its capacity, its offer, and the quality and variety of services delivered to visitors. The traditional island product is beach, sun, lagoon, and other natural riches, water sports (including diving), and a large range of wellbeing and relaxation products. According to Monsieur Kwok, there is still a lot to do as the island seeks to more effectively promote a riche variety of natural and cultural assets (including museums, UNESCO World Heritage Sites, etc.) and the richness of a unique culture at the crossroads of Indian Ocean civilizations. This would help to seduce a new clientele, and diversify the island's offer.

In terms of positioning, Mauritius is developing sustainable tourism in the upscale segment. Seventy-five percent of the hotel room capacity of the island is in either five-star (or five-star luxury), and four-star hotels. Long established local groups developed their brand in Mauritius, and expanded their name to other Indian Ocean islands and other markets. Most hotels, owned and/or managed by groups or independently, focus on the upscale segment. Focusing on environmental issues is the other main objective of Mauritius. More than half of hotels in Mauritius have reported some form of voluntary commitment toward environmentally-friendly practices, many of them having already been certified by independent bodies and labels (Green Globe, Earth Check, Travellife, Green Key). The key target markets for Mauritius, are France and the neighboring island of La Réunion (one-third of arrivals), the United Kingdom (about 10%), and South Africa. However, new markets are emerging from Europe (for instance, Germany and Switzerland) and Asia. The most significant growth comes from the financially healthy middle-class travelers from India (growth rate 2014/15: + 17.9%), South-East Asia, and China (growth rate 2014/15: + 41.4%).

Source: AHRIM – Association des Hôteliers et Restaurateurs – Ile Maurice, Report 2017.

and by therefore being attractive), all this and at the same time making themselves different from the competition. Successful positioning is the key to success. The challenge is to stay linked to the reality of the products (a high quality positioning must correspond to a real quality of services provided), while at the same time proposing a positioning corresponding to an inclination identified on the market. For example, adopting an eco-friendly approach works well these days, as this trend is now strong in the market. However, many companies and destinations have adopted the same criteria to reinforce their positioning, which reduces the attractive and differentiating nature of the criteria. Every characteristic of the positioning, must be reviewed regularly, in line with the strategy of the company or the destination, as today's trends are most likely not those of tomorrow.

## REVIEW QUESTIONS

1. What are the key principles of market segmentation?
2. Are socio-demographic, economic, and geographic criteria limited to segment description or do they also provide in-depth information on travelers' behaviors, and therefore, might be considered as significant segmentation criteria?
3. To what extent is psychographic segmentation different from traditional segmentation?

## YOUTUBE LINKS

### "Positioning The Tri-Cities (Washington): branding, product development and marketing"

URL: www.youtube.com/watch?v=nvP1y7EiC8w

Summary: TRIDEC, the Tri-Cities Visitor and Convention Bureau and Tri-City Regional Chamber of Commerce have been leading efforts to develop a new brand identity for the Tri-Cities. Destination marketing expert, Roger Brooks, has been facilitating the process of creating a unified, distinct, and sustainable regional brand.

### "Customer segments"

URL: www.youtube.com/watch?v=QlfKUfv1vyM

Summary: Explanation of the benefit of market segmentation by Professor Sara Dolnicar, University of Queensland, Australia.

### "Fáilte Ireland domestic segmentation workshop – connected families"

URL: https://www.youtube.com/watch?v=Ma-Jj5lcf6s

Summary: FÃilte Ireland recently conducted research into the domestic market which provides new and unique insights into three priority consumer segments – those with the most potential for growth. Based on consumer values – all of those things that are most important to people when choosing how, when and where to holiday – these segments can be categorized as: "Connected Families," "Footloose Socializers," and "Indulgent Romantics." Learn more about Connected Families in this video.

## REFERENCES, FURTHER READING, AND RELATED WEBSITES

### References

Frochot, I., & Morrison, A.M. (2000). Benefit segmentation: A review of its applications to travel and tourism research. *Journal of Travel & Tourism Marketing, 9*(4), 21–45.

Haley, R.I. (1968). Benefit segmentation: A decision-oriented research tool. *Journal of Marketing, 32*(3), 30–35.

Legohérel, P., Poutier, E., & Fyall, A. (2013). *Revenue Management for Hospitality and Tourism.* Oxford: Goodfellow Publishers Limited.

Legohérel, P., & Wong, K.K. (2006). Market segmentation in the tourism industry and consumers' spending: What about direct expenditures? *Journal of Travel & Tourism Marketing, 20*(2), 15–30.

Le Serre, D., & Chevalier, C. (2012). Marketing travel services to senior consumers. *Journal of Consumer Marketing, 29*(4), 262–270.

Le Serre, D., Weber, K., Legohérel, P., & Errajaa, K. (2017). Culture as a moderator of cognitive age and travel motivation/perceived risk relations among seniors. *Journal of Consumer Marketing, 34*(5), 455–466.

Rokeach, M. (1973). *The nature of human values.* New York: Free Press.

### Further reading

Jin, X., & Wang, Y. (2016). Chinese outbound tourism research: A review. *Journal of Travel Research, 55*(4), 440–453.

Kang, S.K., Hsu, C.H.C., & Wolfe, K. (2003). Family traveller segmentation by vacation decision-making patterns. *Journal of Hospitality and Tourism Research, 27*(4), 464–465.

Leask, A., Fyall, A., & Barron, P. (2014). Generation Y: An agenda for future visitor attraction research. *International Journal of Tourism Research, 16*(5), 462–471.

Legohérel P. (1998). Towards a market segmentation of the tourism trade: Expenditure levels and consumer behavior instability. *Journal of Travel and Tourism Marketing, 7*(3), 19–39.

Legohérel, P., Hsu, C.S., & Daucé, B. (2015). Using the CHAID segmentation approach in analyzing the international traveler market. *Tourism Management, 46* (February), 359–366.

Levy, P. (2011). Segmentation by generation. *Marketing News, 15*(May): 20–23.

Moutinho, L., & Vargas-Sánchez, A. (Eds.). (2018). *Strategic management in tourism, Cabi tourism texts.* Wallingford: Cabi.

Pesonen, J.A. (2015). Targeting rural tourists in the internet: Comparing travel motivation and activity-based segments. *Journal of Travel & Tourism Marketing, 32*(3), 211–226.

Pyo, S. (2015). Integrating tourist market segmentation, targeting, and positioning using association rules. *Information Technology & Tourism, 15*(3), 253–281.

Swinyard, W.R., & Struma, K.D. (1986). Market segmentation: Finding the heart of your restaurant's market. *Cornell Hotel and Restaurant Administration Quarterly, 27*(1), 88–96.

Trout, T. (2005). Branding can't exist without positioning. *Advertising Age,* March0.

Walters, G., & Ruhanen, L. (2015). From white to green: Identifying viable visitor segments for climate-affected Alpine destinations. *Journal of Hospitality & Tourism Research, 39*(4), 517–539.

Websites

Explorer quotient
https://www.destinationcanada.com/en/tools#explorerquotient

Hospitality Market Segmentation
https://www.hsmai.org/knowledge/summary.cfm?ItemNumber=4640

Hotel segmentation
https://www.hvs.com/article/6583/market-segmentation-identifying-where-hotel-demand-comes/

What is your travel type?
https://quiz.canada.travel/us/traveller-types/ttFS

## MAJOR CASE STUDY
## GUIDING THE "COMING TO LIFE" OF DESTINATION CANADA'S BRAND IDENTITY THROUGH MARKET RESEARCH

Also known as the Canadian Tourism Commission (CTC), Destination Canada is a specialized agency of the Government of Canada whose core mandate under the CTC Act is to promote Canada as a desirable tourism destination. With the support of a comprehensive research program, Destination Canada (DC) uses data-driven marketing strategies to stimulate international demand and tourism export revenue for Canada in ten countries: Australia, China, France, Germany, India, Japan, Mexico, South Korea, the UK and the USA.

In 2007, Destination Canada launched a new brand identity – "Canada keep exploring/Explorez sans fin" designed to position Canada as a premier four-season tourism destination for travelers to explore and create extraordinary stories all of their own. Marketing efforts were thus shifted from a focus on tourism products to a focus on tourism experiences, experiences to remember.

To support the deployment of its new brand strategy, DC required a way to track and provide insights on the "coming to life" of the new brand identity in its markets, along with a segmentation mechanism appropriate to the experiential focus of the new brand identity. The two main research programs initiated to guide the "coming to life" of the new strategy were the explorer quotient psychographic segmentation tool and the Global Tourism Watch, which is an annual survey providing consumer-based intelligence in eleven 11 around the world, including Canada.

The explorer quotient (EQ) is a social and value market segmentation system developed for DC that is specifically designed for the travel market. Instead of segmenting travelers into groups based on age, income, gender, family status, or education, the EQ takes a deeper look at travelers' social value and views of world. EQ breaks each geographic market into different psychographic groups, called explorer types. Each type is profiled by particular characteristics derived from social and travel values, travel motivations, and behaviors. How people interpret a travel experience and what experience means to them is directly related to their fundamental outlook on life, their value system. For instance, people that view the world as a dangerous and chaotic place may be looking for security, reassurance, and familiarity when traveling. Others may view the world as an intriguing and exciting place, triggering in them a desire to explore other cultures and ways of life when vacationing. EQ combines these values with travel habits, motivations, and attitudes toward travel to create a deeper profile of the traveler.

The segmentation work conducted by DC across global markets revealed a total of 13 EQ types, with each market comprising between eight and nine types. DC selects its best explorer type in each market based on their affinity for the "*Canada Keep Exploring*" experiential brand, as well as love of travel, potential for being high-yield customers, and propensity for word-of-mouth advocacy. DC generally targets its marketing toward two or three EQ types in each market. For example, the EQ types targeted in the United Kingdom are the Free Spirits, which can be

**Image 13.2**

Source: https://www.pexels.com/photo/freestanding-letters-near-fountain-1048010/

described as enthusiastic indulgers traveling in style that want to see and do everything, and the Cultural Explorers along with the Authentic Experiencers, which can be best described as learners seeking immersive travel experiences, keen to explore other cultures and absorb the natural beauty of destinations they visit.

DC has developed an EQ Traveller Quiz *to* identify the explorer type of travelers. This quiz consists of 20 questions and is easy to administer directly to visitors at tourism centers and other venues, and ready to be incorporated in other market research surveys deployed by DC or its partners. In order to fully leverage insights from its surveys and from EQ, DC includes the EQ battery of 20 questions in most surveys it commissions around the world, including the Global Tourism Watch.

The Global Tourism Watch (GTW) is a tracking program conducted annually in all DC markets. First fielded in 2007, it was initially conceived as a brand monitor to track the "coming to life" of DC's new brand identity and how it resonated with travelers during its initial entry into key markets and in subsequent years. In a global environment where competitive destinations are aggressively investing more resources into tourism marketing, a monitor was – and continues to be required on an ongoing basis to keep a pulse on the markets and to track the evolution of travel consumer perceptions with respect to the Canada brand and competitive destinations.

The GTW consist of a 20-minute online survey administered to long-haul travelers that captures a series of performance metrics including:

- destination awareness and travel considerations toward Canada, its regions and of competitive destinations;
- Canada brand positioning with respect to brand image, value, and price perceptions;
- purchase cycle;
- travel outlook, intensity, and barriers;
- sources of information and appeal; and
- target market demographics detailed by region, past, and future travels and by EQ type.

While a core aim of the GTW as a monitor is to track key performance indicators over time, the survey also provides flexibility to delve into current issues of importance to the Canadian tourism sector (e.g. perceptions and attitude toward tourism sustainability, awareness of major events such as the 2010 Vancouver Winter Olympics and Paralympics) or to support research initiatives such as understanding resources and devices used to plan a trip (Figure 13.1), which provide information on the marketing channel reach, and which devices are taken on trips (Figure 13.2), which can be used to better understand visitor flows associated with mobile phone data.

A powerful feature of the GTW as a source of business intelligence is its link to EQ as it provides information on how EQ type-targeted segments are differentiated from other long-haul travelers in the perceptions and intentions toward Canada and competitive destinations (Figure 13.3).

Market research initiatives are valuable instruments to provide guidance in the management of destination brands and the development of marketing strategies. For Destination Canada, the integration of GTW and EQ programs has since 2007 provided Destination Canada and its provincial and territorial partners with stable, yet flexible research platforms to monitor DC's markets over

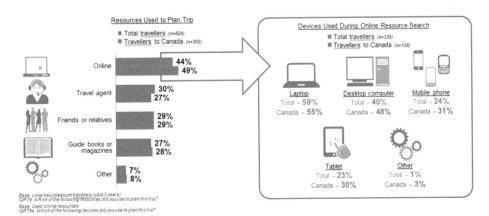

Figure 13.1 Resources and devices used by long-haul French leisure tourists to plan trips

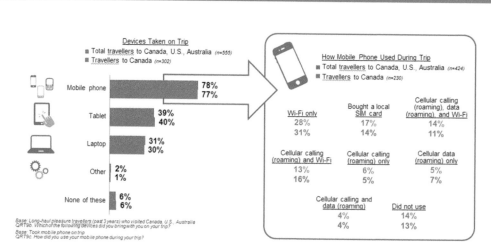

**Figure 13.2** Devices taken in trip and mobile phone usage of long-haul leisure tourists from France

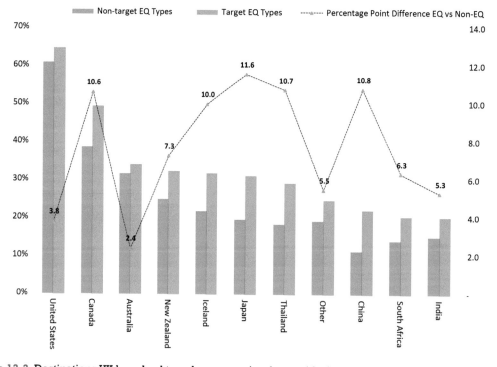

**Figure 13.3** Destinations UK long-haul travelers are seriously considering visiting in the next two years

time and provide information on current issues to support the development of global marketing strategies and other research endeavors.

Source: Michel Dubreuil, Destination Canada.

## Major case study questions

1.  What were the drivers behind Destination Canada's changing approach to market segmentation?
2.  How sustainable do you think such an approach based on consumer experiences is when considering the intense competitiveness of the international destination marketplace?
3.  What may be some of the challenges of adopting an approach based on traveler experiences?
4.  What is the EQ and how would it assist a hotel or airline in their segmentation strategies?

# International marketing strategy

## Learning outcomes

By the end of this chapter, students will:

*   Be aware of the ongoing internationalization of the tourism industry
*   Be aware of the need for companies and destinations to understand fully the international environment and more specifically the cultural gap between markets
*   Be able to consider the issue of adaptation of the marketing mix, in line with the various markets and clienteles targeted by the company or the destination.

## Introduction

Tourism and hospitality activities are inherently international. Both business and leisure tourism, the main segments, are affected in the same way by the growth in cross-border and international trade. The internationalization of business tourism merely reflects the interdependence of social environments and the globalization of the economy. Increased trade and people movements benefit the transport, accommodation, and catering sectors and conference and business centers. The leisure industry is characterized by various phenomena such as falling transport costs and the proliferation of destinations. Increased destination competition incites regional and national tourism authorities to establish development and communication strategies that are fully integrated in the international environment.

Statistics from several international organizations show evidence of the ongoing trend of the growth of international tourism activity: the number of international tourists increased by 3.9 % between 2015 and 2016, and a similar growth is expected in 2017 (Source: WTO). The World Tourism Organization (WTO) expects 1,230 million tourists in 2017, and 1,800 by 2030. The International Air Transportation Association (IATA) statistics show the growth of international travelers over a number of years (even during the severe economic crisis in 2008 and 2009) and forecast more international travelers in the future.

# International development strategies

The notion of developing the business activities of a company on the international level usually involve the desire to sell the company's products and services beyond the national frontiers to a foreign clientele. Since a tourism product or service is consumed in the production site, the notion of commercial relations with a foreign clientele is carried out in domestic markets as well.

## *Explanatory factors*

The first explanatory factor relates to a straightforward situation. As explained above, people move from one place to another, and tourism and hospitality businesses (hotels, restaurants, etc.) may attract clients from both their own domestic market and foreign markets. Dealing with foreign clients may be desired (arising from a company-determined strategy) or unwanted. The issue of integrating the presence of foreign clients into companies' decision making is closely linked with the importance of this segment in terms of volume and financial contribution. For instance, if 5% of the clients of a golf-focused hotel in Brittany (a French region close with a Celtic heritage, across the channel) are British, no specific action will be taken. Conversely, if the British clientele accounts for 70% of the clientele in terms of volume or revenue, the hotel manager will undertake specific actions (e.g. adapting certain features of the services on offer, strengthening communication activities targeting this market segment).

Tourism and hospitality businesses that voluntarily embark on activities targeting foreign markets do so for various reasons. One standard reason is the identification of an economic potential in one of the foreign markets. For instance, an Italian region may decide to target, as it does in its own market, the families living in a nearby European country with a slightly different school calendar; the purpose of the strategy is thus to attract mid-season tourist traffic. The region may also select a specific segment that is underexploited in the domestic market (e.g. seniors or golfers seeking hotels blending charm and the pleasures of Italian gastronomy).

Another explanatory factor is when a business has established that its market has reached saturation point, and any hope of development must be based upon gaining access to new markets. This situation is illustrated by the case of the Accor Group in the low and mid-range hotel market. Despite its significant potential, the French hotel market is already a very dense network. Hence, its rapid development was followed by a shift in perspective, and growth prospects came from close European markets and distant foreign markets. Thus, Accor, which occupied a dominant position on the French market (with chains such as Hotel F1, or Ibis Budget), decided to move into the low-cost US market through the take-over of Motel 6 and Red Roof Inn. In 2009, Accor abandoned Red Roof Inn and continued developing Motel 6.

Finally, political and/or economic factors constitute yet another significant element. The recent removal or lessening of political and administrative constraints has opened up new development perspectives for the tourism sector. For instance, in the early 2000s, China signed agreements with countries that became "politically authorized" tourist destinations, even for individual traveling. Most tourism stakeholders worldwide now favor this type of new clients. Thus, in 2010, Chinese tourists became the biggest spenders in terms of average daily spending. The latest statistics confirm the potential of Chinese tourists in the French market. Similar statistics demonstrate the benefits of Chinese visitors in other European destinations, and in other counties. In 2015, WTO estimates 120 million "international Chinese exits" representing a volume of spending of $194 billion ($165 billion in 2014 – to be compared with $110 million from US travelers, $50.4 from Russian travelers, $99.2 from German travelers, $47.8 from French travelers, and $25.6 from Brazilian travelers). Chinese tourists are young (82% are from 26 to 45 age group), come from urban areas, with increasing financial resources. According to the World Tourism and Travel Council, some 60 million should earn up to $70 000 per annum by 2023, making them potential upscale travelers. In addition, 8.9 million Chinese tourists have visited Europe, with a quarter of them having visited France. This first generation of Chinese tourists focuses on cities that have a concentration of historic buildings, cites, and shopping. The average spending of a Chinese tourist is more than $1,500 per day, and can rise up to around $2,000 in Europe and in the United States. Around 60% of the budget of a Chinese tourists is dedicated to shopping, to the detriment of other expenses, including hotels and restaurants. In the mid-term, it will be interesting to analyze and understand the behavior of repeat Chinese visitors, or first-time second generation of Chinese tourist. They will have increasing revenue, but may have different needs and expectations, and different spending structures.

## The internationalization process and strategic decision making

The first decision companies must take is whether to develop their commercial activities in foreign markets. This process involves determining specific goals: seeking mid-season tourist traffic, pursuing the development and growth of a group, identifying the opportunity factor that shows genuine economic potential.

Second, companies must conduct a thorough examination of the potential client base (e.g. cultural approach, analysis of consumer expectations and consumption patterns) and of all the features of the social environment that would bring increased understanding of the people involved (e.g. language, religious observance, standard of living). Equally essential is an examination of the market and of the country concerned, should the companies wish to establish a production site (e.g. hotel, restaurant) or simply a sales branch in the country (e.g. laws and hygiene, security, or quality standards; administrative and financial structures; social norms; overall safety requirements).

This thorough market analysis enables companies to determine the product-market pairs and the marketing segments that are potentially commercially profitable. They then select their targets. It should be noted that the company-defined segmentations and positioning are not necessarily the same in the companies' domestic and targeted foreign markets. The issue then becomes one of selecting the most appropriate market entry strategy. For instance, in the 1990s, Accor had not tried to develop its Formule 1 product in the US low-cost hotel sector. Not only was the product unknown to American consumers, but it didn't correspond to the motel model and ran the risk of being rejected by American clients. Instead, Accor developed its Sofitel product in the high-end hotel sector. This segment meets the needs of an American and international clientele who are more open and used to staying in different hotels in the various countries they visit. Moreover, in this particular segment, the so-called "French touch" may be an asset.

At an international level, and not only in the US, Accor has decided to use the French touch as a symbol of the spirit of the brand. This cultural signal sent to customers is not utilized for communication purposes only, but also at all stages of the product/service design.

The final decision needs to be made in the operational arena. The marketing policy that has been determined for each client segment and targeted markets must be tailored to the consumers' expectations. The central issue in international marketing is the following: should services be tailored to the new clients? Answering this question is based, to a large extent, upon the analysis of the notion of cultural influence.

## Adaptation, globalization, or glocal-ization?

Culture refers to various consumer characteristics that are reflected in consumers' social behaviors, particularly their acts of consumption. Hence, it stands to reason that products or services will not be consumed in the same way in one cultural environment or in another.

For instance, when French and American people exchange their business cards, they immediately slip the cards into their pockets, whereas in Asia, each person takes the card into both hands and reads it carefully before putting it away, as a sign of politeness towards their interlocutor. Another example is the following: bowls containing soup or rice are placed on the table in China and Korea. In China, as in other Asian countries, it is common practice for people to raise the bowl to their mouth, whereas the same bowl remains on the table or in people's hands in Korea, and people must use chopsticks or spoons. These differences, which may appear insignificant, are representative of our "cultural foundation." They are found in a multitude of behaviors and signal the differences between individuals.

These differences can also be viewed as characteristic features of a consumer universe and the hallmark of a cultural environment. Thus, the French "art of living" characterized by the enjoyment of good food and drink, gastronomy, luxury, etc., is associated with French culture. These cultural characteristics are well known (though often limited to a few clichés) and sought after by foreign tourists.

## The notion of cultural environment

A comment regarding method in the examination of the notion of cultural environment: marketing studies in various sectors, including tourism, tend to consider geopolitical boundaries as marking the frontiers of a cultural environment. For the sake of simplicity, mention is made of French cuisine or Chinese consumers, without further differentiation. However, it is well known that there are cultural differences within the same country and cultural similarities across different countries.

For instance, there are more similarities in olive oil consumption between consumers in Nice, France, and Barcelona, Spain, than between people living on the Côte d'Azur and consumers in northern France. What about, then, geopolitical entities such as India or China encompassing widely diverging realms and cultural environments? Hence, when European tourist authorities say that it is necessary to adapt to Chinese tourists' expectations, it is perhaps even more essential to keep in mind the notion of differences between Chinese consumers. However, we acknowledge that it is difficult for tourism sites to accommodate the diversity of nationalities in, for example, signage or restaurant menu translation, or the adaptation of catering products. From an operational perspective, it is thus often impossible to take into account the cultural differences within a nationality.

This issue brings us back to the key question in international marketing related to globalizing marketing policies or adapting services to the specificities of each tourist, in line with the latter's cultural characteristics. The logical approach would be that in order to meet performance objectives on the one hand and achieve compatibility between customers' expectations and the service delivery dimensions on the other, these service dimensions be systematically adapted to the target market. The advantage of a marketing policy of adaptation is, by default, to avoid shocking or annoying in any way the foreign consumers. For example, Tourism Australia launched in 2006 an advertising campaign created by the Sydney office of the London advertising agency M&C Saatchi. The advertisements feature Australians preparing for visitors to their country. One advertisement ends with model Lara Bingle at Fingal Spit stepping out of the ocean and asking "So, where the bloody hell are you?" This commercial caused controversy as the words "hell" and "bloody," not shocking in Australia, were not accepted by advertising authorities in some other countries. In the UK, the television version was banned, and the roadside billboards bearing the slogan removed. In Singapore and other countries, the television version was modified, and the words "bloody hell" removed.

An issue remains, however, concerning the relevance and feasibility of adaptation policies. Foreign tourists visiting France will be partly motivated by the desire to discover

French cuisine. They should thus be able to explore this cuisine without necessarily being entirely cut off from their own food habits. American consumers will appreciate not eating their evening meal too late, even if they eat French-style food. Hence, the role of service providers is to adapt services entirely or partly depending upon clients' expectations and consumer situations.

## The limitations of globalization

Globalization strategy involves the will to offer the same product across different markets whereby consumers will be able to identify this product easily and consume it in the same way, regardless of the country they are in. This strategy is appropriate particularly when it is known that cultural differences are lessened within a segment. This is true of luxury items or, to a lesser extent, products intended for the young consumer segment. Companies seeking international recognition with a well-known brand also tend to use globalization policies. Reference is often made to extremely well-known US products such as Coca-Cola or McDonald's.

It would be inaccurate, however, to talk about complete standardization of the products and their marketing policy. Products and services might give the impression of similar marketing, but there are adaptations designed for drinks or meals to fit more closely with the prevailing tastes and consumption patterns within each market. Some dimensions of the product known as "McDonalds" are identical, such as the visuals (colors, logo, mascot, etc.), target segments, or the brand's commitment to support charities. There are variations from one market to another, however, regarding positioning and pricing schemes, distribution channels (adapted to the structures of each country's urban and commercial areas), and, of course, the actual food and drink products.

In each country, there are special features: coffee is served in a 60 ml cup in France, but in bigger containers in Scandinavia where milk is also offered because people are used to drinking milk at meal times. Salads are found on the menu in France and in some European countries, but not in US restaurants. In Israel, the McShawarmas on offer correspond to a type of sandwich consumers are used to. In Israel, as in many other countries, McDonald's restaurants are adapted to religious practices; for instance, some are exclusively *kosher* while others offer a mix of products. The façade and exterior design of some restaurants (like the restaurant located in the historical center of the city of Rome, Italy) have been modified to fit in with the architectural style of the surrounding buildings. This strategy is called glocal-ization. This marketing term originates in the saying "Think global, act locally."

From a managerial perspective, companies determine a specific strategy that will be applied to all target markets. However, to be in line with a particular market and to meet their customers' expectations, the companies may adapt all or part of their marketing policy. If we take McDonald's example again, we see that some of their catering services are adapted to each market (with specific new offerings). The distribution and pricing

**Image 14.1**
Source: Pexels.

positioning are partially adapted in line with the market structure, the competitive envir-onment, and the consumers' purchasing power, and the communication strategies remain as homogeneous as possible with a view to ensuring international brand recognition.

To a certain extent, large international hotel chains appear to follow this strategy. When a product is aimed at an international business clientele, regular customers should be able to find it, or something very similar, regardless of the geographical location of the hotel. Products are thus very similar and similarly positioned on the market from one country to the next. Nevertheless, each product is culturally embedded in the local com-munity, usually through catering services providing a regional or national touch. Various services concerning accommodation and customer reception can also be adapted. Travel and hospitality insights 14.1 explain how a French group and a Chinese group, having decided to build closer relationship between their markets and hotel chains, started to adapt their hotel services to the expectations of their respective customer.

## International destination marketing strategies

In this section, we focus on international marketing strategies of tourist destin-ations. We first consider the evolution of destination promotion on an international

## TOURISM AND HOSPITALITY INSIGHTS 14.1
## LOUVRE HOTEL GROUP AND JINJIANG INTERNATIONAL

Created in 1976, the French Louvre Hotel Group developed its activities on an international scale in the 2000s. Merging with the Dutch group Golden Tulip in 2009, it has become the second largest hotel group in Europe. At the same time, closer relations with the Chinese group JinJiang International developed gradually. In February 2015, JinJiang International finalized the take-over of the Louvre Hotel Group. JinJiang aimed to increase the development of hotel tourism between France and China and enhance the international expansion of the brands of both groups.

In the economy segment, a first partnership was established between both groups in 2011 to increase their visibility in their respective markets. In France, 15 hotels of the Campanile brand, located in the five cities most frequently visited by Chinese tourists, were co-branded, which entailed the following:

- Both trade names (Campanile and JinJiang) displayed at the entrance;
- Brochures and information signs in Mandarin Chinese;
- Helpline in Chinese;
- Buffets with Chinese dishes and products;
- Green tea placed on the welcome tray in the rooms;
- Chinese television channels in the rooms.

Presenting this partnership at a press conference, Xu Zurong, Chairman of JinJiang said:

We are proud to become a partner of the Louvre Hotels Group to introduce JinJiang Inn in France through a brand alliance, which is a new model for the overseas expansion of Chinese budget hotel brands. By adapting to the habits of the respective customers of our two brands, we are improving customer experience further.

The JinJiang group then converted existing JinJiang Inn hotels in China into Campanile hotels, with the aim of developing the brand in the Chinese market while maintaining the concept and the strong identifying attributes of the Campanile brand.

Source: Patrick Legohérel.

scale over a few decades. Then, we provide two examples of how a destination may consider and define its international marketing strategy, depending upon it is a local destination, or a country and how a destination should apprehend the new technological and digital environment when building its international marketing strategy and promotion.

## Evolution of international marketing and promotion strategies

Destinations have moved from an old promotion model to a new one, looking for more efficiency and notoriety, in an environment characterized by stiff and intense competition. Destinations also have to adapt to the new digital environment, and the use of destination branding at both domestic and international level. Tourism and hospitality insights 14.2 explains how destinations moved from old practices to new era of branding and promotion on an international scale.

## Examples of destination international marketing strategies at a local level and at the country level

The two examples of Indonesia and the city of Angers (France) illustrate the challenges destinations are facing when developing their international marketing strategy, targeting international markets and clienteles, and promoting themselves in a new digital environment.

---

### TOURISM AND HOSPITALITY INSIGHTS 14.2
### TERRITORIAL BRANDING, POOLING, AND OUTSOURCING: THE NEW PARADIGM OF COUNTRY BRANDING AND PLACE MARKETING

National Tourist Offices (NTOs) have evolved substantially from their initial function of tourism and diplomatic representation towards their current, fully-embraced, behaviors of marketing agencies, much to the satisfaction of the world tourism industry (tour operators, distribution, air transport, etc.). There was a time when 20-odd major destinations worldwide, at most, were vying to attract holiday-makers from ten major markets, at most, in Europe, North America, and North-East Asia, this time is well and truly gone. At that time, market characteristics induced NTOs to invest in lavish showcase offices manned by an army of expatriates in a dozen cities (London, Berlin, Paris, New York, Tokyo, Milan, Madrid, Los Angeles, Sydney, etc.).

This time has now gone. There are very few countries left where public finances are used to establish a successful wholly-owned presence network in each tourist-generating country. The information counter has been replaced by the Internet. By 2020, the number of territories (cities, resorts, regions, countries, country groupings, etc.) that are fully established as tourist destinations, hence running fully-fledged marketing operations, will have grown considerably.

Five years ago, who would have thought that Qatar would become a leading tourist destination? Tomorrow, it will be Sharjah, North Korea, and Kazakhstan among others. Competition is soaring on the supply side, from the perspective of countries, regions, or cities that are now entering the marketing arena. On the demand side, whereas the global pie to be shared is over 1 billion tourists today, it will top 1 billion 800 million by 2030 according to the World Tourism Organization. Could the increase in air transport costs induce less optimistic scenarios? If so, the marketing guerrilla warfare between destinations will be even more ruthless to attract the happy few global travelers.

**Image 14.2**
Source: Pexels.

At the same time, the emerging economies of Africa, Asia, and Latin America will also enter the leisure era, which will increase the number of target markets worth exploring. In short, the destination supply is soaring, and the global demand is going to be increasingly geographically diversified, sociologically segmented, technologically complex, and brand-zapping by necessity or desire. Destination promotion budgets then need to be shared among an increasing number of target markets, and it is quite clear that the funds will not increase proportionally to the increase of potential markets. This difficult financial issue can only be resolved by developing marketing investments at the expense of the structural overheads (e.g. offices, personnel) of the tourist offices in each of the markets involved. Pooling resources and outsourcing the marketing of destinations to private companies under result-based contract renewal terms is the way to go. It is both possible and desirable that policymakers ensure the common good should remain at the helm of the strategic marketing of destinations. However, these politicians are under pressure from their tourist sectors, aware of the increasing yield demands, and from their citizen taxpayers, increasingly vigilant about the proper use of public funds. Hence, their only choice is to move towards promotion structures that are more flexible, successful, adaptable, fast, and fully focused on the notion of return on investment.

Concomitant with the increased outsourcing of marketing in international markets, there is yet another major change, involving global territorial brands, or what is also known as country branding or place marketing. The tourism component is still the largest item of expenditure for the external global territory promotion. However, the tourism image is essentially both cross-sectional and identity-laden; it fuels, strengthens, and brings credibility to the other attractiveness elements of the territories through being included in the selection criteria when it comes to the development of economic and investment activities, the settling in of talented people (expatriates, students), and the hosting of media events (sporting, economic, or diplomatic events). The good tourism image of a territory will work wonders to convince students to choose one university rather than another of similar level, to incite investors to build a new plant and persuade the expatriates' spouses to adopt a new life, to help agri-food sectors distribute their products globally, and to attract star film producers to shoot their next blockbuster. In short, seeking the synergy of images and means leads all the institutions responsible for the attractiveness of a territory (tourist offices, export offices and chambers of commerce, cultural centers, cinema promotion agencies, diplomatic networks, event organizers, universities, etc.) to work better together, under the umbrella of a common, holistic, and identity-laden territorial brand name.

This awareness of the power of brand names in a globalized and digital economy causes upheavals in the missions, structures, and governance modes of the traditional tourist offices. One local example, inspired by similar approaches in Amsterdam or New York, is the territorial brand OnlyLyon led by the Lyon Area Economic Development Agency (ADERLY), created in 2007 by 20 partners and economic institutions in the Lyon area. Overseas, London & Partners, the official promotional organization for London is joined by over 1,000 partners to drive the attractiveness policy of the city to promote London and attract businesses, events, congresses, students and visitors. On a regional level, the CRT Alsace and Alsace International have merged since January 2014 to create the Regional Agency for the Attractiveness and the Development of Alsace to develop the brand ImaginAlsace. On the French national level, no fewer than four State departments joined forces in 2013 to create the brand France. Tourist marketing has thus integrated the core of attractiveness issues that go far beyond the simple economic stakes of the travel industry alone. Hence, tourist offices at all levels (local, regional, national) are often the starting point and the first partners of global projects of country branding or place marketing.

A new paradigm is thus emerging, encompassing the notions of shared brands, pooling resources between various institutions, and outsourcing the marketing of territory attractiveness on external markets.

Source: Philippe Mugnier – Founding President of ATTRACT, Consulting, strategy, and marketing agency for attractivity (www.attract-pr.com). In Frochot I., and Legohérel P. (2014), *Marketing du Tourisme*. Paris: Dunod.

## TOURISM AND HOSPITALITY INSIGHTS 14.3
## DIGITAL MARKETING IN PROMOTING TOURISM IN INDONESIA

Tourism in Indonesia is an important component of the Indonesian economy and has brought considerable economic progress and community prosperity. Data from the Ministry of Tourism Republic of Indonesia shows that the number of foreign tourist arrivals to Indonesia increased from 9,435,407 in 2014 to 10,406,759 foreign tourists in 2015 with a growth of 10.09%. Until November 2016, the number of foreign tourist arrivals to Indonesia was 5,981,743 foreign tourists and the average growth was 13.38%. Figures show that the number of international foreign tourists arriving in Indonesia exceeded the target of 10 million in 2015. Hence, the growth of tourism in Indonesia has surpassed the world's tourism growth of 4.4% and the tourism growth of 6% of the Association of Southeast Asian Nations (ASEAN). It has also been reported that favorite tourist attractions were cultural tourism (60%) followed by nature-based tourism (35%) including marine tourism, agri-tourism, and adventure tourism, Meetings, Incentive, Conventions, and Events (MICE) tourism, and others (5%) including sport tourism and culinary tourism. The average length of stay of foreign visitors in Indonesia was 8.5 days and the average amount of money spent was US$ 1,190 per foreign tourist (the Ministry of Tourism, Republic of Indonesia, 2015).

Image 14.3

Source: Pexels.

The Government of Indonesia, through the Ministry of Tourism, aims to reach about 20 million foreign tourist arrivals by the year 2019. To reach this target, the Government of Indonesia has implemented a massive tourism marketing strategy by giving priority to ten tourist destinations in Indonesia; Bali is used as an example and reference. Bali has been the iconic tourist destination in the world, with all its natural beauty including beautiful beaches, the hospitality of the Balinese people, and unique art and cultural richness, such as the amazing Ubud as the center of traditional culture and art, the Jatiluwih rice field terrace as one of the nature-based tourist areas in Bali that has been well managed for centuries by traditional farmers' organizations called "subak" and has been in the UNESCO World Heritage List since July 2012. There were approximately 10.41 million foreign tourists visiting Indonesia in 2015, and Bali is deemed to have remained the favorite.

Promoting a destination requires different approaches for the different segments of a heterogeneous market regarding the content of the message and the use of communication channels (Baggio et al., 2010; Buhalis, 2000; Middleton et al., 2009). The Ministry of Tourism Republic of Indonesia has implemented a three-fold marketing strategy to boost the number of foreign visitors to Indonesia, involving the DOT strategy, the BAS strategy, and the POS strategy, outlined as follows:

### The DOT strategy

The DOT strategy is the marketing strategy based on destination, origin, and time. Destination involves the development of a marketing strategy aimed at positioning an attractive image of destinations of interest, such as Great Bali, Great Jakarta, and Great Batam. Origin refers to the country of origin of the international visitors, such as Singapore, Malaysia, Australia, Japan, etc. Time refers to the seasonal market patterns that should be understood. An illustration of the DOT strategy can be seen in Figure 14.1.

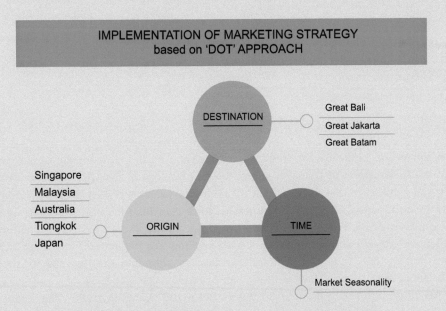

**Figure 14.1** Illustration of marketing strategy based on destination, origin, and time

Source: The Ministry of Tourism Republic of Indonesia, 2015

## The BAS strategy

The BAS strategy refers to branding, advertising, and sales. The Ministry of Tourism Republic of Indonesia has implemented a BAS approach by allocating a promotional budget to three international regions, namely:

1.  The ASEAN market. The budget was allocated about 50% of the marketing budget broken down into 25% for branding, 15% for advertising, and 10% for selling;

2.  The Asia Pacific market. The budget was allocated about 30% of the marketing budget broken down into 15% for branding, 10% for advertising, and 5% for selling;

3.  The Europe Middle East market. The budget was allocated about 20% of the marketing budget, broken down into 10% for branding, 5% for advertising, and 5% for selling;

Table 14.1 shows the implementation of the BAS strategy by allocating the promotional budget for three international regions.

Table 14.1 Implementation of the BAS strategy by allocating a promotional budget to three international regions

| Market | IMPLEMENT OF MARKETING STRATEGY based on 'BAS' APPROACH | | | |
| --- | --- | --- | --- | --- |
| | Budget Allocations | Branding | Advertising | Sales |
| ASEAN | □ 50% | □ 25% | □ 25% | □ 10% |
| ASIA PACIFIC (NON PASIFIC) | □ 30% | □ 15% | □ 15% | □ 5% |
| EUROPE MIDDLE EAST AFRICA (EMEA) | □ 20% | □ 10% | □ 10% | □ 5% |
| | 100% | 50% | 50% | 20% |

Source: The Ministry of Tourism Republic of Indonesia, 2015

The implementation of the BAS strategy was undertaken by the Government of Indonesia when invited by the Government of China to attend the celebrations of the Chinese New Year 2015 in Beijing. At the same time, the Government of Indonesia promoted *Wonderful Indonesia* together with the Garuda Indonesia (Indonesian airlines) through launching the new route Beijing-Denpasar (Bali) three times a week. These events were broadcast by the Beijing TV channel and other local media in Beijing, either online or offline. In terms of selling, the implementation of the BAS strategy was undertaken by the Government of Indonesia when attending the Internationale Tourismus-Borse (ITB) Berlin in Germany. Moreover, the Bali Beyond Travel Fair 2016 took place in Nusa Dua, Bali, on June 22–26, 2016 with the theme "Where the world comes to meet." This event is one of the international prestigious tourism market events in Indonesia. It was enthusiastically greeted by many potential buyers from around the world desiring to buy tour packages in Bali and tourist destinations in the eastern part of Indonesia, called Bali Beyond. It was also reported that this event has generated high economic value, bringing about 300 potential buyers and 75 new buyers (the Ministry of Tourism Republic of Indonesia, 2016).

## The POS strategy

Given the current trend and the future of digital marketing, many destinations are now using digital marketing; offline marketing, however, is found to be still useful (Middleton et al., 2009). The Government of Indonesia through the Ministry of Tourism has implemented a massive campaign to promote Indonesian tourism with the brand "Wonderful Indonesia," using a digital marketing and offline marketing approach. This strategy responds to the challenges of the Information Communication and Technology (ICT) revolution that has enabled potential visitors to search for destinations worldwide more easily. The Government of Indonesia has devised a model of promotion through the media called POS, namely paid media, owned media, and social media, as shown in Figure 14.2.

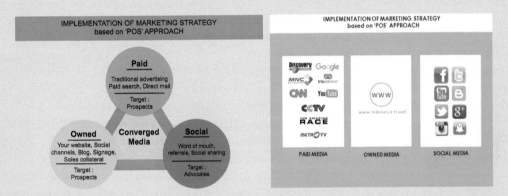

**Figure 14.2** Implementation of a marketing strategy based on paid, owned, and social media

Source: The Ministry of Tourism Republic of Indonesia, 2015.

*Paid media*: This segment of the strategy involves: (i) promoting *Wonderful Indonesia* through global TV channels such as the Discovery channel, CNN, Nat Geo, and other global TV Channels; (ii) promoting the country through online paid media, such as Google, YouTube, TripAdvisor, etc.; and (iii) promoting the country through offline paid media such as a big banner Wonderful Indonesia in the center of London or on a few city buses in Paris, France.

*Owned media*: The Government of Indonesia uses its own website to promote Indonesian tourism, namely www.indonesia.travel/, which focuses on celebrating the experience of five wonder of Indonesia, namely: (i) the natural wonders; (ii) the sensory wonders; (iii) the cultural wonders; (iv) the modern wonders; (v) the adventure wonders. Tourism Indonesia has also highlighted a few chosen destinations such as Exotic Bali, colorful Medan, Natural Wakatobi, Raja Ampat and Bunaken, stunning Bandung, majestic Banyuwangi, enjoy Jakarta, friendly Lombok, and explore Makasar.

*Social media*: This segment of the strategy presents a wide range of opportunities for the hospitality industry to make greater contact with customers. The social media provide other options for the hospitality industry since they provide new opportunities to manage and present business contents (Middleton et al., 2009). Facebook, Google, LinkedIn, Skype, and Twitter are examples of preferred social media. Hotels, restaurants, travel agencies, destinations, etc. need to build their websites in such a way as to make sure that the sites are optimized for search engines, have mobile apps, and keep customers involved in a conversation about the operation. The tourism industry in Indonesia is also intensively promoting its products and services through Google, TripAdvisor, Twitter, Facebook, etc. in order to reach the target of 20 million foreign tourists visiting Indonesia.

The Government of Indonesia now strongly focuses on the development and promotion of ten emerging tourist destinations including: (i) Mandalika in West Nusa Tenggara; (ii) Morotai island in Maluku; (iii) Tanjung Kelayang in Bangka Belitung islands; (iv) Lake Toba in North Sumatra; (v) Wakatobi in Sulawesi; (vi) Borobudur in the Middle of Java; (vii) Thousand islands in Jakarta; (viii) Mount Bromo in East Java; (ix) Labuan Bajo in East Nusa Tenggara; (x) Tanjung Lesung in Banten. The list of ten priority new destinations shows the importance of promoting people's experience of the natural wonders of Indonesia (e.g. marine tourism). Indonesia is the biggest archipelago in the world, with approximately 17,504 islands with beautiful white sand beaches and a variety of interesting marine attractions, such as diving, snorkeling, and other water sports. The involvement of the government to develop adequate infrastructures such as roads, sea ports, and airports to open access to the tourist destinations is crucial to support the tourism stakeholders and the community.

eTN, the global travel industry news, reports that travel expenditure will increase in developing countries such as Russia, Brazil, India, and Indonesia. The sales of travel products will also increase worldwide through the effects of new technologies and business models. In addition, it has been predicted that China will be positioned as the biggest travel market in 2017; the expenditure of Chinese people will continue to increase through increasing gross national product, employment, and consumption rates. Online and mobile technologies will continue to impact the tourism industry on a large scale (eTN: Global Travel & Tourism News (http://etn.travel/willtourism trends201710072/). Hence, there is a need to improve the ICT quality of Indonesian tourism in order to fine-tune the offer of personalized package tours. To reach this potential market, the Government of Indonesia also needs to improve the development of an adequate infrastructure such as roads, sea ports, and airports to open access to the tourist destinations.

## References

Baggio, R., Scott, N. & Cooper C. (2010). Improving tourism destination governance: A complexity science approach. *Tourism Review, 65*(4), 51–60.

Buhalis, D. (2000). Marketing the competitive destination of the future. *Tourism Management, 211,* 97–116.

eTurbo News (eTN). (2017, Jan 25). What will be the tourism trends for 2017. *Global Travel Industry News*. Retrieved from http://etn.travel/willtourismtrends201710072/.

Middleton, V.C.T., Fyall, A., & Morgan, M. (2009). *Marketing in travel and tourism* (4th ed.). Oxford: Elsevier.

The Nation. (2017, Jan 25). Indonesia to focus on ten tourist destinations. Retrieved from http://www.nationmultimedia.com/news/business/aec/30268888.

The Ministry of Tourism Republic of Indonesia. (2015). Marketing of International Tourism in Digital Era. 2015.

The Ministry of Tourism Republic of Indonesia. (2016). Bali & Beyond Travel Fair 2016. Retrieved from http://www.kemenpar.go.id/asp/detil.asp?c=16&id=3155.

Source: I Gusti Ayu Oka Suryawardani and Agung Suryawan Wiranatha; Doctorate Program in Tourism Udayana University, Bali, Indonesia (gungdani@gmail.com).

## TOURISM AND HOSPITALITY INSIGHTS 14.4
## INTERNATIONAL STRATEGY OF THE CITY OF ANGERS (FRANCE)

Angers Loire Tourisme acts as the organizer and tourism engineering expert in several areas: welcoming and providing information to French and foreign visitors, enhancing development (sites and events), promoting, advertising, and marketing for individual clients, groups, or business visitors.

As the central player in the promotion of the destination, Angers Loire Tourisme has defined an overall strategy involving both leisure and business tourism. French tourists remain the main source of the Angevin tourist economy, but the contribution of foreign clients has prompted Angers Loire Tourisme to identify a few foreign priority markets. This strategy works at operational levels through annual action plans. The end purpose is to increase the economic benefits of tourism in the area.

### The foundations

#### Demand marketing

Defining the strategy is first and foremost based upon understanding our visitors and their expectations. Numerous sources of information are used to establish their profile and motives: we use the internal data of the tourist office (e.g. geographical origin and typology of the clients who come to the office, Google Analytics data) and external data, such as accommodation and visit statistics, complemented by the local observatory and customer surveys. To date, almost 90% of foreign visitors are Europeans from neighboring countries, mostly couples. Rapidly changing markets make regular monitoring necessary to obtain up-to-date information.

### The major tourism assets of Angers from an international perspective

#### The Loire Valley

The destination can capitalize on its key position in the Loire Valley, classified as a UNESCO World Heritage Site since 2000. On an international level, the Loire Valley is a brand that evokes both the Loire châteaux and a French way of life, not to mention the strong growth of cycling along the Loire on the EuroVelo route that sees nearly 1 million cyclists annually. The Anjou vineyard, located right outside Angers, is yet another Loire-related asset promoted by Angers Loire Tourisme in all its international publicity campaigns.

**Image 14.4**
Source: Vignoble_et_château_Brissac©Jean-Sebastien_Evrard.

#### An attractive city

Rich in heritage, the urban destination of Angers, labelled "city of art and history," also attracts foreign visitors. Angers castle, with its well-known Apocalypse Tapestry, receives the most visitors, about 30% of whom are foreign. Discovering the city center involves the Angers museums (the Beaux Arts museum, Jean Lurçat, David d'Angers gallery) and the quality built heritage of the city. As far as accommodation is concerned, the urban community of Angers Loire Métropole includes almost 50% of the hotel capacity of the Maine-et-Loire *département* (county) and offers a wide variety of hotels.

**Image 14.5**

Source: Château_d'Angers©Jean-Sebastien_Evrard.

## Business tourism

In the heart of the Great West region of France, Angers enjoys a geographical situation conducive to the development of business events. Owing to quality structuring facilities (conference center, exhibition center, etc.) and its unique tourism offering, trade fairs and large scale professional events take place annually in Angers, related to the main economic sectors of the territory such as SIVAL, the show for the Loire wines, or recently the World Electronics Forum.

## Targets and markets

Through combining information regarding the existing tourism demand and the territory offering, targets were identified and actions planned to reach potential clients. Several parameters were used to prioritize markets: their current weight, development potential, consumption period, the marketing budgets needed for action, and the prospect of successful leverage, and their potential compatibility with the destination.

This is why Great Britain has been chosen as THE priority foreign market, despite the uncertain post-Brexit context, ahead of other countries close to France: Germany, Spain, the Netherlands, Belgium, and Italy. When considering visitors' profiles, visitors whose main motivation is cultural were selected, and offerings were focused upon visits of tourist sites, the discovery of a particular life style (through gastronomy, wines, local specialties), and walks in the city center.

**Image 14.6**

Source: Cremet_d_Anjou©Jean-Sebastien_EVRARD

## The strategy

### *A reception strategy*

The current number of tourists in Angers and its region is estimated at over 1 million a year in commercial and non-commercial accommodation, 80% of whom come for leisure and entertainment. With an average of 170,000 visitors (of whom 25% are foreign) going through its doors, the tourist office necessarily enlists considerable human and financial means to meet the demands of its international clientele. In particular, multilingual reception staff and trained holiday consultants do their utmost to meet the visitors' requests and make their visit to the tourist office (often the very first stop of foreign visitors in Angers) a pleasant experience that brings them real added value in their discovery of the destination.

The tourist office also devises paper or digital materials to provide information and enrich foreign visitors' discovery of the destination. The website www.angersloiretourisme.com and the external terminal, both accessible 24 hours a day, are available in four foreign languages: English, German, Spanish, and Italian. City maps are also available in these languages, plus Dutch. Other documents are available in French and English; these include the Angers Loire Valley magazine, the Loire à Vélo (Loire by bike), and vineyard maps, etc.

### A commercial conquest strategy

In an environment of fierce competition from other French or European cities and dynamic or better-known neighboring cities (e.g. Nantes, Le Mans, Tours), Angers Loire Tourisme demonstrates its determination to break into the main foreign markets, using diverse and complementary actions. Every year, Angers Loire Tourisme is present at several trade exhibitions or general public events targeting specific audiences, such as IBTM or IMEX for business tourism, or the annual Workshop France that receives over 800 tour operators from around the world.

Press relations are yet another strand that generates excellent spillover effects. In 2016, the territory hosted nearly 100 journalists and bloggers. The quality and content of the subsequent articles or publications confirms the value of the return-on-investment of press relations. Educ-tours are organized each year to show the destination to tourism industry professionals: tour operators, travel agencies, coach operators, professional congress organizers, etc. Angers Loire Tourisme is also seeking to increase its visibility through print or Web-based publicity inserts or by improving the natural referencing of its websites www.angersloiretourisme.com and www.meetinangers.fr

### Collaborations

On an ad hoc basis, Angers Loire Tourisme undertakes individual actions in the European markets (UK, Germany, Belgium), but most of the time, operations are conducted in partnership with other institutional stakeholders: Atout France offices, clusters to which Angers Loire Tourisme is affiliated (Urban Tourism and Business Tourism), the Pays de la Loire Regional Agency and the Anjou Departmental Agency. The destination can also rely upon the current concern of the city to promote Angers territory on an international level.

### Perspectives

#### Successfully integrating the impacts of the digital transition

Tourist offices have to rethink their reception and information services, particularly in terms of the complementarity between the physical and digital reception of visitors. The same principle applies to the issue of promoting the territory: the marketing strategy is based upon the social networks, websites, and mobile applications, but it also includes actions on the ground with the various prescribing agencies such as tour operators, professional congress organizers, etc. Tourism is a sector based upon human relations to which it would be dangerous to bring solely technological responses.

#### Relying upon ambassadors already highly appreciative of the destination

In an effort to focus the message on the client experience, Angers Loire Tourisme intends to involve more closely the inhabitants or foreigners living in Angers so that they can share their knowledge of the place in a more authentic fashion than through institutional presentations. For instance, over 3,000 foreign students (representing over 150 nationalities) constitute a genuine potential advocacy resource among their family and relatives and, later, their professional circle.

Source: Olivier Bouchereau, Marketing Department, Angers Loire Tourisme.

## Conclusion

The tourism and hospitality industry is becoming increasingly international. The international economy implies more travel. Almost all countries are tourism destinations. Few political regimes prevent citizens from traveling, and many countries have seen their financial resources increase (e.g. China and other important markets). Many other factors show additional evidence of the ongoing trend of internationalization of the tourism sector and activity. For 50 years (roughly from the early 1950s to 2000), the tourism sector was located mainly in Western Europe and the North American markets, with a couple of other destinations; it is now definitely a worldwide industry, encompassing three main areas: North America, all of Europe, and the most dynamic "new" area, the Asian region, spearheaded by China, the key player in the field.

Does this mean that we all live in a global village (if we refer to Marshall McLuhan's 1968 prophecy), and all travelers are clones with the same expectations and habits? Not at all. The world is still made of significantly different cultural environments. Hence, at company level, the management has to contend with consumers who come from different countries and different cultural environments, with a considerable number of different expectations, habits, and requirements. The main marketing issue is therefore whether you should adapt your marketing mix (or not!) and to what extent. Part of the answer is that yes, we have to adapt to consumers' needs, expectations, and habits. At the same time, we should not forget that leisure tourists are more inclined to experience and discover local cultures, whereas business travelers are more focused on service efficiency and quality. Hence, it is clear that international marketing remains a main concern for managers in the tourist and hospitality industry who have to identify the best balance between customers' expectations and their willingness to experience different elements of local culture to a greater or lesser extent. In the end, decisions must be taken regarding the product/service design and other dimensions of the marketing mix.

### REVIEW QUESTIONS

1. What is the benefit for a company to develop its business in international markets?
2. Is there any specific marketing methodology when a company expands its business internationally on several markets? What are the main challenges the company or the destination will face?

3. What is the importance of culture in the context of international marketing?
4. Why do most tourism and hospitality companies select an adaptation of their marketing mix instead of a globalized marketing approach?

## "Tourism Australia, 2006 advertising campaign: where the bloody hell are you"

URL: http://www.youtube.com/watch?v=rn0lwGk4u9o&feature=player_detailpage

Summary: In 2006, Tourism Australia launched an advertising campaign created by the Sydney office of the London advertising agency M&C Saatchi. The advertisements feature Australians preparing for visitors to their country. The advertisement ends with model Lara Bingle at Fingal Spit stepping out of the ocean and asking "So, where the bloody hell are you?" This commercial caused controversy as the words "hell" and "bloody," not shocking in Australia, were not accepted by advertising authorities in some other countries. In the UK, the television version was banned, and the roadside billboards bearing the slogan removed. In Singapore and other countries, the television version was modified, and the words "bloody hell" removed.

## "Visit Britain marketing show reel 2012"

URL: https://www.youtube.com/watch?v=_pHz01dYYwY&t=2s

Summary: Twenty twelve saw the launch of a four-year $150 million marketing campaign designed to capitalize on the Diamond Jubilee, the London 2012 Festival,,and the Olympic and Paralympic Games to attract millions of additional visitors to Britain by 2015.

## "Hilton and non-digital marketing"

URL: https://www.youtube.com/watch?v=9c-edfKCAcU

Summary: Hilton CMO explains the continual importance of non-digital marketing in the international "digital" age and the emerging role of purpose-driven marketing.

## "International expansion of Norwegian Airlines"

URL: https://www.youtube.com/watch?v=-I_P9zQ3jzs

Summary: Norwegian Airlines is the first low-cost operator to fly the Atlantic and it's already driving an aggressive expansion plan. To support it, it's upping its spend on international marketing to increase brand awareness.

## REFERENCES, FURTHER READING, AND RELATED WEBSITES

### References

Gillespie, K., & Riddle, L. (2015). *Global marketing* (4th ed.). London: Routledge.

### Further reading

Das, D., Eisner, A.B., & Korn, H.J. (2015). Tata Starbucks: How to brew a sustainable blend for India. *Journal of the International Academy for Case Studies, 21*(3), 43.

Hofstede, G. (1994). The business of international business is culture. *International Business Review, 3*(1), 1–14.

Keegan, W.J., & Green, M.C. (2013). *Global marketing* (7th ed.). Harlow: Person Education.

Legohérel, P., Hsu, C.S., & Daucé, B. (2015). Using the CHAID segmentation approach in analyzing the international traveler market. *Tourism Management, 46*(February), 359–366.

Levitt, T. (1983). The globalization of markets. *Harvard Business Review, 61*, 92–102.

Liu B. S. C., Furrer, O., & Sudharshan, D. (2001). The relationship between cultures and behavioural intentions towards services. *Journal of Service Research, 4*(2), 118–129.

McCort, D.J., & Malhotra N.K. (1993). Culture and consumer behaviour: Toward an understanding of cross-cultural behaviour. *Journal of International Consumer Marketing, 6*(2), 91–127.

Okumus B., Okumus F., & McKercher, B. (2007). Incorporating local and international cuisines in the marketing of tourism destinations: The case of Hong Kong and Turkey. *Tourism Management, 28*(1), 253–261.

Reisinger Y. (2009). *International tourism: Cultures and behaviours.* Oxford: Elsevier.

Usunier, J.C., & Lee, J.A. (2012). *Marketing across cultures* (6th ed.). Harlow: Pearson.

Zhang, J., Beatty, S.E., & Gwalsh, G. (2008). Review and future directions of cross-cultural consumer services research. *Journal of Business Research, 61*(3), 211–224.

### Websites

Tourism Australia
http://www.tourism.australia.com/en/about/our-campaigns/theres-nothing-like-australia.html

Tourism Ireland
https://www.tourismireland.com/Marketing/Marketing-Highlights/Marketing-Catalogue/Autumn-Campaign-2017

Tourism New Zealand
https://www.tourismnewzealand.com/about/what-we-do/campaign-and-activity/

Visit Britain
https://www.visitbritain.org/introducing-great-tourism-campaign

Vogue magazine
https://www.vogue.com/article/effortless-cool-fall-destinations-with-a-french-touch

# MAJOR CASE STUDY
## TUNISIA – INTERNATIONAL TOURISM STRATEGY: FOCUSING ON TOURIST EXPERIENCE, DIGITAL MEDIA AND SOCIAL NETWORKS

Tunisia post January 14, 2011, is a new Tunisia, a plural Tunisia, a country that is reborn and has decided to take the path of learning democracy. Undoubtedly, this path is going to be long and arduous; nevertheless, it is essential to join the ranks of democratic, developed countries and to develop a new glorious national image. In this endeavor, the whole Tunisian economy is called upon to carry out the necessary reforms and contribute to the establishment of a new image. This new image is essential, particularly in the tourism sector, which has already been suffering from structural problems for about 15 years in addition to various mishaps resulting from morose international and domestic conditions.

January 14, 2011, was a turning point for Tunisian tourism. Tunisia was mentioned in international news as the country that hosted the first revolution of the 21st century, and the 2015 Nobel Peace Prize was awarded to the Tunisian National Dialogue Quartet for the efforts made by civil organizations to contribute to building a pluralistic democracy and restore socio-political stability. The country's visibility in the world was considerably increased.

Consequently, the Tunisian tourism administration, tourism professionals, and organizations in the Tunisian civil society rallied to review the situation and to establish a new marketing and communication strategy, especially at a time of high security concerns. The issue was not simply the task of promoting and communicating, but rather that of communicating in different ways to invent new, efficient, and effective communication methods. The twofold goal was first to restore the image of the destination, reassure, and regain the confidence of partners and foreign customers, and second, to evolve towards a new image that was closer to the country's reality and in phase with the current international trends of tourism consumption.

The major objective was therefore to promote the tourism potential of Tunisia, away from the beaten track and clichés of the seaside and a cheap destination intended for mass tourism. The issue was to broadcast a nuanced image of Tunisia externally and internally, through a new branding campaign based on the human experience in the digital age; the strategy was to combine both digital technologies and traditional story-telling to arouse the emotions of our targets. Given the low visibility of Tunisia on the Internet and an uncontrolled and haphazard use of various digital tools, it seemed wise to set up a consistent content strategy (brand content) focusing on the emotions of the potential tourists who are looking for a special, even unique, experience in the country. An Internet-based strategy has the advantage of reaching millions of worldwide online users instantly. The Internet is easy to access and has become the most important tool for people who search information before selecting their holiday destination. The various social media developed in recent years represent a huge source of information; they allow online users to learn, exchange, and influence others and consequently, to intervene in the selection process.

Hence, word-of-mouth in the digital age is one of the most powerful tools we choose to build our content strategy.

Concretely, we opted for an international communication strategy designed to promote the diversification of the Tunisian tourism product. Key goals were to showcase the different elements of the destination, to focus on the travel experience, and the notion of forming human connections while taking into consideration the impact of the 2011 revolution on the tourists. Most tourists experienced the surprise, emotions, wonder, expectations regarding the Tunisian process of learning democracy, but they were aware of the bitter reality related to the emergence of terrorism while understanding that Tunisia did not collapse like other Arab and Muslim countries, owing to the neutrality of the army and the proper functioning of its administration.

Thus, in addition to the conventional campaigns through print, television, and radio, we launched a few digital campaigns and organized events with high media impact in Tunisia and abroad. In particular, we focused on social networks (YouTube, Facebook, Twitter, and Instagram) and developed a brand content highlighting the dynamism, energy, freshness, hospitality, optimism of youth, and the joy of living in Tunisia. We made much of the country's cultural activities but also of the international events held in Tunisia, and we gave extensive media coverage to the testimonials of opinion leaders and simple tourists. The selection of social networks depends on the tourist's profile, given that people's search strategies and behavior on the Internet differ from one market to another. The French, for example, have a high penetration rate on Facebook, unlike the Chinese who have their own networks. Therefore, we knew we had to adopt a market-based approach with "personalized" content in order to connect Tunisia to its source markets, link up Tunisians to their fellow world citizens, thereby creating an emotional connection between transmitters and receivers. In this spirit, we conducted the following campaigns and actions:

- Producing 15 videos lasting between seven and nine minutes, translated into ten languages, to reach the majority of our markets. Each video makes online viewers feel part of the trip made by a tourist called "Deborah Gysen." The videos focus on three broad areas: welfare (food, body care, relaxation), beautiful stories (the UNESCO Heritage Sites, natural landscapes), and sport (water sports, golf, trekking, motor sports). This strategy was designed to reach the various profiles of our target markets: the adventurer in search of extreme sensations, the romantic in search of exotic places, etc. The launch of this campaign included a teaser of 30 seconds summarizing the main highlights of Deborah's visit to Tunisia. All the videos were broadcast throughout Europe under the hashtag #TrueTunisia, using digital display, social networks (YouTube, Facebook, Teads, and LinkedIn), and print.

**Image 14.7**

**Image 14.8**

Image 14.9

- Launching the Nobel Peace campaign in ten European countries (Norway, Sweden, France, Germany, Italy, Great Britain, Spain, Belgium, Poland, and Russia) through a promotional film lasting one minute and 30 seconds highlighting the success of the democratic transition in Tunisia. The film, shot in Tunisia and in seven other countries, was broadcast under the hash-tags #UnitedForPeace, #UnitedForTunisia in major search engines and social networks (You-Tube, Facebook, Twitter, and Instagram). Over 1.5 million people saw this video on YouTube after just one day of being posted.
- Producing the "Talents d'ailleurs" (Talents from elsewhere) mini-series of 16 videos for the French market in collaboration with the TV channel M6. The series is designed to promote Tunisia through Tunisian talents, people known for their success stories in various domains (e.g. sports, entrepreneurship, gastronomy, fashion). These people are shown as ordinary human beings who, owing to their strong will, self-confidence, and determination, have overcome obstacles and followed their dreams. The purpose of this campaign was to convey a youthful, dynamic, lively, fresh, modern, educational, cultural, determined image of the destination through its human potential, to reassure would-be French tourists and restore their desire to become acquainted with Tunisian people. The historic, cultural, and linguistic affinities binding France and Tunisia are strengthened through these videos broadcast on M6 at prime time and found on the social networks.
- Producing the second season of the #TrueTunisia campaign. A total of seven videos adapted to the specificities of five major social networks (YouTube, Facebook, Twitter, Instagram, and Pinterest) were produced to attract people to come and enjoy the experience of the "true"

Image 14.10

Tunisia. A teaser summarizing the strong moments of the season was mediatized in 14 priority markets in terms of tourist flows (Russia, Germany, France, Italy, Great Britain, Belgium, Poland, the Czech Republic, Switzerland, the Netherlands, Spain, Portugal, Sweden, and Denmark) in a campaign including film, publicity, displays, digital signage, and social networks.

- Conducting the campaign "Live from Tunisia" in five European capitals (Paris, Berlin, Milan, Brussels, and London) to reassure potential visitors by showing the "normality" of the country and to invite them to share Tunisian everyday moments. This is a major operation in the tourism communication field; through viewing a few scenes of Tunisian everyday life (Sidi Bou Said, Hammamet, Tozeur) on billboards, French or Italian pedestrians could enjoy a welcome break, a "breath of fresh air," a few minutes of complete change of scene and escapism.

Image 14.11

**Image 14.11 (Cont.)**

**Image 14.12**

Source: Feriel Gadhoumi, Tunisian National Tourism Office

Major case study questions

1.  What was the rationale underpinning the creation of Tunisia's new international marketing strategy?
2.  How was this strategy differentiated between different European markets?
3.  How easy (or difficult) is it to move the market away from traditional tourism stereotypes?
4.  How has Tunisia tried to differentiate itself from other competing North African destinations such as Egypt?

# 5 Marketing destinations

## Learning outcomes

By the end of this chapter, students will:

- Understand the variety of definitions of tourism destinations, their influence and impact
- Become familiar with the destination life cycle, the specific phases of touristic development, and the marketing responses required to sustain destination competitiveness
- Understand the influence of the experience economy on the marketing of destinations
- Be familiar with the various roles within DMOs, the environments they operate in, and the challenges they face
- Understand the importance of destination branding and positioning and their contribution to destination competitiveness.

## Introduction

For tourism destinations, the experience economy has been driving radical change in marketing procedures over the past two decades. Destinations have now realized that what is being sold is not a combination of various goods and services in a geographical unit; rather, it is a single experience of visiting a specific destination. It is important to reiterate that it is the experience that has been purchased and consumed, even though what has been purchased is not the tangible parts of the tourism experience such as a hotel room but the right of use for a period of time, and what is left after the consumption of the single experience is only memories. Prior to the introduction of the experience economy, it was argued that service is perishable, intangible, inseparable, and variable; these four service characteristics having tremendous effect on marketing strategies and techniques as outlined back in Chapter 8. However, the most recent consensus is that the traditional 4P marketing mix toolbox (i.e., product, place, price, and promotion) is necessary but insufficient for an experience based service economy, hence three new Ps of people, process, and physical evidence have been integrated to the 7P service marketing mix.

These changes are extremely useful in helping managers to create better and more successful marketing plans in service settings. However, it should be noted that in using the 7P approach, marketers still need to manage each and every service process in a tourism destination separately and sometimes independently. Owing to the impact of a single failure on the whole experience for visitors, some destinations such as Austria, Denmark, New Zealand, and Switzerland have introduced the concept of quality management programs. However, the nature of service management makes the successful implementation of quality standards extremely difficult. Quality management procedures for geographically-large destinations (e.g., the US) are especially harder to standardize. In addition, coordination among different businesses makes quality control at a destination very challenging. By nature, all businesses at a destination are pursuing their own benefits and most of the collaborations among these businesses are destined to a failure. In fact, more than 70% of business collaborations end up failing before achieving the goal of collaboration. Behavioral conflicts among the players are the prime reason for collaboration failure with self-interest playing its part. On the other hand, history has showed that the free market notion represents a failed mechanism for destinations due to the complex and amalgamated nature of the products and services offered at a destination. For a long time, there was no remedy for this issue and all destinations were just trying to follow key performance indices (KPIs) of those successful destinations. However, without successful collaboration and decentralized service and product management, more destinations everyday were getting on the edge of failure in the tourism system.

With the paradigm shift as a result of the experience economy, destination management/marketing organizations (DMOs) have become important players in the success of a destination. Since the whole period of a tourist's visit to a specific destination is considered as a single experience, there is a need for an authority to manage/heavily influence the whole process of the experience. DMOs can create shared vision among all the players in a destination to increase the chance of success for destination level collaborations. In addition, they can manage issues such as free riders, competition among the collaborators, and distribution of the benefits among the collaborators in a way that the distribution of the benefits is fair and stable (i.e., the paradox of equity vs. equality). In tourism destination marketing, the purpose is to create a distinctive and memorable identity using the principles of the experience economy and experiential marketing. DMOs usually do so by using the principles of destination branding and positioning. Accurate implementation of these principles leads to creating and sustaining competitive advantages that can guarantee economic prosperity for these destinations.

## Destinations

Destination can be defined as a location or geographic unit other than an individual's usual place of residence that an individual travels to (spatial movement is necessary) to spend some time for various reasons, which are mostly related to touristic motivations. The majority of tourism activities are expected to take place at destinations, hence, the destination is the major element in any modeling of the tourism system and is introduced as the fundamental unit of analysis in tourism. Based on the above conceptualization of destination, destination marketing and management can be defined as a proactive, visitor-centered approach to the economic and cultural development of a destination, which balances and integrates the interests of visitors, service providers, and the community. Understanding the concept and scope of the tourism industry in general and destination marketing and management in particular is a necessity for effective and integrative marketing and management strategy development. Destination marketing and management, however, is a complex issue that demands a comprehensive, holistic, and systematic approach to its understanding. Globalization and standardization are two processes that largely make tourism products and services homogeneous. Increase in homogeneous products (e.g., Disney theme parks all around the world) makes standardization an easier task than before. As a result, destinations become interchangeable in the visitors' minds and travelers have a variety of choices of available destinations. On the other hand, DMOs at different levels are trying their best to compete for attention from a highly competitive marketplace. Consequently, destination competitiveness and attractiveness are more important than ever in creating integrative marketing strategies for the DMOs to survive in a harsh competitive environment of today's market. In this chapter, we will discuss some of the most important competitiveness issues that DMOs are facing.

Boundaries of destinations are not necessarily tied to visitors' travel patterns, but destination marketers and managers tend to operate on administrative boundaries that often limit an accurate conceptualization of a destination. Destination "boundary" is rather flexible and usually context based. A destination can be as small as a single attraction or as massive as a large continent like Asia and anything in between (e.g., a theme park, village, city, county, state, country, and region). This flexibility makes it difficult to define a destination; there are various discussions in the tourism literature about the concept of destination but a uniform and standard definition of destination has proven to be elusive and slippery owing to the different permutations and implications associated with such an attempt and subsequently it is difficult to conceptualize appropriate marketing activities owing to a confusing concept. Many geographical units, however, have been around for a long time and not all of them become destinations. Tourism and hospitality insights 15.1 provides some contemporary examples of how VisitBritain markets the UK as a "holistic" tourism destination internationally.

The rise, development process, and fall of destination is an interesting process. Knowing about this process is a must for DMOs to successfully intervene in the development of destinations. Destinations follow a timeline in their development that is more or less similar to each other. Tourism Area Life Cycle (TALC, also known as destination life cycle) is probably the best-known tourism model among tourism scholars. Following the product life-cycle (PLC), Butler in 1980 carefully studied tourism destinations in various development stages and suggested a model that is shown in Figure 15.1. According to TALC, in the initial stages of destination development, which is also known as exploration, the number of tourists is very low, visitation pattern is irregular; there is no establishment specifically for

## TOURISM AND HOSPITALITY INSIGHTS 15.1
## VISITBRITAIN – MARKETING THE UK INTERNATIONALLY

Building on Britain's rich heritage, strong cultural assets and varied countryside, our campaigns promote the best of Britain, bringing in additional visitors and encouraging them to explore our country. We work in partnership with a range of organizations across the public and private sectors, maximizing government investment, providing strong returns for our partners and attracting ever-increasing numbers of visitors.

(Visit Britain, n.d.a, np)

Inbound tourism to the UK has grown steadily from 2010 in number of visits, overall spending, and average spent per visit (VisitBritain, n.d.d). VisitBritain uses a mixture of avenues to market the UK internationally and capture a variety of market segments.

### Technology

- Honor 10 smartphone: Utilizing Chinese and British influencers to explore "the unexpected in Britain" through custom itineraries, in the manner of VisitBritain, and image posts taken on the Honor10 phone to various social media outlets accompanied by #AIMAZING.

### Airline partnerships

Partnerships with various airlines to target various traveler markets and promote new routes to the UK.

#### The American market

- British Airways and American Airlines worked in conjunction with VisitBritain on a series of four videos which promoted various destinations throughout Great Britain. The series acted as a platform for turning video-inspired trips into bookings. The partnership between the two airlines also focused on the promotion and offering of more routes and flights to Britain than any other airline partnership.

#### The European market

- Targeting travelers from key cities across Europe, this campaign worked with EasyJet and utilized a variety of marketing channels including radio, digital platforms, influencers, and 360 videos.

### The Chinese market

- Working with British Airways, a two-phase marketing plan ran from November 8–Dec 8, 2017, targeting travelers in Shanghai and Beijing. The first phase used digital and social media with flash ticket sales and special discounts to target Millennials and the second phase utilized targeted promotion within financial media to attract business class travelers.

## Film tourism

The UK has been home to a variety of big screen events and VisitBritain smartly utilizes the entertainment industry as a way to market various parts of Great Britain.

- King Arthur: legend of the sword: A six-week international film tourism campaign which ran across Facebook, Instagram, Snapchat in several countries, and VisitBritain's owned channels. The campaign worked in conjunction with #OMBGLegends (Oh My Great Britain "Home of Legendary Moments") to inspire bookings for film-inspired holidays to Britain.
- #OMGB (Oh My Giant Britain) – "where giant dreams come to life": This campaign worked with both the hundredth anniversary of British novelist and screenwriter Roald Dahl with the launch of the remake of the film "The BFG." The campaign was significant as it was the first partnership between VisitBritain and Disney and included #OMGB in conjunction with the "Oh My GREAT Britain" campaign (VisitBritain, n.d.a).

## Sport tourism

Football (soccer) tourism attracts the largest volume of inbound tourists to Britain (VisitBritain, n.d.c). VisitBritain has capitalized on this with several campaigns including "Bring football home with the Premier League" and "Search for the biggest Premier League fan."

Outside of football, VisitBritain showcases Wimbledon as part of the #OMGB campaign. Wimbledon, which streamed to over 24.1 million viewers via BBC Sport and BBC iPlayer in 2017, allows VisitBritain to highlight an experience unique to Britain and gain exposure across social media with both the hashtags of "OMBG" and "Wimbledon", is in addition to a dedicated Wimbledon page within the VisitBritain site (VisitBritain, n.d.c; Wimbledon, n.d.).

## References

Visit Britain. (n.d.a). Global partnership campaigns. Visit Britain Visit England. Retrieved from https://www.visitbritain.org/global-partnership-campaigns

Visit Britain. (n.d.b). Inbound football tourism research. VisitBritain VisitEngland. Retrieved from https://www.visitbritain.org/inbound-football-tourism-research

VisitBritain. (n.d.c). It's time for Wimbledon! Retrieved from https://www.visitbritain.com/gb/en/campaigns/wimbledon#7JqOdr5YkrMllSgU.97

VisitBritain. (n.d.d). 2016 snapshot. VisitBritain VisitEngland. Retrieved from https://www.visitbri
tain.org/2016-snapshot

Wimbledon. (n.d). Facts and figures. Retrieved from https://www.wimbledon.com/en_GB/atoz/
faq_and_facts_and_figures.html

Source: Amanda Templeton.

tourists, and the destination is not well known in tourism markets. In the involvement stage, locals start to participate in tourism activities and provide services and products to tourists. At this stage, some regular patterns start to emerge in the visitation behaviors and low/high seasons gradually appear. Usually, involvement is the stage in which DMOs are founded and public interest in tourism increases. In the development stage, heavy advertisement and other types of promotions are on the agenda for destinations. The level of involvement and development control decreases significantly. Attractions are growing

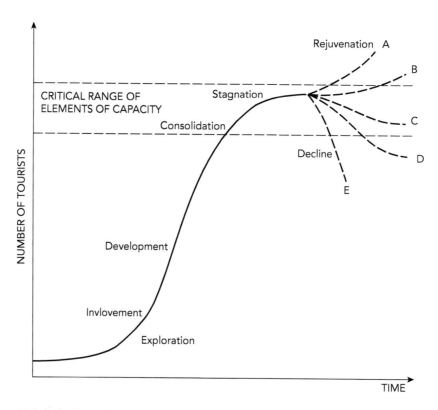

**Figure 15.1 Butler's tourism area lifecycle model of destination development**

and supplementary attractions are developed to complement the main attractions. The number of visitors grows exponentially. In the development stage, the rate of increase in the number of tourists is at its maximum possible value.

In the consolidation stage, the rate of growth is reduced significantly and the number of visitors has reached to the level that is usually more than the number of locals. At this stage, development is slowing down and tourism becomes the major economic force in the local economy. In stagnation, the destination has reached its maximum capacity from various aspects and negative effects of tourism (traffic, increase rate of crime, price increase for locals, etc.) starts to emerge. Locals become dissatisfied with large visitor presence. The destination has a well-established image in the stagnation stage, patterns of re-visitation can be clearly observed, and return visitors become regular to the destination. After stagnation, two possible scenarios exist. In the first scenario, destinations enter into a decline stage in which tourism-related facilities decline, local involvement increases again, some of the negative effects such as high consumer price indices are mitigated, and the area either becomes a veritable tourist slum or other economic activities completely eradicate tourism. In the second scenario, rejuvenation might be an option for the destination. It should be noted that the purpose of rejuvenation is different, however. Sometimes, rejuvenation is just to delay or modify the decline process, while other times the purpose is to reestablish (rebrand) the destination as a new tourism area with different attractions. Generally, almost all the attractions should be transformed in order to have a new destination. For example, for some destinations, man-made attractions such as casinos are necessary parts of rejuvenation either for a remedy purpose until transformation is completed or for permanently creating differentiation from neighboring destinations. Each stage of the development needs its own proper strategies to be adopted by DMOs. Some of these strategies are discussed in the other sections of this chapter.

## Systems approach to destination marketing and management

It can be argued that a destination is a geographical space in which a cluster of tourism resources exist. A tourism cluster is an accumulation of tourist resources and attractions, infrastructures, equipment, service providers, other support sectors and administrative organizations whose integrated and coordinated activities provide customers with the experiences they expected from the destination they choose to visit. Using such a cluster approach, three major destination cluster types can be identified: (1) a destination as a part of a political boundary (e.g., the French Quarter in New Orleans; Fisherman's Wharf in San Francisco; and Darling Harbor in Sydney); (2) a destination as a political boundary (e.g., The Gold Coast in Australia, and The Strip in Las Vegas); and (3) a destination across political boundaries (e.g., the Alps in Europe, the Grand Canyon in the USA, and the Mekong Tourism Area in Southeast Asia).

From a geographical perspective, spatial movement is a key factor defining the tourism industry, which contributes to the understanding of destination marketing and management. One of the earliest, simplest, yet most effective definitions of tourism as a geographic system is offered by Leiper in 1980 (Figure 15.2). Understanding the tourism system enhances our understanding of tourism destinations that leads to better formulation of marketing strategies. The tourism system is composed of three components, traveler-generating region, transit route region, and tourist destination region within human, socio-cultural, economic, technological, physical, political, and legal environments. The traveler-generating region (or origin region), refers to the place where the tourists come from. It is the generating market, which stimulates and motivates travel. From a geographic perspective, tourism generator is any region except for the destination with individuals that have the potential to depart from their usual habitat to visit the destination. The transit route region includes the time and space boundary in between generating and destination regions. It includes all the transportation activities, visitors, and monetary flows. The tourist destination region is a key element in the whole tourism system. It emphasizes what the suppliers can do for the tourists. Of course, this includes not only the physical equipment, which is crucial to attract tourists, but also the management and service, which are helpful to enhance the image of the destination and motivations to visit the destination. The tourist destination region is where the tourists can realize their temporary goal of travel and go through a memorable tourism experience. It provides them with attractions of various types and creates a stage on which planning and management strategies can be carried out.

Inputs and outputs can be defined from different stakeholders' perspectives. For example, visitors' money in exchange for a memorable experience or an exchange of visitors' flow with income flow can be defined as the inputs and outputs of the system. It should be understood that the tourism system is not an independent or closed system. Its development relies on the support of other external or environmental systems, such as socio-cultural, economic, political, physical, etc. Following the same line of reasoning, destination marketing, and management has been, and will continue to be, affected by multiple external factors, which serve as the driving forces. It is imperative to understand the effect of these environmental forces on management and marketing activities of destinations. According to a report of the 2008 Future Studies conducted by KAI for Destination

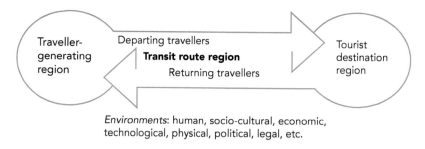

*Environments*: human, socio-cultural, economic, technological, physical, political, legal, etc.

**Figure 15.2 Tourism system from a geographical perspective**

Marketing Association International (DMAI), the following eight "super trends" have been identified as the driving forces for destination marketing and management:

*The customer environment:* Travel customers increasingly seek and respond to a diversified set of value clusters (i.e., combinations of experiences, products, and prices that suit their individual preferences). Destinations must design, promote, and coordinate a satisfying total visitor experience that maximizes the economic contribution to the destination, and one that stimulates return intention and referral behavior. Destination marketers must create an ever-richer palette of options and target their value packages more skillfully to various preference patterns.

*The competitor environment:* As the travel market continues to evolve toward greater fluidity, complexity, disintermediation, and re-intermediation, visitors and the businesses that sell services to them face a bewildering set of information choices. The proliferation of free online content, especially, creates an intense "noise level" that makes it difficult for destinations to make themselves the preferred information providers. Destination marketers must become the most popular information source for visitors and the businesses that sell services to them. This will mean becoming more visible to them in all media, and especially capturing a significant share of the web traffic that involves travel decisions.

*The economic environment:* The increasingly volatile and uncertain economic environment makes it necessary to plan flexibly, and with various economic shocks and even catastrophic contingencies in mind. The possibility of another major terrorist incident such as 9/11, an international health pandemic, a rapid and irreversible rise in oil prices, or other such events that could strike without warning must now be seriously taken into account. Destinations must form their strategic plans and development agendas around alternate economic scenarios, and must have contingency plans for responding to previously unthinkable economic upheavals.

*The technological environment:* As technology advances in sophistication, functionality, and intelligence, destination marketers will become less visible to visitors. They will not be able to sell services to visitors if they fail to keep pace by developing competing digital platforms that teach, inform, entertain, advise, support, and assist the prospective visitor with various features. Destination marketers must build, maintain, and continually improve state-of-the-art technology resources that visitors can rely on for their travel decisions. This includes implementing "social technologies" such as social networking, community building, and user-generated content. This also includes constant attention to search engine optimization and careful analysis of website traffic patterns.

*The social environment:* At the same time, human relationships and communities are becoming ever more physically "de-localized," atomized, and transient. A growing multitude of information experiences and channels connects people to one another, to their various virtual clans, and to the media culture at large. Modern cultures are increasingly defined in terms of proliferating numbers of relationships of a more shallow and transient nature. Social networking is becoming a significant method of reaching customer populations by creating specialized communities of interest. User-generated content is also rapidly becoming an important feature of the electronic culture. These trends in technology and interaction offer opportunities for the meetings business, as well as for consumer marketing, with methods such as spontaneous formation of affinity groups. Destinations must promote travel and travel-related benefits they offer for the purpose of personal enrichment, mutual appreciation between cultures, and reduction of political tension through a sense of community and connectedness. At the same time, they must make their messages viable within the saturated media environment that envelops the prospective of travel customers they hope to attract. They can employ various Internet technologies and strategies, such as blogging, web communities, virtual visits, and social networking programs that differentiate their destinations to specially targeted demographic and psychographic populations.

*The political environment:* Destination marketers such as DMOs continue to face confusion, uncertainty, and doubt from their local governments, stakeholders, and partners regarding the roles they can play and the value they can offer. For many, this results in the perpetual "pie fight," with an increasing number of contenders seeking a portion of local taxes and municipal forms of funding for non-tourism-related purposes. In very popular destinations, leaders of the political process may question the need to market the destination at all, and citizens may view tourists as an intruding nuisance rather than contributors to the economic development of the community. DMOs risk being left out of the important strategic conversation that drives important decisions about the development of the community. DMOs must proactively catalyze and lead the local strategic conversation with regard to the role and importance of visitor commerce in the sustainable development of the entire destination. They must also diligently advocate their role in making that visitor commerce a reality.

*The legal environment:* Governments at a variety of levels in many countries may increasingly impose taxes, laws, and other restrictions upon travel-related commerce, as part of their political, social, economic, and ecological agendas. Some of these legislative interventions work to the advantage of certain destinations and to the disadvantage of others. Some may lead to competitive retaliation by other governments. In some cases, policies at various political levels may conflict with one another, and may even reflect conflicting policy theories within certain governments. Destination marketers must vigorously oppose unilateral governmental actions that threaten to balkanize the travel sector, and advocate shared solutions that balance economic, ecological, social, and political benefits for all involved.

*The geophysical environment:* The intensifying focus on global warming, climate change, and related ecological concerns will create pressure at many levels of society and government, and in many economic sectors, to be "seen as green". Common sense may be in short supply during this "hype" phase, and strong leadership will be needed to focus on the "green conversation" along rational pathways for long-term impact. Destination marketers must advocate a realistic balance in the green conversation, promoting intelligent trade-offs and synergistic solutions that combine a rewarding travel experience with sustainable economic development.

## Roles of DMOs in destination marketing and management

Coordination, strategy formulation, stakeholders' management, economic development, marketing, product development, lobbying, information provision, research, and the host community management are among the common themes identified as the key roles of DMOs all around the world. Taking a more holistic perspective, nine areas can be identified as the main function of a DMO (Wang, 2008):

*Information provider.* At the destination level, the DMO is charged with the responsibility to do research, identify their target markets, meet visitors' expectations, and share the information with the local constituents. They are a source of information for businesses who want to enhance what they are doing. From a visitor's perspective, the DMO is a contact point for people who want to visit the area and it provides information to tourists through various channels, such as publicizing information on websites, sending out an information packet to potential visitors, and providing information at facilities people visit. The information provision function has also been extended to local residents.

*Community brand builder.* In general, the DMO is the destination marketing organization responsible for marketing the whole destination as one entity. Because of the partnerships the DMO has at the local and regional level, they can market the destination in larger geographical scope as well as in bigger business scale than the individual businesses can afford to do. This view is supported by the following comment. The DMO's role is to work in collaboration with the local businesses to market and promote the destination to a multitude of different markets, bring in corporate business, bring in conventions and meetings, group tours, leisure travelers, and act as the marketing representative of the local area. The DMO is the entity which is responsible for marketing the whole destination by treating the destination as one entity and positioning the destination as one place for people to visit. This role cannot be easily replaced by other entities in the community, as if the DMO doesn't brand and market the entire destination, individual businesses will not take that role. They (individual businesses) are more invested in their own private businesses so it's very challenging for them to think outside of their individual partners. If the DMO doesn't exist, there is no organization which can fill that void.

*Convener, facilitator, and liaison of community tourism activities.* The DMO often plays the role of community convener on significant issues that may, or may not, result in further community action. The convening role usually includes a highly visible public discussion of community issues. These discussions are often related to data gathering or studies which provide information intended to highlight a common understanding of the issues at hand. Such discussions are important prerequisites for collaborative community problem-solving. From a marketing perspective, the DMO is the facilitator for the local destination by offering a number of different marketing programs in different markets. In this role, the DMO attempts to help make collaborative destination problem-solving efforts among non-profit, government, business, and other organizations possible and effective. When it works well, convening or facilitation is valued as a source of fairness, encouragement, and a resource to all those who might need it in the collaborative process. The DMO is also the liaison between the visitor and the community, between the local tourism industry and the government. They convey information back and forth between visitor and community to keep the visitors happy. They are also the liaison between the visitor and visitor industry and the government, and facilitate communications between them.

*Catalyst of the collaborative initiative.* The DMO uses the convening role to stimulate discussion with a longer-term strategy in mind. When an organization is catalytic, it makes an early and clear commitment to participate in longer-term community problem-solving that begins with an initial discussion of issues. In this way, it uses its influence and resource base to make the collaborative initiative real in the minds of various other potential partners who may be waiting for leadership before making commitments to an action agenda. The DMO is also the catalyst for economic development relative to the tourism industry.

*Advocate of the tourism industry.* The DMO is the advocate to the tourism industry in that it conveys the message of the importance of tourism, and its impact on the area and on the local economy, as well as the advantages of tourism to the local economy. The DMO is also viewed as an advocate either for individuals or groups that are the primary focus of the collaboration activities. Since partners may be viewed as problematic by other partners in collaboration, therefore, it is important for DMOs to develop frameworks and internal processes within which advocacy efforts can emerge with support from as many partners as possible. In general, it can be argued that most of the marketing efforts seeking commitments from its partners require DMOs to play an advocacy role. Without such advocacy, collaboration will be limited only to data gathering, information sharing, and public education, being unable to put any proposals into action.

*Organizer of destination marketing campaigns.* The DMO has a primary interest in understanding what marketing activities are viable for the local destination, how the constituents proceed with the marketing activities, which should be at the decision-making table and, in particular, how to include as many partners as possible. This marketing role often includes the ongoing search for good marketing and promotion ideas, welcoming and sustaining of participation by community-based, destination-based, and constituency-based organizations and individuals. The DMO is the organizer of different marketing activities. They put things into perspective and work with dominant industry players to bring travelers in.

*Funding agent for collective marketing activities.* The DMO encourages a variety of collaborative marketing activities by providing supporting and matching funds, especially for marketing and promoting the local destination collectively at a larger scale, either alone or with other funding sources. This is an increasingly common practice in the past few years and has been accepted by the local tourism industry, especially the small and medium-sized businesses. For example, for art and event programs, many DMOs have grant matching programs in which local businesses can get a "dollar to dollar" matching fund support from the DMO to promote their events. Obviously, such programs are usually well accepted by the local tourism industry and become one of the incentives for them to work with the DMO. Such a model allows industry partners to expand their marketing dollars.

*Partner and team builder.* This appears to be the most obvious role of the DMO in the destination, and the way this role is played greatly affects the quality of the marketing activities and the likely outcomes of such activities. The DMO's role is to make sure that the empowering partners share risks, responsibilities, resources, and rewards in collaborative marketing efforts so that they establish mutually respectful, trusting relationships, take the time to understand each other's motivations and expectations, and state problems in a manner that provides opportunities for all the others involved in the process. The DMO is also the central focus to create the team at different levels (i.e., at the local, regional, and the state levels). In other words, the DMO creates the interest for the tourism industry to work together, and that's where the partnership between the tourism industry and the DMO starts to interact. Whenever the local businesses think they need to put a partnership together, they look to the DMO.

*Network management organization.* In the domain of destination marketing, it is widely agreed upon that marketing networks in which individual businesses that consciously collaborate and cooperate with one another are more effective at providing a complex array of community-based services than the same organizations are able to do when they go their own way. In other words, such marketing networks are vehicles that provide value to the local community in ways that could not have been achieved through uncoordinated provision of services by fragmented and autonomous businesses. From a production perspective, the joint production of marketing activities may satisfy stakeholders with multiple needs, but it may also raise substantial problems regarding resource allocation, benefits sharing, agreement on goals, expected outcomes, and the like. While such a marketing network may benefit the community in which it is embedded, especially the pool of stakeholders it serves, it must become a viable interorganizational entity which can coordinate the marketing activities. It has to gain considerable legitimacy and external support by satisfying the needs of stakeholders and other community interest groups. The DMO is regarded by the local tourism industry as the network management organization, acting in its capacity as agent for the community and as principal to its network members to guide, coordinate, and legitimize marketing network activities. Besides marketing, promotion, and visitor services, the DMO's mission is about managing and coordinating a diverse group of industry stakeholders in the community. It is a network management organization. Without the support of the stakeholders in the network, no destination marketing activities are possible.

There are several important action agendas for DMOs in order for them to claim leadership and relevance. According to DMAI (2008, pp. 79–83), these key agendas include:

*Building identity.* This is the ongoing effort to build a brand identity for the DMO itself, separate from but related to the brand identity of the destination. Presumably based on the concept of the DMO as the official face and voice of the destination, the actions in this category can position the DMO as objective, unbiased, and having no commercial "taint" to its role as the "friendly concierge" for visitors and event organizers. This may also include making the DMO CEO a high-profile spokesperson in and for the community. It is clear that a comprehensive strategy is needed to define the optimum brand identity for destinations that preserves the positive perceptions held by some visitors and meeting planners, establishes the DMO as the premier visitor expert and preferred source of information, and enhances the DMOs' perception for exceptional service and one-of-a-kind experiences. Tactics include drawing attention to the DMO and its CEO with high-profile community events, industry meetings, and newsworthy events; using visits by celebrities – entertainers, political leaders, star speakers – to put the DMO in front of the news media; emphasizing, at every possible opportunity, the DMO's unique role as the official face and voice of the destination, and defend it aggressively against encroachment by other entities; reflecting it in the advertising message, the slogans, the mission statement, and the business name; abandoning any activities, programs, relationships, or commercial arrangements that contradict the DMO's role as the unbiased, "can't be bought" provider of the best travel information available.

*Building coalition.* This is the systematic and continuous process of building connections and coalitions to the many community leaders, stakeholders, industry partners, client entities, and opinion shapers who can be instrumental in the DMO's success. Establish strong, trust-based connections to every key stakeholder, industry partner, and advocacy group within the destination community. Some of the tactics can include reviewing and updating the media-relations program by expanding the range of media contacts to include national, international, and web-based media; become the "go-to" source for travel writers, publishers, and other mavens who form public opinion, including independent online sources; building cooperative and supportive relationships with travel agencies and other intermediaries that can send business to their destination and becoming their preferred information source and help them sell the destination to their clients.

*Building commitment.* This is the continuous and never-ending practice of teaching, preaching, promoting, and modeling a visitor-centered doctrine to all stakeholders in the destination community. It includes defining service standards for all providers associated with the destination, as well as monitoring and reporting performance against the standards; profile the destination's appeal against primary visitor motivations; measuring and reporting on visitor perceptions of value – the "end-to-end" visitor experience; measuring and reporting on perceptions of value by out-of-town organizers, such as associations, conference organizers, and event promoters; utilizing in-town organizers as a source of information, influence, and relevance building; building a "voice of the customer" program for collecting and publicizing visitor contributions; spotlighting any service categories such as taxi services, tour operators, public transport, and others that might deliver substandard service levels, and pressing for local government initiatives to force improvements.

*Building vision and leadership.* This is the practice of spotting critical issues and policy questions relating to the development of the destination, leading the strategic conversation within the community around these key issues and questions, and helping the community leadership make wise and well-informed policy decisions. Some of the tactics can include: educating the entire DMO team about the key strategic trends, super trends, strategic themes of the industry; patiently and persistently build access routes to the inner offices of the elected political leaders of the community and making the DMO's knowledge, know-how, and ideas valuable to them; delivering an annual "state of the destination" report to community leaders, presenting the competitive standing of the destination and recommending areas of opportunity or improvement; developing an issues agenda for the travel, tourism, meetings, and hospitality dimension of the community's development and promoting it widely to all stakeholders and to the general public; actively engage in discussions about the community's priorities (beyond the hospitality industry) and create a role for the industry to be represented in achieving those priorities; taking a leading role in the "green conversation," helping community leaders see the value to economic development of sustainable development and ecologically responsible policies.

Most of the destination marketing and management activities are coordinated and facilitated by DMOs and there are various types of DMOs in different countries but they can be broadly categorized into three distinct types of tourism organizations:

*National tourism office/administration (NTO/NTA):* The WTO (1979) introduced the term national tourism office/administration as: "the authorities in the central state administration, or other official organization, in charge of tourism development at the national level." The term "NTA" was used to distinguish it from national tourist organization. The national tourism office (NTO) is used to represent the entity with overall responsibility for marketing a country as a tourism destination, whether purely a DMO or an NTA.

*State tourism office (STO):* The organization with overall responsibility for marketing a state (e.g., in the USA), province (e.g., in Canada), or territory (e.g., in Australia) as a tourism destination, in a country that has a federal political system.

*Regional tourism organization (RTO):* The term region here represents concentrated tourism areas such as cities, towns, villages, coastal resort areas, islands and rural areas. This level of DMO is also known by other titles in different parts of the world, such as convention and visitor bureau (CVB) in the USA, regional tourism board (RTB) in the UK. A regional tourism organization can be defined as the organization responsible for marketing a concentrated tourism area as a tourism destination.

*Local tourism office (LTO):* LTO can represent both a local tourism administration and a local tourism association. The former may be the local government authority, while the latter is a form of cooperative association of tourism businesses.

## Destination positioning

Owing to the crucial importance of competitiveness, which was pointed out earlier, DMOs should be familiar with destination branding and positioning. In other words, to achieve destination competitiveness, destinations need more than sales and promotion. As a result, DMOs are becoming involved in more managerial roles in recent years to integrate the marketing and managing activities from an operational perspective. A great deal of destination marketing efforts is directed toward positioning activities. Positioning of a product refers to its cognitive placing in consumer's mind. In other words, positioning of a brand is the collective perception that the customers form about the identity of the company/product/brand. The desired position should be feasible, communicable, and create sustainable competitive advantage. There are various types of positioning errors such as under-positioning, which is lack of enough information to differentiate the destination from other similar destinations; over-positioning, which is restraining the image of a destination to a limited level that many potential opportunities are being lost because of the limitations; or confused positioning, which is sending mixed signals to customers. Nevertheless, correct and effective positioning can create competitive advantage for the destination. For example, quality beaches for a Caribbean destination can be considered as under-positioning as this property is the characteristic of all Caribbean destinations and would not help a specific island (i.e., destination) to successfully differentiate itself from the rest of the islands in Caribbean.

Previous practices have shown that the starting point for positioning is destination branding. In order for a destination to position itself in the minds of customers, the destination needs first to create an appropriate brand. As in the case of product, destination brand has multiple components that together form consumer-based destination brand equity which, if correctly defined, is the initial starting point for a differentiation process. Such a brand equity is composed of destination brand awareness, destination brand associations, destination brand resonance, and destination brand loyalty. Tourism and hospitality insights 15.2 shows how user-generated content in the form of TripAdvisor can be used to help position an international tourism destination; in this case Cape Town in South Africa.

## TOURISM AND HOSPITALITY INSIGHTS 15.2
## USING TRIPADVISOR TO MARKET A DESTINATION

TripAdvisor works with more than 600 global DMOs and offers a comprehensive suite of content products (free and for purchase) that allow DMOs to enhance their websites with user-generated content and drive more traffic (Craig, 2012).

One means of utilizing TripAdvisor is that it allows DMOs to see the destination from the traveler's perspective and transform that information into a means in which to enhance and manage the private DMO website content. However, TripAdvisor offers various tools and features that allow it to be a valuable means through which to market destinations. Free content tools such as badges and widgets that can be uploaded to the destination site and provide fresh traveler-generated content on the site are readily available to DMOs. Wiki features allow for editorial information to be uploaded and edited to the page and DMOs have the option of reporting incorrect information to TripAdvisor or respond to posts directly (Craig, 2012).

Cape Town, South Africa, one of many destinations featured on TripAdvisor, highlights many of the features available on the site allowing for the destination to be showcased to perspective travelers. TripAdvisor provides easy access to ideas, and corresponding reviews, for hotels, vacation rentals, flights, things to do and activities within the destination. Webpage content will often include sections highlighting "Top questions asked" and access to traveler photos and videos, interactive maps, and topics from the TripAdvisor community.

Forums provide a medium for engaging travelers, sharing information, and gaining insight into topics and issues related to the destination. Forums are useful for those considering travel to the destination as well as for those who have already booked their vacation. Topics range from questions regarding airport transfers to ideas on the best companies to utilize for tours and adventures.

Destination experts, members who are knowledgeable about the destination and volunteer to answer questions regarding the destination (TripAdvisor, n.d.b), are featured on forum pages as a reference source for the destination. Often these are members who are either from the destination or live and work in the area. These TripAdvisor members offer peer-to-peer knowledge and can give the "inside scoop" on a destination. Cape Town features two destination experts, both having been born and raised in the city.

Travel guides, some of which are commissioned by TripAdvisor while others are written by destination experts, offer a variety of itinerary ideas based on travelers' interests, locations, and length of stay.

In addition to user-generated content, paid advertising, from banner campaigns to advertorials are often utilized on destination pages and come with analytic packages allowing for performance to be monitored.

Tourism sponsorship, available exclusively to DMOs, allows for photos, videos, and an events calendar which is sold in the form of an annual subscription and priced based on traffic to the page (Craig, 2012).

### References

Craig, D.E. (2012). TripAdvisor for destination marketing organizations. *ReKNOWN*. Retrieved from http://reknown.com/2012/02/tripadvisor-for-destination-marketing-organizations/

TripAdvisor. (n.d.a). Cape Town travel guide. Retrieved from https://www.tripadvisor.com/Travel_Guide-g1722390-Cape_Town_Western_Cape.html

TripAdvisor. (n.d.b). Cape Town travel forum. Retrieved from https://www.tripadvisor.com/ShowForum-g1722390-i15573-Cape_Town_Western_Cape.html

TripAdvisor. (n.d.c). Cape Town, South Africa overview. Retrieved from https://www.tripadvisor.com/Tourism-g1722390-Cape_Town_Western_Cape-Vacations.html

TripAdvisor. (n.d.d). Cape Town destination expert. Retrieved from https://www.tripadvisor.com/members-forums/divacape

TripAdvisor. (n.d.e). Sponsored attraction. Retrieved from https://www.tripadvisor.com/Tourism-g1722390-Cape_Town_Western_Cape-Vacations.html

Source: Amanda Templeton.

Brand awareness as previously explained in TALC, is automatically created by the end of the development stage and in stagnation stage. That being said, the awareness established naturally in stagnation stage might not be the type of awareness that the destination desires. Hence, it is always safer to make sure that the awareness can be created by premeditated marketing plans. Brand awareness can be explained by the hierarchical AIDA (attention, interest, desire, action) advertising axiom. Various types of promotional tools including advertisement, public relations, direct marketing, etc., can be employed to create the awareness. Marketers, however, should consider the attractiveness of the message that is created by the brand, as this attractiveness can grab the attention of potential visitors, thus creating interest towards the destination. The promotional message should also be persuasive to engender desire to visit the destination and strong enough to inspire action. Even if the action is not visiting the destination, it should be in line with visitation behavior such as looking for more information. Selecting the right combination helps in forming a positive attitude towards the destination of interest, that is, the potential visitor achieves cognitive components of awareness which is knowledge (familiarity) about the destination and positive judgment of the destination attributes. The cognitive aspect of the attitudes will lead to the affective component that is the stage of emotional reactions such as liking and preferring the destination of interest over other similar destinations. The affective component along with the cognitive component of attitude results in conative component, which is intentional behaviors and desires to visit the destination. In the conative stage of the attitude, visitors are convinced that the destination of interest is the most appropriate choice to visit and if situational/environmental factors become favorable, visitors will be acting upon their decision to make the purchase and visit the destination of interest.

Destination brand association is dealing with any linkages in the memory that are representing a brand. Associative memory plays an essential role in brand association. Since human beings memorize the concepts in relation to each other, activation of a concept in memory means activating the associated concepts from the closest to the furthest connected concept. These linkages can be in any forms from sensory inputs to celebrities, from personality traits to identity symbols. For example, studies have showed that Orlando, Florida, as a tourism destination is associated with concepts like magic, colors such as blue and orange, and theme park elements with Disney on top of them (e.g., mouse ear, white castle, the written form of Walt Disney, etc.). Brand association is important since positive connotations create positive sentiments regarding destination which helps the visitor store more positive memory compared to previous failures or bad news regarding the destination.

Destination brand association is in a close relationship with another concept known as destination image (i.e., brand image). Destination image is rather a dynamic construct that is continuously transforming. There are various types of destination image such as organic image which is formed as a result of personal experience or trustable resources such as friends and relatives; or projected image, which is the image communicated by the agency (i.e., DMO) as a result of advertisements or other sources of promotion; or perceived image, which is the image formed by potential visitors as a result of direct perception of the visitor from various information sources such as online reviews or advertisement. Previous practices have shown that destination image is under the strong impact of media including news agencies and social media. Especially when the visitor has no previous visitation, the media forms most of the image. Since destination image is closely related to destination brand association, the effect of media might create a spillover effect meaning that neighboring destinations' image can contaminate the destination of interest's image. For example, most of the Americans when being asked about Caucasus mention countries like Russia, Turkey, and Iran, but none of the three countries is part of the Caucasus. It is the neighboring countries that are part of Caucasus. Another example can be Orlando in the eyes of potential visitors. It has been perceived as having nice beaches but Orlando does not have access to sea as it is in the middle of Central Florida. The image of Orlando, however, can be contaminated with neighboring destinations such as Daytona, Tampa, etc. As a result of close relation with brand association, a contaminated image can be in favor or against the destination of interest (depending on the content and neighbor). Nevertheless, even positive contamination might end up harming the image by increasing and/or changing the expectations. Managing destination image is one of the toughest responsibilities of any DMO.

Destination brand resonance deals with supportive events, evidence, and feedback that intensifies the specific stance that one may have regarding a specific brand. In other words, questions like how relatable the brand is, are the questions that can be answered by brand resonance, as this concept shows the psychological connection a customer has with a brand. This stage of relatedness is a necessity in order to have loyal customers, which is the next and last stage of branding. Destination brand loyalty reduces the risk for the destination. In this stage, visitors have developed a high level of attachment to the destination that makes them become advocates of a specific destination. As a result, if a service failure occurs at any stage of experience, depending on the severity and weight of the failure on total experience, visitors most likely will try to forgive the destination. Again, as mentioned in TALC, most of the destination brand loyalty occurs in the stagnation stage of destination life cycle. Nevertheless, planning to create loyalty in early stages can create competitive advantage to the destination at a time that is most needed (early stages).

It should be noted that in positioning, especially for temporary plans, the promotion of the destination is not always the purpose. Sustainability of the tourism development sometimes encourages de-marketing of a destination. There are various strategies for de-marketing including:

- increasing prices
- increasing advertising that warns of capacity limitations
- reducing promotion expenditure
- reducing sales reps' selling time
- curtailing advertising expenditure
- eliminating trade discounts
- reducing the number of distribution outlets
- separate management of large groups
- adding to the time and expense of the purchaser
- reducing product quality or content
- provision of a virtual tour

Sometimes de-marketing is targeting a specific segment of the market. For example, Mauritius eliminates low-expenditure visitors by not allowing charter flights. Cambridge discourages same day visitors by controlling parking processes. De-marketing activities are also crucial part of destination positioning and should be carefully designed and planned by DMOs. Tourism and hospitality insights 15.3 introduces the recent challenge of "overtourism," a phenomenon wherein de-marketing may be one of the solutions.

## TOURISM AND HOSPITALITY INSIGHTS 15.3
## COMBATING OVERTOURISM

UNWTO forecasts that by 2030 1.8 billion trips will be taken internationally (Pylas, 2017). In a world where tourism accounts for approximately 10% of the world's annual GDP, this doesn't sound like a bad thing. However, many destinations are struggling to deal with the side effects, such as congestion increase of housing prices, and long-term environmental damages, resulting from the substantial growth in tourism (Pylas, 2017; Quintos, 2017). Overtourism has become a prominent topic of debate within the tourism industry. Destinations are incorporating a variety of solutions to reduce the strain that tourism is placing on the destination and lessen the tension between residents and visitors.

## Limiting visitation

Several destinations have imposed restrictions both on the number of visitors within the destination as well as the length of time a visitor can spend at a particular site. In the Cinque Terre a ticketing system was introduced to cap visitation to 1.5 million tourists in the area at any given time and the Galapagos Islands and Machu Picchu limit the number of visitors per day via permits (Coffey, 2017; Sheivachman, 2017).

## Technology

Amsterdam has utilized technology to assist in spreading visitation evenly within the city. The launch of an app called "Discover the City" notifies travelers when attractions are busier than normal and provides suggestions for alternative sites (Coffey, 2017). The city is also using Facebook Messenger to gather data from user profiles and, based on post likes and dislikes, provide suggestions for things to see and do within the city, with the goal being to drive tourists away from heavily populated sections and into lesser visited areas (Coffey, 2017).

## Limiting transportation options

The availability of cheap airfares and the docking of mega-cruise ships has been cited as one of the culprits attributing to overtourism (Pyals, 2017). Destinations like Santorini have imposed caps on the number of cruise visitors at 8,000 daily. There is speculation that if destinations made accessibility more difficult, by limiting cruise ship tenders or the access of low-cost carriers, then the number of visitors to the destination would decrease (Sheivachman, 2017).

## Marketing (de-marketing) and education

Taking a proactive approach in educating travelers to the reality of the location, experience, and cultural norms can help provide a more pleasant experience for both the traveler and the residents in the destination. Quintos (2017) offered several suggestions for marketing and education measures to counter-balance overtourism: 1) utilize destination expertise to help travelers figure out what they really want; 2) tap into the traveler trend of seeking a deeper experience; 3) come up with unique products to lesser-known destinations; and 4) use past clients and owned media to market trips. These suggestions are seen in the long-term tourism plans for destinations like London, which is currently working to market its outer areas to tourists, and New York, with recent announced marketing plans that include capitalizing on travel trends to Brooklyn (Sheivachman, 2017).

The CEO of the World Travel and Tourism Council stated that "there is no one solution for all, every destination is different" (Pylas, 2017, np). As visitors continue to increase the solutions to managing it, visitation will continue to diversify and the success will involve the joint efforts of all destination stakeholders.

## References

Coffey, H. (2017, Oct 23). Amsterdam has a new solution for overtourism. *Independent*. Retrieved from https://www.independent.co.uk/travel/news-and-advice/amsterdam-overtourism-solution-tourists-technology-van-gogh-museum-canal-boat-rides-a8015811.html

Pylas, P. (2017, Nov 15). Managing overtourism an increasing feature of global travel. *CTVNews*. Retrieved from https://www.ctvnews.ca/lifestyle/managing-overtourism-an-increasing-feature-of-global-travel-1.3678953

Quintos, N. (2017, Sept 26). Can destinations and tour operators divert travelers from over-visited destinations? *Adventure Travel News*. Retrieved from https://www.adventuretravelnews.com/can-destinations-and-tour-operators-divert-travelers-from-over-visited-destinations?utm_source=ATTA+%26+AdventureTravelNews&utm_campaign=d14550c4fc-ATN_9_27_2017&utm_medium=email&utm_term=0_1e08e536bd-d14550c4fc-412918029

Sheivachman, A. (2017, Oct 23). Proposing solutions to overtourism in popular destinations: A Skift framework. *Skift*. Retrieved from https://skift.com/2017/10/23/proposing-solutions-to-overtourism-in-popular-destinations-a-skift-framework/

Source: Amanda Templeton.

## Conclusion

Destination marketing and management has become a critical component of tourism competitiveness since the introduction of the experience economy as the new paradigm for service and hospitality tourism businesses. It is essential for practitioners to have a clear understanding of tourism geographic systems as these systems define the role of the destination component in the whole system. In this chapter, the popular model of Leiper is explained to define the structure of a destination. In order to understand the operations and performance of the whole system, it is crucial to have a clear understanding of its environment. In this chapter, various environments for tourism systems such as customer, competitor, economic, technological, social, political, legal, and geophysical are scrutinized. Furthermore, roles and procedures of DMOs are explained in detail and four categories of expected responsibilities (i.e., building identity, coalition, commitment, and building vision and leadership) are introduced. Finally, positioning and branding as the major and most challenging responsibilities of a DMO are explained with a focus on contemporary issues of destination branding.

### REVIEW QUESTIONS

1. What are some of the reasons given for why the marketing and management of tourism destinations is so challenging?

2. How has the incorporation of the experience economy concept changed the way(s) in which destinations are marketed today rather than 20 or even ten years ago?
3. How has TripAdvisor changed the manner in which destinations are marketed today?
4. What are the three most relevant roles of a DMO in a destination of your choice?

**YOUTUBE LINKS**

## *I travel for...*"

URL: https://youtu.be/5vXQjzFuVzQ

Summary: Launched in February 2018, VisitBritain's digital campaign that uses short films and story-telling to showcase experiences that can only be experienced in Great Britain and encourage inbound tourism.

## *Inspired by...Manchester*"

URL: https://youtu.be/njM7Qru1L84

Summary: One of the short films from the "Inspired by..." series. This two-minute film shows how the city of Manchester has inspired creative illustrator Stanley Chow.

## *Working at TripAdvisor – tour the headquarters*"

URL: https://youtu.be/nfl8Kx_2AQY

Summary: An inside look at the TripAdvisor headquarters office.

## *The growing problem of overtourism*"

URL: https://youtu.be/-iD5XyeRdcA

Summary: Peter Greenberg discusses the growing problem of overtourism.

## *Skift Lens: Barcelona and 21st century overtourism*"

URL: https://youtu.be/8fj3ttmRBIo

Summary: Explore the impact of overtourism on the popular destination of Barcelona.

## *National Geographic: immerse yourself in the rugged beauty of Ireland's west coast*"

URL: https://youtu.be/ujHxOrBrK7g

Summary: The Wild Atlantic Way, on the west coast of the Republic of Ireland, is like stepping into another world. It boasts rocky coastlines, green hillsides, land and sea adventures, and lots of local characters.

## REFERENCES, FURTHER READING, AND RELATED WEBSITES

### References

Leiper, N. (1980). The status of attractions in the tourism system a reply to Clare Gunn. *Annals of Tourism Research, 7*(2), 255–258.
Wang, Y.C. (2008). Collaborative destination marketing: Roles and strategies of convention and visitors bureau. *Journal of Vacation Marketing, 13*(3), 187–203.

### Further reading

Butler, R. (2004). *The tourism area life cycle in the twenty-first century. A companion to tourism,* 159–169.
DMAI (2008). The future of destination marketing: Tradition, transition, and transformation. Washington DC: Author.
Dredge, D., & Jenkins, J. (2007). *Tourism planning and policy.* Brisbane: Wiley.
Gartrell, R.B. (1992). Convention and visitor bureaus: Current issues in management and marketing. *Journal of Travel and Tourism Marketing, 1*(2),71–78.
Heath, E., & Wall, G. (1992). *Marketing tourism destinations: A strategic planning approach.* New York: Wiley.
Khalilzadeh, J., & Wang, Y. (2018). The economics of attitudes: A different approach to utility functions of players in tourism marketing coalitional networks. *Tourism Management, 65,* 14–28.
Leiper, N. (1995) Tourism management. Melbourne: RNIT Press.
Pike, S. (2008). *Destination marketing: An integrated marketing communication approach.* London: Routledge.
Rubies, E.B. (2001). Improving public-private sectors cooperation in tourism: A new paradigm for destinations. *Tourism Review, 56*(3/4), 38–41.
Tasci, A.D. (2009). A semantic analysis of destination image terminology. *Tourism Review International, 13*(1), 65–78.
Tasci, A.D., Khalilzadeh, J., Pizam, A., & Wang, Y. (2018). Network analysis of the sensory capital of a destination brand. *Journal of Destination Marketing & Management, 9,* 112–125.
Tasci, A. D., Khalilzadeh, J., & Uysal, M. (2017). Network analysis of the Caucasus' image. *Current Issues in Tourism,* 1–26.

### Websites

Atout France
http://www.atout-france.fr/

California
https://www.visitcalifornia.com/

Destinations International
https://destinationsinternational.org/

Dubai
https://www.visitdubai.com/en

London and Partners
http://www.londonandpartners.com/

New York City: the official guide
https://www.nycgo.com/

Singapore
http://www.visitsingapore.com

Amazing Thailand – Tourism Authority of Thailand
https://na.tourismthailand.org/home

## MAJOR CASE STUDY
## INNOVATION IN MARKETING THE WILD ATLANTIC WAY

The Wild Atlantic Way (WAW), Ireland's first long-distance-drive tourism route developed by Fáilte Ireland (National Tourism Development Authority), stretches 2,500km, approximately 1,550 miles, along the Atlantic coast from Donegal to West Cork. The WAW project was developed with the aim of achieving greater visibility for the west coast of Ireland in overseas tourist markets.

The Wild Atlantic Way is one of Fáilte Ireland's signature projects to rejuvenate Irish tourism and was developed in six stages, wherein the first three have been completed and the second three stages are being developed in parallel:

- Stage 1: Develop brand proposition and identity, and key market segments.
- Stage 2: Identify the route.
- Stage 3: Way-finding strategy including directional signage.
- Stage 4: Delivery of "discovery points."
- Stage 5: Selling Wild Atlantic Way experiences.
- Stage 6: Marketing and communications.

(Fáilte Ireland, n.d.a)

Once fully-realized, the WAW will provide the following benefits to the west coast of Ireland:

- assist in increasing visitor numbers, dwell time, spend, and satisfaction along all parts of the route;
- re-package the Atlantic seaboard as a destination for overseas and domestic visitors;
- improve linkages between, and add value to, a range of attractions and activities;
- improve on-road and on-trail interpretation, infrastructure. and signage along and around the route;
- direct visitors to less-visited areas;
- build on the work completed in these areas already and assist businesses, agencies, local groups and other stakeholders along the area to work together;
- reinforce the particular strengths and characteristics of all of the areas located along the west coast, while offering the visitor one compelling reason to visit.

(Fáilte Ireland, n.d.a)

### Marketing the Wild Atlantic Way

A variety of approaches have been implemented to maximize how the Wild Atlantic Way is marketed to tourists and to develop and nurture lasting partnerships with local businesses that enhance the story behind the Wild Atlantic Way.

## Tourism businesses

*Food tourism and Wild Atlantic Way food story*

Collaboration between the WAS and Ireland's development of food tourism is one marketing avenue. The tourism board provides tourism businesses with a toolkit of information that can help them market their business and "tailor [their] food story and create a sense of place by capturing the wild, raw beauty; our distinctive climate – where land meets sea; traditional pubs, turf fires, freshest seafood and of course the warmth of the people" (Fáilte Ireland, n.d.b). Food tourism functions under six main themes:

- simple and fresh;
- strong sense of place;
- local rules;
- warm people;
- new news; and
- experiences that make memories.

The website provides examples of how the themes can be personalized to reflect the Wild Atlantic Way and for businesses that register with the Fáilte Ireland's content pool access to download quality images and video clips to help promote the food business become available for use.

*New horizons grant scheme*

In order to support the development of "world-class visitor experiences," a grant scheme is available that provides funding between €30,000 and €200,000 to new and operating visitor attractions along the Wild Atlantic Way within the defined geographies of the Connemara Coast and Aran Islands and the Skellig Coast (New Horizons Grand, n.d.).

## Tourists

*Wild Atlantic Way passport*

A Wild Atlantic Way passport is available to tourists, at a cost of €10, and can be obtained at any Post Office or Tourism Information Office. The idea behind the passport is to provide tourists with a unique souvenir. Each passport has a unique identification number and can be stamped, with a unique stamp, at 188 possible sites. The Wild Atlantic Way is divided into six zones, allowing tourists to explore the route in one trip or multiple trips. Upon gathering the first 20 stamps, a special gift can be collected at any Tourist Information Office providing additional tangible mementos for the tourists.

*The Wild Atlantic Way social media*

The WAW utilizes Facebook, Instagram, Pintrest, Twitter, and YouTube to promote the route via images, videos, suggested itineraries, and communicate and share visitor experiences.

*Website features*

*360 degree/virtual reality videos*: A variety of videos are available throughout the website. Graphics are used to capture the imagination of tourists and provide opportunities for travelers to be drawn in visually to what the Wild Atlantic Way has to offer. The videos can be used with both virtual reality technology and on any smartphone/laptop/notebook for 360-degree viewing.

*Interactive route planner*: This feature allows visitors to create a profile, save events, things to do, inspirational articles and save items of interest throughout the site for easy reference at a later date.

*Trip planning by days available*: A variety of suggested itineraries are available based on the number of days travelers have to spend on the Wild Atlantic Way. Itineraries can be filtered by location and activities and are often accompanied by traveler quotes and insights.

*Highlights*: Sites of special interest are highlighted within a section of the website. Highlights include promoting film tourism sites, such as locations filmed in recent Star Wars movies, and providing information on the 188 discovery points where passports can be stamped. Visitors are encouraged to share their stories via the website as well as the various social media outlets.

*Useful traveler information*: In addition to providing the expected "how to get here" and "where to stay" information, the website also has a section dedicated to "travel tips." The section provides tips that cover everything from signage to expecting the unexpected (i.e. like sheep in the middle of the road).

(Wild Atlantic Way, n.d.)

References

Fáilte Ireland (n.d.a). The Wild Atlantic Way. Retrieved fromhttp://www.failteireland.ie/Wild-Atlantic-Way.aspx

Fáilte Ireland (n.d.b). Support and training. Retrieved from http://www.failteireland.ie/Supports/Food-Tourism-in-Ireland/Telling-Ireland-s-food-story/Wild-Atlantic-Ways-food-story.aspx

New Horizons Grant (n.d). Retrieved from http://www.failteireland.ie/NewHorizonsGrantsScheme.aspx.

Wild Atlantic Way. (n.d). Home. Retrieved from https://www.wildatlanticway.com/home

Source: Amanda Templeton.

Major case study questions

1. How does working with local tourism businesses benefit the Wild Atlantic Way?
2. Explore the Wild Atlantic Way social media sites. Are they utilized effectively? Are there any unique components? Are there additional social media outlets that would be beneficial?
3. Based on the information available in this case, are the strategies in place able to deliver the benefits to the west coast of Ireland? Explain.

# Innovation and new tourism and hospitality products, services, and experiences

## Learning outcomes

By the end of this chapter, students will:

*   Be aware of the challenges service providers are facing in a constantly evolving world, with a new generation of consumer expectations and behaviors
*   Understand the process of innovation
*   Be aware of the opportunities, but also the challenges, the new technological environment and the emerging virtual reality technology create.

## Introduction

Any company has to develop new products and services when entering a market, or when updating their offer, in line with changing consumption and market trends. Offering new services may simply be refreshing existing products by bringing slight changes in order to address an evolution in guests' expectations, or it might be a more challenging process requiring the company's engagement in innovation development. For instance, most companies focus on Millennials' new behaviors and expectations, which are significantly different from the previous generations (see Tourism and hospitality insights 13.2). This requires companies to create and imagine new and different offers, in order to satisfy these demanding new customers. Not forgetting that in the meantime, all customers of all generations are willing to discover new experiences when it comes to tourism and hospitality consumption; not just for pleasure but also in a business context. In addition, all of this is to be considered in a rapidly-evolving technological era with the market well used to using digital devices, social networks, virtual and augmented reality, among others. There is, thus, no place to hide from the ever-present need to engage in challenging innovation.

# Innovation: conceptual approach and process

This section presents the concept of innovation, related processes, and methodologies. Thereafter, three Tourism and hospitality insights illustrate: the development of an innovation lab in a hotel group; an innovative process to develop a product and a brand through a virtual world; and schools' and universities' contributions to the innovation process.

## New-product and new-services development

Two key questions were asked before any evolution or innovation processes had been started:

1.  What would you like to see evolve or created?
2.  To what extent would you be looking to engage in the process?

### Elements of the service offered

The service offer is diverse, combining a main product (for example a hotel room), with subsidiary offers (for example food or a mini bar, room service, hotel restaurants and bars, a health center which could include a fitness room or a spa, etc.) and a myriad of secondary services associated with the main or subsidiary offer (for example electrical appliances such as a WiFi connection or making electronic devices available to customers). Finally, the hotel- restaurant service offer is associated with an atmosphere, a concept, a design, etc. Associating evolution or creation with a service offer first of all requires the need to establish what is being looked at to change. Is it the service offer in general, or just certain aspects?

### Make the existing service offered evolve or innovate

The service providers must be able to adapt offers constantly to the new requirements of their customers. The permanent contact with customers, keeping up to speed with advances in marketing, and being knowledgeable about ad hoc marketing studies, equip a company with the elements required in order to understand their market. This understanding will enable companies to make the decisions aimed at developing the existing service offered. However, in some circumstances, simply evolving or adapting the service is insufficient and a real innovation process becomes a better option allowing a profoundly modified or a truly different service to be offered to customers.

## Innovation process and methodology

Innovation is defined as all the activities that a company carries out having a research and development objective with the aim of launching new products. The engagement in an innovation process often implies an organizational initiative in order to prepare the team who will be in charge of executing the innovation and who will be most focused on this mission. Big companies dedicate large budgets to innovation departments, often called "Innovation Labs." These structures also work with training institutions (schools and universities which run courses in tourism and hospitality) who inform students about the innovation work going on within companies and who, for some, also contribute to innovation development within the hotel industry directly.

The innovation process is based on a perfect understanding of customer expectations which is made possible through intelligent marketing, social studies, and other sources of data. Company staff (as in hotel directors, headquarters staff, or a board of managers) contributing to the progression of the innovation lab's work, also participate in innovation creation, or give feedback and test the innovative ideas in progress. Even the most random ideas can end up being implemented like Starwood who developed the hotel product "Aloft," which asked Internet customers (real customer using avatars) in the online virtual world "Second Life" for their opinions after a virtual tour in order to help with development and innovative ideas (virtual crowdsourcing).

The initial phase of creation aims to generate, but also rejects, many ideas. An operational reflection must be carried out in parallel in order to verify the feasibility of the project whether that be technical of financial. Then, when the ideas have been validated, the final concept is developed and tested. Going back to the Aloft example, a real-life hotel test had been established, first to allow an exchange with the creative phase carried out in the virtual world, and then it was used to test the best concepts. The company can then proceed to building the final product, at a defined development speed. More often than not, the validated product is then developed fairly quickly to avoid anyone copying the product too rapidly on the market and therefore keeping a strategic advantage over competitors. The company can also choose a more progressive phase of development and consider the first hotel as part of the test phase, studying its performance with the objective to improve later hotels. Several Tourism and hospitality insights below illustrate the ways different hotel groups and training institutions consider innovation and new-product development. Tourism and hospitality insights 16.1 explains further how innovation is considered and developed within a major hotel group (Accor Hospitality), Tourism and hospitality insights and 16.2 tells the story of the hotel brand Aloft innovation process. Insight 16.3 illustrates the priority hotel and hospitality schools give to innovation process and new hotel service development (such as the Tomorrow's Guestrooms Lab at the School of Hotel and Tourism Management in Hong Kong).

## Innovation in tourism and hospitality, new services, and new customers' experiences

Innovation is present in all sectors of tourism and hospitality and across all products. In the following section we concentrate more particularly on the hospitality sector in order to illustrate the way this industry changes and its innovation.

## TOURISM AND HOSPITALITY INSIGHTS 16.1

## INNOVATION LAB IN THE HOSPITALITY SECTOR: INTERVIEW WITH FREDÉRIC FONTAINE, ACCOR HOTELS

**Hospitality ON:** How did innovation lab develop at AccorHotels?

**F. Fontaine:** The lab was created by the group in 2016 in order to have a structure dedicated to innovation and eliminating day-to-day management tasks. Its creation resulted from a survey of Millennials to define the new concept Jo&Joe in 2016. Accor focused on this purpose and today it has entered phase two to provide support either to staff for brands as they redefine their respective concepts, or to projects based on the observation of new customers' habits in terms of hotel use and even more generally.

**Hospitality ON:** In what way have you inherited the internal structure of Research and Development which previously developed each brand's next generation?

**F. Fontaine:** At the time, this R&D structure focused its work on the room and furnishings within a module predetermined to fit building restrictions. His work was more like that of an architect on an experiment limited to the available space. It had the great merit of making initial concepts evolve, but the innovation lab now goes well beyond those limitations. The room is just one of the elements that constitute the innovation the same way digital applications, services, and experiences, and interaction between clients and personnel do. We reverse the proposal by starting with habits, and customer expectations with respect to our offers. The design problem is solved after choices are made that are determined by use.

**Hospitality ON:** How does creativity work in the lab?

**F. Fontaine:** We firmly believe in the collective intelligence and a collaborative approach. The process began with a fairly intense study of Millennials' expectations by working with sociologists, design agencies, and operations staff who are already in contact on the field. The goal was to work fairly quickly, going back, exploring options and abandoning them. We have conducted a lot of testing with customer targets, particularly in the 400m$^2$ showroom on the sixth floor of the Accor Hotels tower in Paris where it recreates the brand universe as closely as possible.

**Hospitality ON:** In an innovative approach, to what extent is self-examination possible when the product is delivered directly to the user?

| F. Fontaine: | Jo&Joe' DNA and our modus operandi include a right to error and need for adaptation. We are committed to "lean management" involving a constant effort to improve. It has already been planned with the designer to organize "hacking sessions" in a year with clients who will share their experiences and recommendations to prepare the next generation of Jo&Joe. Each new opening will be of the moment, with a bias toward permanent evolution. Through social networks, we will also invite the community of travelers, to present us with their ideas of a Jo&Joe in Berlin, Bordeaux, and Paris, a graphic view, materials, colors, ambience … Our designer's mission will be to take inspiration from this material to meet his reasoning. The designer will thus never start with a white sheet or an outlook that is too personal. |

Source: The collective intelligence encouraging new practices, *Hospitality ON*, 258–259, pp. 30–33.

## TOURISM AND HOSPITALITY INSIGHTS 16.2
## FROM VIRTUAL TO REAL INNOVATION: THE CASE STUDY OF THE HOTEL BRAND "ALOFT"

The group Starwood Hotels & Resorts created the hotel brand Aloft. Before opening the first hotel at Montreal International Airport, the brand was presented during two years on the virtual reality universe, Second Life. The virtual customers, stayed in the hotels though their avatars/online characters and then evaluated the 3D version of the project. Each virtual customer could use all the services and rate all the aspects of the hotel (the design, the layout, etc.). The Starwood Hotel project was made to evolve constantly by observing the virtual customers and their suggestions. The prototype hotel was developed on the Second Life virtual reality site, but also its advertising amongst the site's community.

**YouTube link**

https://www.youtube.com/watch?v=-OVXF83Q7lA

At the same time, a "real" prototype was constructed in a warehouse in New York, near the Starwood Hotel's headquarters. These two prototypes, one virtual and one real, were developed together and received visits from the Starwood staff. It was the first time that a hotel group created replicas of a hotel, one in the real world and one in the virtual world. The hotel concept was tested as a whole, not just one room, but at the same time this method saved money, as many customer choices were validated online (for example the choice of colors, etc.). The reflection and test time lasted two years before the first official Aloft hotel was opened in Montreal. After that, the team in charge of the Aloft development project, became an innovation laboratory (innovation lab), and were based near the Starwood Hotel's headquarters with the aim of testing new concepts (rooms, applications, etc.) such as room-service robots, the digital room key for smartphones. When the Starwood Hotel was bought by Marriott International, the innovation laboratory evolved into an experimental site in Los Angeles where the public were invited to discover and test the hotel's innovations for the brands Aloft and Element. Marriott International reached another level by going on to create a test hotel for all their new innovations (opened in Charlotte, North Carolina in November 2016). The tests, carried out on site, enabled the company to verify that the innovations complied with customer expectations.

Source: *Hospitality ON*, 258–259, pp. 40–44.

## TOURISM AND HOSPITALITY INSIGHTS 16.3

## INNOVATION LAB AND SCHOOLS: THE CASE OF TOMORROW'S GUESTROOMS AT THE SCHOOL OF HOSPITALITY AND TOURISM MANAGEMENT (SHTM), HONG KONG POLYTECHNIC UNIVERSITY

**Image 16.1**

Source: School of Hospitality and Tourism Management (SHTM), Hong Kong Polytechnic University.

An SHTM initiative, Tomorrow's Guestrooms has been established by STHM in its teaching and research hotel – Hotel Icon – with a view to setting new standards for hotel rooms of the future. The

Tomorrow's Guestrooms are purposely built to serve as an exceptional platform to innovate, develop, and showcase new technologies, hotel designs, and business concepts in hotel management for the advancement of the entire industry.

Through Tomorrow's Guestrooms, the SHTM is creating a "House of Innovation" for the global hotel industry, where new products and services can be researched and tested. Tomorrow's Guestrooms also serves as a platform for both undergraduate and postgraduate students to realize their ideas developed in hospitality design classes. Students of these classes will put together their plans for soft renovation under the three dedicated themes planned for Tomorrow's Guestrooms: design, technology, and wellbeing.

There now follows an interview with Pr. Kaye Chon, Dean, School of Hotel and Tourism Management, addressing our questions (March, 2018), and explaining the importance of the innovation lab for the School of Hotel and Tourism Management:

| | |
|---|---|
| *P. Legohérel:* | What was the idea behind the creation of an innovation lab for the school/SHTM? |
| *K. Chon:* | We wanted to bring innovations to the hospitality industry so our teaching and research hotel can serve the role of creating new knowledge and practices which can help develop the hospitality industry. This would also benefit students' learning. |
| *P. Legohérel:* | What is the importance of the innovation lab for the industry, and more specifically Tomorrow's Guestrooms lab for Hotel Icon? |
| *K. Chon:* | The Tomorrow's Guestrooms (TGR) focus on innovations in three areas – technology, design, and wellbeing. We believed these three areas are important aspects which will define the future of the hospitality industry. The TGR can be used to develop new technologies and new design ideas which will be more difficult to be implemented in a typical commercial hotel due to the potential risk associated with such experiments. |
| *P. Legohérel:* | Could you give one or two examples of innovation developed in the lab and applied to the Icon Hotel (or other hotels in Hong Kong)? |
| *K. Chon:* | Hotel Icon has been instrumental in conceiving innovative ideas which have been adopted or are considered by other hotels such as: |

1. A paperless check-in and check-out system;

2. A complimentary lounge for use by those guests who arrive before their rooms become available for check-in;

3. Complimentary (free) mini-bars in guestrooms;

4. Provision of a 24-hour Internet connected phone for guests' use during their stay in Hong Kong;

5. Late night supper at 10:45pm until 1:00am on Fridays served in addition to breakfast, lunch, and dinner in order to address the demand of those who prefer to have late night dinners;

6.   Partnering with the electric car maker Tesla to supply all electric vehicles for use in the hotel

**YouTube links**
https://www.youtube.com/watch?v=wacBBCcP-rg
https://www.youtube.com/watch?v=5_GsyyNhO7E

Source: Patrick Legohérel and P. Kaye Chon, Dean, School of Hotel and Tourism Management, Hong Kong Polytechnic University.

The new generation of hotels which are springing up, with their new way of approaching customers, are changing the traditional concept of the hospitality industry. The aim of this new type of hotel is to appeal to the Millennial generation and small groups of travelers, such as families and friends, but also people traveling for business purposes with the groups often catering for the nomadic and hyper-connected populations. These types of customers are looking for a "carefree" experience at a low price. By changing the day-to-day practices of the hotel, these unprecedented new concepts are also used to bring about new business models, re-inventing the traveler experience and customer relations. All the novel brands present themselves as innovation laboratories for the hospitality industry of tomorrow.

In the new hotels, the real change comes from the fact that the lobby and other communal areas became the heart and soul of the hotel, whereas before they were the area that received the most attention. Multi-use areas with a bar that could be used as a de-contracted seating area, a venue for events, co-working, and even a meeting room would allow the hotel not only to appeal to hotel customers, but also the surrounding neighborhood. This reciprocity between the hotel and its environment is another aspect specific to the new concept hotels. The hotel has become not just a place to sleep but also a place where one lives, shares experiences, and shares emotions. These different characteristics have become an integral part of many of the new hotels' business models. The ability to absorb trends increases their attractiveness but also allows them to generate potentially large additional revenues, particularly due to food and drink.

Evolution of all dimensions of our societies, including social, political, economic, and technological issues, implies a deep transformation of the behavior of all stakeholders (consumers, companies, public authorities and governments, etc.). This context might be described as follows:

The physiognomy of the hospitality industry is gradually transforming depending on the fundamental trends that are affecting corporate life, consumer behavior, investment trends, the appearance of new practices and new concepts. The perception of these trends at the right time is key to being able to stay ahead, stay in control of them, and make them a competitive advantage rather than submit to their pressure and run after lost time. The most delicate is undoubtedly to distinguish between fads and deep-set transformation that is not always evident.

*(Hospitality ON, 256–257, p. 106)*

This context favors both the emergence of new consumption trends, and the development of new products and services offered on the market by companies.

In the next section, a couple of interesting new concepts and products are introduced, in line with some significant emerging trends.

## New hospitality concepts adapted to Millennials

Millennial customers have a different approach to commercial accommodation. New concepts are needed to meet their expectations, including the "hybrid concepts, new versions of youth hostels, that associate several accommodations (dormitory, individual room, suites) with a festive F&B offer (bar with live shows and a variety of entertainment) complementary services, related to travel" (*Hospitality ON*, 256–257, p. 108). The context of the emergence of the hybrid hotel concept is explained by the evolution of customer needs and the new generation expectations. Traditional hotels are made for specific targeted clientele, with distinct profiles and needs: a resort, made for leisure, versus a hotel business chain, or an economic hotel versus a luxury, distinguished by the quality of service and level of comfort. "Those properties that have stayed with ancestral marketing traditions are seeing barriers collapse depending on the needs of the moment and the market realities" (*Hospitality ON*, 250–251, p. 49).

Several principles are expressed in these new types of accommodation:

1. The diversity of clientele can prevent imbalance relying on a single segment;
2. The sharing of common areas represents an effort to optimize space that must be experienced differently depending on the time of day;
3. Functions are de-compartmentalized for more flexibility and ready to create new jobs;
4. The boundary between private and professional life is increasingly upheld, particularly for new nomadic workers who need "only" a computer and a good WiFi connection to be efficient (*Hospitality ON*, 250–251, p. 50).

Tourism and hospitality insights 16.4 is an illustration of the new hospitality concept adapted to Millennials.

## TOURISM AND HOSPITALITY INSIGHTS 16.4
## JO&JOE (ACCOR HOTELS)

To seduce the Millennials, the trendy Jo&Joe (Accor Hotels) are neither youth hostels, nor hotels, nor rental, rather all of these at the same time with a choice of either staying in revisited dormitories or private rooms. The central part of the hotel, is the "playground" where many events are organized. An application enables this community to contact others for meetings, to comment, or participate in events but also to pay their bills.

The Jo&Joe concept is not just about accommodations. It is also a place where events take place that are connected to the city, and has an original food and beverage offer, Hence the idea of breaking away from traditional forms of hotel development. All the work was in finding an original positioning that could be built around three ideas: first, the appropriation of spaces with a certain autonomy that is possible with apartment rentals. This involves changing the roles played between the hotelier and the client. The second idea is socialization between the concept's followers, meeting other people at events and happenings. This is what makes this new "hostelry" successful and leads to the development of the first chains. The third idea is that of a reassuring and comforting product thanks to its cleanliness, comfort, and the variety of its offers.

Source: Accor Hotels, Frédéric Fontaine's interview, *Hospitality ON*, 258–259, p. 32.

### *Generalization of the sharing concept*

The sharing economy is invading all aspects of everyday life: accommodation, transport, food and drink, skills, and even workplace and the growing strength of independent workers, consultants, technicians, programmers, have led to another concept of the workplace. After Internet cafÕs, Starbucks has become the leader of informal co-working spaces with dozens of "clients" sitting in armchairs with their computer for the price of an exorbitant cup of coffee and a muffin. Since then, the market has become more refined with co-working spaces in lobbies, replacing former business centers that have become obsolete. It is an opportunity to transform unprofitable surface areas into profit centers through creative packaging such as Á la carte, light meals. Many brands such as Holiday Inn, Le MÕridien, Marriott, Hilton, Westin have already reorganized their social spaces. Other innovations in this area are expected. Shared spaces have opened the way to new practices, derived from co-working that leans into co-living. Why not share an apartment to work for a few days or weeks in a city? WeLive, CommonSpace, PodShare are the first networks for these concepts that offer the possibility of living together around a shared kitchen, spaces for relaxation, and work to create a "temporary community." These are just the beginning of a new market just looking to follow the rise of the sharing economy (*Hospitality ON*, 256–257, p.108).

The next four Tourism and hospitality insights illustrate various contexts in which the sharing concept has been implemented, from hotel lobbies (Hilton's Corner), places to live (PodShare concept), shared work spaces (WeWork concept), to shared working spaces and cafÕs (AnticafÕ concept).

## TOURISM AND HOSPITALITY INSIGHTS 16.5
## HILTON'S CORNER AND NEW LOBBY

Hilton has transformed its public spaces into friendly areas that are also sources of profit. The new experience has been introduced at Hilton McLean Tysons Corner in the United States. It offers a flexible layout that encourages a social atmosphere where guests can interact, work, and collaborate. The centerpiece of the lobby is an 18-hour bar that develops throughout the day serving coffee, select grab'n go specialties, shared dishes, and specialty cocktails. A dedicated Technology Lounge, integrated into the lobby experience, updates the traditional business center concept, bringing the space front and center with PC and Mac workstations, and a communal work table. The check-in experience has also been transformed with a pod-style front desk allowing team members and guests to interact more directly with personalized service.

Source: *Hospitality ON*, 250–251, p. 57.

## TOURISM AND HOSPITALITY INSIGHTS 16.6
## PODSHARE

Founded in 2012 by Elvina Beck in Los Angeles, the network has now three different locations in the city with 50 or so pods and the community already has 5,000 members who are regular or occasional users. The principle is simple: the user buys a "pass" for half day or 24 hours (at around $40), which gies the podestrian access to installations, such as the shared kitchen to prepare and eat meals, a single or double bed in a compartment closed by a curtain that is a modern cross between military bunk beds, a sleeping compartment on a train, and a high-tech space cockpit, and especially, a co-working space with high-speed Internet, chargers, and printers. After a few years of operation, Elvina Beck identified three categories of regular users: travelers in transit who wish to explore the city differently by joining a community of locals of the same generation with the same aspirations; people in transition who arrive in the city for a new job and a new life but have not yet found the apartment to fit their dreams or budget; temporary residents who are seasonal workers, doing an internship, or on a specific mission. Probably because of its location in California, which is still rife with hippie and bohemian culture, the model for economic development also relies on community involvement.

Source: *Hospitality ON*, 250–251, p. 50.

## TOURISM AND HOSPITALITY INSIGHTS 16.7
## WEWORK

Joint tenancy for a few months or a few days, formalized in a commercial concept, is the foundation of a project launched a few years ago by Miguel McKelvey, founder of the WeWork network of shared work spaces that already exist in 50 or so large American cities, but also in Asia and Europe (London, Berlin, Amsterdam, and soon Paris). In buildings in New York and Arlington, he had the idea of extending the shared work space concept with a residence, hence the WeLive.com concept. The space available on 20 floors of the Wall Street tower in New York allows a higher turnover of studios and makes it possible to implement an experimental day concept. WeLive in New York offers different sized apartments, from studios to three-rooms with shared services: a large shared kitchen, a yoga studio, an automatic laundry, cable, and high-speed WiFi, room cleaning as well as a concierge service for tenants.

The link for facilitating connections between the 55,000 members of the network is developing thanks to a dedicated app called WeLive, and festive events that are organized for tenants. They naturally have access to the WeWork installations located in the same building a few floors down. Wherever possible, Miguel McKelvey wants to associate the temporary joint-tenancy dimension with each co-working installation.

> We host a lot of young people who have created their own start-up in the WeWork spaces, sometimes they spend the night there. But that has its limits... And there is nothing like a good night's sleep and equipment adapted to social life. That's what we want to offer.

As the young president explained, this depends on the physical availability in the building and the profitability of the economic model at select destinations.

Source: *Hospitality ON*, 250–251, p. 53.

## TOURISM AND HOSPITALITY INSIGHTS 16.8
## ANTICAFÉ

Anticafé is first and foremost a concept, which comes from an idea of Leonid Goncharov. When arriving in France, he realized that there was nowhere that could accommodate travelers, students, families, and groups of friends all at the same time!

As an answer to the evolving working methods, the expectations of neo-workers and the new Millennial behaviors, he created the first Anticafé in 2013 in the center of Paris at Beaubourg, a different friendly place, where people could meet depending on their activities. Here one pays for the time one spends and everything else: hot drinks, snacks but also other services and even board games to play on site are all free of charge. And it works because in less than five years, 12 Anticafés were opened in Paris (Louvre, République, Station F, La Défense, etc.), and outside of Paris (Aix, Lyon, Bordeaux, and Strasbourg) and abroad (Rome).

**Image 16.2**

Source: Anticafé

This corresponds to the transformation of customary ways of working and the approaching death of the traditional office working environment: 42% of French workers find the nomad working style appealing and would like to see the end of the office as the principal place of work. Anticafé presents itself as a perfect solution to this new trend. These places can accommodate workers without fixed offices (people working freelance, start-ups, etc.) but also company employees, agencies, or practices of all types, looking to modify their way of working.

Each person organizes their day as they see fit, their breaks, their professional, or personal meetings, to be with others or to isolate themselves in a private room. Broadband, WiFi, video projectors, printers. and scanners are all freely available for the day's clients use in the best conditions. This also encourages open innovation! A real Anticafé community has formed around these different addresses and a "common" spirit has developed. The collaborations between people and their talents flows naturally. Relationships grow between people who find themselves sitting at the same table, for a day, for a week, or even longer. This is no virtual social network. Instead, Anticafé is placing itself as a real social network, human and physical. Anticafé real place to meet people, create connections and nurture socialization.

Here, the actors are the customers free to organize events, conferences, workshops, and other memorable events as they wish. Therefore, it isn't rare to be able to participate in a yoga lesson at

Beaubourg, to brush up on foreign languages at République, or to be able to have a lesson in "digital coaching" in Lyon, ideal for team working even if one works alone!

The coffee comes from the coffee roasting company "Coutume" and is a unique blend created especially for Anticafé, with a nutty aroma. At break time, the counter is free access and you can have as much as you want with different types of snacks: savory, sweet, and healthy, all-inclusive at €5 per hour.

**Image 16.3**

Source: Leonid Goncharov, CEO, Anticafé company.

## Technology evolves toward a more intelligent hotel

In the future, hotels will be more connected and high-tech. The increasing power of new technologies already resonates and is certain to become widespread. Such hotels will multiply like Best Western by using enhanced reality to offer a virtual visit of its hotels. This type of service should be more extensive in order to offer guests an experience even before they arrive.

The smartphone will become an inescapable tool, making it crucial to strictly control the data stored in it. Interactivity will also be essential in the coming years mainly for young generations who are used to being surrounded by them. In order to adapt to their customers' need, some groups developed their own mobile app. This system allows direct exchanges with hotel staff, or the "digital concierge" via a chat platform. The hotel of the future will also give major importance to social networks and will have to offer selfie spaces like those at the 1888 Hotel Sydney (*Hospitality ON*, 258–259, p. 57).

## TOURISM AND HOSPITALITY INSIGHTS 16.9
## 1888 HOTEL SYDNEY

An Australian four-star hotel, the 1888 Hotel has a following of 10,000 people on Instagram. In Sydney, the hotel was created by the chain "8 hotels" and the directors decided to use the social networks to promote it. The brand offers a free visit in exchange for free photos. The hashtag #1888hotel can be found on Twitter 'People take photos of everything, that they then send to their friends. So we decided to make the most of it." These are the words of Paul Fishman, CEO of the brand "8 Hotels" creator of the 1888 Hotel.

It is photography that shaped the hotel because it was created with the intention of being photographed in the first place. Also, the name 1888 Hotel refers to the first camera created by Kodak in 1888. With this advertising philosophy based on the influence of the social networks and photographs in mind, this Instagram hotel was created so that each room has mirrors, paintings, and other details designed to increase the number of clicks. An "insta-map" was even added to the entrance with the areas labeled "not to be missed." As far as the decoration is concerned, two years of work were necessary to create a cinematic atmosphere. And as Instagram could not exist without "selfies," a selfie area was created to allow people to feed their narcissism.

Source: Patrick Legohérel.

## New positions in the community

The emergence of the boutique hotel phenomenon is derived from the hotel's wish to become part of the local spirit and become a neighborhood reference, a lively center with its own personality even if it is part of a chain. This is what W does in its success at being unique while integrating with the city and yet projecting a similar image throughout its global network. This logic is reproduced by many brands in their battle against the standardization of concepts whilst proclaiming themselves the ambassador of each destination. This commitment may be found in new generation concepts, youth hostels and hybrid hotels, which are first and foremost bases from which to explore the city, to meet the local community. The next step is for the hotel to draw in the local community, so they adopt it as the local watering hole, as the place to go work, as a platform offering services that is always open. This is precisely what a group like Accor Hotels has in mind when it presents the challenge to transform its 4,500 addresses worldwide into as many local concierges and new profit centers (*Hospitality ON*, 256–257, p.110)

## Designed hotels and other new concepts

Tens of brands and new concepts have arrived on the market in the past ten years, either independent small groups or new brands belonging to international groups. They are similar in a way that they all shake up habits, and bring some fresh, new service offer on the market. As a result, travelers have a larger choice of products, from traditional hotels, to new concepts and new experiences. Tourism and hospitality insights 16.10 provides one example (CitizenM), among many, of these hotel new concepts recently developed.

## Environmental concerns

Any green label, and green attitude, will increasingly be a natural given in the customers' eye. Its absence will be more evident than its presence. Companies may engage in more or less sustainable development, through different means, including energy positive buildings, energy savings and natural resources, waste treatment, etc.

Environmental concerns and a green attitude are no longer just a new major consumer trend. It might also be considered as a strategic tool for companies focusing on these issues, and leading to the development of new concepts and innovation. Tourism and

## TOURISM AND HOSPITALITY INSIGHTS 16.10
## CITIZENM

"Luxury for all," is the ambition of the Dutch company CitizenM. The brand was created in 2007 by Ratta Chadha. His idea is the result of an observation he made during his business trips: "the world has evolved and there is a new type of traveler, a world citizen who wants to share his experience."

Rattan Chadha decided to launch what can be considered a hybrid concept: a midscale offer at a very reasonable price by eliminating the superfluous. According to him, this concept existed in the fashion industry (Zara, H&M, Uniqlo) but not in the hotel industry. Thereupon, he decided to focus only on what is essential in a hotel: bedding, sanitary equipment, and social life in the common areas (libraries, TV rooms, co-working areas). The rooms were reduced to their minimal size (around 10m$^2$) with identical pricing within a single property, subject to variations depending on the type of reservation.

The establishments are designed like modules, factory manufactured and self-assembled. The conception was initiated in partnership with Philips, Swisscom, and the Swiss Design Company in order to integrate automation, communications, technology and aesthetics from the outset.

The group targeted an autonomous clientele that requires minimal assistance and maximum availability of all installations. First launched in airports, the concept works 24/7offering great user freedom. Digital progress and the RFID technology allow automatic check-in and check-out as well as dematerialized money management with a card to open rooms which may also be used for payment in the bar or the cafeteria. Rooms are equipped with a lighting system and music on demand which allow individual customization.

Source: "Newcomers are shaking up hotels habits," *Hospitality ON*, 258–259, pp.53–57.

hospitality insights 16.11 tells the story of a company (Huttopia) which has developed the innovative concept of sustainable camping in the very traditional sector of camping and outdoor hospitality.

## TOURISM AND HOSPITALITY INSIGHTS 16.11
## HUTTOPIA

Huttopia (a contraction of hut and utopia) is a particularly innovative French company who developed a sustainable camping concept. The Huttopia product is positioned along the central values of camping (outdoors and respect for the environment) and is well placed in the outdoor leisure trends of the moment. Seventy percent of the campsite consists of bare tent pitching areas and the rest is made up of four other types of accommodation: Canadian tents (wooden structures covered with canvas), roulottes (wooden caravans), wood and canvas tents (a wooden chalet part tent) and some wooden chalets. These accommodation choices are turnkey, that's to say that they offer a certain level of comfort (cooking stove, fridge, comfortable beds, outside furniture etc.). Tourists rent the accommodation ready to use without having to pitch a tent.

The company decided to develop two different brands, Huttopia and Indigo, in order to keep a clear image of the different brand values. Huttopia is created from land (on seven different sites in France) that has never been used as a campsite before. The brand Indigo is present on 15 campsites that have been taken over. These sites were completely renovated before adopting the brand Indigo, with the same philosophy as Huttopia but offering a more traditional campsite, using the existing installations.

The campsites are aimed at a middle-class family clientele, living in cities, who are curious, with small children and are 45% French (other clients come mainly from Benelux, the United Kingdom and Germany). Customers are loyal to the concept and many enjoy outdoor activities. They are also looking for comfortable and high quality accommodation and often they are not used to camping. Far from the idealism often associated with the sustainable development concept, Huttopia ingeniously has been able to apply the environmental respect aspect that is dear to the brand. The company is present on natural sites that it has tried to change as little as possible. For example, since site maintenance is reduced, weeds grow freely and dead leaves are left on the ground to improve the soil.

Cuttings from trees are reused on site and all the wood use is untreated. A partnership with the ONF (French National Forestry Commission) enables efficient management of the forest, present on some sites leading to the creation of forest camps (Huttopia-ONF) (the first one opened in 2013). The sustainable management of the site includes other sustainable actions (such as recycling rubbish, heating the cabins with wood burning stoves, etc.). For the comfort of their customers, no vehicles are allowed on site.

Céline and Philippe Bossanne founded the company in 1999 and now it consists of 25 sites in France, 15 sites in national parks in Quebec, and employs 200 people all year round with up to 500 people in season. The strategy is to integrate skilled workers for conception, maintenance, marketing and even an industrial aspect, the management of these sites requiring a finesse on a daily level. The development through a network and different brand names provides a stable profitability for this company, in a very capitalistic sector.

The future projects of Huttopia include the creation of new sites and to develop the company internationally: Huttopia is developing in Canada in the National Parks but also its unbranded sites and Indigo, which will soon open its first site in China.

**Image 16.4**

Source: Bossanne, C. (2013 [2018]). In L. Frochot & P. Legohérel (Eds.), *Marketing du tourisme* (4th ed). Paris: Dunod.

## Innovation and virtual reality (VR)

This section starts with the technology insight, written by Giberson and Dimanche (below), explaining differences between virtual reality (VR), virtual environment (VE) and augmented reality (AR). Others examples of applications of VR and AR in various sectors are discussed in the second part of this section.

## TOURISM AND HOSPITALITY INSIGHTS 16.12
## VIRTUAL REALITY

Virtual reality (VR) is becoming a technology of interest to travel marketers as a medium that offers a high level of sensory immersion for those looking to share destination attributes and influence visitor decision-making. VR transports a person to a new or virtual environment (VE), in which they are not physically present, but feel as though they are there through the stimulation of multiple senses (Guttentag, 2010). One can experience a VE, for example, through an immersive head-mounted-display (HMD) or more simply, through navigating a 360° video or image displayed on a desktop computer. An extension or variation of VR is augmented reality (AR). While VR technology completely immerses users in a synthetic world, AR technology superimposes virtual objects and cues upon the real world in real time (Carmigniani et al., 2011).

## VR and travel & tourism

A list of potential applications and impacts of VR in tourism include planning and designing places and experiences, reducing barriers that increase accessibility and open up access to remote places, educating, and guiding visitors in real time, preserving fragile sites, enhanced entertainment, and the ability to broaden global interaction among travelers. An additional application that many are already starting to implement is the opportunity VR presents as a communication and promotional tool.

As the travel industry is often faced with promoting intangible tourism products, VR as immersive visual imagery can help convey experiences, increase awareness, and quite possibly affect purchase intention. It can potentially improve destination image and may also have the ability to positively differentiate a destination in an increasingly complex and competitive global marketplace.

## Applications

With regard to destination marketing, the travel and tourism industry has been implementing VR in varying ways to capitalize on the technology's ability to more accurately depict a destination, airline, hotel, or travel experience. The use of VR in tourism is still relatively limited but fast growing. Some travel agencies have equipped agents in their brick and mortar stores with HMDs to give prospective buyers, through VR, a "try before you buy" experience. For example, Thomson UK, a travel operator and division of the TUI Group, has opened a store in Dudley, UK, featuring VR HMDs where travel agents can showcase premium airline seats or cruise holidays.

Thomas Cook is another travel agency that tried out VR HMDs in store. In 2015, customers planning holidays were able to visit flagship stores in the UK, Germany, and Belgium, and experience a range of VR content from a helicopter tour of Manhattan to a visit to the pyramids in Egypt. According to the content provider, Visualize, there was a 190% uplift in New York excursion bookings after people tried the five-minute version of the holiday in VR.

Other ways companies in the travel sphere are using VR is through in-field marketing activities. For example, Marriott hotels set up a VR brand activation in New York outside City Hall. They wanted to provide newlyweds the opportunity to teleport to honeymoon destinations, like their exotic beachfront resort in Hawaii (Jawbone Brand Activations, 2017). Contiki, a tour operator for young adults, has also invested heavily in the creation of VR content to engage with their target Millennial demographic, showcasing VR videos on their website, at expos and throughout various universities.

Destination Marketing Organizations such as Tourism Australia, Destination BC (British Columbia, Canada) and Fáilte Ireland (to name a few) have all, in one way or another, harnessed and used VR technology.

### Challenges

Though much of the narrative on VR and tourism has focused on its potential, there are of course challenges that come with adopting the technology. Though it is anticipated that the use of VR will grow as the cost of immersive systems declines, making VR more financially accessible to consumers, it is still unclear how households may use the technology in relation to travel. For example, VR as a substitute for travel can be seen as a possible threat to the industry. As a result, tourism destinations will need to provide compelling reasons for visitors to actually travel, visit, and experience the places, people, and culture in real life (Giberson et al., 2017).

With an anticipated 200 million HMDs to be sold by 2020 (Gaudiosi, 2016), VR is certainly expected to become increasingly prevalent. The number of VR applications within travel and tourism continues to grow, with innovative implementations constantly emerging. As it pertains to tourism marketing, the phenomenon is there to stay and marketers need to think about to make the best of this technology.

### References

Carmigniani, J., Furht, B., Anisetti, M., Ceravolo, P., Damiani, E., & Ivkovic, M. (2011). Augmented reality technologies, systems and applications. *Multimedia Tools and Applications, 51*(1), 341–377.

Gaudiosi, J. (2016). *Over 200 million VR headsets to be sold by 2020*. Retrieved from http://fortune.com/2016/01/21/200-million-vr-headsets-2020/.

Giberson, J., Griffin, T., & Dodds, R. (2017). *Virtual reality and tourism: Will the future of travel be virtual?* Ryerson University HTM Research Working Paper No. 2017/1. Retrieved from http://www.htmresearch.ca/wp-content/uploads/2017/09/Sep-25-WORKING-PAPER.pdf

Guttentag, D. A. (2010). Virtual reality: Applications and implications for tourism. *Tourism Management, 31*(5), 637–651.

Source: Juleigh Giberson, BSc. and Frederic Dimanche, Ph.D., Ted Rogers School of Hospitality and Tourism Management, Ryerson University, Canada.

## TOURISM AND HOSPITALITY INSIGHTS 16.13
## BEST WESTERN VIRTUAL REALITY EXPERIENCE

Best Western Hotels & Resorts developed virtual reality tours for all of its North American hotels. Best Western Virtual Reality Experience provides an immersive 360°, three dimensional look at nearly 2,000 properties. Videos range from 50 seconds to two minutes and include narration and music, aiming to provide an engaging storytelling experience. The objective of Best Western for its VR program, is to provide valuable resources to promote the brand, to connect with today's travelers seeking technology, and to be transparent with consumers and offer them a detailed and honest overview of the product before their stay.

**Interview with Olivier Cohn, CEO, Best Western® Hotels & Resorts France (March, 2018)**

P. Legohérel: What is the actual development stage of the virtual reality (project BWVRE) in Europe and/or more specifically on the French market?

O. Cohn: In Europe, the virtual reality development projects are behind the US. Several tests have been carried out especially in France and in Italy but these technologies are not used so much as there is less of a sales dynamic for the virtual reality headsets. The American market is more receptive to this technology than the European markets. The projects have come up against the low sales and high prices of the equipment.

P. Legohérel: What is your impression concerning the use of these new technologies on consumers, for the development of these hotel products and brands?

O. Cohn: These technologies are clearly extremely useful for our sector because they enable the customer to be totally immersed in the accommodation that they are looking to book. It is a strong argument in the reservation process. Unfortunately, they are much slower at implementing the virtual reality tool than the estimations suggested. The expectation of affordable brands was clearly the reason for the actual hesitance. Recent service offers at less than €300 could however restart an interest for these technologies. For the moment, the investments are more focused towards artificial intelligence technology.

Source: Interview with Olivier Cohn, CEO, Best Western® Hotels & Resorts France (March, 2018).

## Conclusion

The new generations of consumers and more especially the break in generations with the Millennials, obliges the tourism and hospitality sectors to re-think their service offers. These profound changes concern just as much the social dimension (seeking somewhere to share and exchange) and the functional dimension (mixing work, restaurants, and reception, mixing work and pleasure), as the other aspects of the service offer (such as the atmosphere, design, communal areas, and less the room where one

## TOURISM AND HOSPITALITY INSIGHTS 16.14
## THE CHÂTEAU OF CHAMBORD, FRANCE

From history....

Unique architectural jewel built from 1519 at the request of François I, a lover of the arts and a passionate hunter, the château of Chambord has become emblematic of the French Renaissance in Europe and throughout the world.

**Image 16.5**

Source: Domaine national de Chambord – Léonard de Serres.

A palace rises up from the heart of the Sologne marshlands. A dashing young king, François I, has ordered its construction. The château of Chambord is not designed as a permanent residence, and François only stays there for a few weeks. It is a remarkable architectural achievement that the king is proud to show to sovereigns and ambassadors as a symbol of his power engraved in stone. The plan of the castle and its decors stem from a central axis, the renowned double helix staircase, inspired by Leonardo da Vinci, an ascending spiral leading to a profusion of chimneys and sculpted capitals on the terraces.

(Retrieved from https://www.chambord.org/)

### ...to new technology

The Chambord estate and the Histovery company are a coproduct of a new tool of mediation at the cutting edge of technology, for interaction, learning, and recreation. The HistoPad is aimed at a large public who can, using a digital tablet and using enhanced reality, rediscover Chambord and explore the château in the sixteenth century.

What can we do with the HistoPad Chambord?

1. Go back in time: immersion visitThe application HistoPad offers above all a virtual visit of the château's rooms at the time of the Renaissance. Thanks to the work of Renaissance experts, the distribution, the décor, the furniture and certain other rooms were re-imagined at the beginning of the sixteenth century. The use of enhanced reality (3D restitutions), offered an immersion experience at the time of the François I, who built Chambord.

2. A digital guide for the visitHistoPad offers digital exploration of the 19 major rooms of the château to discover its history and collections. Nearly 150 pieces of furniture, artifacts, and decorations are described and analyzed thanks to simple texts or animated graphic elements. The images in high definition, are integrated into the application and allow users, amongst other things, to zoom in to look at the most noteworthy objects closely, to discover the object in every detail.

3. An automated geolocation in the castleHistoPad automatically comes on when the visitor takes it into to a room, thanks to the geolocation tags implanted in the castle. Animated maps are accessible at any moment on the reception screen of the rooms, allowing visitors to find their way and organize their visit by themselves. The application shows visitors their exact position in the castle and the circuit that they have visited and the rooms still to visit.

**Image 16.6**

Source: Domaine national de Chambord.
https://youtu.be/-goE_n3sSVo
https://www.chambord.org/en/agenda/histopad/

sleeps). How it is created, at least, the evolution of the actual products, or more often, the real innovation process are driven by a regeneration of the offer (new concepts, brands, etc.).

## REVIEW QUESTIONS

1. What benefit does a company achieve by adapting to new consumption trends?
2. What is the difference between a basic adaptation of the product or service, and a real innovation and new concept?
3. What are the key factors for a successful innovation process?
4. How can service providers use new technologies, such as virtual reality or augmented reality?

## YOUTUBE LINKS

### *"Arne Sorenson, President and CEO of Marriott International, on Marriott's culture, innovation"*

URL: https://www.youtube.com/watch?v=gnLbGi_-4ic

Summary: Hotel News Now speaks with Arne Sorenson, president and CEO of Marriott International, about the company's culture and innovation following its acquisition of Starwood Hotels & Resorts Worldwide.

### *"The world's first virtual reality travel search and booking experience"*

URL: https://www.youtube.com/watch?v=Ax0BmO3DrTc

Summary: This virtual reality travel search and booking experience allows travelers to spin a globe of the world, visit a destination, search for flights, walk through a plane to select their seat, check out different rental cars, and pay for their entire trip – all without leaving virtual reality.

### *"Tourism takes up artificial intelligence and virtual reality"*

URL: https://www.youtube.com/watch?v=3LANOd0Evho

Summary: Virtual reality glasses as brochures, a hotel room that is automatically personalized according to the client's tastes. New technologies are emerging in the tourism sector, which hopes to benefit from the gold mine that is personal data.

## "These virtual reality apps Let You Travel The World Without Ever Leaving Home | Mach | NBC News"

URL: https://www.youtube.com/watch?v=2XTklBA8Rkk

Summary: Virtual reality apps for travel are becoming more realistic, as VR hardware and software gets more advanced. If you like the idea of travel and exploration, but would rather do it from the comfort of your own home these five apps might offer you the perfect weekend getaway.

## "YU virtual – The future of hospitality"

URL: https://www.youtube.com/watch?v=H_VxlcdP0Kk

Summary: What will the hotel room of the future look like? Discover a concept combining two ideas addressing current challenges faced by the hospitality industry. The video illustrates ways technology and ultra-personalization could be used to enhance guest experience and wellbeing.

### FURTHER READING AND RELATED WEBSITES

#### Further reading

Anderson, J.C., & Narus, J.A. (1995). Capturing the value of supplementary services. *Harvard Business Review, 73*, 75–83.

Bitner, M.J. (1992). Serviscape: The impact of physical surroundings on customers and employees. *Journal of Marketing, 56* (April), 57–71.

Booms, B., & Bitner, M.J. (1992). Marketing services by managing the environment. *Cornell Restaurant and Hotel Administration Quarterly, May*, 35–39.

Frochot, I., & Wided, B. (2013). *Marketing and designing the tourism experience*. Oxford: Goodfellow Publishers Limited.

Fuchs, C., & Schreier, M. (2011). Customer empowerment in new product development. *Product Innovation Management, January*, 17–32.

Grissemann, U., Plank, A., & Brunner-Sperdin, A. (2013). Enhancing business performance of hotels: The role of innovation and customer orientation. *International Journal of Hospitality Management, 33*(June), 347–356.

Hall, C.M., & Williams, A. (2008). *Tourism and innovation*. London: Routledge.

Hirschman, E.C., & Holbrook, M.B. (1982). Hedonic consumption: Emerging concepts, methods, and propositions. *Journal of Marketing, 46*(3), 92–101.

Hjalager, A.M. (2010). A review of innovation research in tourism. *Tourism Management, 31*(1), 1–12.

Ottenbacher, M., & Gnoth, J. (2005). How to develop successful hospitality innovation. *Cornell Restaurant and Hotel Administration Quarterly, 46*(2), 205–222.

Storey, C.D., & Easingwood, C.J. (1998). The augmented service offering: A conceptualization and study of its impact on new service success. *Journal of Product Innovation Management, 15*(4), 335–351.

Sullivan, E.A. (2010). A group effort: More companies are turning to the wisdom of the crowd to find way to innovate. *Marketing News, February 28*, 22–29.

Stamboulis, Y., & Skayannis, P. (2003). Innovation strategies and technology for experience-based tourism. *Tourism Management, 24*(1), 35–43.

Victorino, L., Verma, R., Plaschka, G., & Dev, C. (2005). Service innovation and customer choices in the hospitality industry. *Managing Service Quality: An International Journal, 15* (6), 555–576.

Williams, A. (2001). Internationalization and innovation in tourism. *Annals of Tourism Research, 38* (1), 27–51.

## Websites

Best Western
https://www.youtube.com/watch?v=7Y4D-EJbCCI

Failte Ireland Virtual Reality
http://www.failteireland.ie/Utility/News-Library/Virtual-Reality-Brings-Wild-Atlantic-Way-to-Life.aspx

The château of Chambord
https://www.chambord.org/en/agenda/histopad/

Tourism Australia Virtual Reality
https://www.youtube.com/watch?v=aszTdBIbfq0&index= 2&list=PLajBrt9lvgr4v5pDW1L5T4 mETnVVyl8dn
https://www.youtube.com/watch?v=MG3EUz3V-5U&list=PLajBrt9lvgr4v5pDW1L5T4mETnVVyl8dn
https://www.youtube.com/watch?v=h7mU7hZ5QZs

# MAJOR CASE STUDY
# LUX*

## Preliminary remarks

The notion of experience is studied in detail in Chapters 6 and 10. Chapter 6 is dedicated to the customer experience and presents a major case study exposing the marketing practices of a group hotel, LUX, which focuses on the customer experience. We present in this chapter a supplementary major case study, proposed by Julian Hagger, Chief Sales and Marketing Officer of the group LUX, which helps to understand the global processes of change and innovation at the heart of the company. It takes us from the bringing of the first thoughts (ideas, concepts) and the strategy that comes from this through new practices of team management and human resources up to the final operational stage and marketing approach; the process as a whole being directed towards a final objective: reinforcing the customer experience.

## Case study

We're called LUX* because light is our very essence – a lighter touch for a happy and fun atmosphere but with a laid-back luxury feel. To make sure our guest experience is enhanced in every way, we moved away from the heavy and dark ambience of traditional resorts, and left the gloom behind. LUX* is light – by name and by nature. But what's the asterisk for? The asterisk links our brand to our strap-line and serves as a reminder that LUX* is * lighter and brighter, and still very LUXurious.

When we created LUX*, we created a luxury hospitality brand with a new spirit and, in doing so, a fresh experience for our guests. How do we do it? By delivering authentic and extraordinary experiences that are simple, fresh, and sensory. By being fun and spontaneous. By celebrating the culture and nature of some of the world's most spectacular locations. In short, we rewrote the rules of luxury hospitality.

To stand out from the crowd – or the "sea of sameness" as we like to call it – we banished thoughtless patterns. In other words, we chose to avoid the pitfalls that have caused many luxury hospitality brands to be almost indistinguishable. With LUX*, we introduced the world to a new kind of luxury.

At LUX* Resorts & Hotels, everything we do stems from a shared vision and a strong belief and common purpose: helping people celebrate life. This seemingly simple motto perfectly sums up what we feel is our mission in the global hospitality industry. Our vision is to make each moment matter and to ensure that our guests smile throughout their stay. We focus on value creation for all the key stakeholders involved and we celebrate differences. With a market capitalization of Rs8 billion (US$235M) on the Mauritian Stock Exchange, we play an important role not only in the financial community in Mauritius, but also within the IBL group. IBL is the largest conglomerate in Mauritius with a lengthy and distinguished record of accomplishment, adding a distinctiveness to us as a leading hospitality brand with an increasingly global footprint.

LUX* is a proud member of the SEM 10, the first hospitality group on the Stock Exchange of Mauritius Sustainability Index. LUX* Resorts have been Travel Life certified, showing they meet a vast range of sustainability criteria. Since LUX* operates in international destinations, we also follow international and national commitments such as the Paris Agreement and the UN Sustainable Tourism Goals, as well as taking into account the growing commitment of tour operators, investors, the local community and owners for responsible and sustainable tourism. Furthermore, LUX* is a member of the Global Reporting Initiative's Gold Community and we work to international standard such as the International Integrated Reporting Council and the UN Global Compact to ensure high quality sustainable operations.

In this context, we take pride in being a socially and environmentally responsible brand as it is of utmost importance for us to maintain our established reputation as a business with a firm commitment to long-term sustainability. We strongly believe in considered resource utilisation and act to the best of our ability to fully respect and protect the environment. We should not and will not run our business by jeopardising the ecosystem and the environment of the communities where we operate, hence the implementation of a number of green initiatives to which all our collaborators adhere. Our targets include reductions in waste, energy, water consumption and carbon emissions. Our strategy also involves gender equality and equal opportunity. We not only value the importance of corporate responsibility but we fully adopt sound ethical practice and proper risk management. We believe in integrated thinking, integrated reporting, integrated action and integrated communication. Over the years, LUX* has grown into a brand with a strong and sustainable financial base. This is no sheer coincidence but the result of the consistent work of all our teams in both our corporate offices as well as in our resorts and hotels around the world. In the years to come, LUX* intends to be at the heart of the hospitality industry and a reminder that commitment and values makes for a lasting success story.

Also at the heart of our business is a set of values that define our brand and our service. High among these values is innovation, which has driven our business since its inception. This constant quest for improvement through creativity has allowed us to elevate our guests' experience in every respect. Our diversified portfolio of products and service, such as Café LUX* and our other reasons to go LUX*, are all ingredients in our success.

We are committed to equipping our individual team members with the tools that bring out the best in them and to ensuring that we provide them with extensive training and continuous learning so that our guests can feel our distinguishing qualities. Coupled with that, our inclusive policy towards our stakeholders helps consolidate our position and build our reputation the world over. At LUX*, it's more than just training. As well as constantly investing in our people, we give them the opportunity to express themselves as individuals and thrive in an environment that is pleasant and enjoyable. To be relevant we have to be relevant to others and the result has been a fantastic increase in team member engagement. After all, the hospitality industry worldwide is in a unique position to contribute to making the world a better place. Moreover, with the growth of the tourism sector globally over the last decade, we have ensured that our people embrace new cultural needs and provide the finest service to meet all guest needs.

Continuous training is one of LUX*'s hallmarks of quality and this is one of the reasons LUX * Resorts & Hotels' management has regularly sought the services of Ron Kaufman, founder and president of "UP! Your Service" since 2011, to ensure the training of our teams whilst supporting us in our strategy to enhance our services and allow our team to become familiar with the innovative concepts implemented. We endeavor at ensuring that excellence becomes synonymous with our brand in all our establishments, hence our partnership with Ron Kaufman's Up! Your Service College continues to bring world-class actionable service education to all our team members. The focus on our personal energy, which began in 2016, continues to be a highlight of our service culture education. Moreover, we also continue to upskill our teams by providing quality hospitality education through our long-term partnership with Lobster Ink, the leading online training company for our sector, with content covering all major aspects of hospitality.

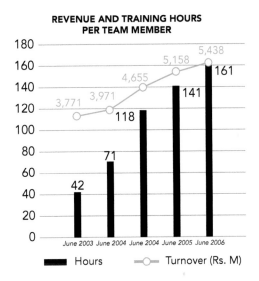

Figure 16.1 LUX* Resorts & Hotels – revenue and training hours for team members

Our Talent Management strategies allow us to manage talent as a critical resource to achieve superior business results. We are very much aware how investment in training and trading success are inextricably intertwined. As a result, with the expansion of LUX* in newer geographic regions, we have earmarked specific resources to ensure we provide for a new range of learning and development requirements. Our target for 2016–17 was an average of 145 man-hours of training per team member and, in fact, we once again exceeded our target as we achieved an average of 161 training hours per individual, an increase of 14% over the previous year.

Creativity is a key driver of the LUX* Brand and, to keep this spirit alive, our teams actively participate in the yearly edition of the LUX* Innovation Challenge which was first introduced in 2013. The Challenge provides an opportunity for all team members to propose innovative ideas, concepts and processes. This initiative serves to prompt our team members to always excel themselves to improve, keep pace and maintain the image of the hotel group. These projects, brought to life, reinforce the feeling of belonging to the group, but also demonstrates our teams' expertise, innovativeness and creativity.

The Challenge has a theme each year and our teams are invited to detail their innovative ideas, which are then presented to a panel of professional jury members, with winning ideas awarded and implemented. Recent innovation themes reflect our priorities: Increasing Loyalty of Guests, Increasing Loyalty of Team Members, Innovate to Increase Revenues and Innovate to Increase Productivity.

Over the last four years, LUX* have been pleasantly surprised by the inventiveness shown by its team members through their projects. While in the beginning, everyone was familiar with the concept of innovation, today we see teams that disregard classic models, challenge standards and redefine the hotel industry. Teams work together with a healthy competitive spirit and are inventive to the point of imagining the unimaginable.

For us at LUX*, our mission is to help people celebrate life, and in this context, our purpose is to make every moment matters. We've therefore banished thoughtless patterns and created simple, fresh and sensory experiences to indulge guests throughout their stay with us. We're here to surprise and delight our visitors with generous touches and creative details that make the apparently ordinary truly extraordinary. After all, they come on holiday to escape the routine of daily life. When they stay at a conventional resort, before long they'll know where everything is. That won't happen at LUX*. We love the impromptu, surprising guests with delightful pop-up treats – an ice-cream cart here, an unexpected prize hiding in a bottle over there, alfresco film shows under a twinkling night sky – there one day, gone the next. LUX* Resorts & Hotels is always in touch with its spontaneous side and with a desire to help guests celebrate moments that may linger in their memories for years to come.

There are, of course, plenty of reasons to choose LUX* for a holiday and, since the ground-breaking brand launched in 2011, our team has been dreaming up ever more reasons to go LUX*, not least when we prepare to open new resorts in some of the world's most sought after locales. As is our way, we love to throw in lots of truly original activities and imaginative twists that give us our distinctive edge. For example, the opening of LUX* Grand Gaube in December 2017 provided us, once more, the opportunity to launch four entirely new ways to ensure time with LUX* is more entertaining and delightful than ever before – and than anywhere else: Beach Bento, Veggie Heaven, Paddle Tennis and the G&T 100 Club.

As ever, expect the unexpected with LUX*! It fits well with our unique brand concept of Locale Light. Locale is all about celebrating the authentic life of a place – its nature, its culture, its music, cuisine, flavours, sights and sounds, while light reflects our new and innovative approach to luxury, an approach that is laid-back and light-hearted. Combine the two and you have Locale Light – a flexible conception that can be adapted to resorts and hotels wherever they are in the world.

Source: Julian Hagger, Chief Sales & Marketing Officer, LUX* Resorts & Hotels, Mauritius.

Major case study questions

1. How would you describe the unique characteristics of LUX*?
2. What role does creativity play in the development of the LUX* brand?
3. How sustainable is both the LUX* brand and its contribution to the green environment?

# Pricing and revenue management

## Learning outcomes

By the end of this chapter, students will:

- Understand concepts and principles of pricing and revenue management;
- Identify some key performance indicators;
- Have a better knowledge of revenue management tools and levers;
- Understand the challenges revenue management is facing (including: big data, distribution, loyalty, etc.), and therefore being in a position to anticipate revenue management trends (including: total RM, profit RM, net revenue).

## Introduction

### From origins of yield management to revenue management

Yield/revenue management was first developed in the 1980s and is associated with the evolution of the airline industry in the United States when the deregulation in the sector brought in by the Airline Deregulation Act of 1978 led to the development of numerous companies, creating a situation of strong competition. In this context, price wars were launched. Yield management contributes to replacing price cutting by finely tuning price variations which are better adapted to the clients' profiles, sales time periods, and product types.

Nowadays, the terms *yield management* (coming from airline sector in the early 1980s) and *revenue management* (which symbolize the idea of revenue optimization) are both used without any real distinction by tourism and hospitality operators.

Yield/revenue management rests on the principle of strong price variation adapted to the market context. It contributes to the protection of high-contributing clients while enabling access at more attractive prices in off-peak periods or for bookings made long before the booking date (early booking). The system pre-supposes client segmentation based on the consumers' sensitivity to price and quality (Legohérel et al. 2013).

Revenue management consists in giving priority to high-contribution clients who will accept higher prices rather than try to serve all clients. Clients are selected according to their profile and their potential contribution, and the door is always kept opened for the best/more valuable clients. Revenue management acts simultaneously on prices and available capacity (inventory management).

Yield/revenue management now plays a key role in service companies' strategic plans, key priorities, collaborations (in the context of alliances and networks), guest relationship and loyalty, and many other key issues.

Tourism and hospitality insight 17.1 explains the importance of revenue management for a mid-sized airlines (MEA) in the context of relationships with partners in an alliance (SkyTeam), while Tourism and hospitality insight 17.2 explain how revenue management can contribute to the new objectives and key priorities of a hotel group (including guest experience and technology), and the consequences for the revenue management department itself, the main evolution being the implementation of a new revenue management system able to address both optimization and marketing objectives of the hotel group.

## TOURISM AND HOSPITALITY INSIGHTS 17.1
## REVENUE MANAGEMENT AND COLLABORATION

Interview with Amina Hachem – Head of Revenue Management Department at Middle East Airlines (May 2016):

Tell us about revenue management, and the value it adds – provide a short history of MEA revenue management/department?

Airlines around the world have faced deregulated competition and globalization of their markets along with an increase in customer power against travel chain. Middle East Airline knew that a new mind-set of management had to be adopted especially on competition side. Competing effectively with the right choice of defensive and offensive strategies effectively will ensure the success and continuity of the airline.

Revenue management is at the heart of an airline's commercial planning department and serves the important function of setting inventory controls to accept the right customer at the right price at the right time to maximize network revenues. There are three important drivers in deriving value from revenue management:

1. Expertise of the personnel in revenue management and pricing;
2. Interaction of the core functions and processes in the airline;
3. Technology and the efficiency/effectiveness of the systems adopted.

The revenue management department started in MEA (Middle East Airlines) and since 2001 has been using a new system called "Sabre revenue management" used by Sabre which was hosted by (AF) Air France. The system objective was to help airlines respond to changing market conditions in real time and maximize multiple revenue streams through advanced decision support for customer segmentation, offering management and pricing optimization. Today, through accurate forecasts of the market and the customer's choice based on historical records, price alignments, and follow-up of the competitor price availabilities we take decisions to best suit our customers with their diverse needs and ensure profitability of the airline.

In 2016/2017, the competition become fiercer between carriers in the Bey hub. MEA knew it had to adapt to more effective and compatible business models. The revenue management department adapted the Amadeus revenue management system (RMS) to be compatible with all Amadeus software across different touch points (reservation, inventory, airport, call center, etc.)

Explain the main objectives of MEA revenue management department?

The primary aim of revenue management is selling the right product to the right customer at the right time at the right price and with the right pack. MEA's fundamental objective is to increase revenue by maximizing passenger value and satisfaction. The main objectives of the revenue management department are to help:

- In demand forecasting and ensure a high level of accuracy to create a bundle of service levels at different prices that best suit the market characteristics and the customer's preference;

- To have a solid background in the competitor's offerings, fares, and responses so that decision-making at the commercial level and top strategic level can be effective.

- To apply the right decision to optimize the revenue of a given sector or flight.

Does the relationship/collaboration with other airlines inside Sky Team alliance impact MEA revenue management?

On May 10, 2011, MEA took a strategic decision to join the SkyTeam airline alliance to increase the revenue generation to save costs, and share knowledge. On the side of revenue management, SkyTeam's alliance objective was to increase revenue for member airlines by expanding the network's coverage on each other's flights. Although MEA, a medium-size carrier, has some limitations due to small revenue management capabilities compared to the larger airlines, there is no doubt that the collaboration and relationships with other airlines were enhanced since MEA joined the SkyTeam Alliance due to the diverse benefits and privileges that MEA gained. For example, block space codeshare agreements, and free space codeshare agreements among the carriers have affected the valuation of seat availability of MEA; we know that some partners benefit more than others. On the other side, the communication and information sharing between partners using dynamic codeshare valuation has a positive impact on the overall revenue and is beneficial.

Does MEA share with/benefit from knowledge of other airlines, practices, tools, technology?

Yes, MEA benefits a great deal from other knowledge of other airlines, practices, tools and technology. This is mainly visible because MEA's revenue management system was hosted by Air France. Moreover, the technological development of airlines encourages other airlines to develop so that they won't fall behind.

Source: Interview with Amina Hachem – Head of the Revenue Management Department at Middle East Airlines (May 2016).

## TOURISM AND HOSPITALITY INSIGHTS 17.2
## THE REVENUE MANAGEMENT CONTRIBUTION TO NH HOTEL GROUP OBJECTIVES AND KEY PRIORITIES

NH Hotel Group (www.nh-hotels.com) is Europe's third-ranked business hotel chain. It operates close to 400 hotels with almost 60,000 rooms in 27 countries across Europe, the Americas, and Africa, including top destinations such as Berlin, Madrid, Amsterdam, Brussels, Paris, Buenos Aires, London, Rome, Vienna, Bogotá, Mexico City, Barcelona, Frankfurt and New York.

In 2013, the NH hotel group launched a big transformation plan supported by a strong five-year plan with the objective to increase profits significantly.

The group defined four key priority areas:

- carrying out a clear brand segmentation of its hotels under a new brand umbrella;
- designing a new value proposition that enhances guest experience;
- driving brand recognition through communications;
- and optimizing management and organization capabilities, particularly with regard to the group's technology systems.

The whole company was in motion towards a common goal, launching more than 20 initiatives from all areas of the company all targeted towards these four areas. The pricing and revenue management initiative played a key role in the transformation. Its main objective was to grow RevPar (revenue per available room) so enabling the group to reach its revenue objectives, but mostly to drive the growth via average daily rate steering revenues directly to the bottom line, achieving net profit targets. The initiative was focused on two main areas: organization and pricing strategy.

*Organization*: Revenue management and pricing relies on many people to succeed. Our people need to make the right decisions at the right time and work closely with all partners. We needed to free people of manual tasks and give them more time to spend on analysis, communication, and coordination with partners. On top of this, our teams had much more information and data needed to make decisions much faster than before.

*Pricing strategy*: Customers today have access to more information and more choices. With such evolution in the market, NH needed to move away from traditional pricing revenue management towards the pricing of the future.

*Technology*: NH's revenue management teams could only achieve their organization transformation and new pricing strategy by investing in new technology: a new revenue management system. This was also only possible thanks to the system transformation initiative.

*System transformation*: Among the initiatives that NH introduced in 2014 to improve the functionality and competitiveness of its systems, a key change was the implementation of a new integrated software platform across all the group's business units in a year. Part of the new integrated platform was the new centralized management and booking systems.

For pricing, the new centralized management and booking systems was a key enabler as it opened to door to much more flexibility in its pricing strategy.

*The new revenue management system (RMS)*. It was time for NH to move away from traditional revenue management. The company launched a request for a proposal in which four RMS providers participated. The new RMS selected offered major benefits. The most important one was open pricing. Traditionally, pricing in hotels was static based on a price grid with often big gaps from €10 to €50 euros between each rate level. With open pricing, the new system would recommend dynamically and independently multiple price points for any segment, channel, and room type, enabling more revenue to be captured. It also allowed the revenue manager to define and automate strategies based on forecast, booking trends, and competition to guide the system in the price setting.

Another key feature was instant data view allowing reactivity. At any time of the day, the system would have up-to-date booking data and adjusted rate recommendations. At this time, traditional revenue management systems would only receive fresh booking data and re-compute forecast and price recommendations once a day just before working hours. The new system also integrated multiple data sets on top of traditional booking data: city–airport traffic, weather forecast, and web shopping. This was not only used in the optimization algorithm but also available for the user as information. The system used cloud-based web servers, allowing infinite computing capacity and thus speed. Revenue managers would then spend more time on analysis and strategy.

In less than a year, the new RMS was implemented across all hotels. NH's revenue management teams were ready to step change the company's pricing strategy in partnership with the hotel operations, sales, distribution and marketing teams.

Source: Mona Maamari, Director of Revenue Management Development, Madrid, NH Hotel Group (June 2016).

## Revenue dilution risk

The notions of perishable service and fixed capacity sales constraints led to the mention of yet another issue: accepting or refusing the client's booking and the risk of price dilution. A "logical" argument would be to assert that any new booking which is accepted will generate new revenue. Strictly speaking, there is indeed revenue increase, but in certain cases, this increase may prove to be lower than that which would have been obtained through another sales decision (for instance, selling to another client, selling at another time, and higher prices). The revenue thus generated, but which is lower than the performance one might have attained, is therefore regarded as revenue loss; also called "price dilution." Price dilution may also result from consumers' using pricing which does not correspond to their profile (Legohérel et al., 2013).

## Application of revenue management

Revenue management is well developed in most tourism and hospitality sectors, including: air transport (both passenger and cargo transport), shipping (ferries and cruises), and railway transport (both passenger and goods); hotel and all hospitality operators (such as Airbnb, campsites); banquet and seminar services offered by many hotels; car rental; convention centers; tour operators; sport arenas and theatres.

Tourism and hospitality insight 17.3 explains the specificity of revenue management implementation in the restaurant sector.

## TOURISM AND HOSPITALITY INSIGHTS 17.3
## RESTAURANT REVENUE MANAGEMENT

Revenue management is particularly relevant in cases where the fixed costs are relatively high compared to the variable costs. Even though restaurants have a higher variable cost percentage than industries where revenue management has traditionally been more important (e.g. airlines and hotels), potential revenue gains can still be substantial. The principles of revenue management can apply to restaurants given that the unit of sale in restaurants is the time required for service, rather than just the meal itself. Unoccupied seat hours represent lost revenue; therefore restaurants should maximize capacity utilization as they attempt to increase revenues.

While many restaurants either defined high table occupancy rates or high average check as their primary business goals to achieve, RevPASH, i.e., revenue accrued at a given time interval divided by the number of seats available during that time, was proposed to measure a restaurant's operations in order to develop revenue management strategies for restaurants. RevPASH measures the rate at which capacity utilization generates revenue. In hotels and airlines, the cost per unit sold, except the intermediary commission, is nearly identical, because the production cost is evenly distributed across all sales units (i.e., seats or rooms). However, the production cost for each restaurant menu varies in restaurants because of the different ingredients for each dish. Thus, restaurants need to consider the contribution margin of each menu item rather than total revenue, because the goal of RRM is to maximize not just revenue but – in the end – profit.

During high demand periods, restaurants should focus on increasing their total gross profit and bottom line by selling more profitable menu items. Although differential pricing has proven to be successful in airlines and hotels, where customers find it to be more acceptable or fair, restaurants are more constrained in their use of differential pricing. Many restaurants believe that using statistical models to optimize prices is difficult for restaurants. Restaurants, however, could offer a special value menu to bring in more customers during low demand periods or special premium menus to increase revenue per customer during high demand periods or apply a differential pricing policy by providing different service levels.

Nanxiang Steamed Bun Restaurant (南翔馒头店) is located in a two-storey building and is one of the most famous steamed dumplings restaurants in Shanghai. It offers different service levels at different price levels. On the ground level, the restaurant sells steamed buns (小笼包) for takeaway only (i.e., no seating is available). On the first floor, partial self-service (i.e., with seating) is provided. First, customers have to find their own seats, and then order food and pay at the cash register. Colored tokens, which indicate the different foods, are given to first-floor customers and the restaurant staff come around with a trolley of food and serves the food while checking the tokens. The second floor is regarded as the premium floor where diners will be ushered to a table and served by the restaurant waiting staff. Regarding prices, on the first floor, the restaurant sells one serving of 16 steamed buns at RMB12 (US$ 1.8; US$ 0.1 per bun) whereas one serving of six steamed buns sells for RMB25 (US$3.8; US$0.6 per bun) on the first floor. On the premium floor, the same serving of six steamed buns is sold for RMB35 (US$5.3; US$0.9 per bun). While there is always a long queue to buy steamed buns on the ground floor, tables on the premium floor are readily available for customers without waiting most of time.

The wide variety of challenges restaurant owners face, such as high labor costs and new competition from indirect and untraditional competitors, have pushed the restaurant industry to look into different solutions to handle today's problems. The success of restaurants' revenue management strategy depends on the availability of historical data regarding demand patterns, customer preferences, sales of specific menu items, and customers' price sensitivity. Therefore, it is important for restaurant operators to have reliable data available to them when they need it so they can analyze these factors correctly. The goal of restaurant revenue management should be to sell the right menu item to the right customer at the right time (and meal duration, as well) and at the right price by using the right table mix in order to maximize profit.

Source: Cindy Yoonjoung Heo, PhD, Assistant Professor of Revenue Management. École Hôtelière de Lausanne, HES-SO/University of Applied Sciences Western Switzerland, June 2016.

Generally speaking, companies which are potentially involved in the application of revenue management approaches are those which share the following features:

- Fixed capacity;
- Fluctuating demand;
- A perishable product;
- A product which can be sold in advance;
- The possibility of price segmentation for price-sensitive consumers;
- The possibility of product segmentation (for instance, an extra service justifies a higher price).

## Total revenue management

The concept of "simple" revenue management is currently being replaced by that of total revenue management which corresponds to a broader approach to a company's revenue optimization. Revenue optimization is similar to the search for commercial performance, which has long-term and all-embracing characteristics.

Total revenue management is based on the integration of all sources contributing to additional revenue generation. Operators have to evaluate overall consumer spending so as to identify clients' real contribution and better select them. The main concern operators are facing, is how to track all data related to a single customer. If a guest has dinner at the restaurant of his hotel, but decides to pay cash, will the hotel collect this information? When information does not appear on the PMS or the guest database, the clients' value is underestimated. Conversely, when the data capture is well done, the data transmitted into the CRM databases feed into the marketing analysis of the company which can then have a comprehensive and up-to-date view of its clients' profile.

The total revenue management practices have been considered by many hotel groups, and tourism companies (theme parks, cruise ships, etc.). Not only is the real contribution of each guest a key factor for a hotel's overall revenue optimization (indeed, there appears to be a movement from the traditional RevPar to new formulae such as GoPar or TotalPar), but the sources of ancillary revenue are often seen to bring revenue maximization opportunities which are greater than those offered by the main product (a room in a hotel, an entrance ticket to a theme park, a cabin, and the transportation on a cruise ship, etc.).

# Revenue management components and metrics

## Pricing

Pricing is a key component of the marketing mix, and plays a significant role since the development of high-price variation practices: its job is to best adapt the services offered to the market conditions and fluctuating demand. A perfect understanding of demand is essential to determine optimal price and relevant pricing variations which are also effective in terms of their impact on demand. It is of great importance to fully understand customers' price sensitivity and their perceived value of services offered. It helps to determine the optimal price, the pricing grid (the various prices for the same product or service), or the numerous selling prices (special offers or other price variations).

It is also essential to monitor competitors' prices and track prices on the market. CompSet (competitive set, that is, a short list of actors defined by a company as its main competitors) provides daily relevant information. Companies may also track public information on the Internet using tracking software in order to collect large volumes of data, or do manual/ad hoc information searches. Such activities are integral to being aware of competitors' pricing positions and promotional offers.

## Differential pricing and dynamic pricing

Depending on clients' different price sensitivities and expectations regarding the services on offer, service firms define not only optimal prices, but also a complex price grid in order to ease price variation and dynamic pricing. For example, attentive companies adjust their prices in real time and use information systems to integrate the new data in order to refine recommendations.

> Pricing decisions also integrate all the opportunities and market characteristics changes, such as event or demand changes and a competitor's action. Flexibility, on which dynamic pricing is based, thus becomes the rule when prices are determined or decisions are taken regarding price grid variations.
>
> (Legohérel et al., 2013)

## Key performance indicators and metrics

Service companies that manage fixed capacity traditionally used to consider two indicators to assess their business efficiency: the occupancy rate (number of units sold divided by the total number of units available), and the average daily rate (revenue divided by the number of units sold). Today, the strategy companies seek is that of finding the right formula between "selling a maximum number of units" and "keeping an acceptable pricing position." Other performance indicators are thus considered. The main one is: the revenue per available unit (RevPar). The revenue per available unit, called RevPAR (revenue per available room) in the hotel industry, is considered a good performance indicator for tourism and transportation companies. It is found by dividing the revenue obtained over a specific period of time by the number of available sales units in the same period or by multiplying the occupancy rate by the average price over a benchmark period to be determined.

Among other indicators, the gross operating profit per available room (GOPPAR) takes into account expenses, and leads to a better analysis of revenue and costs, and of profit. It provides a better indication of the overall firm performance. It is equal to total revenue less the total departmental and operating expenses. As the trend is to move from revenue management to profit management, and net revenue analysis, GOPPAR is now considered as a better key performance indicator of hotel performance than the still relevant, but basic, RevPar indicator (Kimes, 2010). Other increasingly important indicators include Total RevPar (or TrevPar) (total revenue per available room) and NRevPar (net rooms revenue per available room).

## Revenue management optimization and levers

Different levers contribute to revenue optimization. We briefly consider some of them in the section below, but invite readers to proceed to further readings to gain a comprehensive view of these traditional revenue management optimization tools and levers.

- Quota restrictions contribute to the effort against revenue dilution. They represent arbitration between unsold units or units sold at too low a price. The principle consists in always protecting the highest prices, hence gradually raising the low-price limit (called *bid price*) beyond which the company no longer sells its rooms or aircraft seats. The bid price is the revenue expected from the last available unit used as the minimum price of access to a price class. A reservation will be accepted or not by comparing the revenue generated (the price paid by the client) to the bid price; the latter has to remain lower.
- Overbooking involves offering for sale a capacity that is higher than the capacity actually available to anticipate the effects of cancelations and no-shows (a client's failure to show up or cancel a reservation). The phenomenon corresponds to revenue loss for the company, that is the opportunity cost of the no-show or late cancelation ticket and the reduced quota of seats offered for reservation. Overbooking limits the risk of facing empty rooms/seats and consequently is part of revenue maximization.
- Other levers include (but are not limited to) group management, length of stay, distribution.

## Revenue management systems: from Excel to sophisticated RMS

The purpose of a RMS is to ensure turnover growth and company margin optimization.

- Purposes of the tool for revenue managers: in general, they enable revenue managers to analyze clientele behavior and market changes. Revenue managers conduct analyses in terms of different detail levels, for a specific date and a fixed goal by:
  - Clientele segments.
  - Pricing levels.
  - Revenue management levels (RM levels) for the hotel industry.

Revenue managers need to access the information enabling them to monitor in highly specific ways the consistency with which the strategy the company has determined is being applied daily. In the hotel industry, for instance, this implies the analysis of the daily revenue management production per class and its comparison with the ideal mix fixed for the day. Moreover, this task enables revenue managers to obtain specific information regarding the market and the clientele behavior, for instance, the comparison of the pick-up of bookings for a specific day with the pick-up of bookings on a similar day in the past (e.g., events day, ordinary day, and holiday day).

- Purposes of the tool for the end users: The tool should enable hoteliers to manage their revenue management classes more effectively in their daily reservations system. The tool should provide four main benefits:

  o   Knowing every day the measures to be taken;
  o   Knowing the value of the client segments to be communicated;
  o   Adjusting the strategy/ideal mix;
  o   Possessing the main portfolio indicators (reservations and geographic area) for the hotel industry.

## The choice of an RMS

Across the tourism and hospitality industry, the main question for a company committed to using RM techniques is as follows: should one buy or lease a RMS? The price of each revenue management solution depends on the complexity of the company network. Current trends tend towards leasing hosted software (software as a service, or SAAS) rather than buying locally installed licenses. As an implementation project generally takes from six months to one year, it is imperative to set up a project and consultant team to carry out the calibration, implementation, and validation of the tool. The critical steps usually concern the real-time interface validation between the RMS and the inventory and the calibration of the revenue management system.

Before this, the first option for the hotel, tourism, air transport, and cultural sectors is to use Excel-based tools that are adapted to their specific needs and developed in-house. An Excel spreadsheet enables revenue managers to carry out a number of missions such as the projection valuation/estimation of the turnover, group and tour operators' quotations, among others. It works from two databases (for Year N and Year N-1) and enables the daily analysis of traditional indicators such as TO, ADR, and RevPar, according to room/seat type and segment type. All the data are calculated for each client segment or for all segments and per room type. It is also possible to forecast the monthly demand without taking into account the pricing class, no-shows, and cancelations so as to obtain a more long-term, overall market forecast when the company's projected budgets are determined.

Another important issue is for all companies, from small and medium-sized operators, to bigger/international group/chains, to have for all their systems (property management system, central reservation system, channel manager, revenue management system) to work together. They also have to choose a revenue management system (RMS). Many companies, especially the small- and medium-sized ones, consider in-house, Excel-based, company-specific software solutions. More sophisticated RMSs exist, but companies must check that they are fully adapted to their products and their market, and have to calibrate and adapt the RMS before being able to fully benefit from their new system.

Tourism and hospitality insights 17.4 explains how the revenue management department at Intercontinental Cannes works, and how all systems are connected.

## TOURISM AND HOSPITALITY INSIGHTS 17.4
## REVENUE MANAGEMENT AT THE INTERCONTINENTAL CARLTON CANNES

The mission of the revenue management department at the InterContinental Carlton Cannes is to maximize the total hotel revenue generated by accommodation, food and beverage outlets, catering as well as other revenues. The Director of Revenue Management at the InterContinental Carlton Cannes assumes a range of tasks and responsibilities. He occupies a key position within the hotel, works with the Regional Director of Revenue Management for Luxury & Boutique Hotels – Europe, based at the headquarters of IHG (InterContinental Hotels Group) in Denham. He reports directly to the General Manager of the hotel. He manages forecasts, pricing, and capacity allocation. The revenue management team is composed of five team members managing reservations and distribution and one revenue analyst.

In cooperation with all profit generating departments, the Director of Revenue Management provides guidelines and tips for selecting the best revenue opportunities for the hotel. He compares the results and performance to the objectives, and modifies the current strategy if necessary. He monitors the competitive environment of the Carlton Hotel, and implements tactics to maximize market share. He participates in building the strategical business and revenue plan.

So, he works closely with the General Manager, the Director of Operations, the Director of Finance and the Director of Sales and Marketing. He is particularly involved in budgeting, a difficult task because it involves predicting the room nights and average price by segment per day (microeconomic forecast) for a period of one year. At the InterContinental Carlton Cannes, the budgeting starts from June until September for the coming year. Once the budget is prepared by the Director of Revenue Management, it must be validated by IHG and presented at a later stage to the Owners and Shareholders.

Once the budgeting is set, the revenue management team will be responsible for forecasting in order to predict the demand, taking into consideration the changes in the market. The forecast is reviewed every day and will allow the revenue management team to practice:

- Yield management by managing demand through differentiating pricing and inventory allocation in order to maximize revenue;
- Group management that permits choosing the right type of business;
- Pricing by using the three pillars (demand, competition, and price sensitivity);
- Channel management with the focus on "book direct."

The number of systems, software, and databases used by the revenue management team is very important. It is therefore essential to ensure that they are interfaced with each other, that the information is current and there are no gaps. For example, if Holidex (central reservation system) indicates that the hotel still has 30 rooms available and Opera (property management system) shows only 15 rooms available there is the risk of 15 rooms being overbooked! The reverse is also true with a risk of loss of income.

Similarly, the connectivity between Opera and Holidex should regularly be checked as this work is particularly important due to the different departments using the systems in order to take decisions (general manager, sales department, reception, housekeeping, finance).

Opera is the PMS (property management system) of the Carlton. It allows different departments to control the activity. All bookings of the hotel must be entered into Opera. It indicates the state of the rooms, who are the customers, etc. Most of the data used for statistics and analysis are derived from the PMS. Opera also offers in its "rooms plan" screen, a presentation of the rooms booked for the date. This screen allows a better inventory management and revenue maximizing.

SBRP or strategic business and revenue plan is the general database of the hotel. It includes all daily sales room and catering data; budgets, forecasts, the sales and marketing plan, statistics by country, distribution channel. It includes important source reports. The advantage of SBRP, developed by IHG, is that it brings all the critical data together in one system.

Holidex is the CRS (central reservation system) that centralizes all reservations in the hotel. It can deliver the unique number for confirmation of each reservation. Regardless of the distribution channel, all reservations are stored in Holidex directly or via an interface. The rate loading and rate changes are directly managed by Holidex.

Finally, Perform is the revenue management software. Its main function is to calculate the bid prices known as "Hurdle points" in real time depending on the availability of rates. Being interfaced with Holidex and Opera, it automatically closes their rates below the Hurdle. To recap, here is a diagram describing how the different revenue management systems communicate together:

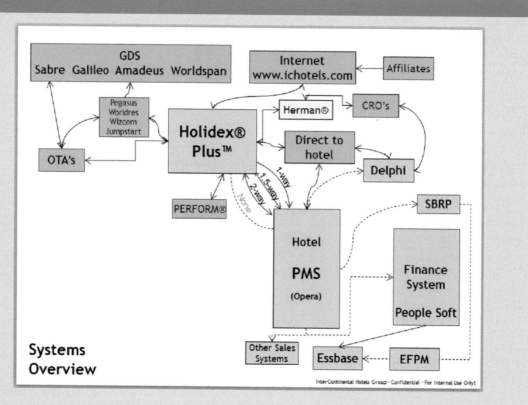

**Figure 17.1 Revenue management systems overview**

Source: Jad Aboukhater, Director of Revenue Management, InterContinental Carlton Cannes, France, June 2016.

## Evolution of revenue management

In recent years, academics and practitioners have raised some key challenges revenue management is facing for the future. Some of these challenges and research prospects are presented in this section (Reference: Wang X.L., Heo C., Schwartz Z., Legohérel P. and Specklin F., Revenue management: Progress, challenges, and research prospects, *Journal of Travel and Tourism Marketing*, 32(7), 797–811, 2015 – reproduced with the kind permission of Taylor & Francis, www.tandfonline.com).

Some of the hot topics considered in this section are as follows:

- Total hotel revenue management;
- Revenue management and distribution;
- Revenue integrity;
- Big data analytics;

- Revenue management and CRM integration;
- Revenue management and social media.

## *Total hotel revenue management*

It was already explained earlier in the chapter that an important issue facing hotel revenue management is the concept of total hotel revenue management, or THRM. It relates to capturing mostly untapped revenue and profit potential associated with the non-room revenue-generating centers of the hotel. Not that long ago, Kimes (2011) reported that, in her survey of industry professionals, the most common response regarding the future of revenue management suggested that RM would become more strategic in nature, and that it would encompass all revenue streams within the hotel. Function space, restaurants, spas, and retail were listed as the most likely non-room revenue centers to be included in revenue management (Wang et al., 2015).

Meanwhile, the industry seems to embrace the concept of THRM and at the same time to acknowledge a gap and a need for better tools. There is a divide between the volume of discussion and buzz around the concept of THRM generated by the industry and the actual level of effective implementation. For several years now, industry leaders and hotel companies have regarded THRM as one of the most desirable advancements in the field. While there seems to be an industry-wide consensus about the necessity to switch to THRM, little is known at this time about how that could be done correctly (Wang et al., 2015).

> Clearly the "Holy Grail" in this regard is the mathematics (Origin World Lab, 2014) as the complexity of the optimization increases considerably once we start adding revenue centers to the equations. While it seems that some RM solution providers are starting to offer integrated models, mostly in the area of casinos, and now meeting space, much more work is needed. Some additional interesting THRM research venues include the question of profit vs. revenue orientation, time horizon and big data analytics. The realization that one should optimize the entire hotel rather than rooms only underscores the need to re-examine the current heavy reliance on revenue optimization. A recent study by Schwartz, Altin, and Singal (2014) provided initial evidence that the assumptions regarding optimal revenue being sufficient to ensure near profit maximization is most probably less likely to hold true when more revenue centers beyond rooms are added to the mix.
>
> (Wang et al., 2015)

## *Revenue management and distribution*

Distribution channels expansion is a mandatory step to develop business growth in the tourism and travel industry: it means dealing with new technologies, worldwide complexity and powerful partners.

For Mauri (2013), channel management has arisen as a crucial component of RM. Whether to differentiate inventory access between direct channel and trade, however, is highly debatable. For the sake of partnering principles and to facilitate sales, dialog inventory access should be strictly the same. However, revenue-speaking, the service producer should offer a wider availability of access to its own direct customers in order to reduce the volume of commissions and distributor fees. RM decisions are usually based on maximizing expected net contribution, and incremental costs are to be incorporated in the inventory control model (Phillips, 2005). Inventory access will be managed differently for direct and indirect channels when fees and costs are integrated in the revenue contribution. Then more availability opportunities will be assigned to the direct channel especially during the constrained periods and when there are few remaining unities to sell. On the other hand, the revenue contribution is calculated in gross revenue when the availability management policy is non-differentiation.

Securing availability access to partners during the most constrained periods is a major consideration. The yearly agreements could include some dedicated allocations to protect capacity for the partners instead of managing it through free sale only. These allocated capacities are managed by the RM team and the contracted capacity allocation is the result of intensive sessions between the RM and the sales division acting as a spokesperson for the partners. Introducing an allotment policy into the reservation inventory is a considerable responsibility and brings with it a weighty additional workload because it implies daily monitoring to comply with the agreed contracts while applying special sales conditions. RM performs the proper analysis to allocate the right level of capacity to trade partners by first assessing the direct channels potential as a basis and then by identifying the forecasted remaining capacities to be proposed for the partners' allocation.

In case of a high-discounted campaign run with a specific partner, the RM function is to steer and limit the demand over the weakest periods. As mentioned in Noone et al. (2003), RM strategy can be adjusted with some partnering efforts including availability guarantees, dedicated pricing, or promotions to support "true friends" partners, according to customer segmentation proposed by Reinartz and Kumar (2002), over a long-term profitability vision that outweighs any short-term rate dilution.

Channel management implies the capability to build mutual agreements based on the proper trade-offs on a yearly basis and the capacity for the RM to perform two-tier performance measurement: traditional RM performance for the direct channel and a second one including Lifetime Value for trade. The long-term risk is not negligible because the cycle of tough negotiations with major partners tends to result in the transferring of significant margins from the services producer to its distributors, and business-to-business (B2B) relationships could turn the service producer into a simple sub-contractor providing raw products with a limited margin. RM plays the role of counterbalancing the pressure by providing revenue and profitability insights, and should be associated more with strategic decisions related to channels management. According to Venkat (2009), this could be through a move from the traditional RM to profit optimization by integrating RM, marketing pricing, and distribution toward consistent data, synchronized analysis, and coordinated actions in response to corporate requirements.

Channel management is finding the right compromise between demand generation and revenue leakage over the long-term horizon. Taking back control over product distribution is becoming a priority and efforts are made to modernize the direct channel devices: web portal designing, smart media development, search optimization engine, and call center streamlining. Improvements may focus on processes and analytical tools for reinforcing the RM role, thus leveraging different fare and availability policies depending on the channel in use.

## *Revenue integrity: practical challenges and research opportunities*

Ten years ago, reports from industry referred to new principles aiming to stem revenue leakage and to yield more revenue improvements and cost reductions. Rose (2007) published one of the first academic papers focusing on revenue integrity (RI) which was described at the time as "an ignored practice in the area of revenue management." Holloway (2008) indicated that RI efforts are to ensure as far as possible that the revenue anticipated when a reservation is accepted does actually materialize. Most pioneer authors were from airlines but, surprisingly, industries, including telecommunications and healthcare, have first taken advantage of RI in order to minimize costs and maximize revenue. RI approaches were developed later in airlines, and then were also implemented in other companies in different sectors (including hospitality and theme parks).

Ten years later, RI is now fully considered by the industry as an option to improve companies' efficiency. IT businesses have developed solutions for service companies to implement RI processes; for instance, Amadeus Revenue Integrity Platform, Sabre Air Vision Revenue Integrity, and others, offer airlines solutions to implement RI processes, and improve global revenue management approaches. Literature also clearly refers to RI and considers that the RI concept and processes should be developed along with global revenue management, in order to reduce cost, stem revenue leakage, and increase benefit (Legohérel, Poutier, & Fyall, 2013).

Niffoi (2013, in Legohérel, Poutier, & Fyall) indicates that the goal of RI is to ensure the integrity of revenue; that is, the consistency of the entire commercial chain from price definition through price charging in booking systems, proper application of price conditions, and respect of yield determined sales recommendations to final invoice clearance. In most services companies, though, failures occur both in the marketing and sales operations. These weaknesses fall into four categories: technical problems, procedure problems, communication problems, and operational/behavioral problems. All weaknesses must be identified and corrected. Then, the expected gain ranges from 1% to 3% in additional revenue.

RI lies at the intersection between several disciplines, including marketing, financial, and cost control issues, management (of sales teams, procedures, etc.), information technology, and systems management, data tracking, human resource skills, and sales, among others. A more global view of revenue and benefit improvement has emerged, and more research is needed to investigate and improve integrated/global revenue management approaches (Steinhardt & Gönsch, 2012).

## Big data analytics

There is a new exciting area of big data analytics. Simply stated, the term big data refers to the fast-growing availability of structured and unstructured data, characterized by large volume, velocity, and variety. Big data can contribute to improving all three phases of the revenue management cycle – consider, for example, how more accurate demand forecast could be if clickstream information is entered into the models and how the hotel's competitive set could be constructed to reflect consumer perspectives rather than the current approach of similarity of hotel characteristics. At the same time, big data analytics presents an unprecedented opportunity for a paradigm shift in the practice of revenue management. Current revenue management systems contrast room inventories with predicted demand by segment. The predicted demand and assessed probability determine decisions such as how the inventory (rooms) are allocated to rate fences, distribution channels, and how many rooms to overbook. As noted by Tim Coleman (2013) big data has the potential to support instantaneous decisions (e.g., on whether to accept or deny a booking request) based on "live information about the guest, the hotel, the city and millions of other data points where available." In economic theory terms, what the industry is so excited about is that big data will support a move away from the less efficient, third-degree, price discrimination model as currently practiced by the industry towards the first-degree, perfect, price discrimination model where the vast majority of the consumer surplus could be extracted by the hotel. A big-data-based system will have immediate and dynamic access to information about each customer. Such information comprises online activity directly or indirectly related to the reservation including search patterns, booking, and post purchase evaluations, rates paid in the past for hotel rooms and other products, guest profile, consumer/psychological profile, time of travel, loyalty patterns, time of booking, the mode of transportation, the customer's response to various marketing efforts in the past and weather at the origin and destination among others.

When this real-time big data information is combined with similar information about other potential future guests' reservation requests, it could be used to individually tailor the product and price combination; that is, the room and room rate quote. With the ability to best assess the individual guest needs, wants, and willingness to pay, the goal of true, most efficient optimization might be within our reach. Academia can and should play a major role in advancing our understanding of these issues and suggesting and testing proper solutions.

## TOURISM AND HOSPITALITY INSIGHTS 17.5
## HOW BIG DATA IMPROVES REVENUE MANAGEMENT

Until fairly recently, a whole night was needed in order to calculate the recommendations of a hotel or an airline, making it practically impossible or at least very costly to optimize in real time. Now the storage and cloud capabilities make real-time big data calculations possible.

Big data is heterogeneous data which, used in conjunction with traditional data revenue management, help provide a predictive and behavioral dimension while RM data are essentially historical and descriptive.

For example, data from social networks, weather forecasting, Facebook, events in a specific area, tweets about a topic or behavior captured by connected devices or mobile devices, can enhance information about the customer and therefore pricing strategies.

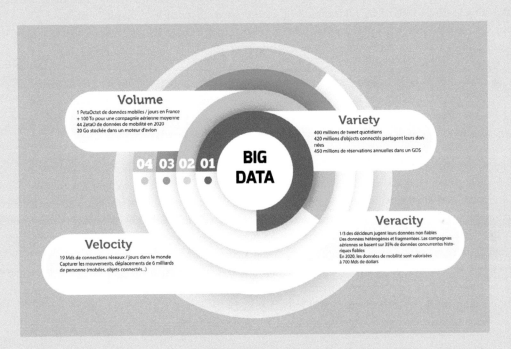

**Figure 17.2** Big data 4 Vs

Big data is summarized by: 1) Enormous amounts of data made possible by the availability of unlimited amounts of storage space. 2) Diverse and heterogeneous data sources from events, social networking, Internet, and connected objects. 3) An unmatched velocity made possible by thanks to "virtualization" which allows masses of simultaneous calculations on billions of individuals. 4) And finally as the trustworthiness of big data is often challenged, the development of proficient algorithms to correct and estimate the data in the best way.

Big data is not just data: it is associated with data science and particularly in the development of artificial intelligence algorithms called "machine learning." Machine learning enables the enrichment of data with the accumulation of knowledge after each iteration. Most tourism stakeholders recruit data scientists, requiring a hybrid profile with a mathematical, statistical, and IT background. Their job is to look out for new data sources, but they spend much of their time developing self-learning algorithms for the enhancement of data in a dynamic way.

### Data scientist for EasyJet: a new profession

In early 2016, EasyJet launched a strategy concerning big data, seeking to utilize 20 years of data. This strategy concerned information from data like the 1.3 billion queries to easyjet.com, the 80 million passengers transported, the 170 million drinks sold on board every year. One of the first big data applications EasyJet put into place was the correlation of repairs with flight delays to better anticipate problems by intervening in a preventive manner to minimize delays.

Big data is also integrated in the RM level at EasyJet with their 25 analysts having recently been trained in data science. According to Rey Villaverde, Chief Data Scientist at EasyJet,

> it is not only to adjust flights using historical data, as 95% of flights are adjusted daily depending on local events. Big Data allows EasyJet to better analyze the behavior of customers, their profiles and know the price that each passenger is willing to pay at each moment of the day.

By tracing clicks on easyJet.com, big data can analyze the purchasing behavior and better understand what transforms a visitor into buyer. The analysis of site data also explains how long the reservation takes or to know which passenger buys additional services beforehand or at the airport (insurance, luggage, etc.). The reconciliation of the Internet site data also allows EasyJet to understand each passenger from the CRM data and segment them into categories and not tariff levels.

For EasyJet and other tourism stakeholders, the promise of big data lies not in the replacement of analysts by computers making artificial intelligence, but rather to enable machine learning and artificial intelligence to improve results by analyzing large volumes of data; something that a human could not do in a short space of time.

For EasyJet, their machine learning is based on three methods:

- Classification: Classification of business customers, purchase behavior of the fight London–Malaga for example;
- Clustering: The analysis of trends when the classifications are unknown. For example, analyzing tea consumption on board;
- Regression: Data from one source are correlated with other data from a different source.

In the learning phase, the algorithm can be based on known variables because we know the relationship between these variables, but it can also be based on the whole set of variables in order to identify the strongest correlations between these variables. It is a new world of opportunity that opens for finding correlations between data set ups until now distinct, never analyzed together, and therefore not exploited to their full potential.

In summary, all tourism stakeholders have much data that is either unexploited or not exploited to its full potential. Technology is no longer a barrier as with the help of a data scientist and some common sense, it is simple to implement a big data approach.

For a hotel chain, big data allows the analysis of 80 Tera Octets of a 4,000 chain of hotels taking into account the competition in a dynamic way. For Airbnb, machine learning allows the prediction of accommodation costs based on data from the competition, online customer reviews, and attributes visible in a photo; and this is not just based on greater volumes of historical data. For transport operators, the geolocation data analysis allows the reconstruction of their customers' journey in order to offer promotions and optimal connections.

Source: Christophe Imbert, RM expert, President, Milanamos Company.

## Revenue management and CRM integration

One of the notable developments in RM in the past ten years is the conceptual development of the RM and CRM interface. Understanding about customer perception towards RM has been greatly enhanced and the notion of integrating RM and CRM has led the hospitality and tourism industry to "a new era" (Mainzer, 2004, p. 285) but not without difficulties. Although RM and CRM should be two complementary practices (Wang, 2012), previous literature offers insufficient guidance on how to integrate CRM with RM at the strategic level (Mathies & Gudergan, 2007; Milla & Shoemaker, 2008; Von Martens & Hilbert, 2011). A significant number of studies have been carried out in recent years to advocate the need for more research into this area and to seek a possible solution. For instance, based on a wide range of interviews conducted with industry leaders worldwide, Milla and Shoemaker's (2008, p. 110) study identifies RM and CRM integration as one of the four major areas of "having the greatest growth potential in hotel RM" and suggests that the customer will become the driver of RM in the future. Pricing, market segmentation, group revenue management, and organizational structure changes to optimize RM potential are key areas that require management attention. Echoing this view, Vinod (2008) suggests that customer-centric RM is a new paradigm for RM.

Customer-value based RM is also proposed to overcome the limitation of transaction-based RM by both utilizing capacity efficiently and establishing profitable customer relationships (Von Martens & Hilbert, 2011). However, in practice, findings from the hotel industry reveal several causes of potential management conflicts that could become hurdles for RM and CRM integration if not addressed (Wang, 2012; Wang & Bowie, 2009). These include management goals, management timescales, perceived business assets, performance indicators, and managers' approaches to achieving individual set goals. In a B2B context, the key account management and RM integration framework developed by Wang and Brennan (2014) is one of the first to amalgamate account management and RM through comprehensive analysis of the relationship and revenue value of an account that facilitates managers to make strategic RM decisions that aim for long-term profit yield.

The importance of recognizing customer value in the RM decision-making process has also been widely advocated by RM professionals. A number of opinion leaders and senior RM practitioners from one of the leading RM professional networks, revenue management and Pricing International (formerly the Revenue Management Society) in the UK suggest that *the ability to comprehend RM implications on online and offline marketing strategies and vice versa, is pivotal for the new generation of RM decision-makers especially in today's fast changing marketplace*. Considering that RM evolves from its originally tactical inventory management to a more extensive role across the company and at a more strategic level, action research addressing relevant issues surrounding this topic area is expected to grow.

## Revenue management and social media

How to capitalize on opportunities offered by the rapid development of social digital marketing strategies such as social media to improve RM is another area of research that has attracted much attention in recent years. The effectiveness of using social networking sites, such as Facebook, Twitter, TripAdvisor, and YouTube, as means to reach prospective customers, understand customer behavior, establish and maintain customer relationships, and influence customers' value perceptions has becoming a popular area for research. The fast growth of SM usage inevitably expands the spectrum of reputation risks and has boosted the risk dynamics (Aula, 2010; Eccless et al., 2007), thereby posing new challenges for RM practitioners. The framework for evaluating social media-related RM opportunities developed by Noone et al. (2011) undoubtedly have made progressive contribution to this relatively new stream of RM research. More sophisticated views of how consumers engage with brands have been revealed in the hospitality and tourism marketing literature, which will have profound implications for RM. For example, Hudson and Thal (2013) argue that social media have fundamentally changed the consumer decision process. They illustrate how social media make the "evaluate" and "advocate" stages of today's "consumer decision journey" increasingly relevant based on the four stages of the consumer decision journey: consider; evaluate; buy; and enjoy, advocate and bond (Court et al., 2009).

The link between SM and RM has been substantiated in recent years, which shows that SM has impacted on revenue performance and reputation matters (Anderson, 2012) although research in this area remains limited. In a first attempt to establish return on investment (ROI) for SM efforts, Anderson's report (2012, p. 5) reveals a number of significant findings. First, the number of reviews that consumers read prior to making their hotel choice has steadily increased over time. Second, a hotel can increase its rate by 11.2% and still maintain the same occupancy or market share if their review scores increase by one point on a five-point scale. Third, hotel pricing power has been influenced by user reviews; 1% reputation improvement could lead up to a 1.42% increase in RevPAR.

Industry leaders such as Patrick Landman, the CEO of XOTELS, an international hotel management company specializing in RM, predicts that a focus on corporate reputation is expected from the RM perspective in the years to come, as it is vital for companies to have a positive reputation and online review score in order to enhance its revenue performance. One of the leading RM system providers, IDeaS Revenue Solutions, launched its Advanced RM system – IDeaS G3 RMS in July 2014, which claims to be the first to allow hotels to use their current online reputations as a criterion for making pricing decisions. It is, therefore, fair to assume that in addition to more traditional pricing factors such as location and demand, future RM pricing decisions are likely to be made also based on a hotel's reputation. More studies in this particular area are needed to explore contemporary issues such as how RM could embrace the opportunities offered by SM and to comprehensively examine the effects of SM, customer reviews and their implications for a company's reputation and subsequently revenue performance.

## Conclusion

The traditional approach to RM developed 30 years ago has probably come to an end. The story started with the objective of the optimization of revenue generated by the main product (i.e. a room in a hotel). Now, the new objective is twofold:

- Have a better overview of the global contribution of the customer. It means, in a hotel, that the first (chronological) expense will be the room, but the remaining expenses may be the restaurant, spa, and other facilities.
- Analyze the real performance of the company, that is, not the revenue, but the profit. Generating more revenue is fine, but as long as you do not control for cost, you can't evaluate the real performance of the firm.

So, the new story is: managing profit, taking into account all customer expenses in order to target the real high contribution customers. Does it mean that we have to forget all that we have learned for 30 years? No, but we must be aware of this new perspective, based on previous concept and principles (still relevant) but with the objective of improving the companies' performance. Also, don't forget that medium-sized and large international groups (hotels and airlines especially) have for a long time improved their revenue management skills, and are studying further improvements. But, many small and medium-sized companies are still in an early stage of RM techniques and system implementation.

What is the most significant challenge for all firms? Is the new technological environment affecting all steps of marketing, pricing policy, and revenue/profit management implementation? Many systems are at the disposal of all companies (PMS, Channel Manager, Reservation systems (RMS), not to forget OTA and their distribution systems). The Internet and social networks offer consumers the opportunity to be major players on the market (easier and more comprehensive searches for information, evaluation of services delivered by companies, opportunities on some systems, to contribute to price definition). And, last but not least, big data is at the same time, the greatest opportunity, and the greatest challenge tourism and hospitality firms have to face. Revenue managers used to build their forecast on historical data, then on more dynamic supply/demand model. The current/next step is/will be to work with more predictive models, integrating customer-based data with the future being made up of models based on the ongoing process of integrating new data, using machine learning. Revenue managers will not just have a forecast based on historical data and a pick-up curve, but many sources of data to visualize more collaborative models fed with data coming from various sources, in order to understand and anticipate the market, and fix their price grid, if not partly decided by customers themselves.

## REVIEW QUESTIONS

1. Yield/revenue management was developed about 30 years ago, and has contributed to a significant optimization of revenue and better performance of tourism, transportation, and hospitality companies. What is next and how will these new techniques and processes evolve in order to further improve the revenue optimization based on the global contribution of customers?

2. Has revenue management come to an end? Companies now consider costs, and therefore profit optimization. Have we moved from revenue management to profit management and net revenue?

3. Customers have been forgotten for years by tourism and hospitality companies, when it comes to the setting of prices. In peak demand periods, customer relationship and guest loyalty are not top priorities for companies. But, as we now have so much data about customers (better knowledge, leading to more granular segmentation), and customers having so many opportunities to be a major player (searching for information and comparing prices on search engines, evaluating companies on social media, sometimes fixing prices by themselves on revenue management systems), do you think that we are entering a new era with marketing concerns to be better linked with pricing and revenue management policies?

4. Big data opens new perspectives to tourism and hospitality companies, including pricing policy and revenue (or profit) management. To what extent will big data revolutionize revenue management?

5.  Will all tourism and hospitality sectors, including the restaurant industry, be able to implement fully, or partially, revenue or profit management in the near future?

## YOUTUBE LINKS

"Understanding flight overbooking"

URL: https://www.youtube.com/watch?v=adShaElbMx4

Summary: The international airline transportation association explains why airlines have to overbook their flights, and the benefit for both passengers and airlines. Added by IATAtv.

### *"What all hotel revenue managers should know"*

URL: https://www.youtube.com/watch?v=9qQCEUu99s8

Summary: Revenue management experts share tips during the 2016 Hotel Data Conference. Added by Hotel News Now.

### *"Helpful advice on hotel revenue management"*

URL: https://www.youtube.com/watch?v=Sr5zrD0NS3A

Summary: Catherine Tremeau, CRME, Manager of Revenue and System Optimization at Sabre Hospitality Solutions, discusses her observations in the field of hotel revenue management. In a recent collaborative webinar, Catherine worked with Professor Sheryl Kimes of Cornell University's School of Hotel Administration to provide a 360 view of total revenue management. Added by SabreHospitality.

### *"The future of hotel revenue management"*

URL: https://www.youtube.com/watch?v=dQJlHYzlzos

Summary: Introductory video to the Future of Revenue Management Hospitality Study by the Cornell Center for Hospitality Research. Linda Hatfield, VP of Product Management at IDeaS, sits down with Sheryl Kimes, Professor of Operations Management at Cornell University, to discuss how the revenue management functions will become more central to hotel operations.

### *"Revenue management under control – the movie"*

URL: https://youtu.be/hCfzVa3Br_U

Summary: First movie on revenue management.

## REFERENCES, FURTHER READING, AND RELATED WEBSITES

### References

Anderson, C.K. (2012). The impact of social media on lodging performance. *Cornell Hospitality Report*, *12*(15), 4–11.

Aula, P. (2010). Social media, reputation risk and ambient publicity management. *Strategy and Leadership*, *38*(6), 43–49.

Coleman, T. (2013, June 20). Look out revenue managers, here comes big data. *Hospitality Upgrade*. Retrieved from http://www.hospitalityupgrade.com/_magazine/MagazineArticles/Look-Out-Revenue-Managers-Here-Comes-Big-Data.asp.

Court, D., Elzinga, D., Mulder, S., & Vetvik, O. J. (2009). The consumer decision journey. Retrieved fromhttp://www.mckinsey.com/insights/marketing_sales/the_consumer_decision_journey on November 22nd 2014

Eccless, R.G., Newquist, S.C., & Schatz, R. (2007). Reputation and its risks. *Harvard Business Review*, *85*(2), 104–114.

Hudson, S., & Thal, K. (2013). The impact of social media on the consumer decision process: Implications for tourism marketing. *Journal of Travel and Tourism Marketing*, *30*(1/2), 156–160.

Kimes, S.E. (2010). The future of hotel revenue management. *Cornell Hospitality Report*, 10 (14), 6–15.

Legohérel, P., Poutier E., & Fyall, A. (2013). *Revenue Management for Hospitality and Tourism.* Oxford: Goodfellow Publishers Limited.

Mainzer, B.W. (2004). Future of revenue management: Fast forward for hospitality revenue management. *Journal of Revenue and Pricing Management*, *3*(3), 285–289.

Mathies, C., & Gudergan, S. (2007). Revenue management and customer centric marketing – how do they influence travellers' choices? *Journal of Revenue and Pricing Management*, 6 (4), 331–346.

Mauri, A.G. (2013). *Hotel revenue management: Principles and practices.* Milan: Pearson.

Milla, S., & Shoemaker, S. (2008). Three decades of revenue management: What's next? *Journal of Revenue and Pricing Management*, *7*(1), 110–114.

Noone, B.M., Kimes, S.E., & Renaghan, L.M. (2003). Integrating customer relationship management and revenue management: A hotel perspective. *Journal of Revenue and Pricing Management*, *2*(1), 7–21.

Noone, B.M., McGuire, K.A., & Rohlfs, V. (2011). Social media meets hotel revenue management: Opportunities, issues and unanswered questions. *Journal of Revenue and Pricing Management*, *10*(4), 293–305.

Origin World Lab. (2014). Tackling the tall tale of total revenue management. Retrieved from http://www.forsmarthotels.com/2014/07/16/total-revenue-management-still.

Reinartz, W.J., & Kumar, V. (2002). The mismanagement of customer loyalty. *Harvard Business Review*, *80*(7), 4–12.

Rose, P. (2007). Revenue integrity: Delivering revenue and cost reduction benefits to airlines. *Journal of Revenue and Pricing Management*, 6, 71–76.

Schwartz, Z., Altin, M., & Singal, M. (2014). Performance measures for strategic revenue management: RevPAR vs. GOPPAR. *Journal of Revenue & Pricing Management*, *16*(4), 357–375.

Steinhardt, C., & Gönsch, J. (2012). Integrated revenue management approaches for capacity control with planned upgrades. *European Journal of Operational Research*, *223*(2), 380–391.

Von Martens, T., & Hilbert, A. (2011). Customer-value-based revenue management. *Journal of Revenue and Pricing Management*, *10*(1), 87–98.

Wang, X.L. (2012). Relationship or revenue: Potential management conflicts between customer relationship management and hotel revenue management. *International Journal of Hospitality Management*, *31*(3), 864–874.

Wang, X.L., & Bowie, D. (2009). Revenue management: The impact on business-to-business relationships. *Journal of Services Marketing*, *23*(1), 31–41.

Wang, X.L., & Brennan, R. (2014). A framework for key account management and revenue management integration. *Industrial Marketing Management, 43*(7), 1172–1181.

Wang, X.L., Heo, C., Schwartz Z., Legohérel, P., & Specklin, F. (2015). Revenue management: Progress, challenges, and research prospects. *Journal of Travel and Tourism Marketing, 32* (7), 797–811.

## Further reading

Belobaba, P. (1987). Airline yield management: An overview of seat inventory control. *Transportation Science, 21*(2), 63–73.

Forgacs, G. (2017). *Revenue management: Maximizing revenue in hospitality operations* (2nd ed.). Orlando, FL: American Hotel & Lodging Educational Institute.

Heo, C.Y., Lee, S., Mattila, A., & Hu, C. (2013). Restaurant revenue management: Do perceived capacity scarcity and price differences matter? *International Journal of Hospitality Management, 35*, 316–326.

Holloway, S. (2008). *Straight and level: Practical Airlines Economics* (3rd ed.). Farnham: Ashgate.

Kimes, S.E. (2011). The future of hotel revenue management. *Journal of Revenue and Pricing Management, 10*(1), 62–72.

Phillips, R.L. (2005). *Pricing and revenue optimization.* Stanford, CA: Stanford University Press.

Smith, B., Leimkuhler, J., & Darrow, R. (1992). Yield management at American Airline. *Interfaces, 22*, 8–31.

Ventkat, R. (2009). The era of convergence in revenue management. In I. Yeoman & U. McMahon-Beattie (Eds.). *Revenue management: A practical pricing perspective.* Basingstoke: Palgrave Macmillan.

Vinod, B. (2008). The continuing evolution: Customer centric revenue management. *Journal of Revenue and Pricing Management, 7*, 27–39.

Vinod, B. (2009). The future of airline distribution and revenue management. In I. Yeoman, & U. McMahon-Beattie (Eds.), *Revenue management: A practical pricing perspective.* Basingstoke: Palgrave Macmillan.

## Websites

Hetras – a Shiji Group brand
https://hetras.shijigroup.com/post/i-have-a-passion-for-revenue-management-do-you-as-well

Hozpitality
https://www.hozpitality.com/browse-jobs/hotels/revenue-management/management/

## MAJOR CASE STUDY
## SMART PRICING: THE DEMAND-BASED PRICING SOLUTION BY ACCOR HOTELS

In a world of full price transparency and unrestricted access to data, hotels deserve better than intuition or a crystal ball to manage their prices. That's why Accor Hotels has recently launched a new pricing solution named SMART pricing for its economy hotels, so far excluded from traditional RM system equipment due to complexity and cost issues.

### Demand-based pricing

The principle is simple, driven by the demand-based pricing theory. The new pricing model (or algorithm) takes into consideration the hotel's historical data, guest input, and level of demanding order to propose the optimal price per day and per booking period (or lead time).

First, Accor Hotels launched a major survey with 40,000 respondents in 17 countries to assess the price elasticity of demand. Through conjoint analysis, Accor Hotels teams were able to assess guests' willingness to pay as well as optimal price range (or "price corridors") for its brands. For example, in Brazil, for one night in an economy hotel, guests are willing to pay a rate from €40 to €70 (price "corridor"). In addition, an optimal demand-based price is defined for each day to maximize the RevPAR (revenue per available room = occupancy × price of the hotel) by using extensive historical data from hotels.

As a result, a pricing algorithm was designed by the Accor Hotels data scientist team to recommend prices per date of stay, level of demand, and lead time. The prices may vary every day and several times for the same date. This is called dynamic pricing, which allows continuous pricing adjustment depending on the level of demand.

The hotel prices change when calculated "triggers" are achieved: pick-up of the demand (or level of the occupancy), the day before arrival. The number of price changes for a given staying date depend on the dynamism of the market and the expertise of the revenue manager. In other words, the more the market is dynamic and competitive, the greater the expertise of the RM, the greater the number of changes in prices. We can see some hotels changing their prices dozens of times for the same date of stay. Is this efficient and does that bring value? For economy hotels, a maximum of five price changes for the same date of stay is already enough. It is key to keep it simple both for guests and for the hotel staff.

Let's take some examples of possible recommendations to understand better the algorithm principle. We are in a business-oriented city during the week end. The demand is low and the elasticity is high, due to significant competition on the market. The pricing algorithm will recommend lower rates to the hotel in order to get more bookings and increase its occupancy rate.

On the contrary, we were in Rio during Olympic Games where the demand was very high. Guests were struggling to find available rooms and the hotels would be full. The elasticity was low. The hotel had an opportunity to maximize its RevPAR through higher prices without threatening its occupancy rate. The correlation between occupancy and price is strong. Therefore, the hotel pricing strategy must be based on the understanding of this relationship.

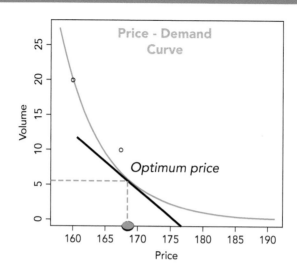

**Figure 17.3** Price-demand curve

## Solution and performances

As of now, the demand-based pricing solution SMART pricing has been deployed in 1,000 Accor Hotel properties worldwide.

Revenue managers steer the solution recommendations, and integrate market and competition price intelligence to make the right decisions. After less than six months, the results are positive

### Price elasticity of the demand

**High**

**2.0**

**HIGH PRICE ELASTICITY OF DEMAND:**
*e.g. Low season, week-end, early booking, etc*
**Customers are more sensitive to price changes**
Possible pricing actions: **Favor** VOLUMES growth
WITH LOWER PRICES / Higher prices may
**1.2** significantly jeopardize volumes

**0.5**

**LOW ELASTICITY:**
*e.g. High season, Event, week days, late booking*
Neither a price increase nor a price decrease
will have a significant effect on OCCUPANCY

**Low**

| SEASON | |
|---|---|
| High Season | L |
| Low Season | H |

| DAY | |
|---|---|
| Monday | L |
| Friday & Sunday | H |
| Tuesday, Wednesday, Thursday & Saturday | H |

| LEAD TIME | |
|---|---|
| Early booking | H |
| Last minute booking | L |

| COMPETITIVE INTENSITY & ENVIRONMENT | |
|---|---|
| High | H |
| Low | L |

**Figure 17.4** Price elasticity of the demand

with an average 5% increase in RevPAR, mainly due to a bolder pricing strategy and higher occupancy rates. Beyond the solution and the associated performance, it is essential to support the teams and the customers to make a shift from a static to a dynamic pricing model. It is necessary to explain over and over again why the price is dynamic to make sure that the hotel team members feel confident about the proposed pricing and to avoid any misperception of the pricing model being considered unfair by the guests.

Source: Agnès Roquefort, Senior VP Global RM, Pricing and Analytics, Data and RM Department, Accor Hotels.

## Major case study questions

1. What is the contribution of the demand-based pricing theory to the new pricing system developed by Accor Hotels for its economy hotels?
2. Is consumer price elasticity similar in various markets and countries?
3. In the light of Accor Hotels' experience, should we consider that implementing dynamic pricing approaches to economy hotels would make sense?

# Image and branding

## Learning outcomes

By the end of this chapter, students will:

* Understand those issues critical to the development and communication of a brand image
* Understand the conceptualization of brand image including its meaning and composition
* Become familiar with those methodologies available to operatively assess brand image
* Understand the formation process of a brand image
* Be introduced to strategies for effective brand communication.

### Key terms

brand image, brand meaning, brand composition, brand communication strategies

## Introduction

The rapid growth of the tourism and hospitality industry, combined with the global trends of globalization and worldwide accessibility has led to a situation where contemporary travelers are faced with endless tourism products to choose from. In order to compare between products, of which they often have only limited knowledge, travelers oftentimes resort to the image and brand associated with each of the products consumed for decision-making. As a result, brand image representation serves as a very important means to differentiate between hospitality and tourism companies and their represented products in the tourist's decision-making process (Pearce, 1982; Sirgy & Su, 2000; Yüksel & Akgül, 2007). Substantial efforts are being directed towards exploring the traveler's image and brand associations as well as the dominant factors that influence it, as this understanding is critical for developing effective planning, development, and marketing strategies for hospitality and tourism companies (Sönmez & Sirakaya, 2002; Tasci, Gartner, & Cavusgil, 2007). For this purpose, it is essential for business managers not only to be concerned about the brand image of their own businesses, but also about that of key competitors (Ahmed, 1991; Bonn, Joseph, & Dai, 2005). The goal of this chapter is to provide a comprehensive overview of critical issues in the development and communication of a brand image. The chapter begins with the conceptualization of brand image, including its meaning and composition, which has attracted much attention in tourism and hospitality marketing. The discussion then moves on to prominent methodologies that were presented to operatively assess brand image. Since the effective communication of a brand image requires a thorough understanding of the mechanism that generates the image, the formation process of a brand image is discussed, including the information agents that affect the mental representation people have with regards to brands. The chapter ends with strategies for effective brand communication by taking advantage of the sensory capital associated with a brand.

## Image and brand in hospitality and tourism: concepts and definitions

A brand is a symbol that identifies goods in a differentiated way; it is a shortcut for consumers. More specifically, it is a "name, term, sign, symbol, or design, or a combination of them intended to identify the goods or services of one seller or group of sellers and to differentiate them from those of the competition" (American Marketing Association). Branding has been a strategic business choice rooted in ancient times, from marking livestock to marking crafts and guilds as a sign of ownership, identification, and differentiation, the purpose evolving from mere protection from stealing, forgery, counterfeiting, and fraud to differentiation with the promise of certain qualities (Keller, 2003). Branding has become a strategic aim as the competition has become fierce in contemporary business life. In many industries, there is almost perfect competition with multiple suppliers of the same or similar products, thus pushing the limits of suppliers to come up with intelligent ways of attracting consumers. The most strategic way of attracting consumers is considered to be distinguishing a product among others by branding, which differentiates the product among many similar others (Aaker, 2001; Keller, 2003). Thus, branding has been a focus of attention, especially for consumer product companies to gain a sustainable competitive advantage (Aaker, 2001).

Marketing and management requires a careful analysis of the brand image transmitted to the market, because it is precisely this image that will affect consumer choice (Dominique & Lopes, 2011). As such, brand management often relies on a medium- to long-term strategy, based on the objectives of the brand (Rial & García Varela, 2008). In the context of modern marketing, brand image becomes a major factor in the success of any organization (Aaker, 1991), and is the result of sensory experiences and internal imitation created by perceptual processes. Keller (1993) defines brand image more succinctly as a set of perceptions about a brand, i.e., the associations that exist in the consumer's memory. Sanz de Tajada (1996) describes image as a set of notes associated spontaneously with a given stimulus which has previously triggered a set of associations that make up a body of knowledge (beliefs) in the consumer.

However, the image of a brand in the market does not always coincide with the image that the company intends to transmit or the actual brand image. As such, organizations tend to consider three different levels for the analysis of brand image:

- The analysis of the perceived image – how the target segment sees and perceives the brand (through a brand image study);
- The analysis of the actual image (strengths and weaknesses), as perceived by the company and based on an internal audit;
- Analysis of the desired image, i.e., how the company wants to be perceived by the target segment.

## The components of brand image

According to Shani and Wang (2012), the study of brand image has a long history, yet it has been acknowledged that the unique characteristics and complexity of the tourism product requires the development of specific conceptual frameworks and methodologies. For example, in the context of destination marketing and management, Gallarza, Gil, and Calderón (2002) stated four main characteristics that represent the nature of destination image: (1) Complex – destination image is a controversial concept with no universally agreed-upon definition or accepted components; (2) Multiple – destination image consists of manifold features that represent its identity, and various interrelated information agents come to formulate the image; (3) Relativistic – designation image is highly subjective and tends to change from individual to individual and is assessed in comparison to other destinations; and (4) Dynamic – destination image is not static but rather likely to change over time and space.

Despite the differences between the various definitions and conceptualizations that have been offered to explain the meaning of brand image, it is generally agreed that it refers to the tourist-based image rather than the marketer-based image (Li & Volgelsong, 2006). It is worthwhile to recognize that what people think about a brand image is strategically more important than what a marketer knows about the brand (Ahmed, 1991, p. 25). The challenge faced by tourism organizations is to bring the image people have in mind as close as possible to the desired image of the brand. Accordingly, various models have been suggested to classify the various types and components of brand image, including the three continuum components model, and the hierarchical model (Shani and Wang, 2012).

## The three continuum components of brand image

Echtner and Ritchie (1991) proposed a conceptual framework for understanding the components of destination brand image. It consists of three image continuums: (1) attribute-holistic; (2) functional-psychological; and (3) common-unique. The first continuum ranges from individual attributes to holistic impressions of a brand image. In other words, some destinations emphasize the individual attributes of the brand image, while others regard brand image as a holistic impression. An example of attribute-based definition of image is "one's perception of attributes or activities available at a destination" (Gartner, 1986), and an example of holistic definition is "the sum of beliefs, ideas, and impressions that people have of a place" (Kotler, Haider, and Rein,

1993). Tasci et al. (2007) state that the former definitions assume high-involvement and piecemeal-based processing on the part of the consumer, who assesses destinations based on attributes and activities. On the other hand, the latter definitions assume low-involvement and category-based processing on the part of the consumer, who does not have the mental capacity nor sufficient information to examine it attribute by attribute, and instead has a Gestalt impression of the destination, based on selected criteria that are relevant to the specific situation. Nevertheless, Echtner and Ritchie (1991) concluded that both dimensions should be incorporated in a conceptualization of a destination image, in order to represent its complexity more accurately and comprehensively.

The second continuum ranges from the functional attributes of an image, which can be directly observed or measured, to its psychological attributes, which cannot be directly measured. Each can be based either on specific traits that are directly observable or on a general impression that represents feelings or aura. Gallarza et al. (2002) summarized the most common image attributes that were utilized, and found that the most used attributes were "resident receptiveness" and "landscape and/or surroundings." The researchers described the traits studied as a spectrum from the most physical (functional) attributes (e.g., activities and nature) to the most abstract (psychological) attributes (e.g., service quality and safety), while some, such as climate and price, fall in the gray area between the two ends.

The third and last continuum in Echtner and Ritchie's (1991) conceptualization ranges from common image attributes, according to which all destinations can be evaluated and compared, to unique image attributes, which are exclusive to the specific destination. Either common or unique attributes can consist of both functional and psychological traits. Examples of common functional attributes often include transportation, infrastructure and accommodation, while frequently-used psychological attributes include residents' friendliness, safety, and quality of service. On the other hand, illustrations of unique functional attributes can be the Taj Mahal for India, the Carnival in Rio de Jeneiro, and the Eifel Tower for France. Unique psychological attributes might include instances such as the image of romanticism for Paris, sacredness for Jerusalem, and mysticism for India.

## *The hierarchical model of brand image*

Gartner (1993), based on the work of Boulding (1956), stated that brand image in the context of destination comprises three hierarchical interrelated components: cognitive, affective, and conative. The cognitive component refers to the knowledge and beliefs about a destination, focusing mainly on its physical attributes. On the other hand, the affective component relates to feelings and emotions about a destination, which are generally neutral, favorable, or unfavorable (Pike & Ryan, 2004). Lastly, the conative component indicates the behavioral intentions in relation to the destination. In other words, "these three components take in what we know about an object (cognitive),

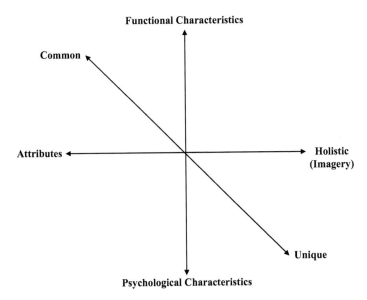

Figure 18.1 The three-dimensional components of destination image (Echtner and Ritchie, 1991).

how we feel about what we know (affective), and how we act on this information (conative)" (Tasci et al., 2007. p. 199). There is a general agreement in the literature, which is supported by empirical evidence, that the affective component is a mediating factor between the cognitive component and the holistic brand image. In other words, the cognitive component is an antecedent to the affective one, while both influence the overall image of the destination (Beerli & Martín, 2004; Lin, Morais, Kerstetter, & Hou, 2010).

While most studies on brand image tend to focus on cognitive image attributes, it should be stressed that the affective image component was found to have a substantial impact on travelers' assessment and selection of tourism destinations (e.g. Yüksel & Akgül, 2007), and thus should be incorporated as an integrative element in the conceptualization of brand image. Moreover, the conative component is also missing in many definitions of brand image, yet it is vital in order to capture the action element in people's perceptions (Tasci et al., 2007). It is suggested that an interactive system of brand image components should be adopted that takes into consideration the cognitive, affective, and conative components. According to Tasci, at the core of this interactive system of components,

> [T]here is cognitive knowledge of common and unique attributes of destination and the affective response toward those attributes. With the interaction between the knowledge of unique and common attributes and feelings toward them, a composite image (holistic or overall) is formed and used by the decision maker to simplify the task of decision making. Assuming the knowledge of common and unique attributes is fact based, the more detailed the core is, the less stereotypical

the holistic synthesis is. This is a dynamically interactive and reciprocal system in which every item could be both cause and effect at any time, and factors cannot be comprehended in isolation; therefore, they should be studied in an integrated manner. Thus, a destination image is an interactive system of thoughts, opinions, feelings, visualizations, and intentions toward a destination.

(p. 200)

## Measurement of brand image

Shani and Wang (2011) argue that in order to conduct effective managerial and marketing activities such as brand positioning and promotion, its image must be accurately assessed. Naturally, the methodology used to measure brand image depends on the way the term is interpreted and conceptualized. Generally speaking, brand image can be measured by applying structured techniques, in which respondents rate a list of image attributes that were specified and incorporated into a standardized instrument (usually on Likert type or semantic differential scale); or unstructured techniques, in which the respondents freely express their perceived images of the brand (Echtner & Ritchie, 1991). By their nature, structured techniques rely on quantitative procedures and statistical analysis, while unstructured techniques are based on qualitative methods such as content analysis, discussions with experts, in-depth interviews, focus groups, integrating questions from a survey, and more (Gallarza et al., 2002).

Traditionally the structured approach was dominant in brand image studies, most likely as a result of their obvious advantages: easier to administrate, simpler data coding, and they offered the ability to apply sophisticated statistical analyses (Echtner & Ritchie, 1991), In addition, structured methods allow the comparison of various destinations across a variety of image attributes included in the survey. On the other hand, the structured approach focuses on general image attributes pre-specified by marketers, and thus does not enable the respondents to state their own impressions regarding the brand. As a result, important holistic and/or unique characteristics of the brand might be neglected. Since unstructured methods measure brand image using free form descriptions, they minimize the researchers' bias in selecting image attributes and yield rich information, and thus are preferable in order to capture the unique and holistic dimensions. Consequently, it is generally agreed upon that a comprehensive investigation of brand image should apply a mixed-methodology approach, that is to say, to incorporate both quantitative and qualitative techniques (Echtner & Ritchie, 1993; Hanlan & Kelly, 2005; Tasci et al., 2007). Broadly speaking, there are two schools that call for applying mixed-methods in brand image studies: the consecutive and the complimentary approaches.

### The consecutive approach

When adopting the consecutive approach, the qualitative phase is initially conducted to elicit the relevant brand image attributes, after which the quantitative phase is applied to measure these attributes in a structured manner (Jenkins, 1999). As an illustration, in the study conducted by Bonn et al. (2005), in order to develop a list of destination attributes to measure the image of the Tampa Bay region in Florida, the preliminary stage included three qualitative methods: (1) using answers from open-ended questions used in an earlier survey among visitors to the region; (2) an expert panel that was formed to assess whether the responses from the previous step were appropriate to represent the image dimensions; and (3) panel and focus group discussions were held with industry and community leaders to gain their perspectives on important image attributes.

Based on the results of this process, the researchers finalized a list of ten attributes that were included in the questionnaire and used in the subsequent quantitative phase. A factor analysis revealed two underlying image dimensions: the service factor (e.g., "ease of getting there" "friendliness of residents," "level of service," "signage," "value of the dollar," and "ground transportation") and the environmental factor (e.g., "variety of things to do," "clean environment," "climate," and "perception of safety"). The quantification of the brand image allowed the researchers to conclude that overall the participants rated the environmental factor higher than the service factor. In addition, international visitors rated both factors lower than domestic visitors, indicating that they had higher service and environmental standards, thus providing important implications for the destination marketers regarding improving these dimensions and emphasizing them in their international marketing campaigns.

## TOURISM AND HOSPITALITY INSIGHTS 18.1
## IMAGE OF CHINA IN THE EYES OF THE INTERNATIONAL TRAVELERS

In measuring brand image, it is important to not only identify the most prominent image components of the brand, but also to examine the relative importance of these components in affecting behavioral intentions. As noted by Lin et al. (2010), more attention should be focused towards discriminating between the roles of the different image components, as they have a different impact on tourists' selection of destinations. For example, Shani et al. (2010) investigated the image of China in the eyes of young international employees in the US. Following the consecutive approach, in order to develop the main study instrument, the researchers conducted several focus group sessions to identify both important common and general image attributes (e.g. pleasant weather and safety) and attributes that are unique to China (e.g. unique historical and cultural attractions, exotic oriental atmosphere, and big and heavily populated). To elicit induced image of China, the respondents also viewed a promotional video that was produced to promote the image of the country. A total of 28 attributes were included in the questionnaire that was used in the quantitative phase. Additionally, a series of behavioral intentions toward China were also investigated, specifically the awareness, desire, likelihood, and interest in visiting China in the future.

**Image 18.1**

Source: https://www.pexels.com/photo/mountains-clouds-historical-great-wall-of-china-19872/

Overall, the results of the study indicated that China was perceived as an attractive destination, exhibiting both cultural and natural qualities, in addition to representations of mixed aspects – on the one hand, traditional oriental images of enormity and exoticism, and on the other hand, modern images of progress and innovation. Nonetheless, the factor of culture and nature tourism was found to have the most significant impact on participants' behavioral intentions. Consequently, the researchers concluded that natural and cultural attributes are the main attractors for visiting the country, and thus should be the focus of promotional campaigns. Despite China's fast modernization, accompanied by the establishment of Western accommodation facilities, shopping facilities, and other tourism infrastructure, the results indicated that emphasizing these attributes is not expected to increase the likelihood of visiting the country. These findings strengthen the suggestion of Li et al. (2010) that "destination managers must develop marketing strategies specific to the character of their specific destinations" (p. 10).

## The complementary approach

The second mixed-method approach in examining brand refers to qualitative and qualitative phases as complimentary rather than consecutive. According to this view, both methods complete each other and are necessary for capturing the entire scope of components of brand image. This approach attributes a higher degree of importance to the qualitative methods than the previous one, which utilizes it only as a means to generate the main research instrument. In this case, the qualitative methods provide insights into image aspects that the quantitative method is unable to reveal, due to its structured nature. Echtner and Ritchie (1993) suggested one of the most popular research frameworks for measuring destination image, using combined structured, and unstructured methods that aim to capture the aforementioned holistic, attributive, functional, psychological, unique and common characteristics of image. According to their suggestion, a list of image items is used to quantitatively measure the common attributes of destination image, both functional and psychological. Additionally, open-ended questions are included in the survey to capture the holistic and unique components of destination image, again along both the functional and psychological dimensions.

### References

Li, X., & Vogelsong, H. (2006). Comparing methods of measuring image change: A case study of a small-scale community festival. *Tourism Analysis, 10*(4), 349–360.

Lin, C.H., Morais, D.B., Kerstetter, D.L., & Hou, J.S. (2007). Examining the role of cognitive and affective image in predicting choice across natural, developed, and theme-park destinations. *Journal of Travel Research, 46*(2), 183–194.

Shani, A., Chen, P.J., Wang, Y., & Hua, N. (2010). Testing the impact of a promotional video on destination image change: Application of China as a tourism destination. *International Journal of Tourism Research, 12*(2), 116–133.

Shani A., and Wang, Y. (2012). Destination image development and communication. In Y. Wang & A. Pizam (Eds.), *Destination marketing and management: Theories and applications* (pp.130–148). Wallingford: CABI.

Source: Youcheng Wang.

# Alternative qualitative methods

It should be noted that when either the consecutive or the complementary mixed method is applied, researchers can employ a wide variety of qualitative methods to elicit DIs. Moreover, in some cases qualitative methods were utilized as the main technique to assess DI, although for the most part they are combined with some form of quantitative investigations (Gallarza et al., 2002). While the typical qualitative methods used in DI are described above, Jenkins (1999) suggested and described other alternative qualitative methods for image construct elicitation: content analysis, free elicitation,

## TOURISM AND HOSPITALITY INSIGHTS 18.2
## DESTINATION IMAGE OF HONG KONG MEASURED BY USING A COMPLIMENTARY APPROACH

Choi, Chan, and Wu (1999) assessed the DI of Hong Kong (HK) among visitors to the island using the three-dimensional image components. The study instrument utilized by the researchers included two main sections. First of all, the participants were asked to state their level of agreement with regard to a series of attribute statements (e.g., "Many places of interest to visit," "Local people are friendly"). These statements were analyzed using statistical procedures, which pointed to the dominant common functional and psychological attributes. The second part of the questionnaire includes three open-ended questions (as specified by Echtner and Ritchie), in which the participants were asked to state the images or characteristics associated with HK, to describe the atmosphere or mood they expected to find in HK, and to list the unique tourist attractions in HK they knew of. The qualitative information was used to assess the holistic images of HK, both functional and psychological, as well as the unique attributes and impressions from the destination.

Image 18.2

Source: https://www.pexels.com/photo/signage-hanging-on-the-street-927485/

Using this method, HK is evaluated positively with regards to the shopping and tourist information, albeit with negative images of crowdedness and stress. Among the unique images of HK are the Peak, the Star Ferry, and the night market. Choi et al. (1999) concluded that the integration of quantitative and qualitative methods in a complementary approach provides a comprehensive DI of HK that could be highly helpful for the destination promoters in understanding its market position.

### References

Choi, W.M., Chan, A., & Wu, J. (1999). A qualitative and quantitative assessment of Hong Kong's image as a tourist destination. *Tourism Management, 20*(3): 361–365.

Echtner, C.M., & Ritchie, J.R. (1991). The meaning and measurement of destination image. *Journal of Tourism Studies, 2*(2): 2–12.

Source: Youcheng Wang.

triad elicitation, and photo-elicitation. Other techniques that were used in research include a sketch map and visitor-employed photography. These techniques are elaborated below, with examples from DI studies.

## Content analysis

Content analysis is a method in which textual information is screened and systematically analyzed to identify patterns and categories. DIs can be inferred from sources such as written information (e.g. guidebooks, newspapers) and visual information (e.g. photos in promotional material). As an illustration, a content analysis was conducted by Xiao and Mair (2006) on articles from 19 English newspapers, in order to analyze China's representation as a tourist destination in the international media. The researchers stated that China has "a paradox of images," as it was depicted with mixed and contrasting images. The negative images of China were associated with issues such as the country's problematic international relations and safety, and the positive images were related to its rich culture and tourist attractions. Based on the study's results, the researchers suggested marketing implications for China's DMO, specifically to emphasize its most positive image dimensions (e.g., culture and outstanding attractions). In addition, it was suggested that in order to correct the more negative aspects, marketing campaigns should highlight the country's growing openness to the outside world and its socio-economic and technological advancements.

## Free elicitation and photo-elicitation

Another qualitative method that was used to assess DI is free elicitation, which refers to word-association. Reilly (1990) demonstrated the usefulness of this technique for DI studies, arguing that it constitutes a fairly simple method that can be used in a variety of survey types (e.g., mail, telephone, and face-to-face interviews). Essentially, free elicitation involves asking participants questions such as "What three words best describe X as a destination for vacation or pleasure travel?" (Reilly, 1999). The recorded responses are then categorized based on similarity, and the frequency of types of responses is assessed to identify the dominant images. This method was advocated by Reilly (1999) since "the responses are sensitive to the subjects' own dimensionalities for constructing an image of the stimulus" (p. 22), in addition to the technique's ability to reflect the lack of a coherent image, when participants cannot respond with clear descriptions. A similar method is photo-elicitation, which also involves presenting photographs of the destination to the participants to investigate their perceptions.

Reilly (1990) empirically investigated the images of the State of Montana, as a whole, among US and Canadian residents, and the Montana Mountain ski area, in particular, among skiers, using free elicitation. The results indicate that the most common descriptors of Montana were its scenic beauty and its large size, while the skiing area elicited descriptions of physical beauty, spaciousness, and enjoyableness. The findings also reveal variations based on the participants' origin, resulting in different marketing implications for different market segments. Accordingly, it was found that respondents from distant areas lacked a clear representation of Montana, in comparison to residents from closer areas. Consequently, Reilly (1990) recommended integrating more informational contents into promotions targeting these areas.

## Triad elicitation

The triad elicitation concept was initially formulated by Kelly (1955), and was adapted to DI studies, as well. On the basis of Kelly's theory, it is assumed that individuals appraise certain phenomena using constructs that are finite and bipolar in nature. For instance, "a tourist might apply the construct 'good value for money' to potential destination A, whereas the contrast 'too expensive' might be applied to destination B" (Coshall, 2000, p. 86). The technique developed to operationalize Kelly's theory is known as the repertory grid approach (RGA), in which elements – represented by names or other symbols – are presented to participants in a series of triads, usually using cards. In the context of tourism, these elements are for the most part tourism destinations or specific attractions. As noted by Jenkins (1999), the participants are asked to evaluate and compare three destinations, and state in what meaningful way two of these destinations are similar and dissimilar from the third. Combinations of three destinations are presented to the participants until no new construct is revealed.

For instance, Pike (2003) applied the RGA to identify important destination attributes for domestic travelers in New Zealand, when they consider going by car on a short vacation. Nine prominent domestic holiday destinations were selected and displayed to the participants in series of three. It was found that the most salient attributes were "lots to do," "within a comfortable drive," "the sea/beach," "water sport," and "good weather." Since the participants' perceptions were akin neither with the views of local tourism practitioners, who were interviewed for the study, nor with attributes used in the literature, Pike (2003) concluded that it is essential to gain the consumer's input directly when defining the salient destination's attributes in image studies.

## Visitor-employed photography

The use of visitor-employed photography (VEP) was advocated by MacKay and Couldwell (2004) as an effective method to communicate the representations of a destination. They stated that "the technique involves distributing cameras to respondents and asking them to photograph aspects of the site that relate to the research objectives" (p. 390) which, in this case, refers to DI elicitation. Since most advertisements and promotions entail the use of pictorial elements, it is suggested that DI studies also incorporate the visitor's visual perceptions of the destination, which can substantially increase the validity of the research. Additionally, understanding the appealing visual elements of a destination in the eyes of the visitors can help assess current pictures used in marketing campaigns and design future projected image.

This method was applied by MacKay and Couldwell (2004) in an image study on a national historic site in the Canadian province of Saskatchewan. Visitor samples were asked to take photos that best represent the site – either positively or negatively. They were also requested to state in their diaries the main theme of each photo, the main motive for taking the photo, and whether the photo represented a positive or a negative image. The analysis revealed two consistent themes that accounted for why respondents took their pictures: "aesthetics," which refers to the tangible facets of the site (e.g., exterior buildings, farming equipment), and "nostalgia," which refers to the intangible elements (e.g., display of a past way of life, personal memories). The researchers concluded that the findings provide evidence that the VEP is a sensitive tool to the multidimensionality of DI since it captures both the site's attributive and holistic images.

## Sketch map

The goal of the sketch map methodology is to comprehend people's mental map, which refers to their knowledge with regard to what is found at a particular location. As noted by Son (2005),

> Mental maps are useful in predicting where people will want to go and what they will want to do when they get there (...) Investigating how well tourists know the areas that they visit, what roads and landmarks they come to know, which areas they want to visit and which areas they consider to be unpleasant, is essential for better understanding of tourists' behaviour and perception.
>
> (p. 280)

This information is necessary in order to gain a proper appreciation of travelers' behavior and perceptions. Son (2005) applied the sketch map technique to assess international students' mental maps of the Australian cities of Sydney and Melbourne. The participants were asked to draw a sketch map of the downtown areas of these cities as they remember them, providing as many details (i.e., paths, districts, and landmarks) as possible. Examples of sketch maps of other locations were provided for illustration. Other sections, aimed at identifying the affective and holistic images of the cities were also included in the questionnaire. The analysis revealed that both destinations are fairly legible cities, while Sydney is perceived as a spatially-dominated city and Melbourne as a path-oriented city. The results also provide useful information concerning dominant landmarks (i.e., buildings, attractions, and monuments) for each city, such as the Sydney Opera House and Queen Victoria building for Sydney, and Nike building and the Parliament House for Melbourne.

## Destination image formation

It is essential for DMOs and tourism managers not only to understand the existing image of their destination, but also to explore the critical factors that influence that image (Tasci, 2011). Such understanding provides valuable information as to the degree of effectiveness of marketing and/or publicity, and assists in decision-making with regard to future marketing campaigns. Owing to the abundance of potential information sources that combine to form a DI, various attempts to classify these sources appear in the literature. To name a few examples, information sources were categorized as (1) symbolic stimuli (destination's promotional efforts) and social stimuli (word-of-mouth communication, including recommendations from friends and relatives); (2) informal (personal) and formal (corporate-based) sources; and (3) commercial, advisory, and social sources (see Choi, Lehto, & Morrison, 2007). Similarly, Phelps (1986) differentiated between primary images, which are based on past experiences, and secondary images, which are based on external sources.

One of the most detailed and cited typologies of information sources was offered by Gartner (1993), based on previous work conducted by Gunn (1972). The typology is presented as a continuum of information agents that act autonomously or jointly to form a DI within the individual. The continuum ranges from sources that are in the full or partial control of destination promoters (overtly and covertly induced) to sources that are much harder to influence (autonomous and organic). Gartner (1993) also stated that the eight formation agents are differentiated along their credibility, market penetration, and destination costs. For example, advertising is often expensive and is characterized by the lowest level of credibility, but also with the ability to reach wide segments of consumers. On the other hand, autonomous and organic sources enjoy high credibility and only imply indirect expenses on the part of the destination, yet market penetration is relatively low as these sources rely on individual communication rather than mass media.

The growing recognition in the significance of DI formation has led to studies that investigate the effectiveness of various information sources to convey the projected image. Investigating the effectiveness of marketing efforts is critical in monitoring whether marketing efforts to enhance DI bear fruit, and in providing stakeholders with

**Table 18.1** Gartner's typology of destination image formation agents

| Information Sources | Description | Examples |
|---|---|---|
| Overt Induced I | Traditional forms of advertising that are generated by destination promoters. | Radio, television, and print media commercials, brochures, and billboards. |
| Overt Induced II | External sources that have a vested interest in marketing the destination. | Travel agents, tour operators and wholesalers. |
| Covert Induced I | Well-known spokesmen who are paid to endorse the destination and participate in advertisement. | Celebrities such as films stars, athletes and fashion models |
| Covert Induced II | Seemingly unbiased sources that are actually influenced by destination promoters to endorse the destination. | Offering familiarization tours for travel writers and other media representatives, to project the desired image of the destination. |
| Autonomous | Genuinely independent sources; mainly news and popular culture. | News reports and articles, documentaries, books and movies. |
| Unsolicited Organic | Individuals who visit or claim knowledge on the destination attributes provide unrequested information. | Voluntary information about vacation destinations generated from conversation with friends or business colleagues. |
| Solicited Organic | Knowledgeable sources without vested interest in promoting the destination provide information on its attributes, in response to explicit requests. | Word-of-mouth information generated from friends and relatives who visited or heard about the destination. |
| Organic | Personal experience | Previous visit to the destination. |

Source: Adapted from Gartner (1993)

reasonable transparency as to the success of tourism organizations' marketing strategies (Govers & Go, 2003). As noted by Shani et al. (2010), since DMOs are often operated and financed through government support, they "are increasingly being held accountable by their stakeholders and selected officials (…) to provide evidence of adequate returns for the often costly marketing expenditures" (p. 3). For example, in an early study that was conducted with an American sample, Bojanic (1991) found that as the level of exposure to advertising increased, the attitudes of the respondents toward a certain south European country were more favorable. Respondents who reported high frequency of exposure to advertising also expressed higher likelihood and interest in visiting that particular destination. It was also noted that the most effective media to reach the target market were newspapers and magazines.

Nevertheless, other studies indicate that the overt induced I sources are not necessarily the ones with the most influence on DI. This is the lower scale of sources as compared to

II – see Table 18.1. The study of Beerli and Martín (2004) revealed that the organic and autonomous sources (e.g., guidebooks), as well as overt induced II sources (i.e., travel agency staff) had positive effects on DI, while induced sources such as brochures and advertising campaigns did not have such an effect. Similarly, Govers, Go, and Kumar (2007) found that advertisements have relatively little importance in the formation of DI, while autonomous and covert-induced information agents such as television, magazines, Internet, books and movies, and organic sources (both solicited and unsolicited) were the most important sources. Finally, Mercille (2005) also discovered that prior to their trip, a substantial number of travelers to Tibet consulted a variety of autonomous sources, such as books, magazines, and travel films (fiction and non-fiction) on Tibet.

These findings call for destination marketers to strengthen their ties with critical distribution channels (such as travel agents), as well as focusing attention on generating positive word-of-mouth communication. Although WOM is regarded as an organic source, Hanlan and Kelly (2004) point to radically new tactics, such as whisper marketing (or in its Internet form, viral marketing), in which opinion makers "plant" positive messages about the destination within specific target markets, to exploit the high credibility of WOM communication. The contemporary shift of focus from word-of-mouth to word-of-mouse has led Shani et al. (2010) to predict that the Internet can "be expected to play an important role for DMOs in the near future, especially in light of the increasing popularity of blogging and online social networks" (p. 118).

## Destination image change

Most DI studies focus on measuring image at a certain point in time. Nevertheless, as noted by Gallarza et al. (2002), image is not static but tends to change over time. Moreover, in most cases people do not formulate a whole new DI, but evaluate information they receive from image agents, based on some existing perceptions they have on the destination. As noted by Tapachai and Waryszak (2000), it is well accepted that "an individual does not face each new stimulus as a completely novel experience but compares the incoming data with prior information or schema stored in memory" (p. 38). Understanding the mechanisms of image change is crucial for monitoring it and adjusting marketing strategies, in response to changing circumstances. Furthermore, destination promoters should not accept the current image as a fixed state, and should apply various activities to improve its weaknesses and maintain its strengths. It should be stressed, however, that an image is slow to change by induced image agents, especially when large entities such as countries or states are considered. Therefore, attempts to alter an image require substantial resources and must be planned for the long term. In addition, promoters should ensure the consistency of the desired image throughout the various information sources that are used (Gartner, 1993).

Several studies were conducted in order to investigate the images of the same destination, over a period of time. For example, Gartner and Hunt (1987) investigated the image of Utah over a 12-year period, and discovered improvements in many of the state's attributes. Similarly, Tasci and Holecek (2007) found improvements in the majority of the image attributes of Michigan between 1996 and 2002, among US respondents, and thus concluded that its overall image had improved. Nevertheless, in both studies the authors raised several potential causes for the image change, while recognizing the difficulty in assessing the exact influence of each cause. More generally, it was suggested that

> [I]n the absence of any catastrophic impact of international importance, image(s) will continue to evolve at a rate contingent on the relative strengths of an area's induced (i.e., advertising or secondary endorsement efforts, etc.) and organic (incidence of travel) factors.
>
> (Gartner & Hunt, 1987, pp. 18–19)

Nevertheless, due to the perceived credibility of autonomous agents, dramatic events that receive wide coverage in information sources, such as news broadcasts, are more prone to generate prompt and drastic change in a DI, at least in the short term. For example, Gartner and Shen (1992) compared the DI of China among US respondents before and after the Tiananmen Square protests in June 1989, where violent confrontations between students and the military resulted in hundreds of dead protestors. The results demonstrated that the incident, which received high attention in the West, led to the deterioration of most touristic attributes of the country, not just the perceptions of safety and security, but surprisingly also unrelated attributes such as service and natural resources.

Note that other studies also showed the harmful impact of negative reporting that covers undesirable facets of a destination. Such situations can include both human-induced security threats (e.g., terrorism and wars) and natural security threats (e.g., hurricanes and diseases) (Timothy, 2006). In the previous decade, natural disasters such as the Asian tsunami and the SARS and the food-and-mouth disease outbreaks, as well as man-made disasters such as the political unrest in Nepal and terrorist attacks in Bali and Egypt, all received wide media coverage and subsequently led to decline in the number of journeys to these destinations (Bhattarai, Conway, & Shrestha, 2005; Henderson, 2007; Uriely, Maoz, & Reichel, 2007). Ahmed (1991) suggested six marketing steps to correct a negative image, which can be applied by using advertising and/or publicity:

1. Capitalizing on the positive images of the component parts – identifying the image components of the destination and emphasizing the most favored ones;
2. Scheduling mega-events – organizing special events (e.g., cultural festivals, sports' contests, food fairs) that attract media attention, for PR purposes;
3. Organizing familiarization tours – inviting key opinion makers that influence tourists' decisions, such as travel writers and tour operators, to experience the destination;
4. Using selective promotion – highlighting the destination's strength and downplaying its weaknesses, in advertising and other promotional campaigns;

5. Bidding to host international travel and tourism conventions – destination representatives should persuade leading travel and tourism organizations (e.g., International Hotel and Restaurant Association; World Association of Travel Agencies) to conduct future conferences at the destination, for the main purpose of getting the industry's attention; and

6. Taking advantage of a negative image – in certain cases destination promoters can spin problematic images into assets.

## Conclusion

Brand image is highly complex and complicated to manage, yet it is one of the most critical factors that determine the competitiveness of the hospitality and tourism industry; thus, brand image should receive high priority on the part of tourism organizations. Generating and maintaining an appealing brand image is more important than ever, as consumers have a wide variety of options to choose from. The worldwide acknowledgment of the economic and other benefits from the tourism industry has led even unknown destinations to seek tourism development, creating fierce competition over the hearts and minds of tourists. Remote and developing countries, which are increasingly seeking recognition as legitimate tourism destinations, have a particular interest in raising awareness and appreciation as to their qualities among potential tourists. Moreover, destinations that share similar attractors (e.g., sun, sea and sand) struggle intensely to differentiate themselves from their competitors, especially in cases where costs of visit are comparable. These challenges require not only the recognition of the importance of brand image, but also the allocation of adequate resources to manage and monitor it.

The current chapter emphasized that the complexity of brand image calls for adopting a comprehensive framework in order to grasp its essence and properly measure it. While most brand image studies focus on the common cognitive and psychological image attributes of destinations, models that depict image components such as the three continuum model (Echtner & Ritchie, 1991, 1993) and the hierarchical model (Gartner, 1993) highlight the significance of taking other aspects into consideration, such as unique and holistic images, and/or the affective and conative components of brand image. Integrating these elements into the image measurements provides a more accurate and comprehensive picture of the representation of the destinations people have in mind. Note that such investigations should also incorporate qualitative research methods to shed light on the aspects of an image that quantitative methods fail to project. Several qualitative methods described in the chapter can be used either solely or jointly with quantitative methods.

Contemporary trends in tourism marketing call for directing more efforts towards understanding the process of image change. This is particularly crucial in light of the considerable sources that are invested by tourism marketers on various types of promotional campaigns. Measurement of brand image changes should be incorporated as an important component in the examination of the effectiveness of marketing activities.

To conclude, this chapter provides a comprehensive review as to the conceptualization, measurement, formation, and change of brand image. The main challenges faced by tourism marketers in effectively managing and communicating brand image are to design and implement comprehensive image assessments, despite the considerable resources that are required, and to effectively monitor and manage the processes of image formation and change. Although brand image study in tourism is relatively young, this chapter's review demonstrates the wide variety of tools and implications that are being generated from the extensive research on the subject.

## REVIEW QUESTIONS

1. What are the four main characteristics that represent the nature of destination image?
2. What techniques are available to measure brand image?
3. For a destination image of your choice, what are those factors or forces that are likely to impact on its future image?
4. Based on your answer to question 3, what strategies do you advocate for a forward looking brand communication strategy?

## YOUTUBE LINKS

### "How Southwest Airlines built its culture"

URL: https://www.youtube.com/watch?v=8_CeFiUkV7s

Summary: Southwest Airlines became one of the world's most honored companies, as proven by the numerous awards, including being named number one in customer satisfaction by the US Department of Transportation, a best place to work by Glassdoor and one of the 100 best corporate citizens by *Corporate Responsibility* magazine. Herb Kelleher, Co-Founder of Southwest Airlines, talked about several ideas through which they have built the culture of employee empowerment that led to the airline's success.

### "Herve Humler, co-founder and president, Ritz-Carlton: ladies and gentlemen, a culture of quality"

URL: https://www.youtube.com/watch?v=mACUOnvSS6c&t=14s

Summary: Herve Humler, co-founder and president of Ritz-Carlton, discussed how their corporate culture and empowered employees enabled the company to provide a high quality of service, which, in turn, brought high brand prestige in the global market as well as high financial performance.

## Acknowledgments

Much of the information in this chapter is based on the following publications: Shani. A., and Wang, Y. (2011). Destination image development and communication. In Y. Wang & A. Pizam (Eds.), *Destination marketing and management: Theories and applications* (pp. 130–148). Wallingford: CABI.

## REFERENCES, FURTHER READING, AND RELATED WEBSITES

### References

Ahmed, Z.U. (1991). Marketing your community: Correcting a negative image. *Cornell Hotel and Restaurant Administration Quarterly*, *31*(4), 24–27.

Avraham, E. (2009). Marketing and managing nation branding during prolonged crisis: The case of Israel. *Place Branding and Public Diplomacy*, *5*(3), 202–212.

Baloglu, S., & McCleary, K. (1999). A model of destination image formation. *Annals of Tourism Research*, *26*(4), 868–897.

Beerli, A., & Martín, J.D. (2004). Factors influencing destination image. *Annals of Tourism Research*, *31*(3), 657–681.

Bhattarai, K., Conway, D., & Shrestha, N. (2005). Tourism, terrorism and turmoil in Nepal. *Annals of Tourism Research*, *32*(3), 669–688.

Bojanic, D.C. (1991). The use of advertising in managing destination image. *Tourism Management*, *12*(4), 352–355.

Bonn, M.A., Joseph, S.M., & Dai, M. (2005). International versus domestic visitors: an examination of destination image perceptions. *Journal of Travel Research*, *43*(3), 294–301.

Boulding, K. (1956). *The image-knowledge in life and society*. Ann Arbor, MI: The University of Michigan Press.

Choi, S., Lehto, X.Y., & Morrison, A.M. (2007). Destination image representation on the web: Content analysis of Macau travel related websites. *Tourism Management, 28*(1), 118–129.

Choi, W.M., Chan, A., & Wu, J. (1999). A qualitative and quantitative assessment of Hong Kong's image as a tourist destination. *Tourism Management, 20*(3), 361–365.

Coshall, J.T. (2000). Measurement of tourists' images: The repertory grid approach. *Journal of Travel Research, 39*(1), 85–89.

Dominique, S., & Lopes, F. (2011). Destination image: Origins, development and implications. *Journal of Tourism and Cultural Heritage, 9*(2), 305–315.

Echtner, C.M., & Ritchie, J.R. (1991). The meaning and measurement of destination image. *Journal of Tourism Studies, 2*(2), 2–12.

Echtner, C.M., & Ritchie, J.R. (1993). The measurement of destination image: An empirical assessment. *Journal of Travel Research, 31*(4), 2–12.

Gallarza, M.G., Saura, I.G., & García, H.C. (2002). Destination image: Towards a conceptual framework. *Annals of Tourism Research, 29*(1), 56–78.

Gartner, W.C. (1986). Temporal influences on image change. *Annals of Tourism Research, 13*(4), 635–644.

Gartner, W.C. (1993). Image formation process. *Journal of Travel and Tourism Marketing, 2*(2/3), 191–215.

Gartner, W.C., & Hunt, J.D. (1987). An analysis of state image change over a twelve-year period (1971–1983). *Journal of Travel Research, 26*(2), 15–19.

Gartner, W.C., & Shen, J. (1992). The impact of Tiananmen Square on China's tourism image. *Journal of Travel Research*, *30*(4), 47–52.

Govers, R., & Go, F. (2003). Deconstruction destination image in the information age. *Information Technology and Tourism*, *6*(1), 13–29.

Govers, R., Go, F.M., & Kumar, K. (2007). Promoting tourism destination image. *Journal of Travel Research*, *46*(1), 15–23.

Gunn, C.A. (1972). *Vacationscape: Designing tourist regions*. Austin, TX: University of Texas: Bureau of Business Research.

Hanlan, J., & Kelly, S. (2005). Image formation, information sources and an iconic Australian tourist destination. *Journal of Vacation Marketing*, *11*(2), 163–177.

Henderson, J.C. (2007). Corporate social responsibility and tourism: Hotel companies in Phuket, Thailand, after the Indian Ocean tsunami. *International Journal of Hospitality Management*, *26* (1): 228–239.

Hsu, C.H.C., Wolfe, K., & Kang, S.K. (2004). Image assessment for a destination with limited comparative advantages. *Tourism Management*, *25*(1): 21–126.

Hudson, S., & Ritchie, J.R.B. (2006). Promoting destinations via film tourism: An empirical identification of supporting marketing initiatives. *Journal of Travel Research*, *44*(4), 387–396.

Jenkins, O.H. (1999). Understanding and measuring tourist destination images. *International Journal of Tourism Research*, *1*(1), 1–15.

Kelly, G.A. (1955). *The psychology of personal constructs*. New York: Norton & Company Incorporated.

Kotler, P., Haider, D.H., & Rein, I. (1993). *Marketing places*. New York: Free Press.

Li, X., & Vogelsong, H. (2006). Comparing methods of measuring image change: A case study of a small-scale community festival. *Tourism Analysis*, *10*(4), 349–360.

Lin, C.H., Morais, D.B., Kerstetter, D.L., & Hou, J.S. (2007). Examining the role of cognitive and affective image in predicting choice across natural, developed, and theme-park destinations. *Journal of Travel Research*, *46*(2), 183–194.

Loda, M.D., Norman, W., & Backman, K. (2005). How potential tourists react to mass media marketing: Advertising versus publicity. *Journal of Travel and Tourism Marketing*, *18*(3), 63–70.

Lubbers, C.A. (2005). Media relations in the travel and tourism industry: A co-orientation analysis. *Journal of Hospitality and Leisure Marketing*, *12*(1/2), 41–55.

MacKay, K.J., & Couldwell, C.M. (2004). Using visitor-employed photography to investigate destination image. *Journal of Travel Research*, *42*(4), 390–396.

Mercille J. (2005). Media effects on image: The case of Tibet. *Annals of Tourism Research*, *32*(4), 1039–1055.

Murphy, L. (1999). Australia's image as a holiday destination – perceptions of backpacker visitors. *Journal of Travel and Tourism Marketing*, *8*(3), 21–45.

O'Leary, S., & Deegan, J. (2003). People, pace, place: Qualitative and quantitative images of Ireland as a tourism destination in France. *Journal of Vacation Marketing*, *9*(3), 213–226.

Pearce, P.L. (1982). Perceived changes in holiday destinations. *Annals of Tourism Research*, *9*(2), 145–164.

Shani, A., Chen, P.J., Wang, Y., & Hua, N. (2010). Testing the impact of a promotional video on destination image change: Application of China as a tourism destination. *International Journal of Tourism Research*, *12*(2), 116–133.

Shani A., and Wang, Y. (2011). Destination image development and communication. In Y. Wang & A. Pizam (Eds.), *Destination marketing and management: Theories and applications* (pp.130–148). Wallingford: CABI.

Tasci, A. (2011). Destination branding and positioning. In Y. Wang & A. Pizam (Eds.), *Destination marketing and management: Theories and applications* (pp. 113–129). Wallingford: CABI.

## Further reading

Chen, J.S., & Hsu, C.H.C. (2000). Measurement of Korean tourists' perceived images of overseas destinations. *Journal of Travel Research*, *38*(4), 411–416.

Connell, J. (2005). Toddlers, tourism and Tobermory: Destination marketing issues and television-induced tourism. *Tourism Management, 26*(5), 763–776.

DiPietro, R.B., Wang, Y., Rompf, P., & Severt, D. (2007). At-destination visitor information search and venue decision strategies. *International Journal of Tourism Research, 9*(3), 175–188.

Fan Y. (2006). Branding the nation: What is being branded? *Journal of Vacation Marketing, 12*(1), 5–14.

Pawitra, T.A., & Tan, K.C. (2003). Tourist satisfaction in Singapore – a perspective from Indonesian tourists. *Managing Service Quality, 13*(5), 399–411.

## Websites

The world's most powerful airline brand? You'll never guess
https://www.telegraph.co.uk/travel/news/aeroflot-most-powerful-airline-brand/

Why branding is as important as ever in the airline industry
https://blog.lsgskychefs.com/spiriant/branding-airline-industry-important-as-ever/

Airline brand strategy
https://www.brandingstrategyinsider.com/airline-brand-strategy

Why Southwest Airlines has the "brand intimacy" major competitors lack
https://www.bizjournals.com/chicago/news/2017/07/26/why-southwest-airlines-has-thebrand-intimacy-major.html

Hotel branding strategy
http://32digital.com/hotel-branding-strategy/

Hotel branding trends
https://www.gourmetmarketing.net/hotel-essentials/hotel-branding-trends/

Hotel branding and marketing tips: how to position your business for growth
https://www.designhill.com/design-blog/hotel-branding-and-marketing-tips/

Build your brand's equity through experiences
https://www.hotelbusiness.com/build-your-brands-equity-through-experiences/

Why place and destination brand strategies fail
http://www.citynationplace.com/why-place-and-destination-brand-strategies-fail

Branding and hospitality: what's your differentiation?
https://www.hospitalitynet.org/opinion/4083490.html

# MAJOR CASE STUDY
# EMPLOYEE BRANDING AT SOUTHWEST AIRLINES

Strong brand service companies purposely utilize their brands to define reasons for their existence, allow their brand images to be internalized by employees, and connect with customers' emotions (Berry, 2000). Southwest Airlines is one such company that builds, develops and utilizes their strong brand to obtain a unique market position in the highly competitive global market. Southwest Airlines has developed into one of the world's most honored and loved brands, as proven by the numerous awards they obtained in 2017: Southwest Airlines was (1) ranked number one in customer satisfaction by the US Department of Transportation, (2) evaluated as the eighth most admired company in the world by *Fortune* magazine, (3) recognized as a best place to work by Glassdoor and (4) named one of the 100 best corporate citizens by *Corporate Responsibility* magazine (Southwest Airlines, 2017). During the five decades since its establishment in 1967, given its strong brand, the company has developed into the world's largest low-cost airline company; it currently operates more than 4,000 flights per day during peak travel seasons in their approximately 100 destination networks in the United States and ten additional countries (Southwest Airlines, 2017). Their success is largely thanks to their competitive brand, obtained by effectively positioning themselves in customers' minds. Based on their extensive research, Southwest found that on-schedule flights with friendly service and low fares were contributing to their customer satisfaction (Ford, Heaton, & Brown, 2001). As such, they have focused on their key concepts of brand image, such as heartfelt, friendly, reliable and low-priced services, to gain their brand positioning. In order to achieve such brand images in their customers' minds, they utilized employee branding, defined as "the process by which employees internalize the desired brand image and are motivated to project the image to customers and other organizational constituents (Miles & Mangold, 2004)."

First and most importantly, the strong and clear Southwest mission and values have contributed to the development of employees' knowledge and understanding of the desired brand image, which can be found on their website: "The mission of Southwest Airlines is dedication to the highest quality of Customer Service delivered with a sense of warmth, friendliness, individual pride, and Company spirit (Southwest Airlines, 2018)." Here, Southwest Airlines focuses on emotional aspects, rather than skill or technology-based aspects of work. They extraordinarily emphasize heart, which translates to caring for their customers as well as employees (Czaplewski, Ferguson, & Milliman, 2001). This explains how far the company has gone to please their customers. For instance, their staff members are renowned in terms of their displays of humor, such as telling jokes and greeting customers by popping out of overhead luggage compartments (Czaplewski, Ferguson, & Milliman, 2001). In addition, interestingly, the foundation of the corporate message emphasizes putting employees first with customers second, expecting, in turn, their employees to extend to their customers the same level of warmth, respect, and responsiveness (Miles & Mangold, 2005). By sharing corporate values that are fun and inclusive, the company has been able to educate their employees about their values and desired brand image as well as motivate them to do their best work to please their customers.

Second, in order to strengthen employees' understanding of desired brand image, Southwest Airlines has sent consistent messages and made every effort to ensure that their messages align with their values and desired brand image (Miles & Mangold, 2005). One example is their advertising and public relations. They utilize these tools in order to not only attract customers, but also communicate their values and desired brand image to their employees. For instance, they introduce stories that focus on how their employees performed heroic acts of customer services, which enables employees to understand their expected level of service (Miles & Mangold, 2005). Customer letters, both good and bad, are also effectively utilized to share their values. For instance, when service mishaps occur, even though service resolutions are made to appease dissatisfied customers and possible solutions are implemented to prevent recurrence, the company doesn't necessarily criticize or penalize their employees (Miles & Mangold, 2005). This manner of dealing with customer issues and employees sends workers an important message: the company put them first, who, in turn, are expected to treat customers as the company treats them (Miles & Mangold, 2005). Recruiting is also a critical component for companies to reinforce their values and desired brand image. The company carefully screens prospective employees in order to ensure that their personal values are consistent with the company's values and desired brand image (Miles & Mangold, 2005): they especially focus on prospective employees' inherent values and attitudes, such as friendliness, sense of humor, and ability to work with others (Czaplewski, Ferguson, & Milliman, 2001).

Last but not least, Southwest Airlines' psychological contract has been playing an important role in order to motivate their employees to project the desired brand image to their customers. This provides employees with the rules about what is expected of them and what they can expect in return (Miles & Mangold, 2005). As Miles & Mangold argue (2005), the fulfillment of employees' psychological contracts has contributed to their high motivation to deliver the desired brand image as well as enhance trust between the company and employees. Furthermore, in order to monitor how well their new employees' expectations have been met (or how well their employees' psychological contracts have been upheld), the company randomly selects and invites them to have lunch with executives (Miles & Mangold, 2005). The company also utilizes these luncheons to obtain improvement ideas in all human resource related processes, including recruitment, selection, training, and orientation (Miles & Mangold, 2005).

Southwest Airlines has obtained their distinctive brand position in consumers' minds through their employee branding. They have consistently and extensively communicated their mission, values, and desired brand image, which has led to employees' knowledge and understanding of the desired brand image (Miles & Mangold, 2005). In addition, upholding employees' psychological contracts plays a pivotal role in gaining a positive emotional connection, which motivates employees to project the desired brand image.

The company introduced new designs, including a new iconic logo, and a new aircraft livery, named "Heart" in 2014 (Southwest Airlines, 2014). Kevin Krone, Southwest Airlines' Vice President and Chief Marketing Officer said, "We already know who we are. The job was to keep the elements of Southwest that our Employees and Customers love, and to make them a bold, modern expression of our future." This was not to change their brand image, but rather symbolize and reinforce that which their employees had already been projecting to customers (Southwest Airlines, 2014).

## References

Berry, L.L. (2000). Cultivating service brand equity. *Journal of The Academy of Marketing Science, 28*(1), 128.

Czaplewski, A.J., Ferguson, J.M., & Milliman, J.F. (2001). Southwest Airlines: How internal marketing pilots success. *Marketing Management, 3,* 14.

Ford, R.C., Heaton, C.P., & Brown, S.W. (2001). Delivering excellent service: Lessons from the best firms. *California Management Review, 44*(1), 39–56.

Miles, S.J., & Mangold, G. (2004). A conceptualization of the employee branding process. *Journal of Relationship Marketing, 3*(2/3), 65. doi:10.1300/J366v03n0205

Miles, S.J., & Mangold, W. G. (2005). Positioning Southwest Airlines through employee branding. *Business Horizons,* 48535–48545. doi:10.1016/j.bushor.2005.04.010

Southwest Airlines. (2014, Sep 8). *Southwest Airlines unveils its new look, same heart.* Retrieved from http://investors.southwest.com/news-and-events/news-releases/2014/09-08-2014-192749904

Southwest Airlines. (2017). *2017 Southwest Airlines one report.* Retrieved from http://southwestonereport.com/2017/about-the-report/

Southwest Airlines. (2018). *About Southwest.* Retrieved from https://www.southwest.com/html/about-southwest/index.html?clk=GFOOTER-ABOUT-ABOUT

Source: Ryuichi Karakawa.

## Major case study questions

1. What role have employees played in the success of the Southwest brand?
2. What are the emotional components of the Southwest brand?
3. How does the recruitment of staff contribute to the overall essence of the brand?

# Customer relationship management
## Loyalty and social networks

## Learning outcomes

By the end of this chapter, students will:

- Understand the importance of building customer relationship programs (in both business-to-business and business-to-consumer contexts); discover the evolution of the tools available from the older tools, that are still used (guest files, marketing databases, etc.) to new tools and processes (big data, artificial intelligence, etc.);

- Appreciate the need for loyalty programs to evolve in order to remain efficient with loyalty programs still widely regarded as key marketing tools;

- Understand the evolution of technology (fast development of digitalized communication and social networks, big data, etc.) and its consequences on the tourism industry, including the expansion of the customer-to-customer relationship and the growth of consumer power.

### Key terms

customer relationship management, loyalty, social networks, loyalty programs

## Introduction

Relationship marketing is presented as a "marketing challenge" for organizations targeting the general public but also business-to-business (B2B) relationships. This marketing approach reflects the evolution of society, technological tools, and marketing practices.

A customer orientation has always been a key concern of hotel and catering business professionals and of tourism professionals. What is a concierge in a luxury hotel? This is a person who holds major responsibilities and whose mission is, with his/her team, to meet all the customers' demands and anticipate some of their expectations. Palaces and luxury hotels have always closely monitored their clients' every whim, gradually increasing their knowledge of each client's profile. If we go beyond this reference to the legendary responsibilities of the Clefs d'Or (the elite professional association of hotel concierges), we need to acknowledge that careful and personalized monitoring of

501

clients is currently occurring on a large scale and in all branches of the tourism and hospitality industry. The tourism industry has been using relationship marketing practices for a long time; these include the airline companies' frequent flyer programs or the reward programs aimed at the loyal clients of hotel groups or car rental companies.

Current marketing policies based upon relationship marketing techniques reflect the evolution of a society that exalts individuals at the expense of groups. Within the new generations, people follow their own path according to each person's wishes and desires. In the world of modern consumption, the challenge of marketing is partly to influence consumers through a relational approach that is based upon closer relations between individuals and the economic entity (company, brand, product, etc.). Accordingly, tourism industry professionals are compelled to use consumer-individualized strategies when designing products, disseminating information, and engaging in commercial communication actions.

To be successful when approaching clients, it is necessary to have access to data that help define the travelers' client profiles. To do so, practitioners use increasingly effective computerized tools to collect, analyze, and disseminate information. They also help to develop marketing techniques such as direct marketing and loyalty schemes. This set of practices forms part of customer relationship management (CRM).

## Information systems in the tourism sector

Information systems are computerized tools designed to collect, use, and disseminate information. In general, they are intended to facilitate and enhance the reliability of organizational decision-making and require endogenous or exogenous data (input) that are stocked, analyzed (creating value), and then transmitted (output) to the different destination depending on the identified requirement. They are used to perform various tasks such as competitive intelligence gathering, macro-environmental monitoring, forecasting, or strategy building. Information systems can be used in the management of reoccurring company transactions (as an example see "PMS in hospitality" below), management tasks (example reporting systems), and decision-making help. More recently, we also talk about "expert" systems (such as artificial intelligence, machine learning, etc.) that often relies on the big data concept, and real-time access and analysis of large volumes of data.

An example of information systems managing reoccurring company transactions is as follows: In the hotel, the PMS (property management system) treats all the customer transactions from bookings to bills. The information systems generate all documents such as bills, and events such as cancelations. All the information concerning the customer is used for the operational management, accounting, and the commercial management (customer relations) of the customer; and are stocked in a data base for future analysis.

*In the marketing sector, information systems serve two major purposes:*

- Gathering competitive intelligence and establishing the marketing and commercial strategy;
- Learning about the company's partners and particularly customers and prospects. The era of empiricism and managers collecting data almost by default is over; hence, computerized tools, namely customer files, databases, and information systems, are now extensively used. Organizations are fully aware of the crucial need to acquire knowledge, analyze, and understand information for any relevant decision-making. However, the managers of small businesses, numerous in the tourism sector, acknowledge that they do not always make the required efforts because they lack the will or, more often, the necessary technical, financial, or human resources. In the tourism sector, computerized tools are brought into play both to process and disseminate tourism information and to use client-related commercial information. Thus, we distinguish two purposes and two types of tools:
- Collecting tourism data and using them through institutional structures and customer information systems. These are the main purposes of tourism information systems;
- Collecting and using strategic and commercial data that underpin organizational decision-making. Among others, these contribute to establishing the company strategy, analyzing the market segmentation, and developing communication and monitoring activities relating to the client relationship, such as direct marketing and loyalty schemes. This is the domain of databases and marketing information systems.

## The tourism information system

The tourism information system is an information system that collects, manages, analyzes, produces, and presents information regarding tourism resources (e.g., accommodation, activities). Hence, it is a database that identifies all or part of the tourism resources in a territory (i.e., the diversity of stakeholders and product types). This information is made available to the territory partners, namely, on the one hand the professionals (e.g., journalists, tour operators, distributors) and on the other the general public, through adapting the contents and the presentation of the resources to the targeted markets and segments.

## The marketing information system

The computerized tools for collecting and processing information may take different forms according to their development level.

- The client file. In its simplest form, the file is a list of names and contact details of clients and prospective clients. It can be enriched with data designed to establish the profile of consumers using behavioral variables related to their tourism practices.

This file is internal when it is designed, developed, and updated by the company. It is external when an organization uses the data marketed by another structure. The latter practice is common during scouting operations in particular. The internal file is mainly used for the analysis of the core target, market segmentation, or retention operations.

- The marketing database. This tool is merely the continuation of the computerized files. Its purpose is to help establish pathways between the different nodes in a company that possesses information regarding its clients. For instance, tour operators composed of a business/marketing division, a reservation center, and distribution agencies need to be able to aggregate all the information they possess on each client at any time. The purpose of this operation is to increase understanding of their client profiles, to avoid duplication of files, to fine-tune commercial propositions, or to standardize communication activities.

- The marketing information system (MIS). It is based upon an overall structured and systematic approach to collect, analyze, and disseminate information. It is a computerized tool but also an information management method that reflects the company's will to give real importance to information processing and control. The goals of a MIS are the following:

  - Identifying the information needs in terms of management levels, information and/or decision types, activity sectors, the information life cycle, etc.;
  - Collecting the information: the collection phase may be ad hoc or ongoing depending upon the various collection sources organizations can tap, such as sales personnel, customer contacts, trade fairs, the press, etc.;
  - Storing and processing the information: storing the data is centralized in a data warehouse; the MIS approach involves both data processing and creating added value to the raw data. Data processing is also called data mining;
  - Disseminating the information: the purpose of the MIS is to allow the company personnel to retrieve raw or processed information depending upon their needs.

Today, companies have access to an almost inexhaustible volume of open data (unstructured data, Cloud, Big Data, etc.). Hence, the same issues that arose at the time of the development of tourism or marketing information systems have come to the fore. These issues are related to data access, storage and analysis, data richness, and the strategic policy issues and the benefits the data can give to those who can use them.

## Convergence of tools and missions

The increasing interrelationship between tools and missions generates tools designed to fulfill all the missions through cross-tabulating tourism and commercial data. It is well to remember that the main types of information systems applied to tourism are the following:

- The tourism information system intended to identify the tourism resources and make them available to the organization's partners, more particularly the general public;
- The marketing information system designed to promote the customer relationship management;
- The reservation system that presents the information related to rates and availability and, in some cases, authorizes business transactions;
- The economic information system destined to observe and analyze tourism activities.

Many organizations responsible for the tourism promotion of a territory seek the integration or simply the interoperability of the various systems. Moreover, organizations do not necessarily share the same missions, and the priorities ascribed to the computerized systems will thus vary. Thus, the reservation center for a local hotel network is designed first to make sales and subsequently, perhaps, to provide tourism information. In general, consumers expect a "good" Internet site to provide both information and operational services regarding distribution and sales.

# Direct marketing

## The goals of direct marketing

Direct marketing is intended to establish direct relationships between tourism organizations and consumers. It is a marketing approach that involves collecting and using in a database individual information regarding a specific target and managing a customized transaction.

## Direct marketing is governed by two central tenets:

- Interactivity: a link is established between the sender and the receiver. Communication is also designed to help consumers or prospective clients contact the tourism business. Overall, all business-related communication is meant to encourage dialogue with the consumers and make it bear fruit.
- Customization: messages are adapted not only to the targeted consumer segment but also to each consumer. The degree of customization can vary. The tourism company that knows a customer's consumption patterns through the information provided in the database can send information and/or commercial propositions relevant to the customer's expectations (e.g., family-oriented accommodation, trips with focused cultural content).

The purpose of direct communication is twofold:

- Disseminating information: for instance, travel producers or distributors send their clients price information and a description of their latest products;
- Getting people to act: for instance, travel producers or distributors send their clients emails informing them of the price reduction for some products. The purpose

is thus to prompt an unplanned acquisition (impulse buying and/or last-minute purchases are on the increase for short stays in particular), to speed up the decision-making process (before competitors propose the same offer), or to steer people towards a product that was not the client's first choice.

Direct marketing has increased considerably over time, which is in part the result of the increased effectiveness of customized business contacts. These contribute to the development of close relationships between companies and their customers. The development of computerized tools has also fully contributed to the growth of direct marketing.

## The channels of direct marketing

Direct marketing actions use specific methods enabling companies to establish a personalized relationship and/or interaction with their clients.

•    Direct mail

The old method of direct marketing involving paper mail sent to post boxes is still being used by companies. Despite its high cost, much higher than that of other vectors of direct communication, mainly because of the costs of production and postage, it accounts for 40% of direct marketing communication budgets. The use of this method is likely to decrease as the younger generations (but also the older ones) are increasingly using electronic media. The use of print media (e.g., paper mail, brochures, catalogues) is also declining year-on-year.

•    Telemarketing

Another historic channel of direct marketing is telemarketing, which has developed owing to reduced costs (e.g., telephone costs, reduced personnel costs when the call center is relocated). Consumers, however, are still viewing business telephone calls made to their home as an invasion of privacy and an annoyance, which does represent an obstacle to the development of telemarketing.

•    Electronic communication channels

Emails, text messages, and other kinds of electronic messages are increasingly being used within relationship marketing and direct marketing activities. All involve text, video, and/or audio documents in digital form. The advantages of this form of communication include a very low cost, numerous digital technical options (e.g., animated pictures, transfer to sites), good visual quality channels, and genuine interactivity. Sending information can be initiated by the tourism organization, but consumers can also register on a mailing list on the company's site. Messages are personalized (e.g., individual letters and commercial offers) or the same for all receivers (e.g., newsletters).

The major phenomenon of this age, the Internet, has crossed all the channel borders and is now accessible (almost) everywhere and on all types of telecommunication devices. Mobile communication channels are growing and becoming dominant. The development of "mobiquitous" tourism involving, for instance, the distribution of tourism information or commercial communication, is part of the powerful evolution of the new forms of communication.

It is essential to remain vigilant, namely:

*   Keeping an eye on technological developments;
*   Understanding how the various customer categories relate to the different communication channels;
*   Determining the relevance of the various types of channels to commercial communication.

For instance, blogs are communication tools developed through individual initiatives. They represent the consumer society of the self where people assert their individualism by personalizing their everyday objects, putting themselves on a stage, or simply sharing their opinions. Tourism industry professionals know the positive or negative effects of word-of-mouth. The information that is distributed on personal websites or blogs (and social networks that are discussed in the next section) may have repercussions on the image and/or the consumption of tourism and leisure services. Just imagine a tourist who is filming a flaw in your accommodation and catering structure, such as a rubbish-strewn beach at the end of the day, contrasting sharply with the photo published in the travel catalogue or posted on the Internet site of the destination! These communication tools, regarded as belonging to the world of individuals, arouse the interest of practitioners. As early as June 2009, Costa Croisières invited eight reference female bloggers to test a cruise on the Baltic Sea and post their comments on their blogs. This type of operation intended to use the comments and opinions of influential bloggers is increasing in

## TOURISM AND HOSPITALITY INSIGHTS 19.1
## VISIT FRENCH WINE

In 2016, Atout France, the public body that is charged with the promotion of France, launched a website/portal for wine tourism "Visit French Wine" in French and in English. In order to communicate with the American clientele, Atout France invited seven bloggers to visit all the French vineyards. On the website www.visitfrenchwine.com/us, the bloggers talked about their experience. ("The best wine tour bloggers are now in our 'Expert Advice' section). This was a very popular idea.")

These examples show that any discussion of direct relationship marketing is closely linked to loyalty issues and increasingly to the notion of information exchange through the Internet and participative communication networks.

Source: Patrick Legohérel.

the tourism sector. Nowadays, bloggers and tourism organizations even have events to develop relationships and business (summit, conferences, and the Travel Blog Exchange – www.tbex.com, or the We Are Travel event – www.salon-blogueurs-voyages.com).

## Securing customer loyalty

### *Objectives*

Loyalty schemes are intended to develop sustainable special relationships with the best customers of companies. Tourism organizations use these programs as part of their customer management practices. For instance, airline customers may enter frequent flyer programs that enable them to accumulate free miles when flying regularly on the same airline. They benefit from various services such as reception lounges in airports or boarding procedures with no waiting time. Regular customers of an airline company or a hotel may also be granted an upgrade (e.g., a room upgrade when checking in at the hotel or going from an economy to a business class seat in an aircraft).

• Loyalty programs

The number of loyalty programs has increased. In the air transport sector, all the airlines, except the low-cost airlines, are offering frequent flyer programs (FFPs). To remain attractive, these programs need to be increasingly "profitable" to customers. For example, several hotel groups have started a double dipping system that enables customers to accumulate both hotel points and airline miles.

• The impact of loyalty schemes

Loyalty schemes are usually reserved for high-spending customers. Companies tend to segment the category of loyal customers, thus instituting differentiated loyalty-building practices. The biggest business benefits are reserved to the best customers. The practice of selective customer treatment has the merit of rewarding those people who contribute the most to optimizing the company's turnover. However, it also runs the risk of causing a "small" frustration to clients who are loyal but not "quite enough" to be granted the most attractive benefits, which then reduces their feeling of being valued.

To make up for this adverse effect and to meet customers' growing demand, hotel groups such as Marriott have decided to speed up access to the higher categories in their reward program and facilitate earning prizes and opportunities. Furthermore, access to the higher categories (going from Silver to Gold to Platinum) has a leverage effect upon consumption. Clients who have reached a particular category and are getting used to all the services and advantages it provides often seek to keep their status, sometimes through overconsumption, in order to reach their annual quota of miles. It is very hard to be refused priority boarding or access to the reception lounge when one was used to these rewards!

## TOURISM AND HOSPITALITY INSIGHTS 19.2
## THE EVOLUTION OF HOTEL LOYALTY PROGRAMS

Hotel group loyalty programs evolve and modify the type of reward scheme for customers. The points reward scheme still exists today but is on the downturn and many places offer advantages instead. For example, the program Hello Rewards (Red Lion Hotel Corporation (RLHC)) offers one free night after seven paid nights as well as other small advantages during the stay, such as free breakfast, or a $5 Uber voucher. The Hilton Honors program, gives points but also offers free WiFi or special member prices.

The new innovative program World of Hyatt, launched at the beginning of 2017, encourages loyal customers to use their points to experience so called "extravagant" or "exceptional" holidays. The InterContinental Hotel Group also offers a rewards scheme in the form of an experience, but during their stay, such as going to a show (or a concert ...).

The loyalty programs, do not neglect the traditional method of rewarding in the form of points. Rather, they tend to integrate the notion of experience more in the promise of a reward for loyal customers.

Finally, there is a generational and context problem. We live in a "now" society, and customers want rewards quickly. Collecting points enables important and loyal customers to be rewarded, but for a majority of customers, and more particularly Millennials, the reward must be almost straight away. They don't want to collect points like their parents did before them.

Source: Frochot I., & Legohérel P. (2018). Marketing du tourisme (4th ed., p. 137). Paris: Dunod.

Loyalty schemes, whose main purpose is to increase sales and turnover, also contribute to the ongoing improvement of customer knowledge. The customer surveys found that the marketing databases provide companies with thorough knowledge of their customers. They are then able to adapt their service offer to each one of their best customers or to homogeneous microsegments of regular high-spending customers.

### Limitations of the traditional loyalty-securing techniques and development prospects

One limitation of an operational nature is that companies have to fulfill their obligations, namely they have to honor their promises and deliver the promised advantages to their customers. For instance, if an airline allows customers to purchase free tickets (through the airmiles, customers have accumulated and won) unrestrainedly, they run the risk of seeing some aircraft take off with too many "free seats" to be profitable. In particular, the airline runs the risk of having customers demand seats that would be sold at the premium price at times of peak demand. Conversely, if the airline applies drastic restrictions to the demand for free tickets (e.g., tickets restricted to specific dates or to conditions that do not correspond to people's purchasing and travel habits),

## TOURISM AND HOSPITALITY INSIGHTS 19.3
## CRM IN THE INDEPENDENT LUXURY HOTEL SECTOR: THE CASE OF L HOTEL IN LONDON

L Hotel (LH) is an independent five-star luxury hotel in London overlooking Kensington Palace and its gardens. The hotel has two restaurants and 394 rooms. The restaurant on the ground floor serves modern British cuisine, while on the tenth floor an authentic Chinese menu is offered with views of Hyde Park and the London city skyline. The hotel's location is a key attraction for customers, being a five-minute walk to High Street Kensington underground station, ten minutes to the Royal Albert Hall, and with Kensington Palace and Hyde Park next door. However, it is LH's service and the long-standing relationships with its guests that have led to the high rate (approximately 43% repeat business) of loyal customers. The hotel has hosted countless high-profile guests from Michael Jackson to presidents such as Vladimir Putin; and as is the case with any regular guests, many of the VIPs appreciate LH's relaxed atmosphere and genuine service. Although it is a luxurious hotel, it forgoes the archetypal high-end, rigid style of service and trains its employees to be friendly and intuitive, always seeking opportunities to unaffectedly engage with their guests.

### Personalized service enabled by CRM aims to enhance customer loyalty

As an independent hotel, LH embraces the freedom to tailor and personalize guest service without adhering to generic brand standards. Employees are empowered to use their own judgments when stepping away from policies and procedures in order to accommodate guests' needs. It is important to LH that all employees, including line staff, are able to distinguish between the rigid requirements behind policies and procedural guidelines which are malleable in order to fulfill any justifiable guest request. In 2016, LH put this goal at the forefront of its objectives, with all departments focusing on a "tailored, personalized guest service." This was predominantly put in place to enhance its customer relationship management (CRM) that aims to enhance customer loyalty as well as to compete with hotel chains' loyalty schemes.

Loyalty schemes often encourage customers to use certain hotels that are part of hotel chains, particularly when all other considerations are equal amongst alternative options. However, they are mostly appealing to highly frequent travelers who accrue enough points/levels to make it worthwhile pursuing. While guests enquire about a loyalty scheme, comparing hotel chains, it has always been considered impractical to implement a loyalty scheme that is predominantly designed to acknowledge loyal guests by offering reward points for independent luxury hotels such as LH. Instead relationships with new and returning guests are developed and fostered through LH the genuine engagement of LH staff and ability to provide a personalized service before, during, and after stays. As earning points and maintaining club levels within loyalty schemes may encourage guests to hotel chains; the genuine and authentic relationships built between guests and all hotel staff encourage loyalty to LH by ensuring that although five-star service is delivered, that "home away from home" feeling is always paramount.

## Putting CRM into practice – royalty rewards program at L Hotel

One of the advantages for hotel chains is the sharing of information collected by their loyalty scheme. Independent hotels have to work harder to obtain information and need to collect it organically by engaging with their guests; one of the foremost ways LH does this is by utilizing its Book Direct campaign. It is a common practice now for hotels to encourage customers to book directly instead of via online travel agents (OTAs). Although OTAs are necessary for independent hotels in terms of distribution, the use of them decreases the hotel's ability to build and manage relationships with its guests. Book Direct was chiefly born out of the need to decrease yearly commissions paid to OTAs; however, it quickly became about much more. LH began rewarding guests who booked directly with complimentary upgrades and early check-ins/late check-outs upon availability, and a welcome amenity from a limited selection (including wine, beer, fruit, and movies). LH was also able to engage with guests to deliver a higher level of service by obtaining estimated times of arrival and purposes of their visit. A year after its launch, Book Direct was evaluated and revamped into the current campaign "Royalty Rewards." It was launched late 2017 with new marketing initiatives, including the new tag line "for a stay as unique as you are." Beyond the tangible changes to both customers and staff, there was a clear change in the driving force behind it. Having significantly decreased commissions, the once supplementary benefits of getting to know guests better, became Royalty Rewards' raison d'être.

Guest Services also went through a major transformation in 2016, becoming the axis of managing customer relationships via tailored, personalized guest service. Luxury customers do not solely rely on traditional factors such as price and location in selecting a hotel, and instead are looking beyond impeccable service towards gaining experiences from their hotel stays. Guest Services launched several initiatives at LH in 2017 for the purpose of providing said experiences and building relationships with its guests. An extension of Royalty Rewards launched in October 2017 was "One Guest, One Day," where Guest Services began celebrating a guest of the day each week, exclusively selected from Royalty Rewards guests. As much as it is about "wowing" the guest, it is about creating and encouraging a hotel culture that lives and breathes tailored, personalized service.

## Training and development of L Hotel staff centered on CRM practices

Training on the importance of CRM exists at every level at LH, from staff completing induction through to senior executives. Its 'Distinctive Service' training program is compulsory for staff and includes a segment lead by Guest Services about engaging, delivering personalized service, and maintaining relationships with guests. Recently, LH's reservations department received additional training encouraging stories to be collected about guests, and, as a minimum, find out the purpose of their stays. Guest Services were able to utilize the information found to provide tailored welcome amenities, ensure rooms were ready on time, and greet each guest with a deeper understanding of their needs. Policies and procedures were amended hotel-wide to ensure consistent compliance with and understanding of LH's new ethos. It merely required minor amendments to procedures that encouraged genuine engagement, intuition, and flexibility, which consistently placed the customer at the center of all interactions.

Also, in place at LH are "Guest Profile Cards," which are kept back of house throughout the hotel on which staff can write down any information they find about the guest. Guest Services sort through them to find ways they can enhance guests' stays and then liaise with the staff who wrote them to encourage collaborative efforts in tailoring guests' staying experience. These cards have helped manage relationships with loyal customers as all the information is stored in the hotel's customer database. This allows LH to continually update profiles each stay and thereby consistently exceed customers' expectations upon their return by staying in tune with their evolving needs. Although there are many ways to manage customer relationships, the aforementioned personalized CRM efforts have proven to be effective and have been well received by both new and repeat customers of LH.

Source: Charlotte Reed and Xuan Lorna Wang, University of Surrey, UK.

consumers then see the loyalty program advantages as a misleading trick. The desired goal (i.e., satisfied and regular customers) is not reached, and the commercial technique may even backfire; feeling betrayed, customers can then spread a poor image of the company. Hence, tourism organizations need to find a good balance between an attractive commercial offer that fosters loyalty and the feasibility of giving customers the promised benefits.

Developing customer relationship management practices is currently a key issue in the various sectors of the tourism industry in terms of both technical concerns (tools, compatibility, services on offer, etc.) and the commercial solutions to be selected.

### Digitalized communication (Internet, social networks, apps, etc.)

The development of the participative web and social networks has modified marketing approaches: the participative web is associated with intermediation/information and comparison of stakeholders and tourism territories. Web 2.0 and social networks are drivers of new relational approaches between organizations and tourists and between consumers.

Internet users move from being passive consumers of information to active creators of information. They can produce and share texts, photos, etc. This is what is known as user-generated content. The tools available are much simpler than before (e.g. wikis, blogs, and social networks). In the tourism sector, the content of such posts involves notices, advice, and tips that travelers worldwide exchange regarding the destinations, good places for accommodation and catering, and the tourist traps to avoid. Web 2.0 enables people to share information on an unprecedented scale. The various principles conveyed by the digital channels and social networks entail the notion that knowledge has to be shared and often, that information provided by an Internet user is more trustworthy than that provided by a supplier. After about 10 years of intense Internet development, digitalized communication and social networks, C2C relationships have become a major phenomenon, upsetting company and organization habits, and dominating all kinds of relationships in the tourism context.

Today, marketing needs to take into account consumers' desire to become fully involved in making purchase decisions. Hence, tourism industry professionals enter into a participative client relationship whereby they have to take tourists' opinions into account while being as transparent as possible.

Practitioners are fully aware of the importance of the information that is traveling on the Internet and social networks. Contact areas are available to customers on the operators' websites, but tourism companies are increasingly opening areas on social networks to capture the information sent by consumers. Some of these sites are managed publicly and in a transparent manner by the companies. Internet users may communicate with one another and with the company, knowing full well what the issues are. The goal of tourism operators is to maintain contact and a privileged informal relationship with their customers. The tool thus falls between a direct marketing method intended to secure loyalty and a more traditional communication activity when, for instance, a specific product offer is made to fans and friends through a Facebook page.

## TOURISM AND HOSPITALITY INSIGHTS 19.4
## SOCIAL NETWORK ADVERTISING BY CUSTOMERS

The guide *Forbes Travel*, announced at the beginning of the year the rating of photos most seen on their Instagram account. These photos or videos are taken by "followers" all over the world during their stay in all types of hotels. At the beginning of 2017, the rating of the "best photos" resulted in a French hotel "La Résidence de la Pinède" in Saint Tropez, also known for its restaurant, taking first place in front of big group hotels in Paris, New York, or other well known-places. The photograph showed a beach owned by the hotel in the background and a Mediterranean countryside, which seemed to have been a significant source of inspiration for many Instagram followers, potential travelers, and customers.

Source: Patrick Legohérel.

Other sites/dialogue areas are also managed in a transparent manner, but this time, by customers. Comments (both positive and negative) and pictures are posted freely, without any obligation to mirror the company's official statements. These comments constitute a rich source of information; each customer becomes a "mystery customer" who shares his/her opinion with a whole community.

Many tourism operators elect to make contact with consumers by opening their own pages and dialogue areas on social networks; they are determined to "be present" and to develop a sustainable close relationship with them. They believe that consumers/Internet users are likely to be more receptive to communication with a company on a Facebook page than to receiving a commercial email or paper mail.

Hence, the community and participative web is of considerable importance for the development of close relationships with consumers. Other benefits include its free-of-charge character, its capacity to identify a database of interested users, its contribution to reinforcing the positioning of the company's official web page, etc.

Destinations and official institutions follow suit: numerous national tourism offices and French destinations are present on Facebook and Twitter. Many tourism organizations use social networks with a view to developing their client relationship. The Côte d'Azur Regional Tourism Committee (CRT) is a case in point as evident in Tourism and hospitality insights 19.5.

## TOURISM AND HOSPITALITY INSIGHTS 19.5
## SOCIAL MEDIA MANAGEMENT: WHEN RELATIONSHIP MARKETING BECOMES LEVERAGE FOR TOURISM PROMOTION!

### Strategic framing

The emergence of Web 2.0 has changed the Internet into a vast space for free speech, which, in the tourism sector, has generated a new phenomenon, namely customer-to-customer (C2C) communication: tourists speak to tourists. Recent years have been marked by the advent of social networks such as Facebook, Twitter, Google+, Instagram, YouTube, to name but a few, with over 1.7 billion users worldwide.

More than ever, e-reputation control is at the heart of the concerns of tourism destination managers. To meet these new marketing challenges and adapt to the changing tourism behaviors (e.g., the overriding power of recommendations and experience sharing), since 2012, the Côte d'Azur RTC has incorporated the social web at the heart of the Côte d'Azur marketing strategy, thus making think social become Think Côte d'Azur!

Today, the appeal of destinations is not based on what institutional bodies can say about them, but rather upon what tourists and Internet users say about them. Thus, the Côte d'Azur RTC is firmly positioned within the framework of multi-channel communication and relationship marketing through optimizing its presence on social networks and collaborative platforms. At the end of December 2013, 170,000 members followed the Côte d'Azur on 2.0 channels; 45% of them were foreign members. With nearly 100,000 new "Côte d'Azur fans" for the year 2013, the Côte d'Azur networks have increased by a phenomenal +134%.

On both national and international levels, the new communication channels strengthen the ties between the Côte d'Azur brand – a destination representing almost 1% of international tourism – and its ambassadors, whether local inhabitants or tourists.

Within this approach designed to consolidate the destination visibility and notoriety, Internet-using tourists have become tourism-promoting actors and Côte d'Azur ambassadors among their friends and networks. A recent survey conducted with the Côte d'Azur Tourism Facebook community shows that 48.6% of respondents see themselves as "absolutely" promoters of the Côte d'Azur among their friends and networks.

## Focus upon the Côte d'Azur social media management strategy on Facebook

Facebook is the social network that incites traveling! Fifty percent of Facebook users say they are influenced by their friends' holiday photos when selecting their holiday destination.

The pages of Côte d'Azur Tourism and Côte d'Azur Mountains account for 80% of the Côte d'Azur members. The RTC has set up a specific Côte d'Azur social media management strategy on Facebook, focusing the destination positioning on eight key points:

1. Capitalizing on the "Côte d'Azur" brand image: creating desire in all seasons!
2. Relying on a successful editorial strategy: selecting high added value content, harnessing the power of the image, emphasizing "exclusivity," geolocating activities, etc.
3. Creating sympathy for the destination: humanizing the relationship and encouraging the spirit of belonging.
4. Highlighting the top contributing fans: photo of the week, monthly top fans.
5. Emphasizing experience sharing: securing loyalty, optimizing the power of recommendation!
6. Using viral applications to increase the audience: competitions, quizzes, instant wins, etc.
7. Developing partnerships with Côte d'Azur stakeholders: sponsorships, games, exclusive deals, etc.
8. Listening, assessing, and self-examining.

A successful community is a committed community. Each Côte d'Azur fan is seen as an opportunity and major opinion leader among his/her friends and networks.

The Côte d'Azur RTC has established several operations designed to foster individual and emotional experience sharing and to reward the loyalty of the highest contributing fans:

- The image, leverage tool for tourism promotion! Launching the operation "Côte d'Azur tourism photo of the week" – with over 6,500 fan photos shared in 2012 and almost 9,000 during the year 2013, every Friday, the Côte d'Azur RTC shares a Facebook album, "The Côte d'Azur seen by its fans." The principle is straightforward: The photo registering the highest number of "likes" is selected the following week to be the official cover page of Facebook Côte d'Azur.

- Highlighting our top contributing fans! In October 2012, the Côte d'Azur RTC launched the operation "Côte d'Azur Tourism top fans." Each month, the most active fan is rewarded for his/her commitment within the community. The fans' "liked" contributions, comments, and "shares" enable them to accumulate points. The fan who has scored the highest number of points at the end of the month wins the special offer from one of the prestigious Côte d'Azur Tourism sponsors.

Patrick M.: This page is a real treat every day, thanks to all of you who post such superb photos! Thank you all, photographers and sponsors, you inspire us in the best possible way! Thanks again to the RTC team who know how to push the right button to make this page live in the best possible way!

Marie-Noëlle A.: Côte d'Azur Tourism moves well ... I love this approach! (...) Thanks to the team and of course the sponsors who take up the challenge (...) As they say, let the best one win (...) although (...) they are all so beautiful!

Choni G.: A superb initiative and wonderful incentive to all amateur photographers.

- Rewarding our fans' loyalty: launching the Côte d'Azur Tourism "special offers." A straightforward principle: offering our fans exclusive benefits through a personalized and limited coupon system. *Seventy-three point five of our fans are very interested in this scheme!* This scheme has been set up so that Côte d'Azur Tourism fans can become our preferred customers!

- 2014: a Côte d'Azur seduction campaign through the Chinese social media! Through setting up a dedicated digital and partnership-based strategy, the Côte d'Azur RTC seizes the opportunity offered in 2014 by the 50th anniversary of Franco-Chinese diplomatic relations to promote the destination through the Chinese social media. China is a fast-growing tourism market and represents an attractive target for the Côte d'Azur, particularly through its low season potential.

## The Côte d'Azur operation is based upon the following goals

- Developing the visibility and image of the destination and its partners on the Chinese web and social web to create a strong Côte d'Azur digital presence!

- Using social media to attract and develop people's interest for the destination by stimulating booking for individual stays on the Côte d'Azur outside the summer season;

- Using partner agencies selling Côte d'Azur products;

- Developing and securing a Côte d'Azur loyal fan community that is influential and committed and collaborating with it;
- Learning about the behavior patterns of Chinese travelers and collecting information regarding their expectations and areas of interest through careful monitoring.

## The strategic pillars of this operation are as follows

Pillar 1: Driving and coordinating a high-end Côte d'Azur social media management strategy through the Chinese platforms Sina Weibo and TripShow > brand strategy, brand content, and showcasing partner commercial propositions. Creating a dedicated mini-site.

Pillar 2: Magnifying the Côte d'Azur image and notoriety through two social web digital campaigns, using the viral effect of the games and competitions in partnership with the Emirates Company and the Côte d'Azur tourism stakeholders (both institutional and professional) and organizing a Côte d'Azur fan trip in the context of the Golden Week 2014 for the four winners of the competitions.

Image 19.1

Pillar 3: Securing customer loyalty and extending the viral effect through organizing two Côte d'Azur offline travel meet-up sessions in Beijing and Shanghai with influential and active Chinese fans.

This 2014 campaign illustrates both the objective of the French Riviera, CRT Côte d'Azur, to target international travelers, including Chinese visitors, and to rely more and more on social media and digital tools to promote the destination. Another example is one of the latest campaigns, when the city of Nice had been facing terrorist attack on July 14, 2016. After this sad period, a new campaign was needed to rehabilitate the image, and the strengthen confidence of regular tourist and new visitors. Again, digital tools and social media have been considered as efficient tools, with bloggers, Instagrammers, YouTubers etc., posting and forwarding messages and photos.

#COTEDAZURNOW
https://www.youtube.com/watch?v=7pzb97rbttc

**Image 19.2**

Source: CRT Côte d'Azur France – Groupe ComPlus.

Source: Nathalie Dalmasso, Digital Communication Officer, Côte d'Azur CRT. In Frochot I., & Legohérel P. (2014). *Marketing du tourisme* (3rd ed.). Paris: Dunod.

# Conclusion

The development of social media has achieved deep-seated and lasting change in the relationships between consumers and practitioners and among practitioners. Disintermediation, commonly related to the disappearance of traditional stakeholders, such as the concrete representations of national tourism offices or travel agencies, is one of the direct consequences of this evolution. For instance, destinations are no longer seeking to develop, in their new markets, relationship marketing and promotion based upon communication with both prescribing practitioners (tourism offices and travel agencies, journalists, etc.) and consumers.

The contribution of communication through computerized networks, in both its traditional (Internet-based) and evolving (social networks, apps, etc.) forms, has changed the rules of the relationship marketing game in a significant and sustainable manner.

## REVIEW QUESTIONS

1. What is the importance, for a company, of building a successful and strong relationship with customers?
2. To what extent have digital communication, and related tools (including blogs, social networks, etc.) impacted customer relationship management?
3. Are loyalty programs still relevant marketing tools across the tourism and hospitality industry?
4. What are the challenges a company may be facing when developing a CRM program at an international level, and for a large hotel group?

## YOUTUBE LINKS

### *"Hotel loyalty programs – are they worth getting locked into?"*

URL: https://www.youtube.com/watch?v=zzxTEv8t0-E

Summary: Hotel loyalty programs have become very popular with chain hotels. They offer various incentives to encourage you to lock yourself into staying with them on an ongoing basis. But are they really offering you any savings over the long-term?

### *"Hotel rewards program: which is the most generous?"*

URL: https://www.youtube.com/watch?v=mHhtuEW0oyY

Summary: WSJ "Middle Seat" columnist Scott McCartney reveals the results of his annual study of hotel rewards programs. He and Lunch Break host Tanya Rivero discuss the most generous programs and the vast differences among numerous hotel companies.

## FURTHER READING AND RELATED WEBSITES

### Further reading

Boulding, W., Staelin, R., Ehret, M., & Johnston, W.T. (2005). A customer relationship management roadmap: What is known, potential pitfalls, and where to go. *Journal of Marketing, 69*(4), 155–166.

Dev, C.S., & Ellis, B.O. (1991). Guest histories: An untapped service resource. *Cornell Hotel and Restaurant Administration Quarterly, 32*(2),29–37.

Fan, Y-W., & Ku, E. (2010). Customer focus, service process fit and customer relationship management profitability: The effect of knowledge sharing. *The Service Industries Journal, 30*(2), 203–223.

Gupta, S., Hansenns D., & Hardie, B. (2006). Modeling customer life-time value. *Journal of Service Research, 9*(2), 139–146.

Lo, A.S., Stalcup, L.D., & Lee, A. (2010). Customer relationship management for hotels in Hong Kong. *International Journal of Contemporary Hospitality Management, 22*(2), 139–159.

Marshall, N.W. (2010). Commitment, loyalty, and customer lifetime value: Investigating the relationships among key determinants. *Journal of Business and Economics Research, 8*(8), 67–85.

Payne, A., & Frow, P. (2005). A strategic framework for customer relationship management. *Journal of Marketing, 69*(4), 167–176.

Rosman, R., & Stuhura, K. (2013). The implications of social media on customer relationship management and the hospitality industry. *Journal of Management Policy and Practice, 14*(3), 18–26.

Sigala, M. (2005). Integrating customer relationship management in hotel operations: Managerial and operational implications. *International Journal of Hospitality Management, 4*(3), 391–413.

Siu, N.Y-M., Zhang, T. J. F., Dong, P., & Kwan, H-Y. (2013). New service bonds and customer value in customer relationship management: The case of museum visitors. *Tourism Management, 36*, 293–303.

Stockdale, R. (2007). Managing customer relationships in the self-service environment of e-tourism. *Journal of Vacation Marketing, 13*(3), 205–219.

Vogt, C.A. (2011). Customer relationship management in tourism: Management needs and research applications. *Journal of Travel Research, 50*(4), 356–364.

Wang, X.L. (2012). Relationship or revenue: Potential management conflicts between customer relationship management and hotel revenue management. *International Journal of Hospitality Management, 31*(3), 864–874.

Weizhong, J., Dev, C.S., & Rao, V.R. (2002). Brand extension and customer loyalty. *Cornell Hotel and Restaurant Administration Quarterly, 43*(4), 5–16.

### Websites

TBEx marketplace
www.tbex.com

The social travel summit
www.thesocialtravelsummit.com

Visit French Wine
www.visitfrenchwine.com/us

Enjoy the Côte d'Azur and the Paris region day and night #Francebynight
www.youtube.com/results?search_query=cote+d%27azur+crt

## MAJOR CASE STUDY
## SODEXO: DEVELOPMENT OF A NEW CUSTOMER RELATIONSHIP MANAGEMENT (CRM) PROGRAM FOR B2B ACTIVITIES

Founded in Marseille in 1966 by Pierre Bellon, Sodexo is the global leader in services that improve quality of life, an essential factor in individual and organizational performance. Operating in 80 countries, Sodexo serves 75 million consumers each day through its unique combination of on-site services, benefits and rewards services and personal and home services. Through its over 100 services, Sodexo provides clients an integrated offering: from food services, reception, maintenance, and cleaning, to facilities and equipment management; from Meal Pass, Gift Pass, and Mobility Pass benefits for employees to in-home assistance, child care centers and concierge services.

Recently, Sodexo On-site Services decided to go through a client relationship management program with the objective to use the same system across all countries and all segments for our

B2B activities. This global initiative was necessarily sponsored by the CEO at group level. Many challenges arose from the idea to the implementation as some countries already had a tool while others didn't have anything.

Why deploy a CRM in a company like Sodexo? What does the CRM bring for a mostly B2B company?

- It enables us to centralize information on clients, and more importantly on prospects: Who is their current provider? What is the potential size of the business? What activities have been conducted with them? Historic information is stored over time and accessible to sales teams spread across different geographies. For instance, when our Business Developer talked to our global client Total, she could almost instantly share our penetration rate with them, including a breakdown by country and type of site (platforms, offices, refineries) and the range of services we were already delivering. This helped us open conversations on how we could standardize our service delivery for them and increase our penetration.

- It helps move away from a reactive approach to a proactive approach. Today, we tend to only respond to tenders when requests for proposals are released. With the CRM, we can now track our opportunities at the beginning of the sales funnel, prioritize the time of sales teams on selected clients, and anticipate the work required to understand customers' expectations and establish trust-based relationships. Overall, we need to improve our current hit rate of 33% to 50%.

- It provides information not only on the company but on the client contacts themselves: we are now able to record our Web of Influence, i.e., decision makers and influencers who will help us grow and retain the business. We have evolved away from business cards piling up on a desk, at worst, or at best Excel sheets (with no version control and inevitably outdated positions or email addresses) to real-time information. More details like areas of interest or response to satisfaction surveys and links to the LinkedIn page of the contact or the Outlook-synchronization function have helped our staff become more efficient and trigger new types of conversations with our client counterparts.

- We can measure the performance of the sales and operations teams with automated metrics and graphs (hit rate, average size of a deal, development rate, etc.). Standardized dashboards have been developed and will trigger bonuses/incentives.

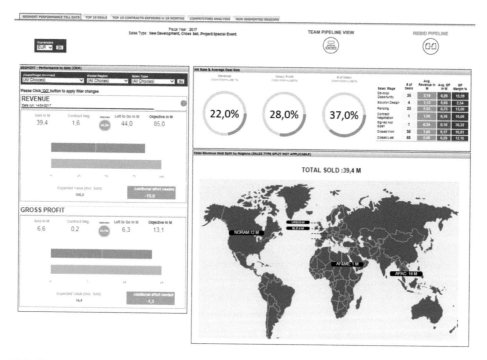

**Figure 19.1  Example of a sales dashboard at global level**

What were the main challenges encountered during the implementation of the CRM?

- *Integration with other systems:* The more we develop the CRM, the more we need to link it to other systems and integrate additional fields (marketing, legal, finance, HR, HSE, operational excellence, etc.). We need to keep it simple so we do not create a monster (what the French would call a "gas factory"). We also need to ensure that the people who ask for additional functionalities understand they are accountable for inputting data (and not expect sales and operations teams to be input everything for everyone).
- *Customization:* how do we balance the need for a global tool while taking country and client segment specificities into account? Here again, we needed to be simple. We made sure that we could get rid of a "my business is different" mindset to think first about similarities and

common objectives/priorities. As a result, we have been able to harmonize the CRM fields and improve consistency in the way we talk about clients and Sodexo services, while leaving just one section open for segment-specific attributes.

- *User adoption:* This is the main challenge because we all know that old habits die hard. At the beginning of the process, old Excel sheets and user-specific templates continued to show CRM date and reporting tended to remain outside of management and business reviews.

    - We need to avoid duplication of work by rationalizing tasks so that using the CRM doesn't add up to the sum of existing tasks and contributes to eliminating unnecessary tasks. As an example, key data such as the "contract end date" used to be entered in four or five different systems (for finance, operations, legal, procurement, etc.). Now the CRM is the one-stop reference for such information.

    - Leadership involvement is mandatory. Top managers need to push their teams to use the system, by making sure, for instance, that their own direct reports set the example. A basic rule which worked well to boost user adoption: consider that "what is not in the CRM doesn't exist," which means that updating the tool has to become a daily business practice. On the other hand, if information is requested by "the boss" that is supposed to be stored in the CRM, the user should systematically refer to it in all appropriate situations.

    - Finally, we have to continuously highlight the value of the tool through appropriate communication and more importantly results: with time, teams will understand that we don't only ask them to "feed the beast" with data but that they

    - will actually get something out of it. Again, developing the right dashboard is critical. Sharing success stories on how consistent use of the tool is paying off is also very important.

In conclusion, it's worth mentioning that the CRM in itself is just a tool. It is only one brick in Sodexo's transformation journey towards improved client-centricity, profitable growth and higher retention. It is embedded in our larger 'Boost our Sales Culture and Effectiveness' initiative which focuses on improving soft skills and revisiting our behaviors.

The B2B component will be enriched by a B2C-oriented CRM program. Sodexo's Quality of Life positioning requires us to focus not only on the buyers of our services but also on the end-users, our consumers. We are already inducting some B2C pilots in Australia, for example. Needless to say, this will be another exciting chapter of Sodexo's CRM deployment and we will draw on the lessons learned from past rollout phases.

Source: Jean-Jacques Laham, Client Relations Manager, Sodexo Energy and Resources.

1. What have been the challenges faced by Sodexo when developing the CRM program, in terms of new managerial and day-to-day practices?
2. What are the lessons learned from the development of a B2B CRM system, when it comes to further develop a B2C CRM program?
3. What have been the challenges faced by Sodexo when developing the CRM system on an international scale, and some markets/places already having their own local tools?

# Channels of distribution

## Learning outcomes

By the end of this chapter, students will:

- Understand the dynamics of travel distribution and the extent to which it is re-shaping the tourism and hospitality industry
- Be introduced to the specific functions of travel distribution intermediaries
- Understand the system and structures of distribution channels
- Understand conflicts in the distribution system
- Understand the emerging role of information and technology in distribution channels.

## Introduction

A marketing channel (also known as a distribution channel) is a system making the product of the company (producer) available to consumers. In other words, a distribution channel takes the product(s) and/or service(s) as an input and transfers it in an available (accessible) state to customers and delivers the outcome to the customers in their convenient space, place, and time. This process is also known as product delivery. Product and service delivery is an important part of any marketing activity regardless of the product or service attributes. The delivery concept's importance is reflected in the core toolbox of the marketing mix by including "Place" as one of four Ps (i.e., product, price, place, and promotion).

In a broader scope, the distribution channel is part of supply chain management (SCM). SCM in a company has upstream and downstream partners, which together with the company shape the value delivery system of the company. Distribution channels are mainly related to downstream partners. These partners are basically intermediaries or middlemen that complete the delivery process between producer(s) and customers. Wholesalers and retailers are two major types of intermediaries that can be distinguished based on their distance from customers/producer(s) in a way that wholesalers are closer to producers whereas retailers are closer to customers. The influence of distribution channels is not only limited to the realms of product and service delivery in that the cost of delivery is a large portion of the total cost for the final goods and services. Adding a distributor (wholesaler or retailer) to the marketing channel, reduces the number of transactions in the network of distribution channels which, in turn, results in a lower cost of product or service delivery. For example, if there are 100 hotels in a city capable of hosting conventions and events, and 1,000 meeting planners looking for contracts with these hotels, there are 100,000 transactions. If each transaction costs $100, then the total cost of the marketing channel is $10 million. In this scenario, if we add one distributor like a convention and visitor bureau (CVB) that all hotels and meeting planners use for the transactions, the total number of transactions becomes 1100 which for $100 each, the total cost of the marketing channel reduces to $110,000 (98.9% reduction in cost). As it is seen in the example, a well-designed, well-operated, well-maintained channel plays an essential role in adding value to customer-company transactions by reducing the cost of transaction. Reducing the cost of transactions is only one of the functions of distribution channels. The rest of the functions are discussed in the next section.

Distribution channels can be described from length and width viewpoints. Channel length in its shortest form is a zero-level channel (also known as direct channels) followed by a one-level channel which a retailer or a wholesaler serves as an intermediary in between producer(s) and customers. A two-level channel is a system that includes both wholesalers and retailers in between producer(s) and customers. According to some resources, there is also a three-level channel that has jobber(s) in between wholesalers and retailers. In each level, multiple firms might be involved. For example, in a one-level channel, a fast food restaurant might have franchised 1,000 retailers in different metropolitan areas around the US. The number of intermediaries in each level, indicate the level of intermediation of a specific marketing channel. On the other hand, channel width refers to the intensity of distribution channels' activities in the system. Three strategies are common when defining the intensity of the activities: exclusive, selective, and intensive. In an exclusive strategy, a company is presented through its exclusive channels to which no other company has access. In selective strategy, apart from exclusive presence, the producer uses few other channels to present the service or product to a wider market that is not available to the exclusive channel(s). For example, a resort that provides reservations on its website (exclusive) might also offer its product (i.e., room reservation) through an intermediary like Expedia (selective). Finally, intensive distribution strategy is to deliver the product and services from every possible channel that a company can afford to involve.

## Functions of distribution channels

As previously explained, distribution channels provide important benefits to both sides of producers and customers. From a business perspective, there are eight functions of marketing channels: information, promotion, contact, matching, negotiation, physical distribution, financing, and risk taking. Distribution channels are two-way communication channels that can provide the information of customers to companies and vice versa. Information is a valuable asset for companies as they can customize their services and products based on the acquired information. Also, information can be used to conduct market segmentation and more precisely target the market(s) of interest. Companies/producers can use distribution channels to promote the product and services. Successful targeting for promotional materials through distribution channels is more probable as these channels are already examined through years of delivering the products and services for the company and other similar producers (competitive set). In addition, distribution channels are established methods of contacting customers that can provide access to potential customers for the companies. Matching is another function of distribution channels as these channels are connected to a diverse set of producers as well as various groups of customers. As a result, these channels can match the right products and services to the right customers at the right time. Companies can increase their bargaining power by using distribution channels as most of the time the channel starts with wholesalers, which usually buy the products and services in bulk. One of the primary functions of distribution channels is transportation, which is to distribute the physical products or bring the service to the customers' environment. Companies might be better off if they deliver their physical products through these channels, as they are expert in efficiently and safely delivering the products. Financing is another function of the distribution channels. As explained in the example of convention hosting hotels, CVB and meeting planners, introduction of distributors to marketing channels reduces the costs significantly for both customers and producers. Finally, distribution channels reduce the risk of product and services from not being sold. For example, if a hotel has sold 50 rooms to a distributor, the risk of no shows, discount of last-minute sales, inventory management, revenue management operationalization, reputation management, etc., are all transferred to the third party (distributor). In the service industries including hospitality and tourism, due to the perishability of products, it is important to minimize the risk of product expiration.

Not all functions are equally available using a distribution channel. It is imperative that companies select the best distribution channel mix to achieve the desirable outcome(s). Market coverage, partnership potential, cost of operations, and capabilities are important factors to consider while selecting a distribution channel mix. Talking about distribution channel mix does not necessarily mean that the company should only select between various combinations of one, two, and three levels of intermediaries with different types intermediation but also various ways of direct marketing (i.e., zero-level such as company's online webpage) should also be included in the distribution channel mix. For example, a theme park might choose to sell the tickets to the park through stands or vending machines in airports and malls, hotel concierges, group sales through various associations and unions such as students' unions, destination management/marketing organizations (DMOs), and CVBs as well as the company's website, and ticket booths at the entrance of the park.

The intermediaries can work through various forms of partnerships. Two strategies of "push," which is using sales force, and "pull," which is using persuasion are the most common ways of involving various intermediaries in the distribution channel. In the push strategy, a company tries to sell the product and services to the closest level of intermediaries and push them to do the same until reaching out to the customers. In the pull strategy, on the other hand, a company tries to persuade (e.g., by advertisement) the potential customers that a specific service or product is worth trying and as a result creates a demand in the customer level from the closest level of intermediaries, which this demand transfers to higher levels until reaching back to the company.

## System approach to distribution channels

The distribution channel is not a collection of different events rather it is a continuous process. To be more specific, the distribution channel is a system, a complex system that adds value to the delivery network. Complexity of distribution channel system depends on the product and service attributes such as perishability, variability, intangibility, inseparability, bulk, frequency of purchase, and type of customer.

Producers of services including hospitality and tourism usually face more complex systems when compared to producers of physical products/goods. The reason behind this complexity is due to the specific characteristics of services. In particular, there is no possibility of storing services for the later consumption. What is delivered is a memory of the service experience usually with no physical product, or with a product, which plays the role of memorial for a specific experience to help recall the memory of the experience. Service cannot be sent. The concept of delivery in service businesses is usually to take the client/guest to the service place (or the service and its operator to the client/guest place) and operate the service on client/guest. Finally, it is difficult to standardize the service process and outcome because human error is part of the process, even if a process is successfully standardized, the perception of the client/guest from the outcome is not going to be without variations.

Understanding the complex system nature of the distribution channels helps us to better explain, predict, and organize its structure and behavior. The behavior of the distribution system is nonlinear and shows emergence characteristics and is barely predictable; the whole system usually does not behave as the sum of its parts. For example, increasing the number of intermediaries and available rooms to twice the previous capacity for a hotel, does not necessarily make the sale volume of the hotel double. Distribution channels are self-organized and show spontaneous order meaning that usually the system does not have any leader unless the channel is administrated or corporate vertical marketing systems (for more information on vertical marketing systems, please see system typology section). Finally, the distribution channels are usually adaptive, meaning that they adjust with market changes and can overcome failures. One of the main reasons behind the resilience of these systems is the hub-structure of the delivery network, which results from the impact of the Internet in reintermediation of distribution channels. For example, if one or multiple online travel agencies are out of reach searching the name of the destination on search engines like Google, results in other options to reserve a flight for the specific destination even with multiple travel agencies being out of reach. In fact, the virtual/online part of the distribution channel in fact can handle more or less 80% random failures of its components and fully operate as all components were working (more explanation about resilience of distribution systems can be found in the information and communication technology section of this chapter).

Network science is shown to be a successful approach studying complex systems. Taking a network approach to distribution channels, the system can be defined as a set of nodes showing different players (e.g., producers, wholesalers, jobbers, retailers, and buyers) in the system, and set of edges connecting these nodes based on their relationship (e.g., who buys from whom). The question is when the structure of the system is identified, apart from the physical goods that are primary reasons for the existence of distribution channels, what will be transferred through the links among the nodes? Generally speaking, five types of flows among the members of distribution channel can be listed: physical goods, ownership, payment, information, and influence (promotion). In the supply chain network, some of these flows such as payment and promotion are unidirectional while some others such as information are bidirectional. In other words, flows such as promotion can be only traced from producers to customers whereas flows such as information can go both ways. Issues related the ownership of service and products in any given time are important legal issues. Specifically, when it comes to damages, tracking the product through the network and identifying the party in possession and ownership of the product in time of damage is critical to keep the errors and failures at minimum. For example, when something is wrong with an airline ticket reservation and customers realize the error in the airport in middle of the connection flight, who is responsible?

## System typology

The traditional distribution channels were linear and hierarchical in nature with separate entities acting independently of each other. These channels are known as conventional distribution systems (CDS) and are useful for ordered, less complicated, and easy to manage environments and products. Contrary to CDS, there are various integrated systems, which are more appropriate for products and services with high complexity and chaotic environments. In a general classification, integrated systems are divided to broad categories of vertical and horizontal. In vertical marketing systems (VMS), producers, wholesalers, and retailers act as a unit. There are three forms of VMS: corporate, contractual, and administered. In corporate VMS, the system has a single ownership while in contractual VMS, involved parties in the system have a formal contract-based relationships. For example, if Marriott International decides to take a corporate forward integration strategy, the company (i.e., Marriott) might by a hotel reservation website (i.e., a retailer like Hotel.com) and integrate it with its distribution channel while keeping the brand and identity of the retailer as a separate company. An example of contractual VMS can be a new franchisee for McDonald's, which as contract franchisor can force a few principles that all McDonald's stores should follow to offer the standard products and services of the company (franchisor). Contrary to corporate and contractual VMS, in administered VMS, involved parties in the system are not integrated by contract or single ownership, rather the leadership of the system is identified through high level of authority of one of the players in the system. For example, Amazon as a major retailer is one of the most powerful retailers in the world. As a result, a new producer wanting to offer its products universally should stick to the rules of the game, which are established by Amazon.

Unlike VMS, in the horizontal marketing system (HMS) players at the same level join together to help each other in terms of keeping or growing market share. The players might be competitors or non-competitors. For example, McDonald's express stores inside Walmart chains or Starbucks inside Target stores can be considered as a form of HMS.

Various target markets of a company might need various distribution mix strategies, and the heterogeneity of these target markets pushed companies to use multichannel distribution systems (MDS), which is mainly the combination of previous systems based on the conditions, necessities, and goals. If MDS is used in one market (one segment), it is what is called a hybrid channel. (For more information on distribution mix strategies, refer to the "functions of distribution channels" explained above).

## Channel behavior

Like any complex organism, the system shows a specific behavior, which is the outcome of individual components' behavior plus the configuration of these components. It should be noted that the systems behavior is neither the linear combination of components' behavior nor the reflection of individual components' behavior, as individual participants' behavior in the systems is based on their goals and motivations that are not necessarily aligned with the whole system. Regardless of the system type, the behavior of the components is under the impact of power mechanisms in the system. Channel power is the ability of a channel or a member of the channel to direct the behavior of other member(s) in a way that these other member(s) would not behave in that specific way without power. There are different types and sources of power. Five types of power are the most prominent, including coercive, reward, expert, legitimate, and referent. Coercive power is a type of power in which the channel or its member forces the other members to behave in a specific way. In reward power, the channel or its members encourage and motivate other members by rewarding instead of forcing them. Rewards can be tangible or intangible and are usually used in a combination with coercive power as they become more efficient. For example, a restaurant can offer a percentage of the sale on each seat after a certain volume of sale as a reward for the central reservation system but at the same time to identify a minimum number of seats to sell in order to pay for the channel's membership. Expert power is all about knowledge and specialization of one of the channel's players. For example, Amazon as the most experienced distribution channel in the world is an attractive option to producers because of the knowledge and specialization of this channel. Legitimate power usually comes from the position of the member in channel. For example, Marriott hotel chains might be able to exert legitimate power in an administrative VMS. Finally, referent power comes from sources such as loyalty, respect, admiration, and friendship. Different types of leverage such as higher utility and scarcity of resources can be employed to exert power. In higher utility cases, other players of the system are willing to follow a specific member because doing business with that specific member creates a higher sales volume or revenue for other members. In scarcity of resources cases, members of a distribution channel might follow a specific retailer because that retailer has a lot of stores in various metropolitan areas close to the channel members' market.

The variation in behavior of components sometimes results in conflicts. Conflicts are types of behaviors of one or more firms in distribution channels that endanger the goal, achievement, and motivations of the other firms in the same distribution channel. Conflicts are not the sign of deficiency in the system but the natural outcome of the interactions among the participants as the participants of the distribution channel are self-centered firms pursuing their own benefits. Even well-designed, well-operated, and well-maintained systems frequently show different levels of conflict.

From a structural perspective, there are two forms of conflicts, namely vertical and horizontal. Vertical conflicts are the conflicts between firms at different levels of the distribution channel's hierarchy whereas horizontal conflicts are conflicts between firms at the same level in the distribution channel's hierarchy. For example, if a Subway franchisee in an area does not follow the codes for fresh ingredients, it might endanger the market share and revenue of other Subway franchisees in the same area, which is an example of horizontal conflicts. From the content perspective, there are three forms of conflicts known as goal, domain, and perceptual conflicts. Goal conflicts are more likely to emerge whenever companies involved in distribution channels follow incompatible goals and lack shared vision. Domain conflicts are results of unclear responsibility definitions and disagreement on rights of various companies involved in the channel. Perceptual conflicts are among the most common forms of conflicts arising from different perspectives and perceptions. If the conflicts are ignored in the system, in the long run and serving multiple target markets with the same distribution channel, the conflict might result in brand cannibalism in the brand portfolio of the producer. For example, if two brands from the Hilton family compete in the same target market for the company as a result of goal conflicts, the mother company (i.e., Hilton) should pay the price of this competition because of the competition within its brand portfolio.

# The role of information and communication technology

The marketing strategies and business models adopted by the various participants in distribution channels and consumers' available choices are both under the impact of the structure of the hospitality and tourism distribution system. By the advent of the World Wide Web in 1969, and later on commercial application of Internet and free access to the public in 1993 the structure of the hospitality tourism distribution channel was transformed and changed substantially. This transformation, particularly facilitated by information and communication technology (ICT), resulted in greater choice for the consumers, increased competition for channel members, and a more complex system structure. Although ICT's role can be traced back to as far as the 1960s, in past two decades the Internet has become more and more popular. ICT has revolutionized the marketing channels as is evident in Tourism and hospitality insights 20.1, 20.2, and 20.3.

---

## TOURISM AND HOSPITALITY INSIGHTS 20.1
## HOTEL ELECTRONIC DISTRIBUTION OPTIONS

In order to maintain occupancy levels and maximize ADR, hotels must work to market and book beyond their local area. Electronic distribution systems allow hotels to expand their reach. However, sales and marketing directors must understand how to properly utilize the various distribution systems in order to maximize the potential for the property. This includes understanding the various electronic distribution options available for utilization.

### The GDS

The global distribution system (GDS) is the most commonly utilized electronic distribution system. It is comprised of four main competing companies: Amadeus, Galileo/Apollo, Sabre and Worldspan, and began as a system of private networks utilized by travel agents (Understanding, n.d.). The GDS began with listing airline and expanded to offer a variety of travel services and has the potential to offer hotels a variety of benefits including:

- Worldwide access
- 24hr/7days a week availability
- Extensive travel agent usage
- A common booking conduit for consortia and negotiated rates
- Low maintenance and information can be easily offered across all four GDS systems

(Understanding, n.d.)

## Websites

Hotels are often contacted by various websites seeking to gain business listings. This means that sales and marketing managers must determine if listing on the site will result in a worthwhile return on investment and deliver bookings. Other things to consider include supplemental promotional opportunities such as preferred placement of property in sites and banner ads.

In addition, hotels must decide where on the Internet is the best fit for their property, be it a "shop and buy" or a specialty sales site, such as those that sell only distressed inventory. There are a variety of options for hotel properties to consider (Understanding, n.d.).

### Internet sites – maintained by property

- Site run and operated by the property;
- Distressed inventory sites (discounted rate): Charge a listing fee and sell the rooms at discounted rates, e.g., Lastminutetravel.com;
- Distressed inventory sites (auction based): Hotels provide a net rate and the site receives profit from the difference between the net rate and the rate that the buyer pays, e.g., Bid4travel.com;
- Distressed inventory (reverse auction): Similar to auction based, e.g., Priceline.com;
- Meeting planner sites: A transaction fee is charged for any business that takes place, e.g., allmeetings.com.

### Internet sites – computer reservation system powered

- Chain branded sites/franchise or representation company site: Can serve as a booking engine for member websites. Often charges a reservation processing fee and commission if a travel agent is part of the booking process, e.g., Hilton.com

### Internet sites – switch powered

- Switch company site: Sites charge a booking fee and possibly commission to travel agents. Limited number of affiliated sites, e.g., TravelWeb.com;
- Distressed inventory – discounted rates: Charges commission, e.g., lastminute.com.

### Internet sites – GDS powered: These are ones that operate from a GDS platform

- Expedia.com: (Worldspan; Pegasus for hotel data) Offers a variety of participating websites for distribution, e.g., earthlink, Washington Post;
- Travelnow.com: (Sabre and Worldspan; Pegasus for hotel data);
- Travelocity.com: (Sabre) e.g., Yahoo Travel;
- Trip.com (Galileo).

(Understanding, n.d.)

**References**

Understanding and maximizing a hotel's electronic distribution system. (n.d). *htc.* Retrieved from http://www.burns-htc.com/articles/understanding-and-maximizing-a-hotels-electronic-distribution-options.html

Source: Amanda Templeton.

## TOURISM AND HOSPITALITY INSIGHTS 20.2
## METASEARCH ENGINES VS. OTAS (ONLINE TRAVEL AGENTS): CLEARING UP THE DIFFERENCES

Determining the difference between an online travel agency and a metasearch engine can be confusing. The role of OTAs and metasearch engines will be explained in order to clear up some of the confusion.

### Online travel agencies

Online travel agencies, or OTAs, for short are travel websites that specialize in the sale of travel products to consumers. Some OTAs sell travel products that include flights, hotels, car rentals, and packages, where other OTAs specialize in tours and activities (rezgo, n.d.). Commonly used OTAs include Expedia, TripAdvisor, Booking.com, etc. OTAs promote hotels at destinations by advertising room rates, descriptions, and photographs and allow customers to book the hotel, or other travel vendor, directly on the site. When comparing an OTA to an independent property, or vendor, the OTA has as much bigger marketing budget that typically puts them at the top of most search engine result pages (Little Hotelier, 2016). Travel agencies have "agency agreements" with suppliers to resell their products wherein the OTA takes payment from the consumer and pays the supplier a net rate (rezgo, n.d.).

### Metasearch engines

A metasearch engine aggregates information and posts it on their site, providing users with the opportunity to view a variety of providers and easily compare prices/routes/etc. (O'Gara, n.d.). The key difference between a metasearch engine and an OTA is that a metasearch engine will display the information necessary for the booking process; however, the inventory is not sold (Little Hotelier, 2016). Hipmunk is a prime example of a metasearch engine. On a metasearch site, the user is generally directed to the OTA or direct booking site (O'Gara, n.d.). In the event that a customer has a question or needs assistance they contact the OTA or vendor directly

### References

Little Hotelier. (2016, October 6). Metasearch engines and OTAs: What's the difference? *Little Hotelier Resource Hub*. Retrieved from https://www.littlehotelier.com/r/distribution/metasearch-engines-otas-whats-difference/

O'Gara, E. (2017, April 7). What is a travel metasearch engine? *TAILWIND*. Retrieved from https://www.hipmunk.com/tailwind/meta-search-engine/

Rezgo. (n.d.). Travel and tourism industry glossary. *rezgo*. Retrieved from https://www.rezgo.com/glossary/ota

Source: Amanda Templeton.

American Airlines launched the first global distribution systems (GDS), Sabre, in the 1960s, which resulted in major competition in this area from other players such as Amadeus, Galileo, Abacus, and Worldspan. The way that GDS was designed, it was more appropriate for homogeneous products and services and successfully worked with some hospitality and tourism subsectors such as air transportation industry. Diversity, however, creates a major issue for most of the hospitality and tourism companies and as a result, Central Reservation Systems (CRS) were suggested to solve the issue. CRSs were designed to be a more centralized system and cater more to local needs; at higher levels, CRS were connected to the GDS for more global market reach. Hotel CRSs were connected to the GDS, which was facilitated by switches. The switch providers had provided another layer of intermediation insofar as hotel bookings were concerned.

The changes after 1993 were especially more critical for the service sector as the physical product and traditional aspects of distribution channels were never the most critical part of the service sector. Diversity of hospitality and tourism products and services along service characteristics such as intangibility, perishability, inseparability, and variability enhanced the role that ICT could play in hospitality and tourism distribution channels. Unlike GDS and CRS which were closed systems, the Internet is an open system and provides a more feasible way of distributing products and services with much less cost and more freedom of action. GDS and CRS were enjoying significant power in an oligopolistic distribution environment that was broken by the popularity of the Internet after 2000. Basically, ICT reduced entry barriers to alternative channels and systems, which resulted in exponential growth of virtual intermediaries all around the web. ICT advances continue to increase the complexity of the hospitality and tourism distribution system from various perspectives. The structure of the system was revolutionized by several disintermediation and reintermediations. Initially, the web added to the width of distribution channels by simply becoming an additional option to wholesalers (e.g., tour operators), retailers (e.g., travel agencies), call centers, etc. Then, most of the traditional retailers such as physical travel agencies were pushed aside as the need for an interface between the customer and GDS was eliminated by the Internet (disintermediation).

As a result, the Internet became a tool for direct or zero-level distribution channel and most experts were expecting the end of intermediaries in the system. On the contrary, as time went by, online travel agencies, Internet travel networks (ITN), search engines, and metasearch engines were added to the system (reintermediation) as new cybermediaries. These cybermediaries are also known as e-mediaries (an inclusive concept including both traditional GDS and new electronic players). These additions influenced both length and width of the distribution channel. In 1996, Sabre, a GDS owner, debuted Travelocity. Also in 1996, Microsoft launched the online travel agent Expedia. Priceline was launched in 1998; it began by selling airline tickets using a "demand collection system" in which demand is collected from consumers and communicated to suppliers. Currently, Priceline offers that system, as well as the traditional retail method of disclosing prices. ITN was eventually rebranded as GetThere, which was later acquired by Sabre in 2000. Of course, distribution channel participants not only need to add value for consumers, but also add value to other participants with whom they have relationships. For example, hotels and airlines would not continue to work with GDS if the latter no longer provided any value to the suppliers. The simultaneous coexistence of multiple categories of intermediaries is a manifestation of the differentiating value that each brings to the distribution system. Also, distribution participants should consider the benefits of cooperating with other participants who might otherwise be considered competitors, and that suppliers can effectively become intermediaries by selling partners' complementary products and services. The collaboration with competitors is known as "co-opetition." Whereas co-opetition is difficult to achieve in traditional systems due to the cost-benefit ratio, in virtual environments, thanks to ICT, it is more feasible to see multiple forms of co-opetition. For example, lastminute. com has partnered with a potential competitor, Expedia, as both can enjoy the larger market share and still compete on the benefits.

While this technology-induced structural change offers more choices to consumers, it also fosters an environment of fiercer competition for channel participants. The structural changes create some serious form displacement compared to previous models. For example, the star network topology is now changing to a hub-based network, which functionally is drastically different from previous topology. The traditional value-chain was radically changed as the structure of the Internet inspired decentralized agencies in all forms of reservation, distribution, and evaluation. There was no further need for a central system such as GDS or CRS. In fact, centralized systems were dangerous to the existence of the distribution channels as these central systems are susceptible to terrorist attacks. Hub systems with multiple hubs around the world replaced star designs. This new design introduces a new characteristic to the system by making it a scale-free network. The technicality of scale-free networks is not related to the objectives of this chapter, however, and can be found in network science texts. Nevertheless, these networks are extremely resistant to random failures of the components of the system. That being said, scale-free networks are still vulnerable to deliberate attacks because if approximately 20% hubs were targeted, the system would easily collapse.

## TOURISM AND HOSPITALITY INSIGHTS 20.3
## TRAVEL AGENTS AND/OR OTAS?

With the Internet and the ease of utilizing the Internet to find information on destinations and book travel, many travelers question the need for travel agents. In this era, there is a place for both OTAs and travel agents based on the circumstances and needs of the travelers.

### Inventory

*OTA*: Access to inventory is limited – OTAs operate on off-peak inventory and often vendors will dump excess inventory on an OTA site. With a rise in the number of OTA premiums, vendors have stopped offering premium commissions and some vendors refuse to sell inventory on OTAs (such as Southwest Airlines).

*Travel agent*: Travel agents will have access to a variety of inventories and have the ability to find the best value available. In addition, most travel agents will have inside information as to what room has a better view for the best price or which seats on a plane are more spacious for the same price, and so on (Stein, 2017).

### Price discrimination and "steering"

*OTA*: Pricing "steering" due to supply and demand and travelers can be directed to sites where there may not be a good deal but rather depends on the quantity demand while the traveler is booking. OTAs utilize technology and algorithms to steer the traveler to potentially more expensive bookings. Price discrimination occurs when the OTA charges different consumers different prices for the same product, which is illegal but does occur (Stein, 2017).

*Travel agent*: Travel agents connect directly using the GDS, the property, or wholesalers, giving them access to fair prices, the ability to bundle products, create packages, and hold tickets/rooms (anywhere from the end of day and up to 48 hours depending on the product) (Stein, 2017). Travel agents may also have access to special discounts depending on the vendor they are working with and will often have knowledge as to when prices are lowest or when special discounts/packages are available.

### Group bookings

*OTA*: OTAs are generally not conducive to group bookings. When booking through an OTA there is no guarantee that the same rate can be applied to all units of the product that the traveler would need to accommodate a group.

*Travel agent*: Travel agents can provide great savings and value for groups. Travel agents have the opportunity to negotiate group rates, build packages that are best for the group while providing the best value and savings for the client.

## Personalization

*OTA*: OTAs have data and automation capabilities. However, while this may be responsive it is not necessarily personalized (Signature Travel Network, 2016).

*Travel agent*: Travel agents have experience and ability to create connections with travelers. This allows them to establish, build, and maintain relationships based on personal communication, which often translates into value added benefits when booking travel for customers.

## Knowledge and time

*OTA*: OTAs can offer suggestions based on algorithms and links to social media sites. However, the traveler must be willing to put in the time and effort to research the destination and determine the best pricing, savings, and value as well as where to go and what to do.

*Travel agents*: With knowledge of the destinations, travel agents will be able to save travelers time in research and offer suggestions based on personalized knowledge. In addition, through relationship building, travel agents are able to match vendors to clients ensuring the best experience possible.

## References

Signature Travel Network, & Skift. (2016, November 10). Online travel agencies vs. travel agents: It's getting personal. *Skift*. Retrieved from https://skift.com/2016/11/10/otas-vs-travel-agents-its-getting-personal/

Stein, M. (2017, October 5). Using a travel agent vs. booking online: An infographic. *Host Agency Reviews*. Retrieved from http://hostagencyreviews.com/travel-agent-vs-booking-online/.

Source: Amanda Templeton.

Advertising is another area that has undergone radical changes. Not only has web technology provided an advertising revenue opportunity for search engines, but it has also opened the door for other tourism distribution participants to earn such revenue. Nowadays, more and more intermediaries are starting to become involved with advertising. Four of the big online travel agencies, Expedia, Orbitz, Priceline, and Travelocity, are looking to expand revenue sources beyond transactions to include advertising revenue streams. The metasearch engine Kayak is planning on doing likewise, having established an ad network. Kayak's SideStep subsidiary obtains advertising revenue by means of the SideStep website, email newsletters, and the SideStep web-browser toolbar plug-in. Expedia signed a deal with InterContinental Hotels Group (IHG) in order to obtain revenue, not only from booking transactions, but also from web surfers' clicks on IHG properties at Expedia.com or Expedia-owned Hotels.com. This represents Expedia's new two-part revenue model, for which IHG is serving as the launch partner. Fast-pace changes continue to affect all parties involved in the distribution system. At each level of distribution channel, its members are competing on different capacities with each other. This intense competition results in improvements of the product and services that consumers are interested. The spending of cybermediaries on marketing can be an indication of this intense competition. In 2017, for example, Expedia spent more than half (about 52%) of its $10.2 billion income on marketing. Comparing these figures to the ones in the era of GDS and CRS reveals that oligopoly in distribution channels is at its lowest state and the free market is now ready to move on to the next stage of technology advancement.

## Conclusion

Distribution channels are in a continuous battle of intermediation, disintermediation, and reintermediation. Incremental continuous changes in technology have picked up a fast pace in recent years which has resulted in drastic changes in structure, functions, operations, and utility of the distribution system. Ownership of the product at each level, order, and payment remain three major issues yet to be discussed in distribution channels as these three areas are at the same time the most influential factors in restructuring the distribution channels and most influenced by the continuous changes of the system. Similar to distribution channels for other products, distribution channels in the service sector are dealing with the impact of technology on the logistics. Complexity of hospitality and tourism distribution channels has been exponentially increasing due to restructuring as a result of Internet, and operation complexity as a result of advances in logistics and flow management. The complex system of distribution channels in hospitality and tourism needs experts who know how the system operates and how to tame the system by using appropriate control mechanisms. Without these trained experts in marketing channels, the system starts auto-cannibalism (also known as autosarcophagy) by wasting the company's investment and disrupting delivery process, which can easily diminish an organization.

The future of marketing channels is tied to the future of intelligent cybermediaries. Development of big data analytics, machine learning, artificial neural network algorithms, and artificial intelligence (AI) are all transforming the distribution channels in a revolutionary manner with each shaping the future of tourism and hospitality marketing (see Chapter 22). Future customers are looking for experiences instead of searching for destinations. Hospitality and tourism companies, in the future, should be prepared to develop a just in time (JIT) production for their product and services. The new JIT, unlike in tangible product situations, will be imagination-based, meaning that companies should be able to produce offers based on the customers' imagination in real-time.

## REVIEW QUESTIONS

1. How has the Internet influenced the role of distribution channels in tourism and hospitality since the mid-to-late 1990s?
2. How may distribution channels vary in importance between leisure and business markets?
3. How may the functions of a distribution channel change in the next three to five years and why?
4. What are "barriers to entry" and how may they impact the future development of electronic channels of distribution?

## YOUTUBE LINKS

### *"The future of hotel distribution"*

URL: https://youtu.be/u_Pu7OUclxY

Summary: How mobile consumers will evolve their booking behavior

### *"How does travel distribution work – the GDS version"*

URL: https://youtu.be/fJPkS7S-02g

Summary: ETTSA explains what travel distribution is, and gives a historical context. It outlines the benefits that the industry brings to business and leisure travelers.

### *"InnTouch forum: GDS, OTAs, and metasearch"*

URL: https://youtu.be/2pgSpSlCbew

Summary: InnLink account manager provides an introduction to GDS, online travel agencies, and metasearch. The video includes suggestions for improving hotel performance in OTAs.

### *"What's the difference between a travel agent and an online agency?"*

URL: https://youtu.be/82Ls9N5sdGg

Summary: The differences between an online agency versus a human travel agent.

## FURTHER READING AND RELATED WEBSITES

Further reading

Anderson, J., & Earl, M.J. (2000). lastminute.com: B2C e-commerce. *Business Strategy Review, 11* (4), 49–60.

Bojanic, D.C., Oh, H., & Pizam, A. (2008). *Handbook of hospitality marketing management.* Oxford: Butterworth-Heinemann.

Buhalis, D. (1998). Strategic use of information technologies. *Tourism Management, 19*(5), 409–421.

Buhalis, D. (2004). eAirlines: Strategic and tactical use of ICTs in the airline industry. *Information and Management, 41*(7), 805–825.

Buhalis, D., & Laws, E. (2001). *Tourism distribution channels: Practices, issues and transformations.* London: Continuum.

Buhalis, D., & Law, R. (2008). Progress in information technology and tourism management: 20 years on and 10 years after the Internet – the state of eTourism research. *Tourism Management, 29*(4), 609–623.

Buhalis, D., & Licata, M.C. (2002). The future eTourism intermediaries. *Tourism Management, 23*(3),207–220.

Buhalis, D., & O'Connor, P. (2005). Information communication technology revolutionizing tourism. *Tourism Recreation Research, 30*(3), 7–16.

CERN. (2003). *CERN celebrates web anniversary,* 29 April. Retrieved from http://press.web.cern.ch

Chircu, A.M., & Kauffman, R.J. (1999). Analyzing firm-level strategy for Internet-focused reintermediation. In R. Sprague (Ed.), *Proceedings of the 32nd Hawaii International Conference on System Sciences – 1999,* Maui, Hawaii, 5–8 January (pp. 181–190) Los Alamitos, CA: IEEE Computer Society Press, 5,.

Chircu, A.M., & Kauffman, R.J. (2000a). A framework for performance and value assessment of e-business systems in corporate travel distribution. Working Paper, Minneapolis, MN: Management Information Systems Research Center, Carlson School of Management, University of Minnesota.

Chircu, A.M., & Kauffman, R.J. (2000b). Reintermediation strategies in business-to-business electronic commerce. *International Journal of Electronic Commerce, 4*(4), 7–42.

Choi, S., & Kimes, S. (2002). Electronic distribution channels' effect on hotel revenue management. *Cornell Hotel and Restaurant Administration Quarterly, 43*(3), 23–31.

Dale, C. (2003). The competitive networks of tourism e-mediaries: New strategies, new advantages. *Journal of Vacation Marketing, 9*(2), 109–118.

Egger, R., & Buhalis, D. (2008). *eTourism case studies: Management and marketing issues.* Oxford: Butterworth-Heinemann.

Expedia, Inc. (2007). *Expedia and IHG sign new long-term agreement,* 15 November. Retrieved from http://press.expedia.com

EyeforTravel. (2008a). *Kayak focuses on developing its own ad network,* 1 May. Retrieved from http://www.eyefortravel.com

Farrelly, G. (1999a). *Search engines: Evolution and Revolution,* July. Retrieved from http://web home.idirect.com

Farrelly, G. (1999b). *Search engines: Evolution and revolution – Part 2,* July. Retrieved from http://webhome.idirect.com

Giaglis, G.M., Klein, S., & O'Keefe, R.M. (1999). Disintermediation, reintermediation, or cybermediation? The future of intermediaries in electronic marketplaces. *Proceedings of the 12th International Bled Electronic Commerce Conference: Global Networked Organizations,* Bled, Slovenia, 7–9 June.

Granados, N., Kauffman, R., & King, B. (2008). The emerging role of vertical search engines in travel distribution: A newly-vulnerable electronic markets perspective. In R. Sprague (Ed.), *Proceedings of the 41st Hawaii International Conference on System Sciences – 2008,* Waikoloa, Big Island, Hawaii, 7–10 January, Los Alamitos, CA: IEEE Computer Society Press, 389.

Hopkinson, G.C. (1997). Channel conflict. In C.L. Cooper & C. Argyris (Eds.), *The Blackwell encyclopedia of management: Marketing.* Oxford: Blackwell.

Kotler, P., & Armstrong, G. (2012). *Principles of marketing*. Boston, MA: Pearson Prentice Hall.

Kotler, P., & Keller, K. L. (2006). *Marketing management*. Upper Saddle River, NJ: Pearson Prentice Hall.

Littler, D. (1997). Channels of distribution. In C.L. Cooper & C. Argyris (Eds.), *The Blackwell encyclopedia of management: Marketing*. Oxford: Blackwell.

Longhi, C. (2008). *Usages of the Internet and e-Tourism. Towards a new economy of tourism*, First Draft, 7 May. Retrieved from http://halshs.archives-ouvertes.fr

McCubbrey, D. (1999). Disintermediation and reintermediation in the U.S. air travel distribution industry: A Delphi study. *Communications of the Association for Information Systems, 1*(18),June, 1–39.

O'Connor, P., & Frew, A. (2002). The future of hotel electronic distribution: Expert and industry perspectives. *Cornell Hotel and Restaurant Administration Quarterly, 43*(3), 33–45.

Palmer, A., & McCole, P. (1999). The virtual re-intermediation of travel services: A conceptual framework and empirical investigation. *Journal of Vacation Marketing, 6*(1), 33–47.

Pearce, D., Tan, R., & Schott, C. (2004). Tourism distribution channels in Wellington, New Zealand. *International Journal of Tourism Research, 6*, 397–410.

Pinkerton, B. (1994). Finding what people want: Experiences with the WebCrawler. *Proceedings of Second International WWW Conference*. Retrieved from http://www.thinkpink.com

Pinkerton, B. (2000). *WebCrawler: Finding what people want*. PhD thesis, University of Washington, Seattle.

Priceline.com. (1998). *Leisure travelers can now name their own price for airline tickets*, Press Release, April, 6. Retrieved from http://phx.corporate-ir.net

Priceline.com. (2009). *Priceline.com 2009 Annual Report*, 30 April.

Reid, R.D., Bojanic, D.C., & Reid, R.D. (2006). *Hospitality marketing management: Student workbook*. Hoboken, NJ: Wiley.

Sabre Holdings. (2009). *Sabre history*. Retrieved from http://www.sabre-holdings.com.

Sheldon, P.J. (1997). *Tourism information technology*. Wallingford: CAB International.

Sheth, J.N., & Malhotra, N.K. (2011). *Wiley international encyclopedia of marketing*. Chichester: Wiley.

Statista (2018). *Revenue of Expedia Inc. worldwide from 2007 to 2017*. Retrieved from https://www.statista.com/statistics/269387/revenue-of-expedia/

Travel Ad Network. (2008). *Online travel agencies pump more resources into advertising*, March, 25. Retrieved from http://www.traveladnetwork.com

Tse, A.C. (2003). Disintermediation of travel agents in the hotel industry. *International Journal of Hospitality Management, 22*(4), 453–460.

Wang, Y.C., & Qualls, W. (2007). Technology adoption by hospitality organizations: Towards a theoretical framework. *International Journal of Hospitality Management, 26*(3), 560–573.

Werthner, H., & Klein, S. (1999). *Information technology and tourism – a challenging relationship*. Vienna: Springer.

Wolf, P. (2008). The perfect storm: Search, shop, buy (Part 2), *Hospitality Net*, July, 18. Retrieved from http://www.hospitalitynet.org

Websites

Expedia
www.expedia.com

Hotwire
www.hotwire.com

Kayak.com
www.kayak.com

Orbitz
www.orbitz.com

Priceline
www.priceline.com

Travelocity.com
www.travelocity.com

Trivago
www.trivago.com

The trouble with travel distribution
https://www.mckinsey.com/industries/travel-transport-and-logistics/our-insights/the-trouble-with-
    travel-distribution

Channel shock: the future of travel distribution
https://skift.com/2017/08/07/channel-shock-the-future-of-travel-distribution/

## MAJOR CASE STUDY
## THE EVOLUTION OF DISTRIBUTION CHANNELS IN TRAVEL AND TRIPADVISOR

Before the development of the Internet, there were only traditional tourism distribution channels, including retail travel agents, corporate travel agents, tour operators, and global distribution systems (GDSs) (Wang & Pizam, 2011). At that time, suppliers, such as airlines and hotels, pursued disintermediation of other channels and sold directly to customers by utilizing their retail outlets and toll-free call centers (McCubbrey, 1999). Companies started to use the Internet in the 1990s, when they became able to leverage the benefits of the communication protocol of the World Wide Web (A&E Television Networks, n.d.). Since then, suppliers began establishing their websites in order to connect directly with customers as well as disintermediate other channels that charged them commission (Wang & Pizam, 2011). In addition, online travel agencies (OTAs), such as Travelocity, Expedia, and Priceline, became big players in distribution channel competition at the same time (Chircu & Kauffman, 1999). Because of the Internet, which led to the development of online travel agencies and enabled suppliers to connect directly with their customers via their websites, the number of accredited travel agencies in the US decreased from 32,000 in 1998 to 21,000 in 2004 (Grossman, 2006). In the 2000s, the new category of electronic distribution channels, metasearch engines, including Kayak, Trivago, and Skyscanner, appeared in the tourism market (Wang & Pizam, 2011). They aggregate all information on rates and availabilities from suppliers and other OTAs' websites and present them to customers. Since there were no channels that provided indepth reviews from real travelers, even though several new electronic travel distribution channels had been established, TripAdvisor was founded to offer valuable user-generated information and consequently became the world's largest travel site, covering the world's most extensive selection of travel listings (TNOOZ, 2013).

Since its establishment in 2000 by Stephan Kaufer and Langley Steinert, TripAdvisor developed into the most-visited travel site by consumers prior to booking, with over 600 million reviews of approximately 7.5 million accommodations, airlines, restaurants, activities and other travel-related services (TripAdvisor, 2018). TripAdvisor-branded sites are currently accessible in 49 markets, and have the world's largest travel community of and average of 455 million unique visitors monthly (TripAdvisor, 2018). The most significant reason for the company's success is their great business model, representing social media and user-generated content (Bussgang, 2012). TripAdvisor's main content is created by travelers who voluntarily write reviews on their website (Bussgang, 2012). These travelers allow their contents, such as reviews and pictures, to be monetized by TripAdvisor without asking for anything in return (Bussgang, 2012). By utilizing a huge volume of these usergenerated contents and excellent manipulation of Google's search algorithm, TripAdvisor attracts many customers to their website and app. Then, when customers click on advertisements and move to booking pages, TripAdvisor obtains revenue regardless of whether they actually book or not (InnovationTactics.com, 2017). These are called cost-per-click (CPC) advertisements. If customers make direct bookings on TripAdvisor's website or app, the company generates a higher margin of revenue, as it gives them 12 to 15% commission on the booking price (InnovationTactics.

com, 2017). The revenue generated by these CPC advertisements and transactions (direct booking) accounts for nearly 70% of TripAdvisor's total revenue. Since contents are free and advertisers are drawn to self-service channels that don't require a large sales force, the company's EBITDA margins are quite high (Bussgang, 2012). In addition, the network-effect works well for TripAdvisor's business model; as the network grows bigger, it becomes more valuable (Bussgang, 2012). As more consumers post more interesting content, more suppliers, such as hotels and restaurants, provide more access to their trip services while, at the time, more advertisers purchase more advertisements. As more vacation options become accessible to suppliers and more valuable reviews are uploaded by customers on TripAdvisor's site and app, more customers are attracted to their services prior to their trips (Bussgang, 2012). This virtuous cycle has enabled them to grow until becoming the world's largest travel site (Bussgang, 2012).

The advance of the Internet has impacted on the travel distribution industry and generated many new types of electronic distribution channels, including TripAdvisor. Within just a decade since its establishment, TripAdvisor has become the most viewed travel site across the world thanks to the development of social media and a sound business model. Having said that, the travel distribution industry remains complex and very competitive. Their future success will depend on whether they are able to keep innovating their services for travelers.

## References

A&E Television Networks. (n.d.). *The invention of the Internet.* Retrieved from https://www.history.com/topics/inventions/invention-of-the-internet

Bussgang, J.J. (2012). The secrets to TripAdvisor's impressive scale. Cambridge, MA: Harvard Business School Cases, 1.

Chircu, A.M., & Kauffman, R.J. (1999). Strategies for Internet middlemen in the intermediation/disintermediation/reintermediation cycle. *Electronic Markets, 9*(1–2), 109–117.

Grossman, D. (2006). A lesson from Portugal, or fighting disintermediation. *Searcher, 14*(4), 45–47.

InnovationTactics.com. (2017, Sep 30). *Business models compared: Booking.com, Expedia, TripAdvisor.* Retrieved from https://www.innovationtactics.com/business-models-tripadvisor-booking-com-expedia/

McCubbrey, D.J. (1999). Disintermediation and reintermediation in the US air travel distribution industry: A Delphi study. *Communications of the Association for Information Systems 1*(18), 1–39.

TNOOZ. (2013, Sep 12). *A brief history of travel technology – from its evolution to looking at the future.* Retrieved from https://www.tnooz.com/article/a-brief-history-of-travel-technology-from-its-evolution-to-looking-at-the-future/

TripAdvisor. (2018, Apr 12). *Majority of global online travel buyers visit TripAdvisor before booking a hotel or flight, according to new study.* Retrieved http://ir.tripadvisor.com/news-releases/news-release-details/majority-global-online-travel-buyers-visit-tripadvisor-booking

Wang, Y., & Pizam, A. (Eds.). (2011). *Destination marketing and management: Theories and applications.* Wallingford: Cabi.

Source: Ryuichi Karakawa.

Major case study questions

1. What are metasearch engines and how have they changed the balance of power (if at all) in travel distribution?
2. What are the benefits and drawbacks of user-generated information (reviews) for suppliers of tourism and hospitality products?
3. How innovative is TripAdvisor's business model and where do they go next in seeking to enhance their competitive advantage?
4. What role does TripAdvisor now play in the entire customer journey?

# Media, public relations, and marketing communications

## Learning outcomes

By the end of this chapter, students will:

- Explain the role of public relations in corporations and outline the main functions of the public relations department
- Name the major tools used by public relations practitioners
- Explain the importance of the departmental role of public relations in collaboration with other organizations
- Elaborate on the impact of technology on public relations and the future of the public relations department
- Describe the process of the evolution of the communication models and discuss the complex systems and network aspects of communication models
- Clarify the role of creative storytelling in public relations activities

**Key terms**

public relations, media, marketing communications, storytelling

## Introduction

Public relations (PR) is one of the elements of the promotion mix (also known as the communication mix), of which the promotion mix itself is one of the elements of the marketing mix (also known as 4Ps, 7Ps, 12Ps, etc. depending on the definition) tool box (Cooper & Argyris, 1997). Three traditional corporate communication goals of informing, reminding, and persuading can be pursued by most of the promotion mix elements including PR as well. That being said, informing is the main focus of PR in terms of traditional goals; hence informing the public and communication models and methods are inseparable parts of PR departments. PR as part of corporate communication strategy manages the attitudes and opinions toward the organization. PR is all about building and maintaining a favorable reputation and publicity to influence attitudes and behaviors and enhance mutual understanding, organization image, and favorable positioning for the organization (McCabe, 2012).

The public relations platforms for an organization can be divided into external and internal PR platforms. The external PR platform includes media such as the press, social media, radio, and TV; communal beneficiaries such as local communities, pressure groups, and general public; and the government, such as local, national, regional, and international authorities as well as non-governmental non-profit organizations and associations. On the other hand, the internal PR platform includes stakeholders such as shareholders, banks, and boards of trustees; representatives such as staff and trade unions; internal commercial units such as suppliers, agents, intermediaries, and current customers (McCabe, 2012). PR departments usually counsel CEO and top management in terms of public speeches, positive programs benefiting the corporation, and best practices eliminating questionable practices. The marketing literature divides the major functions of PR departments into the following seven categories (Kotler & Keller, 2016; Kotler & Wood, 2005):

- Press relations: To present a positive image of the organization by creating newsworthy stories;
- Product publicity: To publicize the products (especially the newly launched ones) through different ways like sponsorship;
- Corporate communications: To enhance the sympathy/empathy of the organization among the external and internal public;
- Public affairs: To build and to maintain local, national, and international relations;
- Lobbying: To deal with legislators and government officials in order to promote/prevent specific legislative activities;
- Investor relations: To maintain a relationship with shareholders and the financial community;
- Counseling: To advise top managers about the public as well as organization position on various issues, brand image, and public policies in both times of crises and prosperity.

According to *The Blackwell Encyclopedia of Management*, publicity is a non-paid and non-personal form of communication from a specific source with the aim of providing information about the company, its products/services, and its position on different issues (Cooper & Argyris, 1997). From the definition then, unlike advertising, PR should be able to produce noteworthy news from the perspective of mass media (e.g., cinema, TV, radio, posters, magazines, newspapers) in order to receive desirable coverage. PR's output is more credible compared to that of advertisements since the output is attributed to an independent information source (media). As a result, advertising does not build brands, whereas PR does (Kotler & Wood, 2005). The main problem is that PR does not have any control on publicity since it is mainly driven by the media. In addition, PR has no control over the content of the message, its timing, and delivery to the public (McCabe, 2012). Even when there is control over the content, the inflexibility of mass media makes it difficult to plan all the details of a PR plan.

Despite PR's potential in increasing the sales and profit by publicizing products, it has been treated, until recently, more like the stepchild of marketing (Kotler & Wood, 2005). The potential reason for this ignorance towards PR might reside in two gaps between PR functions and marketing tactics: (1) among promotion mix elements, PR compared to other elements is the most loyal pure communication model that disseminates information with uncommon practices such as storytelling. (2) PR is so preoccupied with other functions such as counseling, lobbying, investors' relations, public affairs, corporate communications, and press relations that there is usually no time to actively become involved with product publicity and, as a result, PR has not always been given enough serious attention as it deserves. It is only recently that PR has become one of the discussion topics in marketing promotional plans. Tragic events and crises such as 9/11, the SARS epidemic, and the Iraq war have brought PR into the limelight. Crises are unpredictable major catastrophic events that threaten the existence of the corporation or otherwise harm the organization in a serious manner. Appropriate PR actions are absolutely necessity in mitigating and reducing the negative impacts of crises on an organization as well as helping the corporation to rebuild its identity after any form of major crisis. PR actions in dealing with crises can be divided into two broad categories. The proactive approach is the use of PR tools to get the situation under control and combat the crisis aggressively. On the opposite end of the spectrum is the reactive approach, which mainly uses the PR tools to react and respond to the strikes of crisis passively. Organizations can have a combination of various proactive and reactive strategies dealing with a crisis, and it should be pointed out that one (i.e., proactive vs reactive) is not necessarily preferred over the other. Based on situational factors, the best possible portfolio including proactive and reactive strategies should be prepared. Regardless of the type of crisis, a few strategies such as being visible to the customer, providing straightforward information, and being internally consistent with that information are helpful in enabling the PR department to successfully handle the situation (Bojanic et al., 2008). No matter which portfolio is adopted, inactivity is the worst response in times of crises, as there are numerous examples of the downfall of large corporations from either being inactive or non-timely in responding to internal or environmental crises (Bojanic, Oh, & Pizam, 2008) That being said, it should be noted that dealing with crises is only one of the functions of PR departments.

Now that there is an understanding of the main PR functions, it is essential, then, to have an understanding of the main tools that PR practitioners use for the major PR functions. The broad list of available tools can be as long as one's imagination and creativity in PR operations. There exist seven distinct categories (Kotler & Keller, 2016):

- Publications: In any media-driven form such as reports, brochures, articles, newsletters, magazines, editorials, and audiovisual materials like video clips, podcasts vodcasts, and films;
- Events: Participation and presence at news conferences, seminars, trade shows, exhibits, contests, and celebrations;
- Sponsorships: Monetary contributions in form of sponsoring mega events, local and national sports tournaments, exhibits, and professional conferences;
- News: Depending on the scope can be from local radio/TV stations to worldwide known news agencies such as CNN, CBS, MSNBC, Fox News, and BBC;
- Speeches: Talks to trade associations, sales meeting, openings, and syndicates, all of which determine the corporate image and position;
- Public service activities: Contributing time and money to good causes and charities;
- Identity media: Creating a distinctive and memorable visual identity that can be easily recognized by the public such as company logo, stationery, brochures, business cards, and uniforms.

PR departments in hospitality and tourism organizations should be able to match the instruments and tools in hand with the intended function(s) and the goal(s)/objective(s) to achieve the promotion plan. In order to do so, most of the time it is beneficial to consider the product life cycle (PLC) stage. For example, for most occasions, launching a new tourism product occurs at a news conference/gathering with ceremonial types of events (depending on how high the product is regarded) that might be covered by one or more news agencies based on the scope of the event. The event might be recorded or live, and participants can be employees, stakeholders, shareholders, media, and influential political/local figures. A party type of gathering with fireworks and a music/food festival can be a plan for opening a new resort. A news conference for Tesla introducing a new car or truck or the gathering for Apple to announce a new product category (cell phones) are examples of introductory PLC. Another instance can be repositioning activities that the PR department might design to alter a rather negative reputation. These types of repositioning are usually only applicable using PR because of its credibility. For example, in the 1970s, before the "I Love New York" campaign, New York was known as a dirty city with a relatively high crime rate. The campaign was so successful in repositioning the image of a mature product as saturated as New York that most of the other destinations started similar campaigns worldwide.

As briefly explained, the main focus areas of PR departments are to build and maintain a promising reputation, to manage public attitude and opinion, to publicize an organization and its products to influence public behavior, and to build and maintain a favorable image and position for the organization. It is imperative to clearly distinguish these focus areas since terms such as image, attitude, identity, and reputation are overlapping concepts that are often used interchangeably. Image is how a corporation and its products are perceived by the public. It is a combination of factual and emotional signals. On the other hand, identity is the sum of all of the actual representations and

## TOURISM AND HOSPITALITY INSIGHTS 21.1
## COLLABORATION MATTERS

Tackling the complex challenges such as climate change, resource depletion, and ecosystem loss poses threats to competitive self-interest organizations that lack shared purposes and trust to each other. Collaboration seems to be the only sustainable solution for dealing with these threats. In order to build trust and reach more substantial collaborative goals, corporations can start with small-group projects that link self-interests to shared interests. The display below shows the matrix of four sustainable collaboration models based on the breadth of organizations involved in collaboration and the desired goals as the focus and outcome of the collaboration process over time.

| | Companies across the value chain | Companies and nonbusiness stakeholders |
|---|---|---|
| **Outcomes** | **KEY STRATEGY** Develop *industry benchmarks and standardized systems* for measuring environmental performance across the value chain<br><br>**EXAMPLE** The Sustainable Apparel Coalition's Higg Index | **KEY STRATEGY** Institute *"payment for ecosystem services"* models in which firms invest in funds that compensate local communities for improving conservation and protection outcomes<br><br>**EXAMPLE** The Latin American Water Funds Partnership between Coca-Cola's largest bottler and upstream farmers and landowners |
| **Operational Processes** | **KEY STRATEGY** Identify and share *industrywide operational processes* that reduce emissions, natural resource consumption, and waste and protect the environment<br><br>**EXAMPLE** Dairy Management Inc.'s efforts to reduce milk's carbon footprint while producing renewable energy | **KEY STRATEGY** Initiate *extended collaborations* that engage the business community and noncorporate stakeholders in the pursuit of operational innovations and best practices that create shared value<br><br>**EXAMPLE** Action to accelerate recycling's collaboration to change consumer behavior |

FOCUS (left axis) — Outcomes / Operational Processes

PLAYERS (bottom axis) — Companies across the value chain / Companies and nonbusiness stakeholders

**Figure 21.1** The collaborative imperative

Source: Nidumolu, Ellison, Whalen, & Billman (2014).

images that an organization holds over time. Unlike image, identity is completely factual and is developed based on the actuality (image can be potential) of the corporation in the long run. Furthermore, whereas image and attitude are all held by the public, identity is more existential and is all about what an organization holds or perceives of itself. Among the above-mentioned concepts, image has the most overlap with attitude. Although they are similar to a great extent, attitude is mainly based on the belief system of a person and is under the impact of motivations. Attitudes are more judgmental in nature and are reflected in three dimensions: cognitive, affective, and conative. The cognitive dimension of attitude is the closest to the belief system. Affective dimension, on the other hand, is emotion-based, and finally, the conative dimension is more of a behavioral tendency. Image is more perceptual in nature without any behavioral intention. Image sometimes is also confused with reputation. Reputation is an intangible asset capable of impacting the organization's performance. Reputation is difficult to imitate and, as a result, in its positive form, can be considered as a competitive advantage. Reputation encompasses all of the above-mentioned concepts; hence it has impact on both stakeholders and customers. Proper positive reputation boosts the sales volume and increases the buying intention of the customers and reduces employee turnover and leaving intentions. In addition, positive reputation brings credibility to the corporation claims. Reputation is the combination of tangible and intangible assets of the organization. It can be in the form of internal and external reputation. A company can have multiple reputations based on the audience of interest. PR departments usually manage the reputation of the organization through a careful identity mix program. Owing to the comprehensive nature of reputation, the PR department cannot successfully manage the corporate reputation on its own. A contingency plan with contributions from all departments in the company is needed in order for PR to successfully manage the reputation of the company (Cooper & Argyris, 1997).

Now that the basic principles, functions, tools, and concepts of PR departments have been explained, it is possible to discuss some changes over the past 20 years that have dramatically influenced PR and its operations as well as the potential upcoming changes that will restructure the future of PR and marketing on the corporate level. Both past and future changes are mainly driven by technological advancements. Specifically, progress in information technology has mainly influenced the PR practices and will be the driving force of any future changes in PR operations. In the next section, these technological changes and trends are briefly discussed, and some potential future directions are projected.

## Changes and trends

Technological changes and digital PR has changed the concept of mass media, both in the way PR uses it (i.e., mass media) and with the additions of new media (e.g., online social media). Technological advancements have changed all aspects of PR operations from message invention, information diffusion, data storage, and data analysis to data

## TOURISM AND HOSPITALITY INSIGHTS 21.2
## UNITED AIRLINES AND POLICY CHANGES FOLLOWING FLIGHT 3411

April 2017, videos went viral of a man being dragged down the aisle of a United Airlines (UA) flight for refusing to give up his seat on an overbooked plane. A public relations nightmare ensued. UA's CEO issued an initial statement two days after the incident, provoking criticism that the airline was slow to respond (Zumbach, 2017).

**Image 21.1**

Source: https://www.pexels.com/photo/air-air-travel-aircraft-airline-175656/

United released a second statement that a thorough review of the incident would be conducted and listed the following primary actions that would be taken.

- Law enforcement officers will not be asked to remove passengers from flights unless it is a matter of safety and security;
- A thorough review of policies that govern crew movement, incentivizing volunteers in oversold situations, the handling of oversold situations and examining the partnership with airport authorities and local law enforcement will be conducted;

- A full review and improvement of training programs to ensure that employees are prepared and empowered to put the customers first (Statement on Press, 2017). The CEO stated:

Every customer deserves to be treated with the highest levels of service and the deepest sense of dignity and respect. Two weeks ago, we failed to meet that standard and we profoundly apologize. However, actions speak louder than words. Today, we are taking concrete, meaningful action to make things right and ensure nothing like this ever happens again. Our review shows that many things went wrong that day, but the headline is clear: our policies got in the way of our values and procedures interfered in doing what's right. This is a turning point for all of us at United and it signals a culture shift toward becoming a better, more customer-focused airline. Our customers should be at the center of everything we do and these changes are just the beginning of how we will earn back their trust.

("United Airlines announces changes," 2017)

Ten substantial changes were announced, some effective immediately and others implemented over the remainder of 2017.

1. Limit use of law enforcement to safety and security issues only;
2. Not require customers seated on the plane to give up their seat involuntarily unless safety or security is at risk;
3. Increase customer compensation incentives for voluntary denied boarding up to $10,000;
4. Establish a customer solutions team to provide agents with creative solutions such as using nearby airports, other airlines or ground transportations to get customers to their final destination;
5. Ensure crews are booked onto a flight at least 60 minutes prior to departure;
6. Provide employees with additional annual training;
7. Create an automated system for soliciting volunteers to change travel plans;
8. Reduce the amount of overbooking;
9. Empower employees to resolve customer service issues at the moment;
10. Eliminate red tape on permanently lost bags by adopting a "no questions asked" policy on lost luggage.

("United Airlines announces change," 2017; Zumbach, 2017)

Additionally, UA expanded roles for three members of the executive leadership team to "accelerate its momentum in elevating the experience it provides to customers and continuing its strong operational performance" ("United Airlines announces expanded," 2017).

- "Executive vice president, chief administrative officer and general counsel": A newly created position which will lead the company's legal, corporate real estate, corporate security, community, and government and regulatory affairs teams, and oversee global communications;

- "Executive vice president, technology and chief digital officer": An expanded role which is responsible for United's technology platforms and analytics and lead the strategy, development and deployment of United's e-commerce, mobile app and commercial web platforms; and

- "Executive vice president and chief commercial officer": An expanded role which oversees the network, commercial and pricing and revenue management strategy, along with marketing and MileagePlus.

("United Airlines announces expanded," 2017)

### References

Munoz, O. (2017, April 11). Statement from United Airlines CEO, Oscar Munoz, on United Express flight 3411. *United Hub*, Retrieved from https://hub.united.com/united-express-3411-statement-oscar-munoz-2355968629.html

Statement on press conference. (2017, April 13). *United*. Retrieved from http://newsroom.united.com/news-releases?item=124756

United Airlines announces changes to improve customer experience. (2017, April 27). *United*. Retrieved from http://newsroom.united.com/2017-04-27-United-Airlines-Announces-Changes-to-Improve-Customer-Experience

United Airlines announces expanded responsibilities for executive leadership team. (2017, June 15). *United*. Retrieved from http://newsroom.united.com/2017-06-15-United-Airlines-Announces-Expanded-Responsibilities-for-Executive-Leadership-Team

Zumbach, L. (2017, April 9). A year after passenger was dragged off a United flight, everyday indignities remain. *Chicago Tribune*. Retrieved from http://www.chicagotribune.com/business/ct-biz-united-passenger-dragging-anniversary-20180405-story.html

Source: Amanda Templeton.

recovery and retention. The Internet and recent improvements in its worldwide coverage and accessibility have revolutionized PR practices simply because already the traditional constraints of time and place with mass media have all been eliminated. The lack of control on the PR side due to excessive media control over the content has been practically eliminated, and now there is a lack of control on the media side, which to a great extent, empowers customers as well as PR departments (although not as much as it does customers). The main causes of this power swing are the decentralized structure of the Internet, the removal of intermediaries, deregulation of the new media, and the interactive (as a result of Web 2.0) capability. Traditional media totally lacked all of the above-mentioned qualities. It is not that traditional mass media have been totally eliminated, but rather they are also changing and integrating the opportunities that the Internet and other technologies are providing (Sheth & Malhotra, 2011). These new technological advancements have expanded the variety of the media channels to a large number of channel combinations which an organization must manage. These radical technological changes are both in the way we use the media channels that have been available for us and the new emerging channels that are evolving on a day-to-day basis. The new channels such as blogs, Wikis, Rich Site Summary (RSS, also known as really simple syndication), podcasting, vodcasting, social bookmarking, social networking websites (SNSs also partially known as social media), video sharing, and photo sharing are only a few examples of these new channels (some of these channels are not even new nowadays and are close to their end of product life cycle) (Brown, 2009). These changes resulted in PR departments being increasingly involved in electronic and/or digital PR operations (Sheth & Malhotra, 2011).

PR is still dealing with the public but in the form of an individual-based public rather than the mass public. Traditional models fail to accommodate the changes in mass media communications and should be substituted with the newer models. Electronic word of mouth (eWoM), if not more powerful than word of mouth (WoM), is equally influential on customers' decision-making. The difference is that eWoM disseminates much faster than does WoM and reaches a much larger audience. As explained, the radical technological changes have resulted in customer empowerment through the process known as user generated content (UGC), in which customers can be involved with companies interactively and provide the organization with different forms of feedback and/or complaints. There are number of different instances of a customer bankrupting large corporations from the use of social media and UGC. For example, Dave Carroll, a Canadian musician and his band, Sons of Maxwell, released a trio of protest songs titled "United Breaks Guitars" in July 2009, as a result of an unpleasant experience with United Airlines in 2008. This led to the song becoming an immediate hit on YouTube. The song had been viewed more than 18 million times by 2018. In fact, this song has its own Wikipedia page, has become a hit on iTunes, and is a huge embarrassment for United Airlines PR. On the other hand, opportunistic customers knowingly abuse the power given by digital media to gain financially from corporations. Fake reviews of negative experiences which never occurred is an example of these deviant behaviors. As a result, PR departments should be in close relationship with other marketing departments of the organization such as customer relationship management (CRM) and direct marketing to handle situations similar to above-mentioned instances. Big data analysis, text mining, semantic and sentiment analysis, and machine learning are among the practices that PR departments employ in order to survive in today's volatile and continuously changing markets. PR departments need to accurately and continuously identify the negative rumors and information disseminating among the public and block any negative information change. Furthermore, it is imperative to have access to the large volume of hourly-based real-time data from consumers in order to have control over trends and online behaviors of the public.

As a result of the above-mentioned changes, the old measurement and evaluation techniques might not be helpful anymore. The sales volume and publicity are valuable measures, but the definitions have changed (especially on publicity) and these measures are not enough by themselves. For example, the page rank and order of name appearance in a Google search for the keywords with both positive and negative sentiments is an important part of the publicity of a corporation which, in turn, is extremely important for the online identity of the corporation. Number of clicks, page rank centrality, number of downloads, eigenvalue centrality measures, number of views, etc. are a few new measures among the numerous measures suggested to evaluate the PR activities in the era of digital PR. Third party evaluation tools such as Google Analytics and Google Trends can also help organizations to evaluate the success rate of PR operations.

Another important change in the PR department operations is that apart from traditional corporate communication goals of informing, reminding, and persuading, recently, the activities of good PR also converged as a reflection of corporate social responsibility (CSR). CSR is increasingly utilized with affluent democracies as an index of corporate caring about the future of humanity. In the future, we might see exponential growth in accepting the practices related to CSR; thus the PR department should be prepared to have specialized personnel on this matter since PR is going to play a key role in CSR in both briefs and consultancies (Goldsworthy & Morris, 2008).

The future of PR departments is woven to the technological advancements specifically in the realm of information technology. Although it seems that the future advancements are going to empower both sides, that of customers as well as companies, there are also threats that can tragically impact PR departments and human society in general. The progress of artificial intelligence in the future is both promising and frightening. The supremacy of artificial intelligence can be employed to reduce the errors in operations, reduce the workload of the PR departments (as a result enhance the PR employees' quality of work-life balance), improve the computational power, and enhance the analytical power. On contrary, the advancements might continue to the point that technology by itself can occupy the position of PR in organizations. As a result, the power balance shifts again to media, but the problem is that media, PR, and decision makers of the information age are all the same authority (i.e., artificial intelligence) with exceptional computational power with the ability to make strategic decisions. There is no need to mention how catastrophic mankind's destiny will become in this case.

PR is rooted in media relations with over half of the practitioners in PR operating public information models, which are mainly focused on dissemination of information among the public (Theaker, 2001). As a result, media relations and information dissemination are the central areas to which PR is dedicated. In practice, a lot of tactical issues should be take into consideration in order to have successful media relations. Nevertheless, good media relations can contribute to long-term strategic goals such as favorable brand image, better media profile, desirable public attitudes of the target audience, enhanced community relationship, increased market share, the ability to influence authorities on the local, national, and international level, better investor relations, and

## TOURISM AND HOSPITALITY INSIGHTS 21.3
## SOCIAL MEDIA 3.0

Social media 3.0 is a concept developed in order to make effective use of social media for mass communications. It is promising to cultivate contagious and memorable messages by consistently differentiating communication with the help of social media. According to social media 3.0, it is important to define the purpose of using social media. Depending on the PR functions, the message is going to be very different both in content and in form. In addition, the appropriate platform should be identified. The question is where (which platform) are the PR department's audience of interest? Although social media has facilitated the communication process, there are communities on social media just as there are in the real-world. Blindly shooting the message would not result in the intended results. PR departments should be able to analyze the platforms (e.g., Facebook, Twitter, YouTube, LinkedIn, Instagram, Pinterest, Google+) to select the platform of interest and then look for the relevant communities in the selected platforms. For example, according to Forbes magazine, 60% of the Snapchat users in the US are under 24, meaning that with 100 million users there is a goldmine for businesses targeting millennials. On the other hand, for the older customers, Facebook might be a better option since 44% of its users check their account several times per day, something valuable for those companies looking for frequency of exposure to a message. Finally, not all social media platforms offer the same capabilities for PR experts. For example, Google+ offers a strong platform for UGC with the possibility of using an enhanced video conference capability that is in line with other Google products and social media such as Google Drive and YouTube. In contrast to Google+, Twitter does not offer most of the above mentioned capabilities and has a character limit in terms of message content. Nevertheless, the extent of exposure, publicity, and reliability are main reasons for PR practitioners to extensively use Twitter as one of the main communication tools between corporations and their audience of interest.

**References**

Butler (2015), Social Media 3.0. https://www.forbes.com/sites/jiawertz/2017/02/18/which-social-media-platforms-are-right-for-your-business/#4eeaeb3a12a2

Source: Youcheng Wang.

improved industrial relationship (Theaker, 2001). Tools are continuously changing but the goals and functions are more or less the same. Information dissemination might follow different purposes and use different tools, but the act of disseminating information is still the same. In its traditional form, media relations were how one organization dealt with the news media (Doorley & Garcia, 2007). The immediate implication of radical technological changes is that media planning as part of a PR job description is becoming more difficult and complicated. As a result, PR departments should start utilizing different optimization techniques (from operation research) to discover the best solution in media planning for PR purposes. Communication is a complex system; the technological advancements have resulted in more complex ways of communication. On the other hand, PR operations add to the complexity, along with the Internet and social media, which are also complex systems. The overlapping complexity is exponentially adding to the complexity level of the system. Consequently, traditional communication theories are unable to explain the complex mechanisms and complexity and, as a result, predict the outcomes. In order to understand the evolution of communication theories and the need to have communication models with complex systems and network aspects, a chronological approach is adopted in the next section.

## Evolution of communication theories

Communications theory is mainly investigated from four different aspects: mechanistic, psychological, sociological, and systems and networks. The mechanistic aspect is mainly focused on transmission of communication from sender to receiver, whereas the subjective process of communication, which includes thoughts and emotions and the way a message is interpreted by a recipient, are the main focus of the psychological aspect. The sociological aspect is looking at socially constructed meanings and the impact of the social construct in the communication process. All three of the above-mentioned aspects fail to explain the complexity of the communication process. As a result, the last aspect of systems and networks has become more popular in recent years. It focuses on the complexity of the communication process and considers the whole process as a complex system (McCabe, 2012).

Schramm (1954), for the first time, suggested the three-step process in which a message is produced by a source and is then transmitted to the receiver (Figure 21.1). While the Schramm model is easy to understand and is effective, there is no explanation as to how the source produces the message, how the message is transmitted, and how the recipient receives the message (McCabe, 2012).

The Schramm model was further developed by Shannon-Weaver in 1962 and is known as one of the early theories of communication (Figure 21.2). Shannon-Weaver's model clarifies most of the unexplained processes in Schramm's model. Shannon-Weaver's approach was to discriminate the information source from the transmitter, which delivers the message. They also discriminate the destination from the receiver, as the receiver only completes the transition process while the destination is the target of the message. In addition, Shannon-Weaver's model used the "signal" as the vehicle of

**Figure 21.2 Schramm process model**
Source: McCabe (2012).

transmission. Introducing signals in communication theories is a milestone for later communication models since they enable us to comprehend the mechanism better and to have a clear understanding of potential physical and semantic noises that can disturb the communication process (McCabe, 2012).

In 1993, the Osgood-Schramm model was introduced as another example of the early theories of communication. Their model took the middle ground between the earlier models of the Schramm process model and the Shannon-Weaver model. The Osgood-Schramm model (Figure 21.3) recognizes the importance of the encoding, decoding, and interpretation process. Nevertheless, these processes are inherently part of the source/sender and receiver in the Osgood-Schramm model. Moreover, the Osgood-Schramm model introduced the new concept of the feedback loop, something which was missing from the previous models. In other words, the receiver of the message sends a new message in response to the sender and their sender/receiver roles swap. As a result of this role change, there is no fixed role as a sender/source or receiver, and both parties play both sender and receiver roles at any given time (McCabe, 2012).

Proposed by Fill (2005), a more recent version of the communication theories, known as the marketing communications transmission model, has received a lot of attention and is widely used in marketing books. The transmission model was simply an adaptive combination of the previous models proposed by Schramm, Shannon, Weaver, and Osgood (Figure 21.4). The marketing communications transmission model, despite its popularity among marketers and PR people, is simply another variation of the traditional mechanistic models, all of which lack the ability to explain the complexity of the communication system and the failure and control mechanisms of real-world events (McCabe, 2012).

Maletzke's model (1992) took the psychological aspect of communication theories into account (Figure 21.5). In Maletzke's model, concepts such as self-image, personality structure, social environment, public pressure, other party's image, pressure and constraints of message and medium, message structure, selective perception (based on experience), and image of the medium are added to the traditional models. While

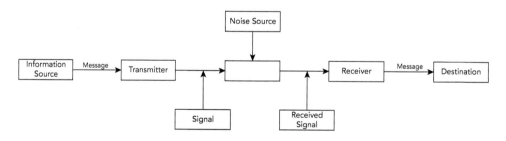

**Figure 21.3 Shannon-Weaver's model of communication**

Source: McCabe (2012).

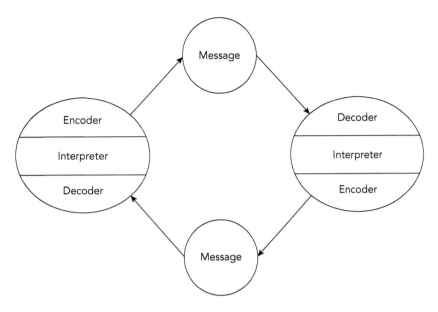

**Figure 21.4  Osgood-Schramm model (1993)**

Source: McCabe (2012).

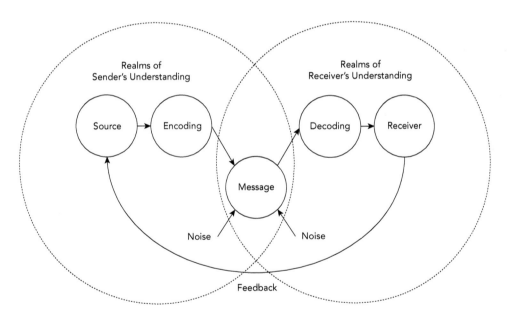

**Figure 21.5  Fill's adaptation model of the marketing communication transmission model**

Source: McCabe (2012).

Maletzke's model seems to offer a better explanation of real-world communication along with the potential disturbance of communication, the model loses a significant amount of parsimony due to being complicated (Theaker, 2001).

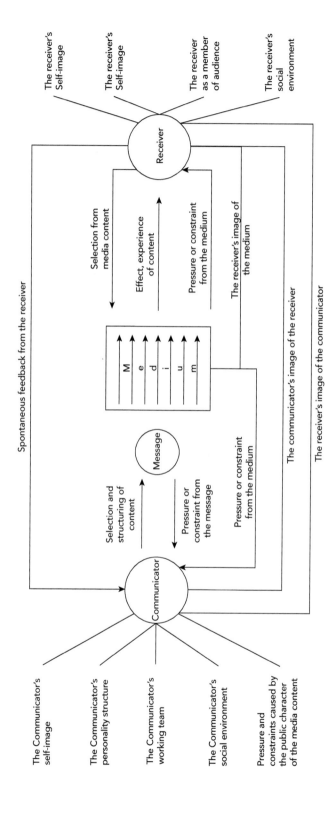

**Figure 21.6  Maletzke's model**

Source: Theaker (2001).

Maletzke's model, despite its complication, was unable to explain the complexity raised from multi-agent (multiple senders and receivers) communication. Multi-modal communication models suggested by Fill (2005) were in opposition to earlier mass communication models, all of which were like blind shots in clusters of a public audience without any specific targeting (Figure 21.6a). In multi-modal communication models (one specific form is also known as the two-step flow model (two-way asymmetric model)), mass media target opinion leaders in the public eye use opinion leaders' dissemination power to publicly spread the message (Figure 21.6b). There are other variations of multi-modal models, some with feedback loops or a reciprocal two-step flow (two-way symmetric) that takes into consideration the mutuality of the communication. Models with reciprocal paths are relatively new since the Internet in general and Web 2.0 specifically has revolutionized mass communication. In the previous two-step flow models, there was less attention on reciprocity since the media was more of a one-way road only acting as the source of information, and the public were only consumers of the information. Multi-modal models were among the early social aspect theories recognizing the importance of social context, the supporting role of peer groups in reinforcing, mediating, transmitting, and the influencing behavior of the public (McCabe, 2012; Theaker, 2001). Multi-modal models also acted like a bridge between the mechanistic, psychological, and social aspects of the communication theories and the newer approach of complex systems.

Complex system models are a large series of models trying mathematically to explain the behavior of a complex system. One of the most successful and most prevalent techniques for studying complex systems is complex networks. Unlike other traditional statistical and quantitative approaches, which are reductionist-based approaches trying to isolate the concept of study and minimize it to the smallest units of analysis to study the concept, network analysis is a holistic computational approach that considers interactions of different units of analysis in their contextual reality. All communication occurs in a context with multiple players that are always dynamically joining and detaching different networks with different boundaries. These players also evolve during this time by making

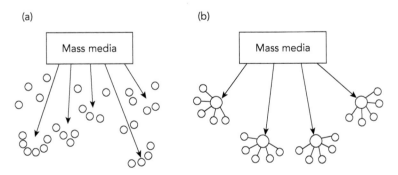

**Figure 21.7** (a) Traditional mass media communication model; (b) Two-step flow model without mutuality

Source: Theaker (2001).

connections to each other or eliminating some existing connections. It is imperative to understand two concepts in any networks called node and edge. Node is the actor or player, and it can be a person, an animal, an organization, an idea, a city, a computer, while the edge is a connection or link between nodes. It can be a physical connection like a road or wire, or it can be an abstract level connection like friendship or organizational hierarchy. Edges in a network can be directed (e.g., from node A to node B) or undirected (e.g., there is a link between nodes A and B).

Studies have shown that the complex systems do not form on random bases. Particularly, most of the complex systems fit in a specific class of network models known as scale-free networks. There are in fact two major mechanisms behind the formation of scale-free networks known as: (1) preferential attachment (also known as rich-get-richer) and (2) the node's fitness. Preferential attachment indicates that nodes with more edges are more likely to connect to the newcomers. Intuitively, nodes with more links are more capable of building new relationships. On the other hand, newcomers are going to find building relationships with these nodes (i.e., nodes with more edges) more attractive. Even from the probability point of view, nodes with more links are over presented in the sample space compared to nodes with fewer edges. According to preferential attachment, nodes which joined the network in the early stages of development are more likely to become nodes with a lot of edges. Again, it is intuitive that early comers have a longer time available to create relationships compared to late comers. In a network, the nodes with more connections compared to other nodes are called hubs and follow the power-law distribution (also known as the Pareto principle or the 80/20 rule). In other words, in any given scale-free network, very few nodes (approximately 20%) reach hub level, while the rest of the nodes are going to become connected to these hubs one way or another (Figure 21.7). The first mechanism, although useful in explaining scale-free network formation, fails to explain circumstances in which the hubs enter the network much later than other nodes. For example, Google was created later than Yahoo but, in a short amount of time, it became one of the main hubs of the World Wide Web. The second mechanism of "node's fitness" indicates that the nodes, which have an inner quality to become a hub, are more likely to become a hub independent from the time of joining the network. This inner quality can be capability/capacity depending on the type of network (Pham, Sheridan, & Shimodaira, 2016). For example, in a friendship sympathy network, a friend with a higher mental capacity of being compassionate towards other friends is more likely to become a hub no matter the time of joining the network. A physical example can be the capacity of a router on a computer network. Irrespective of the time the router is added to the network, if it has a higher capacity compared to other routers, it is going to handle most of the traffic on the network (i.e., becoming a hub).

Studying the network and the complex systems aspect of communication, one might take any of two common approaches: (1) studying the topology and structure of the network in terms of who is where and connected to whom, or (2) studying what can be transmitted in what rate through the connections that can be also studied in the context of communication by using any of the above-mentioned

**Figure 21.8** Scale-free network of a hypothetical social group with 400 members and their professional (work-related) relationship in terms of who is reporting

Source: Author.

approaches. For example, due to the small number of hubs, scale-free networks show resilience to random errors. It means that in any given time, if we randomly eliminate a worker from Figure 21.7, it is more likely going to be one of the small nodes, which would not have a serious impact on the whole network flow in terms of who is reporting to whom. On the contrary, scale-free networks are vulnerable to deliberate attacks (Albert, Jeong, & BarabÃsi, 2000). For example, in Figure 21.7, knowing that larger nodes are hubs and more critical for the work flow, if we start eliminating large nodes, in a short time frame, the whole network collapses and there are a lot nodes singled out with no connection to the rest of the system. If the network in Figure 21.7 was the connections of the audience of interest (public) for a PR department, the hubs will be the opinion leaders and, by identifying the opinion leaders (hubs) with much less spending, the PR department could more efficiently spread a message about the company or product. On the other hand, if negative publicity in form of rumor is disseminating on the network, instead of running after people and suing them for character defamation, organizations could simply target the hubs and try to provoke them against the negative publicity. As a result, the rumor will be eliminated shortly. There are statistical/mathematical techniques developed to estimate the controllability level of the scale-free networks. It is possible to estimate what percentage of nodes are required to be controlled (driving nodes) if we want the whole system to reach the desired state (from a PR perspective). These techniques also can help the PR department to gain specific outputs they are looking for in time of repositioning. Knowing the current outcome (undesirable image or position in market) and knowing that by controlling which nodes the company can use to create the desirable outcome (the desired position and image that company is willing to have), companies create competitive advantage and efficiency regarding publicity management. It should be noted that the latter concept (controlling the outcome through driving nodes) is different from the former one (disseminating information or targeting unfavorable rumors through opinion leaders (hubs)) since driving nodes usually shy away from hubs (Liu, Slotine, & BarabÃsi, 2011).

## TOURISM AND HOSPITALITY INSIGHTS 21.4
## EXPERIENCE AND STORY

A worldwide leader in customer experience management, SDL, has selected a public relations agency PAN Communication as their partner for the technology, consumer, and healthcare industries. This is a partnership, which will provide the opportunity to work with more than 40 top global brands in more than 30 countries. "We recognized PAN's capabilities to leverage our assets and product strengths and turn our public relations efforts into an ongoing news cycle," said Jessica Hohn-Cabana, vice president of global communications at SDL. "PAN has been a diligent partner, committed to setting metrics and applying measurement to our PR initiatives. We have already seen tremendous value and results from the partnership."

SDL PLC maintains a global infrastructure across 38 countries and is publicly traded on the London Stock Exchange. The partnership leverages customers' social data to build loyalty and through experience management make customers brand advocates. SDL and PAN Communications are trying to engage customers across different languages and cultures to turn their buying behavior into a pleasant experience.

### About PAN Communications (from PAN Communication website)

With an expertise in driving industry-leading visibility and engagement programs for innovative businesses, PAN Communications is an award-winning public relations agency that utilizes all media and disciplines to increase awareness and opportunities to achieve our clients' business objectives. As an integrated communications partner to companies that lead their industries or those that aspire to, PAN leads strategic public relations for consumer, technology and healthcare brands.

### References

https://www.pancommunications.com/news-item/customer-experience-management-leader-sdl-
    selects-pan-communications-global-strategy-content-development-influencer-marketing/
The company website: https://www.pancommunications.com/

Source: Youcheng Wang.

In addition, approaching communication theories from the network and complex systems perspective enables researchers to apply dynamic models of information diffusion. Information diffusion models follow the logic of SIR (susceptible-infectious-recovered (immune)/removed (deceased)) S-shaped models of epidemics. SIR models on networks have been proven to be accurate models both in predicting the contagious spread pattern of behaviors and explaining the technology acceptance of the individuals in the community. Information dissemination models would be useful for studying public behavior in publicity of the corporation and technology acceptance models would be useful in studying employees' (including the PR department) behavior in dealing with changes resulting from technological advancements (Newman, 2011).

## Conclusion

This chapter is dedicated to PR management in tourism organizations and their relation with media. The chapter started with basics of PR departments and their role in organizations. Seven main functions of traditional PR were elaborated along with the related tools to perform PR operations. The impact of technology is briefly discussed and major changes from traditional PR to digital PR are highlighted with some potential future directions. The level of complexity that PR departments are facing nowadays is daunting. In order to fully understand the complexity that PR is dealing with, a chronological evolution of communication models is provided with a focus on complex systems and network approach to communication models. Three case studies are also provided to signify the role of collaboration, technology, and experience in PR activities. The main approach in explaining the key points was mainly focusing on the general and context-free principles with discussions and examples from hospitality and tourism industry. Hospitality and tourism industry is a strongly heterogeneous industry, in which, a prescription for a successful restaurant PR might be a total failure in a resort PR, or a destination PR approach might not be applicable for a theme park.

### REVIEW QUESTIONS

1. What is the role of PR departments in dealing with climate change, resource depletion, and ecosystem loss in hospitality and tourism contexts? Specify at least five important contributions regarding the PR functions.
2. Can you think of any examples of corporate collaboration in terms of the four collaboration models in hospitality and tourism? If not, what are the possible reasons?
3. Discuss the importance of storytelling in experience enhancement by PR departments.
4. Discuss which social media platform is appropriate to what PR functions. Elaborate on your opinion.

5.  Think about the differences of using social media as a PR tool in hospitality and tourism compared to its use in other industries such as health services, energy, insurance, and the automotive industry.

## YOUTUBE LINKS

### *"United Airlines apologizes for removal of passenger"*

URL: https://www.aljazeera.com/news/2017/04/united-ceo-apologises-passenger-removed-170412012733328.html

Summary: Airline practice of overbooking flights is in focus after the video of man dragged off plane goes viral

### *"Seeing through the eyes of others"*

URL: https://youtu.be/Ced5P7proZE

Summary: Hyatt employees offer a perspective of the world through their eyes in the #worldofunderstanding campaign.

### *"The reason they won't do it is always the reason they should do it"*

URL: https://youtu.be/zb1u9vgbLBE

Summary: Shari Levitin discusses handling objections in the sales process of selling timeshares.

### *"Tourism training live: SEO strategies and best practices for travel brands"*

URL: https://youtu.be/UoKJSNm39gw

Summary: A Tourism training live session for travel and tourism industry professionals looking to make SEO a meaningful part of content marketing efforts, and shares practical steps and techniques that can be implemented to make SEO a key part of the marketing success for a tourism business.

## REFERENCES AND RELATED WEBSITES

References

Albert, R., Jeong, H., & Barabási, A.-L. (2000). Error and attack tolerance of complex networks. *Nature, 406*, 378. Retrieved from http://dx.doi.org/10.1038/35019019

Bojanic, D.C., Oh, H., & Pizam, A. (2008). *Handbook of hospitality marketing management*. Oxford: Butterworth-Heinemann.

Brown, R. (2009). *Public relations and the social web: How to use social media and Web 2.0 in communications*. London: Kogan Page.

Butler, D. (2015). Social media 3.0. *Principal, 94*(5), 20–23. Retrieved from https://login.ezproxy.net.ucf.edu/login?auth=shibb&url=http://search.ebscohost.com/login.aspx?direct=true&db=eft&AN=103197624&site=ehost-live&scope=site

Cooper, C.L., & Argyris, C. (1997). *The Blackwell encyclopedia of management. Marketing Volume IV*. Oxford: Blackwell.

Doorley, J., & Garcia, H.F. (2007). *Reputation management: The key to successful public relations and corporate communication*. London: Routledge.

Goldsworthy, S., & Morris, T. (2008). *PR – a persuasive industry? Spin, public relations, and the shaping of the modern media*. Basingstoke: Palgrave Macmillan.

Kotler, P., & Keller, K.L. (2016). *A framework for marketing management*. Boston, MA: Pearson.

Kotler, P., & Wood, M.B. (2005). *Principles of marketing. European edition*. Harlow: Pearson

Liu, Y.-Y., Slotine, J.-J., & Barabási, A.-L. (2011). Controllability of complex networks. *Nature, 473*, 167. Retrieved from http://dx.doi.org/10.1038/nature10011

McCabe, S. (2012). *Marketing communications in tourism and hospitality: Concepts, strategies and cases*. Abingdon: Routledge.

Newman, M.E.J. (2011). *Networks: An introduction*. Oxford: Oxford University Press.

Nidumolu, R., Ellison, J., Whalen, J., & Billman, E. (2014). The collaboration imperative (cover story). *Harvard Business Review, 92*(4), 76–84. Retrieved from https://login.ezproxy.net.ucf.edu/login?auth=shibb&url=http://search.ebscohost.com/login.aspx?direct=true&db=buh&AN=95094105&site=ehost-live&scope=site

Pham, T., Sheridan, P., & Shimodaira, H. (2016). Joint estimation of preferential attachment and node fitness in growing complex networks. *Scientific Reports, 6*(1). https://doi.org/10.1038/srep32558.

Scott, J., & Carrington, P.J. (2014). *The SAGE handbook of social network analysis*. London: Sage Publications. https://doi.org/10.4135/9781446294413

Sheth, J.N., & Malhotra, N.K. (2011). *Wiley international encyclopedia of marketing*. Chichester: Wiley.

Theaker, A. (2001). *The public relations handbook*. London: Routledge.


Websites

American Marketing Association
https://www.ama.org/

Chartered Institute of Marketing
https://www.cim.co.uk/

Institute for Public Relations
https://instituteforpr.org/

## MAJOR CASE STUDY
## TECHNOLOGICAL COMMUNICATION DURING NATURAL DISASTERS

Destinations affected by natural disasters such as hurricanes and earthquakes often have a crisis management plan in place. Crisis communication has seen changes recently due to the influence of social media, which was showcased in both Florida and Texas recently with Hurricanes Irma and Harvey.

Emergency management officials have recognized that social media is a means through which to target a larger audience and many emergency management officials and local emergency managers have taken a more proactive approach to utilizing social media outlets (FEMA, 2018).

FEMA has adapted a variety of social media outlets such as Facebook, Instagram, and Twitter, both on national and regional specific levels. When Florida was declared a major disaster, FEMA utilized digital communication specialists to monitor social media to monitor references to the organization on social media, share survivor posts with experts to answer questions, and post information on the FEMA Facebook and Twitter pages (FEMA, 2018).

In Florida, first responders and government officials heavily utilized social media to communicate with residents and coordinate relief efforts (MacMillan, 2017). The Florida tourism office utilized Facebook to send targeted messages to visitors and residents advising them to take the appropriate storm precautions. Alphabet Inc and Google worked in partnership with the state to quickly update road closures within the state on Google Maps (MacMillan, 2017). Twitter was utilized by various agencies to communicate the risks and location of the storm. The Coast Guard in Florida realized that social media could help to alleviate stress on dispatchers, who were receiving over 1,000 calls per hour (Meadows-Fernandez, 2017).

Following Hurricane Irma, local officials in Florida have tapped into new technology to communicate with different groups of residents. One county is working with Nextdoor, a neighborhood social media site, to create a map of every residence inside the county and unincorporated area. The map would then allow the county to send notices to those residents who would be affected by delayed services, such as trash, after a storm (MacMillan, 2017).

In both Florida and Texas, residents were asked to utilize Zello, a smartphone app that works as a digital walkie-talkie and has since reached the top of the iTunes store charts. In Houston, Zello was utilized by volunteers in relief coordination efforts. The app is also used by police officers in some parts of Texas, as the app is secure and works in areas with minimal cell coverage (MacMillan, 2017; Meadows-Fernandez, 2017). Another popular app being utilized is GasBuddy, an app that crowdsources prices at the pump allowing users to determine where fuel is available (MacMillan, 2017). Facebook's safety-check tool was used in both states, and is being more commonly used across a variety of disasters, to allow users to mark themselves as safe within their profiles. Crowd-Source Rescue is a smaller site that works on from an online platform to connect users who need rescuing and those with the resources to help; CrowdSource Rescue was utilized in Hurricane Irma to coordinate over 7,000 rescues (MacMillan, 2017).

### References

Meadows-Fernandez, R. (2017, Sept 15). What Harvey and Irma taught us about using social media in emergency response. *PacificStandard*. Retrieved from https://psmag.com/social-justice/what-harvey-and-irma-taught-about-using-social-media-in-emergency-response

MacMillan, D. (2017, Sept. 11). In Irma, emergency responders' new tools: Twitter and Facebook. *The Wall Street Journal*. Retrieved from https://www.wsj.com/articles/for-hurricane-irma-information-officials-post-on-social-media-1505149661

FEMA. (2018, April 16). Social media and emergency preparedness. *FEMA*. Retrieved from: https://www.fema.gov/news-release/2018/04/16/social-media-and-emergency-preparedness

Source: Amanda Templeton

### Major case questions

1. What are some of the benefits to emergency management personnel of using social media technologies before, during, and after natural disasters?
2. How may you differentiate your use of the above between local residents and tourist markets; especially in the case of Florida which receives approximately 120 million visitors per year?
3. What are some of the disadvantages to emergency management personnel of using social media technologies before, during, and after natural disasters?

# The future of tourism and hospitality marketing

## Learning outcomes

By the end of this chapter, students will:

- Understand the contemporary drivers for change in the wider environment shaping the future of tourism and hospitality marketing
- Be cognizant of the future direction of marketing and its impact on the future of tourism and hospitality marketing
- Comprehend the skill set for those wishing to succeed in the future as marketing moves from an experiential domain to one driven by big data, predictive analytics and artificial intelligence.

## Introduction

This book set out to provide a contemporary, accessible, and useful resource for students who are encountering, possibly for the first time, the intricacies and complexities of tourism and hospitality marketing and the very real challenges that lie ahead in the real and dynamic world of marketing. What hopefully has become obvious having now reached the final chapter in the book, is how fascinating and how challenging marketing is today and how competitive the wider environment is in which marketing is being conducted. As the old saying goes, the only constant in life generally is change with this always having been the case. However, the speed of change over the past two decades has been phenomenal with advances in technology underpinned largely by the emergence of the Internet in the mid-to-late 1990s contributing so much to the world we know today. The early chapters of this book set out the wider context and environment within which marketing is now conducted with a brief synthesis provided in the next section.

What remains true to this day though, despite all the change in disruption in the world, is the extent to which marketing's core questions remain the same. For example, despite the considerable forces at play nationally, regionally, and globally, marketers still need to understand the needs, wants and desires of individuals and groups of individuals who make up the markets that consume the products manufactured and supplied in order to ensure that those products and services delivered are those that the market wishes to consume. In Chapter 1, Middleton et al. (2009, p. 24) argued that for the user or buyer marketing is concerned with six key questions:

1.  What are the needs, wants, and desires of existing and prospective users and their interactions with suppliers?
2.  Which products or services do they wish to buy or use and at what price?
3.  What information do they obtain to make their purchasing or consuming decisions, and how do they process that information and what type of communication influences their decision?
4.  Where do they obtain their preferred products and services (i.e., where do they buy them from)?
5.  What level of post-sales service is required (if any)?
6.  What is their level of satisfaction with their purchase or consumption and how likely are they to make such a decision again?

These six questions remain as valid today as they did in the 1950s when marketing as a subject discipline started to emerge. Likewise, for the producer or supplier organization, six different questions remain equally as valid today as in previous decades:

1.  Which products and services do they need to supply and why?
2.  How many of the products or services do they need to produce?
3.  At what price or cost do these products and services need to be made available for?
4.  How should they communicate their products and services to users and buyers?
5.  When, where, and how do they make them available to the market?
6.  What level of service is required before, during, and/or after purchase has taken place?

What on the surface seem like very simple and ordinary questions, however, are not so easy to answer in practice. There thus remains a strong need for a management decision process and the adoption of a marketing orientation that ensures that the real needs of the market are met. In reality, the management process remains very similar albeit with a different set of forces at play and a different set of tools to utilize than was previously the case. Likewise, different marketing situations require different approaches with some former orientations of marketing, such as the selling orientation, still relevant in particular circumstances (for example, see Tourism & hospitality insights 1.1). For any company to effectively utilize marketing management properly, they must go through a very specific process that helps them develop an identity, analyze their market potential, identify and select their target audiences, formulate a strategy, implement tactics and reflect on their efforts to date as outlined in Chapter 12 with market segmentation, targeting and positioning (see Chapter 13) continuing to underpin modern marketing theory and practice.

Although the above is true for any industry or sector, the tourism and hospitality industry continues to demonstrate a distinct set of characteristics that are worthy of revisiting, all of which are in addition to the generic service characteristics of inseparability, heterogeneity, intangibility and perishability (all of which are discussed in more depth in Chapter 8). The key characteristics that continue to underpin tourism and hospitality marketing are: seasonality; the high fixed cost of many products, services and experiences; the overall interdependence of the industry. This latter characteristic in part, explains why collaboration is such an important characteristic of the tourism and hospitality industry and why it features so strongly throughout this book. Marketing strategies have been implemented ad nauseam to remedy the challenges of seasonality in particular, most notably in small-island destinations. However, climate, school vacation patterns, geo-politics and transportation networks (many of a deeply historical nature) continue to serve as impediments to change with seasonality a perennial challenge for so many companies and places. This is also true for those wishing to reduce the high fixed-cost nature of the industry with revenue management, originating in the airline industry as introduced in Chapter 17, continuing to advance in sophistication and accuracy as a means to combat the biggest challenges of this particular characteristic. And finally, although the concentration of power and influence in some sectors of the industry such as international tour operations and cruising benefit from vertical and horizontal integration, the vast majority of the industry is made up of smaller players where collaboration is highly beneficial if wishing to deliver a seamless, integrated, and satisfying consumer experience. Before analyzing the future of tourism and hospitality marketing, however, a short revisit to the driving forces for change is necessary as a means to really highlight the strength of the forces at play.

Chapter 2 provided a thorough overview of the external challenges being faced by all industries as the world experiences a myriad of forces at play. Although there have always been a multitude of challenges at any one time in different parts of the world, what is different today is the speed with which so many of the world's population know what is going on with social media driving global communication at a rate and speed not witnessed before. Although this has many positive impacts, the sense of insecurity from migrants in many parts of the world, the fear of losing jobs to cheaper "source" countries, and the threat of personal and nationwide security from day-to-day crime and more extreme forms of terrorist action all of a sudden become "real" for many people ... whether they are likely to be impacted or not, with not being the most common answer. The global distribution of information at a press of a button has, for many, become a source of fear when in reality the world is much safer than at any time in its history.

# Change and the emerging experiential phenomenon

More problematic for most markets is not change itself but the speed with which change is occurring, much of it driven by new technologies and automation, and our ability to accommodate it into our daily lives and work. After all, it is only 20 years ago that Google was launched in California, an event that in reality changed the entire dynamic of the marketplace and marketing with the balance of power very much shifting from the supplier to the consumer. In response to this scenario, Chapter 1 introduced a series of generic consumer trends by Pride (2016) with far-reaching implications for the tourism and hospitality industry. Pride's "Yourism" agenda highlights the trend towards accessible and personalized experiences with the "mass marketing" of old no longer working for many in the tourism and hospitality industry as guests, visitors, passengers, or users expect individual or personalized experiences and a degree of tailored authenticity with "one size" most definitely "not fitting all." With consumers now more impatient than ever before, providing a proactive (co-creative) input into their own experiences, and experiencing information "overload" in many areas of life, the need for marketers to be more precise with the communication of their message and actual channels of communication and distribution are real. Personal safety is also a concern for many as implied previously with many longer-haul destinations and destinations in parts of the world where political instability, natural disasters, or terrorist activity are becoming the norm struggling to compete. Finally, in a world dominated by virtual agendas, there is a growing trend toward consumers seeking a degree of social capital or "sense of belonging" in their pattern of consumption of tourism and hospitality products. This is evidenced by the increasing number of people visiting places of significance whether it be as a result of family connection and places of birth, religious sites, or places deemed significant to their self-worth.

What all of the above demonstrates is the continuing influence of the experience economy and the means by which it has reshaped the way businesses across the tourism and hospitality industry have looked to position themselves in the consumers' minds. As outlined in Chapter 6, Pine and Gilmore identified five key components to the design of memorable experiences: theming the experience; harmonizing impressions with positive cues; the elimination of negative cues; mix in memorabilia; engagement with all five senses in the form of aauditory, tactile, olfactive, gustative marketing and visual marketing. At roughly the same time, Shmitt (1999) was advocating the need for strategic experiential modules (SEM) to create successful experiences with sensory, affective, cognitive, physical, and social-identity experiences necessary to meet and exceed the needs and wants of the modern consumer. The need to escape from the rigors and challenges of daily life remains with Hetzel back in 2002 advocating the need among many consumers to be transported into a different universe. Hetzel identified four experience pillars that constitute what he named the "experience wheel" with their being the need to create an element of surprise, the need to offer something truly extraordinary, the need to stimulate the five senses and to create "proximity" via a strong and personal relationship with customers.

This book is replete with case examples of companies, destinations, and organizations throughout the tourism and hospitality industry responding to the experiential demands of the market with customer-produced experiences continuing to accelerate in the 21st century. The phenomenon of corporations creating goods, services, and experiences in close cooperation with experienced and creative consumers, tapping into their intellectual capital, and in exchange giving them a direct say in (and rewarding them for) what actually gets produced, manufactured, developed, designed, serviced, processed or experienced will increasingly become the norm across many business sectors including the tourism and hospitality arena (Cova et al., 2011). It is thus clear that the new emergent empowered tourist consumer enabled by the Internet – no longer alone, digitally connected and well informed – will seek out authentic, customized, environmentally aware, and friendly tourism experiences; specialist niche interest activities and independently customized tourism will flourish (Gilmore & Pine, 2007). The experiential dimension was first introduced in the book in Tourism & hospitality insights 1.2 with the example of the French Ministry of Tourism; an example of how even in traditionally-conservative organizations the need to address the experiential demands of visitors, and customers, is necessary. So much so that "pro-sumption" is the "new-normal" with its focus on: the customer-company interaction as a new value creation; co-creating value through customer and company collaboration; the consideration that value is unique to each customer and is associated to personalized experiences; and that, in reality, products and services are only a means to an end.

# Looking to the future

So, looking to the future, what are the six key trends driving the future of tourism and hospitality marketing:

## Contextual marketing and a sense of purpose (mission)

The major case study on Destination Canada in Chapter 13 represents a perfect example of the growing need for purpose-driven marketing and the need for it to be contextualized by aligning with conversations that consumers care about. Rather than segment travelers into groups based on age, income, gender, family status or education, the experience quotient (EQ) takes a deeper look at travelers' social value and views of the world. EQ breaks each geographic market segmented into different psychographic groups, called explorer types. Each type is profiled by particular characteristics derived from social and travel values, travel motivations and behaviors. How people interpret a travel experience and what experience means to them is directly related to their fundamental outlook on life, their value system. Thus, where some people view the world as dangerous and a chaotic place and are thus seeking security, reassurance, and familiarity when traveling, others view the world as an intriguing and exciting place, triggering in them a desire to explore other cultures and ways of life when vacationing.

What is clear that in so many markets now, the target audience frequently cares more about just the product being purchased. Marketing of the future thus needs a sense of empathy and compassion with the views of its audiences and content that touches the emotions of its customers. The need for content that connects with people has now become a marketing necessity that requires investment in time and people capable of communicating the necessary story that is truly compelling to the desired market. For brands seeking to grow either their offline and/or their online presence and stand out in a crowded and competitive marketplace, effective content marketing with a sense of purpose is obligatory. The user experience remains critical but the need for messaging that resonates carries far more weight than was previously the case. Social media is particularly adept at this with their complex algorithms taking users to those posts that are contextual to them at that moment. Thus, with no context to the moment, messages (marketing) fail to get through all the clutter and noise and reach the desired destination.

Tourism and Hospitality Insights 7.9 represents another good example of a major organization, this time Disney, creating a new tourism experience with a very strong sense of overall mission; Disney Nature Village. With a strong underpinning theme of sustainability and "one planet" living, Disney clearly recognizes the changing experiential demands in the wider environment and has delivered a first-rate experience that clearly connects with its target markets. As with the Destination Canada example, Disney is strong on content with creative video content critical vis-à-vis connection with new markets.

## Meaningful engagement and avoidance of superficiality

Related to the above, and particularly among younger markets (see for example Tourism & hospitality insights 2.2), there is a growing need for a more meaningful less fake experience. For example, to now reach out to your audience there is a need to focus on their real needs and challenges. Connectivity to issues that are truly relevant is vital with avoidance of any form of superficiality at all costs. The pressure on many traditional brands can be explained by this emerging trend with the phenomenal growth in food trucks, craft beers, and parts of the sharing economy matching the changing dynamics of the marketplace. For many parts of the market now, and not only younger markets, quality of life, work-life balance, lifestyle and less short-term hedonistic experiences are becoming the norm with marketing efforts needing to touch consumer hearts and souls to really connect and generate engagement. The major case study on Tunisia in Chapter 14 demonstrates the level of meaningful engagement that can be achieved, this in response to a very difficult period after the terrorist attacks that took place on a Tunisian beach back in 2015. In a very different way, the employee branding strategy of Southwest Airlines also represents a very proactive and engaging approach that enables customers (or in this instance passengers) to see and experience the tangible elements of the brand rather than merely colors, shapes, and logos!

## Peer-to-peer (influencer) marketing

The rise of the Millennial and omnipresence of social media have together served to shape consumer opinions and highlight the growing influence of peer-to-peer or influencer marketing. Trust is central to peer-to-peer marketing with all forms of social media, but especially YouTube, instrumental in disseminating trusted communications throughout the market. So-called bloggers, vloggers, and other influencers today exert much power in shaping opinion with many traditional brands struggling to remain "genuine" and "trustworthy" in this new social-media driven competitive climate. More and more brands are now appreciating the power of cooperation with influencers and are beginning to engage opinion leaders in their campaigns and general marketing communication. That being said, loyalty to older brands is decreasing, especially among younger markets, with a general degree of cynicism caused by poor levels of believability, limited emotional engagement and a misunderstanding of how smaller details do now matter. Marketing generally, and branding in particular, is now an immersive experience driven by peer-to-peer communication with trust at its core.

## One-to-one relationships and the customer journey

As with the previous trend, technological advances have fueled the ability of marketers to target consumers on a one-to-one with the availability of big data providing a lake of data that contains everything you ever need to know about consumer behavior, their preferences, and interests. Through the analysis of big data, market analysts are able to develop personalized marketing messages to individuals and really engage on a one-to-one basis, something that although desirable in the past was not achievable due to the limitations of technology. Tourism & hospitality insights 3.3 represents a perfect example of this trend. Given its robust characteristics, volume (amount of data), velocity (speed of data), and variety (variety of data types and sources), big data provides valuable insights for marketers' practitioners' decision-making processes by allowing them to track and analyze consumer behaviors, such as transaction, purchasing patterns, and recommendations. In turn, marketers can provide better targeted services and products to travelers through personalized marketing and targeted product designs.

## Marketing automation

It was not that long ago that automation in a marketing sense took place across two established platforms, namely email and websites. Today meanwhile, integration and automation across dozens of channels, data sets, and applications (commonly referred to as a hyper-connected network or marketing automation 2.0) are required for the delivery of customer experiences. Staying abreast of developments in automation is far from easy with many smaller companies, very typical in the tourism and hospitality industry, struggling to compete. Intelligent automation is very much beneficial to the larger organizations who have the resources to employ suitably-qualified people to analyze what works, what doesn't, and those remedies necessary to ensure benefits from the cutting-edge technology can be leveraged fully. Across all technological platforms, knowing in detail the customer's buying journey is now possible with marketers having far greater accuracy as to when, where, and at what level communication and engagement needs to be applied to generate a return on marketing investment. This is especially true for those working to maximize search engine optimization (see major case study in Chapter 1) in that they need to know who their customers are, what they are looking for, and where they are in the buying journey.

One of the outcomes of all of the above shifts in technological and analytical advances is the extent to which they themselves will shape the changing patterns of future behavior and consumption. By being "ahead of the game," consumer expectations will simply become more and more demanding with the marketing "chase" continuing forever. Virtual reality (see Tourism & hospitality insights 16.13 and 16.14), augmented reality, artificial intelligence, automation and robots … yes, robots … are all now part of the marketing toolkit with a recent study concluding that high-performing marketing leaders now spend one-third of their budget on channels they didn't know existed only five years ago! As identified with the first trend, the future of marketing is driven by context. To achieve this, marketers will require a network of tools capable of executing intentions across many different mediums with implications for the guest experience, marketing and all forms of consumer behavior. And although digital marketing has now become mainstream, artificial intelligence and machine learning are just at the beginning of their contribution to modern marketing. The future is certainly not dull.

## Mobile and the app

Although mobile marketing is not new, the extent to which it is central to future marketing initiatives is such that it warrants some attention. Where previously mobile marketing was very much targeted to millennial markets, the spread of smartphones across all age groups combined with the ways in which artificial intelligence is changing the way consumers are interacting with their devices which, in turn, is changing their buying patterns and the need for marketing at different stages of the buying journey. Google Assistant, for example, is a virtual assistant powered by artificial intelligence that is primarily available on smart phones and devices which, unlike some of its competitors, can engage in two-way conversations. The marketing implications of such an innovation are huge and in many cases game-changing but … necessitate exploration in another book!

In conclusion, what all of the above trends demonstrate is that marketing generally, and specific to tourism and hospitality, is changing at a rapid pace. Keeping abreast of these and future trends is going to prove fascinating yet challenging as all corners of the tourism and hospitality industry seek to maintain, and ultimately enhance, their competitive standing. To survive and prosper in this new world of marketing, marketers of the future need to be analytically-intelligent, data-confident and technology-smart with a need to understand the customer journey in its entirety. They also need to be able to anticipate, accommodate, and thrive on disruption as this will be a constant in the future as at the same time continuing to focus on those six questions raised by Middleton et al. (2009) highlighted at the beginning of this chapter. Marketing of tourism and hospitality in the future is going to be a roller-coaster of a ride in that it will be fast, furious, fun, and fearsome ... are you prepared and ready to get on board? Hopefully this is the case with this book providing you with the knowledge, information, and toolkit to succeed!!

## REFERENCES AND FURTHER READING

### References

Cova, B., Dalli, D., & Zwick, D. (2011). Critical perspectives on consumers' role as "producers": Broadening the debate on value co-creation in marketing processes. *Marketing Theory, 11*(3), 231–241.

Gilmore, J. H., & Pine, B. J. (2007). *Authenticity: What consumers really want.* Cambridge, MA; Harvard Business Press.

Middleton, V.T.C., Fyall, A., Morgan, M., & Ranchhod, A. (2009). *Marketing in travel and tourism* (4th ed.). Oxford: Elsevier Butterworth Heinemann.

Moutinho, L., Ballantyne, R., & Rate, S. (2014). Futurecasting the tourism marketplace. In McCabe, S. (Ed.), *The Routledge handbook of tourism marketing* (pp. 561–569). Abingdon: Routledge.

### Further reading

Avraham, E., & Ketter, E. (2017). Destination marketing during and following crises: Combating negative images in Asia. *Journal of Travel & Tourism Marketing, 34*(6), 709–718.

Buhalis, D., & Neuhofer, B. (2017). Service-dominant logic in the social media landscape: New perspectives on experience and value co-creation. In *Advances in social media for travel, tourism and hospitality* (pp. 13–25). Routledge.

Day, J. (2017). Collaborative economy and destination marketing organisations: A systems approach. In *Collaborative Economy and Tourism* (pp. 185–202). Urbana-Champaign: Springer.

Dixit, S. K. (Ed.). (2017). *The Routledge handbook of consumer behaviour in hospitality and tourism.* Abingdon: Taylor & Francis.

Fletcher, J., Fyall, A., Gilbert, D., & Wanhill, S. (2018). *Tourism: Principles and practice* (6th ed.). Harlow: Pearson.

Griffin, T., Giberson, J., Lee, S.H., Guttentag, D., Kandaurova, M., Sergueeva, K., & Dimanche, F. (2017, June). Virtual reality and implications for destination marketing. In *48th Annual Travel and Tourism Research Association (TTRA), International Conference, 20–23 June 2017.*

Hudson, S., & Hudson, L. (2017). *Marketing for tourism, hospitality and events: A global and digital approach.* London: Sage.

Jung, T.H., tom Dieck, M.C., & Chung,N. (2018). Determinants of hotel social media continued usage. *International Journal of Contemporary Hospitality, 30*(2), 1152–1171.

Kim, M., Vogt, C.A., & Knutson, B. J. (2015). Relationships among customer satisfaction, delight, and loyalty in the hospitality industry. *Journal of Hospitality & Tourism Research, 39*(2), 170–197.

Leung, X.Y., Bai, B., & Erdem, M. (2017). Hotel social media marketing: A study on message strategy and its effectiveness. *Journal of Hospitality and Tourism Technology, 8*(2), 239–255.

Line, N.D., & Wang, Y. (2017). Market-oriented destination marketing: An operationalization. *Journal of Travel Research, 56*(1), 122–135.

Litvin, S.W., Goldsmith, R.E., & Pan, B. (2018). A retrospective view of electronic word-of-mouth in hospitality and tourism management. *International Journal of Contemporary Hospitality Management, 30*(1), 313–325.

McCabe, S. (Ed.). (2014). *The Routledge handbook of tourism marketing.* Abingdon: Routledge.

Morgan, M., Lugosi, P., & Ritchie, J. B. (Eds.). (2010). *The tourism and leisure experience: Consumer and managerial perspectives.* Clevedon: Channel View Publications.

Neuhofer, B., Buhalis, D., & Ladkin, A. (2014). A typology of technology-enhanced tourism experiences. *International Journal of Tourism Research, 16*(4), 340–350.

O'Connell, J.F., & Williams, G. (2016). Ancillary revenues: The new trend in strategic airline marketing. In *Air Transport in the 21st Century* (pp. 195–220). Abingdon: Routledge.

Shaw, S. (2016). Aviation marketing and the leisure market. In *Aviation and tourism* (pp. 65–76). Abingdon: Routledge.

Sterne, J. (2017). *Artificial intelligence for marketing: practical applications.* Hoboken: Wiley.

Tanford, S., Shoemaker, S., & Dinca, A. (2016). Back to the future: Progress and trends in hotel loyalty marketing. *International Journal of Contemporary Hospitality Management, 28*(9), 1937–1967.

Torres, E.N., Fu, X., & Lehto, X. (2014). Examining key drivers of customer delight in a hotel experience: A cross-cultural perspective. *International Journal of Hospitality Management, 36*, 255–262.

Torres, E.N., & Kline, S. (2006). From satisfaction to delight: A model for the hotel industry. *International Journal of Contemporary Hospitality Management, 18*(4), 290–301.

Williams, A. (2006). Tourism and hospitality marketing: Fantasy, feeling and fun. *International Journal of Contemporary Hospitality Management, 18*(6), 482–495.

Xu, F., Buhalis, D., & Weber, J. (2017). Serious games and the gamification of tourism. *Tourism Management, 60*, 244–256.

# Index

Information in figures is indicated by page numbers in *italics*. Information in tables is indicated by page numbers in **bold.**